NOVELS
for Students

Advisors

Susan Allison: Head Librarian, Lewiston High School, Lewiston, Maine. Standards Committee Chairperson for Maine School Library (MASL) Programs. Board member, Julia Adams Morse Memorial Library, Greene, Maine. Advisor to Lewiston Public Library Planning Process.

Jennifer Hood: Young Adult/Reference Librarian, Cumberland Public Library, Cumberland, Rhode Island. Certified teacher, Rhode Island. Member of the New England Library Association, Rhode Island Library Association, and the Rhode Island Educational Media Association.

Ann Kearney: Head Librarian and Media Specialist, Christopher Columbus High School, Miami, Florida, 1982–2002. Thirty-two years as Librarian in various educational institutions ranging from grade schools through graduate programs. Library positions at Miami-Dade Community College, the University of Miami's Medical School Library, and Carrollton School in Coconut Grove, Florida. B.A. from University of Detroit, 1967 (magna cum laude); M.L.S., University of Missouri–Columbia, 1974. Volunteer Project Leader for a school in rural Jamaica; volunteer with Adult Literacy programs.

Laurie St. Laurent: Head of Adult and Children's Services, East Lansing Public Library, East Lansing, Michigan, 1994–. M.L.S. from Western Michigan University. Chair of Michigan Library Association's 1998 Michigan Summer Reading Program; Chair of the Children's Services Division in 2000–2001; and Vice-President of the Association in 2002–2003. Board member of several regional early childhood literacy organizations and member of the Library of Michigan Youth Services Advisory Committee.

Heidi Stohs: Instructor in Language Arts, grades 10–12, Solomon High School, Solomon, Kansas. Received B.S. from Kansas State University; M.A. from Fort Hays State University.

NOVELS
for Students

**Presenting Analysis, Context, and Criticism on
Commonly Studied Novels**

VOLUME 26

Ira Mark Milne, Project Editor

Foreword by Anne Devereaux Jordan

THOMSON

GALE

Detroit • New York • San Francisco • New Haven, Conn. • Waterville, Maine • London

Novels for Students, Volume 26

Project Editor
Ira Mark Milne

Editorial
Jennifer Greve

Rights Acquisition and Management
Margaret Chamberlain-Gaston, Leitha Etheridge-Sims, Kelly Quin, Tracie Richardson

Manufacturing
Drew Kalasky

Imaging and Multimedia
Lezlie Light

Product Design
Pamela A. E. Galbreath, Jennifer Wahi

Vendor Administration
Civie Green

Product Manager
Meggin Condino

ISBN-13: 978-0-7876-8683-3
ISBN-10: 0-7876-8683-2
eISBN-13: 978-1-4144-2933-5
eISBN-10: 1-4144-2933-9
ISSN 1094-3552

Printed in the United States of America
10 9 8 7 6 5 4 3 2 1

Table of Contents

The Informed Dialogue: Interacting with Literature

When we pick up a book, we usually do so with the anticipation of pleasure. We hope that by entering the time and place of the novel and sharing the thoughts and actions of the characters, we will find enjoyment. Unfortunately, this is often not the case; we are disappointed. But we should ask, has the author failed us, or have we failed the author?

We establish a dialogue with the author, the book, and with ourselves when we read. Consciously and unconsciously, we ask questions: "Why did the author write this book?" "Why did the author choose that time, place, or character?" "How did the author achieve that effect?" "Why did the character act that way?" "Would I act in the same way?" The answers we receive depend upon how much information about literature in general and about that book specifically we ourselves bring to our reading.

Young children have limited life and literary experiences. Being young, children frequently do not know how to go about exploring a book, nor sometimes, even know the questions to ask of a book. The books they read help them answer questions, the author often coming right out and *telling* young readers the things they are learning or are expected to learn. The perennial classic, *The Little Engine That Could, tells* its readers that, among other things, it is good to help others and brings happiness:

"Hurray, hurray," cried the funny little clown and all the dolls and toys. "The good little boys and girls in the city will be happy because you helped us, kind, Little Blue Engine."

In picture books, messages are often blatant and simple, the dialogue between the author and reader one-sided. Young children are concerned with the end result of a book—the enjoyment gained, the lesson learned—rather than with how that result was obtained. As we grow older and read further, however, we question more. We come to expect that the world within the book will closely mirror the concerns of our world, and that the author will *show* these through the events, descriptions, and conversations within the story, rather than *telling* of them. We are now expected to do the interpreting, carry on our share of the dialogue with the book and author, and glean not only the author's message, but comprehend how that message and the overall affect of the book were achieved. Sometimes, however, we need help to do these things. *Novels for Students* provides that help.

A novel is made up of many parts interacting to create a coherent whole. In reading a novel, the more obvious features can be easily spotted—theme, characters, plot—but we may overlook the more subtle elements that greatly influence how the novel is perceived by the reader: viewpoint, mood and tone, symbolism, or the use of humor. By focusing on both the obvious and more subtle literary elements within a novel, *Novels for Students* aids readers in both analyzing for message and in determining how and why that message is communicated. In the discussion on Harper Lee's *To Kill a Mockingbird* (Vol. 2), for example, the mockingbird as a symbol of innocence is dealt with, among other things, as is the importance of Lee's use of humor which "enlivens a serious plot, adds depth to the characterization, and creates a sense of familiarity and universality." The reader comes to understand the internal elements of each novel discussed—as well as the external influences that help shape it.

"The desire to write greatly," Harold Bloom of Yale University says, "is the desire to be elsewhere, in a time and place of one's own, in an originality that must compound with inheritance, with an anxiety of influence." A writer seeks to create a unique world within a story, but although it is unique, it is not disconnected from our own world. It speaks to us *because* of what the writer brings to the writing from our world: how he or she was raised and educated; his or her likes and dislikes; the events occurring in the real world at the time of the writing, and while the author was growing up. When we know what an author has brought to his or her work, we gain a greater insight into both the "originality" (the world of the book), and the things that "compound" it. This insight enables us to question that created world and find answers more readily. By informing ourselves, we are able to establish a more effective dialogue with both book and author.

Novels for Students, in addition to providing a plot summary and descriptive list of characters—to remind readers of what they have read—also explores the external influences that shaped each book. Each entry includes a discussion of the author's background, and the historical context in which the novel was written. It is vital to know, for instance, that when Ray Bradbury was writing *Fahrenheit 451* (Vol. 1), the threat of Nazi domination had recently ended in Europe, and the McCarthy hearings were taking place in Washington, D.C. This information goes far in answering the question, "Why did he write a story of oppressive government control and book burning?" Similarly, it is important to know that Harper Lee, author of *To Kill a Mockingbird,* was born and raised in Monroeville,

Alabama, and that her father was a lawyer. Readers can now see why she chose the south as a setting for her novel—it is the place with which she was most familiar—and start to comprehend her characters and their actions.

Novels for Students helps readers find the answers they seek when they establish a dialogue with a particular novel. It also aids in the posing of questions by providing the opinions and interpretations of various critics and reviewers, broadening that dialogue. Some reviewers of *To Kill A Mockingbird,* for example, "faulted the novel's climax as melodramatic." This statement leads readers to ask, "Is it, indeed, melodramatic?" "If not, why did some reviewers see it as such?" "If it is, why did Lee choose to make it melodramatic?" "Is melodrama ever justified?" By being spurred to ask these questions, readers not only learn more about the book and its writer, but about the nature of writing itself.

The literature included for discussion in *Novels for Students* has been chosen because it has something vital to say to us. *Of Mice and Men, Catch-22, The Joy Luck Club, My Antonia, A Separate Peace* and the other novels here speak of life and modern sensibility. In addition to their individual, specific messages of prejudice, power, love or hate, living and dying, however, they and all great literature also share a common intent. They force us to *think*—about life, literature, and about others, not just about ourselves. They pry us from the narrow confines of our minds and thrust us outward to confront the world of books and the larger, real world we all share. *Novels for Students* helps us in this confrontation by providing the means of enriching our conversation with literature and the world, by creating an *informed* dialogue, one that brings true pleasure to the personal act of reading.

Sources

Harold Bloom, *The Western Canon, The Books and School of the Ages,* Riverhead Books, 1994.

Watty Piper, *The Little Engine That Could,* Platt & Munk, 1930.

Anne Devereaux Jordan
Senior Editor, TALL (Teaching and Learning Literature)

Introduction

Purpose of the Book

The purpose of *Novels for Students* (*NfS*) is to provide readers with a guide to understanding, enjoying, and studying novels by giving them easy access to information about the work. Part of Gale's "For Students" Literature line, *NfS* is specifically designed to meet the curricular needs of high school and undergraduate college students and their teachers, as well as the interests of general readers and researchers considering specific novels. While each volume contains entries on "classic" novels frequently studied in classrooms, there are also entries containing hard-to-find information on contemporary novels, including works by multicultural, international, and women novelists.

The information covered in each entry includes an introduction to the novel and the novel's author; a plot summary, to help readers unravel and understand the events in a novel; descriptions of important characters, including explanation of a given character's role in the novel as well as discussion about that character's relationship to other characters in the novel; analysis of important themes in the novel; and an explanation of important literary techniques and movements as they are demonstrated in the novel.

In addition to this material, which helps the readers analyze the novel itself, students are also provided with important information on the lit-

erary and historical background informing each work. This includes a historical context essay, a box comparing the time or place the novel was written to modern Western culture, a critical essay, and excerpts from critical essays on the novel. A unique feature of *NfS* is a specially commissioned critical essay on each novel, targeted toward the student reader.

To further aid the student in studying and enjoying each novel, information on media adaptations is provided (if available), as well as reading suggestions for works of fiction and nonfiction on similar themes and topics. Classroom aids include ideas for research papers and lists of critical sources that provide additional material on the novel.

Selection Criteria

The titles for each volume of *NfS* were selected by surveying numerous sources on teaching literature and analyzing course curricula for various school districts. Some of the sources surveyed included: literature anthologies; *Reading Lists for College-Bound Students: The Books Most Recommended by America's Top Colleges*; textbooks on teaching the novel; a College Board survey of novels commonly studied in high schools; a National Council of Teachers of English (NCTE) survey of novels commonly studied in high schools; the NCTE's *Teaching Literature in High School: The Novel*; and the Young Adult Library Services Association

(YALSA) list of best books for young adults of the past twenty-five years.

Input was also solicited from our advisory board, as well as from educators from various areas. From these discussions, it was determined that each volume should have a mix of "classic" novels (those works commonly taught in literature classes) and contemporary novels for which information is often hard to find. Because of the interest in expanding the canon of literature, an emphasis was also placed on including works by international, multicultural, and women novelists. Our advisory board members—educational professionals—helped pare down the list for each volume. If a work was not selected for the present volume, it was often noted as a possibility for a future volume. As always, the editor welcomes suggestions for titles to be included in future volumes.

How Each Entry Is Organized

Each entry, or chapter, in *NfS* focuses on one novel. Each entry heading lists the full name of the novel, the author's name, and the date of the novel's publication. The following elements are contained in each entry:

Introduction: a brief overview of the novel which provides information about its first appearance, its literary standing, any controversies surrounding the work, and major conflicts or themes within the work.

Author Biography: this section includes basic facts about the author's life, and focuses on events and times in the author's life that inspired the novel in question.

Plot Summary: a factual description of the major events in the novel. Lengthy summaries are broken down with subheads.

Characters: an alphabetical listing of major characters in the novel. Each character name is followed by a brief to an extensive description of the character's role in the novel, as well as discussion of the character's actions, relationships, and possible motivation.

Characters are listed alphabetically by last name. If a character is unnamed—for instance, the narrator in *Invisible Man*—the character is listed as "The Narrator" and alphabetized as "Narrator." If a character's first name is the only one given, the name will appear alphabetically by that name.

Variant names are also included for each character. Thus, the full name "Jean Louise Finch" would head the listing for the narrator of *To Kill a Mockingbird*, but listed in a separate cross-reference would be the nickname "Scout Finch."

Themes: a thorough overview of how the major topics, themes, and issues are addressed within the novel. Each theme discussed appears in a separate subhead and is easily accessed through the boldface entries in the Subject/Theme Index.

Style: this section addresses important style elements of the novel, such as setting, point of view, and narration; important literary devices used, such as imagery, foreshadowing, symbolism; and, if applicable, genres to which the work might have belonged, such as Gothicism or Romanticism. Literary terms are explained within the entry but can also be found in the Glossary.

Historical Context: this section outlines the social, political, and cultural climate *in which the author lived and the novel was created*. This section may include descriptions of related historical events, pertinent aspects of daily life in the culture, and the artistic and literary sensibilities of the time in which the work was written. If the novel is a historical work, information regarding the time in which the novel is set is also included. Each section is broken down with helpful subheads.

Critical Overview: this section provides background on the critical reputation of the novel, including bannings or any other public controversies surrounding the work. For older works, this section includes a history of how the novel was first received and how perceptions of it may have changed over the years; for more recent novels, direct quotes from early reviews may also be included.

Criticism: an essay commissioned by *NfS* which specifically deals with the novel and is written specifically for the student audience, as well as excerpts from previously published criticism on the work (if available).

Sources: an alphabetical list of critical material used in compiling the entry, with full bibliographical information.

Further Reading: an alphabetical list of other critical sources which may prove useful for the student. It includes full bibliographical information and a brief annotation.

In addition, each entry contains the following highlighted sections, set apart from the main text as sidebars:

Media Adaptations: if available, a list of important film and television adaptations of the novel, including source information. The list also includes stage adaptations, audio recordings, musical adaptations, etc.

Topics for Further Study: a list of potential study questions or research topics dealing with the novel. This section includes questions related to other disciplines the student may be studying, such as American history, world history, science, math, government, business, geography, economics, psychology, etc.

Compare and Contrast: an "at-a-glance" comparison of the cultural and historical differences between the author's time and culture and late twentieth century or early twenty-first century Western culture. This box includes pertinent parallels between the major scientific, political, and cultural movements of the time or place the novel was written, the time or place the novel was set (if a historical work), and modern Western culture. Works written after the mid-1970s may not have this box.

What Do I Read Next?: a list of works that might complement the featured novel or serve as a contrast to it. This includes works by the same author and others, works of fiction and nonfiction, and works from various genres, cultures, and eras.

Other Features

NfS includes "The Informed Dialogue: Interacting with Literature," a foreword by Anne Devereaux Jordan, Senior Editor for *Teaching and Learning Literature* (*TALL*), and a founder of the Children's Literature Association. This essay provides an enlightening look at how readers interact with literature and how *Novels for Students* can help teachers show students how to enrich their own reading experiences.

A Cumulative Author/Title Index lists the authors and titles covered in each volume of the *NfS* series.

A Cumulative Nationality/Ethnicity Index breaks down the authors and titles covered in each volume of the *NfS* series by nationality and ethnicity.

A Subject/Theme Index, specific to each volume, provides easy reference for users who may be studying a particular subject or theme rather than a single work. Significant subjects from events to broad themes are included, and the entries pointing to the specific theme discussions in each entry are indicated in **boldface**.

Each entry may include illustrations, including photo of the author, stills from film adaptations, maps, and/or photos of key historical events, if available.

Citing Novels for Students

When writing papers, students who quote directly from any volume of *Novels for Students* may use the following general forms. These examples are based on MLA style; teachers may request that students adhere to a different style, so the following examples may be adapted as needed.

When citing text from *NfS* that is not attributed to a particular author (i.e., the Themes, Style, Historical Context sections, etc.), the following format should be used in the bibliography section:

> "*Night.*" *Novels for Students.* Ed. Marie Rose Napierkowski. Vol. 4. Detroit: Gale, 1998. 234–35.

When quoting the specially commissioned essay from *NfS* (usually the first piece under the "Criticism" subhead), the following format should be used:

> Miller, Tyrus. Critical Essay on "*Winesburg, Ohio.*" *Novels for Students.* Ed. Marie Rose Napierkowski. Vol. 4. Detroit: Gale, 1998. 335–39.

When quoting a journal or newspaper essay that is reprinted in a volume of *NfS,* the following form may be used:

> Malak, Amin. "Margaret Atwood's *The Handmaid's Tale* and the Dystopian Tradition." *Canadian Literature* No. 112 (Spring 1987), 9–16; excerpted and reprinted in *Novels for Students,* Vol. 4, ed. Marie Rose Napierkowski (Detroit: Gale, 1998), pp. 133–36.

When quoting material reprinted from a book that appears in a volume of *NfS,* the following form may be used:

Adams, Timothy Dow. "Richard Wright: 'Wearing the Mask.'" In *Telling Lies in Modern American Autobiography*. University of North Carolina Press, 1990. 69–83; excerpted and reprinted in *Novels for Students,* Vol. 1, ed. Diane Telgen (Detroit: Gale, 1997), pp. 59–61.

We Welcome Your Suggestions

The editorial staff of *Novels for Students* welcomes your comments and ideas. Readers who wish to suggest novels to appear in future volumes, or who have other suggestions, are cordially invited to contact the editor. You may contact the editor via e-mail at: **ForStudentsEditors@thomson.com.** Or write to the editor at:

Editor, *Novels for Students*
Gale
27500 Drake Road
Farmington Hills, MI 48331-3535

Literary Chronology

1820: Anne Brontë is born on January 17, the sixth and last child of Patrick and Maria Branwell Brontë. She was born in the village of Thornton in West Yorkshire, England, but the family moved to Haworth just a few months later so that her father could take a higher paying position as the local parson.

1848: Anne Brontë's *The Tenant of Wildfell Hall* is published.

1849: Anne Brontë dies on May 28.

1882: James (Augustine) Joyce is born on February 2 in Dublin, Ireland, the eldest of ten children.

1885: D. H. (David Herbert) Lawrence is born on September 11 in the mining town of Eastwood in the English Midlands.

1890: Boris Pasternak is born in Moscow to professional artists.

1892: J. R. R. (John Ronald Reuel) Tolkien is born January 3 in Bloemfontein, South Africa, of English parents.

1915: D. H. Lawrence's *The Rainbow* is published.

1915: Saul Bellow is born Solomon Bellows in Lachine, Quebec (a suburb of Montreal), the youngest of four children. His original birth certificate is lost in a fire, but his birthday is generally recognized as June 10. His parents, Abraham and Liza, emigrated from Russia to Canada not long before Bellow was born.

1921: Yoshiko Uchida is born in Alameda, California, the daughter of Japanese immigrants.

1922: James Joyce's *Ulysses* is published.

1928: Philip K. (Kindred) Dick and his twin sister, Jane Charlotte, are born six weeks prematurely on December 16 in Chicago, Illinois, to Joseph Edgar, a fraud investigator for the U.S. Department of Agriculture, and Dorothy Kindred Dick. Jane dies several weeks later, and the loss of his twin has a residual impact on Dick's life and the themes in his writing.

1929: Michael Shaara is born on June 23 in Jersey City, New Jersey, the son of Italian immigrants.

1930: D. H. Lawrence dies in Venice, France.

1941: James Joyce dies after surgery for a perforated ulcer.

1950: Edward P. Jones is born on October 5 in Washington, D.C., and raised by his single mother, to whom Jones will dedicate his first two books.

1954-1955: J. R. R. Tolkien's *The Lord of the Rings* is published.

1955: Geraldine Brooks is born in Sydney, Australia.

1957: Boris Pasternak's *Doctor Zhivago* is published.

1958: Boris Pasternak is awarded the Nobel Prize in Literature for "his important achievement both in contemporary lyrical poetry and in the field of the great Russian epic tradition." Russian authorities force Pasternak to decline the prize. In 1988, the Union of Soviet Writers reinstate Pasternak, which opens the path for Pasternak's son to officially accept his father's Nobel Prize the following year.

1960: Boris Pasternak dies of lung cancer.

1964: Philip K. Dick's *Martian Time-Slip* is published.

1973: J. R. R. Tolkien dies in Bournemouth, England.

1974: Michael Shaara's *The Killer Angels* is published.

1975: Michael Shaara is awarded the Pulitzer Prize in Fiction for *The Killer Angels*.

1975: Saul Bellow's *Humboldt's Gift* is published.

1976: Saul Bellow is awarded the Pulitzer Prize in Fiction for *Humboldt's Gift*.

1976: Saul Bellow is awarded the Nobel Prize in Literature "for the human understanding and subtle analysis of contemporary culture that are combined in his work."

1982: Philip K. Dick dies in Santa Ana, California.

1987: Yoshiko Uchida's *Picture Bride* is published.

1988: Michael Shaara dies of a heart attack.

1992: Yoshiko Uchida dies in California.

2003: Edward P. Jones's *The Known World* is published.

2004: Edward P. Jones is awarded the Pulitzer Prize in Fiction for *The Known World*.

2005: Geraldine Brooks's *March* is published.

2005: Saul Bellow dies in Brookline, Massachusetts.

2006: Geraldine Brooks is awarded the Pulitzer Prize in Fiction for *March*.

Acknowledgements

The editors wish to thank the copyright holders of the excerpted criticism included in this volume and the permissions managers of many book and magazine publishing companies for assisting us in securing reproduction rights. We are also grateful to the staffs of the Detroit Public Library, the Library of Congress, the University of Detroit Mercy Library, Wayne State University Purdy/Kresge Library Complex, and the University of Michigan Libraries for making their resources available to us. Following is a list of the copyright holders who have granted us permission to reproduce material in this volume of *NFS*. Every effort has been made to trace copyright, but if omissions have been made, please let us know.

COPYRIGHTED EXCERPTS IN *NFS*, VOLUME 26, WERE REPRODUCED FROM THE FOLLOWING PERIODICALS:

Contemporary Literature, v. 19, 1978. Copyright © 1978 by the Board of Regents of the University of Wisconsin System. Reproduced by permission.—***The D. H. Lawrence Review***, v. 7, spring, 1974. Copyright © by *The D. H. Lawrence Review*. Edited by James C. Cowan. Reproduced with the permission of *The D. H. Lawrence Review*.—*Journal of Modern Literature*, v. 27, summer, 2004. Copyright © Indiana University Press. All rights reserved. Reproduced by permission.—***Modern Fiction Studies***, v. 25, spring, 1979. Copyright © 1979 by the Purdue Research Foundation. All rights reserved. The Johns Hopkins University Press. Reproduced by permission.—***Science Fiction Studies***, v. 2, March, 1975; v. 32, July 5, 2006. Copyright © 1975, 2006 by SFS Publications. Both reproduced by permission.—***Studies in English Literature, 1500-1900***, v. 39, autumn, 1999. Copyright © 1999 The Johns Hopkins University Press. Reproduced by permission.—***War, Literature & the Arts: An International Journal of the Humanities***, v. 14, 2002 for "Vietnam, Survivalism, and the Civil War: The Use of History in Michael Shaara's *The Killer Angels* and Charles Frazier's *Cold Mountain*," by Kevin Grauke. Reproduced by permission of the author.

COPYRIGHTED EXCERPTS IN *NFS*, VOLUME 26, WERE REPRODUCED FROM THE FOLLOWING BOOKS:

Carrère, Emmanuel. From *I Am Alive and You Are Dead: A Journey into the Mind of Philip K. Dick*. Translated by Timothy Bent. Metropolitan Books, 2004. Copyright © 1993 by Emmanuel Carrère. Translation copyright © 2004 by Metropolitan Books. All rights reserved. Reproduced by permission of Henry Holt and Company, LLC.—Grice, Helena. From "Yoshiko Uchida," in *Dictionary of Literary Biography, Vol. 312, Asian American Writers*, edited by Deborah L. Madsen, Gale, 2005.—Johnson, Sarah Anne. From "The Image You Woke Up With," *In the Very Telling: Conversations with*

American Writers. Copyright © 2006 by Sarah Anne Johnson. Reprinted by permission of University Press of New England.—Rudova, Larissa. From *Understanding Boris Pasternak*. University of South Carolina Press, 1997. Copyright © 1997 University of South Carolina. Reproduced by permission.—Widmer, Kingsley. From "D. H. Lawrence," in *Dictionary of Literary Biography, Vol. 36, British Novelists, 1890–1929: Modernists*, edited by Thomas F. Staley, Gale Research, 1985.

COPYRIGHTED EXCERPTS IN *NFS*, VOLUME 26, WERE REPRODUCED FROM THE FOLLOWING WEBSITES:

Koornick, Jason. From "*Martian Time-Slip*," *www.philipkdickfans.com*. Reproduced by permission.

Contributors

Susan Andersen: Andersen is an associate professor of English literature and composition. Entry on *The Lord of the Rings*. Critical essay on *The Lord of the Rings*.

Bryan Aubrey: Aubrey holds a Ph.D. in English. Entry on *The Killer Angels*. Critical essays on *The Killer Angels* and *Picture Bride*.

Joyce Hart: Hart is a freelance writer and published author. Entries on *Doctor Zhivago* and *Picture Bride*. Critical essays on *Doctor Zhivago* and *Picture Bride*.

Lois Kerschen: Kerschen is an educator and freelance writer. Entry on *Martian Time-Slip*. Critical essay on *Martian Time-Slip*.

Melodie Monahan: Monahan has a Ph.D. in English and operates an editing service, The Inkwell Works. Entry on *Ulysses*. Critical essay on *Ulysses*.

Wendy Perkins: Perkins is a professor of twentieth-century American and British literature and film. Entries on *March* and *The Rainbow*. Critical essays on *March* and *The Rainbow*.

Scott Trudell: Trudell is a doctoral student of English literature at Rutgers University. Entry on *The Known World*. Critical essay on *The Known World*.

Carol Ullmann: Ullmann is a freelance writer and editor. Entries on *Humboldt's Gift* and *The Tenant of Wildfell Hall*. Critical essays on *Humboldt's Gift* and *The Tenant of Wildfell Hall*.

Doctor Zhivago

BORIS PASTERNAK

1957

Boris Pasternak's *Doctor Zhivago* was first published in 1957, not in Pasternak's homeland, the Soviet Union, but rather in Italy. Pasternak's manuscript for this novel had to be written in secrecy and then smuggled out of the Soviet Union because of government censorship of Pasternak's work. Pasternak, as the author espouses through his protagonist, Yuri Zhivago, in this his only novel, believed that art should not be enslaved by politics and thus criticized his oppressive government through his writing.

Doctor Zhivago is an epic work that provides several fictionalized eye-witness accounts of the upheaval in Russia as the tsar is deposed, communism rises from the revolution, and a Marist government attempts to take control. *Doctor Zhivago* is also a love story of a man torn between two women—his wife, Tonia, and the beautiful Lara with whom Yuri has an affair. This novel explores the idealism of its protagonist, which is contrasted with the brutal reality of war and its effects on ordinary citizens. This work of fiction is also a philosophical treatise on life, religion, and art as expressed by its protagonist. Finally, Pasternak, who was also a poet, wrote *Doctor Zhivago* in a particularly lyrical style. Much of the text reads like poetry.

Critics, over the years, have had trouble classifying the work since in certain ways it does not conform to the conventions regarding novels. Pasternak often introduces characters

who quickly disappear. The author often jumps forward in the story before solving present mysteries and sometimes focuses more on language and philosophical thought than on developing the plot line.

Despite some of these characteristics, *Doctor Zhivago* draws readers inside the lives and thoughts of its characters, their hopes and frustrations, their disappointments and their passions as they live through the Bolshevik Revolution and the creation of the Soviet Union, as a new world order under communism is attempted. One of the messages that *Doctor Zhivago* delivers is that some dreams are never realized.

Pasternak was awarded the Nobel Prize for this novel. First published in Italian, the work was translated into many different languages and its story served as the basis for film and television dramas. After Pasternak died in 1960, the novel was finally accepted into the Russian literary canon.

AUTHOR BIOGRAPHY

Boris Pasternak was born in 1890 in Moscow to professional artists. His father was a painter who illustrated the works of famed Russian novelist Leo Tolstoy, and his mother was a concert pianist. Pasternak grew up surrounded by outstanding artists; for example, the poet Rainer Maria Rilke was a frequent visitor in his home.

Pasternak was well educated in the liberal arts. He studied art, music, and philosophy, but his first love was poetry. His first collection of poetry was published in 1914 but went unnoticed. Almost a decade later, however, Pasternak gained the public's attention with his poetry collections *Sestra moya zhizn* (My Sister Life, 1922), and *Temy i variatsii* (Themes and Variations, 1923). Although his novel received more attention in the United States, Pasternak is mostly remembered in Russia for his poetry.

Pasternak was fascinated by the Russian Revolution of 1905, and unlike many of his contemporaries, he did not emigrate to another country to escape the violence. He had studied philosophy in Germany and was inspired by the writings of Karl Marx (1818–1883), made famous by his book *Communist Manifesto* (1848), and the political activist and writer Maxim Gorky (1868–1936). Details of the war and some of his own

Boris Pasternak (Hulton Archive / Getty Images)

experiences during the revolution found their way into Pasternak's poetry, as well as his only finished work of fiction, *Doctor Zhivago*. However, as the revolution continued and the brutality of the new government became obvious to him, he slowly retreated from politics. In addition, the Leninist attitudes present in the Russian government ran contrary to Pasternak's. Leninists believed that art should glorify and bolster the government, whereas Pasternak believed that art should seek the higher truths in order to benefit society. After Lenin's death in 1924, when Stalin came to rule, the clamp down on artists became more severe. The communist leaders demanded adherence to their rules and banned writers who did not agree that all art was to be used to promote communist ideals. Pasternak wrote an autobiography in 1931 called *Okhrannaya gramota* (Safe Conduct).

Pressure from government censorship intensified, so that when Pasternak decided to write his anti-Marxist novel, he had to do so in secrecy. When it was finished, he had it smuggled out of

MEDIA ADAPTATIONS

- David Lean directed Robert Bolt's screen version of *Doctor Zhivago* in 1965, which was a box office hit. Omar Sharif played Zhivago, and Julie Christie played Lara. The movie won five Oscars.

- In 2002, *Doctor Zhivago* was adapted to a television script for British television.

- In 2003, *Masterpiece Theatre* presented a television version of *Doctor Zhivago*. Scottish actor Hans Matheson played Zhivago, and Keira Knightley played Lara. This version is available on DVD.

- As of 2007, a Spanish audio tape, *El Doctor Zhivago* (2005), was available. It was narrated by Philip Madoc.

- The Nobel Prize committee maintains a Pasternak web page at http://nobelprize.org/nobel_prizes/literature/laureates/1958/index.html with links to other interesting sites.

the country to Italy, where it was first published in 1957. The following year, Pasternak was awarded the Nobel Prize for Literature, but he was forced to refuse the award by the Russian government. He was thrown out of the official Union of Soviet Writers that same year and was threatened with exile. Instead, Pasternak pleaded with officials to allow him to remain in his beloved homeland. He lived out his remaining years in a colony of artists outside Moscow.

Pasternak was married twice. In 1922, he married Evgeniia Vladimirovna Lourie. They had one son. The marriage ended nine years later. In 1934, he married Zinaida Nikolaevna Neigauz, upon whom the character of Lara in Pasternak's novel is based.

Pasternak died on May 30, 1960, of lung cancer. In 1988, the Union of Soviet Writers reinstated him, which opened the path for Pasternak's son to officially accept his father's Nobel Prize the following year.

PLOT SUMMARY

Chapter One: The Five-O'clock Express

Paternak's *Doctor Zhivago* begins with the funeral of the protagonist's mother. Yura Zhivago (who is called Yurii once he becomes an adult) is taken away by his maternal uncle, Nikolai Vedeniapin (or Uncle Kolia), whom Yura admires. Nikolai is a defrocked priest, cast out of the priesthood supposedly for his radical political views. He becomes, later in this book, a well known author, mostly of philosophy tinged with political theories.

Background information is given. Yura's father, a businessman, was very wealthy. Many buildings and streets in the town where Yura lived with his mother were named Zhivago, illustrating the influence that his father once had. Yura's father, however, was seldom at home. Yura discovers later that his father had a mistress and squandered the family's wealth. Yura's sickly mother often traveled in southern European countries in an attempt to cure her consumption. Yura, by the time of his mother's death, was used to living in the homes of many different people.

The chapter jumps ahead to 1903. Yura is still with his uncle. They visit another author whose work Uncle Nikolai has edited. Nikolai reminds Yura of his mother, "his mind moved with freedom and welcomed the unfamiliar." In this chapter, Pasternak initiates one of the main themes of this novel: the importance of the individual. Uncle Nikolai explains his belief that only the individual can express truth. But political thought in Russia at the time so subscribes to the group that Nikolai fears that outcome will be mediocrity. Uncle Nikolai suspects that many people grab on to one idea and stick with it regardless of its value.

Also introduced in this chapter is Misha Gordon, a boy about the same age as Yura who becomes Yura's lifelong friend. Misha is traveling with his father on a train. On this same train is Yura Zhivago's father, who eventually throws himself onto the tracks, committing suicide. Also on this train is a character that prevails in the novel, Victor Komarovsky, a lawyer. It is suspected that Komarovsky affected Yura's father's suicide, by fostering the older man's excessive drinking and leading him to financial ruin.

Chapter Two: A Girl from a Different World

An indeterminate amount of time has passed. Larisa (Lara) Guishar and her family, the widowed Amalia Guishar (Lara's mother) and Rodia (Lara's younger brother), are introduced. Russia is involved in a war with Japan (which Russia will lose) and the somewhat unorganized and sporadic revolutions of its citizens. The Guishars have just arrived in Moscow. Amalia has some money left from her husband's estate, but the sum is fast dwindling. She has asked Victor Komarovsky (who was at one time her husband's lawyer) to help her invest the money. Amalia buys a sewing shop and lives in one of the poorest sections of the city in order to extend her funds. She also has an affair with Komarovsky.

Lara, sixteen years old and just coming into her womanhood, notices the way Komarovsky looks at her, and this makes her very uncomfortable. However, as Komarovsky continues to focus on her, Lara is torn between hating him and being flattered by his attention. Komarovsky takes her out to dinner one night and makes a sexual pass at her. She turns him down initially but later gives in. Komarovsky is fascinated by Lara for her beauty, her intelligence, and her wild nature. Komarovsky scares Lara, and she despises herself for giving in to him.

Later in the chapter, Kuprian Tiverzin is introduced. He will later become a revolutionary. At this point of the story, Tiverzin becomes involved in one of the first labor strikes as the revolution gains momentum. Tiverzin has been identified as one of the leaders of the strike, and his mother warns him to run away. Pasha Antipov, the son of one of the managers of the railroad, seeks Tiverzin's mother, asking her to give him shelter since his father has been imprisoned.

A mass demonstration is organized; throngs of people crowd the streets, intent on rallying and protesting in front of the tsar's winter quarters. Tiverzin's mother takes Pasha with her as she joins the marchers. Cossacks, the tsar's military guard, surround the demonstrators and shoot indiscriminately into the crowd. Tiverzin's mother is punched in the back but not seriously injured.

Yura's uncle Nikolai has been published and is now very much in demand, giving lectures and teaching courses. He has left Yura in the care of the Gromekos. Alexander Gromeko is a chemistry professor. His wife, Anna, is the daughter of Ivan Krueger, a rich industrialist. The Gromekos have a daughter, Antonina (Tonia). Misha Gordon has also been left with the Gromekos, so Yura, Tonia, and Misha all live together through their adolescent years. Nikolai comments on how the three teens share beliefs about sexuality, how they think it is vulgar. Nikolai believes the youths have gone too far in their condemnation of sex.

Lara meets Pasha and notices that the boy has a crush on her. She watches him play with friends as if they are soldiers.

Lara hears that the area of Moscow where she and her mother live will soon be under attack. She and her mother pack their things and move to a cheap hotel outside the district. Lara is happy about the move because she hopes this will keep Komarovsky away from her. Her mother, however, is disheartened when her workers go on strike. Lara fears that her mother may attempt suicide if she learns that her daughter is having an affair with Komarovsky.

One night, a doctor who is visiting the Gromekos (where Yura is living) is called to the hotel. Amalia Guishar has indeed attempted suicide by swallowing iodine. No motive is mentioned. Since the doctor was at the Gromekos when he was called, Yura and Misha ask to go to the hotel with the doctor for the adventure of it. This is the first time that Yura sets eyes on Lara, and he is taken by her, although he does not speak to her. Yura also senses that there is some dark secret between Lara and Komarovsky, but this intuition only makes Lara more intriguing. Yura also realizes that his physical response to Lara is related to what he, Misha, and Tonia have been talking about, the vulgar or sexual side of human interactions. Misha tells Yura that Komarovsky acted as Yura's father's lawyer, the man who might have been responsible for Yura's father's suicide.

Chapter Three: The Sventitskys' Christmas Party

Yura is in college studying medicine. He tries to improve the health of Mrs. Gromeko, who has become bedridden. During one of the last talks she has with the two young adults, Anna Gromeko tells Tonia and Yura to become engaged. They are made for one another, Tonia's mother tells them.

Lara has moved in with a friend's family, the Kologrivovas, in an attempt to get away from her mother and Komarovsky. She is working as a tutor for the Kologrivovas's youngest daughter. While there, Lara's brother shows up and asks Lara for money. The only source of help that Lara can think of is Komarovsky. She finds out that he is at a Christmas Party, and Lara goes there uninvited. She has a gun with her. She sees Komarovsky playing cards with some other men. Lara shoots at him but misses, the bullet grazes another man's hand. Komarovsky later goes to court with Lara and helps to clear the case. Yura and Tonia were at the Christmas party, too. Yura is once again startled by and attracted to Lara. When Yura and Tonia return home, they find that Tonia's mother has died.

Chapter Four: The Hour of the Inevitable

Lara and Pasha marry. Both have now graduated from college and decide to take jobs in a small town, Yuriatin, in the Ural Mountains in western Russia. Meanwhile, Yura has his medical degree. Referred to as Doctor Zhivago or Yurii, he is working at a hospital on the front lines of World War I, where Russian and Hungarian troops are fighting. Yurii is married to Tonia, and she is about to have their first baby, a son.

Lara and Pasha also have a child, a three-year-old daughter, Katenka. Pasha is uncomfortable in his married life and decides to join the army. After joining, Pasha realizes he has made a mistake but it is too late to turn back. Later, rumors spread that Pasha has been taken prisoner. Other rumors state that he is dead. Lara, in the meantime, has decided to go to the frontlines to look for Pasha, to discover the truth of his whereabouts. She ends up working as a nurse in the same hospital as Yurii. At this point in the story, the human cost of war is unveiled as wounded soldiers flood the base hospitals. When Yurii is hit with shrapnel, Lara takes care of his wounds.

Chapter Five: Farewell to the Old

Chapter five begins in the town of Meliuzeievo. Lieutenant Galiullin is working with Yurii and Lara. Galiullin was once a friend of Lara's husband, Pasha. He has told Lara that Pasha was taken prisoner, but Lara does not believe it.

In a letter to Tonia, Yurii has mentioned Lara. In Tonia's reply, she insinuates that Yurii has fallen for Lara. Yurii is embarrassed about leading Tonia to feel this way, and he decides to make sure that Lara does not believe the same thing. Yurii appears unaware of his own emotions.

Meanwhile, revolutions and counter-revolutions occur all over the country. Government officials become increasingly ruthless, determined to stop the insurgencies. Court martials and death penalties that had once been rescinded are now in practice again. There are thousands of deserters: Soldiers are tired of war. Dissention brews among the Bolsheviks and between the Red and the White armies.

Yurii is distracted by wanting to confront Lara and make sure that she has not interpreted any of their conversations as his having an interest in her. In the midst of a philosophical discussion with Lara, however, Yurii exposes his true feelings toward her, as if the words just come out through their own will. He is embarrassed. Lara tells him to stop talking. She is about to leave to go back to Yuriatin. Yurii plans to return to Moscow. They part without further discussion.

Chapter Six: The Moscow Encampment

Yurii is home at last in Moscow. He must reacquaint himself with his son. His wife and her father are living in an old family home. Food is scarce and so is fuel; sporadic fighting breaks out in the streets. Yurii is reunited with old friends, but he is disappointed by how dull everyone looks. They are afraid of new ideas. Misha Gordon is there, playing a role that seems artificial to Yurii. Even Yurii's uncle Nikolai appears detached from what is happening around him. Yurii feels like a stranger in Moscow, someone who cannot fit in.

Much of this chapter deals with the everyday experience of hunting for wood for the furnace and whatever food Yurii and Tonia can find. The struggles are ongoing. However, Yurii holds out hope that this is part of the process of creating a new world order. He still has dreams that the communist system will adjust, and life will become easier.

Yurii contracts typhus, a disease carried by the ticks and fleas on rats. While he is unconscious with fever, his half-brother, Evgraf, brings the family food and other supplies. Yurii does not even know Evgraf. However, Evgraf is well aware of Yurii, having heard of Yurii's good works. Evgraf admires him. When Yurii is healthy again, he realizes that his time in Moscow has come to an end. It is now about 1917, and he does not accommodate the restrictions and the group-think style of the new Soviet Union. Yurii is an individual, and his forward-thinking ideas come up against the prescribed communist values. He and Tonia decide to leave. They plan to live at the estate of Tonia's grandfather, which is close to the town of Yuriatin.

Chapter Seven: Train to the Urals

The train ride is long, uncomfortable, and dangerous. Paranoia reigns everywhere in the government, in the military, and among the citizens. Yurii and his family must travel in a boxcar. The passenger cars are reserved for soldiers who are being taken to the frontlines.

Just before they arrive at Yuriatin, Yurii decides to take a walk at night when the train stops. Guards suspect him of being a spy or a deserter and take him to the man in charge. This man is known by the name Strelnikov. He is feared by everyone. He is a fierce fighter and renowned military strategist. He is also known as a cold-blooded killer. Yurii is interrogated by Strelnikov, who later muses about a wife and daughter who live in Yuriatin. Strelnikov wonders if they are still there. Yurii believes this man is Pasha, Lara's lost husband.

Chapter Eight: Arrival

Yurii is told that the old Krueger place where he and Tonia were heading is now occupied by a man named Mikulitsyn, who was once a manager at Krueger's ironworks. Yurii is warned that Mikulitsyn might turn Yurii and Tonia away. Both Yurii and Tonia are viewed suspiciously because they come from a moneyed class at a time when the labor class and peasants are in power. Yurii also finds out about the partisans, a group of fighters who infiltrate foreign forces (Hungarian and German, for instance) who are attacking the outer fringes of the Soviet Union. One band of the partisans in the area of Yuriatin is called the Forest Brotherhood because they camp in the thick woods in that area. The leader of the Brotherhood is Livka (or Liberius), the son of Mikulitsyn, the man living in the old Krueger estate.

Yurii and his family must go by horse from Yuriatin to the smaller town of Varykino, where Tonia's grandfather's house and factory are located. When they first meet Mikulitsyn in Varykino, Yurii and Tonia are a bit dismayed. Mikulitsyn is afraid that Yurii and Tonia will only bring trouble upon his family. However, he offers to allow them to stay in what used to be an old manager's house behind the main estate.

Yurii and Tonia prepare to spend their time there as farmers, producing their own food, and generally keeping to themselves.

Chapter Nine: Varykino

Yurii and his family have happily settled in Varykino. They are living quietly as farmers, dependent only on the land. One day, while Yurii is visiting the library in Yuriatin, he recognizes Lara, sitting across the room. He decides not to approach her. After she leaves, Yurii walks over to the pile of books that Lara had been reading and notices her address on a piece of papers. Time passes, and one day Yurii decides to find Lara's house on another visit into town. He runs into her and admits that he had seen her earlier. She confesses that she saw him, too. As they drink some tea together in Lara's house, Lara confirms that the man called Strelnikov whom Yurii had met while on the train was indeed Pasha, Lara's husband. She and Pasha have not been together, however, since the day that Pasha left to join the army. Lara has accepted that for some unknown reason, Pasha believes he must not give away his identity. Yurii decides to spend the night, making some excuse to Tonia for not coming home. He feels like a criminal, but he cannot help loving Lara. On his way home one night, a few months later, Yurii is kidnapped by soldiers of the Forest Brotherhood.

Chapter Ten: The Highway

Yurii is taken to a place in Siberia where the Soviet government has been overthrown by banned Cossacks, former political prisoners, and other forgotten soldiers in the Soviet armies. At one time, this far northern area was under the control of a Siberian provisional government, but Yurii learns that it is now under the loose direction of an Admiral Kolchak. This chapter presents background regarding the politicians who are struggling to rule this part of Russia. There are partisans, whose members are loyal to the Red Army, who include Liberius, Tiverzin, and Pasha's father. There are members of the White Army, the more conservative wing of landowners and merchants. One faction fights another. As one citizen puts it, all the good young men have been lost. Those who are left are merely the garbage. Various divisions within these groups argue about what direction they should take.

Chapter Eleven: The Forest Brotherhood

Yurii has been gone from his family for over a year. He is with the partisans, acting as the group's physician. He is not treated as a prisoner, but he knows he cannot leave. He has tried to escape three times. He is constantly on the move with this group. Yurii spends several nights, sleeping in the same trench as Liberius, who keeps him up all night with his chatter. Liberius is addicted to cocaine, which Yurii has kept as a medical treatment for wounded soldiers. Yurii tries to keep his political comments to himself, but at one time, he tells Liberius, who is a zealous communist, that the theory of communism and the practice of it are far different things. Liberius then tells Yurii that rumors have it that Varykino has been attacked and destroyed by the White Army. Yurii fears for his family.

Time passes. Russia experiences the October Revolution on October 25, 1917, during which the Bolsheviks, led by Vladimir Lenin, take over the government.

Chapter Twelve: The Rowan Tree

The White Army has completely surrounded the partisans, who rally and break through the White Army's ranks. Refugees from the villages pour in before the White Army recuperates and cuts off the path, leaving part of the partisans stranded. News arrives that the newest revolution is over. The White Army is in retreat. The partisans join ranks with the Red Army, which is demolishing Kolchak's grip on Siberia. Yurii learns that most of the inhabitants of Varykino escaped before the White Army destroyed the village. Yurii hopes that his family has returned to Moscow and imagines the struggle that Tonia must have endured. Before he was kidnapped, Yurii had learned that Tonia was pregnant. He wonders about her having given birth. Yuriatin, where Lara is, however, appears to be still in tact. Yurii decides one night that he must escape from the partisans.

Chapter Thirteen: Opposite the House of Sculptures

Yurii finally arrives in Yuriatin, a "wild-looking, emaciated man." He has been walking for months. He finds Lara's house empty, but a note from her suggests that she is still in the area. He finally collapses there, falling in and out of dreams. When he finally regains consciousness, he finds he has been unconscious for many days. Lara has been taking care of him. After he

regains his strength, he works at the local hospital. Yurii sends several letters to Tonia and finally receives a reply. She has given birth to a daughter, but the family will soon be deported.

Chapter Fourteen: Return to Varykino

Komarovsky arrives in town. He has come to warn both Lara and Yurii that their names are on a list of suspicious people. They will be imprisoned, maybe even shot, if they do not get away. Komarovsky is in a position of power with the government. He offers to take them away. Lara and Yurii refuse. Instead they decide to move back to the old Krueger place in Varykino, where Yurii and Tonia used to live. They stay there for a month or so, before Komarovsky comes again. Yurii suggests that Lara go with Komarovsky for her daughter's sake. Yurii promises to join them soon. After Lara leaves, Strelnikov (Pasha) shows up. Yurii tells him that Lara loves Pasha above all else. Pasha tells Yurii to run. Government forces are shooting anyone they fear is against them. In the night, Yurii hears a shot. In the morning he finds Pasha dead in the snow, an apparent suicide.

Chapter Fifteen: Conclusion

At the beginning of the New Economic Plan (NEP), Yurii returns to Moscow. The NEP is what the narrator calls "the most ambiguous and hypocritical of all Soviet periods," a time during which the ban on private enterprise is lifted in order to increase Soviet productivity. It is 1922, and Yurii returns to the city a broken man. At his side is a young man, a survivor of all the wars in Siberia, Vasia Brykin, who helps Yurii on their long walk toward Moscow. As time passes, Yurii and Vasia find means of making money. Yurii turns to writing. Vasia watches as Yurii turns more and more inward, away from life and passion.

After settling in, Yurii is further disappointed by his former friends, who are, in Yurii's eyes, mere shadows of the people they once were. Yurii lives with a common-law wife, Marina Markel, who bears him two children. At one point, unable to fit into society and wanting to refresh himself, Yurii goes into seclusion, leaving notes behind to explain his need for privacy. He works on his writing, and one day collapses on the streets, dead. At his funeral, Lara reappears for a few days and then vanishes. The narrator suggests that Lara is taken away to a concentration camp.

Chapter Sixteen: Epilogue

In the summer of 1943, Misha Gordon is involved in World War II. He is talking to a friend about a young girl who has suddenly appeared in his life. The girl's name is Tania, and she has a smile that Gordon finds similar to Yurii's. She tells her story to Gordon and to Evgraf Zhivago, Yurii's half-brother, who is now a general. Tania is an orphan of the war. She never knew her father and was long since separated from her mother, either because her mother was kidnapped or because her mother gave her away. She is not sure. Both men realize that Tania is the daughter of Yurii and Lara. Evgraf promises to take care of her.

Chapter Seventeen: The Poems of Yurii Zhivago

The last section is a collection of Yurii's poems, unaccompanied by narrative or explanation.

CHARACTERS

Pasha Antipov

Pasha Antipov develops a crush on Lara at a very early age. Eventually he marries her in Moscow then shortly afterward they leave for the village of Yuriatin in the Ural Mountains. After fathering a daughter, Pasha becomes restless and believes that joining the army will revive his passion for life. Rumors spread of his death or possible imprisonment. Pasha later turns up as the mysterious Strelnikov, leader of a group of extremists of the new Russian government.

Pasha has decided to completely disconnect from his former life and never sees Lara or his daughter again, although he is often stationed close to Yuriatin, where they live. At the end of the story, Pasha and Yurii meet. Pasha knows that Yurii has had an affair with Lara. But Yurii tells Pasha that Lara admitted to him that it was Pasha to whom she owed her allegiance. Shortly after this, Pasha kills himself.

Vasia Brykin

Vasia Brykin is a young man, the victim of war. He comes across Yurii as the doctor is walking back to Moscow at the end of the story. Vasia becomes disappointed in Yurii as he watches the doctor withdraw from life. Vasia represents the generation of young people who have learned to make a life for themselves in the midst of war, poverty, and stringent government regulations.

Lieutenant Galiullin

Lieutenant Galiullin appears when Lara and Yurii are working in the hospital on the front-lines. He tells Lara that Pasha was not killed but rather was taken prisoner. Galiullin works with Lara and Yurii for awhile then disappears. Later he reappears as a leader of the White Army. Whereas he had at one time considered himself a good friend of Pasha, he ends up the leader of an army that is opposed to Pasha's group.

Misha Gordon

Misha Gordon grew up with Yurii at the Gromekos' house. He is in and out of Yurii's life throughout the novel, one of the few acquaintances of Yurii's still alive at the end. Yurii was once very close to Misha, but as they mature, Yurii finds Misha artificial, willing to go along with the dictates of the government and too afraid to challenge them.

Alexander Gromeko

Alexander Gromeko is Tonia's father. Yurii greatly admires this man, a chemistry professor, who raised him. Alexander comes to live with Yurii and Tonia after they are married. Yurii often turns to Alexander, appreciating the way his father-in-law thinks.

Anna Gromeko

Anna was Tonia's mother and Alexander's wife. She is very loving toward Yurii and suggests that Tonia and Yurii become engaged. Anna dies early in the novel.

Antonina Gromeko

Antonina Gromeko, called Tonia, is Alexander's and Anna's daughter. She is also the granddaughter of Ivan Krueger, the rich industrialist from Varykino, to whose house Tonia and Yurii escape when Moscow's economy collapses. Tonia bears Yurii a son and persuades Yurii to escape from Moscow, fearful that because they both come from moneyed families, they will be persecuted by the new communist regime. Tonia bears up well, knowing that Yurii has fallen in love with Lara, sending notes to Lara when she needs to find out where Yurii is. Tonia spends two uninterrupted periods with Yurii, but for the rest of the novel, Yurii is often absent from her. Tonia becomes pregnant with a second child and gives birth after Yurii is kidnapped by the partisans. She escapes to Moscow but is later deported with the rest of her family, presumably ending up in Paris. She is never heard from after that.

Amalia Guishar

Amalia Guishar, the widow of a rich, French businessman, is the mother of Lara and Rodia. Amalia arrives in Moscow to begin a new life with the help of her husband's old lawyer, Victor Komarovsky. She opens a sewing shop, but when the women in her shop go on strike and when Amalia finds out that Lara is having an affair with Komarovsky, Amalia tries to commit suicide.

Larisa Guishar

Larisa Guishar, called Lara, is sixteen years old when she first appears in this story. She begins an affair with Komarovsky and is both attracted and appalled by it. Later, after she has broken away from his control over her, she tries to kill him.

After graduating from college, Lara asks Pasha to marry her. She then suggests that they get away from Moscow and go to the village of Yuriatin in the Urals. She gives birth to Pasha's child. When Pasha enlists in the army and goes missing, Lara goes to the frontlines to look for him. She meets Yurii there and is drawn to him. The passion she feels for Yurii is almost out of her control, despite the fact that she truly still loves Pasha.

Strong, independent, and intelligent, Lara thrives on her own. However, when Yurii turns up several years later, she cannot resist him. She helps to nurse him back to health and continues her affair with him, even though Yurii's family lives close by. When Yurii goes missing for almost two years, Lara waits for him. She is there when he returns, a sick man, and nurses him back to health again. She lives with Yurii, but she knows that she and he are marked people and could likely be imprisoned or put to death. When Komarovsky comes to Lara and offers her a way out of her predicament, Lara refuses to go with him. Only when she believes that Yurii will follow does Lara leave to preserve her safety and that of her daughter.

Lara reappears at the story's end. By this time Pasha is dead and so is Yurii. Then Lara disappears, supposedly accused of being an enemy of the Soviet government and taken to a concentration camp for women. Readers learn in the epilogue that she gave birth to Yurii's daughter, Tania.

Rodia Guishar

Rodia Guishar is Lara's younger brother. His role in this story is minimal. He gets into trouble and needs money, which forces Lara to turn to Komarovsky.

Uncle Kolia

See Nikolai Vedeniapin

Victor Komarovsky

Victor Komarovsky is portrayed as a cold-blooded businessman who takes advantage of women, especially young ones. It is suggested that he might have caused Yurii's father to lose his fortune and commit suicide. Victor does whatever he needs to do to survive, without consideration of morals or a twinge of conscience. He has an affair with both Lara's mother and Lara. Later he appears in the story when Lara and Yurii have been placed on a list of suspicious persons who will be arrested and imprisoned if not executed. Victor pleads with Lara to go to the farther boundaries of Siberia where he will protect her. Lara does go with him after she is tricked into believing that Yurii will follow. Victor lives with Lara for several years.

Ivan Krueger

Ivan Krueger is Anna Gromeko's rich father and Tonia's grandfather. Ivan made his money in iron and owned a large factory and huge family estate, to which Tonia and Yurii escape when Moscow collapses during the Bolshevik Revolution.

Livka

See Liberius Mikulitsyn

Marina Markel

Marina Markel is the daughter of a man who used to work for Yurii. Upon returning to Moscow at the end of the story, Yurii shares a house with Markel, who treats Yurii as being beneath him. Marina takes pity of Yurii and eventually falls in love with him. They live together as man and wife and Marina bears him two children.

Mikulitsyn

At one time Mikulitsyn was a manager in Ivan Krueger's iron factory in Varykino. When Yurii and Tonia run away from Moscow, they find

Mikulitsyn living in the old Krueger estate. Mikulitsyn is a small time political official in the town and agrees to shelter Yurii and his family.

Liberius Mikulitsyn

Liberius is Mikulitsyn's son, who becomes the leader of the Partisans who kidnap Yurii.

Strelnikov

See Pasha Antipov

Tania

Tania shows up in the Epilogue, when the Soviet Union is fighting in World War II. Misha Gordon comes across her and is drawn to her because of her smile, which Misha compares to the type of smile Yurii had. Tania is interrogated by Evgraf Zhivago, Yurii's half brother, who is now a general in the Soviet military. Upon listening to Tania's story, he realizes that she is the daughter of Yurii and Lara. Evgraf promises to take care of the young girl. Tania remembers her mother but never knew her father.

Kuprian Tiverzin

Kuprian Tiverzin appears in the beginning of the story, one of the instigators of the strikes that sweep across Russia right before the collapse of the Russian tsar. He becomes a leader in the Red Army.

Nikolai Vedeniapin

Nikolai Vedeniapin is Yurii's maternal uncle. In the beginning of the story, Nikolai is Yurii's hero. Nikolai is responsible for the boy after Yurii's father and mother die. However, by the time Yurii is a teen, Nikolai has given Yurii to the Gromekos.

After Nikolai has become a famous author, Yurii is proud of him and the way he thinks. Nikolai has taught Yurii to open his mind to new possibilities, a concept that Yurii develops. However, Nikolai is ultimately a victim of the newly established communistic government that discourages individual thought. In the end, Yurii is disappointed with his uncle.

Andrei Zhivago

Andrei Zhivago, Yurii Zhivago's father, was, at one time, a very rich and influential industrialist. He deserted his family and lived with another woman. Yurii very rarely saw his father. In the first chapter of the story, Andrei commits suicide by throwing himself off a train.

Evgraf Zhivago

Evgraf Zhivago, Yurii's half-brother, is the product of Yurii's father's affair. Evgraf appears at times when Yurii is in trouble, such as when he falls sick with typhus. He also appears at the end of the story as an influential general in the Soviet army. He promises to take care of Tania, the daughter of Yurii and Lara.

Maria Zhivago

Maria Zhivago is Yurii Zhivago's mother. The novel begins with Maria's funeral.

Yura Zhivago

See Yurii Zhivago

Yurii Zhivago

Yurii Zhivago is the protagonist. The novel encompasses Yurii's development from young boyhood to professional doctor. Yurii has high ideals and expects much from what he perceives as the changing political mode of communism, which he expects to take over the world. As the story progresses, however, Yurii sees the ravages of war and the brutal behavior of the leaders. His initial ideals and optimism do not match the reality of how practitioners of communism plan out the lives of the Russian citizens. As the story progresses, Yurii withdraws more and more into himself.

Just as Yurii is torn between the ideals of political theory and the reality of its practice, he is torn between the love for Tonia, his wife, who represents the conventional relationship in marriage, and his love of Lara, which inspires a illicit passion that Yurii likens to natural urgings. Unable to choose between the two women, Yurii eventually withdraws from both of them.

By the end of the story, Yurii has withdrawn from society, from the two women who matter most to him, and from his children and his friends. He has withdrawn from society and into his writing. In the end, he lives in a small room where he sorts through and records his thoughts. He dies on a public sidewalk away from everyone he has ever known.

TOPICS FOR FURTHER STUDY

- Watch any of the televised versions or the 1965 movie adaptation of *Doctor Zhivago* with your class. Then lead a class discussion on how the adaptation varies from the written text. Use some of the following questions to get the discussion going. Then add some of your own questions. What themes are emphasized in the adaptation? Does the movie elicit different responses than the book? Is the characterization of Yurii different in the movie than it is in the novel? What role does the affair between Yurii and Lara play in the movie? How does that differ from the novel? At the end of the discussion, take a poll. Ask your peers which presentation they like best, the novel or the movie, and have them discuss the reasons behind their preference.

- Do a historical presentation in which you compare the timeline in Pasternak's novel, which sometimes runs counter to actual historical events, with the history of the Bolshevik Revolution. Compare a map of old Russia with one of the Soviet Union, and explain the changes in the country. Locate the major battles and explain who fought in them, so your classmates better understand such groups as the Cossacks, the Partisans, and the White and the Red Armies.

- Research communism as a political theory. How is the communist economy supposed to work? Why was there widespread starvation and lack of supplies as Lenin, and then Stalin, tried to set up a communist state in the Soviet Union? Present your findings to your class.

- Take what little description that Pasternak gives his readers of the main characters, Yurii, Lara, and Tonia, and draw sketches or portraits of them as you imagined them. Present your drawings to your class. Ask them how your images compare to what they imagined.

THEMES

Revolution

Revolution effects the violent and sudden change of political order, and Pasternak's novel shows its all-encompassing effects. Various uprisings and civil and world wars create the backdrop for and determine much of the action. The characters' lives are shaped by political upheaval. Revolution heightens the ironic contrast between the initial ideal and the harsh outcome. Revolution causes destruction and suffering and illustrates the contest between powerful groups and individuals. Revolution shows how the ordinary individual is swept along by group action. The characters fall for the hypnotic promise in political rhetoric, and they suffer the ruthless havoc that follows. Pasternak's portrait of revolution and the destruction it caused prevented his novel from being published in his country. He was called a traitor because he presented a critical view of this troubled time in Russian history. This more negative view was not permitted.

But Pasternak also depicts some positives in his portrait of revolution. He shows how passionately people believed in bringing about change and how willing they were to make sacrifices. Although he describes massacres, he also depicts the undying hope that some of the people involved in the revolution could maintain in spite of constant fighting.

Ideal versus Real

When the ideal clashes with the real, which it often does, alternative plans or concepts must be made. One of Pasternak's criticisms of the communist revolution in Russia was that these alternative plans were suppressed. The ideal, as Pasternak demonstrates in this novel, remains a concept or idea; it cannot be realized in actual circumstances. Pasternak presents the ideal in politics, economics, love, and friendship. When his characters attempt to bring the ideal into their lives, they show that it is impossible. Political upheaval brings death as citizens attempt to reshape their government in accord with the highest ideals of socialism and communism. When confronted or obstructed, reform leaders were brutal and resorted to dictatorship. When economic ideals were put in place, businesses dried up, people went hungry, and corruption spread. Even those intellectuals who first discovered and promoted the ideals got lost in their own ideas and stagnated. Zhivago himself discovers that his love relationships are not ideal; with one person he knows the dryness of an intellectual love and with the other the emotional and moral chaos of an illicit affair. People have flaws, Pasternak seems to imply, and ideals may spur them to act, but ideals themselves are not realized in actual experience.

Destruction and Suffering

Destruction and the suffering it causes can bring out the best or the worst in characters, either forcing them to rise as heroes or reducing them to beggars. The war touches everyone; suffering is universal. Characters suffer the loss of loved ones, homes, and basic needs for survival such as food and shelter. Wars provide the most obvious mode of destruction but not all destruction happens on the battlefield. The death of his parents destroys Zhivago's inner peace and security. The loss of wealth leads Zhivago's father to commit suicide. Health is destroyed when rats infest dwellings and easily contaminate the paltry food supply, which spreads disease. There is also the destruction of hope as brutal leaders, drunk on power, make extreme demands on the common people. Throughout all the destruction and suffering, however, Pasternak demonstrates how people adjust. Death of a loved one occurs, but those who are left behind learn to live without that person. Wealth of the bourgeois is stripped, and people learn to live on much less.

Individual versus Group

Socialism and communism promote the group over the individual. Although some ideas in socialism and communism seem to recommend

Actor Omar Sharif as Yuri Zhivago in the 1965 film adaptation of the novel (Hulton Archive / Getty Images)

helping the poor, the country peasants, and the working class, Pasternak, through his protagonist, shows that thinking as a group rather than as individuals leads not only to stagnation but also to poorly conceived ideas. As communism spreads throughout his country, Zhivago feels more and more isolated from his former intellectual friends. They wear masks or enact prescribed roles rather than moving forward, independently. They begin thinking as a group rather than as individuals. As individuals, Zhivago believes, they might have thought up productive solutions. They might have found answers for starvation or ways to avoid or cope with the typhus epidemic. Perhaps these catastrophes could have been avoided if people had not been afraid to think for themselves, Zhivago concludes.

STYLE

The Classic Russian Novel

Pasternak's *Doctor Zhivago* was written at the end of what many critics refer to as the golden

COMPARE & CONTRAST

- **1910s:** Russia suffers through a series of civil revolutions as the people attempt to gain democratic rights and overthrow the rule of the tsar. The country suffers from devastating losses in World War I.

  1950s: Russia (now called the U.S.S.R.) is involved in a cold war with the United States.

  Today: Russia has witnessed the dissolution of the Soviet Union and struggles between communist rule and capitalism. The Russian Orthodox Church declares Nicholas II, the last Russian tsar, a saint.

- **1910s:** Lenin takes Marxist ideas and creates a political philosophy upon which the Soviet Union's Communist Party is based.

  1950s: Mao Zedong is established as the leader of a new communist government in China. In the United States, meanwhile, the U.S. House of Representatives, under the influence of Joseph McCarthy who heads its Committee on Un-American Activities, attempts to purge any communist sympathizers from the country.

  Today: Kim Jong Il, leader of North Korea, struggles to maintain control in his communist country, whose military is one of the world's largest but whose people suffer from starvation.

- **1910s:** There is a political revolution in Russia as the people rebel against the monarchy.

  1950s: Europe and the United States witness the beginnings of a cultural revolution as the younger generation rebels against the ideals of the older generation.

  Today: Many countries witness acts of terrorism, some of which are based on or prompted by particular religious beliefs.

age of Russian literature. Although the novel differs in some ways from the works of Tolstoy and Dostoyevsky, there are enough similarities to see it as following the form of the traditional nineteenth-century Russian novel.

The classic Russian novel provides extensive historical details. It also tends to explore religion and depict its influence on the characters. The large nineteenth-century Russian novel is realistic; it determines to present the authentic truth of real life. Often there are discussions of philosophy and contrasts drawn between the lives of those who dwell in the city and those who make their homes in the country. These novels also distinguish between romantic ideals and brute realism. The story of families is told, their ancestry and their progeny.

Journal Writing

Often in this novel, the narrator or some of the main characters reveal their thoughts as if they were writing in a journal. Quotation marks are even used to imply that the entries were taken directly from the journal. This adds a personal or introspective look into the characters' minds and also adds legitimacy to their comments or observations. It makes readers feel privy to the inner thoughts of the characters. It also helps the reader to imagine that the characters are real. The journal writings add complexity to the characters, as they are not just reacting outwardly to what is happening to them in the story but are also taking the time to think privately through the larger issues that define their experiences.

Some critics have argued that the entire text of *Doctor Zhivago* is one large journal, the exposition of the author's thoughts, thinly clothed in characterization and plot. In other words, the novel does not fit into the expected form. The characters are not fully developed and the plotline barely exists. The main purpose in the novel is to express the ruminations of the author. The dialogue is not so much a form of communication between two characters as it is a monologue that the author records, perhaps for readers, maybe just for himself, as one might write to oneself in a diary.

Epic

Many people have called Pasternak's novel an epic. Traditionally, an epic refers to a long poem, but in modern times, this term has been used to describe novels and even movies. In general, an epic is a large work that encompasses a complex, huge subject. While it may focus on particular individuals, an epic generally tells the story of a people or a race, often including the story of how a given civilization or society had its beginning.

In an epic, the hero represents or endures the challenges that the people of his country face. While Zhivago, toward the end of this novel, feels more like an outsider than a hero leading his people, readers may envision him as a man of or before his time. Zhivago suffers much like most of the people in his country and is not afraid to speak his mind. He sees the foibles of the newly empowered leaders as well as the weaknesses and fears that paralyze many of the intelligentsia. In many ways, Zhivago predicts the fall of the Soviet Union, and in that sense, he may be considered heroic.

An epic may also cover a large geographic area and time. The timeframe of this novel, especially when read in the twenty-first century, adds to its epic quality. Also, the protagonist travels the vast landscape of the Soviet Union from its famous cities of Moscow and St. Petersburg to the remote regions of the Ural Mountains and Siberia.

However, *Doctor Zhivago* fails to meet the definition of an epic in the fact that it does not focus on great, majestic heroes or fantastic kings and warriors, but rather on the ordinary citizen, the true subject of an idealized communist state.

HISTORICAL CONTEXT

Karl Marx (1818–1883)

Pasternak studied philosophy in school while he was in Germany and was interested, as many students were at that time, in the writings of Karl Marx, a German philosopher who supported the working class and whose ideas fueled

the socialist movement that began in the early twentieth century and swept across the world.

In *Economic and Philosophical Manuscripts* (1844) Marx contrasted the different approaches to labor under a capitalist government and a communist one. In Marx's ideal communist environment, laborers worked in a cooperative in which all shared equally in the benefits. Together with Friedrich Engels (1820–1895), Marx published a book from which many revolutionists took their ideas. The *Communist Manifesto* (1847) contained all of Marx's beliefs about the nature of a communist society. This book was written in a simple language, unlike some of Marx's other works. The publication quickly became very popular and was said to be one of the instigations of revolutions that began sweeping across Europe. Marx's most extensive work, on which he devoted the latter years of his life, was the three-volume *Das Kapital* in which Marx delineated a capitalist society and its effects upon workers. Volumes one and two were published in 1885. After Marx's death, Engels put together Marx's notes and published the third volume in 1895.

Maxim Gorky (1868–1936)

Pasternak was also influenced by the political works of Maxim Gorky. Gorky was the pseudonym, taken from the Russian word that means "bitter," used by Aleksei Maksimovich Peshkov. Gorky began as a journalist and spent many years traveling across the vast territory of Russia, and what the standards of living he saw agitated him. To make sense of his experiences and to sort through his responses to them, he began writing fiction, which became instantly popular. His first work, *Sketches and Stories* (1889) tells of the hardships of the working class, of social outcasts, and the poor. Gorky's best known work is a play that he conceived after being encouraged by famed Russian playwright Anton Chekhov. Gorky's play, *The Lower Depths* (1902), received a lot of attention in Russia and also found appreciative audiences in Europe and in the United States.

In the same year that his play was positively received, Gorky was banished to northern Russia because of his political activism and his revolutionary ideas. He joined the leftist group, the Social Democratic Party led by Lenin. Then in 1906, Gorky traveled to the United States to raise money for the Bolsheviks. Later, he would find both the Bolsheviks' and Lenin's theories too harsh, and he placed himself in voluntary exile from his homeland. Gorky returned to Russia, however, before his death. By then Stalin's regime was in full force. Under Stalin, intellectuals and artists, along with many other citizens, were considered suspicious and thousands were executed. When Gorky died suddenly in 1936, rumors spread that he had been poisoned.

Vladimir Lenin (1870–1924)

The first head of the Soviet Union, Vladimir Lenin (whose real name was Vladimir Ilyich Ulyanov) was the son of a Russian official who worked to improve the education of the masses. Lenin's brother was hanged as a terrorist, and his sister, who was considered an accomplice, was exiled. These events are said to have radicalized the intelligent Lenin, turning his thoughts to revolution. A student of Marxism, Lenin was himself exiled in 1895 for five years for contributing to propaganda in favor of revolution. His most famous propaganda pamphlet, "What Is to Be Done," is said to have sparked the 1903 split between the two factions of the Russian Social-Democratic Labour Party. The Mensheviks disagreed with Lenin's philosophy, while the Bolsheviks completely embraced it and made Lenin their leader. Another important and influential writing was Lenin's *Materialism and Empiriocriticism* (1909), which espoused the basic tenets of the Marxist-Leninist political philosophy. Lenin led the October Revolution in 1917, which overran the provisional government and then took power. He was elected chairman of the Council of People's Commissioners. After two assassination attempts on his life, in 1918, Lenin took a heavy handed and deadly approach to suppressing any rebellion against him and his government. Censorship prevented counterrevolutionary publications, and many people suspected of being against Lenin's revolution were executed, deported, or imprisoned. Known as the Red Terror, this systematic abuse of human rights continued for years. Some scholars estimate that approximately 6,300 were killed the first year; by 1921, an estimated 70,000 had been imprisoned in what came to be called the Gulag, a network of labor camps and prisons across remote areas of the country.

Lenin died of a stroke in 1924, and his body went on permanent display in the Lenin Mausoleum in Red Square in Moscow. Later, he was revered as the first leader of a communist state and was honored by statues in almost every Russian city. The name of St. Petersburg was changed to Leningrad until the fall of the Soviet Union in 1991.

Alexander Pushkin (1799–1837)

Considered Russia's greatest poet (and often referred to in Pasternak's book), Pushkin is also credited with establishing Russian literature. Pushkin was the first to use the language of the people in his poetry, thus making it accessible to the general public. He was the child of aristocrats, born in Moscow, and was a published poet by the age of fourteen. His earliest writings were influenced by old Russian fairytales. Pushkin was a radical politically and was later banished from his town because of his philosophy expressed in some of his writing. In 1833, Pushkin published what is considered his most influential work, a novel told in verse, titled *Evgenii Onegin*. His writings, with their mix of satire and drama continued to influence Russian literature for generations.

First Russian Revolution, 1905

Dissatisfaction among Russian workers was festering before 1905. Revolutionaries and those who called for democratic reform were carefully watched and if necessary suppressed, which caused a large emigration of intellectuals, artists, and students from Russia to other European countries. Many of these self-exiled people learned about Karl Marx while living in Germany, France, and Italy, and incorporated his ideas into their own beliefs about political change. In 1898, the Marxist Russian Social-Democratic Labour Party was formed. This party split into two factions in 1902, the Bolsheviks and the Mensheviks. In the following few years, many top Russian officials were assassinated, causing the government to crack down even harder on anyone suspected of being a revolutionary. During this same time, Russia was involved in a losing war with Japan. The people became more and more dissatisfied with the poor conditions of their lives, and even peasants began burning down farms. As a result, a large part of the Russian Army was involved in suppressing fellow citizens.

On January 22, 1905, a quiet protest march in St. Petersburg to complain about the poor living conditions and to ask for voting rights began moving down the streets toward the winter residence of Tsar Nicholas II. The crowd was confronted by armed men on horseback who shot out indiscriminately. In the end, around one thousand people were killed with many more thousands injured. This confrontation and massacre, which became known as Bloody Sunday, sparked even more widespread protests across the country. Workers organized strikes, peasants looted the homes of gentry, and even landowners demanded access to more land. The government made slight concessions, reducing forced labor and insubstantial payments for work and setting up a powerless representative arm of the government, which only infuriated the people further. In October of 1905, the people presented their October Manifesto, which demanded more civil rights.

Nicholas II reluctantly signed the manifesto, giving the people the right to form political parties and take part in the government. Their role was minor, and the Duma (the political house of representatives) was completely suppressed by the tsar a year later. The police and the military quickly took up arms against anyone suspected of political activism, yet the political activists increased their attacks on government officials. However, nothing really changed. The tsar continued his absolute rule, the peasants and laborers continued to suffer and go hungry, and the unrest simmered without a leader or powerful organization to focus its energy.

Russian Revolution of 1917

By 1917, the Russian people were dismayed. Thousands of people had died in Russia's disastrous involvement in World War I. Soldiers were deserting from the army by the thousands. Many returned home and used their weapons to take land they did not own. Food was scarce, and riots broke out in St. Petersburg. Soldiers united with the rioters, and this time they were successful in removing Nicholas II from power. Nicholas was forced to abdicate; he was assassinated the following year, along with all members of his immediate family and some members of the staff. He was the last Russian tsar.

With the tsar gone, a provisional government was established, which leaned toward a democratic form. However, the provisional government only lasted until October when the Bolsheviks, led by Vladimir Lenin, took power and established the Soviet Union in a nearly bloodless coup. This became known as the October Revolution. The Bolsheviks were popular but did not represent the majority of Russian citizens; the Bolsheviks knew that they could not maintain rule by democratic vote, so they declared a dictatorship.

Russian Civil War, 1918–1920

The Bolsheviks were in power in 1918, having created the Union of Soviet Socialist Republics (U.S.S.R.). The Bolsheviks were members of the Russian Social Democratic Workers Party, which supported the political philosophy of Marx and the leadership of Lenin. The army that supported the Bolsheviks was called the Red Army. There was, however, an anti-Bolsheviks group that was referred to as the White Army, which represented the conservative wing of Russian political activists. The Russian Civil War was fought between these two groups. The Red Army had control of the cities of St. Petersburg and Moscow, while the White Army found support in the outlying areas. In order to counter the anti-Bolshevik movement, the Bolsheviks created a secret police organization that captured, imprisoned, and killed anyone suspected of allegiance with the White Army. This became known as the Campaign of Red Terror. The fight between the two armies lasted for two years, then ended when the Red Army was successful in completely putting down the White Army in 1920.

CRITICAL OVERVIEW

Boris Pasternak was awarded the Nobel Prize for literature in 1958, but he was forbidden by the Russian government from accepting it, and *Doctor Zhivago* was initially banned from Russia. Pasternak's novel, however, won widespread acceptance and appreciation all over the world.

In his introduction to the 1991 edition of *Doctor Zhivago*, John Bayley attributes the great force of the novel to the "poetic power of the hero," Yurii Zhivago, and to Pasternak's skill in being "able to fill the book with that richness and minutiae of life which distinguish[es] a great novel." In the 1980s and 1990s, Bayley writes, readers and critics enjoy Pasternak's fiction more for its art than for its politics, while during the 1950s cold war between the Soviet Union and the United States the politics mattered most. "Thirty years or so after the book's first publication in English," Bayley writes, "it is the feeling of poetry it gives which now makes its strongest impression, an impression of continuing vitality and greatness. . . . No longer the explosive cry of freedom and protest from the heart of Stalin's Russia, the book has been published in its own country and been soberly valued and appraised, taking a distinctive and distinguished place in the tradition of Russian literary art." Bayley then explains the novel's uniqueness: *Doctor Zhivago* "is one of those rare works—whether we consider it fiction, poetry, or a kind of imaginary autobiography—which makes no attempt to protect itself against the reactions of the reader. It does not seem to care whether we are moved or unmoved by it; whether we criticize its sentiment and its discourse or whether we surrender to them. Like life itself it goes on its own way, indifferent to the conflicting responses of those who are, as it were, living it. This is an extremely rare quality in a modern novel, for modern fiction is the most self-conscious of art forms."

In *Pasternak: A Critical Study*, Henry Gifford comments on the fact that Pasternak was a poet who wrote a novel. Gifford states, "Though Pasternak would have liked it to be otherwise, he was 'first and last a poet, a lyric poet.' Dramatically, his novel lacks power; it is not everywhere realized with the same adequacy." Yet Gifford praises Pasternak for his "extraordinary keenness and fertility of perception," concluding that "*Doctor Zhivago* is a poet's novel." Finally, Gifford writes: "That intensity is focused finally in the poems proper that form the last section of the book, and for which the novel has provided an elaborate context."

Angela Livingstone, in her critical study of *Doctor Zhivago*, reviews the praise and the troubles that Pasternak experienced when his book was first published. "In 1958," she writes, "people started talking about Pasternak all over the world. Journalists, literary critics, people in public life, writers and readers, all suddenly became interested in this Russian who had written a novel which his own country refused to publish." In Pasternak's own country, *Doctor Zhivago* "was denounced as an anti-Soviet work by large numbers of Soviet citizens who had not read it. Its author was attacked as a traitor and condemned in the Press and at writers' meetings in the most vituperative language." Livingstone adds: "While persecuted by his fellow-countrymen, Pasternak found himself winning friends in the rest of the world, receiving up to seventy

WHAT DO I READ NEXT?

- Pasternak thought of himself primarily as a poet. A selection of his poetry appeared in *Pasternak: Selected Poems*, published in 1992.

- *War and Peace*, first published in a series between 1863 and 1869, covers the lives of several characters and the Russian culture during the Napoleonic wars. Tolstoy, a friend of Pasternak's father, is a Russian literary legend. This novel is an epic recollection of five families and how they were affected by the wars.

- *Crime and Punishment* is another classic Russian novel, written by Fyodor Dostoevsky and first published in 1866. The story takes place in St. Petersburg, Russia, and centers on a rebellious young student who commits a murder. This novel is much more than a murder mystery, however, as Dostoevsky uses the crime and the criminal to portray the ills of society.

- Alexander Solzhenitsyn's novel *One Day in the Life of Ivan Denisovich* (1962) relates the story of a man caught in the oppressive Stalin years in Russia. Like Pasternak, Solzhenitsyn was awarded a Nobel Prize for literature but was forbidden by his government from accepting it.

- A more contemporary award-winning Russian writer is Ludmila Ulitskaya, whose 2005 novella and collection of short stories *Sonechka* relates stories of love, often turned bad. Ulitskaya tells stories of families who try to make their lives work in a terribly dysfunctional society.

foreign letters a day, most of which expressed admiration." Livingstone points out that critics have had trouble categorizing Pasternak's work, not knowing for sure what to call it. She lists various descriptions: "It has been called 'a rhapsody,' 'a kind of morality play,' 'an intro-spective epic,' 'a poet's novel,' 'an apocalyptic poem in the form of a novel,' yet also 'a political novel par excellence,' 'a love story for all time,' as well as 'one of the most original works of modern times.'"

> BUT LARA POINTS OUT TO HIM, JUST THROUGH HER EXISTENCE IN THE SAME ROOM WITH HIM, THAT EMOTIONS ARE NOT THE SAME AS THE INTELLECT AND ARE NOT SO EASILY RULED."

CRITICISM

Joyce Hart

Hart is a freelance writer and published author. In the following essay, she examines possible reasons why Pasternak's protagonist, Yurii, has trouble loving the women in his life.

Pasternak opens his novel *Doctor Zhivago* with the funeral and then the suicide of his pro-tagonist's parents. From the beginning to the end of this story, the author then explores the slow fracturing that tears apart his protagonist, and his protagonist's dreams and relationships. As the outer world of Russian politics falls apart, so too does Zhivago, to the point that he is unable to deal with his society and is incapable of loving the women who affect and support him. The process is slow but devastating.

When readers come to this novel, they quickly become aware of the political struggles that provide the background of the story. The main theme is the struggle between the ideal and the real. The concepts of socialism and commu-nism provide lofty ideals that fill those who believe in them with hope. However, when these same people attempt to put these concepts into practice, the lofty ideals fall apart. There is a disconnect between what people can imagine and what people actually experience.

Examples of failed ideals include the stories about the laborers who strike for better benefits. Other citizens join in when the laborers plan a march, taking their protest to the streets. The main impetus behind the protest is the ever-widening gap between the moneyed class and the working class. To fill this gap, the workers hope to push the people with money out of their positions of power. However, as the story pro-gresses and members of the working class take over, new gaps appear. The new political party splits into two factions, and later another crack appears between party members from the city and their counterparts who are from the distant countryside. These cracks divide again, just like the cracks in a sheet of ice, splitting in pairs that

split again, fracturing what at one time appeared solid. By the end of the novel, the fissures have created chaos, brutality, and a complete break-down of morals, human decency, and common sense. Instead of an equalizing distribution of wealth, the economy is completely destroyed. Starvation engulfs the population. Diseases such as typhus spread through the entire population. Social order, political structure, and the economy crumble. Moreover, familial and psychic frac-tures take place, too. These internal breaks in psyche are particularly noticeable in the protag-onist, Yurii Zhivago.

Zhivago's familial disconnections begin quite dramatically right in the beginning of the novel. Zhivago is orphaned. Then he is abandoned by his beloved and admired uncle. Although he is placed with a considerate and supportive family, Zhivago has no one who claims him as their own. Zhivago's early family situation explains some of his later problems.

While a young boy, Zhivago's intellectual development is encouraged. So on this level, he does quite well. His college work earns him a degree in medicine, which he uses as a profes-sion. He is satisfied with his work, and it pro-vides him the freedom to travel and, for awhile, a fairly comfortable lifestyle. Throughout most of this story, Zhivago's intellect shows no fissures. However, his emotional side is quite weak.

One emotional disconnect in Zhivago is noticed by Nikolai. Nikolai mentions that Zhi-vago and his friends Misha Gordon and Tonia, while they are all still adolescents, declare that everything associated with sexuality should be considered vulgar. Passions are to be controlled by the mind. "It was right," Nikolai thinks to himself, "for adolescents to go through a frenzy of purity, but they were overdoing it a bit." Then Nikolai adds, "For some reason, they called the domain of the sensual, which disturbed them so much, 'vulgar.'" This term, Nikolai states, "was applied to instinct, to pornography, to exploitation of women, and almost to the whole physical world." With this description, Nikolai emphasizes how Zhivago tried to use his well developed intellect to control his emotions.

Later in the novel, readers witness the cracks in Zhivago's thinking when he first comes upon Lara. Zhivago see her when Lara's mother has attempted suicide. Death and suicide are not new experiences for Zhivago, but sexual passion is. When Zhivago encounters Lara, he feels his own sexuality aroused and is startled by it. "His heart was torn by contradictory feelings of a strength he had never experienced before." The narrator then adds: "Here was the very thing which he, Tonia, and Misha had endlessly discussed as 'vulgar,' the force which so frightened and attracted them and which they controlled so easily from a safe distance by words." What Zhivago experiences at that moment when he finds himself aroused by Lara is the beginning of the cracks in his psyche. His emotions are starting to tear him apart. On one side is his rational self, the philosopher and the scientist. This is his intellectual side that has, up to this point, driven him forward. On the other side are his emotions, which have been suppressed in his attempt to look at them, to define them, then to place them on some interior shelf as if he could then forget about them. But Lara points out to him, just through her existence in the same room with him, that emotions are not the same as the intellect and are not so easily ruled. Just like the ideals of political thoughts, the actual implementation of those ideals is a lot more complex than the language that attempts to explain them.

Shortly after this scene, Tonia's mother dies. On her deathbed, she tells Zhivago and Tonia that they should marry because they are made for each other. What is interesting to note here is that Zhivago feels passion when he sees Lara, not Tonia. The relationship that Zhivago has with Tonia is rational or intellectual. They are definitely made for one another, at least on one level. They make the perfect Russian couple, on the outside. They can provide one another with the conventional comforts of marriage. They can set up a home and have children. They can work toward ensuring the health and success of this marriage. They might say that they love one another, but there are those words, again. The words of love do not necessarily imply deep feelings. Somewhere in their psyches, Tonia and Zhivago have defined their relationship and their love, just as they had previously defined passion and then placed it somewhere safe, hoping it remains undisturbed by emotional pangs. After all, they both have defined passion as vulgar—too commonplace or too far beneath the level of their strong intellects. Here readers may surmise from these descriptions that Tonia represents the ideal, while Lara symbolizes the real.

Although Zhivago attempts to suppress his feelings for Lara, Tonia recognizes them in him. Zhivago sends letters to Tonia while he is at the frontlines of the war. Zhivago believes that all he has done is mentioned Lara in his correspondence, as one would mention a colleague. But Tonia senses something underneath the few details that Zhivago presents. Surprised, Zhivago is thrown off balance. If Tonia sees an emotional connection in what he has written, Zhivago worries that Lara might also interpret his friendship in that emotional way. Zhivago appears to be the last one to know his own feelings. Instead of questioning himself, though, he runs to Lara to explain. Then, in the middle of talking to Lara about mundane things, he blurts out how much concern he has for her. Apparently Zhivago's emotions are so tired of being repressed that they come out without his intending it. In spite of his rational attempts to keep his emotions under control, his passion is expressed. He does not understand himself because he has split himself into two—his rational self and his emotional self, strangers to one another.

This split in him plays out through the rest of the novel. Zhivago believes that he loves two women, but in fact, as the story unfolds, readers discover that he really loves neither of them. Zhivago is incapable of loving because he is not a whole being. On the one side he has chosen Tonia, the perfect wife. Tonia stabilizes Zhivago, giving him what he, as a child, never had. On the other side is Lara, who represents freedom, excitement, and eroticism. Whereas Tonia grounds Zhivago in the commonsensical, Lara makes him explode with possibilities. Lara inspires him and renews him, wakes him up. Unfortunately, Zhivago needs both of these women to make him whole, and ironically, because he needs both Tonia and Lara, he will never be whole. He has placed himself in the middle of a contradiction. When he is with Tonia, his relationship with Lara is eclipsed. When he is with Lara, his guilt keeps him from fully engaging in the relationship. So in the end, he separates himself from both of them. He lies to Lara, then sends her away with a man that both of them despise. When he is in a position to reunite with Tonia, he uses only half-hearted measures to find her.

Without a woman in his life, Zhivago becomes not much more than a decrepit beggar. Unable to live alone, he takes a common-law wife, with whom he attempts to replicate his relationship with Tonia. Once again he has a wife and two children. Once again, he has no passion. Marina is a lot like Tonia. She provides him with shelter and makes sure that he is fed. There is no mention of love or even companionship.

It is only at the end of the story, as well as the end of Zhivago's life, that Zhivago attempts to gain some congruence. Just as the fellow countrymen begin to compromise in the political structure in order to regain social health, so too does Zhivago. He makes sure that Marina and the children are taken care of and then he goes off on his own. He must withdraw from his women, his friends, and his society in order to empty his mind of all its random thoughts. He lives in a small room, which appears to him as a "banqueting room of the spirit, a cupboard of mad dreams, a storeroom of revelations." Here Zhivago hopes he can bring his intellect and his emotions together. He has so many thoughts to explore, however, that they constantly compete with one another, trying to come out at the same time. Some of these come out only as brief notes, interrupted sketches, or scribbles in the margins of books. Some, it is suggested, come out in the form of poetry, which is found at the end of this book.

More telling than the poetry, though, might be the thoughts of Lara, who returns during Zhivago's funeral. Lara, who for some unexplained reason has abandoned the child that is the product of her relationship with Zhivago, believes that what she and Zhivago shared was love. However, that love was not so much made up by their own passions as it was willed upon them, as if they were love's insignificant vessels. Maybe she is correct. However, as a vessel, Zhivago is imperfect. He held as much as he could, but that love could not be contained. Lara reveals her thoughts beside Zhivago's casket: Maybe that love was not for them alone to enjoy. Lara thinks, "Perhaps their surrounding world, the strangers they met in the street, the wide expanses they saw on their walks,

the rooms in which they lived or met, took more delight in their love than they themselves did."

As in the beginning of this novel, so too in the end, the outer world and the inner world reflect and affect one another. As chaos reigns outside, so, too, does it rule the inner workings of the psyche. If Zhivago could have healed himself, so too might have his country.

Source: Joyce Hart, Critical Essay on *Doctor Zhivago*, in *Novels for Students*, Thomson Gale, 2008.

Larissa Rudova

In the following chapter excerpt, Rudova offers a general introduction to the novel and gives an overview of its historical context.

On 23 October 1958 Pasternak was awarded the Nobel Prize for Literature for "important achievements both in contemporary lyric poetry and in the field of the great Russian epic tradition" (Conquest 1966, 85). But the award was not altogether a happy event in Pasternak's life because his joy and pride at receiving this high honor were overshadowed by the expectation of imminent trouble with the Soviet authorities and subsequent personal and professional isolation. In his conversation with Max Frankel, the *New York Times* correspondent in Moscow at the time, Pasternak expressed his mixed feelings about the award: "I am extremely happy, but you must understand that I am confident that I will move immediately into this new lonely role, as though it had always been so" (Conquest 1966, 88). Indeed, the Nobel Prize played a double role in Pasternak's literary career: on the one hand, it established his international literary stature, while on the other it made him the target of a slanderous ideological campaign unleashed against him by the Soviet authorities. In order to understand the "Pasternak affair," as it came to be labeled, it is necessary to back up and trace the events that precipitated the new ideological absurdities and excesses triggered against the poet after the recognition of his achievements by the Nobel Committee. Although no Soviet publisher had been willing to publish *Doctor Zhivago*, the Soviet authorities were profoundly irritated by its release in the West and its overwhelming success with the public. It appeared to the party ideologues that the Nobel Prize was awarded to Pasternak solely for his politically provocative interpretation of the revolution in *Doctor Zhivago*, as a part of the West's politics of cold war. The fact that the poet was nominated for the Nobel Prize

PASTERNAK APPROACHES HISTORY AS 'AN IMPRESSIONIST PAINTER,' DE MALLAC WRITES: 'MANY STROKES CREATE THE TOTAL IMPRESSION IF ONE JUST STANDS BACK FAR ENOUGH.' ..."

for his poetry alone first in 1947 and again in 1953 did not seem to bear any significance for the cultural bureaucrats.

Pasternak wrote his novel between 1945 and 1955, but in a sense he had been working on it all his life. Most of his short stories and unfinished fiction in one way or another were geared to culminate in a novel. The first prominent piece that anticipated Pasternak's major project was the short story "Liuvers's Childhood," discussed earlier in this book. The immediate correspondence between *Doctor Zhivago* and this short work lies mainly in the place of the action, the Urals, where Zhenia Liuvers grows up and many of the events of the novel take place. But "Liuvers's Childhood" was also conceived by Pasternak as a chapter of the never-realized novel "Three Names." Important for *Doctor Zhivago*'s genesis is also a prose sketch, "Bezliub'e" ("Without Love"), published in 1918. In this short piece Pasternak outlines one of the essential questions of *Doctor Zhivago* regarding the individual's role in society. The story's two Tatar names, Gimazetdin and Galliula, reappear in the novel. The protagonists of another one of Pasternak's stories, "Aerial Ways," Lelia and Polivanov, anticipate *Doctor Zhivago*'s Lara and Antipov-Strel'nikov. In "Aerial Ways" the theme of the revolution—one of the central themes of the novel—enters Pasternak's fiction for the first time. Both the novella "The Tale" and the novel in verse *Spektorskii* develop around the character Sergei Spektorskii, a writer whose artistic nature and undefined political beliefs make him akin to Iurii Zhivago. By writing "The Tale" Pasternak hoped to develop one of the last chapters of *Spektorskii*, which he tentatively entitled "Revolutsiia" ("Revolution"). He also cherished the dream of using "The Tale" as the beginning of yet another novel. But besides these prose pieces, it is the poet's autobiography *Safe Conduct* that is most profoundly linked with the

themes and central issues of *Doctor Zhivago*. The key questions that Pasternak addresses in *Safe Conduct* reappear in the novel. The concept of art as a fresh and original representation of reality, freedom of the artist in society and his role in it, as well as the artist's moral responsibility before himself and others are among the questions that guide both works. There are also the evolution and fate of his own generation that Pasternak is concerned with in both his autobiography and the novel. But whereas *Safe Conduct* spans the period from Pasternak's childhood to 1931, *Doctor Zhivago* expands and diversifies the historical background against which the ideas and ideals of Pasternak's generation are portrayed. The juxtaposition of two poetic types, the more withdrawn and aesthetically distant Pasternak and the politically involved Mayakovsky, anticipates a similar juxtaposition of characters in the novel, represented by Zhivago and Antipov-Strel'nikov. And finally, *Doctor Zhivago*, like *Safe Conduct*, is autobiographical and informed by Pasternak's personal life experiences.

After *Safe Conduct* Pasternak had not altogether given up his hope of writing a novel, and throughout the 1930s he had made further sketches for one, among them "The Notes of Patrick." Although this piece starts with World War I and then jumps back to the events of 1905, other chapters of the novel that Pasternak worked on were supposed to present a wider historical scene than that. Unfortunately, all this material perished in a fire in 1941. What survives is the cover of Pasternak's projected novel with two crossed out titles on it: "Kogda mal'chiki vyrosli" (When the Boys Grew up) and "Zapiski Zhivul'ta" (The Notes of Zhivul't). It is probably not accidental that the very sound of the name Zhivul't is close to that of Zhivago and that both names are related to the Russian word *zhivoi* (living). This similarity becomes especially meaningful if readers take into account that one of Pasternak's early prose sketches, "Smert' Reliquimini" ("The Death of Reliquimini"), has a variant name, Purvit—for Reliquimini, derived from the distorted French phrase *pour la vie* (for the sake of life, 3:645). The three names, Zhivago, Zhivul't, and Purvit, are then united by their common life-affirming symbolism.

"The Notes of Patrick" contains a range of themes that links it with *Doctor Zhivago*. Its heroine Evgeniia Istomina is reminiscent of Lara. Istomina is married to a teacher of physics and mathematics in the Ural town of Iuriatin, one of the major sights of action in *Doctor Zhivago*. After her husband disappears at the front during World War I, Istomina, like Lara, raises her daughter Katia alone. There are further characters in "The Notes of Patrick" that could be considered models for *Doctor Zhivago*. Among them are Anna Gubertovna (in *Doctor Zhivago* her patronymic is Ivanovna) and Aleksandr Aleksandrovich Gromeko, in whose house Patrick grows up. As in the novel, the Gromekos in "The Notes of Patrick" have a daughter, Tonia, whom Patrick/Zhivago marries. Other similarities that reach beyond the scope of this discussion further enhance the closeness between the two works.

Pasternak began work on *Doctor Zhivago* in the winter of 1945–1946, and his correspondence of that period reflects his intensive work on the novel. On 1 February 1946 he wrote to Olga Freidenberg that he was writing a "large prose" in which he wanted to express things most important to him. By October 1946 he informed her that he had already written a part of novel titled "Mal'chiki i devochki" (Boys and Girls), which spans the period 1902–1946. The degree of involvement with and excitement about this piece of writing is reflected in a letter to Freidenberg of 13 October 1946, in which Pasternak calls "Boys and Girls" his "first real work" and outlines some issues it was going to address: Christianity, nationalism, and the Jewish question. Despite his intense translation work at that time, Pasternak made progress on his novel, which later was titled *Doctor Zhivago*. In the fall of 1948 he reported to Freidenberg that the first part of the book was finished and he was planning for the second, which would cover the period from 1917 to 1945. The letter contains major points of the plot development that indeed later fully materialized in the completed novel: the characters Gordon and Dudorov were to survive their friend Zhivago, who was to die in 1929, leaving behind a notebook filled with poems, which would appear in a separate chapter.

Although the literary-political situation in the Soviet Union continued to be oppressive and Pasternak was systematically attacked in the press despite the fact that he was not publishing new works, on 27 December 1974 he signed a contract with the journal *New World* for the novel with the working title "Innokentii Dudorov," earlier called "Boys and Girls." The work on the novel did not progress as fast as he had hoped because of the bulk of commissioned translations he had to finish first and because of unexpected personal circumstances. In the fall of 1946 he met Olga Ivinskaia, who worked at the publishing house of *New World* and who soon became his new love. His intimate relationship with Ivinskaia lasted for the rest of his life, and once again he was caught in the moral dilemma of making a choice between his wife and his mistress. The problem was never resolved; he was torn between the two women until his death. Ivinskaia began to play a growing role as Pasternak's literary agent during his lifetime, and she also significantly influenced his creation of the image of Lara. Pasternak's liaison with Ivinskaia became known to the secret police, and in the fall of 1949 she was arrested, charged with anti-Soviet activities, and sentenced to five years in prison camps. She served practically the full term and was released in 1953 under the first amnesty for political prisoners. A few months before her return Pasternak suffered a serious heart attack from which it took him months to recover. On 14 March 1953 Stalin died, and a brief relaxation of the political climate, known as the "thaw," followed. In the April 1954 issue of the literary journal *Znamia* (*Banner*), ten poems from Pasternak's novel-in-progress were published with a short authorial introduction, and Iurii Zhivago's name was mentioned as the "author" of the poems for the first time. Also in 1954 Pasternak's *Hamlet* premiered at the Leningrad Pushkin Theater. But liberalism was never a lasting phenomenon in the Soviet Union, and a swift return to the ideological control of culture and literature was inevitable. When *Doctor Zhivago* was finally finished in 1955, Pasternak encountered the usual obstacles of censorship to publishing his novel.

The history of the publication of *Doctor Zhivago* could well serve as the plot for a political thriller. The general controversies have been aptly described by Robert Conquest in his book *Courage of Genius*. A brief review of them may suffice here in order to provide the background of the reception of the novel in the Soviet Union and abroad. Initially Pasternak submitted the manuscript to the journals *Literaturnaia Moskva* (*Literary Moscow*) and *New World*, but both found problems with its ideological overtones and refused to publish it. Despite the "thaw" and signs of some social criticism in newer works of Soviet literature, Pasternak's novel was an oddity because it challenged "the very theoretical basis of Marxism on which the Soviet state was built" and also seemed to demonstrate that Stalinism was the inevitable result of "the nature of the Bolshevik Party and Soviet power" (Fleishman 1990, 278). In addition to its oppositional ideology, the novel was also unacceptable because it contained "no statement of ultimate truths or prescriptions" (Fleishman 1990, 279).

The decision not to publish *Doctor Zhivago* reflected the government line on preventing any political controversy over intellectuals' desire for more freedom. The party also feared an emergence of antigovernment movements that were fermenting in Eastern Europe at the time (the East German uprising in 1953, the Hungarian struggle, and the unrest in Poland in 1956). What precipitated the liberal moods in Eastern Europe and the Soviet Union was the so-called "secret speech" delivered by the new first secretary of the Communist Party, Nikita Khrushchev, at the Twentieth Party Congress in 1956. At a closed session Khrushchev exposed Stalin's crimes and denounced his cult of personality. The content of the speech became widely known and was viewed by Eastern European as well as Soviet intellectuals as a sign of liberalization. But all such hopes were shattered when the political oppositions in Poland and Hungary were quickly suppressed. Especially after the Hungarian rebellion the Soviet Government had to make sure that the dangerous spirit of freedom did not infect its own ranks and thereafter its stability. Among the first targets of the Khrushchev government in its preventive campaign to purge literature of the dangerous moods of liberalization were the journals *New World* and *Literary Moscow*, known for their liberal inclinations. Under these circumstances the publication of *Doctor Zhivago* in either of these periodicals or any other Soviet publication was out of the question, and in March 1956 Pasternak gave the manuscript to a visiting Italian journalist, Sergio D'Angelo, a member of the Italian Communist Party who was working in Moscow and visited Pasternak in Peredelkino. With Pasternak's permission, D'Angelo sent the manuscript to an Italian publisher with pro-Communist sympathies, Giangiacomo Feltrinelli, who offered to publish the book in an Italian translation. Pasternak was well aware of the consequences of his acceptance of such an offer, but in view of the near impossibility of publishing *Doctor Zhivago* in the Soviet Union and the urgency with which he wanted to see the manuscript published, he was willing to face the wrath of the authorities after the book's publication in the West (Fleishman 1990, 278). Since

Pasternak made no secrets about his plans, the news of the novel's foreign release on 22 November 1957 spread rapidly among the literary circles and alarmed Soviet officials. The entire Soviet press mobilized its forces in a slanderous campaign against him. Pasternak was subject to enormous pressure from the authorities to stop the publication, and the Soviet officials requested that Feltrinelli abandon the book's production. Feltrinelli, however, was determined to publish the novel and pointed out to the Soviets that the English and other editions were already well under way (Conquest 1966, 66).

The rage of the Soviet authorities against *Doctor Zhivago* had been building even up before the novel was published in Italy. What was especially offensive to them was the publication of excerpts from the novel in a Polish literary journal, *Opinie* (*Opinion*), and of a few of Zhivago's Christian poems in the anti-Soviet émigré journal *Grani* (*Landmarks*). Soviet authors were not allowed to publish abroad without permission from the authorities, and so the fact that Pasternak's writing appeared in print in the West without official approval and on such a forbidden topic as Christianity was seen as a slap in the face of the Soviet literary institutions.

The success of the novel following its publication in Italian was sensational. Its first printing of six thousand copies was sold out on the first day. Over the next two years the novel was translated into twenty-four languages. After Pasternak was awarded the Nobel Prize the Union of Soviet Writers, the Communist Party, and various public organizations began systematic attacks against Pasternak. He was expelled from the Union of Soviet Writers and accused of betraying his country and negatively portraying the socialist revolution and Soviet society—despite the fact that the vast majority of the people participating in the campaign had never even read the novel. Some demanded his expulsion from the country. Privately, however, Pasternak received many letters of support and encouragement from admirers. Yet the psychological pressure on him mounted, and he seriously feared deportation to the West. Compared to other options—prison or labor camps—that dissident Soviet writers had to face, deportation to the West seemed to be a mild punishment. Yet Pasternak did not want to leave Russia. These circumstances forced him first to decline the Nobel Prize and then to write a letter to

Khrushchev with a request not to be deported. In this letter he wrote: "I am linked with Russia by my birth, life, and work. I cannot imagine my fate separate from and outside Russia.... A departure beyond the borders of my country would for me be equivalent to death ..." (Conquest 1966, 178). Pasternak was also forced to write to *Pravda* a letter of renunciation of the Nobel Prize. This letter is an interesting document. Despite its generally apologetic tone, it contains lines that can be read as a defense of the views expressed in the novel: "It seems that I assert that any revolution is a historically illegitimate phenomenon, that the October Revolution was one of such illegitimate events, that it brought Russia misfortunes and led the Russian traditional intelligentsia to its destruction. It is clear to me that I cannot accept such assertions carried to absurdity" (Conquest 1966, 181). Although Pasternak was allowed to stay in Russia and retain both his apartment in Moscow and the house in Peredelkino, the attacks against him never stopped. His last collection of verse, *Kogda razguliaetsia* (*When the Weather Clears*), includes a poem, "Nobelevskaia premiia" ("The Nobel Prize," 1959), that describes his feelings about that hard time: "I am lost like a beast in its bay. / There are people out there, freedom, light, / But behind me there is the noise of the hounds, / There is no escape for me. / ... How did I dare to write such malicious offense, / I, a murderer and evildoer, / Who make the whole world weep / At the beauty of my native land."

Whereas the official Soviet press presented *Doctor Zhivago* as an artistically weak novel noted in the West solely for its political content, the reaction of Western critics, although not unanimous, was for the most part enthusiastic. Particularly favorable reviews came from such distinguished writers as the American Edmund Wilson, the Italian Alberto Moravia, and the French Albert Camus and François Mauriac, to name but a few. But the book was also attacked on both artistic and political grounds in the West. Vladimir Nabokov found it weak, and one American Slavic scholar bluntly called it mediocre in his 1959 review "Courage But Not Excellence" (Cornwell 1986, 11–13). There were also opinions voiced by the European orthodox left agreeing with the official Soviet views on history and politics. These critics presented the novel as ignoring or maliciously distorting facts of Soviet history and life (Conquest 1966, 52–53). There was another reason, beyond politics, however, why the case of Pasternak's novel attracted so much attention in the West. In Fleishman's opinion, Pasternak's frame of mind in *Doctor Zhivago* demonstrated "the organic, indissoluble tie with European culture," a feature that Stalin consistently had tried to destroy in the Soviet intelligentsia during his rule (Fleishman 1990, 286–87). Pasternak appeared to Westerners as a symbol of the old culture that had almost completely vanished in the Soviet Union. His refined education and open-mindedness, resistance to official culture, advocation of humanism, and original interpretation of Christianity—"all this was out of keeping with stereotypical portraits of the Soviet intellectual" (Fleishman 1990, 287). These features of *Doctor Zhivago* go against the grain of ideology and cultural assumptions and present a different, older world of free thinking and originality that the Soviet party apparatus was systematically trying to kill in its writers. ...

In *Doctor Zhivago* readers see Russian history from the beginning of the twentieth century to the mid 1950s. Pasternak takes his characters through the turbulent events of the first Russian revolution of 1905, World War I, the February revolution of 1917 that overthrew the monarchy, the October revolution of the same year that installed the Bolshevik regime, and the civil war that followed it. In the conclusion he further, however briefly, treats the first years of building socialism in Russia, and finally, in the epilogue World War II and the postwar situation up to the 1950s are touched upon. This historical sweep and breadth of the novel makes Pasternak's approach to representing history seem problematic for some readers and critics. Isaac Deutscher, for instance, in a highly critical article titled "Pasternak and the Calendar of the Revolution," accuses the author of *Doctor Zhivago* of placing his characters "in the backwoods and backwaters" of history. Deutscher's comparison is to Tolstoy, who, in his celebrated historical epic, *War and Peace,* throws his characters "right onto the stream of history" (Deutscher 1969, 244). Deutscher also points out that whereas in *War and Peace* Tolstoy introduces real historical figures (for example, Czar Aleksandr, Napoleon, and the head of the Russian army, Kutuzov) and describes places of historical significance, Pasternak "has no eye for the historic scene. He runs away from history, just as all the time his chief characters flee from the scourge of revolution" (Deutscher 1969, 245). Deutscher's notion is indeed correct that Pasternak presents his heroes mostly on the periphery of the revolutionary events and introduces no real historical figures into the narrative (the White Army admiral Kolchak fighting in Siberia is perhaps the only historical figure to make a brief appearance in the book). But the critic fails to see that Pasternak was hardly concerned with writing a traditional historical novel or a "political novel *par excellence*" (Deutscher 1969, 241). Pasternak is neither attempting to chronicle history in *Doctor Zhivago,* which is obvious from his somewhat careless use of dates, nor does he intend to write a political indictment of the Soviet regime in a dissident vein à la Solzhenitsyn a short time later. Above all, he is writing "a philosophical novel, a testimony of thought and experience." The focus of Pasternak's exploration is primarily on the individual and, only through the individual and his existential and psychological situation, on history. It is because of this that Pasternak's novel projects a very different sense of history than Tolstoy's—more intimate, personal, and emotionally intense than Tolstoy's, whose philosophical views on the nature of war permeate the novel, and who at the end of *War and Peace* adds an essay on his understanding of the meaning of history. Pasternak approaches history as "an impressionist painter," de Mallac writes: "many strokes create the total impression if one just stands back far enough" (de Mallac 1981, 307).

The impressionistic perception, conceptualization, and projection of history are consistent features of the novel. Although views on history and the revolution are expressed by many characters in the book, the voice that readers hear most prominently is Pasternak's own. Through Iurii, a thinly veiled persona of the author himself, readers follow the evolution of Pasternak's views on Russia's revolutionary history, the view through the eyes of a sophisticated, sensitive, and talented artist, very much like Pasternak himself.

When the provisional government assumes power in Russia after the abdication of the czar, Iurii is at the front, in Meliuzeevo, far away from the events of the revolution. He responds to it with enthusiasm and idealism. The joy of freedom is reflected in his conversation with Lara: "Just think of it, the roof has been torn off Russia and we, with all the people, are out in the open.... Freedom! Real freedom...out of the blue, beyond our expectation, freedom by accident, through a misunderstanding." The language of

Zhivago's welcoming of the revolution is significant both for understanding his views as well as the novel's whole meaning. What Iurii's words emphasize is the elemental nature of the events, their accidental occurrence and ambiguity, in fact a possibility of their being a misunderstanding. These aspects stand behind much of the novel's own plot progression. For Zhivago the revolution has a providential quality, and he elevates it almost to divine status in his vision of universal harmony ("mother Russia ... is talking and she cannot stop. ... And it is not only people that are talking. Stars and trees got together and are talking, and night flowers are philosophizing, and stone houses hold meetings"). In his interpretation the revolution acquires an abstract quality. Indeed, with Zhivago on the periphery of the events in Meliuzeevo, readers do feel far removed from the violent historical reality. This feeling is intensified by Zhivago's "double vision" of the revolution: "Everyone has been through two revolutions: first his own, personal as well as another, the general one." It is the personal one that readers are mostly exposed to, and the general one reveals itself through the multiplicity of the characters' voices in the novel.

Pasternak does not in any way promote Zhivago's ideas about the revolution as the correct ones. On the contrary, he emphasizes the fact that his protagonist expresses the view of the Russian professional middle class, which constituted the core of the intelligentsia. He makes it clear in the novel that Zhivago's response to the revolution has two sides. The first could be described as the "poetics of home," comfort, stability, "goodheartedness and purity." Zhivago is very concerned that this cozy life might vanish and "wanted it safe and whole." The second side reveals his naive and romantic attraction to the revolution, identifying it with the freedom-loving ideals of his youth and at the same time being fascinated by its new, unknown drifts. For Zhivago these new elements, while associated with blood and violence, also symbolize real life and a real change for Russia. With fascination and respect, he describes the Bolsheviks as heroes and "experts of [this] elemental power" of the revolution, guiding the people to the future.

In part 2 Zhivago's prerevolutionary world of comfort and high values is juxtaposed to the world of the revolutionary railroad workers. Once again it is an individual perception that Pasternak focuses on. Untouched by good fortune, the railroad worker Kupriian Tiverzin lives in a world of injustice, "of ignominy and fraud." In his revolutionary dreams, in the name of the workingmen, he rises against his oppressors, among whom Zhivago (by virtue of his class) might very well be placed.

Iurii's initial desire to include himself with the "people" is problematic from the very beginning. The people—like Tiverzin—are not eager to include him in their ranks. Later in the novel the growing polarization of the two worlds after the socialist revolution—the working class on the one hand, professional and industrial bourgeoisie on the other—is explicitly commented on by the author: "Old life and the new order did not correspond to each other. They were not yet openly hostile to each other, as when the civil war broke out a year later but there was a lack of connection between the two. These were two sides confronting each other.... " The gap between the social classes is tangible even before the October revolution, and therefore, it is not surprising that Zhivago senses it and, while preaching socialism as the road toward an amelioration of society, foresees the imminent death of his class ("he considered himself and his own class doomed"). This, however, does not change his deep spiritual commitment to the people and their future well-being. A Christian touch of self-sacrifice, reminiscent of *Lieutenant Schmidt,* sounds in his words when he is talking about his fate, which he is willing to accept without resistance in the name of the suffering Russian people: "[He] was ready to sacrifice himself for the general good." In these words readers hear an echo of Vedeniapin' revolutionary utopianism ("[it] will lead people toward the light") and his total inability to connect theory with real life. In fact, both uncle and nephew preach the radical and complete liberation from the old system but have only a vague idea of the new one. Vedeniapin's metaphor of the complete destruction of the old building corresponds in its essence to the medical language of Zhivago's ecstatic welcoming of the October revolution. Zhivago marvels at the Bolsheviks;ap ability to "cut out the old stinking ulcers" at once Vedeniapin's and Zhivago's attitudes toward the revolution are romantic and idealistic. Their political naïveté points to Pasternak's earlier hero Lieutenant Schmidt and even to Pasternak himself at the time of the February revolution.

As the narrative develops, external events are given more attention and gradually influence Zhivago's attitude toward the new regime. As his hardships worsen, the pulse of history is felt more and more strongly and "manifests itself as civil war and domestic strife, in a 'permanent revolution' which is at once material and spiritual warfare, a total struggle without quarter or truce" (Poggioli 1958, 551). Material deprivations, hunger, epidemics, brutality, and the new bureaucracy of the Bolshevik regime all inexorably lead Zhivago to change his views on the revolution. Assuming that he was ready for self-sacrifice and suffering, is his subsequent disappointment with Bolshevism inevitable?

The answer to this question lies in Zhivago's philosophy and his idealistic expectations of new freedoms and enlightened liberalism for all people of Russia. Unfortunately, however, liberalism was scarcely on the Bolsheviks' agenda. Their priorities were the establishment of their dictatorship by means of a victorious class struggle and reshaping the new society according to their uniform ideological pattern. The October revolution that actually took place was not Zhivago's revolution, and he was quick to realize it. During his trip to the Urals he comes in contact with people outside his own social circle for the first time in his life. What he sees in the Russian provinces and hears from people only confirms his view that Marxism, which lies at the foundation of Bolshevism, is an abstract, self-centered teaching, far removed from life, and as handled by the new regime it becomes not a tool of liberation but an effective means of political suppression. Ordinary people have been fooled by it as much as the intellectuals. As Zhivago's cotraveler, the co-operativist Kostoed observes, the hope of the people for land and freedom was deceived, and instead, "from the fetters of the old government oppression, the people fell under the much harsher yoke of the new revolutionary superstate." The omnipresent oppression under the new regime is a major blow to Zhivago's liberal attitudes and leads him to reject the dictatorship of the Bolsheviks as a form of transition to a happier socialist society: "nothing can be gained by brute force. One should be drawn to good by goodness."

After the horrors of the civil war, which he experienced during his forced service with the partisans, Zhivago's sense of history and the revolution undergoes a drastic change. Now he clearly sees that his hope for freedom will not materialize in a state based on political dogma and oppression.

He cannot expect anything from those "active, limited and fanatical geniuses," as he calls the revolutionaries, who are determined to transform Russia according to their will. From now on they will perpetually be called "bright heroes," whereas he will be stigmatized as a "petty soul that sides with obscurantism and the oppression of the people." This hurts and angers Iurii. But he is not the only one disturbed by the new people in power. Along with Iurii, the author himself responds to the powerful revolutionary force that from now on is going to determine the destiny of the Russian people. And therefore the portraits of the old revolutionaries Tiverzin and Antipov appear in a telling grotesque light: "Counted among gods at whose feet the revolution laid its gifts and sacrifices, they sat silent, as strong idols from whom political conceit annihilated all life and humanity."

After the true nature of the Bolsheviks begins to emerge even more clearly, Zhivago justifiably expects that in the process of altering the social order, they will eradicate any hint at individuality in the building of their monolith ideological state. The threat to his humanistic ideal of freedom is real, and he sees only two outlets for himself: art and love. Reality itself forces him to create his own castle, a world within the world of the revolution. To preserve his value system, he must reject the historical context. In that, Zhivago can be perceived as both "the weakest victim" and the most "elusive enemy" (Poggioli 1958, 551) of the Bolshevik regime. Art and love become his islands amid the hostile stormy waters. But despite his proud isolation as an artist without any political cause, he remains a threat to the new regime as long as he speaks his idiom and exists on the margins of the social system. While readers may interpret Zhivago's retreat from the world of socialism into the world of his ideas as a capitulation before the revolution and therefore pronounce the death of his whole class, there is an optimistic message in the novel that must not be ignored. Even under Soviet socialism Zhivago remains spiritually free and faithful to his moral and intellectual principles. It is these principles that Pasternak was interested in presenting in his novel and for the sake of which he avoided the presentation of history through dates, facts, and actual personalities. Instead, he foregrounds the individual perception and experience of history. Pasternak's novel is "a spiritual document of great significance" (Poggioli 1958, 551) in which the self occupies center stage and is elevated above history. ...

Source: Larissa Rudova, "*Doctor Zhivago*," in *Understanding Boris Pasternak*, University of South Carolina Press, 1997, pp. 137–42, 160–65.

SOURCES

Bayley, John, "Introduction," in *Doctor Zhivago*, Pantheon Books, 1991, pp. xii, xiii.

Gifford, Henry, "*Doctor Zhivago*," in *Pasternak: A Critical Study*, Cambridge University Press, 1977, p. 197.

Livingstone, Angela, "Reception, Importance, and Position of *Doctor Zhivago*," in *Doctor Zhivago*, Cambridge University Press, 1989, pp. 1, 2. 5.

Pasternak, Boris, *Doctor Zhivago*, Pantheon Books, 1958.

FURTHER READING

Barnes, Christopher, *Boris Pasternak: A Literary Biography*, Cambridge University Press, 2005.
Using both personal accounts and family archives, Barnes depicts in this two-volume work both the personal and the political side of this great Russian writer.

Fitzpatrick, Sheila, *The Russian Revolution*, Oxford University Press, 2001.
The Russian Revolution was supposed to bring about a model Marxist political form of government. Instead, the revolution caused great suffering among its intended beneficiaries. The research done by Fitzpatrick occurred after the fall of the Soviet Union, which opened up archives that had been closed to all historians, including Russian researchers, until this time.

Fleishman, Lazar, *Boris Pasternak: The Poet and His Politics*, Harvard University Press, 1990.
Having researched Pasternak's politics in preparation for writing this book, Fleishman gives the reader an understanding of the times in which Pasternak lived and an appreciation of the courage Pasternak displayed in speaking his mind and standing up to government censorship.

Reid, Christopher, *From Tsar to Soviets: The Russian People and Their Revolution, 1917–21*, Oxford University Press, 1996.
Reid presents the Russian Revolution through the eyes of the people, their struggles and their dreams. With a very readable style, Reid presents the political, economical, and social environment during the time of the Russian

tsars and how the pressure built up in the citizenry, leading them to revolt. This book also attempts to explain how the Bolshevik goals differed from those of the citizens during the ensuing revolution.

Rudova, Larissa, *Understanding Boris Pasternak*, University of South Carolina Press, 1997.

In this book, Rudova expands on the merits of Pasternak, claiming that Pasternak's literary ability and claim to fame extend well beyond this one publication. After all, in Russia, Pasternak is known first as a poet. Rudova explores Pasternak's proficiency and artistry foremost in this genre.

Humboldt's Gift

SAUL BELLOW

1975

Humboldt's Gift (1975), by Saul Bellow, is the eighth novel published by the celebrated and prolific Jewish-American author. *Humboldt's Gift* won the Pulitzer Prize in 1976 and contributed to Bellow's winning the Nobel Prize for Literature in the same year. This novel takes place in Chicago, like many of Bellow's works, and is widely recognized as a *roman à clef*—a fictional story about real events—concerning Bellow's friend, Delmore Schwartz, a Jewish-American poet who lived and died in New York City. Humboldt's infamous life of brilliant success and crashing failure closely parallels that of Schwartz. His name appears to be a reference to Alexander von Humboldt, a famous nineteenth-century Prussian naturalist and explorer.

At its heart, *Humboldt's Gift* is less about Humboldt and more about the narrator, Charlie Citrine, who is a dear friend to Humboldt and strongly contrasts with the poet's personality. Charlie drifts through life, lost in his own thoughts, which are often philosophical and high-minded. He is an accidental success and now preyed upon by any who wish to use him or his money in the twilight of his literary career. *Humboldt's Gift* is a novel about transformation: bereft of his fortune, Charlie finally finds the strength of spirit—which Humboldt said he had—to stand up to his users and do exactly what he wants to with his life.

Saul Bellow (*Hulton Archive / Getty Images*)

AUTHOR BIOGRAPHY

Saul Bellow was born Solomon Bellows in Lachine, Quebec (a suburb of Montreal), the youngest of four children. His original birth certificate was lost in a fire, but his birthday is generally recognized as June 10, 1915. His parents, Abraham and Liza, emigrated from Russia to Canada not long before Bellow was born. Just like Charlie in *Humboldt's Gift*, Bellow suffered from tuberculosis at age eight and stayed at a hospital for many months. In 1924, his family moved from their impoverished neighborhood in Quebec to a tenement in Chicago. Eight years later, at age seventeen, Bellow was devastated by the death of his mother, to whom he was close. He started college in 1933 at the University of Chicago, later transferring to Northwestern University. He graduated with honors in 1937 with a bachelor's degree in sociology and anthropology. Bellow started graduate work at the University of Wisconsin, but over Christmas vacation, he married Anita Goshkin and abandoned his studies. He really wanted to be a writer instead of an anthropologist. Bellow took a number of

editorial and teaching jobs until the outbreak of World War II. He served in the Merchant Marine from 1944 to 1945 after being rejected by the Army due to a hernia.

Bellow wrote his first novel, *Dangling Man* (1944), while he was waiting to be drafted into military service for World War II. His second novel, *The Victim*, was published three years later. Most of Bellow's books are connected to or based in Chicago, where his roots run deep. Bellow received a Guggenheim Fellowship in 1948 and spent two years traveling around Europe. There he began work on one of his most famous novels, *The Adventures of Augie March* (1953), which won him the National Book Award in 1954. *Humboldt's Gift* won Bellow the Pulitzer Prize in 1976. He also won the National Book Award for *Herzog* (1964) and *Mr. Sammler's Planet* (1970). Bellow was awarded the Nobel Prize for Literature in 1976 "for the human understanding and subtle analysis of contemporary culture that are combined in his work," as described on his Nobel diploma. He received the National Medal for the Arts in 1988.

Bellow was a prominent Jewish-American postwar writer, but he considered himself an American writer who happened to be Jewish. He moved to Boston in 1993 to get away from the houses of his dead friends in Chicago. He taught at New York University, Bard College, Princeton University, the University of Minnesota, the University of Chicago, and Boston University. Bellow was married five times and had three sons and one daughter. Until his death, Bellow remained an active presence in contemporary literature and politics. He died on April 5, 2005, at age eighty-nine, at his home in Brookline, Massachusetts.

PLOT SUMMARY

Chapters 1–3

Humboldt's Gift begins with an introduction to Von Humboldt Fleisher, who published a popular avant-garde poetry book in the 1930s. Charlie Citrine, fresh out of college and in love with literature, is so moved by this work that he relocates to New York City in 1938 and becomes friends with Humboldt. Humboldt is a famous talker and manic depressive. In the 1940s, Humboldt marries Kathleen, and they move from Greenwich Village to rural New Jersey.

MEDIA ADAPTATIONS

- *Humboldt's Gift* was adapted as an unabridged audio book in 1992 by Blackstone Audiobooks. It is read by Christopher Hurt. As of 2007, it was available on cassette or as an audio file download from online book retailers.

Charlie spends a weekend with Humboldt and Kathleen in September 1952 when Humboldt's mania is in full swing. Humboldt's success is dissipating just as Charlie hits it big with a Broadway play a couple years later. They are estranged, and Humboldt pickets his show, arguing that real intellectuals do not make money.

Humboldt dies of a heart attack at a hotel in the early 1960s. Charlie reads his friend's obituary in the paper and is deeply moved. Humboldt is one of the few people Charlie loves, and he dreams of him often. In the present day, ten years later, Charlie's life is not going well. He has a beautiful girlfriend and is physically fit, but his ex-wife and the IRS are taking all of his money, and he is mentally unchallenged. But it is all about to change, thanks to Humboldt.

Chapters 4–7

Charlie leaves for an appointment and finds his Mercedes-Benz 280 SL smashed up. He is stunned. He knows Rinaldo Cantabile did it because he has been harassing Charlie with late night phone calls. Charlie lost to Cantabile in a poker game but stopped the check he paid him with when he found out that Cantabile was cheating. Charlie asks his doorman, Roland, to flag down a cop and returns to his apartment. Charlie is overwhelmed by the mess this has made of his day. He thinks on his past success; most of his money is gone, the money that came between him and Humboldt. The cops show up and seem amused by Charlie's smashed up car. They also hint that it is mob-related, but Charlie plays dumb.

Around noon, Cantabile calls Charlie, and they set a time and place to meet for Charlie to pay him back in cash. Charlie manages to drive his wrecked car to the bank and from there calls to make an appointment with the dealership. Charlie leaves a message for George, asking him to stay away from the Russian Bath today. He is worried Cantabile will go after George for telling Charlie to stop the check. George set up the poker game to give Charlie a chance to hang out with "real people." Cantabile and his brother Emil crashed the party and openly cheated; everyone noticed, except Charlie. Charlie thinks about asking his gentleman hoodlum friend, Vito Langobardi, at the Downtown Club what he thinks of Cantabile. But at the last minute, Charlie changes his mind because he does not want Vito to think less of him for mixing business and pleasure.

Chapters 8–10

Charlie takes a taxi to the Russian Bath. Inside, Mickey, who runs the concession, assures Charlie that George has already paid his weekly visit. Cantabile pulls up in a white Thunderbird, and Charlie tries to pay him but Cantabile has other plans. They get into the Thunderbird. As Cantabile is driving, Charlie remembers visiting his birth home in Appleton, Wisconsin. Charlie knocked on the door but no one answered so he peeked into the bedroom where he was born. He saw an old fat woman in her underwear. Her husband accosted Charlie, who managed to talk his way out of a beating.

Cantabile takes Charlie to the Playboy Club. They sit at a table with Mike Schneiderman, a gossip columnist, and Bill Latkin, who owes Cantabile a favor. Charlie is supposed to pay Cantabile back publicly, but he fumbles the cue, angering Cantabile. Their next stop is a jewelry dealer's apartment in the Hancock Building. Charlie successfully pays Cantabile this time. They go to a construction site, and Cantabile flies all but two of the fifties from a girder high off the ground. They have dinner at a steakhouse, and Cantabile asks Charlie to help his wife Lucy with her doctoral thesis on Humboldt. Charlie refuses.

Chapters 11–12

Charlie takes the next morning off to recuperate. His latest big work is a series of essays on boredom. He is also increasingly fascinated with Dr. Rudolph Steiner's anthroposophy philosophy.

Charlie takes out all of his Humboldt papers and lies down on his green sofa to think. He now knows that Humboldt was sane at the end of his life and regrets that he ran away that day on 46th Street. He recalls how the *Times* published a two-page obituary for Humboldt. Humboldt lived like Americans expect their poets to live: his great work was followed by personal decay and decline. Americans see poets as essentially useless; however, Humboldt would have been pleased to see his prominence temporarily renewed with such a long obituary.

Chapters 13–17

In November 1952, Humboldt is depressed that Stevenson lost the presidential election. He reveals a scheme to get himself a chair in modern literature at Princeton. Humboldt needs this stability because he is off-balance and cannot write poetry. Charlie agrees to help, and at Humboldt's insistence, they form a blood-brother pact by exchanging blank checks.

Charlie makes the pitch to Professor Ricketts for Humboldt to be given a chair. Ricketts agrees wholeheartedly but says that there is no money. Defeated, Charlie reports this answer to Humboldt. Humboldt is inexplicably elated and leaves immediately for New York City. He visits Wilmoore Longstaff, head of the very rich Belisha Foundation. Longstaff likes Humboldt's plan and promises him the money. Humboldt's chair lasts a few months before the trustees of the Belisha Foundation reject Longstaff's budget. Ricketts offers to find money to keep Humboldt on staff, but Humboldt resigns.

A month later, in March, Humboldt tries to run Kathleen down on a back road in New Jersey. They had all been at a party, and Humboldt became insanely jealous and beat up Kathleen and tossed her into the car. At a stoplight, Kathleen jumped out and then had to leap into a ditch to avoid being run over by her husband. No one yet knew, except Humboldt and Ricketts, that Humboldt was losing his chair.

In May, Humboldt and Kathleen visit Charlie at the cottage where he is rewriting his play, *Von Trenck*, for production. Humboldt warns Charlie not be taken in by the glamour and money. He is extraordinarily paranoid about Kathleen and will not let her out of his sight. Kathleen soon disappears from a restaurant, and Humboldt goes crazy. Just before Labor Day, Humboldt is hauled off to Bellevue Hospital for psychiatric treatment.

He accuses Charlie of breaking his blood oath. Meanwhile, *Von Trenck* is a Broadway hit. Just before Christmas, Demmie and her father die in a plane crash in Colombia, and Charlie spends months looking for her body. Humboldt cashes his blood-brother check, while Charlie is gone and grieving.

Chapters 18–19

In the present day, Cantabile shows up at Charlie's apartment with a woman named Polly Palomino. Cantabile and Polly check out Charlie's apartment and ask about a movie he and Humboldt wrote at Princeton. While they are in the bathroom shaving, Cantabile offers Charlie help with his money and divorce problems, but Charlie is appalled at his suggestions of threats and kidnapping. Polly privately warns Charlie that Cantabile's investments are failing.

Renata picks up Charlie in an old yellow Pontiac. While she drives, Charlie remembers Doris Scheldt, a woman he dated while Renata was mad at him. Though he is attracted to Renata, Charlie knows that she is a gold-digger and her mother is a schemer. His friend George encourages him to settle down with Renata. She lets him off at the county courthouse building for his meeting.

Chapter 20

Charlie remembers how he and Renata met in this building while serving jury duty. Charlie's friend and Renata's divorce lawyer, Alec Szathmar, set them up. On their first date, at a hotel bar, Charlie runs into Naomi Lutz and her father, Doc Lutz. Charlie is sentimental with Naomi, but she says, with affection, that he was too cerebral for her. Renata drinks too much and passes out.

Chapters 21–22

At the courthouse, Charlie meets his legal team, Tomchek and Srole. Charlie insists that he will not give in to Denise anymore. He goes to an empty courtroom to work on his meditation. After a while, Denise appears. They are "dear enemies." She thinks she can fix Charlie and so asks him to marry her again, for the children's sake. Charlie is astonished. Denise gives him an opened letter from Kathleen.

Tomchek, Srole, and Charlie meet Judge Urbanovich in his chambers. Urbanovich says to Charlie, "Now you've had a taste of marriage, the family, middle-class institutions, and you want to drop out. But we can't allow you to dabble like that." The judge threatens to put a bond on Charlie's money. When the meeting is over, Charlie wishes he could take a vow of poverty. But Renata would leave him. Charlie escapes to the bathroom to read Kathleen's letter.

Chapter 23

Kathleen writes to tell Charlie about the death of her second husband, Frank Tigler. She also tells him that the executor of Humboldt's estate is looking for him because Humboldt left him a gift. Charlie meets Pierre Thaxter outside the Art Institute, and they are accosted by Cantabile who forces Charlie into his car. Thaxter goes along for fun. They go to see Stronson who has been caught defrauding the Mafia. Cantabile threatens Stronson's life. An undercover cop arrests Cantabile and Charlie, but Stronson's receptionist, who happens to be Naomi's daughter Maggie, gets Charlie's charges dropped.

Chapter 24

Before leaving town, Charlie visits his anthroposophist mentor, Dr. Scheldt, and they talk about the Exousiai, spirits of form in Jewish mysticism. He takes his daughters to see *Rip Van Winkle*, which he finds very moving. Lish gives her father a note from her mother—Denise has been threatened. Charlie hopes Cantabile gets killed in prison. Lastly, Charlie visits Naomi. They reminisce and catch up. Naomi asks Charlie to help her son, who has no good male role models.

Chapters 25–26

Renata and Charlie stop over in New York City to pick up Humboldt's gift. Renata thinks that this is a prank. But Charlie declares his affection for Humboldt and the poetry he wrote; he comments, "Some say that failure is the only real success in America." They stay at the elegant Plaza Hotel, but Renata can only complain—about their room, about being unmarried, about Humboldt's gift. Charlie arranges to meet Huggins, the executor, at a gallery opening. Huggins tells Charlie that Humboldt's uncle Waldemar has all the papers and that Waldemar is cranky, but Charlie understands that he is just holding out for a visit.

Chapter 27

Charlie makes Renata go with him to Coney Island. She is sore at him for a lot of reasons, mostly for not marrying her. At the retirement home, Charlie is unexpectedly reunited with Menasha Klinger, his family's boarder from the 1920s. Waldemar is glad to have visitors. He is hoping Humboldt's papers are valuable so that he can afford to rebury Humboldt properly and rent a flat. Charlie's gift from Humboldt constitutes a personal letter and two sealed envelopes.

Chapter 28

Humboldt's letter is sane and affectionate. In the letter, Humboldt declares: "For you are, at one and the same time, no good at all and a darling man." He says that he wronged Charlie when he cashed the blood-brother check. His gift is a copyrighted screenplay treatment for a movie about a character loosely based on Charlie's personality. He has also included a copyrighted version of their Princeton idea. Humboldt believes these are worth a lot of money.

Chapter 29

Over lunch, Renata picks on Charlie for being sentimental. She still thinks Humboldt's gift is a joke. He is thrilled that Humboldt still cared for him. The waiter brings Charlie a telephone. Szathmar is calling to warn Charlie that Urbanovich is impounding Charlie's money and that Julius is going to have open-heart surgery soon. Charlie tells Renata that he has to go to Texas. He gives her one thousand dollars to keep her happy in Milan for a week. They go to meet Thaxter in the hotel lobby. Thaxter and Charlie talk about their projects and agree to meet in Madrid. Renata goes to see a movie, and Thaxter leaves for a party.

Chapter 30

Kathleen visits Charlie in the hotel lobby. They discuss the movie treatments that Humboldt has left each of them and realize that they have the same treatment, the one written by Humboldt. Charlie wonders to himself if Humboldt did this to bring them together. Kathleen has already been paid an option for first movie scenario, and she wants to split the money with Charlie.

Chapters 31–32

In Houston, Charlie sees that Julius does not look well and eats too much. He is a very successful real estate investor. Julius is appalled that Charlie does not have any money hidden away. Julius takes Charlie on an excursion to look at some new property he is planning to buy and develop. When they return, Julius says goodbye until after the surgery. He tells Charlie to marry his wife, Hortense, if he dies. After the surgery, Hortense calls to tell Charlie that Julius is fine. Charlie goes to visit him, and Julius asks Charlie to buy him a seascape while in Europe, which is his way of offering money to help his brother. Charlie tells Julius he will be working on his own projects again soon. Hortense and Julius agree to take care of Charlie.

Chapters 33–37

Charlie is troubled by what Renata might be up to in Milan. They agree to meet in Madrid. When Charlie arrives at the Ritz Hotel, he is very eager to reunite with Renata. She is not there. Señora and Roger arrive unannounced to stay with him, while Renata is nowhere to be found. Charlie spends Christmas caring for Roger, who has the flu. After a few days, Señora leaves without warning, and Roger remains in his care. Unable to afford the hotel any longer, Charlie moves with Roger to a *pensión* and pretends to be a widower. Renata has disappeared from Milan, and Charlie is heartbroken by her silent rejection.

Charlie and Roger settle into life at the *pensión* where they get a lot of help and sympathy because they are pretending to grieve. A Danish woman named Rebecca takes a liking to Charlie and tries to convince him to sleep with her. Renata writes to officially tell Charlie that she and Flonzaley married in Milan and are now on their honeymoon. Her letter is both affectionate and scathing. No word is given as to how long he is expected to watch her son.

Charlie sends a letter to Kathleen, hoping she will remember her promise to give him his share of the movie option she sold. His finances in Chicago have worsened to the point that debtors are coming after him. He writes to George asking for help. While he waits, Charlie spends a lot of time alone in his room experimenting with his ability to communicate with the dead, especially his parents, Demmie, and Humboldt. He hopes that Renata will change her mind and return to him, but she only sends postcards to her son. Kathleen replies that she will be stopping in Madrid on her way to Almería. George writes to Charlie from Africa in mid-February. He has not received Charlie's letter yet. George says the Africa trip was miserable. He took Naomi's son, Louie, who whined the whole time. Also, the beryllium deal fell through because there is no mine.

Chapters 38–40

Cantabile shows up at the *pensión*. He tells Charlie about a current movie hit, *Caldofreddo*, which seems to be made from the idea that Charlie and Humboldt wrote at Princeton. Cantabile wants Charlie to sue the producers. Charlie refuses until Cantabile reminds him of Uncle Waldemar. Charlie and Cantabile go to see *Caldofreddo* in Paris, and Charlie affirms that it his and Humboldt's movie idea. Charlie presents his evidence to lawyers the next morning. Charlie offers them an option on the second movie scenario. Cantabile wants in on this deal too, but Charlie refuses him.

Charlie learns that Thaxter was kidnapped in Buenos Aires. He writes to Carl Stewart, Thaxter's editor, stating that he will pay to free his friend. Back in Madrid, the Señora finally picks up Roger.

Kathleen arrives in Madrid. She is on her way to Almería to shoot a historical film. Stewart writes back, informing Charlie that Thaxter is not in danger. Kathleen urges Charlie to choose what he really wants to do now that he does not have any pressing worries. He says that he wants to spend time at the Goetheanum, a center for anthroposophical study in Switzerland. The *Caldofreddo* settlement is eighty thousand dollars plus five thousand dollars to read the other movie treatment. Charlie turns down a lucrative script-writing job to pursue a different life.

Chapter 41

In April, Charlie, Waldemar, and Menasha attend the reburial of Humboldt and his mother at Valhalla Cemetery. Waldemar and Menasha now live in a flat on the Upper West Side because of the *Caldofreddo* settlement. On their way back to the limousine, Menasha spies an early flower, and he asks Charlie what kind it is. Charlie does not know but thinks it must be a crocus.

CHARACTERS

Barbash

Barbash is the American lawyer hired by Cantabile to represent Charlie in the nuisance settlement against the producers of *Caldofreddo*.

Rinaldo Cantabile

Rinaldo Cantabile is a hoodlum with minor Mafia connections who enters Charlie's life after a fateful game of poker at George Swiebel's house. Cantabile chases Charlie down for stopping a check on him and then, seeing a potential cash cow, sticks close to Charlie, trying to help him in his own rough way. Cantabile is married to a well-to-do woman named Lucy who is attending Harvard's Radcliffe College and writing a doctoral thesis on Humboldt. Cantabile hopes to get privileged information from Charlie for his wife, but Charlie refuses to help.

Part of Cantabile's motivation to be tough is the result of an incident fifty years before when his uncle Moochy killed a young man and embarrassed the Cantabile family to the rest of the Mafia. Since then his family has been a laughing stock and mistrusted by other mobsters. Cantabile shows some forethought when he tries to convince the undercover cop at Stronson's office that Charlie has nothing to do with the threats being made on Stronson's life. But Cantabile's efforts are all, in the end, for his own benefit.

Cantabile's energy turns to mania toward the end of the novel when he sniffs out the potential earnings to be had off Charlie. He realizes Charlie's old movie scenario has been made into a smash hit film and, in his own argumentative and abusive fashion, helps Charlie settle the matter and get the failing writer some much needed money. But money is Cantabile's primary objective at all times, and he is angry when Charlie refuses to let him in on the second movie deal. Cantabile's greed is blind: greed for greed's sake. He is obsessed with money, much like Renata, Thaxter, and Denise.

Charlie Citrine

Charlie Citrine loves literature and has made it his life. He struggles throughout the novel to escape the mess his life has become. He believes he has failed as a writer and dwells on the success and failure of his dear friend Humboldt as he meditates upon anthroposophy and seeks deeper meaning from his life. Charlie's golden age is in his youth when he befriends Humboldt and falls in love with sweet and supportive Demmie Vonghel. All at once, dreamy Charlie's support network is yanked away: he and Humboldt are estranged over a misunderstanding, and Demmie dies in a plane crash. Left on his own, Charlie loses his direction, his motivating force as a writer to do something that will make a difference to the world. Charlie makes a lot of money off his Broadway hit, *Von Trenck*, which attracts all

sorts of people who do not have his best interests in mind. He marries Denise and lets her direct his work. For the next twenty years, Charlie is surrounded by vultures (Denise, Renata, Thaxter, Cantabile) who are attracted to his status and money. Approaching sixty years of age, Charlie withdraws even further from reality into his thoughts (on boredom, on anthroposophy) as his career and life slide slowly toward failure. But Humboldt writes to him, "You are lazy, disgraceful, tougher than you think but not yet a dead loss." Humboldt's gift to Charlie is not just the money-making movie scenario but also his passion to do something significant for the world. Charlie's sense of failure does not stem from an inability to make money from his writing (none seems to doubt that) but from his failure to make a difference for the betterment of humankind.

Denise Citrine

Denise Citrine is Charlie's ex-wife. She and Charlie have two daughters, Lish and Mary. Denise and Charlie met on the set of his play, *Von Trenck*, when she was living with the star actor. Denise is intelligent, politically savvy, intense, status-conscious, greedy, manipulative, and beautiful, with large violet eyes. She burdens Charlie with her endless divorce suit. He keeps giving her what she wants, and she renews the suit to ask for more. She despises his girlfriend, Renata, and everything connected with her.

Hortense Citrine

Hortense Citrine, Julius's wife, is loud, short, and attractive, with blue eyes and chub lips. Charlie finds her gruffness off-putting, but Julius convinces him that she is actually very sensitive and affectionate.

Julius Citrine

Julius Citrine is Charlie's older brother; his family nickname is Ulick. He is a successful real estate developer in Texas, living just as richly as his brother only on a grander scale. Julius is married to Hortense and has two sons. He is Charlie's polar opposite: practical, unsentimental, and ambitious. At age sixty-five, he has open heart surgery probably because his poor eating habits have led to heart disease.

Lish Citrine

Ten-year-old Lish Citrine is Charlie's older daughter.

Mary Citrine

Eight-year-old Mary Citrine is Charlie's younger daughter. She shares his taste for literature and language.

Von Humboldt Fleisher

Von Humboldt Fleisher, called Humboldt, is a poet modeled after Delmore Schwartz, one of Bellow's friends. Like the real-life figure, Humboldt is a legendary talker, a social creature, and a schemer. Born to an immigrant family in New York City, he eschews a life of labor for the love of poetry. Humboldt makes a name for himself when his book of avant-garde poems is published in the 1930s.

Humboldt does not live life quietly. Although he does not produce any other significant work, he stays active and inquisitive. His relationships with women are awkward, even adolescent. Humboldt abuses pills and alcohol and suffers from manic depression and paranoia. He is obsessed with money, litigation, and power. He loves deeply, and even when that love is betrayed, he does not cast the person out of his heart. In this subtle way, he and Charlie are much alike. This affection is what moves him to secure a legacy for Charlie, Kathleen, and, by extension, his uncle Waldemar.

Harold Flonzaley

Harold Flonzaley owns a chain of funeral parlors and is very wealthy. Renata hooks up with him when she is angry with Charlie. In the end, Flonzaley and Renata get married in Milan.

Maître Furet

Maître Furet is the French lawyer hired by Cantabile to represent Charlie in their nuisance settlement against the producers of *Caldofreddo*.

Orlando Huggins

Orlando Huggins is a radical bohemian who manages to be savvy about money and also avant-garde. He is the executor of Humboldt's estate.

Ben Islovsky

Ben Islovsky is a geologist at Chicago's Field Museum. He identifies George's ore as beryllium and is invited to join George and Charlie in beryllium speculation in Africa.

Menasha Klinger

Menasha Klinger lived with Charlie's family as a boarder when Charlie was a child in the 1920s. An amateur physicist, Klinger worked at Western Electric as a punch-press operator. His true love is opera, and as a young man, he takes voice lessons. He is a poor but ardent singer. Menasha Klinger is from Ypsilanti, Michigan, and he marries his high school sweetheart, a fat girl who cries all the time.

Gaylord Koffritz

Gaylord Koffritz is Renata's ex-husband and Roger's father. Like Renata's new husband, Koffritz is in the funerary business.

Renata Koffritz

Renata Koffritz, Charlie's girlfriend, is young, beautiful, and amply proportioned. Renata wants to marry a rich man, and she thinks her future husband will be Charlie for much of the book. She was raised by a single mother, the Señora, and feels strongly about having her father, Signor Biferno, acknowledge her. Renata was once married to Koffritz, but they divorced. They have a child together, Roger.

Renata is often selfish and impatient. She tries to bully Charlie into doing the things that she thinks are most important, and she complains a lot when she does not get what she wants, such as a better room at the Plaza hotel. Although Renata never knows about Charlie's financial problems, she gets tired of waiting for him to marry her, so she runs off with and marries Flonzaley while she is in Milan, waiting for Charlie to finish his business in Houston.

Roger Koffritz

Roger Koffritz, son of Renata and Gaylord Koffritz, is a sweet, quiet child who stays with Charlie for a few months in Madrid while his mother is traveling with her new husband.

Vito Langobardi

Vito Langobardi is a gentleman hoodlum with whom Charlie often plays racket ball at the Downtown Club.

Doc Lutz

Doc Lutz, a podiatrist, is the father of Charlie's childhood sweetheart, Naomi.

Magnasco

Magnasco is a critic whom Humboldt imagines is having an affair with his wife, Kathleen. Magnasco complains to the police when Humboldt persists in harassing him.

Polly Palomino

Polly Palomino is Cantabile's mistress and Lucy's old college roommate. She is very pale with red hair, and she does not wear a bra. Although she goes along with Cantabile's schemes, she makes an effort to warn Charlie away from the Stronson affair.

Professor Ricketts

Professor Ricketts is Humboldt's and Charlie's colleague at Princeton.

Scaccia

Scaccia is a sleazy private investigator who fleeces Humboldt for most of his Guggenheim grant by lying and saying that Kathleen is still in New York City.

Doris Scheldt

Charlie dates Doris Scheldt while he and Renata are fighting. Doris is sweet but has hang-ups about sex. She makes a needlepoint pillow for Charlie. Doris's father is a practicing anthroposophist, and even after Charlie breaks off with the daughter, he continues to consult with the father.

Dr. Scheldt

Dr. Scheldt is an academic and a specialist in anthroposophy. Charlie consults with Dr. Scheldt on a regular basis as he attempts to gain a deeper understanding of this spiritual science.

Señora

Señora is Renata's mother. She is a single mother and unsure which of two men may be her daughter's father. She teaches Spanish at a secretarial school, but Charlie is fairly certain that she is actually Hungarian. Señora is a schemer, and Charlie does not like her in the least. When Renata decides that Signor Biferno must be her father, Señora files a paternity suit, despite the fact that her daughter is a grown woman. Without asking, she makes Charlie pay for everything while they are staying in Madrid.

Billy Srole

Billy Srole is Charlie's lawyer's associate. He is pale and chubby with long hair.

Carl Stewart

Carl Stewart is Thaxter's editor in New York City.

Roland Stiles

Charlie's doorman, Roland Stiles, is an elderly black man who is ceaselessly entertained by Charlie's life. Renata pays Stiles occasionally to watch Roger, so she and Charlie can be alone.

Stronson

Stronson is in a lot of trouble with both the government and the hoodlums for defrauding the Mafia. Before the end of the book, he tries to run away to Costa Rica but gets caught and sent to jail.

Alec Szathmar

Alec Szathmar is a lawyer and Charlie's childhood friend. He helps Charlie out with legal advice as well as setting him up with women because Szathmar is a matchmaker at heart. Szathmar has white hair and gloomy eyes. He is very sexual, but his health is poor. He had a heart attack a few years earlier, and Charlie worries that he is not taking care of himself.

Pierre Thaxter

Pierre Thaxter is a man who talks big but acts little. He is rumored to be a CIA agent, which may explain why he travels so much and continues to stay a step ahead of his creditors. Charlie has loaned Thaxter a great deal of money in an effort to produce a literary journal called *The Ark*. Thaxter has nine children. He is kidnapped while working in Buenos Aires but concern for his well-being lags as he publishes from captivity several Op-Ed pieces in the *New York Times*.

Theo

Theo is a cousin of Ezekiel Kamuttu and acts as George's guide while he is in Nairobi. Theo and George get along well, but Theo is driven to extreme rage when Louie Wolper, George's traveling companion, translates English cuss words into Swahili.

Frank Tigler

Frank Tigler is Kathleen's second husband. He and Kathleen were married for twelve years. He runs a derelict dude ranch in Nevada and is an abrasive and unpleasant person. He is shot in a hunting accident and dies.

Kathleen Fleisher Tigler

Kathleen Fleisher Tigler and Humboldt marry in the 1940s. She is a beautiful, fleshy, mild-mannered woman who lets Humboldt lead in their relationship. Despite her easy-going nature, Humboldt becomes paranoid and suspects that Kathleen is carrying on secret affairs with other men. When his paranoia gets so bad that he will not let her out of his sight, she decides she must leave him. Kathleen slips away while they are eating at a restaurant. She runs to Nevada where she files for divorce and eventually meets Frank Tigler, whom she is married to for twelve years. After Frank dies, Kathleen goes into the movie business. Humboldt has left Kathleen the same gift he left Charlie. At the end of the novel, Kathleen is shooting a historical film in Spain, and Charlie gets a job from her as an extra. Charlie and Kathleen enjoy talking to each other as a substitute for the conversations they used to have with Humboldt.

Forrest Tomchek

Forrest Tomchek is Charlie's divorce lawyer. He is very expensive but seemingly ineffective despite the fact that Szathmar promised he was the best in the city.

Judge Urbanovich

Urbanovich is a Croatian American lawyer who gives Charlie a hard time over his divorce suit.

Miss Rebecca Volsted

Rebecca Volsted is a gimpy blonde who works at the Danish Embassy and lives at the pension. She is in her fifties and tries to convince Charlie to sleep with her.

Anna Dempster Vonghel

Anna Dempster Vonghel, called Demmie, was Charlie's girlfriend when he was a young man. She comes from a large, tight-knit family. She is tall and blonde with knock-knees that rub together slightly. Demmie is simultaneously elegant and country-rough. She wants to marry Charlie, but he is intimidated by her parents who are very religious. Demmie, like Humboldt, self-medicates with different pills and has trouble sleeping. She dies with her father in a plane crash over Colombia, leaving Charlie heartbroken.

Waldemar Wald

Waldemar Wald is Humboldt's uncle and has the same wide-set grey eyes. He is an only son and was doted on by the women in his family, so that he never learned to take care of himself and instead became a lay-about and a gambler. Humboldt eventually becomes one of his caretakers as well. After Humboldt dies, Waldemar is left in a shoddy nursing home. He needs Charlie to find value in Humboldt's papers so that he can afford to rebury his nephew and move into his own flat.

Louie Wolper

Louie Wolper, Naomi's son, is on the cusp of adulthood. He has recently kicked a drug habit but still engages in infantile behavior, underlined clearly by his unceasing request for milk while in Nairobi.

Maggie Wolper

Maggie Wolper, Naomi's daughter and Stronson's receptionist, is a beautiful twenty-five-year-old woman, and her tears over Charlie's near imprisonment speak to a more sentimental sensibility than her mother has.

Naomi Lutz Wolper

Naomi Lutz Wolper is Charlie's childhood sweetheart. As teenagers, they loved deeply but when Charlie went to college, Naomi realized that she wanted a man with both feet planted firmly on earth. She also wanted charge accounts to Field's and Sak's. Her husband eventually left, but Naomi is satisfied with her life. She has a boyfriend, enjoys watching sports, and drinking beer. She works as a crossing guard for a school.

THEMES

Money, Success, and Happiness

Money is a significant entity in *Humboldt's Gift*. At the time this story is told, Charlie has been a successful writer and rich from his successes, but his wealth is drying up due to poor financial management and exploitations he has suffered by friends, family, and strangers. Numb and unhappy, Charlie is at a loss for how to transform his life. He trusts everyone so much that other people have repeatedly made off with his money and property.

By contrast, in the first part of the book, Charlie reflects on an earlier period in his life, when he was poor and happy. At that time, he was filled with ideas, energy, literature, conversation, rhetoric, and the love of beautiful Demmie Vongel. But just as Charlie's *Von Trenck* is becoming a wildly successful Broadway show, his friendship with Humboldt crumbles, and his girlfriend dies in a plane wreck. Over and again, Bellow's

TOPICS FOR FURTHER STUDY

- Saul Bellow set a lot of his fiction in the city of Chicago, where he himself grew up. Research the history of this vibrant city, focusing on arts, literature, music, or drama and write a paper on what you learn.

- Charlie takes his daughters to see a performance of "Rip Van Winkle," adapted from the short story by Washington Irving, which was first published in 1819. Read this story and write an essay about why "Rip Van Winkle" is significant within the novel *Humboldt's Gift*.

- Write a short story about Charlie Citrine that takes place after the end of *Humboldt's Gift*. Is he happier? Does he ever find someone to love again? Does his gift from Humboldt continue to affect his life? Is he still writing or is he doing something completely different?

- The Mafia, through Rinaldo Cantabile, plays an important role in Bellow's novel. What presence does the Mafia have in contemporary culture (in the news, entertainment, politics, business, etc.)? Does the Mafia contribute to society or do it harm? Defend your position in a poem.

- *Humboldt's Gift* is a semi-autobiographical novel. Not only is Humboldt based on Delmore Schwartz, but Charlie is based on Bellow himself. How many correlations between the novel's plot and Bellow's real life can you find? Work together as a class to come up with a list.

- Read a short story by Delmore Schwartz. Did you like the story? Does his writing style evoke the character of Humboldt? In what way? Write a one-page response to the story that you read, connecting it to Bellow's novel.

- In *Humboldt's Gift*, Charlie and Thaxter want to start a journal of literature and ideas named *The Ark*. It fails to get going in part because of the expenses involved with printing. With the explosive popularity of the Internet in the 1990s, online literary journals became more prevalent. Find a literary journal that is exclusively online or has web-only content. Read through the current issue and then write a review about what makes this journal unique, what you liked and did not like, and why.

- Write a poem inspired by the novel—its characters, events, or themes. For extra credit, write it in an avant-garde style, like Humboldt composed his poems.

---

commentary, via the character of Humboldt, is that money and success are not tied to happiness and may, in fact, be the antithesis of happiness.

Thaxter, for example, obsessively wastes other people's money, and although he seems jolly, he is a fair-weather friend. Renata is also fair-weather, concerned only with marrying a rich man. Although she never learns of Charlie's destitute finances, she grows impatient with him and quickly marries someone else. Denise, Charlie's ex-wife, got everything in their divorce—the house, the children, and a lot of his money. But it is not enough because, as Urbanovich and others point out, Charlie has an excellent potential for making more money so long as he does some work. By way of his money, Charlie has attracted a pack of jackals, none of whom has Charlie's interests in mind. He can only be rid of them by giving up his money.

Humboldt's message is lost on Charlie until the end of the book. Charlie comes into a great deal of money via Humboldt's legacy but focuses instead on finally leading the life that interests him rather than pursuing greater riches. Money is blinding to creativity, which is partly why Humboldt is so angry with Charlie and his flashy success with the play. Charlie was not being true to his artistry; he was just being popular.

Insanity and Artistry

It is a long-held assumption in Western culture that artists are eccentric and passionate because their creativity and talent stems from their abandonment of societal norms. Sometimes this behavior adds up to unconventionality, but popular perception of artists emphasizes their destructive traits, such as alcoholism, drug abuse, and mental illness. This theme is explored in *Humboldt's Gift*, in which the eponymous Humboldt struggles with manic depression, paranoia, and drug and alcohol abuse. The picture Bellow paints for the reader shows a troubled man whose afflictions derail his ability to be creative and produce new work. The one big success of Humboldt's lifetime is his first book, *Harlequin Ballads*, which he wrote as a young man. Later, he is distracted by his wife, schemes for various jobs, and suffers from substance abuse and mental and financial problems. As a result, Humboldt produces no work of significance until late in his life and even those works are not recognized until ten years after his death. There are, of course, many creative individuals who do not have destructive lifestyles. Charlie appears to have no vices, and he is quite capable of producing creative work when he applies himself. His eccentricity, if any, is his distracted air—he lives inside his thoughts so much and is so often disconnected from real-world concerns that many people call him a snob.

Friendship

The greatest friendship in *Humboldt's Gift* is between Charlie and Humboldt. Like Humboldt's manic depression, the friendship of these two men goes through extreme highs and lows, and together they talk about subjects that few people have the patience to discuss with Charlie, when he is older. Despite the estrangement that develops between Humboldt and Charlie, their affection for each other persists, as seen in Charlie's dreams about Humboldt and in Humboldt's posthumous gift to Charlie.

Amidst the tumult of girlfriends, marriages, and divorce, it is Charlie's true friends who help hold him together and get through the rough parts. His real friends are George, Szathmar, Kathleen, Humboldt, and Demmie. But no one Charlie has met since he and Humboldt were estranged has proven to be a real friend to Charlie. On the contrary, Cantabile, Thaxter, Renata, and Denise, among others, have taken far more than they are willing to give, both financially and emotionally, to support this person they supposedly care about. In his novel, Bellow underlines the significance of friendship beyond material possessions. Friendship is not measured solely by a show of affection but also by how one's friends weather the good and the bad experiences.

Materialism

Materialism is obsession about money and/or possessions. Charlie seeks over the course of the novel to free himself from materialistic concerns. In the courthouse, he declares to his lawyers that he wants to take a vow of poverty, and by the end of the book, having earned enough money to devote himself to studying anthroposophy, he turns down a lucrative scriptwriting offer. Before his Broadway hit, *Von Trenck*, Charlie's means are modest—he borrows money from his girlfriend to buy a bus ticket to New York City, and fourteen years later, when he and Humboldt exchange blood-brother checks, Charlie has only eight dollars in his bank account. A year later, *Von Trenck* is a success, and Charlie is bankrolling more money than he ever dreamed of having. With that money comes its baggage. Charlie marries Denise and is swallowed up with her elite ideas of who his friends should be, how his house should be decorated, and what assignments he should take. Even after they are divorced, Denise continues to harangue Charlie for more money. He also falls in with people, such as Thaxter, Renata, and Cantabile, whose lives revolve around money. Thaxter borrows heavily and abandons his debts. Renata wants to marry into wealth. Cantabile is a thug who wants to have control over Charlie and an ability to tap into his income.

Charlie is most concerned with his meditation. He sees how Americans are consumed with materialism and ignore their inner lives. He hopes through his meditations to come up with a way to help people—no small feat since first one must convince people that there is a problem. Charlie has the most difficulty with communication. Many of his friends and family find Charlie's meditations ridiculous, boring, and circuitous. *Humboldt's Gift* may thus be seen as Bellow's wake up call to Americans about the evils of materialism.

Spirituality

Spirituality is a sense of connection to something greater than oneself. Spirituality differs from religion, although they can and often do overlap. Charlie is concerned about spirituality because of the distinct lack of it that he sees in the world. His meditation is his deepest concern throughout the book. He is fixated on anthroposophy, a spiritual science created by Dr. Rudolph Steiner in the nineteenth century. Charlie attempts to understand spiritual phenomena (such as communication with the dead) with his methodical meditations on aspects of anthroposophy. His spirituality, instead of connecting him to something greater, distances him from those who are nearby.

STYLE

Point of View

Humboldt's Gift is told in first-person point of view, which means the reader sees the events of the novel through the eyes of one character who speaks in his own voice. Charlie spends a lot of time thinking about abstract concepts, which is weakly communicated in the first person. The benefit of first-person point of view is that the close proximity between reader and narrator makes the story more directly engaging. When Charlie is stood up by Renata in Madrid and left to care for her son, Roger, while she honeymoons with her new husband, the reader feels his heartbreak more keenly because of the immediacy between reader and narrator.

Foil Characters

Foil characters are delineated in part by the contrast they pose to one another. An author uses this literary device to highlight by contrast characteristics of the juxtaposed characters. This juxtaposition helps the reader to see something about the character via the contrast. In *Humboldt's Gift*, the protagonist, Charlie, is contrasted with Humboldt; they are foil characters. In some ways their friendship is both unlikely and makes perfect sense because they are very different in their personalities, mannerisms, and, occasionally, tastes. Bellow shows that Charlie's passive nature makes him an easy fit in many unlikely relationships, such as with his ex-wife Denise; his hoodlum shadow Cantabile; his fair-weather girlfriend Renata;

and his irresponsible friend Thaxter. By the end of the novel, as the full extent of Humboldt's character is revealed—his thoughtfulness and affection for those he truly loved—it is apparent that he was a true friend to Charlie.

The juxtaposition of the women in Charlie's love life is particularly interesting. Naomi and Demmie were Charlie's first loves and both were sweet young women. By contrast, Denise and Renata are concerned with status and money and ultimately ill-suited to Charlie. Just as the two halves of Charlie's life are in stark contrast—happiness and fulfillment turned to discontent and frustration—so are the women from those periods in his life in contrast.

Conflict

Conflict is an aspect of the plot in which struggle occurs between two forces, such as character versus character or character versus nature. The end of the story often provides a resolution of conflict. A novel, because of its length and variety of characters, is often comprised of various kinds of conflict. In *Humboldt's Gift*, the primary conflict is character versus society, in which Charlie struggles to free himself from the bonds of money, bad people, and material goods, all of which he is grown to despise. Wealth has not brought him any happiness and continues to drag him deeper into a meaningless existence. At the end of the novel, Charlie has given up his wealthy lifestyle to focus on the study of anthroposophy and to search for a solution to what ails society. Character versus character also recurs in this novel on a more minor level. Charlie struggles with Tomchek, Srole, Denise, Cantabile, Renata, Thaxter, and the Señora. On a more abstract level is the conflict between materialism and spirituality represented by Charlie's efforts against the agents of materialism, such as Renata and Cantabile.

HISTORICAL CONTEXT

Feminism

Feminism is a political and social theory that argues for equality of men and women with an understanding that women have not historically been given equal opportunities and that these shortcomings must be acknowledged and repaired. First-wave feminism includes nineteenth-century and early twentieth-century feminist activity leading

COMPARE
&
CONTRAST

- **1970s:** Divorce rates are on the rise world-wide with approximately 50 percent of marriages in the United States ending in divorce by 1975.

  Today: Approximately 41 percent of marriages in the United States end in divorce, a rate that has gradually been decreasing since the late 1970s. At the same time, marriage rates have also been declining.

- **1970s:** Congress passes the Racketeer Influenced and Corrupt Organizations Act to give federal investigators and prosecutors the power to defuse organized criminal activity.

  Today: Identity theft, online extortion, and human trafficking are common transgressions for organized crime. Organized criminal activity that utilizes the Internet is difficult for the police to trace but advances in security technology are closing the gap in protection.

- **1970s:** The cold war between communist and democratic world powers eases. Economic concerns and an arms race stalemate (acknowledged mutually assured destruction) drive the United States, the Soviet Union, and other nations to improve trade relations and thaw tensions.

  Today: Well over a decade after the fall of the Berlin Wall and the end of the cold war, regime change and economic hardship in former communist countries significantly redraw the map of Europe and Asia. China, Laos, Vietnam, and North Korea remain under communist rule.

- **1970s:** A decade after the Cuban Missile Crisis (1962), world nuclear powers, such as the Soviet Union and the United States, sign arms control agreements to limit arsenals and ban nuclear weapons. The Nuclear Non-Proliferation Treaty, signed by one hundred and eighty-eight sovereign nations, is enacted in 1970.

  Today: The U.S. invasion of Iraq is justified by a concern that Iraq is stockpiling weapons of mass destruction. As of 2007, the stockpile is not discovered. Meanwhile, Iran conducts nuclear research in keeping with the Nuclear Non-Proliferation Treaty, to which some countries, particularly the United States and the United Kingdom, object on the grounds that they believe the research is for weapons and not for power plants.

---

up to extending the franchise to women, which occurred in Great Britain in 1918 and in the United States in 1920. Second-wave feminism lasted from approximately 1960 through 1989. Radical feminism took hold in Western nations in the 1970s. Radical feminists take an extreme viewpoint, which some criticize as being misandrist, or man-hating. In the 1970s, two significant milestones in the mainstream feminist movement were achieved. Passed in 1972, Title IX Education Acts forbade discrimination in education for women. In the 1973 case of *Roe v. Wade*, the U.S. Supreme Court legalized abortion. The Equal Rights Amendment was a big cause in the 1970s for many groups, including feminists, but despite its popularity, it failed to achieve ratification in 1982. Third-wave feminism began in the mid-1980s, alongside second-wave feminism, with a different theoretical approach. Third-wave feminists emphasize a close examination of gender and how gender is defined, among other applicable interpretations. The women in Bellow's novel do not overtly represent ideals of feminism, but Denise and Renata, as single mothers, are less marginalized by society because of advances made by feminists. Renata's flagrant sexuality is also more acceptable because of the social effects of some feminist thought.

Vietnam War

The Vietnam War was a long, violent, and controversial clash between North and South Vietnam from 1945 to 1975. The United States was heavily involved in Vietnam's struggles from 1965 through 1973 as part of U.S. participation in the cold war between communist and democratic nations. The United States allied with the anticommunist government of South Vietnam and joined forces with it to overcome communist (and U.S.S.R.-backed) North Vietnam. But this was a conflict unlike any the United States had ever fought because the Viet Cong (North Vietnam soldiers) engaged in guerilla warfare, a style of combat that relies on ambush and sabotage and is very difficult for opposing forces trained in traditional battlefield engagement to counter. South Vietnam and its allies sustained heavy casualties because they were unprepared for guerilla warfare. Back in the United States, people protested U.S. military action in South East Asia, and these demonstrations, which sometimes turned violent, led to accusations that protestors were unpatriotic, lazy, and self-indulgent. When U.S. forces pulled out of Vietnam in 1973, over seventy thousand American soldiers had died or were missing in the line of duty. Civilian casualties across South East Asia numbered more than ten million.

Realism in Literature

Post–World War II literature is marked by a trend toward realism in the United States. Bellow was a realist author although already established in his career and style by the 1970s. The turbulent politics of the 1960s influenced a development in the realism literary movement toward more experimental forms (such as blending fact and fiction or atypical narrative techniques) as well as content that focused on minority groups and their concerns. Significant experimental novels of the 1970s include *Chimera* (1972) by John Barth, *Childlike Life of the Black Tarantula by the Black Tarantula* (1973), by Kathy Acker; *Gravity's Rainbow* (1973), by Thomas Pynchon; and *Breakfast of Champions* (1973) by Kurt Vonnegut. Important African-American fiction and poetry from the 1970s include *I Know Why the Caged Bird Sings* (1970), by Maya Angelou; *Mumbo-Jumbo* (1972), by Ishmael Reed; *Roots* (1976), by Alex Haley; and *Song of Solomon* (1977), by Toni Morrison. Minority literature became even more mainstream in the early 1980s.

Film Industry

In the United States, the New Hollywood period lasted from approximately 1967 until 1980. Young directors in the 1970s, such as Steven Spielberg, George Lucas, Francis Ford Coppola, Roman Polanski, and Martin Scorsese, made a huge impact on the American film industry, developing the current blockbuster movie model, which was the foundation of the film industry at the turn of the twenty-first century. Early blockbuster movies include *Star Wars Episode IV* and *Jaws*. Counterculture subjects and unusual techniques, often borrowed from foreign films, were also popular with young American audiences, giving rise to the independent film industry. Independent films are generally produced on a small budget and outside direct control of a major studio.

CRITICAL OVERVIEW

Humboldt's Gift is filled with references to literature and philosophy and, on the whole, focuses more on thinking than on action. Although *Humboldt's Gift* took the Pulitzer Prize in 1976, critics have given it mixed reviews. Anatole Broyard, writing for the *New York Times*, gives a tepid review:

> While the random contents of Saul Bellow's mind make better reading than most novels, they do not make for a good novel in this case because they are not integrated into the action, such as it is.

Richard Gilman, in a more favorable *New York Times* review, compliments Bellow's examination of American views on art and culture: "Its length is a function not so much of copious incident as of slow accretion of recognitions, a painstaking working-out of a plan of escape." Gilman identifies the central theme as misdirected intelligence. John Leonard also gives a favorable review of both the book and the author in the *New York Times*. He describes *Humboldt's Gift* as "a fierce, energetic comedy about postwar Jewish intellectuals trying to come to terms with American popular culture." Louis Simpson puts it succinctly in his article on Delmore Schwartz and *Humboldt's Gift* for the *New York Times*: "The interest of *Humboldt's Gift* does not lie in the plot, it is in Bellow's ideas." As other critics have pointed out, the plot is weak in comparison to the characters and the ideas.

WHAT DO I READ NEXT?

- *In Dreams Begin Responsibilities*, published in 1938, is Delmore Schwartz's seminal book of short stories and poetry.

- *The Adventures of Augie March* (1953) is Saul Bellow's most famous work. It is a bildungsroman (a novel about growing up) about a young man in Chicago during the Great Depression.

- William Faulkner's *Absalom! Absalom!* was published in 1936. It follows the life of a poor man who becomes rich with a huge plantation but loses his sons and fails to establish his dynasty in the fashion he envisioned.

- *American Pastoral* (1997) is a Pulitzer Prize–winning novel by Philip Roth, one of Bellow's protégés. This book is about a man trying to live the American dream and how that dream is shattered and then re-envisioned.

- *The Sun Also Rises* (1926), by Ernest Hemingway, is a roman à clef, like *Humboldt's Gift*. It follows the exploits of a group of American expatriates in Europe during the

1920s, mirroring Hemingway's own life and friends at that time.

- *Best American Essays of the Century* (2001), edited by Robert Atwan and Joyce Carol Oates, is a collection of important essays from North America's twentieth century by such authors as Mark Twain, Stephen Jay Gould, and Maya Angelou.

- *Moby-Dick* (1851), by Herman Melville, is a famous novel about a ship captain who is obsessed with hunting down an elusive white whale. Bellow is often considered the Melville of the twentieth century.

- *The Closing of the American Mind* (1987), by Allan Bloom, is a critique of the American university educational system by an accomplished philosopher and close friend of Bellow.

- *Gimpel, the Fool* (1957), by Isaac Bashevis Singer, is a collection of short stories about an individual's search for guidance in life. It is Singer's first book to be translated into English. The title story was translated by Bellow.

CRITICISM

Carol Ullmann

Ullmann is a freelance writer and editor. In the following essay, she investigates accusations from Charlie's friends and acquaintances that Charlie is a snob.

Saul Bellow's Pulitzer Prize-winning *Humboldt's Gift* is a novel of much thought and little action, a lot like its main character, Charlie Citrine. Charlie spends a great deal of time inside his own head, exploring anthroposophy, thinking about the blight of boredom in contemporary culture, worrying about his girlfriend, worrying about money, trying to communicate with the dead, and reminiscing about the past. As the novel progresses and his reality worsens,

Charlie withdraws all the more from society. Despite the reader's proximity to the narrator through the first-person point of view, most knowledge of Charlie's character actually comes from what other people say about him, often right to his face. What many people say is that Charlie is a snob.

Charlie does not seem to be a snob from the first-person perspective, where the reader is as lost in Charlie's thoughts as Charlie is. He does not treat others with obvious superiority. In his private mind, he only finds fault with people who do not mean him well, such as Denise, Cantabile, and Urbanovich, and that can hardly be considered a sign of a superior attitude.

When Charlie fumbles his cue to repay Cantabile at the Playboy Club and inadvertently offends

> CHARLIE IS AS SENTIMENTAL AS HE IS INTELLECTUAL; THE ONE MAY TEMPER THE OTHER, BUT BOTH STILL LEAVE HIM REMOVED FROM REALITY."

Mike Schneiderman, Cantabile says, "You have contempt. You're arrogant, Citrine. You despise us." Although Charlie's actions are unintentional, Cantabile is not wrong. Throughout *Humboldt's Gift*, Charlie condemns people who have invested too heavily in the American dream. His worst reproach is reserved for lawyers, as if they are the grease that keeps the whole ugly machine running. Even Naomi, Charlie's childhood sweetheart, is not spared. Although he is excessively sentimental about her, Charlie sees Naomi's transformation into a common American as something Naomi gives up—never mind that she is probably the most content person in the whole novel. Charlie pities Cantabile's earnest desire to be a successful hoodlum; of course, when Charlie tells Cantabile that he likes to sit in his room and think for hours, Cantabile comments, "A hell of an egotistical thing to do." Schneiderman and his gossip column mean nothing to Charlie, although he pretends to care in order to satisfy those around him, those who are living in reality. Denise calls Charlie a snob when she senses his disdain for the intelligentsia with whom she surrounds herself—and Charlie does not disagree. Although he has always disdained Denise's friends, he has never bothered to expend any energy in explaining himself. Renata writes to him, "I admit you're smart. . . . *You* should be as tolerant toward undertakers as *I* am toward intellectuals." His singular pursuit of some undefined truth seems to provide the dividing line between those whom Charlie deems worthy and those who are not.

At their kindest, Charlie's friends and associates tie his snobbishness to a dreamy, detached attitude that goes along with his long and tangled thought processes. To some degree, he is forgiven his distracted air because he is a writer, but the less Charlie publishes, the fewer people consider his rambling thoughts to be useful to his work. Charlie's lifelong friend George says to him, "This abstract stuff is poison to a guy like you. . . . You're too exclusive, you're going to dry out!" Renata and Naomi do not consider Charlie to be a snob as much as intolerably boring and long-winded. Their focus is on the material world; spiritual matters are worthless and overly romantic. Downright hostile, Renata and Naomi are unsupportive of Charlie's mental aerobics, which may belie Bellow's own experience and prejudice against women (he was married five times). Kathleen and Demmie are exceptions. Kathleen, who was once married to Humboldt, misses the poet's ecstatic, intellectual conversations, even if she does not participate in them herself. Readers do not know Demmie's opinion explicitly, but in all of Charlie's remembrances, she is the model of a supportive partner. Kathleen and Demmie, of course, were never expected to participate in intellectual conversation because Charlie and Humboldt had each other to talk to.

Charlie also spends a great deal of time reminiscing. He fondly remembers Humboldt and with sadness recalls his dear, dead Demmie. He also touches ever so lightly, as if to a wound, his childhood: the tuberculosis sanatorium, his birth house in Wisconsin, playing in the streets of Chicago, and working for Doc Lutz. Charlie is as sentimental as he is intellectual; the one may temper the other, but both still leave him removed from reality.

Charlie was most successful in the real world when he was young and well-matched to the devoted Demmie, who took care of him, loved him as he was, and encouraged his artistry. As Charlie gets older and experiences a series of failures, such as his marriage, his journal of ideas *The Ark*, and the loss of his fortune, he starts to fumble and fail much as Humboldt did, only more quietly. Humboldt went down in a blaze of insanity; Charlie is fizzling slowly and irrevocably.

Humboldt, who knows Charlie's soul best, even calls him a snob:

> You're too lordly yourself to take offense. You're an even bigger snob than Sewell. I think you may be psychologically one of those Axel types that only cares about inner inspiration, no connection with the actual world. . . . You leave it to poor bastards like me to think about matters like money and status and success and failure and social problems and politics. You don't give a damn for such things.

What Humboldt and others consider snobbery on Charlie's part may be more accurately described as self-involvement. Having taken Humboldt's advice that success is not about the money, Charlie is in a spiral of failure, having been unable to make a difference to the world through his work. As he searches for an answer, lost in his thoughts, Charlie does not place himself above others so much as completely ignore the fact that he needs to function in reality just like everyone else. Later in life, he does not have anyone to engage his mind as Humboldt once did, and it wears away at Charlie like overworked gears being stripped of their usefulness. Charlie hungers for mental stimulation, for conversations like he used to have with Humboldt and sometimes has with Thaxter or Dr. Scheldt. He is drawn to anthroposophy because he is looking for a cure: he believes all original ideas have been used up, and culturally, people are entering an era of boredom. "[Y]ou don't spend years trying to dope your way out the human condition. To me that's boring," Renata tells Charlie. Perhaps, it is only Charlie who is bored, having fallen into the rut of an existence lacking in stimulation. People comment to him that anthroposophy is bogus, but Charlie is undaunted and does not mind being labeled eccentric. He is gradually breaking free of his material bonds, selling his Persian rugs, losing his Mercedes, and losing most of his money to Denise. Humboldt, who understands Charlie's pursuit, accuses him, "You're always mooning in your private mind about some kind of cosmic destiny." Charlie hopes to someday reach a conclusion that will help humankind recover from its boredom of ideas.

Stuttering, Huggins asks Charlie: "[W]hat were you re-re-reserving yourself for? You had the star attitude, but where was the twi-twi-twink." Charlie's biggest problem is his failure to connect with people. He admits to Huggins that he once considered himself intellectually superior to most people but that he has given that up. If he is to be believed, he still has not given up the practice of solitude that has turned to obliviousness. Charlie seems not to hear Renata's pleas to marry, even with the threat of Flonzaley always on the horizon. He repeatedly pours his sentimental nostalgia on Naomi even though she hates it. Naomi is clear with Charlie why they did not work out, but her words do not seem to penetrate his fog of thought. While they are married, he allows Denise to push him around and make him work on the assignments she thinks are worthwhile even if he is disinterested. Despite their great affection for each other

as childhood chums, Charlie and Szathmar often seem on the verge of a fight. Charlie fails to connect partly because whenever he is in an unpleasant or boring situation, he withdraws into himself to think: the bathroom stall with Cantabile, in Cantabile's car, in Renata's car, waiting in the courthouse, on the airplane with Renata, at the Ritz in Madrid, at the pensión. Renata writes to Charlie in her farewell letter, "You always said that the way life happened to you was so different that you weren't in a position to judge the desires of other people. It's really true that you don't know people from inside or understand what they want ... and you never may know."

Charlie's growth as a person over the course of the novel is double-edged. He regains control of his life but takes the not-wholly-unexpected option of pursuing a life of pure intellect at the Anthroposophy Institute in Switzerland. Near the end of the novel, he is fixated on communicating with the dead, which necessitates that he ignore all the vibrant, fully alive individuals around him, from the lovely Renata to the eager Rebecca Volsted to even his own daughters. His self-involvement holds no malice, but his grand plan to do something beneficial for society by way of deep thought may be unrealistic. By the conclusion of *Humboldt's Gift*, Charlie has grown up but not out.

Source: Carol Ullmann, Critical Essay on *Humboldt's Gift*, in *Novels for Students*, Thomson Gale, 2008.

Ben Siegel

In the following essay, Siegel explores Bellow's comment on the precariousness of the artist in America and the obsession, guilt, and metaphysical experimentation of his protagonist prompted by the death of a friend.

Easily the novelist most successful in capturing contemporary life's realistic and grotesque aspects has been Saul Bellow. Now past sixty, he has for more than three decades proved himself this country's most profoundly serious and exuberantly comic observer. If many writers today resort to "impressionistic journalism and innovative fantasy," he retains a "Tolstoyan appetite" for serious ideas. Indeed, ideas are Bellow's primary material, and usually they entangle themselves in his characters' perceptions and emotions. Despite his intellectual concerns, however, Bellow is basically a storyteller, and one who remains in the major tradition of conscious realism, with its

"MORE TO THE POINT, SAUL BELLOW AND CHARLIE CITRINE PRESENT THE READER WITH COMIC YET MOVING INSIGHTS INTO THOSE CRUCIAL ISSUES CONFRONTING EVERY SENSITIVE INDIVIDUAL BETWEEN HIS CRADLE AND GRAVE."

intense characterizations and detailed, textured descriptions of its heroes' every physical and mental action.

He has been described as having emerged from an "ancient Jewish tradition of alarm wedded to responsibility." His social concepts and interpretations bear this out. His fiction derives much of its strength from his grasp of the cultural implications of his characters' behavior and emotions. His central Jewish loners and lamenters are perceptive, critical, overextended urban beings; they tend to separate themselves from families and friends while they strain to bring order and coherence to their private lives. For these bedeviled seekers, the pressures and constraints come as often from without as from within. Most suffer not only from minds tormented by personal fears but also from an unfeeling society's frequent indignities. As a result, their lives often become desperate battles against not merely their own capricious, self-serving appetites but also against the wants and wishes of family members and intimates, friends and strangers.

Yet despite their antic involvements, his characters reassert Bellow's unflagging humanism. Every individual, he insists, should adhere to a human measure or mean. Even his least cerebral heroes seek to convert America's social chaos into coherent traditional notions about character, morality, and fate. Some critics have accused Bellow—especially with *Mr. Sammler's Planet*—of souring in his humanism, liberalism, and social expectations. "There can be little doubt," notes Malcolm Bradbury, that the "high ironies" of recent Bellow fiction "betoken a sceptical withdrawal from ... contemporary consciousness ... and a cold eye ... [toward] the contemporary circus." Bradbury is only half-right. For if Bellow does view present social and moral disorders with a skeptical or "cold eye," he has hardly withdrawn from current happenings or ceased to care about those affected by them. Moses Herzog and Artur Sammler, for example, express concern not only for the cultural drift evident at every turn but for their own urges toward detachment or withdrawal as well.

Bellow is even more deeply involved with contemporary life in *Humboldt's Gift*. Here narrator Charlie Citrine is nagged by guilt at having immersed himself in personal pursuits. He has closed his eyes, he laments, and "slept" through momentous historical events. Citrine's troubled ruminations enable Bellow to explore again, directly and unequivocally, American morals and expediencies—this time as they operate in the 1970s. He does not fit, admittedly, current definitions of the "experimental" novelist. He retains instead specific and basic literary commitments to realism; in short, his plot structures derive from story and character, and his people exist in a tumultuous but recognizable world. Yet Bellow is hardly a static thinker or writer. In each novel he not only records meticulously his evolving responses to setting and culture, but he also ventures beyond his previous imaginative perimeters to make playful use of shifting narrative styles and forms. His realism often shades into romanticism and the absurd, into social comedy and black humor, into psychology and the picaresque, into philosophy and satire. These elements enrich *The Adventures of Augie March, Henderson the Rain King, Herzog, Mr. Sammler's Planet*, and now *Humboldt's Gift*. In these novels Bellow reaffirms that the comic view offers the most valid means of grasping an American scene by turns tragic or absurd, or both. But laughter alone, he makes clear, is never enough. In *Humboldt's Gift*, therefore, as in his earlier novels, he mixes historical speculation and "metaphysics" with his vivid pathos and "mental farce."

Here his turbulent world overflows as usual with things and noises and human needs. If he evokes again his fierce love of Chicago, he leavens his nostalgia with recollections of life among such New York literati as Philip Rahv, Sidney Hook, and Lionel Abel—and especially of his troubled friendship with the poet Delmore Schwartz. Moving along the periphery of that life are such political or social figures as Adlai Stevenson, the brothers Kennedy, Jacob Javits, and Harry Houdini. Others, like Dwight Macdonald, Richard Blackmur, and Carlos Baker, are thinly disguised, but play more central roles. These people, appearing in real and imagined events and places, present two familiar interlocking Bellovian themes. The first theme details the dangers posed to the artist in America by worldly success, with its inevitable attachments of money and fame, sex and excitement, and, often now, crime. Bellow has emphasized repeatedly in his fiction the gap between America's professed ideals and practiced compromises, between its high aspirations and low opportunism. The artist or writer's function, as he sees it, is not merely to expose but to help mend the rift between these divided value areas.

Centering on a live writer and a dead poet, Bellow tries to define the artist's role in a society lured away by its massive material substance from its cravings for mind and beauty. In a culture so fragmented the artist too often meets professional failure, if not personal disaster. For despite his early dreams and plans, he—no less than businessmen and lawyers—generally ensnares himself in a typical American compromise, as Charlie Citrine puts it, of "crookedness with self-respect or duplicity with honor." This moral confusion, Bellow suggests, is caused primarily by the artist's refusal to confront "the main question ... the death question." In other words, the artist, like his fellow Americans, frequently fails to consider the moral or ethical—much less the spiritual—aspects of his goals and behavior. As so often in the past, Bellow is following (albeit more cynically) Walt Whitman, here the Whitman of *Democratic Vistas* and of "Out of the Cradle Endlessly Rocking."

Saul Bellow embraces moral, ethical, and spiritual problems. His second theme is vintage Bellow: the comic pathos of a vain intellectual's efforts to age with style and dignity. Bellow writes of the deeply felt loss of dead kin and friends, focusing primarily on that sharpest of human anxieties, the fear of death. Probing this and related areas, he fashions a long, loose, funny/sad narrative of a crucial five months, in 1973–74, in the life of an embattled writer. During that December-to-April span, Charlie Citrine seeks higher significance in his life and possible ways for his soul to transcend or defeat death. Bellow shapes his hero's untiring monologue not into chapters but into unnumbered segments brimming with social details and philosophic speculations, narrative flashbacks and quick transitions. Charlie Citrine is the picture of the successful American man of letters. He is a cultural historian and biographer who has won Pulitzer Prizes for books on

Woodrow Wilson and Harry Hopkins. He has rejected academic rewards to garner fame and money for a hit Broadway play. Top magazines have commissioned him to write articles on the Kennedys and other national leaders, and the French government has made him a Chevalier of the French Legion of Honor. Clearly, his is a life to admire in a success-loving age. Yet if he is so successful, why is he so blocked, Charlie wonders, in his joy and work? Why is he so accomplished in several worlds and at ease in none?

A major reason is his character. History may intrigue Charlie and literature and art fascinate him, but daily life baffles him. Indeed, unhappy events have in recent years been shattering his lengthy "slumber" of money, fame, and middle-class comforts. At fifty-six, he is losing his looks, his hair, and his paddle ball game. He owes his publishers $70,000 for advances on books he will never write. His ex-wife and a battery of lawyers, judges, and tax experts are stripping him of funds. So is his old friend Pierre Thaxter, a flamboyant literary con artist with a scheme for launching an intellectual quarterly. In short, despite his subtle, perceptive intelligence, Charlie is an easy mark for crooks and cranks and greedy friends.

Material problems are not his only worry. Of late, Charlie has been experiencing pangs of guilt and responsibility. He feels he should help alleviate the modern day's spiritual and cultural shortcomings—as if they were his personal obligation. He is also haunted by recollections of his close friend and mentor, the poet Von Humboldt Fleisher. Now seven years dead, Humboldt had been the big, blond, new bard whose thin volume of early lyrics, *Harlequin Ballads*, had helped shape the literary landscape of the 1930s and 40s. But his book's title suggests the clownish aspects of Humboldt's character and fate. Charlie had read Humboldt's first poems while still a University of Wisconsin graduate student. Charlie is a native of Appleton, Wisconsin, the home of Harry Houdini, "the great Jewish escape artist." The magician's feats are repeatedly evoked and prove to be a paradigm of Charlie's dreams of escaping middle-class life and pressures. For Moses Herzog, the wily bankrobber Willie Sutton had served a similar emblematic role. Houdini and Sutton appeal to Bellow and his heroes as sly illusionists who evade nature and society's laws.

Yet Von Humboldt Fleisher had been the direct agent of Charlie's escape efforts. Eager to enter New York's heady world of high intellect,

Charlie had fled the Midwest. He had found his idol in Greenwich Village enjoying, he later recalls, "the days of his youth, covered in rainbows, uttering inspired words, affectionate, intelligent." A generous if disoriented patron and guide, Humboldt had launched Charlie's academic and literary career and filled him with manic, improbable dreams. Exhilarated by life, art, thought, Humboldt was an irrepressible creative force, "a hectic nonstop monologuist and improvisator" and an unending source of wit and wisdom and paradox. If he warned Charlie, for example, to view the dangerous and beautiful rich only as they are mirrored in the "shield of art", he hungered also for wealth and fame. He lusted to be artist and oracle, culture czar and celebrity, and a living link between art and science.

His desires filled Humboldt with "high-minded low cunning" and turned him into a scheming mix of sage, publicist, and tavern prophet. A masterful wheeler-dealer in literary politics, he garnered fellowships and faculty appointments, consultancies and grants. Combining talent and drive, he fashioned himself into one of the exemplary literary successes of the 1930s and 40s and won acceptance as a major American poet. What he wanted for himself, he wanted—or thought he wanted—for others. Convinced that culture was on the rise in America, and that the imminent presidency of Adlai Stevenson would make all things possible, he dreamed of transforming the nation, through its art and wealth, into a new Athens. In such a state, American social forces would be reconciled with Platonic concepts of truth and beauty.

Humboldt could not sustain his "youthful dazzle," and subsequent disappointments and the opposing tensions of poetry and politics exacted a cruel toll. Expending his creative juices on the grant-and-fellowship game, writing little and orating long into the night fueled by gin and barbiturates, Humboldt began to crack. Slipping steadily into paranoia, detecting acts of betrayal everywhere, he lashed out repeatedly at his wife and friends. His special target was Charlie. As the latter's career rose and his own sank, Humboldt turned on his old chum in envy and depression. While Charlie, his writing in demand (and propelled by an ambitious wife), visited at the White House and shared helicopters with the Kennedys, Humboldt was in and out of institutions, feeding his rancor and resentment at his pal for not impeding his fall. Once, from Bellevue, Humboldt

phoned Charlie at the Belasco Theater. "Charlie, you know where I am, don't you?" he yelled. "All right, Charlie, this isn't literature. This is life." He even filled in and cashed for over $6700 a blank check Charlie had signed years before at his urging as a friendship bond. The greatest shock for Charlie, however, came years later when he spotted Humboldt—broken, dirty, forlorn—on a New York street corner, a shambling, mumbling derelict. Confused and embarrased, Charlie hid and then rushed back to his own bustling world. Two months later, he read that Humboldt had dropped dead in a Times Square flophouse.

Now Humboldt is much on Charlie's mind. Haunted by his bad conscience, Charlie mourns his friend's accomplishments and follies and lonely death. He dwells obsessively on his last glimpse of the poet, appraising him less as an individual than as a "cause" or "mistreated talent" meriting "posthumous justice." Humboldt had tried "to drape the world in radiance," Charlie decides, "but he didn't have enough material"; and he died essentially of "unwritten poems." Even worse, Humboldt had lain unidentified and unclaimed for three days. The morgue, Charlie muses sardonically, harbored "no readers of modern poetry." Yet Humboldt had died, Charlie observes, as a poet in America is expected to die. He had gratified the public's conviction of the superiority of the practical over the ideal, the material over the aesthetic. Charlie tries, however, to see his friend's death in more positive terms; he wonders, therefore, if Humboldt had not made a "Houdini escape" from the world's madness and distractions. Had he also not embodied, in his personal and professional turmoils, the confusing talents, visions, and drives of a nation committed historically to opportunity and success?

For these and other reasons, Charlie regrets not having been more tolerant and understanding of Humboldt. He wishes now to redeem his friend's reputation and even in some way to carry out his ideas. He would also like to discover why so charged and talented a figure produced so little. By unraveling that riddle he hopes to find answers to his own creative and social dilemmas. For Charlie is as much a victim of his emotional needs and success drives as Humboldt. He is another of Bellow's versatile but aging Jewish intellectual innocents, marked by their "talent for absurdity." Caught up in this cra of urban violence and public assassinations, uneasy family life and moral cynicism, he finds his vast knowledge of dusty volumes and esoteric authors of little practical value. "I knew everything I was supposed to know," he complains at one point, "and nothing I really needed to know." His lack of devious, pragmatic strategies leaves him desperately protecting his dignity and principles from a familiar Bellow array of greedy, dissatisfied women, voracious lawyers, and societal demands, diversions, and clutter. These pressures move Charlie to take cynical measure of his country and countrymen. The American had overcome his land's "emptiness," he observes, but "the emptiness had given him a few good licks in return."

Chicago offers ample evidence. The city is Charlie's testing ground. He had grown up there and been drawn back to it. He is, he admits sardonically, "a lover of beauty who insists on living in Chicago." Why? Well, New York may have better talk, he reasons, but in "raw Chicago" one can best "examine the human spirit under industrialism." He is also intrigued by the phenomenon of boredom, and this element pervades his city in a pure, near-mystical state. New York, on the other hand, dilutes its boredom with culture. So anything significantly revealing of the boring human condition, Charlie is convinced, will more likely befall him in his hometown. Ironically, Bellow presents a vibrant, pulsating Chicago that offers quite a stimulating microcosm of the USA. He fashions the city into a living metaphor for the violent, mad, real world that differs so sharply from Humboldt's ideal, aesthetic one. Here Charlie confronts his turbulent muddle of lawyers and alimony hearings, past and present girlfriends and vengeful ex-wife, petty gangsters and greedy friends.

Here also, as so often in Bellow, criminality takes comic forms. Amid his confusions Charlie entangles himself with Rinaldo Cantabile, a small-time Mafia operator, and the plot acquires overtones of black humor. If New York's intellectual ferment had spawned a Von Humboldt Fleisher, Chicago's material turmoils have thrown off the opportunistic Cantabile. "One of the new mental rabble of the wised-up world", as Charlie describes him, this petty racketeer lives totally in the here and now; he is always "one thousand percent" with the action. Meeting and cheating Charlie in a poker game, Cantabile is furious when his victim stops payment on a check written to cover game losses. In revenge, he clubs Charlie's Mercedes Benz into a shapeless wreck. When Charlie does offer the money, he is ritualistically humiliated and insulted. To make matters worse, Cantabile not only tries to replace Humboldt as Charlie's mentor and guide, but he has a Ph.D.-candidate wife who is writing her dissertation on the poet and wants Charlie's help.

Cantabile, like Humboldt and Charlie Citrine himself, proves one of Bellow's great comic figures. He is literally Charlie's "nemesis"—a satanic spirit fated to shatter Charlie's slumber of success and smugness and to compel him to move away from "dead center" and confront his true self. He also personifies the tightening bonds between an upwardly mobile middle class and a shady world of confidence men and mobsters. Charlie's friends view this new social comradeship with indifference. They nourish, like most Americans, a steadily higher gratification threshold and an intense need to escape boredom. One major result of such attitudes is a morally and intellectually uncertain age in which "culture and corruption" are symbiotically entwined. The effects of this turbulent partnership are strongly visible. "What a tremendous force," Charlie observes, "the desire to be interesting has in the democratic USA."

Charlie is fighting hard to shake off both his own boredom and the incessant demands of others. Like Tommy Wilhelm and Moses Herzog before him, however, he is enmeshed in a web of domestic court battles. Denise, his ex-wife, bitter at his having rejected her, has separated him from their two young daughters; now she, her lawyers, and a cooperative judge are determined to teach Charlie some hard, practical lessons by draining him of money, energy, and time. His own lawyers, accountants, and friends prove equally insatiable "reality instructors." Yet, as his name suggests, Charlie Citrine, with ironic, slightly soured, self-deprecatory humor, is wryly amused at his repeated victimizing by these frenetic business toughs, literary con men, and divorce court hustlers who envy his fame and covet his money. For the money, he decides, is the world's money. A capitalist society, for its own darkly comic motives, has granted him temporary loan of huge sums and now is taking its own back. He views his mounting losses, therefore, with bemused detachment, even seeing virtue in the process.

Time and disappointment, however, are having their effect. At fifty-six, Charlie is nearing exhaustion. Yet, exhausted or not, he remains a dedicated womanizer who fights aging by frantic devotion to yoga postures, paddle ball, and body exercises. His current mistress, the young and voluptuous Renata Koffritz, demands marriage, money, respectability. But if she pressures Charlie to marry her, Renata fears his unreliability and imminent loss of wealth. She takes the precaution, therefore, of sleeping periodically with the wealthy undertaker Harold Flonzaley. So blocked and confused are Charlie's relationships here and elsewhere that he is repeatedly tempted to lie down and go to sleep.

Yet he fears already having slept through the high moments of his era and his life. The novel's latter half is suffused with "sleep" images that suggest both Charlie's "bemused worldliness" and his hunger for a higher awareness or consciousness. For if Humboldt had succumbed to high-voltage graspings for fame and success, Charlie has been given to lethargy and self-absorption. While those about him, especially the relentless Cantabile, scheme to destroy his peaceful slumber, Charlie himself now resolves to concentrate his "whole attention" on his time's "great and terrible matters"—those same matters that for decades he had filtered out by turning inward. But he must ponder first Humboldt's blunted career and life. Charlie is not certain how much sympathy either Humboldt or he merits. They both had enjoyed, after all, the best America had to offer: fame, money, audiences, women. If they had gone sour, where lay the fault? Had they misdirected or misapplied their intellectual and creative gifts? Or does fault lie with this country, so rich in diversity and distraction that it ignores or downgrades its creative talents and rewards mediocrity? Whatever the root cause of its dulled aesthetic sensibilities, American society has to answer for its blatant adoration of material success.

Bellow's central figures are never mere passive, blameless victims. The novelist makes clear that the artist in America bears at least partial blame for his failures. Many problems derive from every artist's acute sense of self or of being special. "Remember," observes Humboldt in a letter he bequeathes Charlie, "we are not natural beings but supernatural beings." But for most sensitized, creative individuals to view themselves as "supernatural beings" in a tough-grained technological world is not easy. For many artists it proves even crushing. If they feel at one with the heavens, they draw their materials from life. If

given to Platonic speculations about truth and beauty, they hunger for acclaim, luxuries, acceptance. If they strive desperately for purity, achievement, art, they become speculators in mind and profit, sinking almost inevitably to performance, caricature, compromise. Delineating these cultural paradoxes, Bellow resists (more in his fiction than in essays or lectures) easy formulations or explanations. Assigning blame is, to him, not only facile but beside the point.

He expresses serious reservations, however, about the aims or motives of the modern artist—at least as exemplified by Von Humboldt Fleisher and Charlie Citrine. Bellow's doubts are hardly new. He has stated them in his recent Nobel Prize address and on many previous occasions. He had criticized in a 1963 Library of Congress lecture those American writers who smugly mix affluence and radical chic. Such middle-class writers "are taught," he charged, "that they can have it both ways. In fact they are taught to expect to enjoy everything that life can offer. They can live dangerously while managing somehow to remain safe. They can be both bureaucrats and bohemians ... [or] conservative and radical. They are not taught to care genuinely for any man or any cause." For this reason Bellow expects the reader to take Charlie Citrine seriously. Charlie does come to care about those close to him and about the artist's place and function in American life.

Despite his faults, the artist hardly bears sole responsibility for his marginal status. Who—if not his American history, culture, and countrymen—has taught him to want the wrong things? Contemporary America for Bellow is a politically expedient, science-and-technology-oriented community uncertain about how to employ—much less celebrate—its artists. Filling them with false values, this society then stirs their anxieties and insecurities. "I don't think we know where we are or where we're going," Bellow has told interviewers. "I see politics—ultimately—as a buzzing preoccupation that swallows up art and the life of the spirit." Charlie Citrine shares these uncertainties. Can a poem, Charlie asks himself, transport you from New York to Chicago? Can a novel plot a condominium or an epic "compute a space shot"? In Bellow's America, therefore, writers generally are frustrated and ineffectual, and often they entrap themselves in social roles and institutions whose managers treat them as irresponsible, ungrateful children.

Writers who seek acceptance compound their problems: they appeal to readers or audiences who value all artists' public images over their creative acts, their personal lives over their paintings or novels, their scandals over their music or poems. Is it even possible, then, Bellow and Citrine seem to ask, for the artist or writer in this country to express his true philosophical, religious, or even aesthetic convictions? Yet what worries Bellow and Citrine had fascinated Von Humboldt Fleisher. The collective disappointments of other artists were of little account to Humboldt. For him, as for Walt Whitman, America was promises, opportunities, excitement. America had been his world, and "the world," Humboldt insisted, "had money, science, war, politics, anxiety, sickness, perplexity. It had all the voltage. Once you had picked up the high-voltage wire and were *someone*, a known name, you couldn't release yourself from the electrical current. You were transfixed."

Where a Walt Whitman or Von Humboldt Fleisher saw opportunities, Saul Bellow and Charlie Citrine see pitfalls, indifference, neglect. "The history of literature in America," Bellow has stated, "is the history of certain demonic solitaries who somehow brought it off in a society that felt no need for them." Charlie Citrine voices similar sentiments. "Poets have to dream," he points out, "and dreaming in America is no cinch." Humboldt, having grown desperate, "behaved like an eccentric and a comic subject." Many poets, declares Charlie (picking up the theme of Bellow's 1971 essay "Culture Now"), have become publicists or promoters, campus politicians or public clowns. Thus, for Charlie, Humboldt's fate raises many questions. Was the poet's deepening disenchantment, his sense of being nothing more than his society's superfluous, comic victim, what drove him to destruction? Were his strivings for power and money less mercenary yearnings than symptoms of his growing fears and frustrations? Or was he little more than a "pathetic wool-gatherer" whose "comeuppance" was not only "inevitable" but "somehow correct"? Does Humboldt's fate prove emblematic, in other words, of the artist's dark destiny in American life?

Whatever its prime cause, his friend's pitiful end saddens and frightens Charlie. He is pained especially by Humboldt's strong contribution to his own failure. He is keenly aware that the poet's self-indulgence and lack of discipline rendered him a "farcical" rather than a tragic martyr.

Humboldt fed in his life and in his death the popular conceptions that poets are kindred spirits to those "drunkards and misfits and psychopaths" who cannot confront the American reality and for whom "the USA is too tough, too big, too much, too rugged." Humboldt, by chasing "ruin and death," performed in the manner expected of him. Americans derive pleasure from such sad happenings, Charlie sighs, because the poet's failure validates their cynicism.

To make matters worse, Humboldt's pitiful finish, alone and muttering in abject poverty, suggests to Charlie the social and moral confusion not merely of "demonic solitaries" but also of prudent, decorous intellectuals like himself. Has not he acted even less commendably than his erratic, disorderly comrade? Did he not reject Humboldt's physical presence on a public street? Is not his own carefully calibrated success a denial of his friend's failed but somehow valiant life, with its heedless, dramatic mistakes and misfortunes? Not even Humboldt's pathetic hunger for success and fame mitigates Charlie's guilt. Haunted by the dead poet's voice, communing with his own "significant dead," trying to withstand his living debtors, and unable to write, Charlie abandons an ambitious essay on boredom for "interior monologues" on life and death, rebirth and immortality.

Ironically, Charlie Citrine (like Saul Bellow) has been a tough-minded realist committed firmly to a cause-and-effect balance between man's past and present and between his inner and outer worlds. Now, painfully aware of an aging body and diminishing lifespan, he refuses to believe that the extraordinary human soul "can be wiped out forever." Charlie disagrees, therefore, with those thinkers and theorists who, having lost their own "imaginative souls," dismiss any possibility that man's consciousness can survive death's oblivion. "If there is one historical assignment for us," he argues, "it is to break with false categories" and to accept an "inner being" separate from physical nature's finalities.

Such metaphysical faith or acceptance, however, requires the individual to confront "the big blank of death." Charlie turns for help to the writings of Rudolf Steiner (1861–1925). One of this century's "Scientists of the Invisible," Steiner had moved from German philosophy to an occultist doctrine he called anthroposophy. Rejecting conventional scientific or even theosophical views, he developed a theory of "spiritual science" that involved the study of the human spirit by "scientific" inquiry. Steiner argued for the transmigration of souls, and he advocated self-discipline of mind and body to achieve cognition of the spiritual world. For guidance through the Steinerian maze, Charlie consults a Chicago anthroposophist, Dr. Scheldt. Their conversations dwell on the soul's connections to "a greater, an all-embracing life outside" the physical one—as well as on the plight of the dead, who surround the living but are "shut out" by modern man's "metaphysical denial" of them.

His spiritualistic musings do not prevent Charlie from enjoying the pleasures of the flesh. Several reviewers have dismissed Charlie's interest in anthroposophy, therefore, as a "highly egoistic" one centering on Steiner's ideas of "transcendence and immortality of the self." Yet Charlie makes clear—as had Walt Whitman—that what is true of him is true of all men. Some readers also have seen in Scheldt a counterpart to Artur Sammler's friend Dr. Govinda Lal. That Indian scientist, too, advocated "extraterrestrial reality." The rationalistic Sammler, however, rejected such fanciful views for life on a troubled earth. Charlie Citrine, on the other hand, driven by "frenzied longings" for existential possibilities beyond this sphere, embraces Steiner's occultist concepts (with their strong Wordsworthian overtones) of the soul's cycle of sleep and wakefulness.

These cogitations are interrupted by more mundane problems. A domestic relations judge rules that Charlie must give his ex-wife most of his money and orders him to post a $200,000 bond. Despite this heavy penalty, Charlie takes off on a European trip, with Renata scheduled to join him in Spain. He makes two stops. He goes first to New York to pick up Humboldt's legacy to him, which consists of a long conciliatory letter, a movie scenario they had collaborated on, and a Humboldt original film treatment. Charlie then heads for Texas, to Corpus Christi (an ironic reference, perhaps, to his physical-spiritual meanderings). He wants to see his older brother Julius through a serious operation. Julius Citrine merits a novel of his own. A heavy-eating, fast-moving real-estate tycoon, he has the dash and drive of a Eugene Henderson or Von Humboldt Fleisher. A maker and loser of fortunes, he wheels and deals on the very eve of open-heart surgery. Charlie, despite his interest in occultist metaphysics, retains the traditional Jew's respect for family, the past, and conventional burial rites. Julius

does not. His views on death and burial reflect both his restlessness and his ease with the American here and now. "I'm having myself cremated," he tells Charlie. "I need action. I'd rather go into the atmosphere. Look for me in the weather reports."

Julius proves a born survivor, however, and Charlie heads for Madrid. There he learns that Renata, having saddled him with her mother and son, has eloped to Italy with her undertaker. Though crushed, Charlie realizes that losing Renata was inevitable. Does not Death (here mortician Flonzaley) always ensnare Beauty? Still he mourns his loss of sexual pleasure and especially those gifts of youth—excitement, stimulation, pride—that Renata had provided to soften the advancing years. Finally alone in Madrid, and nearly broke, Charlie resumes his meditations. He hopes to reorganize his life and to reconcile his mystical readings with his rationalistic "head culture." His growing sense of the tight interplay between man's inner and outer worlds, of the soul's power to escape into the supersensible, convinces him that the respected Western thinkers of the last three centuries offer little guidance. Most bothersome is the seeming exhaustion of modernist ideas of art and the poetic imagination so cherished by Humboldt and himself. These ideas, centering on art's ultimate value, have emphasized metaphor, language, and style as the basic purveyors of truth, beauty, and immortality. Such concepts, Charlie now feels, have lost validity in this America of horrendous distractions and temptations. As a result, the sensitive individual finds it difficult to sustain an ethical imaginative life amid the materialistic erosions of science and art.

Charlie also finds it difficult to age and die—much less fail—with dignity in a society cherishing youth, money, and sex. His attempts to establish rapport with the accepted representatives of modern intellect and high culture have left him few solid, conventional beliefs, and his future efforts to reconcile mind and spirit will not be easy. He can expect little help, he realizes, from a "learned world" that disdains anthroposophy. Undaunted, he rejects all rationalist denials of communication between physical and spiritual worlds, as well as all arguments against the continuing life of the soul. Charlie is convinced that it is modern man's failure to interpret the cosmos, to read its subtle, suggestive signs, that has turned the world turbulent. "Real life," he insists, derives from the singular "relationship between *here* and *there*." But how, he wonders, is he to get *there* from his tangled *here*?

Despite his doubts and uncertainties, Charlie determines to leap beyond tangible human facts and passions. "I meant to make a strange jump," he declares, "and plunge into the truth. I had had it with most contemporary ways of philosophizing. Once and for all I was going to find out whether there was anything behind the incessant hints of immortality that kept dropping on me. ... I had the strange hunch that nature itself was not *out there* ... but that everything external corresponded vividly with something internal, ... and that nature was my own unconscious being." Charlie is attracted, therefore, to Steiner's "explanations" of the interplay of each person's outer setting and inner self—to those ideas, in other words, expanding man's awareness of self and cosmos. His readings convince Charlie that the individual's "external world" often blends with the internal to become indiscernible to him. He and it are one. "The outer world is now the inner," he states. "Clairvoyant, you are in the space you formerly beheld. From this new circumference you look back to the center, and at the center is your own self. That self, your self, is now the external world."

Reviewers have expressed surprise at Saul Bellow's visionary turn. This "worldly Chicagoan," they point out, hitherto has been immersed in social realities. How seriously, some ask, does Bellow expect his readers to take Charlie Citrine's "dubious quasi-mysticism"? The more incredulous reviewers have looked for quibbles or qualifications, ironic jokes or subtle satire. But his public comments emphasize that Bellow is strongly taken with Steiner's ideas on the immortal spirit and on the possibilities of the living communicating with the dead; Charlie Citrine, he makes clear, speaks for him as well as for himself. "Rudolf Steiner had a great vision," Bellow states flatly, and he "was a powerful poet as well as philosopher and scientist." He discovered Steiner's anthroposophy, he adds, through the work of British writer Owen Barfield. Both Steiner and Barfield not only exemplify "the importance of the poetic imagination," but they also have convinced him "that there were forms of understanding, discredited now, which had long been the agreed basis of human knowledge." We believe "we can know the world scientifically," Bellow declares, "but actually our ignorance is terrifying."

Bellow's confidence in the occult is reminiscent of Yiddish novelist Isaac Bashevis Singer and his stated acceptance of demons and spirits. Like Singer (and, for that matter, Harry Houdini), Bellow does disparage most occultist practitioners, as well as the "many cantankerous erroneous silly and delusive objects actions and phenomena [that] are in the [physical] foreground." Both novelists are, however, intrigued by the great unknown—by death, rather than by miracles, tricks, or wonder workers. Bellow, despite his basic realism, has often displayed a mystical turn of mind. A careful review of his fiction reveals not only a persistent determination "to break with false categories" but also repeated references to the "illusory" nature of a "successful" life in America. From the dangling Joseph to Artur Sammler, his protagonists are "seeker[s] after cosmic understanding," spiritual pilgrims convinced life can offer them more than meets the eye. Both Moses Herzog and Artur Sammler, for instance, though tough-minded rationalists committed to confronting "the phony with the real thing," are readers of such mystics as William Blake, Meister Eckhart, John Tauler, and Jacob Boehme; they, too, attempt to satisfy yearnings toward a higher, intuitive awareness. Augie March's earthy friend William Einhorn, it will be recalled, subscribed in the 1930s to the Rudolf Steiner Foundation publications. Charlie Citrine speaks for all Bellovian heroes, therefore, when he reasons that "*this* could not be *it*." One earthly turn is not enough. "We had all been here before," he insists, "and would presently be here again." Though obstructed repeatedly by greedy and unscrupulous "reality instructors," Bellow's stubborn questers are merely slowed, not deterred, in their search for higher knowledge or illumination.

Yet how does Saul Bellow treat the occult here? What precisely does Charlie Citrine's anthroposophy do for him? Clearly, he does enjoy some positive results. If nothing else, Charlie's theosophical readings and reflections calm him; they lift his mind and attention from immediate tribulations to more permanent questions of matter and spirit. Equally clear, however, is Bellow's flexible, even ambiguous, attitude toward "the great beyond." For if Von Humboldt Fleisher indeed "speaks" to Charlie from beyond the grave, he does so in a surprisingly clearheaded, practical fashion. It is the dead poet who rescues the live but floundering historian from his financial problems. He has bequeathed Charlie a film treatment that is a fable of the latter's own life—the tale of an artist destroyed by the pursuit of success. Humboldt has also left him a legally protected but seemingly worthless movie scenario on cannibalism and survival in the Arctic the two of them had concocted years earlier as a joke. Charlie puts it aside, but Rinaldo Cantabile, ever the hyperactive operator, arrives with news that this plot outline has been plagiarized and developed into a currently popular film. The ensuing settlement eases Charlie's financial pressures and provides him a modest security. If no longer wealthy, Charlie is in a position—thanks to Humboldt's gift—to contemplate serenely both past errors and future possibilities; he can look to a life without ambitious struggles or self-loathing, or even boredom.

Through their scenario, therefore, and his own film idea (which also proves lucrative), Humboldt has repaid Charlie money taken in life. More significantly, by "communicating" with Charlie, he has, like Harry Houdini, "defied all forms of restraint and confinement, including the grave," and given substance to Charlie's speculations about an existence beyond this sphere. In this limited sense at least, Rudolf Steiner's claims of a possible dimension transcending the here-and-now exhibit some merit. Yet Charlie's occult speculations are merely that; they are provisional meditations or possibilities to challenge his mind and imagination. They do not carry the novel's thematic burden, and their validity or nonvalidity alters neither Charlie Citrine's nor Von Humboldt Fleisher's character, or the relationship of the two men to each other or to their society. At most, Charlie views anthroposophy as a possible aid in perceiving internal or external truths. If he reveals a mystical bent, Charlie Citrine is otherwise a familiar Bellovian figure whose successes and failures, betrayals and humiliations are clearly "separable from his spiritual pilgrimage."

In fact, he resembles strongly a number of recent literary figures. Solvent again, and seeing himself at a late station in life, Charlie decides to lie fallow for a time and to concentrate on his search for a higher selfhood. Thus he proves to be another "underground man" awaiting the proper moment for a return to an active life. Further, if Charlie is more mystically inclined than either Herzog or Sammler, he shares their conclusions on man's moral contract; like them, he believes the individual, when confronted by death, should respond with dignity and style. Indeed, he has himself long been "dying to do something good," and so he now returns temporarily to

America to square accounts with the living and dead. Despite his spiritualism (or perhaps because of it), he views the traditional ritual of Jewish burial as a symbolic act giving order and meaning to the most disorderly life. With his share of the film profits, therefore, he has Humboldt's body exhumed from a large public cemetery for a family reburial. He retrieves also from an old-age home Humboldt's uncle, Waldemar Wald, and a longtime mutual friend, Menasha Klinger, and he helps the two old men set up their own apartment.

The novel's final scene finds Charlie, accompanied by the old men, witnessing the transfer of the coffins of Humboldt and his mother from the public cemetery (Deathsville, New Jersey) to the Fleisher family plot. Here, as in scenes closing his other novels, Bellow brings his narrative concerns into sharp focus. For as Charlie Citrine watches the bulldozing crane tearing the soil and whirring noisily among the dead, his thoughts epitomize Bellow's views on the continuing confrontation of death and life, society and individual, collective technology and solitary artist. "The machine in every square inch of metal," thinks Charlie, had resulted from the "collaboration of engineers and other artificers." Any system derived from the discoveries of numerous great minds has to overwhelm and dominate anything produced by the working of any single mind, "which of itself can do little." The crane raises, then lowers Humboldt's coffin, and Charlie adds: "Thus, the condensation of collective intelligences and combined ingenuities, its cables silently spinning, dealt with the individual poet."

Bellow's narrative endings have come in for much debate. He closed *Seize the Day* also with a "burial scene"—a strongly promising or optimistic one. He is given to taking leave of his heroes amid nature's invigorating currents: Augie March philosophizing his way through Normandy's frozen terrain, Moses Herzog meditating in his old Massachusetts country house among freshly picked summer flowers, Eugene Henderson running in circles through the Newfoundland snow bearing a young orphan. Each scene suggests a future better than the past. Is there reason, therefore, to doubt a positive intent in his present conclusion?

Certainly here, as elsewhere, Bellow does not rule out redemption. Yet if many readers are confident that better days lie ahead for Charlie Citrine, both Bellow and Charlie now seem less certain and more ambiguous about his future, in this life or the next. Charlie looks into Humboldt's grave, for instance, to see the poet's coffin placed within a concrete casing. "So the coffin was enclosed," he muses, "and the soil did not come directly upon it. But then how did one get out? One didn't, didn't, didn't! You stayed, you stayed!" Bellow may be paying homage to James Joyce, whom he admires, for Charlie here echoes the Irish novelist's meditative Jewish hero, Leopold Bloom. "Once you are dead," sighs Bloom, gazing at the gravestones surrounding Paddy Dignam's burial plot, "you are dead." Charlie finishes his narrative with a wry joke and a graveyard pun that underscores his doubts—and most likely would have pleased Joyce. Menasha Klinger points out a sight unexpected in a New Jersey cemetery even in April: spring flowers. "What do you suppose they're called, Charlie?" Menasha asks. "Search me," Charlie replies. "I'm a city boy myself. They must be crocuses."

Most reviewers have accepted Charlie's response, along with others of the scene's implications, as purposeful signs of rebirth. Admittedly, these blooming flowers—the new season's first pastoral signs of renewal—seem indeed a gift from the dead; they seem to provide more evidence that Von Humboldt Fleisher's true gift is his ability to touch and affect the living even after death. Yet a close attention to Charlie's mocking urban tone and ironic play on words suggests he is certain not that the flowers are *crocuses* but only that all of *us croak*. The need to listen intently for Bellow's mood and meaning has resulted in reviewers and critics differing more sharply in their interpretations and evaluations of *Humboldt's Gift* than of any previous Bellow novel. They can not agree, for example, whether Saul Bellow here extends his familiar themes and ideas or departs sharply from them.

Most critics and readers should agree, however, that no modern novelist moves as effectively or authoritatively as does Bellow between "allusive metaphysical speculation and racy low-mimetic narrative." Nor do many writers fictionalize with as cutting a comic wit the "competing urges" of flesh and spirit, "money-making and truth-seeking." For that matter, few writers today will risk the critical mockery stirred by hints of man's redemptive possibilities—or by challenges to intellectual fashions of cynicism and predictions of crisis and doom. More to the point, Saul Bellow and Charlie Citrine present the reader with comic yet moving insights into those crucial issues confronting every sensitive individual between his cradle and grave. If their impressions and conclusions fail to convince totally, they can hardly be faulted for failing where no one has succeeded. Certainly they render the human journey more open and challenging than before.

Source: Ben Siegel, "Artists and Opportunists in Saul Bellow's *Humboldt's Gift*," in *Contemporary Literature*, Vol. 19, No. 2, 1978, pp. 143–64.

Sarah Blacher Cohen

In the following essay, Cohen considers the ardor of Bellow's guilt-ridden protagonist and his response to the intense feelings that torment him.

In Saul Bellow's recent novel, *Humboldt's Gift*, the protagonist, Charlie Citrine, and Von Humboldt Fleisher, the dead poet he mourns, have been readily identified by some readers as Bellow himself and Delmore Schwartz. Bellow denies these simple identifications, claiming that "Von Humboldt Fleisher is a composite" and that it "never was true that a character in a novel must be true to a historical person. There is a difference between a portrait and a picture. A picture allows more freedom." Thus Bellow denies that *Humboldt's Gift* is autobiography and that he is Charlie Citrine: "When the character of Charlie needed some quality I happen to have, I gave it to him from myself. It was only charity and enabled him to do his job in the book." Despite these disclaimers, however, Bellow has bequeathed an unduly generous portion of his emotional, intellectual, and physical self to Citrine. He even has him awarded the same public honors—the Pulitzer Prize and the *Croix de Chevalier des Arts et Lettres*—while having Citrine's dearest friend, the poet Von Humboldt Fleisher, meet with the same tragic fate as three of Bellow's closest writer friends. As Bellow's fame escalated, Isaac Rosenfeld died at 38 of a heart attack in a seedy Chicago hotel, his talent waning and unappreciated. Delmore Schwartz at 53 suffered a fatal coronary in a Manhattan flophouse, poetically and emotionally bankrupt. John Berryman jumped off a University of Minnesota bridge, "praying," in Bellow's words, "to the ruined drunken poet's God." Undoubtedly, these destroyed men are the partial models for the doomed Von Humboldt Fleisher. Their sorry ends must have diminished the happiness Bellow received from his mounting acclaim and made him suffer guilt over his good fortune in light of

ALONG WITH COMICALLY *IN*FLATING
HUMBOLDT'S IDIOSYNCRASIES, CITRINE, AS GUILTY
SURVIVOR, COMICALLY *DE*FLATES HIS OWN
ACHIEVEMENTS."

their misfortune. Since Bellow has Citrine comically undermine his success because of Humboldt's decline, it would seem that one of the principal traits Bellow has taken from himself and given to Citrine is his own survival guilt over certain defeated friends and his mocking attitude toward his own fame.

This same deprecation of success figures prominently in the works of other Jewish-American writers. Prosperity and recognition are outwardly the goals of their characters, but inwardly they are reluctant to give up their imposed identity as victims, to abandon the historically designated role of *schlemiel*. If they manage to become successful, like Abrahan Cahan's David Levinsky, they turn into sad millionaires, readily sacrificing their lonely affluence for the poverty and solidarity of the *shtetl*. Like Malamud's heroes, they feel more at home in tomb-like grocery stores, decrepit tenements, and squalid jail cells. Like Wallant's Sol Nazerman, they prefer to reconstruct pawnshops into their own private concentration camps. Wedded to suffering and accustomed to its pain, they are not likely to divorce themselves from it.

Bellow's earlier protagonists do not find success a compatible bedfellow either. It is not so much that they dislike the plush surroundings, but that they imagine they are interlopers, taking someone else's reservations. No matter how long they reside there, they never feel they have the proper credentials. Even when their rightful occupancy is without question, they cannot enjoy themselves because of the destitute who have no shelter and the dissatisfied who covet their privileged position. In *Dangling Man*, Joseph, the young intellectual, cannot endure being a civilian while so many innocent men have been killed in the war. To compensate for not being a casualty on the front lines, he becomes a psychological casualty in his own room. In *The Victim*, Asa Leventhal, editor of a minor trade journal, feels

unworthy even of this minimal good fortune, since so many were outcast, ruined, effaced. He thus allows Allbee, an anti-Semitic derelict who blames him for his job loss, to invade his premises, absorb his thoughts, and almost destroy him. Eugene Henderson is also one of those "people who feel they occupy the place that belongs to another by rights." Outliving a favored brother, he considers himself the unentitled heir of the family estate. Similarly, in Africa Henderson helplessly witnesses the death of King Dahfu, his Reichian therapist and lion coach. To atone for not sharing his fate, Henderson resolves to carry on Dahfu's good works and become Dr. Leo Henderson in America. Moses Herzog regards himself an unfit heir as well, since he has spent his father's hard-earned patrimony not on promised land, but on dilapidated property in the Massachusetts wilderness. Only in recollecting the priceless values of his Napoleon Street childhood does Herzog compensate for his prodigality. Artur Sammler is, of course, Bellow's most obvious survivor, who has come through the worst ordeal: the Holocaust. Crawling out of a mass grave where his wife has been murdered, he is the "old Jew whom they had hacked at, shot at, but missed killing somehow." Sammler also outlives his nephew, physician Elya Gruner, his benefactor in America. In a final eulogy for Gruner, Sammler contrasts his own selfish character with Gruner's unselfish one. He mourns the loss of Gruner and the loss of his own humanity.

In all of these Bellow novels, the most grievous crime his protagonists believe themselves to have committed is to have survived and, in varying degrees, prospered. In *Humboldt's Gift* the crime is the same, but the confession of the precise wrongs is more elaborate, the self-condemnation more harsh, and the desire for atonement more earnest. Also, the self-professed criminal frequently resorts to a more self-ironic humor to cope with his transgression and remorse. This prevalent self-irony may have something to do with Roger Shattuck's explanation as well: "the more closely Bellow projects himself into Citrine, the more mocking his voice seems to become." It's as if Bellow must employ his own form of comic censure to chasten himself for his sins of commission and omission.

In his own life Bellow has confessed to being delinquent toward cherished friends now dead. In a foreward to a posthumous collection of Isaac Rosenfeld's essays, he acknowledged: "I love

[Isaac], but we were rivals, and I was peculiarly touchy, vulnerable, hard to deal with—at times, as I can see now, insufferable, and not always a constant friend." Bellow felt he was not always loyal to his friend Delmore Schwartz either. A few weeks before Schwartz's death, he admitted to seeing him on the street but ran away from him because he could not face Schwartz in his extreme destitution. After Schwartz's death, Bellow began a memoir, he claims, so that "Delmore would not be *spürlos, versenkt* [sunk without a trace]," which after eight years of reworking became *Humboldt's Gift*. According to Schwartz's biographer, James Atlas, the novel came into being because "Bellow, tormented by the dead, was compelled to resurrect an image of Delmore Schwartz."

It is impossible to know the full extent of Bellow's torment or to understand Bellow's complexity of motivation for the genesis of the novel. Since I cannot get into Bellow's head to analyze the intricate dynamics of his survival guilt, I shall examine his imaginative transformation of it in *Humboldt's Gift,* or what he has termed the fictional working out of his "private obsessions."

Professionally, Charlie Citrine is one of Bellow's most fortunate heroes. A celebrated historian, biographer, and playwright, his talents are appreciated in the major centers of influence: Washington, Broadway, and the academy. He is wealthy enough to indulge himself in the pleasures of the affluent: a Mercedes-Benz, a magical Persian carpet, numerous trysts, and an expensive divorce. As he says, it was his turn "to be famous and to make money, to get heavy mail, to be recognized by influential people, to be dined at Sardis and propositioned in padded booths by women who sprayed themselves with musk ... " But Charlie cannot enjoy his renown because Von Humboldt Fleisher, his former mentor, died impoverished and in obscurity. Though Citrine was not in danger of death himself, he suffers from what Robert Lifton terms "survivor priority," the sense of being given preferential treatment to go on living while the next person's life is, for no good reason, terminated prematurely. Citrine also resembles those Holocaust and Hiroshima survivors whose "unconscious sense of an organic social balance makes them feel that their survival was purchased at the cost of another's." Especially in the concentration camps where the practice of selection intensified the competition for survival, survivors felt they

were responsible for the deaths of those chosen to be annihilated in their place. Indeed, the literary market place is by no means the concentration camp, but to the desperate artist struggling to make or preserve his reputation, the competition for survival seems almost as fierce. He may view the person who does triumph as somehow destroying his opportunities, of usurping his place. Humboldt, for example, accuses Citrine of gaining recognition at his expense, of not reimbursing him for providing the inspiration for Citrine's highly acclaimed Broadway play, *Von Trenck.* Humboldt also blames Citrine for his own decline on the "cultural Dow Jones" when in fact his alcoholism, insomnia, and paranoia have destroyed his native talent.

Yet Citrine believes that his meteoric rise has in some way been responsible for Humboldt's steady descent. Citrine sees himself as a latter-day Joseph selected to wear the artistic coat of many colors and Humboldt as one of the other brothers chosen to wear the shroud of death. Citrine feels uneasy about appearing in such a splendid coat, but at the same time he doesn't want to wear Humboldt's shroud. In this respect, Citrine is like the Holocaust survivor who, Lifton claims, is "torn by a fundamental ambivalence: he embraces the dead, pays homage to them, and joins in various rituals to perpetuate his relationship to them; but he also pushes them away, considers them tainted and unclean, dangerous and threatening." Even during the final stages of Humboldt's deterioration, when he is dead in life, Citrine hides from him. He fears that Humboldt's failure and approaching mortality are infectious and that he must quarantine himself from him. Just as Herzog avoids greeting the abject poet, Nachman, his boyhood friend from Napoleon Street, so Citrine crouches behind parked cars to avoid meeting Humboldt in Manhattan. Citrine cannot confront his old friend whose face was now "dead gray" and whose "head looked as if the gypsy moth had ... tented in his hair." So Citrine rushes back to Chicago, repelled by Humboldt and himself. To mask his horror and shame, Citrine flippantly bids Humboldt a silent farewell: "Oh kid, goodbye, I'll see you in the next world." But when he reads Humboldt's obituary two months later and sees his "disastrous newspaper face staring at [him] from death's territory," he is overwhelmed with grief and doesn't want to let go of Humboldt. Indeed a good part of the novel is a protracted elegy, with Citrine weeping for Humboldt and cursing materialistic

America for driving the brilliant poet to ruin. But if *Humboldt's Gift* is elegaic, it is a comic elegy. Bellow criticized reviewers for treating the novel "with a seriousness which was completely out of place. They didn't seem to realize that this is a funny book. As they were pursuing high seriousness, they fell into low seriousness." They failed to grasp that the "root of the light is in the heavy and the source of all humor is in the grave."

Citrine is one of Bellow's graveyard school of comics. To perpetuate his connection with the dead poet, Citrine stresses Humboldt's antic qualities as a way of resurrecting him, of making him more vivid. In Citrine's thoughts, Humboldt appears as Borscht Belt *tummler* and academic lecturer whose "spiel took in ... Goethe in Italy, Lenin's dead brother, Wild Bill Hickok's costumes, the New York Giants, Ring Lardner on grand opera, Swinburne on flagellation, and John D. Rockefeller on religion." Citrine also remembers Humboldt's Pagliacci routines where he stars in what Delmore Schwartz had called the "vaudeville of humiliation," the ridiculing of his faulty artistic talents and his fumbling attempts to gain recognition. Citrine calls attention to the Bergsonian comic battle of Humboldt's gross body warring with his refined sensibilities so that for Citrine Humboldt resembles the "caricature," the "stupid clown of the spirit's motive" of Schwartz's poem, "The Heavy Bear." By focusing on the risible dimensions of Humboldt, Citrine makes him amusingly eccentric rather than pathetic. Thus he does not have to feel guilty for abandoning such a funny fellow whose suffering he can dismiss as zany histrionics. After all, the recriminations of a clown need not be taken seriously, nor are his threats of vengeance menacing. Even his death does not seem real. Transforming Humboldt into an indestructible comic archetype, Citrine can look forward to his reappearance in the next act.

Along with comically *in*flating Humboldt's idiosyncrasies, Citrine, as guilty survivor, comically *de*flates his own achievements. He ridicules his fame, agreeing with Humboldt that the "Pulitzer Prize is for the birds, for the pullets ... a dummy newspaper ... award given by crooks and illiterates." Or Citrine likens his green Legion of Honor medal from France to the one "they give to pig-breeders." He jests about being a physical culture freak and would-be sexual superman. Contrasting his physical fitness with Humboldt's decaying remains, he wryly states: "Strengthened in illusion and idiocy by these proud medical reports, I embraced a busty Renata on this Posturepedic mattress," while Humboldt's bones had probably "crumbled in Potter's Field." Like Herzog, Citrine punctures his intellectual ambitions. Of his plans to write the definitive study on boredom, he claims he can't finish the work, because he gets "overcome by the material, like a miner with gas fumes." His project, which he mock-earnestly calls "a very personal overview of the Intellectual Comedy of the modern mind," he assigns to his more capable young daughter to complete. Like Herzog, Citrine makes light of his humanitarian aspirations, his sense of mission. He refers to himself as a letter which has been "stamped ... posted and ... waiting ... to be delivered at an important address." Citrine castigates himself for his psychic numbness, a common defense of many survivors. Like Henderson, Citrine wants "to burst the spirit's sleep," but as he playfully remarks, "I have snoozed through many a crisis while millions died." In all areas Citrine comically undercuts his stature to make himself equal in size to the diminished Humboldt. It is as if the hyperbolic recounting of his flaws is the price he must pay to remain alive. A life foolishly lived, he imagines, would not incur the jealousy of the dead Humboldt. Thus dwelling on the fatuity of his earthly pursuits gives Citrine permission in effect to go on in his bungling mortal state.

Like many of Bellow's protagonists, Citrine is comically obsessed with death, both dreading and anticipating it. Schopenhauer called death "the muse of philosophy," and for Citrine it, too, is the catalyst of most of his philosophizing. He shares Henderson's view that the "greatest problem of all" is how "to encounter death." However, Citrine does not flee to a mythic Africa to grapple with the problem. He does not sob incoherently, like Tommy Wilhelm, before the corpse of a stranger, or, like Herzog, ruefully accept the limitations of his mortality. Rather, Citrine immerses himself in Rudolph Steiner's anthroposophy in search of an alternative to the finality of death. Since Citrine and Bellow are both well beyond the middle of the journey, *Humboldt's Gift* insists more vehemently than any previous Bellow novel that there is another destination: "the soul's journey past the gates of death." Also, because Citrine has wronged Humboldt in this world, he believes in the existence of an after world where he can make amends to Humboldt and give him the respect due him. Thus, Citrine often mentally vacates his soporific state for Steiner's realm of the super-sensible. Indeed, Citrine, less geocentric than any of Bellow's other heroes, is more intoxicated with Steiner's visionary after-life than with the distracting spectacles of this earth. But he is not always sure that Steiner's heady brew is the draft that refreshes. He is intrigued with its doctrine of transcendence and the immortality of the self, yet reels from its theosophical ingredients. As an intellectual, suspicious of the occult, he mocks himself for swallowing it; yet it seems to quench his spiritual thirst.

Though Citrine is a biographer who earns his livelihood from writing about the dead, he is more interested in profiting spiritually than monetarily from his relationship to them. To obtain their otherworldly knowledge, he creates connections with the deceased which they would not permit when alive or which he was not capable of sustaining during face to face confrontations. Like Henderson, who frantically plays the violin to make contact with his dead parents, Citrine reads Steiner's texts aloud to the departed as a way of communicating with them. As for the dead he values most, he attempts, like the distraught Holocaust survivor, to "incorporate within himself an image of the dead, and then to think, feel, and act as he imagines they did or would. He feels impelled, in other words, to place himself in the position of the person ... maximally wronged." For Citrine that person is Humboldt. Citrine feels so loyal to the dead that he starts leading their lives and acquiring their characteristics. Thus, in the course of the novel Citrine becomes "absurd in the manner of Von Humboldt Fleisher." During his lifetime Humboldt relished being the solitary, misunderstood poet, but he wanted money/and acclaim as well. Similarly, Citrine, caught up in his mysticism, seems unconcerned about worldly possessions, yet he becomes highly distraught over the wreckage of his Mercedes-Benz. Humboldt blamed America for exploiting his talent, mass-producing his insights. Citrine, in turn, accuses Rinaldo Cantabile, Mafia thug and culture huckster, of capitalizing on his intellect: trying to book him as a high-brow act at Mr. Kelly's and wheedling information from him for his wife's Ph.D. thesis. Humboldt thought his friend Citrine was conspiring to ruin him just as Citrine believes his lawyer friend is profiting from his pain. Humboldt sapped his poetic energies chasing women just as Citrine's womanizing

drains his intellectual powers. Humboldt went to psychiatrists to entertain them with his lurid confessions: Citrine visits a psychiatrist to be entertained by his lurid analyses. Humboldt performed encyclopedic arias before culture-deaf audiences, and Citrine lectures on spiritualism to uninterested materialists. Like Humboldt, Citrine knows "everything [he] was supposed to know and nothing [he] really needed to know." Clearly, Citrine has become Humboldt's comic double, the not-so secret sharer of his folly. Internalizing the manic Humboldt within him, Citrine does not feel so bereft. He finds comfort in imitating his idiocy.

Though Citrine is addicted to the past and ill-equipped to live in the present, Humboldt's gift rather than his presence enables Citrine to live in the here and now. Humboldt's two film scenarios provide Citrine with enough money to take up the contemplative life in Europe. But a tidy sum for retirement from crass America is the least benefit he derives from Humboldt. The film scenarios characterize Citrine's relationship to Humboldt and provide Citrine with Humboldt's opinion of him. One scenario concerns a fastidious author who exploits human relationships for his art and is then successful, though unfulfilled. The other, already made into a popular movie, concerns an old man who in his youth resorted to cannibalism to survive a doomed North Pole expedition. When he is forced to confess his misdeeds, the townspeople forgive him. The old sinner is likened to Oedipus at Colonus, who in old age acquired "magical properties" and at the time of death had "the power to curse and bless." Obviously, Citrine is meant to be that exploitative, unfulfilled author. He is also the old cannibal whom Humboldt with the passage of time can forgive, thereby enabling Citrine to bless rather than curse his lot. In a farewell letter, Humboldt tells Citrine that he is redeemable in this world and the next, even though he still labors "in the fields of ridicule." But the message from Humboldt which most heartens Citrine is that "we are not natural beings but supernatural beings." With such assurances, Citrine's terror of non-being is diminished. He no longer strains against the grave as did the great death-defier, Harry Houdini, his fellow escape artist. Humboldt gives Citrine faith to believe that "so extraordinary a thing as a human soul" cannot be destroyed forever. Humboldt also absolves Citrine of his guilt so that he no longer has to berate himself for injuring or neglecting the dying. Citrine can now transform his destructive self-blame into a constructive concern for others. Or, as Robert Lifton has shown, negative survival guilt can lead to an "energizing or animating guilt" and ultimately to a redefinition of survival guilt as the "anxiety of responsibility." Thus Citrine comes to realize that "he had responsibility not only to fulfill his own destiny, but to carry on for certain failed friends like Von Humboldt Fleisher." "The dead and the living still formed one community."

Like Bellow's other keepers of the covenant, Citrine meets his obligations. He tries to retrieve the body of his lover killed in a South American plane crash. He postpones a pleasure junket to help his brother cope with fears of death the day before his open-heart surgery. Citrine shares with Humboldt's near-dead uncle the money from his legacy and moves him and an old family friend from an old age home to a comfortable apartment. More significantly, he disinters Humboldt and his mother from one of those crowded necropolitan developments and reburies them in ample graves of their own. The funeral service he performs is his formal way of seeking true forgiveness from Humboldt, since Jewish law prescribes that the only way to obtain genuine atonement is to visit the grave of the wronged person and there ask his pardon. The funeral service also functions, as all such ceremonies do, to "speed the dead on their 'journey' to another plane of existence" and to "'incorporate the deceased into the world of the dead.'" Indeed for Citrine the ceremony confirms that the dead are really dead, that dust has returned to dust. But it also keeps the buried Humboldt alive for Citrine and holds out the hope for immortality. Although "Humboldt's flowers were aborted in the bulb" during his lifetime, Citrine's discovery of crocuses at his grave suggests that his spirit is flowering elsewhere.

The novel's end is in keeping with the conventions of the pastoral elegy: "expression of grief at the loss of a friend," "praise of the dead," "a statement of belief in ... immortality," and the presence of flowers as symbols of renewal. The heart of the novel, Citrine's copious reminiscences of Humboldt, is also a form of reparation and restoration. Like the Holocaust survivors who are compelled to act as witnesses for those slain, Citrine feels obliged to tell the ruined Humboldt's tale, to redress personal and public wrongs against him. By recapturing his unique essence,

Citrine is able to give Humboldt a kind of permanence. If it is true that art is a "recreation of a once loved and once whole, but now lost and ruined object," then Bellow, through Citrine, is able to give Humboldt an eternal life in his work. The title of the novel, then, has a double meaning. It refers to Humboldt's gift to Citrine, but it also represents Citrine's gift to Humboldt. And if we rely on the psychoanalytic wisdom of aesthetician Hanna Segal, the book could represent Bellow's gift to himself. "Writing a book," claims Segal, can be for the author like "the work of mourning in that gradually the external objects are given up, they are re-instated in the ego, and recreated in the book." Thus, Bellow is able to resurrect his dead friends through his literary revival of them. Since they are a part of his internal world and have become immortalized through him, he is encouraged to believe in his own immortality.

But Bellow does not make this meaning apparent. His *animal ridens* leads him rather into the more circuitous route of comedy. He has Citrine caught up in what has become a typical humorous situation—the frenetic evasion of death. Like Bellow's other protagonists, Citrine desperately clings to childhood, frantically seeks refuge in sex, and anxiously theorizes about death to circumvent it. He travels great distances to hide from death or races and connives to meet up with it. He zealously shuns the dead Humboldt or communes exclusively with him. He feels unworthy of living, yet would not exchange places with the dead. He wants to escape the ennui of this life, yet dreads an eternity of boredom.

While Citrine plays hide-and-seek with death, he is immersed in the circus of this life. He accompanies Mafia freaks in pursuit of thrilling low life. He chases voluptuous younger women who abandon him on romantic merry-go-rounds. He loses out to cannibal divorce lawyers who strip him of his possessions. He harbors madman vendettas against his exploiters. Yet Citrine doesn't end up as a side-show grotesque. Though he is another of Bellow's "higher-thought clowns," he finally recognizes the folly of his escapist actions and wayward beliefs. Aware of how precious his limited time on earth is, he resolves to be an "entity," an autonomous individual who listens to the voice of his own soul, and not an "identity," a self which is socially determined. By choosing his authentic self over the presentation self, he intends to stop being a creature of "foolishness, intricacy, wasted subtlety." He also refuses to allow a world which is hostile to or oblivious of poetry to shape his values or restrict his tastes. Thus, like Tolstoy, Citrine advocates that we put an end to the "false and unnecessary comedy of history and begin simply to live." This emphasis upon life rather than death does not rule out a divine comedy, since Citrine vows to "listen in secret to the sound of the truth that God puts into us."

Source: Sarah Blacher Cohen, "Comedy and Guilt in *Humboldt's Gift*," in *Modern Fiction Studies*, Vol. 25, No. 1, Spring 1979, pp. 47–57.

SOURCES

Bellow, Saul, *Humboldt's Gift*, Penguin Books, 1996.

Broyard, Anatole, "Books of the Times: Lion or the Anthroposophist?" in *New York Times*, August 14, 1975, p. 29.

Gilman, Richard, "Saul Bellow's New, Open, Spacious Novel about Art, Society, and a Bizarre Poet," in *New York Times*, August 17, 1975, p. 209.

Leonard, John, "A Handsome Gift," in *New York Times*, September 7, 1975, p. 268.

Nobel Foundation, "The Nobel Prize in Literature 1976," in *Nobelprize.org*, 1976, http://nobelprize.org/nobel_prizes/ literature/laureates/1976/index.html (accessed September 14, 2006).

Simpson, Louis, "The Ghost of Delmore Schwartz," in *New York Times*, December 7, 1975, p. 308.

FURTHER READING

Atlas, James, *Delmore Schwartz: The Life of an American Poet*, Farrar, Straus, Giroux, 1977.

> This biography covers Schwartz's life and death, focusing on his writing career. Atlas's fluid writing style makes this biography read like a novel.

Cronin, Gloria L., and Ben Siegel, eds., *Conversations with Saul Bellow*, University Press of Mississippi, 1994.

> Cronin and Siegel have collected interviews with Bellow from 1953 through 1994. Some biographical information is included.

Phillips, Robert, ed., *Delmore Schwartz and James Laughlin: Selected Letters*, Norton, 1993.

> This book collects correspondence between American poet Delmore Schwartz and his publisher, James Laughlin of New Directions, from the time of Schwartz's fame until mental illness incapacitated him. The two were good friends and shared a love of poetry.

Pifer, Ellen, *Saul Bellow against the Grain*, Penn Studies in Contemporary American Fiction, University of Pennsylvania Press, 1991.

> Pifer argues that Bellow was a radical writer. In this book, she examines ten of his novels within this new framework of assessment.

Steiner, Rudolph, *Knowledge of the Higher Worlds and Its Attainment*, translated by George Metaxa, Anthroposophic Press, 1947, http://wn.rsarchive.org/Books/GA010/ English/GA010_index.html (accessed October 11, 2006).

> Steiner's major text on anthroposophy presents meditation exercises for the attainment of higher consciousness. It is available free on the Internet courtesy of the Rudolph Steiner Archive.

The Killer Angels

MICHAEL SHAARA

1974

Michael Shaara's novel *The Killer Angels* (1974) covers a four-day period (June 29, July 1–3, 1863) during which the Battle of Gettysburg, the turning point of the American Civil War, was fought in Pennsylvania. Shaara describes the battle from the points of view of several of the main participants, the most important being, on the Confederate side, General Robert E. Lee, commander of the Army of Northern Virginia, and Lieutenant General James Longstreet, commander of the Confederate First Army Corps and Lee's second in command, and on the Union side, Colonel Joshua Lawrence Chamberlain, commander of the Twentieth Maine Infantry regiment. Shaara reveals the thoughts and feelings of these and other soldiers as they play out their parts in the historic battle: why they fight, what motivates them, what their beliefs are, what decisions they make and why. Through dialogue and inner monologue, the author explores the great issues of the day, including slavery, states' rights, and theories of war and how they are applied to the battle at hand, as well as religious and philosophical issues such as the role played by chance and destiny in the great battle. In vivid prose that recreates the sights, sounds, and smells of battle, *The Killer Angels* makes readers feel that they are right there in the midst of the action. *The Killer Angels* won the Pulitzer Prize for Fiction in 1975 and was the basis for the film *Gettysburg* in 1993.

AUTHOR BIOGRAPHY

Michael Shaara was born on June 23, 1929, in Jersey City, New Jersey, the son of Italian immigrants. He attended Rutgers University and it was there that he realized his goal was to become a writer. He wrote his first published story while he was still an undergraduate, even though his creative writing teacher was less than enthusiastic about his work and suggested he aim for a more literary style.

Shaara graduated from Rutgers with a Bachelor of Arts degree in 1951 and then pursued graduate study at Columbia University (1952–1953) and the University of Vermont (1953–1954). He also began to publish science fiction short stories in popular magazines.

Shaara married Helen Krumweide in 1950, and in 1954, he moved with his wife and young son to Florida, where Shaara was for a short time employed as a police officer in St. Petersburg. After this he began to teach English, literature, and creative writing at Florida State University in Tallahassee. He was associate professor at that university from 1961 to 1973.

Shaara continued to write and published more than seventy short stories in magazines such as *Playboy*, *Galaxy*, *Redbook*, *Cosmopolitan*, and the *Saturday Evening Post*. His first novel, *The Broken Place*, about a soldier who returns home from the Korean War and becomes a boxer, was published by New American Library in 1968.

The origins of Shaara's second novel, *The Killer Angels*, was a visit Shaara made with his family to Gettysburg, the site of the famous Civil War battle. Shaara worked on the manuscript for seven years, only to see it rejected by fifteen publishers. It was finally accepted by a small independent publisher, the David McKay Company, and published in 1974. It did not attract great attention from reviewers, but this did not prevent it from being awarded the Pulitzer Prize for Fiction in 1975. The novel was the basis for the 1993 television miniseries *Gettysburg*.

During a difficult process of recovery following a serious motorcycle accident, Shaara continued to dedicate himself to his writing. His third novel, *The Herald*, was published by McGraw in 1981. It is about a scientist who wants to create a master race and plans to kill

MEDIA ADAPTATIONS

- *The Killer Angels* was adapted by Turner Pictures and aired as the television miniseries *Gettysburg*, in 1993.

- The novel was also recorded, in an unabridged audio version by Books on Tape and published in 1985.

millions of people in order to accomplish his goal.

The following year, a selection of Shaara's previously published short stories, *Soldier Boy*, was published by Pocket Books.

During the 1980s, however, Shaara's health was in decline. He had already, in 1965, suffered a major heart attack, and on May 5, 1988, in Tallahassee, he died of a second heart attack.

After Shaara's death, his children discovered an unpublished manuscript by their father. Called *For Love of the Game*, it is a story about an aging baseball pitcher. It turned out that during the 1980s, Shaara had tried but failed to find a publisher for this novel, which was eventually published in 1991 by Carroll & Graf. In 1999, *For Love of the Game* was released as a major motion picture by Universal Studios.

PLOT SUMMARY

Foreword: June 1863

The Killer Angels begins with a foreword that sets the scene for the action that follows. It is divided into two sections. The first section describes the two armies. The Army of Northern Virginia, consisting of seventy thousand men commanded by Robert E. Lee, has on June 15, 1863, crossed the Potomac at Williamsport and invaded the North. Its aim is to draw the Union army out into the open and crush it. In late June, the Union army, the Army of the Potomac, numbering eighty thousand men, turns north to begin its pursuit of the rebels that ends at Gettysburg. The second section of the foreword briefly describes the main characters: on the Confederate side, Robert Edward Lee, James Longstreet, George Pickett, Richard Ewell, Ambrose Power Hill, Lewis Armistead, Richard Brooke Garnett, J. E. B. Stuart, Jubal Early; on the Union side, Joshua Lawrence Chamberlain, John Buford, John Reynolds, George Gordon Meade, Winfield Scott Hancock.

Monday, June 29, 1863

1: THE SPY

Harrison, a spy sent by Longstreet from Virginia to locate the position of the Union army, looks down from a high position in the woods upon two Union corps, twenty thousand men moving fast. He slips away on horseback and reaches Confederate headquarters after dark. He is taken to General Longstreet and to whom he gives detailed information about the position of the Union army. Longstreet did not even know that the Union army was on the move and certainly not as close as two hundred miles away. He is skeptical about the accuracy of Harrison's report, but Harrison insists he is right. Longstreet knows that if Harrison's information is correct, his army is in great danger, with the Union army so close. He takes Harrison to see Lee, who is doubtful whether he should make a move on the word of a spy. But he does decide to move quickly, aiming to get behind the Union forces and cut them off from Washington. Lee gives the order to move at dawn in the direction of the small town of Gettysburg.

2: CHAMBERLAIN

Colonel Joshua Chamberlain, commander of the Twentieth Maine regiment, is awakened by his aide Buster Kilrain. Kilrain informs him that they are being sent 120 mutineers from the Second Maine regiment, men who have refused to serve the final year of their three-year enlistment. There is a message signed by General Meade, the new Union commander, to the effect that these men are to fight. If they refuse, Chamberlain is authorized to shoot them. The ragged, tired mutineers are presented to Chamberlain by a captain from a Pennsylvania regiment. Chamberlain allows their leader, Joseph Bucklin, to express their grievances. Bucklin complains about the incompetence of the officers they have served under. After Chamberlain receives

orders to move west into Pennsylvania, he gives what he hopes will be an inspirational speech to the mutineers about the cause of freedom they are fighting for. He says he needs them because the regiment is under strength, but he will not shoot them if they refuse to fight. As the regiment moves in the direction of Gettysburg, Chamberlain is pleased to hear from his brother Tom that all but six of the mutineers have agreed to fight.

3: BUFORD

At noon, from the top of a hill outside Gettysburg, Union commander John Buford observes rebel troops on the far side of the town. There is at least a brigade, but no cavalry in sight. Buford has two brigades with him; the big infantry is a day's march behind him. Buford watches as the rebels withdraw then sends scouts to gather information about the rebels' movements so he can know what the Union forces are facing. Next, he sends a message to John Reynolds and General Meade explaining that he expects the rebel army to be there in force in the morning. He worries that they will occupy a strong position in the hills, and he does not know whether his forces will be able to hold their ground until Reynolds arrives with his infantry. After dark, the scouts return and report that the whole Confederate army is on its way to Gettysburg. Later, Buford receives a note from Reynolds, who promises to come in the morning as early as possible.

4: LONGSTREET

In Longstreet's camp, thirty miles from Gettysburg, Longstreet worries because he does not know the position of the Union army. He was expecting to hear from General Stuart, who has been gone for several days but has sent no information. General Hill disbelieves reports of Union cavalry in Gettysburg, and Lee accepts Hill's judgment. Longstreet is not so sure. General Pickett, an old friend of Longstreet's, arrives. Pickett and his forces are bringing up the rear; he is desperate to see some action and asks Longstreet if he can be moved forward. Longstreet tells him his time will come. Longstreet then talks to Armistead, who is confident of victory in the forthcoming battle. They discuss military strategy, including the merits of offensive and defensive war. Other officers discuss why the war is being fought. Just before dawn, Confederate soldiers approach a Union picket, and one of the pickets fires the first shot of the battle.

Wednesday, July 1, 1863: The First Day

1: LEE

Lee arises at dawn. He has heart trouble and does not feel well. His aide Major Taylor informs him that nothing has been heard from Stuart. He also informs Lee of Hill's skepticism about the presence of Union cavalry at Gettysburg. Lee knows that if cavalry is present, there will be infantry close by. He tells Taylor that he does not want to fight until his entire army is concentrated. Lee deals with some civilians and consults further with his aides. Marshall wants to court-martial Stuart for his continued absence, but Lee offers him no support. Longstreet arrives, and Lee tells him to stay in the rear, since he cannot afford to lose him. They discuss tactics; Longstreet favors defense, but Lee wants to attack. When the army gets on the move, Lee and Longstreet ride several miles together. At about ten in the morning, they hear the first sounds of artillery in the distance.

2: BUFORD

At dawn, Buford deals with the first rebel attack and expects another more organized one imminently. His forces are dug in and he is confident, but he writes to Reynolds saying he expects relief. Another rebel attack is repelled, and prisoners are taken. Buford knows that the rebels are there in force, and the Union position is precarious against such numbers, even when Reynolds arrives. When the big attack comes, Union lines are tested, and Buford considers pulling out. Then Reynolds arrives with two corps of fresh Union infantry, and their prospects look good. But when Buford and Reynolds ride out together, placing their troops, Reynolds is shot and killed.

3: LEE

Lee has issued orders to Heth not to force a major engagement. He frets about not having heard from Stuart and, therefore, not knowing the disposition of Union forces. He soon realizes that Heth has taken on more than he can handle and has been repulsed. Heth arrives and explains that he was surprised by the presence of Union infantry. He thought he was faced only by local militia. He apologizes. Rodes and Early continue the attack, and Heth requests permission to do so also. Lee is unsure but then tells Heth

to go ahead and tells Pender to do the same. The battle rages. Heth is wounded, but then a courier from Early brings the news that the enemy is falling back. Lee instructs Early to take Cemetery Hill, unless he is faced with a superior force, since he does not want Union forces established on high ground. Longstreet arrives, and he and Lee disagree over tactics. While Lee wants to press the attack, Longstreet wants to disengage, swing the army round, and get a good defensive position on high ground between the Union army and Washington, so that Union forces will have no option but to attack. Lee is worried that he sees no sign of an assault on Cemetery Hill. Longstreet again pushes for withdrawal, but Lee says he will attack the next day if Meade is there with all his forces.

4: CHAMBERLAIN

Chamberlain and the Twentieth Maine make their way north across the Pennsylvania border to Hanover. Tom Chamberlain, Joshua's younger brother, teaches one of the men from Second Maine the regiment's bugle call. Chamberlain reflects on the battle of Fredericksburg, in which he participated; the characteristics of Maine; his mother and father; his home. When they reach Hanover, the townspeople are delighted to see them. As evening comes they go to rest; they have marched a hundred miles in five days. But soon they hear their bugle call and are ordered to march on through the night to Gettysburg; they hear rumors about the battle that has just taken place and also the false information that the popular General McClellan is back in charge of the Union army. They reach Gettysburg at midnight.

5: LONGSTREET

In the evening after the first day of battle, Longstreet rides back from Gettysburg to his camp. He knows that Lee will ignore his advice and attack in the morning. He thinks back to the previous winter, during which his three children died of fever. He discusses the day's events with the Englishman, Fremantle, who is there as an observer of the battle. Fremantle speaks of his admiration for Lee and his hope that England will ally itself with the Confederacy. Longstreet relates some memories of Stonewall Jackson, the Confederate general who was killed before Gettysburg, and argues the case for defensive rather than offensive war.

6: LEE

That evening Lee receives congratulations for the Confederates' success in battle. Ewell explains that he did not attack Cemetery Hill, because it did not seem practical. Early, to whom Ewell defers, confirms the reasons for their decision. Lee explains Longstreet's preferred strategy, but Ewell and Early favor attack rather than defense. Lee rides off and encounters General Trimble, who is angry with Ewell for not attempting to take the hill. He believes it could have been done. Lee returns to his headquarters, where Ewell apologizes for being too careful during the battle. Lee realizes Ewell is not up to the task, but he speaks kindly to him. Alone later in the night, Lee resolves to attack the following afternoon.

7: BUFORD

At two o'clock in the morning, Buford rides along Cemetery Hill as his men dig in. He is in pain from an arm wound. He goes to a farmhouse where officers are gathered and sees two majors arguing about who is in charge. Buford learns that Howard, who was in charge of the Eleventh Corps that did not perform well, has complained that Buford did not support Howard's right flank. Buford explains to Hancock how much he was involved in the previous day's action. Meade arrives. Buford has received his orders, cannot get close to Meade, and rides back towards the cemetery, where he talks to the dead Reynolds, saying that they held the ground.

Thursday, July 2, 1863: The Second Day

1: FREMANTLE

At three o'clock in the morning, Fremantle eagerly awaits the coming battle as he joins the other officers at breakfast. He feels at home, thinking of the Confederate army as transplanted Englishmen. He is certain they will win. The officers observe the Union lines through field glasses. A bit later, Fremantle rides with Longstreet then goes off to talk with some of the European officers; he thinks about how he supports the traditions of the South rather than the democracy favored by the North.

2: CHAMBERLAIN

Kilrain informs Chamberlain that just before dawn they found a wounded black man. Chamberlain has rarely seen a black man before. They cannot communicate with him and think he must have been a slave who tried to run away

from the Confederates and was shot. They feed him and treat his wound. They conclude he has not long been in the country. It later transpires that he was shot by a woman in Gettysburg after he came into town looking for directions. Bugles blow and the division forms itself. Colonel Vincent informs Chamberlain that they will probably be held in reserve that morning. The call comes to advance, and the corps begins to march. Then they are ordered to stop, and they rest in a field. Chamberlain talks with Kilrain about black people; Chamberlain says that he sees no essential differences between the races, only the humanity and the "divine spark" they share. He regards slavery as a terrible thing. Chamberlain sits against a tree, waiting for the battle to begin.

3: LONGSTREET

Lee seeks Longstreet's agreement on tactics. He points out that neither Ewell nor Early favors withdrawing. They believe they can take Cemetery Hill and Culp's Hill, which are held by Union forces. Poring over a map, the generals plan their moves as Lee gives orders. Johnston is given responsibility for moving Longstreet into position, and Longstreet insists that his men are not seen by the enemy. Johnston confesses he knows little about the roads, which causes Longstreet to curse at the continued absence of Stuart, who would have been able to supply information. They begin the march at noon. Lee and Longstreet ride together; they recall past battles, and Lee hopes the coming one will be the last. After Lee rides off, Johnston informs Longstreet that if they continue their present course, they will be seen by the enemy. Furious, Longstreet orders a change of direction. They find another route, but Longstreet knows that the extra march will tire his men. When they reach the front, they unexpectedly find Union soldiers in the peach orchard. Hood wants to shift the plan and go right, behind the Big Round Top. He says otherwise he will lose half his division. Privately, Longstreet agrees this is the wisest course but refuses to deviate from Lee's orders. The attack begins.

4: CHAMBERLAIN

Chamberlain hears artillery fire and knows the battle has begun. It is nearly 4 p.m. Vincent informs them that the rebels are attacking the Union left flank and places Chamberlain's regiment on Little Round Top, the extreme left of the

Union line. He instructs him to hold the line at all costs. Chamberlain places his men; he can see the battle raging below. Three of the Maine mutineers agree to join the fight. The rebels come in full force, and the Union line holds. The rebels come again. There are many dead on both sides; Kilrain is wounded, and Chamberlain is wounded in his right foot. He continues to direct his forces effectively, but they are running low on ammunition, and the rebels are still coming. He directs his brother Tom to fill a gap in the line. One man says they cannot hold the line and should pull out. Chamberlain refuses. He orders his men to fix bayonets, and they charge down the hill, routing the rebels and taking five hundred prisoners. Kilrain is wounded for the second time, but he saves Chamberlain's life by shooting a rebel who was aiming his rifle at Chamberlain. Tom brings news that they fought off four rebel regiments, perhaps two thousand men. The Twentieth Maine takes 130 casualties, which is nearly half the regiment. Chamberlain feels great joy at the victory.

5: LONGSTREET

In the evening, Longstreet visits the wounded Hood in the hospital. Then he learns from Sorrel that Hood's officers blame Longstreet for the failure to take the hill. Longstreet knows that no one will blame Lee, even though they were following Lee's orders. Longstreet learns that Hood's division suffered losses of 50 percent and knows they no longer have the resources for another major assault. Then he hears that General Pickett has arrived with five thousand fresh men. He goes to headquarters to talk to Lee and finds that at last Stuart has returned. Lee tells Longstreet they almost succeeded, but Longstreet knows that is not true. He informs Lee that there are three Union corps dug in on the high ground. When Longstreet moves off into the crowd he sees Marshall, who wants to court-martial Stuart but says Lee refuses to sign the papers; Longstreet says he will speak to Lee about it. He rides with Fremantle, who is full of praise for Lee, but Longstreet speaks of Lee and his tactics in a way that he immediately realizes might be thought disloyal. He returns to camp and listens to the officers singing, drinking, and telling stories. An emotional Armistead recalls a time back in 1861 when he sang a particular song with his close friend Win Hancock, who is now on the opposing side.

6: LEE

Lee works all night. He reflects on why he had to break his vow to defend the Union; he feels he had no choice, since he could not take up arms against his own people. He now has to decide whether to move to higher ground in another place or stay and fight. Stuart visits him; Lee rebukes him for letting the army down, and Stuart offers to resign, but Lee says he needs him in the coming fight. Lee decides he must attack. He plans to use Pickett's forces in a drive to the center of the Union line that will split the enemy in two, and then he wants to use Stuart's cavalry at the rear to complete the rout.

Friday July 3, 1863

1: CHAMBERLAIN

At dawn, Chamberlain climbs a tree and surveys the scene. His foot is still bleeding, and the men are out of rations. He thinks the rebels will come again that day; he has only two hundred men left, but they are in a good position. The battle has begun, to the north of them, on the opposite flank. An aide from Colonel Rice arrives and tells Chamberlain he is relieved; Colonel Fisher is to take over their position. Chamberlain does not want to leave, and the Union lieutenant takes them to their new position, which is right in the center of the Union line.

2: LONGSTREET

Longstreet and Lee ride together; Longstreet says he has discovered a way south and wants to move, but Lee will hear none of it. He explains his attacking strategy. Longstreet protests, saying a frontal assault will be a disaster. Lee insists there is no alternative. Word comes that Union forces are attacking Ewell. Lee is surprised. Lee talks to Wofford, who tells him his men cannot break the Union lines because the enemy has brought in reinforcements. Lee still believes that his fifteen thousand men can do it. The plan is for a heavy artillery barrage on the center of the Union line, followed by a charge at the center by Pickett's division, which will break the line. Longstreet says he believes the attack will fail. They will have to march for a mile over open ground under constant artillery fire. Lee, however, is confident of victory. Longstreet says nothing about his doubts as he explains the battle strategy to the officers, including Pettigrew, Trimble, and Pickett. Longstreet waits for the 140 guns to begin firing and for the Union reply. It will be the greatest artillery barrage ever fired.

3: CHAMBERLAIN

Lieutenant Pitzer guides Chamberlain and his men to their position, near Meade's headquarters. They are to be held in reserve. Chamberlain is called over to meet General Sykes, who is impressed by what he has heard of Chamberlain's bayonet charge. Sykes promises he will get rations to Chamberlain's men. Chamberlain walks back to his men, troubled by his injured foot. Tom reports that Kilrain has died not from his wounds but of a heart attack. The artillery battle begins, and shells fall very close to Chamberlain and Tom. Chamberlain sleeps intermittently while he waits for action.

4: ARMISTEAD

Armistead watches the artillery barrage begin just after one o'clock in the afternoon. He sees Pickett writing a poem for his sweetheart and gives him a ring from his finger to send to her. Pickett is joyfully awaiting the action. Garnett rides up on horseback and says he intends to ride into the battle, even though that is against orders. His leg is injured, and he cannot walk. Armistead tries to get Pickett to order Garnett not to make the charge, but Pickett refuses. The artillery barrage slackens, and the Confederates begin their charge, moving through the woods and then into the open fields beyond. Armistead encounters Garnett still on horseback and knows he will die. The Union artillery opens up once more, and a wave of fire rolls down on the advancing men who form a line a mile long. Many men fall, and the gaps in the line are closed up. Armistead permits himself to hope that they may succeed. They face devastating canister fire—millions of small metal balls. Armistead yells encouragement to Kemper. He is wounded in the leg, but he still goes forward and manages to reach the stone wall that is the object of their charge. He is hit in the side and knows he is dying. The dead are all around him, most of them Confederate soldiers. He asks a Union officer if he can send a message to his old friend General Hancock. He is informed that Hancock is wounded; he prays that Hancock may survive, then he dies.

5: LONGSTREET

Longstreet sits watching the battle and then sees his men retreat. He orders Pickett to retreat. He thinks that all his men have died for nothing. Lee appears, and the retreating men slow at the sight of him. Longstreet thinks he will never forgive Lee. Lee says he expects a counterattack, but the Union troops pull back. Longstreet rides back towards the camp. He learns that of the thirteen colonels in Pickett's division, seven are dead and six wounded. Lee tells Longstreet they must withdraw that night. He says they will do better next time, but Longstreet disagrees. Lee admits he was wrong in his battle strategy and that Longstreet was right.

6: CHAMBERLAIN

In the evening, Chamberlain goes off to be on his own. He looks over the battlefield. Tom joins him and remarks on the courage the rebels showed. Tom does not understand how they could fight so hard for slavery. Chamberlain feels pity for the dead men whose corpses are being laid out on a nearby field, but he feels a thrill at the thought of fresh battles to come.

Afterword

A brief Afterword describes what happened to some of the main characters in the months and years after the great battle.

CHARACTERS

Brigadier General Lewis A. Armistead

Brigadier General Lewis A. Armistead is one of Pickett's brigade commanders. He is a shy, courtly, honest man, with a strong sense of duty. A widower, he is nicknamed Lo (short for Lothario) as a joke. He is a close friend of General Hancock, who is now fighting on the Union side, and this gives Armistead much cause for reflection. He had once said to Hancock, "if I ever lift a hand against you, may God strike me dead." He takes part in Pickett's charge, against positions defended by Hancock, and is killed.

Major General John Buford

Major General John Buford is a tall, blond cavalry soldier, born in Kentucky. He is a veteran of the Indian wars in the west and many Civil War battles. He tends to proceed slowly and carefully. Conscious of class divisions, he does not care for "gentleman" Confederates. Buford is a professional soldier who has acquired the latest weaponry for his men and taught them how to dig in and hold off any force for a while. Once he held off Longstreet's army for six hours, and he is proud of the fact that they hold their ground against the first wave of Confederate attacks.

Colonel Joshua Lawrence Chamberlain

Colonel Joshua Lawrence Chamberlain commands the Twentieth Maine regiment with distinction. He is not a career soldier or politician; before the war he was a professor of rhetoric at Bowdoin University. He is tall, with "a grave boyish dignity," and he has a gift for making speeches. Chamberlain is always concerned with the welfare of his men and leads by example. He treats even the mutineers well, feeding them, listening to their grievances, and explaining to them the cause for which they are being asked to fight. He speaks to them in the same calm, pleasant manner that he used to deal with rebellious students. It is because of Chamberlain's decent attitude that most of the mutineers agree to fight. Chamberlain would not shoot them even though he is authorized to do so. He is also chivalrous to captured prisoners, on one occasion offering his own water flask to a rebel who requests water.

Chamberlain is a strong believer in the Union cause. He believes in the dignity of man and the equality of all men, and he has faith in the United States and in the individual. He loves his brother Tom, but he is willing to put Tom in harm's way when necessary because of his belief in the cause. Chamberlain loves army life; he finds it "a joy to wake in the morning and feel the army all around you and see the campfires in the morning and smell the coffee." He feels exhilarated after the victory that follows the bayonet charge; his ordering of the charge shows his ability to instinctively do the right thing in an emergency. After the final battle of Gettysburg is over, he is eager for future battles.

Lieutenant Tom Chamberlain

Tom Chamberlain is Joshua's younger brother. He has been recently promoted to lieutenant, and he is Chamberlain's aide. He practically worships his older brother.

Major General Jubal Early

Major General Jubal Early is the commander of one of Ewell's divisions. He is "a dark, cold, icy man, bitter, alone." Longstreet dislikes him.

Lieutenant General Richard Ewell

Lieutenant General Richard Ewell is the commander of the Union's Second Army Corps. He has "the look of a great-beaked, hopping bird. He was bald and scrawny; his voice piped and squeaked like cracking eggshells." He lost a leg in an earlier battle and has just returned to the army. Ewell has been a good soldier, but he is not a success as a commander. He is too cautious and unsure of himself and defers to the judgments of Early. He apologizes to Lee for failing to attack Cemetery Hill on the first day of battle. Lee realizes that appointing him as a corps commander, in charge of twenty thousand men, was a mistake.

Lieutenant Colonel Arthur Lyon Fremantle

Lieutenant Colonel Arthur Lyon Fremantle is an Englishman who is present with the Confederates at Gettysburg as an observer. Described as "a scrawny man, toothy, with a pipelike neck and a monstrous Adam's apple," Fremantle is an officer of the British Coldstream Guards. He admires Lee and the Confederacy because their respect for tradition reminds him of England.

Brigadier General Richard Brooke Garnett

Brigadier General Richard Brooke Garnett is Pickett's brigade commander. He is a man who has something to prove, since Stonewall Jackson accused him of cowardice. This seems to have been a false accusation, since Garnett is respected by his fellow officers, including Longstreet and Armistead. He insists on riding into battle during Pickett's charge, even though he is wounded and cannot walk. He has to prove his honor and his courage. He is killed during the assault.

Major General Winfield Scott Hancock

Major General Winfield Scott Hancock is the commander of Second Corps. He is known as an excellent soldier. Longstreet thinks of him as "dashing and confident," and Chamberlain, when he sees him, observes that he is "tall and calm, handsome, magnetic." An old friend of the Confederate Armistead, Hancock is wounded on the third day of the battle, but he recovers.

Harrison

Harrison is the Confederate scout, or spy, sent by Longstreet to report on the position of the Union army. He is distrusted by the Confederates, who treat him with disdain. By profession, Harrison is an actor.

Major General Henry Heth

Major General Henry (Harry) Heth is a commander of one of Hill's divisions. He is "a square-faced man, a gentle face." On the first day of battle, he gets into a major fight with Buford's forces, even though he was under orders not to start a major engagement.

Lieutenant Colonel Ambrose Power Hill

Lieutenant Colonel Ambrose Power Hill has recently been put in charge of the Confederate Third Army Corps. He is a "nervous, volatile, brilliant man" and was a superb division commander, but Lee has his doubts about whether Hill will be as effective now that he is in command of an entire corps.

Major General John Bell Hood

Major General John Bell Hood, known as Sam, commands one of Longstreet's divisions. He is a "tall slim man with an extraordinary face, eyes with a cold glint in them, erect in posture even as he sat, cutting a stick." He is a competent soldier.

Major General Oliver O. Howard

Major General Oliver O. Howard is the commander of the Union's Eleventh Corps that does not perform well on the first day of battle. Howard allows his line to be broken as he had also done at the battle of Chancellorsville. Hancock takes command and reforms Howard's men, after which men go to him rather than Howard for orders. This greatly angers Howard who outranks Hancock.

Brigadier General James Kemper

Brigadier General James Kemper serves under General Pickett. Formerly, he had been Speaker of the Virginia House. He is wounded in the Confederate charge on the last day of the battle.

Private Buster Kilrain

Private Buster Kilrain is an aide to Chamberlain. He is much older than Chamberlain and is described as "a white-haired man with the build of an ape." He has a fatherly attitude toward Chamberlain, and Chamberlain depends on him. Kilrain is a former sergeant who was demoted for striking an officer when drunk. He is twice wounded in battle, saves Chamberlain's life by killing a man who was taking aim at Chamberlain, and finally dies of a heart attack.

General Robert E. Lee

General Robert E. Lee is the commander of the Army of Northern Virginia. He is fifty-six years old and is not in good health, showing early signs of heart disease. He is often weary, but his appearance is impressive: "regal, formal, a beautiful white-haired, white-bearded old man." Lee is known as an honest man and a gentleman without vices. He does not drink, smoke, gamble, or chase women. He does not complain, and he is always in control. Lee is loved by his men who regard him with respect and awe. Fremantle tells a story going round that when Lee was asleep, and the army was marching by, fifteen thousand men went by on tiptoe to ensure they did not wake him. Lee's men have faith in their commander, and this is what has made the Confederate army, up to Gettysburg, so successful.

Lee has a great deal of patience. He speaks formally to his officers and does not betray his irritation at Ewell for being too cautious, and he refuses to court-martial Stuart for letting him down. He listens calmly to Trimble as he rages against Ewell. Lee's practical nature means that he deals with the situation as it is rather than worrying about how things might have been better. His practice is to give the orders and let his men get on with the job, but he is sometimes let down by the poor performances of his officers. He does not always coordinate his orders by assembling his officers in one place, and he gives no written orders.

Lee loves Virginia and believes he had no alternative but to take up arms in the Confederate cause. Throughout the battle he shows great faith in God. He believes his strategy is the way God would have it, and he believes everything rests in the hands of God. He is prepared to take risks, and he dislikes defensive warfare. Committed to attack, he ignores Longstreet's advice to withdraw. In Longstreet's eyes, Lee appears stubborn, persisting in a strategy of attack when it is clearly doomed. However, like all the other officers, Longstreet greatly admires and respects Lee.

Lieutenant General James Longstreet

Lieutenant General James Longstreet is the commander of the Confederate First Army Corps and Lee's second in command. Longstreet "gave an impression of ominous bad-tempered strength and a kind of slow, even, stubborn, unquenchable anger." He talks and moves slowly and some of the officers regard him as not much fun. But he is acknowledged to be a magnificent soldier, and he is a brilliant man. Now that Stonewall Jackson is dead, Longstreet is regarded as "the rock of the army." He is Lee's most trusted commander and confidant. Lee respects Longstreet because Longstreet always says what he thinks and tells him the truth. In return, Longstreet respects Lee as the finest commander he has served under. However, he comes into conflict with Lee over battlefield tactics. Longstreet has invented a theory of defensive warfare, but he cannot convince his officers or Lee of its virtues. He is convinced that Lee's insistence on attack is a tragic mistake. But Longstreet is also a loyal soldier who follows orders.

The previous winter, Longstreet's three children died of fever, and he has since become more withdrawn than usual, not taking part in the poker games that he used to love. Unlike most of the officers, he is not from Virginia, and he does not feel quite at home with many of them. He thinks he does not belong. But he is an old comrade of Pickett and Armistead, from many previous military campaigns, and he is extremely fond of them both. He dislikes Stuart, however.

Major General George Gordon Meade

Major General George Gordon Meade is the recently appointed commander of the Union army. He took charge only two days before the battle of Gettysburg begins. He is described as "Vain and bad-tempered, balding, full of self-pity." Lee expects him to be a cautious commander and is surprised when Meade attacks on the third day.

Brigadier James Johnston Pettigrew

Brigadier James Johnston Pettigrew is Heth's brigade commander. He is one of the few intellectuals in the army. When Heth is injured, Lee gives his division to Pettigrew. Pettigrew suffers a minor hand wound during the Confederate charge on the third day of battle.

Major General George E. Pickett

Major General George E. Pickett is Longstreet's division commander. He is described as "Gaudy and lovable, long-haired, perfumed." He loves adventure and romance. Pickett finished last in his class at West Point, and Longstreet regards him as not particularly bright but knows that he is a fighter and can be relied upon. Pickett is an exuberant, entertaining man who knows how to tell a good story. He and his men missed out on the action at Chancellorsville and Fredericksburg, and he is desperate to see action now. He gets his wish, but his division suffers 60 percent casualties in the charge on the third day.

Major General John F. Reynolds

Major General John F. Reynolds is the commander of the Union First Corps. He is a fine soldier, giving the impression of being completely in charge of the situation. He is killed on the first day of battle.

Colonel James M. Rice

Colonel James M. Rice is the commander of the Forty-fourth New York regiment in Vincent's brigade.

Major General Daniel Sickles

Major General Daniel Sickles is the commander of the Union Third Corps. He was formerly a politician from New York, and he is notorious for having shot his wife's lover. He is nicknamed "The Bully Boy."

Major Moxley Sorrel

Major Moxley Sorrel is Longstreet's chief of staff.

Lieutenant General J. E. B. Stuart

Lieutenant General J. E. B. Stuart is a cavalry division commander on the Confederate side. He was sent out by Lee to bring back information about the movement of the Union army, but he fails to do this. Some officers want him court-martialed for his failure, but Lee, although he speaks to Stuart sternly, takes no action against him. Stuart is a flamboyant man, "carefree . . . languid, cheery, confident."

General Sykes

General Sykes is a general on the Union side. He is a "small, thin, grouchy man, [with] a reputation of a gentleman, though somewhat bad-tempered." He congratulates Chamberlain on his bayonet charge.

Major Walter Taylor

Major Walter Taylor is an aide to General Lee. He is already a major at the young age of twenty-four.

Brigadier General Isaac Trimble

Brigadier General Isaac Trimble is nearly sixty years old. He is a fiery kind of man who is so angered by Ewell's indecision that he refuses to serve under him any longer. He is appointed division commander under Pender and is wounded in the charge on the final day of the battle.

TOPICS FOR FURTHER STUDY

- Watch the movie *Gettysburg* and make a class presentation, using video clips, in which you discuss to what extent the main characters in the film resemble the characters as created by Shaara in the novel. Do you notice any major differences between the movie and the novel?

- Read two or three nonfiction historical accounts of the third1 day of the battle. Also study the sections in the novel in which Lee and Longstreet disagree about tactics. Then write an essay in which you discuss the different ways in which the relationship between the two men at Gettysburg has been interpreted. Do your sources give any clue as to whether the Confederate defeat was due to Lee's flawed judgment or to Longstreet's lack of support for his commander's tactics?

- Write an essay in which you analyze how the attitude toward war expressed by the participants, especially Chamberlain after the battle, and Pickett, before the final charge, differ from modern attitudes toward war. Would it be fair to say that the characters in *The Killer Angels* have a romantic view of war and battle? What role does the concept of honor and glory play in this novel? How have attitudes toward war today been altered by the experience of the United States in Vietnam and Iraq?

- Make a class presentation in which you analyze two characters from the novel, comparing and contrasting them. You may choose two characters from the same side, such as Lee and Longstreet, or from different sides, such as Longstreet and Chamberlain. You may also select less central figures, such as Buford, Armistead, or Pickett. Make sure you discuss important traits such as leadership qualities. What type of leadership does each man show?

Colonel Strong Vincent

Colonel Strong Vincent is Chamberlain's new brigade commander. He has a good reputation and the air of a man who knows what he is doing. He is killed on the second day of battle.

THEMES

Different Beliefs about the Cause of the War

The Union men all believe that the Civil War is about freeing the slaves in the South. They subscribe to a democratic ethos that asserts the equality of all men. This is made clear early in the novel by Chamberlain, who is probably the most idealistic character in the novel. He believes he is fighting for freedom, the right of every individual to "become what he wished to become," free from oppression by tradition or the old European-style aristocracies and royalties. He explains to the mutineers that the Union army is a different kind of army than any in the past. It does not fight for land, for king, or for booty, but with the purpose of "set[ting] other men free." For Chamberlain, the Confederacy represents a new kind of aristocracy that is perpetuating tyranny through the institution of slavery.

The Confederates, however, mock the Union belief that the war is about slavery. For them it is a matter of states' rights. As Kemper says to Fremantle, the Englishman who just seems to assume the war is about slavery, "We established this country in the first place with strong state governments . . . to avoid a central tyranny." This point is echoed by the rebel prisoners who are captured by Chamberlain's men. They insist they are fighting for their rights, not for the continuance of slavery. But Chamberlain is not convinced. When he sees the wounded black man, he believes he sees the cause of the war, the enslavement of blacks, very clearly.

Offensive versus Defensive War

A recurring theme is the disagreement between Longstreet and Lee over strategy. Longstreet is a pioneer of defensive warfare, and he thinks Lee is misguided in his insistence on attack. Longstreet consistently argues for setting up a sound defensive position and luring the enemy into an attack. He tries to convince Armistead of the virtues of his theory, but Armistead insists that neither Lee nor his army is suited for "slow dull defense." Lee is not to be convinced, either. He loathes the nickname of "King of Spades," which was given to him when he ordered tunnels dug for the defense of Richmond, Virginia. Defensive warfare goes against his training. He has confidence in the pride of his men; they have been outgunned before, as they are now, but have still won great victories. He thinks only of attacking and getting the battle won. For Longstreet, however, Lee's attitude is out of date. The entire war, Longstreet thinks, is old-fashioned, with tactics dating back to the Napoleonic era, as well as outmoded notions of chivalry and glory. "They all ride to glory, all the plumed knights," he thinks bitterly as he looks at the Confederate officers. In the end, Longstreet is proved correct, and Lee acknowledges this to him.

On the Union side, Buford espouses theories similar to those of Longstreet. He has had much experience in the Indian Wars, and he speaks disparagingly about how ineffective is "that glorious charge, sabers a-shining" against the Indian, who will hide behind a rock and then shoot you as you go by. Putting his experience to good use, Buford has schooled his men in defensive tactics, which is how they are able to dig in and hold off the attacking Confederates until relief arrives.

Divided Friendships

The nature of the Civil War is brought home by frequent references to the fact that it has split up old friends and comrades and placed them on opposite sides in the conflict. Longstreet remembers the shock of realizing that "the boys he was fighting were boys he had grown up with." Before the war, the Confederate Armistead was close friends with the Union man, Hancock. In an emotional scene, Armistead recalls his last meeting with his friend, when after dinner at Hancock's home, they stood around the piano, singing. Now, two years later, at Gettysburg, Armistead must take part in a charge on a position defended by Hancock.

When Longstreet and Lee look back on their exploits in the U.S. war against Mexico (1846–1848), Longstreet speaks admiringly of the men who served with them, noting that "Some of them are up ahead now, waiting for us." When Chamberlain thinks about the ethics of putting his brother in grave danger by getting him to plug a gap in the line, he reflects: "Killing of brothers. This whole war is concerned with

the killing of brothers." John Gibbon, of Hancock's corps, has three brothers on the Confederate side. The emphasis on brother against brother presents an image of the United States as a family divided against itself.

God's Will, Human Will, or Chance?

Lee is a religious man who sees the hand of God at work in events: "He believed in a Purpose as surely as he believed that the stars above him were really there." When he hears news of the Confederates' victory on the first day, he thinks it was God's will and offers a prayer of gratitude. He also feels that the location of the battle at Gettysburg, even though it was not consciously planned, was nonetheless a part of the divine "Intention," even though earlier he had thought, as it became apparent that a battle was looming, "We drift blindly toward a great collision."

Just before the final charge begins, Lee says, "It is all in the hands of God." But Longstreet, with his practical, down-to-earth nature, thinks differently. After Lee's remark, Longstreet thinks, "[I]t isn't God that is sending those men up that hill." In other words, it is a human decision, one that could have been made differently. Not everything is predestined or fated to be the way it is. Humans also have responsibility.

The theme that events are working themselves out, for good or ill, according to God's will, can also be seen in the fact that Lee and other Confederate officers are troubled because they broke their oaths to defend the Union. There is a certain fatalism on the Confederate side, the idea that since they broke their oaths, and also since they invaded the North, God may have turned against them.

STYLE

Recurring Metaphor

The title of the book points to a metaphor that recurs in the book. Before the first battle, Buford notices in the cemetery, among the gravestones, a statue of a "white angel, arm uplifted, a stony sadness." After the first battle, Buford stops in the cemetery but cannot find the white angel. It is as if the brutality of the battle has driven away this divine image.

The metaphor recurs, but with a shift in meaning, later in the novel, when Chamberlain recalls learning a speech from Shakespeare's play,

The historical Joshua Lawrence Chamberlain. In The Killer Angels, *the Union side of the story is told through his character* (*Brady National Photographic Art Gallery. Courtesy of The Library of Congress*)

Hamlet, in which man in action is compared to an angel. On hearing his son recite the passage, Chamberlain's father remarked, "Well, boy, if he's an angel, he's sure a murderin' angel." Chamberlain then gave a speech at school entitled "Man the Killer Angel." The image recurs after the final battle ends, when Chamberlain surveys the battlefield, sees the corpses being laid out, and thinks again of man as the killer angel. The image conveys the paradox of man: he is blessed with noble feelings and high ideals, as shown in the soldiers' devotion to a cause that transcends their individual selves. This higher aspect of man's nature links him to God; it is what Chamberlain calls the "divine spark," and yet man also has another side to his nature: He is aggressive and destructive, prepared to slaughter his own kind in terrible battles.

Music

Music is a recurring motif in the novel. The sound of military bands playing is an almost constant background to the movement of troops and the battles. As Chamberlain's men enter Hanover, a band plays the "Star-Spangled Banner"; Buford hears the Sixth Wisconsin band playing "The Campbells are Coming" as they move to take up battle positions. The music is described as "an eerie sound like a joyful wind." At Confederate headquarters, a band plays "That Bonny Blue Flag" in honor of Lee. This kind of stirring, patriotic music is designed to fill the soldiers with pride and steel their hearts for battle, but there is music of another kind that plays a key role in the novel, too. An Irish song sung by a tenor in the Confederate camp on the night before the final day of battle evokes tender emotions in all who hear it. The song is called "Kathleen Mavourneen," about the sadness of old friends when the time comes to part, whether for years or forever. The officers who hear it are deeply touched, and stillness descends on the camp. For Armistead, the song recalls the last time he was with his close friend, Hancock, who is now fighting on the Union side. Music thus creates moments of reflective sadness when men feel the pain of loss and separation. Another moment comes earlier that same night, when Longstreet hears a boy playing a harmonica, a "frail and lovely sound," and Longstreet thinks immediately of a comrade who rode off into battle and was killed. Music can therefore fortify the men for battle, or it can sadden their hearts by making them aware of the human price paid in war.

Music is also referred to in a metaphoric rather than literal sense in the description of the battles. In the midst of battle, Chamberlain hears the incredible variety of sounds, "like a great orchestra of death"; later, another unusual musical metaphor occurs: "Bullets still plucked the air; song of the dark guitar."

HISTORICAL CONTEXT

The Civil War Begins

The American Civil War pitted the United States federal government, under President Abraham Lincoln, against a group of initially seven southern states (South Carolina, Mississippi, Florida, Alabama, Georgia, Louisiana, and Texas) that seceded from the Union in February 1861, and formed the Confederate States of America, under President Jefferson Davis.

The main cause of the Civil War was slavery; states' rights were also an issue. The Confederate

COMPARE
&
CONTRAST

- **1860s:** Advances in weaponry lead to high casualty rates during the American Civil War. Muskets are deadly at ranges of hundreds of yards; rapid-firing rifles are common, and artillery becomes more mobile and lethal.

  1970s: In the Vietnam War, the most common weapon issued to American troops is the M16A1, 5.56mm assault rifle, a gas-operated, magazine-fed rifle capable of semi-automatic and automatic fire with an effective range of three hundred meters and a practical rate of fire of sixty rpm.

  Today: U.S. troops in Iraq are equipped with M16A2 semiautomatic rifles. The maximum effective range of this weapon over an area target is eight hundred meters; for a point target, the range is 550 meters. It fires forty-five rounds per minute and can also fire 40mm grenades when equipped with a M203 grenade launcher.

- **1860s:** The United States endures its most bitter and deadly conflict. The Civil War results in the deaths of about 646,000 soldiers. Two-thirds of the deaths are due to disease.

  1970s: The Vietnam War comes to an end. In 1973, a ceasefire agreement is signed and the last U.S. forces leave Vietnam. Over 58,000 U.S. servicemen die in the war.

  Lasting eleven years, the war is the longest in U.S. history. In 1975, Saigon, the capital of South Vietnam, falls to North Vietnamese forces.

  Today: The United States is engaged in a costly war in Iraq. As of January 2007, the United States has lost over 3,000 servicemen since U.S. forces invaded Iraq in 2003; Iraqi dead are estimated to exceed 600,000.

- **1860s:** After the Civil War ends, Lee campaigns for reconciliation between the North and South. In 1865, Lee becomes president of Washington College in Lexington, Virginia, a position he retains until his death in 1870. Lee makes a point of recruiting college students from the North as well as from the South.

  1970s: In 1975, following a vote in Congress, President Gerald Ford issues a posthumous pardon for General Lee and a restoration of his U.S. citizenship. Ford issues a statement that the pardon corrects a one-hundred-year-old oversight in U.S. history.

  Today: In 2006, *The Atlantic*, in its list of the hundred most influential Americans of all time, places Lee in fifty-seventh position, and states, "He was a good general but a better symbol, embodying conciliation in defeat."

---

states believed they had a right to continue slavery and to expand the practice into the territories. Citing the Tenth Amendment, they argued that the federal government did not have the power to curtail states' rights and so could not prevent slavery being exported to the territories. The South also argued that northern states were failing to honor their obligations to the Constitution by assisting slaves to escape via the Underground Railroad and refusing to enforce the Fugitive Slave Law, which required

the capture and return of slaves who escaped into northern free states. The South also feared long-term changes in the demographic and political structure of the United States. The northern population was growing and would soon control the federal government, leaving the South in a permanent minority.

Although abolitionist sentiment was strong in the North, the abolition of slavery was not an original goal of the federal government. The

North regarded secession as an act of rebellion and initially fought simply to preserve the Union.

In the early months of 1861, the Confederacy took charge of federal forts within its boundaries, and in April, Confederate forces bombarded and captured Fort Sumter in Charleston, North Carolina. This marked the beginning of the Civil War. The North immediately moved to recapture Fort Sumter and other forts; Lincoln called for seventy-five thousand volunteers. The following month, four more states, Arkansas, Tennessee, North Carolina, and Virginia, joined the Confederacy. The Confederate capital was moved to Richmond, Virginia.

In May 1861, Lincoln blockaded southern ports, cutting off exports vital to the South. On July 21, 1861, the Confederate army fought off Union forces at the first Battle of Bull Run. The following year, the war intensified. The Union Army of the Potomac, under Major General George B. McClellan, attacked Virginia but was halted at the Battle of Seven Pines and then defeated by General Robert E. Lee in the Seven Days' Battles. Lee's army recorded another victory, against General John Pope's Union Army of Virginia, in the Second Battle of Bull Run in August. The Confederacy then invaded the North and fought the Union army at the Battle of Antietam, near Sharpsburg, Maryland, on September 17, 1862. The result of the battle was inconclusive, but it did have the effect of halting the invasion and prompting Lee to return to Virginia.

Confederate successes followed, with victories for Lee's army at the Battle of Fredericksburg on December, 12, 1862, and the Battle of Chancellorsville in May 1863. Lee then decided to once more invade the North.

The Battle of Gettysburg

Lee's army began its invasion on June 15. He learned on June 28, 1863, that the Union army had crossed the Potomac in pursuit, and he concentrated his forces at Cashtown, eight miles west of Gettysburg. The stage was set for the most decisive battle of the war. On the first day of fighting, July 1, federal troops were outnumbered, since not all their forces were assembled. The rebels, led by Major Generals Robert E. Rodes and Jubal Early, forced the Union army to retreat from their positions just north and west of Gettysburg to the high ground known as Cemetery Hill, south of town. Lee ordered Lieutenant General Richard Ewell to take the hill if possible, but Ewell decided not to attempt it. That night Major General George Meade arrived with two divisions and set up a strong defensive position on Cemetery Hill.

On July 2, the second day of battle, Lee ordered General Longstreet's forces, led by Major General John Bell Hood, to capture the area south of Cemetery Hill, known as Big Round Top and Little Round Top, on the Union left flank. Union forces, enduring heavy casualties, managed to hold their ground. The Federals also held their positions on Culp's Hill and Cemetery Hill, despite determined Confederate assaults by Ewell's divisions.

On July 3, Lee attempted to capture the center of the Union line on Cemetery Ridge. The assault was preceded by a heavy artillery bombardment, after which 12,500 Confederates marched three-quarters of a mile across open terrain, during which they were subject to intense Union rifle and artillery fire. This is popularly known as Pickett's Charge, although Pickett led only one of the three divisions involved; the others were led by Brigadier General James Johnston Pettigrew and Major General Isaac R. Trimble. The charge was repulsed, with Confederate forces suffering heavy casualties.

Lee regrouped his army into a defensive position, thinking that the Union forces would attack. The counterattack never came, and on July 5, Lee's army headed back to Virginia.

The Battle of Gettysburg resulted in an estimated twenty-three thousand casualties on the Union side and twenty-eight thousand on the Confederate side.

The Final Years of the Civil War

After Gettysburg, the tide turned against the South. Northern forces, under General Ulysses S. Grant, formed and executed a comprehensive strategy to destroy the Confederate army and its economic base. A series of battles forced Lee's army to retreat to the Confederate capital of Richmond, Virginia. At the Siege of Petersburg, trench warfare lasted for over nine months. In April, 1864, Richmond fell to the Union army.

Meanwhile, General William Tecumseh Sherman marched through Georgia, capturing

An illustration of the Battle of Gettysburg (© *Bettmann* / *Corbis*)

Atlanta in September 1864 and Savannah in December. Lee, realizing that the Confederate position had become hopeless, surrendered to Grant at Appomattox Court House on April 9, 1865.

The Thirteenth Amendment, abolishing slavery, took effect in December 1865.

CRITICAL OVERVIEW

Published by a small independent publisher in 1974, *The Killer Angels* at first attracted little attention from major review sources. In a very brief review in *Atlantic Monthly*, Phoebe Adams notes that Shaara had taken "a novelist's liberty of invention with [selected officers'] motives and reactions." Adams concludes that the novel was "an unusual project and has worked out well, with excitement and plausibility." The reviewer for *Publishers Weekly*

comments that Shaara "fashions a compelling version of what America's Armageddon must have been like." The reviewer concludes that *The Killer Angels* is "a novel Civil War buffs will relish for its authenticity and general readers will appreciate for its surefire storytelling." In *Library Journal*, Ellen K. Stoppel comments that "Although some of [Shaara's] judgments are not necessarily substantiated by historians, he demonstrates a knowledge of both the battle and the area. The writing is vivid and fast-moving."

The novel received more attention when it won the Pulitzer Prize in 1975. Edward Weeks, in a longer review in *Atlantic Monthly*, comments that "The best way to write about battle is to tell it as the men who went through it saw it and felt it, and that is what Michael Shaara has done in this stirring, brilliant interpretive novel."

When the television miniseries, *Gettysburg*, based on *The Killer Angels*, was screened in 1993, the novel achieved popular success,

WHAT DO I READ NEXT?

- *The Last Full Measure: A Novel* (1998), by Jeff Shaara, takes up the story of what happened after the Battle of Gettysburg. Shaara, who is Michael Shaara's son, covers Lee's retreat from Pennsylvania and continues through the end of the war. He tells the story through the eyes of Lee, Joshua Lawrence Chamberlain, and Ulysses S. Grant. Readers may also be interested in Jeff Shaara's novel, *Gone for Soldiers* (2000), which covers the action prior to Gettysburg.

- *The Red Badge of Courage* (1895), by Stephen Crane, is one of the most famous novels set in the Civil War period. The hero, Henry Fleming, is a young farm boy who comes under fire in battle for the first time and runs away in fear. The battle is unnamed but may have been Chancellorsville. Henry rejoins his regiment, which does not know about his cowardice, and in a later battle shows great courage.

- *Cold Mountain* (1998), by Charles Frazier, is an epic novel about the return of a wounded Civil War veteran to his home in North Carolina following the Battle of Fredericksburg in 1862. The soldier travels three hundred miles, struggling with physical hardship and despair.

- Carol Rearden, in *Pickett's Charge in History and Memory* (1997), examines Pickett's Charge through the lens of memory and reveals why the charge endures so strongly in the American imagination. Over the years, soldiers, journalists, veterans, politicians, orators, and others have shaped and revised the facts of the charge to create versions that met shifting needs and deeply felt values. Rearden shows that the story of Pickett's Charge as told in the late twentieth century is really an amalgam of history and memory.

reaching number one on the *New York Times* bestseller list, nineteen years after its publication. On publication in England in 1997, the reviewer for the *Times Literary Supplement* noted that the novel concentrates entirely on the battle, rather than ranging into social territory. Commenting that "the reader becomes involved in the decisions which had to be taken and the conditions of combat, harrowingly described," the reviewer concludes that the novel is a "moving, dramatic tale."

CRITICISM

Bryan Aubrey

Aubrey holds a Ph.D. in English. In this essay, he argues that in The Killer Angels, *Shaara presents his historical material in a manner that clearly favors the northern cause in the Civil War.*

Michael Shaara's riveting novel about the Battle of Gettysburg presents in novelistic form some of the political and social factors that divided the North from the South during the Civil War years, and in the dialogue he carefully selects spokesmen on both sides who argue that their cause is the just and right one. In writing the novel, Shaara states in his note "To the Reader," the author went back to the actual words of the men who participated in the battle, as recorded in letters and other documents. He states that to his knowledge, he changed no facts, and he adds, "Though I have often had to choose between conflicting viewpoints, I have not knowingly violated the action. ... The interpretation of character is my own." There is no reason to quibble with Shaara's words; however, he does appear to have decided to present his material in a way that clearly favors the northern cause.

The northern cause is presented almost exclusively through the viewpoints of Colonel Joshua Chamberlain and his aide Buster Kilrain. Chamberlain adheres passionately to the American democratic ideal, the belief that all men have the right to freedom and the pursuit of their own destiny without coercion from the ruling powers. Chamberlain, who evokes the cause eloquently to the Maine mutineers, believes the North is fighting for the dignity of man in a country, unique in the world, where the individual matters more than the state. He is proud of the fact that in the United States, no man has to bow down to another. He regards an aristocracy as a "curse," something that belongs to old Europe, and he is horrified to see what he thinks of as a "new aristocracy" transplanted from Europe into the South. For Chamberlain, the cause for which he is fighting transcends simple patriotism and attains a universal meaning: "The Frenchman may fight for France, but the American fights for mankind, for freedom; for the people, not the land."

The other man who gives expression to the Union cause is Chamberlain's devoted aide, Kilrain. The rough-and-ready former sergeant is a complete contrast to the eloquent, former professor Chamberlain. But as comrades in arms, their mutual respect and affection, coupled with the difference in their ages, enables them to be like father and son to each other. Separated by rank and education they may be, but they relate to each other with generosity and affection, an example of the ideal for which they are fighting, the basic equality of all men. Kilrain even attains a rough eloquence of his own in expressing his beliefs. Like Chamberlain, he dislikes aristocracies, and he expresses himself with venom that is foreign to his commanding officer: "It's the aristocracy I'm after. All that lovely, plumed, stinking chivalry. The people who look at you like a piece of filth, a cockroach, ah." He also says, "There is only one aristocracy, and that's right here—" (he taps his skull with his finger). The rights of all men to make of their talents what they can rather than being born into a rigid social and cultural system in which who a man's father is matters more than who a man is.

The only other Union character presented in any detail is Buford. Like Kilrain, he shares a dislike of a social system based on class. He is irritated by "the cavaliers, the high-bred, feathery, courtly ones who spoke like Englishmen and treated a man like dirt." When a Confederate officer he sees in the distance takes his hat off to him, Buford grimaces; "a gentleman," he thinks.

The southern attitude that Buford, Chamberlain, and Kilrain dislike can be seen right at the beginning of the novel in the way the Confederates treat their spy, Harrison, who was sent out personally by Longstreet to report on the movement of the Union army. As shown by his colloquial speech, Harrison is a lower-class individual, a former actor who likes Shakespeare but gets his quotations muddled up (he slips in a quotation from *King Lear* thinking it is from *Hamlet*). Harrison does the job he was asked to do, but there is not much of the famed southern chivalry in the way he is treated when he returns to the Confederate camp with the required information. Sorrel gazes at him distastefully; Longstreet and Lee distrust him. The point is that Harrison may be a small cog in the wheel of war; he may not be a particularly admirable character, but he doggedly gets his job done, and he does it with skill and cunning and even bravery. He is implicitly contrasted with the flamboyant, cavalier officer J. E. B. Stuart, who was also charged with the task of tracking the Union army. Whereas the humble Harrison does what he was asked to do, the glamorous Stuart conspicuously fails in the task Lee entrusted to him, and as a result he endangers the entire Confederate army. The little man did his job; the great man failed.

Compounding the subtle message imparted by this comparison between Harrison and Stuart is the fact that in this novel, the South has no spokesman who presents the southern cause with anything approaching the eloquence of the North's Chamberlain. This is not for want of conviction on the part of the rebels, since the justifications for the war are so important to them that the word "Cause" is capitalized whenever the subject comes up. Nor is the lack of eloquent defense of the Confederacy due to a lack of possible spokesmen. The reader learns the Union point of view only from Buford and Chamberlain, with a little help from Kilrain, whereas the bulk of the novel is told from the point of view of the Confederate men, Lee, Longstreet, and Armistead, and the Confederate sympathizer Fremantle. Lee fights not from some grandiose notion of states' rights but simply because he refused to take up arms against Virginians, his own kith and kin; his reasons are deeply personal, not political or philosophical. Longstreet, the professional soldier, simply wants to get on with the business of fighting and winning; he is impatient when he hears the other officers discussing the Cause, as is Armistead. It is left to the English observer Fremantle to put the southern case best. He is in favor of tradition and "breeding"; he regards democracy as advocated in the North as the "equality of rabble"; equality, he thinks, is "rot." In the South that he admires so much (in part because it reminds him of England) he finds a pleasing homogeneity; there is for the most part one religion and one way of life, but in the North there are those "huge bloody cities and a thousand religions" in which "the only aristocracy is the aristocracy of wealth." Snobbish and bigoted he may be, but Fremantle has hit on something that was indeed one of the underlying causes of the war: the modernizing, industrializing, urbanizing North, with its rapid development of free-market capitalism, was perceived with dismay and suspicion by the predominantly rural, agrarian, tradition-bound South.

Another defense of the southern cause is given by Colonel George E. Pickett. He likens the United States before the war to a gentlemen's club. But then some members of the club (the North) started interfering with the private lives of southern members (their right to do as they pleased, according to their own traditions) so the South resigned from the club, only to be told they had no right to resign. In Pickett's eyes, then, the war resulted from a breaking of a gentlemen's agreement as enshrined in the Constitution. For Pickett and the other Confederate officers, the war has nothing to do with slavery, and everything to do with their states' rights. (Longstreet knows better and privately thinks that the war is indeed about slavery, although he does not care to talk about it.) But this defense of the Confederate cause is almost comically undercut later—in a way the northern cause never is in this novel—by the incident involving Confederate prisoners that Tom Chamberlain reports to his elder brother, Colonel Joshua Chamberlain. Tom has been chatting with three rebel prisoners, farm boys from the

South, who insist they are fighting for their "rats." Tom finally manages to figure out that they mean "rights," but when he questions them further, trying to find out what rights they feel have been violated, all one man can say is that "he didn't know, but he must have some rights he didn't know nothin' about."

The undermining of the Confederate cause is also apparent in the story Chamberlain tells about his encounter with a southern Baptist minister who resented the North in the same way he would if someone had asked him to free a fine stallion from one of his fields. When Chamberlain tried to point out that a man is not a horse, the minister replied that "a Negro was not a man." Coming just after the incident in which Chamberlain's men treat the frightened black man who has strayed into town seeking directions and been shot by a woman from her porch, Chamberlain's story reinforces the simple moral basis of the northern cause. By turning the spotlight on slavery and the plight of black people, Shaara tries to ensure that—the fundamental decency of the rebel officers and the courage of their men notwithstanding—the reader realizes that this was a war in which the northern cause, the cause of democracy, equality of opportunity, and human rights, on which the United States of America prided itself then as now, was the just and honorable one.

Source: Bryan Aubrey, Critical Essay on *The Killer Angels*, in *Novels for Students*, Thomson Gale, 2008.

Kevin Grauke

In the following essay, Grauke argues that the novel should be read in terms of the social and political effects that the Vietnam War had on American society. Focusing on Shaara's interpretation of character, Grauke interprets the novel as a defense of the United States' involvement in Vietnam.

In his book, *The Civil War in Popular Culture*, Jim Cullen examines a number of Civil-War-inspired twentieth-century works in light of how they, to varying degrees, rewrite history, thus revealing the influence of a "social or political stress" present at the time of their creations. To Cullen, the sentimental, panegyric qualities of Carl Sandburg's biography of Abraham Lincoln should be understood within the context of the Great Depression, "a time of enormous social and psychological instability, [during which] Lincoln could simultaneously represent ideals of freedom and equality, order and democracy, ordeal and victory." On the other hand, *Gone with the Wind*, particularly its protagonist, Scarlett O'Hara, should be read in terms of having been created at a "time when it finally seemed that modernity might allow women to escape, or at least restructure, the bonds of womanhood that had circumscribed their hopes for so long." To Cullen, the Confederacy-infused music of Southern rock bands of the 1970s such as Lynyrd Skynyrd and the Allman Brothers Band should be heard as a reaction to the "Civil Rights movement and the fear and guilt that movement engendered in white men." Along the same lines, I would argue that Michael Shaara's *The Killer Angels* (1974) and Charles Frazier's *Cold Mountain* (1997) should be read in terms of the social and political stress exerted upon the nation by, in Shaara's case, the Vietnam War, and in Frazier's case, the approach of the millennium.

Despite being awarded the Pulitzer Prize in 1975, and despite selling nearly three million copies as of 1996, very little has been written about *The Killer Angels* except for the reviews that were published at the time of its initial printing and at the time of the release of its film adaptation, *Gettysburg* (1993). Praise for the novel was nearly unanimous in these reviews. The elements of the novel that were repeatedly singled out for acclaim were its multiple points of view, which present perspectives from both the North and South, its authentic and detailed descriptions of battle scenes, and its strict reliance upon correspondence and other historical documents. Thomas LeClair, in the *New York Times Book Review*, praised Shaara's ability to capture the "terror and the bravery, the precarious balance of machine and man that made Gettysburg one of the last human battles," as well as his ability to provide the "minutia that give the immense motions of intellect and men their reality."

Although I agree with the accolades that these facets of the novel have received, most of these reviews ignored the more interesting—and more important—question of the novel's ideological perspective. The few that have addressed it mistakenly have praised the novel for its non-judgmental treatment of both sides. Shaara "doesn't attempt to glorify [. . .] the causes of either North or South," wrote one reviewer (Stoppel 2092). This may seem the case at first, simply because the majority of the novel is

> DURING A TIME OF DRAFT DODGERS, ANTI-WAR DEMONSTRATIONS, AND A GROWING FEAR THAT THE U. S. HAD ENTERED AN UNWINNABLE WAR, SHAARA TURNS TO THE CIVIL WAR, A WAR THAT, AT LEAST IN HISTORICAL RETROSPECT, HAD A CLEARLY DELINEATED MORAL CONFLICT, PARTICULARLY IN COMPARISON TO THE DUBIOUS NATURE OF THE VIETNAM WAR."

presented from the South's—particularly Lee and Longstreet's—point of view. However, if one carefully compares how each side is presented—particularly how the novel presents the reasons for which each side believes it is fighting—one inevitably will come to realize that *The Killer Angels* forwards the Union's cause at the expense of the Confederacy's.

In his disclaimer to the reader, Shaara states, "I have not consciously changed any fact. [. . .] I have not knowingly violated the action." However, at the end of this disclaimer, he adds, "The interpretation of character is my own." In light of the praise that has been heaped upon *The Killer Angels* by such respected historians as James M. McPherson, author of *Battle Cry of Freedom*, it seems fairly safe to assume that the novel does do an excellent job of accurately portraying the facts and action of Gettysburg; however, it is through Shaara's "interpretation of character" that the novel reveals the anxieties peculiar to the United States during the 1970s.

During the ten years that Shaara spent crafting *The Killer Angels* prior to its publication in 1974 ("Pure Primacy" 58), the American public's discontent with the United States' involvement in Vietnam steadily intensified, particularly after the 1968 Tet Offensive and Nixon's escalation of the war into Cambodia in 1970. An increasing number of people were coming to question not only the possibility of an American victory, but the very involvement of American forces in a conflict that some viewed as a Vietnamese civil war. By 1970, two out of every three Americans believed the war to be a "brutal, dehumanizing, and pointless affair from which the United States should withdraw" (Taylor).

In direct opposition to the consensus of public opinion, Shaara—a former paratrooper in the 82nd Airborne Division of the U. S. Army (1946–49) and a former sergeant in the U. S. Army Reserve (1949–53) ("Shaara" 463)—puts forth in *The Killer Angels* what should not be read merely as an attempt to portray "what it was like to *be* [at the Battle of Gettysburg], what the weather was like, what men's faces looked like," as Shaara claims as his reason for writing the novel, but as a defense of the United States' involvement in Vietnam. To see this, one needs only to examine the distinctions that exist between the words and thoughts of Colonel Joshua L. Chamberlain, the heart and voice of the Union at Shaara's Gettysburg, and the words and thoughts of Generals Robert E. Lee and James Longstreet, the foremost Confederate figures at the battle.

Early in the novel, before the Battle of Gettysburg commences, Chamberlain must speak to one hundred and twenty mutineers from the disbanded Second Maine in an effort to persuade them to fight with his regiment. While preparing himself for this speech, the narrator states Chamberlain's reasons for being there, for fighting against the Confederacy:

> He had grown up believing in America and the individual and it was a stronger faith than his faith in God. This was the land where no man had to bow. In this place at last a man could stand up free of the past, free of tradition and blood ties and the curse of royalty and become what he wished to become. This was the first place on earth where the man mattered more than the state. True freedom had begun here and it would spread eventually over all the earth.

This passage, particularly the final two sentences, speaks as loudly against the perceived threat of communism toward democracy as it does against the Confederacy's threat toward the Union. The mention of the word "state" brings to mind both the Confederate States of America as well as the communist state that, according to the foreign relations policy of the United States government during the Cold War, threatened, via the domino effect, the free world more and more with every country it consumed.

Chamberlain's thoughts continue:

> If men were equal in America, all these former Poles and English and Czechs and blacks, then they were equal everywhere, and there was really no such thing as a foreigner; there were only free men and slaves. And so it was not even patriotism but a new faith. The Frenchman may fight for France, but the American fights for mankind, for freedom; for the people, not the land.

This jingoistic passage is intended to cause the chests of readers to swell with pride at the mention of such all-American sensibilities as freedom and equality, not only in contrast to the South's institution of slavery, but also in contrast to communism's "slavery" of individuals to the state.

In his note to the reader, Shaara claims to have "gone back primarily to the words of the men themselves, their letters and other documents." The actual Joshua Chamberlain may very well have held the beliefs that Shaara has placed in the head of the fictional Joshua Chamberlain, but if we look at what the actual Chamberlain said regarding the cause of the Civil War at the dedication of the Maine monuments at Gettysburg in 1889, it seems as if Shaara took considerable license with the true sentiments of the hero at Little Round Top. Says Chamberlain:

> It was, on its face, a question of government. There was a boastful pretense that each State held in its hands the death-warrant of the Nation; that any State had a right, without show of justification outside of its own caprice, to violate the covenants of the constitution [sic], to break away from the Union, and set up its own little sovereignty as sufficient for all human purposes and ends; thus leaving it to the mere will or whim of any member of our political system to destroy the body and dissolve the soul of the Great People. This was the political question submitted to the arbitrament arms. But the victory was of great politics over small. It was the right reason, the moral consciousness and solemn resolve of the people rectifying its wavering exterior lines according to the life-lines of its organic being.

According to this passage, the reason Chamberlain felt the Civil War was fought was not to further the cause of democracy via the crushing of the South's peculiar institution and the aristocratic impulses that forged it, but simply to bring back into the Union the rebellious southern states that unlawfully considered themselves able to disengage from it. But this reasoning does not allow itself to be applied to the contemporary situation in Vietnam. The Vietnam War was not an attempt to bring back into the fold a mutinous constituent; it was an attempt, at least theoretically, to free an innocent people from the bondage of communism. Hence the transformation of Chamberlain.

As for the Confederacy, the novel paints both Lee and Longstreet as tragically heroic figures, but it does not allow them to fight for reasons they believe in; they merely fight because they are soldiers. In the first section dedicated to Longstreet's perspective, the narrator says that Longstreet "did not think much of the Cause. He was a professional: the Cause was Victory." Then, after Pickett's Charge fails and the battle is known to be lost, Lee echoes these words in a conversation with Longstreet: "You and I we have no Cause. We have only the army." By disallowing these men a legitimate reason for fighting, the South's heartfelt cause is condemned in the same manner that the cause of Ho Chi Minh's Viet Minh movement and the National Liberation Front of South Vietnam was condemned to the American public by its government.

This denigration of the South's cause exists in other parts of the novel, as well, particularly in a section in which Tom Chamberlain conveys to his brother Joshua a conversation he has had with a group of Confederate prisoners. Says Tom:

> They kept on insistin' they wasn't fightin' for no slaves, they were fightin' for their 'rats.' It finally dawned on me that what the feller meant was their 'rights,' only, the way they talk, it came out 'rats.' Hee. Then after that I asked this fella what rights he had that we were offendin', and he said, well, he didn't know, but he must have some rights he didn't know nothin' about.

Granted, many of the men fighting for the South—as well as the North—probably did not have a firm grasp of what exactly they were fighting for, but no Northern equivalent of this lack of sophistication exists in the novel (nor is any Northerner ridiculed as is this soldier). Instead, we are shown soldiers such as Buster Kilrain, Chamberlain's brave and loyal man Friday, who says, "What matters is justice. 'Tis why I'm here. I'll be treated as I deserve, not as my father deserved. I'm Kilrain, and I God damn all gentlemen. I don't know who me father was and I don't give a damn." The Northern soldiers, like the U. S. government of the 1960s and 1970s, are to be seen as fighting for a righteous cause, whereas the Southern soldiers, like the Viet Cong, are, at best, sadly misled by their leaders, or, at worst, thoroughly un-American in their beliefs.

According to the historian Robert Brent Toplin, regrets about American involvement in World War I affected the manner in which historians of the period perceived the Civil War, causing them to see it as a conflict that was avoidable. But this opinion changed after World War II. "America's fight for freedom against fascist oppression evidently had its impact on the interpretations of history. The 'Good War' had involved a struggle against the evils of racism and territorial aggrandizement, and in this context consideration of ethical questions seemed to take on heightened importance." Shaara's *The Killer Angels* fits well within this sort of reasoning. During a time of draft dodgers, anti-war demonstrations, and a growing fear that the U. S. had entered an unwinnable war, Shaara turns to the Civil War, a war that, at least in historical retrospect, had a clearly delineated moral conflict, particularly in comparison to the dubious nature of the Vietnam War. By doing this, he attempts to transmit the artistically enhanced gloriousness and patriotism of the Union Army of 1863 to the U. S. armed forces of the 1960s and 1970s that were fighting the red scare in Southeast Asia. Had the Confederacy won, the novel implies, the America of the late twentieth century would not have come to pass. Slavery would have continued and spread, as would have the aristocratic mindset that stresses the blood of the father over the achievement of the son.

And if we extend this implication to the situation contemporary to the writing of this novel, we see that we are to understand that the America of the 1970s had reached a similarly crucial crossroads. The America that the Union affirmed with the victory over the South was in peril. If communism were allowed to sweep through Vietnam—if it were not fought militarily—it subsequently would sweep through neighboring countries, spreading until it reached the United States, where it would annihilate all the freedoms and rights we had struggled to maintain. Thus, in "one of the few effective defenses of military culture in [the Vietnam era]" (Cullen 154), *The Killer Angels* stands up against the tide of contemporary popular opinion, and via the seemingly unrelated topic of the Battle of Gettysburg fought in 1863, subtly forwards the United States' unpopular campaign against the spread of communism.

Now skip ahead to 1993, the year *Gettysburg*, the film adaptation of *The Killer Angels*, is released. Upon seeing the name of the distribution company, Turner Home Entertainment, one might be suspicious of *Gettysburg*'s interpretation of *The Killer Angels*. After all, Turner Home Entertainment is owned by the Atlanta business mogul/Southern gentleman, Ted Turner, and its logo is an antebellum plantation house. Would the bias shift somehow from the North to the South? Would Chamberlain be portrayed as less heroic? Would Lee be portrayed as less stubbornly and foolishly arrogant? Oddly enough, if anything, the biases of the novel are intensified in the film. Overbearing, triumphalist music accompanies every move made by the Union army, while Martin Sheen's Robert E. Lee seems on the verge of senility.

Why did this film come out when it did, so long after the initial publication of *The Killer Angels*? Undoubtedly, one reason was the popularity of Ken Burns' 1990 eleven-hour documentary, *The Civil War*, as well as the popularity of Edward Zwick's 1989 film, *Glory*. But another probable reason was the "popularity" of the Persian Gulf War a few years before. Times—and sentiments—had changed. The American public's cynical distrust of the government and military that had been bred by the U. S. military's involvement and subsequent defeat in Vietnam had withered away significantly during the Reagan dynasty of the 1980s. Once again, public opinion supported the U. S. military's involvement in world affairs as the global policeman, the peace-maker. Operation Desert Storm, the United States' response to Iraq's invasion of Kuwait, inspired a sense of nationalistic pride not experienced since World War II, a sense that maintained itself in the years following Saddam Hussein's defeat. It is within this context that *Gettysburg* should be viewed. Even the reprint of the novel is aimed toward such a reading; the only blurb present on the cover is from General H. Norman Schwarzkopf, the chief military officer of the Persian Gulf War: *The Killer Angels* is "the best and most realistic historical novel about war I have ever read."

In less than twenty years, *The Killer Angels*, which had once threatened the commonly held beliefs of the status quo, had come to embody them. The South, the enemy, the region that fought to continue slavery, could now reflect upon—and be reflected upon—Saddam Hussein, the despot who used his country's own people as human shields to protect his palace.

Four years after the release of *Gettysburg*, Charles Frazier published *Cold Mountain*. The patriotic atmosphere of the Gulf War had faded in the face of intensifying cultural anxieties emerging with the steady approach of the millennium, anxieties that reveal themselves from within *Cold Mountain* in much the same way that the cultural anxieties inspired by the situation in Vietnam reveal themselves in *The Killer Angels*. Like *The Killer Angels*, *Cold Mountain*, too, was a critical and commercial success. This story of Inman, a wounded Confederate veteran, and his struggle to return to Ada, the woman whom he wants to make his wife, and his home on Cold Mountain in North Carolina, sold 1.6 million copies within nine months of being published and won the National Book Award. Rick Bass's hyperbolic dust jacket blurb typifies much of the reaction this novel received: It "seems even possible to never want to read another book, so wonderful is this one."

What was it about this novel that caused such a furor? Some mentioned its realistic detail, its authentic rendering of nineteenth-century life. Others pointed to Inman and Ada's romance, the love that impels each of them to overcome numerous obstacles. "The genuine romantic saga of Ada and Inman is a page turner that attains the status of literature," wrote one reviewer (Jones, Jr. 73). Wrote another, "The author's focus is always on Ada and Inman. It is their movement toward each other that always remains central, and that finally makes *Cold Mountain* such a memorable book" (Polk). Still others referred to its setting during Civil War times, which continued to remain popular with the culture at large. One reviewer called it this generation's version of the Civil War, as were Michael Shaara's *The Killer Angels* and Stephen Crane's *The Red Badge of Courage* for each of their respective generations (Breslin 33). But unlike Shaara's and Crane's novels, Frazier's novel provides very little battle; what combat it does provide comes to us distilled by Inman's memory. In addition to this, we get virtually no mention of the usual elements we have come to expect of Civil War novels—slavery, the Union, or states' rights.

So what kind of Civil War novel is this? Like *The Killer Angels*, *Cold Mountain* takes the Civil War and manipulates it in order to approach a contemporary issue. Where *The Killer Angels* concerns Vietnam, *Cold Mountain* alludes to the phenomenon of survivalism, as well as the ideology that encompasses survivalism, millennialism. As a cultural phenomenon, millennialism originated in the ancient Hebrew and Christian apocalyptic prophecies that foretold God's destruction of evil and his raising of the righteous to his kingdom, where they would live for a thousand years. It tends to gain popularity "during periods of intense social change, coinciding with the end of an age or era" (Lamy viii). But millennialism does not necessarily have to be of a religious order; it can be secular, as well. As we approached the year 2000, we saw the evidence of both religious and secular millennialist thought in such diverse individuals and groups as the Branch Davidians, the Unabomber, Timothy McVeigh, Aum Shinrikyo (the perpetrators of the Tokyo subway bombings), Randy Weaver (Ruby Ridge), the Montana Freemen, the Heaven's Gate cult, and the countless numbers of people who stockpiled living necessities in fear of fallout from the universal computer glitch famously known as Y2K. A world populated by such individuals and groups was the context from which *Cold Mountain* emerged, a world not too unlike the world which Inman passes through in his quest for home and in which Ada struggles to gain the knowledge necessary to allow her to survive in Inman's and her father's absence.

According to Philip Lamy in his book, *Millennium Rage: Survivalists, White Supremacists, and the Doomsday Prophecy*, the survivalist philosophy, which can generally be thought of as the pragmatic aspect of millennialist thought, grew specifically from the cold-war paranoia of the fifties and gained popularity throughout the years of the Korean and Vietnam Wars. It "speaks of mass destruction and death. It is not interested in reforming the system; the collapse of civilization is imminent. However, it does offer a plan of action, a kind of 'redemption' or 'salvation,' in the manner of surviving the great destruction of the current order and living on to build a new one" (Lamy vii).

In *Cold Mountain*, the end of the world seems to have already occurred. The landscape—nearly post-apocalyptic in its bleakness—is blighted, blasted. On the second page of the novel, as Inman looks out the window from his hospital bed where he is recovering from a wound to his neck, before he has even begun his treacherous trek back home, the narrator tells us that "he had seen the metal face of the age and had been so stunned by it that when he thought into the future, all he could vision was a world from which everything he counted important had been banished or had willingly fled." Traveling primarily by night, Inman passes through a cruel and inhospitable landscape inhabited by vicious hounds, vipers, moths that look like ghosts, tree stumps that look like people, mosquitoes, ticks, gnats, horseflies, butterflies that drink from the stream of a man's urine, poison ivy, Venus fly traps, foul rivers, scythe-wielding attackers, "root doctors" (read: witches), the not-yet-dead picked apart by buzzards, lecherous preachers, and roving bands of murderous looters. In order to provide himself with at least the illusion of luck as he makes his way through this Godless world that "spoke of nothing but strife, danger, [and] grief", he "daubed on the breast of his jacket two concentric circles with a dot at the center and walked on, marked as the butt of the celestial realm, a night traveler, a fugitive, an outlier."

This image of the loner determined to prevail in an environment that is, at best, indifferent, and at worst, hostile, is the quintessential image of the survivalist hero: he wants only to survive in order that he may be left alone to make a modest life for himself. Cold Mountain, the destination of his trek, becomes for him the embodiment of his ideal, his isolationist Heaven (or, if you prefer to read Inman's journey from a non-secular perspective, his true Heaven). "He thought of getting home and building him a cabin on Cold Mountain so high that not a soul but the nighthawks passing across the clouds in autumn could hear his sad cry. Of living a life so quiet he would not need ears."

This desire for isolation and self-sufficiency is a common characteristic of the survivalist (and also of the retro-Confederate), who generally fosters an intense dislike and distrust of others. Inman "wished not to be smirched with the mess of other people," says the narrator. This dislike and distrust particularly applies to governments, which are considered a tyrannical threat to personal freedom. Many survivalists "refuse to pay federal taxes, purchase an automobile license, or vote in nationalist elections" (Lamy 124). A very distinct strain of anti-governmental thought runs throughout *Cold Mountain*. For Inman, the Civil War began as a fight "to drive off invaders", but it becomes for him just as much of a fight against the defenders of the South as embodied by the Home Guard, whose purpose is to round up defectors and return them to the front lines but who more often than not merely murder those whom they find. At one point, Inman is forced to kill several Federals after they have stolen everything from a widowed mother of an infant and left her to starve; at another point, he is caught and driven for days by the Home Guard, then shot and left for dead. Both sides are equally horrible, leaving Inman with no allegiances but to himself.

But Inman's story is only half of the novel. The other half concerns Ada, a former Charleston socialite who finds herself alone, helpless, and poor on a farm that she doesn't know how to maintain after the death of her wealthy and impractical father whom she had completely depended upon her entire life. Upon introduction to her, we are told that she

> was perpetually hungry, having eaten little through the summer but milk, fried eggs, salads, and plates of miniature tomatoes from the untended plants that had grown wild and bushy with suckers. Even butter had proved beyond her means, for the milk she had tried to churn never firmed up beyond the consistency of runny clabber. She wanted a bowl of chicken and dumplings and a peach pie but had not a clue how one might arrive at them.

Eventually, in exchange for room and board, a world-weary but thoroughly capable woman named Ruby teaches her the art of subsistence. Grudgingly, Ada puts away her novels as well as her art materials and begins to learn everything that she needs to know to survive, from when to plant what in the garden to how to butcher and process a hog. Gradually, she grows to appreciate her newfound knowledge and respect these aspects of life that she once had disparaged. In a letter that she writes to her sister near the end of the novel, she describes the transformation, both physical and spiritual, that she has experienced: "I am brown as a penny from being outdoors all day, and I am growing somewhat ropy through the wrists and forearms. [. . .] Working in the fields, there are brief times when I go totally without thought. Not one idea crosses my mind, though my senses are to all around me. [. . .]

You would not know [my new mien] on me for I suspect it is somehow akin to contentment."

By the end of the novel, when she and Inman reunite, Ada has come to be as self-sufficient as Inman has always been. Inman is pleasantly surprised by her metamorphosis. In their newfound harmony, the social barriers that had existed between them before Inman left to fight in the war have disappeared; the couple is able to come together naturally, without artifice. But, just as it seems they soon will begin an idyllic life together upon Cold Mountain, Inman is killed by the Home Guard, ending their hopes for the future promised by their first sexual encounter.

Despite this calamity, however, as we see in the epilogue that moves us ahead in the story nine years, Ada, without Inman, prospers in her life on Cold Mountain. Along with Ruby, Ruby's father, and Ada's daughter by Inman, Ada has come to realize that society at large is not necessary to be content; in fact, it is a hindrance. All that is needed is the community of the family and the knowledge needed to live off the land. In the final scene, we are shown a sentimental tableau: the group sitting outside around a campfire, listening to Ada read a story. "The night was growing cool, and Ada put the book away. A crescent moon stood close upon Venus in the sky. The children were sleepy, and morning would dawn early and demanding as always. Time to go inside and cover up the coals and pull in the latch string." No mention is made in the epilogue of the world beyond Cold Mountain; having completely isolated themselves within their self-sufficient sphere, they are oblivious to the struggles associated with Reconstruction that the rest of the South is experiencing.

For the South, the Civil War was the millennium, the end of the world. As we approached our own millennium (at least in the calendar sense of the word), we did not have to look through too many newspapers to find the values held by Inman and Ada reflected by a growing number of individuals and constituents in this country. Like Randy Weaver's wife and son at Ruby Ridge and David Koresh at the Branch Davidian compound in Waco, Inman dies a martyr's death in defense of his beliefs, leaving behind him a small but fervent group that is adamant in its desire to continue what he had started. All that he wanted was to be left alone, "to exist unmolested somewhere on the west fork of the Pigeon River drainage basin." But the government (first the government of the United States, then the government of the Confederate States of America) that once served his interests had stopped doing so; in fact, it had come to oppose him actively as he attempted to make it through the wasteland to his home.

Cold Mountain can be read as a paean to survivalism and anti-governmentalism; it is a novel that accurately reflects a small but distinct population of the United States that either believes that it must protect itself from its government by arming itself and becoming self-reliant, or believes that it must isolate itself in preparation for the end of the world (or believes a combination of both). Like some conflation of the Four Horsemen of the Apocalypse and the Bureau of Alcohol, Tobacco, and Firearms, the Home Guard strikes down Inman (Henry David Thoreau as portrayed by a *Josey Wales*-era Clint Eastwood), leaving him to burn in our memories as a symbol of what we have to fear from these times of ours. The comparatively clear-cut morality of the Civil War as observed by Shaara in the Vietnam era has transformed. No government—neither North nor South—can now be trusted. All that we can depend upon is ourselves.

How we tell the story of the Civil War structures the cultural narrative of the United States; it is the American sacred text, the American *ur*-text—or, at the very least, the New Testament to the Declaration of Independence's Old Testament. All that came before it in this nation can best be understood by thinking in terms of how each significant decision made or action taken influenced subsequent decisions and actions that would finally culminate in the 1860s. And all that has come after it has been influenced by how it resolved. Because of the fundamental role that the Civil War has served and continues to serve in the creation and maintenance of our nation's notion of itself, the significant attention that it continues to be paid should come as no surprise. But, like anything so monolithic, it should also come as no surprise that its meaning remains utterly protean. It is frequently interpreted in manners that drastically conflict with each other, as well as frequently referenced to buttress any number of diverse ideologies. Even the very naming of the conflict itself (The Civil War, the War Between the States, the War of Northern Aggression) tellingly exposes the divisiveness that has marked all aspects of discourse about

it. The very fact that it refuses to be completely understood and explained goads us to attempt to infuse it with our own concepts of what is significant and important to our contemporary lives. In the 1970s, *The Killer Angels* recast the Civil War as a parable of Vietnam; in the 1990s, *Cold Mountain* recast it as a backdrop to the political and spiritual concerns that faced a growing number of individuals as the millennium approached. In the future, the concerns and fears of the populace of the United States will again make themselves known through the manner in which the decisions and actions made by the likes of Lincoln and Lee are recast.

Source: Kevin Grauke, "Vietnam, Survivalism, and the Civil War: The Use of History in Michael Shaara's *The Killer Angels* and Charles Frazier's *Cold Mountain*," in *War, Literature & the Arts: An International Journal of the Humanities*, Vol. 14, Nos. 1–2, 2002, pp. 45–57.

SOURCES

Adams, Phoebe, Review of *The Killer Angels*, in *Atlantic Monthly*, Vol. 234, No. 4, October 1974, p. 118.

Douthat, Ross, "They Made America," *The Atlantic*, Vol. 298, No. 5, December 2006, p. 74.

Review of *The Killer Angels*, in *Publishers Weekly*, Vol. 206, No. 2, July 8, 1974, p. 69.

Review of *The Killer Angels*, in *Times Literary Supplement*, No. 4916, June 20, 1997, p. 25.

Shaara, Michael, *The Killer Angels*, David McKay, 1974.

Stoppel, Ellen K., Review of *The Killer Angels*, in *Library Journal*, Vol. 99, No. 15, September 1, 1974, p. 2092.

Weeks, Edward, "The Peripatetic Reviewer," in *Atlantic Monthly*, Vol. 235, No. 4, April 1975, p. 98.

FURTHER READING

Chesnut, Mary, *Mary Chesnut's Civil War*, Yale University Press, 1993.

    Wife of a Cabinet member under Jefferson Davis, Chesnut describes the Civil War, much of which she witnessed. She was in Charleston during the firing on Fort Sumter, for example, which began the conflict. The 1982 edition of this book received the Pulitzer Prize for History.

Foote, Shelby, *The Civil War: A Narrative: Fredericksburg to Meridian*, Random House, 1963, pp. 467–581.

    This is one of the best accounts of the Battle of Gettysburg written to date. It brings the personalities of the soldiers to life and clearly recreates the ebb and flow of battle as it really was, not as legend has made it.

Hartwig, D. Scott, *A Killer Angels Companion*, Thomas Publications, 1996.

> Hartwig is a historian at Gettysburg National Military Park, and in this book, he examines the extent to which Shaara's novel reflects the truth about the Battle of Gettysburg and its key figures. He also discusses what happened to the major characters after Gettysburg.

Lewis, Clayton, "The Civil War: Killing and Hallowed Ground," in *Sewanee Review*, Vol. 103, No. 3, Summer 1995, pp. 414–25.

> Lewis argues that in many respects the novel is quite conventional. Its achievement, however, is the use of modern fictional technique to convey the immediacy of Civil War combat.

The Known World

EDWARD P. JONES

2003

The fact that free African Americans used to own other blacks as slaves is an ironic oddity of U.S. history that Edward P. Jones pondered for a long time. This perplexing detail about life before the Civil War eventually inspired him to write an eloquently crafted, Pulitzer Prize-winning novel entitled *The Known World*, published in 2003. Beginning with the life and death of Henry Townsend, a black slave master, Jones's novel explores a fictional county in antebellum Virginia over several decades. With its community-narrative approach and its patchwork storytelling style, the work gets to the heart of the moral dilemma that surrounds the institution of slavery. Jones delves into fundamental questions of human ownership and power over others while exploring views on justice, religion, and morality in the antebellum South.

An astute analysis of a tense era in U.S. history and a critical and literary success, *The Known World* carries an aura of historical accuracy and gravity even though it is entirely fictional. The novel's frequent allusions to the twentieth-century descendents of its characters and its fabricated references to twentieth-century historical scholarship suggest that Jones is also interested in how slaveholding bears on contemporary life. Jones's other work focuses on blacks living in late-twentieth-century Washington, D.C., and *The Known World* enters a fictional chapter of black history which is not necessarily so distant from the frequently desperate conditions that many blacks face in urban U.S. society.

AUTHOR BIOGRAPHY

Edward P. Jones was born in Washington, D.C., on October 5, 1950, and raised by his single mother, to whom Jones dedicated his first two books. He grew up well aware of the widespread poverty and desperation in the U.S. capital, particularly among African Americans, and this problem was a frequent subject of his writing in the 1990s and early 2000s. Jones himself was homeless for a period in the 1970s, and he struggled with depression. He did well at school and earned a scholarship to Holy Cross College, and he took care of his mother when she became ill and died in 1975.

Jones went on to earn a Master of Fine Arts degree at the University of Virginia, where he studied with authors James McPherson, John Casey, and Peter Taylor. He held a variety of jobs, including summarizing business articles, working as an assistant at *Science Magazine*, and teaching writing at universities, including Princeton and Georgetown. For most of his life, he has resided in or near Washington, D.C., and for twenty years preceding the publication of *The Known World* (2003), he lived in the same flat in Arlington, Virginia.

Jones's first book, a collection of short stories entitled *Lost in the City*, was published in 1992 to critical acclaim; it won the Ernest Hemingway Foundation/PEN Award and received a nomination for the National Book Award. The stories vividly portray African Americans coping with confusion and decay in poverty-stricken, inner-city Washington, D.C., during the 1950s, 1960s, and 1970s. Though they tend to portray bleak circumstances, the stories generate sympathy for their characters, many of whom are warm-hearted. Jones won a Lannan Foundation grant in 1994 and another in 2003, the same year he published *The Known World*. In 2004, Jones won the Pulitzer Prize for Fiction for *The Known World*.

Jones has published short stories in journals, including the *New Yorker* and *Ploughshares*. He won a MacArthur Fellowship in 2005, and in 2006, he published a collection of short stories, entitled *All Aunt Hagar's Children*, which focuses on characters living in Washington, D.C., many of them from the rural South. As of 2006, he

MEDIA ADAPTATIONS

- HarperAudio released an unabridged audio version of *The Known World*, narrated by Kevin Free. As of 2007, it was readily available in compact disc and audio cassette formats.

continued to live and write in the Washington, D.C., area.

PLOT SUMMARY

Chapter 1

The Known World begins with a description of the 1855 evening when Henry Townsend, the black master of a Virginia plantation, dies. Henry's slave overseer, Moses, wanders into the rainy woods and masturbates, while Henry's wife, Caldonia, sits with her husband as she has done for the previous six days and nights.

When Henry's father, Augustus, bought himself out of slavery, he left his wife Mildred and his son as slaves to William Robbins until he could earn enough money to free them. Although he freed his wife shortly afterwards, it was many years before he earned enough to free his son. During this time, Henry curried Robbins's favor, learned about Robbins's family with a black woman named Philomena, and helped his master suffer through "storms," or mental breakdowns, on his returns from Philomena's house.

Chapter 2

John Skiffington was a deputy to Sheriff Giles Patterson when he married Patterson's niece Winifred. Skiffington's cousin Counsel and his wife gave the newlyweds a slave named Minerva as a wedding present, and although Skiffington and his wife agreed that they wanted nothing to do with slavery, they kept Minerva and treated her like a daughter. Meanwhile William Robbins was worried that Patterson was not doing enough to keep slaves from running away, and after his slave Rita escaped (with secret help from Augustus), Robbins used his influence to force Patterson to retire. Skiffington took over as sheriff and hired twelve poor white and Native American slave patrollers to ensure that no more slaves escaped.

Chapter 3

After Henry dies, Caldonia's maid Loretta tells Moses to break the news to everyone and deal with all problems. Augustus, Mildred, Fern Elston, and all of the slaves come to the house and listen to Caldonia's words of comfort, which imply that the slaves will not be set free. Calvin, Louis, and Augustus help the slaves dig Henry's grave. That night, Alice goes out wandering, singing and dancing, but the slave patrollers leave her alone. The night of the day Henry is buried, Elias finishes the doll he has been whittling for his daughter Tessie and begins to whittle a horse for his son.

Celeste caught Elias staring at her shortly after Henry purchased him, and she resented this, thinking that he was staring at her limp. She was mean to him whenever possible afterwards, although she began to pity him when he became ill. After he recovered, Elias attempted to escape, but he grew ill on the journey and William Robbins caught him. Henry had Elias chained and resolved to have Elias's ear chopped off. This decision troubled Henry, who became enraged when Ramsey Elston insulted him at dinner that night, but the next morning he paid Oden Peoples to cut off a third of Elias's ear.

A slave boy named Luke befriended Elias while he was recovering, and later Celeste resolved to look after the boy. Elias carved her a wooden comb, and they fell in love. Elias told Henry that he would like to live with Celeste, and Henry agreed, pleased that this would prevent Elias from running away again. The couple lived with Luke until Henry hired the boy out as a harvest worker to a white man who worked him so hard that the boy died.

Chapter 4

In 1881, a Canadian pamphlet-writer called Anderson Frazier comes to Manchester County in order to interview Fern Elston about the "oddest" thing he had ever come upon as a journalist: the fact that blacks used to own black slaves.

Fern tells him that, contrary to his impression, it was not the same as owning members of one's family, and she tells him about Henry.

Henry was always devoted to Robbins, and after Augustus bought his freedom, Henry continued to visit Robbins and travel with him. When Philomena ran away to Richmond for the second time, Robbins took Henry with him to help bring her back. Robbins got into a violent fight with Philomena when he found her, in which he punched her brutally while Henry screamed. Henry followed Robbins's instructions and calmed the children, however, and then drove them to Manchester the next day.

One day when Henry was building his house with Moses, Robbins rode up and saw them wrestling in the dirt. Furious, Robbins told Henry that he must act as a master, not a slave. Henry walked back and slapped Moses twice, telling him that he was leaving and that Moses must be "doin right" when he returned. He rode to his parents' house, but the news that he had purchased a slave horrified them. Augustus beat Henry with a walking stick, breaking his shoulder, and Henry left for Robbins's house. Meanwhile, Robbins had gone to Fern and asked if she would educate Henry. Fern agreed because Robbins protected her from any trouble with the slave patrollers. Henry was Fern's most intelligent, darkest-skinned, and oldest student. He met Caldonia at Fern's house and married her soon afterwards.

Chapter 5

In 1844, Skiffington went to the house of Clara Martin, his wife's cousin, to ease her fears about her slave Ralph. After dinner at Clara's, Skiffington rode out to settle a dispute between his slave patrollers Harvey Travis and Clarence Wilford over a cow flowing with milk. Travis sold the cow thinking it would not give milk, but now he wanted it back and was threatening violence. Skiffington told him that he could not have the cow back and warned him about making trouble. When Skiffington arrived at the jail the next morning, William Robbins came to complain that Travis hit Henry, and while he was there Robbins bought Moses from Jean Broussard, a French prisoner. Moses pleaded for Robbins not to separate him from his wife, but Robbins ignored him. The money went to Broussard's widow in France, however, because the jury decided to hang

Broussard, disbelieving his story because he had a foreign accent.

Chapter 6

Caldonia's mother Maude comes to the plantation two days after Henry's death and urges Caldonia not to waste her "legacy" by selling or freeing her slaves. Moses puts the slaves back to work, but Calvin tells them to return home. Stamford tries anxiously to find a young woman and gets into a fight which leaves him unable to work for a week and a half. Meanwhile, an insurance salesman attempts to sell Caldonia a policy on her slaves.

Stamford becomes depressed and starts drinking a strange brew. He makes a pass at Delphie, and she tries to help him but then turns him out into a storm. Stamford finds a little girl named Delores trying to collect blueberries, and he insists on sending her inside and doing it for her. He sees lightening strike a tree and kill two crows and their nest, and this experience affects him deeply. He gives a bucket of blueberries to Delores and her brother and resolves to look after the plantation's children. During this time, Moses begins to meet with Caldonia and tell her about the slaves' activities that day, and he begins to fabricate stories about Henry and the slaves.

One night when Augustus is traveling home, he meets slave patrollers Harvey Travis, Oden Peoples, and Barnum Kinsey. Travis eats Augustus's free papers and sells him to a speculator named Darcy. Barnum protests, but Travis spits on him, pushes him down, and threatens to shoot him. Darcy and his slave Stennis drive away with Augustus, and Travis burns Augustus's wagon.

Chapter 7

Counsel Skiffington's creditor Manfred Carlyle spreads smallpox to Counsel's estate. The epidemic kills everyone except Counsel, who sets fire to the entire plantation and starts traveling southwest with no destination in mind. Eventually Counsel makes his way to Georgia, where he hires himself out as a laborer, and to Louisiana, where he stays in a barn and has sex with a married woman. Counsel then meets a group of mixed-race migrants in Texas who frighten him, and he shoots his horse when it will not follow him into a thicket. Dismayed, he asks what God wants of him, and then he decides to go back to Virginia.

Chapter 8

Maude is the first to leave Caldonia after Henry dies, and when she returns she becomes intimate with her slave Clarke. Calvin and Fern leave afterwards, and on her way home Fern meets Jebediah Dickinson, who claims that her husband owes him five hundred dollars. Fern refuses to give him the money, but Jebediah stays there waiting until his horse dies, and then Oden Peoples arrests him for vagrancy. Skiffington telegraphs the sheriff of Jebediah's town, and Reverend Wilbur Mann comes to Manchester claiming that Jebediah has written false papers and is his property. Mann threatens to bring Jebediah home and torture him, but Fern buys him.

When Jebediah sees Ramsey, he shouts that Ramsey owes him money and was unfaithful to Fern. Fern keeps Jebediah as a slave, but soon he starts leaving her plantation with passes that he has forged. Fern has him flogged for making a sexual comment towards her, and afterwards he steps on a rusty nail and needs to have his right foot amputated. Fern frees him, and he corrects her spelling of "*manumit*" in his free papers.

Moses continues to meet Caldonia each night and tell her stories. He begins to have ambitions about being a free man, and he asks the house slave Bennett for a new set of clothes without Caldonia's permission. He also begins to act more harshly towards his wife and the other slaves and to have suspicions that Alice is not actually crazy. He starts following Alice on her nightly wanderings and has a near run-in with slave patrollers. One night Caldonia kisses Moses, and a week later they begin making love.

Chapter 9

Darcy and Stennis drive with Augustus and the other people they have stolen to South Carolina. A child dies and they dump her on the side of the road, and they start to sell black people who used to be free. They try to sell Augustus, but he pretends to be mute. Augustus asks Stennis to let him slip away or escape with him, but Stennis refuses. Counsel arrives at John Skiffington's house after his long travels, and Skiffington asks him to be his deputy. Two weeks after Augustus's disappearance, Mildred, Caldonia, and Fern tell Counsel that he is gone, but Counsel does not pass the message along to Skiffington.

Meanwhile, Caldonia's relationship with Moses intensifies, and she goes to Henry's grave and asks for forgiveness. Fern, Louis, Dora, and Calvin come to dinner, and they talk about abolition and the possibility of slave uprisings. After Caldonia arranges for him to have supper with her in the kitchen, Moses feels increasingly confident. He goes to Alice and asks her to run away on Saturday night, taking his wife and son with her. Moses tells Priscilla and Jamie that he will join them later, and Moses goes with them to the edge of the plantation. Priscilla is worried, but Alice slaps her and talks to her in a new, perfectly sane voice. The next day at noon, Moses tells Caldonia that the three slaves are missing, and Caldonia tells Bennett to report their "'disappearance'" to Skiffington on Monday.

Skiffington begins to suspect Moses of murder, and he comes to Caldonia's plantation to investigate. Two days later, Barnum comes to Skiffington while he is drunk and tells him that Travis and Oden sold Augustus. Skiffington rides to Mildred's house and finds out that she had already told Counsel about Augustus's disappearance. He goes to Counsel's boardinghouse and tells him that he has "but one more time to do this." Then Skiffington warns Harvey and Oden, and he writes to the Richmond authorities about the matter. Meanwhile, Darcy and Stennis continue to try to sell Augustus.

Chapter 10

Caldonia begins to worry about the missing slaves and to cool to Moses' affection. Skiffington visits Caldonia and Mildred and then goes to William Robbins's plantation. Robbins tells him that he will pay for a five-hundred-dollar bounty on the head of the speculator Darcy. That night, Moses makes love to Caldonia and then asks her to free him, but she says she does not want to talk about it. The next day, Moses forces Celeste to work even though she is six months pregnant and not feeling well, and she loses her baby. Elias says he will kill Moses.

Moses confronts Caldonia again about his freedom, and after he leaves, Loretta begins protecting the house with a pistol. The next day, Moses refuses to come out of his cabin, and that night he runs away. In the confusion, Gloria and Clement also run away. Elias becomes the new overseer, against Celeste's wishes. Bennett rides to tell Skiffington that Moses has run away then returns to say that Gloria and Clement are gone

as well, and Skiffington worries that the world is falling apart.

Chapter 11

A wealthy man in Georgia develops resentment for a poor woman named Hope Ulster because she refuses to see him about marrying his son, and he ensures that she and her family stay poor. Hope's husband, Hillard, buys Augustus from Darcy for fifty-three dollars, but Augustus starts to walk away from him and Hillard shoots him in the shoulder. Augustus dies, and his ghost walks rapidly to let Mildred know that he has died.

Skiffington develops a painful toothache and sends his patrollers and deputy all over to look for the missing slaves. Stamford plays with Elias's son Ellwood, who later helps Stamford and Delphie run the Richmond Home for Colored Orphans. Ray Topps, the insurance salesman, returns and sells Caldonia a policy for her slaves which covers incidents that are not "'ordinary act[s] of God.'"

Chapter 12

Skiffington decides that Moses must be hidden in Mildred's house, and he and Counsel travel there. Mildred points a rifle at them when they arrive, and Skiffington tells her to surrender the property. He shoots her in the heart, and then he tells Counsel to get Moses out of the house. Inside, Counsel finds five gold pieces, and when he comes out he shoots Skiffington with Mildred's rifle and puts the rifle in Mildred's hands. He notices Moses watching him and threatens to kill Moses if he says anything. Counsel meets Elias and Louis, and then Barnum, Travis, and Oden on the road, and he tells them that Mildred shot Skiffington. Oden offers to hobble Moses or cut his Achilles tendon, and Counsel tells him to go ahead, over Barnum's and Louis's protests.

Barnum takes his family to Missouri but dies not long after they cross the Mississippi River. Robbins enters the dispute over what should happen to Mildred and Augustus's property, and this conflict escalates a feud between him and Robert Colfax which leads to the dissolution of the county of Manchester. Darcy and Stennis are caught and imprisoned. Winifred and Minerva move to Philadelphia, and one day Minerva meets a handsome black man and marries him. She never returns to tell Winifred why she left.

The novel ends with a letter from Calvin to Caldonia, which describes his life in Washington, D.C., and tells her that Alice, Priscilla, and Jamie live there as well. Caldonia has married Louis, even though seeing Moses continues to make her heart stop. Celeste continues to make meals for Moses until he dies.

CHARACTERS

Alice

Alice is Henry's slave, "a woman people said had lost her mind" because a mule kicked her in the head. Moses suspects that she knows what she is doing after all, however, and Alice confirms this when she leads Moses' wife and son to freedom in Washington, D.C.

Tom Anderson

Tom Anderson is the name that a preacher shares with his slave. The 1842 disappearance of the slave Tom Anderson worries William Robbins, even though he was probably sold by Tom Anderson the preacher.

Bennettt

Henry's house slave, Bennettt, is Zeddie's husband. He goes on errands for Caldonia and handles other odd jobs on the plantation.

Jean Broussard

Jean Broussard is an amiable Frenchman who is imprisoned after killing his Scandinavian partner. He loves the United States and plans to take his family there, but he is executed because the jury does not trust his accent.

Morris Calhenny

Morris Calhenny, a rich man from Georgia, is prone to bouts of melancholy. He resents Hope Uster because she does not marry his son and resolves to make life difficult for her and her husband.

Manfred Carlyle

Manfred Carlyle, who is in love with Saskia Wilhelm, is one of Counsel Skiffington's creditors. He contracts smallpox from Saskia and spreads it through Counsel's plantation, though he shows no symptoms and does not know that he carries it.

Cassandra

Cassandra, or Cassie, is Delphie's daughter and Henry's slave. Stamford tries to court her, but she is not interested.

Celeste

Henry's slave and Elias's wife, Celeste has a severe limp and is dedicated to caring for children. She resents Elias at first, but grows to love him.

Clarke

Clarke is Maude's slave, with whom Maude becomes intimate after she kills her husband.

Clement

Gloria's boyfriend, Clement, is a strong and protective man.

Robert Colfax

The second-wealthiest man in Manchester County, Colfax is friends with Robbins until Robbins angers him by purchasing Clara Martin's estate.

Darcy

Darcy is a corrupt speculator who buys and sells free men and women as slaves.

Darr

Darr is Counsel Skiffington's overseer and the first of his slaves to come down with smallpox.

Delores

Delores is a little slave girl who looks for blueberries in a storm.

Delphie

Delphie is Henry's slave and Alice's cabin mate. She is used to nursing and healing people, and later in life she marries Stamford.

Jebediah Dickinson

Jebediah Dickinson is a literate and extremely intelligent black man who comes to the Elton's house determined to collect on Ramsey's gambling debt. He is proud and resourceful and even corrects Fern's spelling when she finally writes his free papers. Later it becomes clear that Fern has fallen in love with him, but he does not return these feelings.

Dora

Dora is the daughter of William Robbins and Philomena.

Elias

Elias is Henry's slave and Moses' antagonist. Elias's loyalties are to his wife and children. He is determined to run away after Henry buys him from two white newlyweds, but William Robbins captures him and Henry orders a third of his ear cut off. Elias develops a hatred of Henry as a result and continues to resolve to escape until he falls in love with Celeste. As Henry puts it, she is the invisible chain which keeps Elias on the plantation.

Ellwood

Ellwood is Elias and Celeste's young son.

Fern Elston

Fern Elston is a well-educated teacher of free African Americans. She is responsible for the education of most of Manchester County's free blacks, and her students include Caldonia, Calvin, Louis, Dora, and Henry. She is black herself or has a small fraction of African American blood, but her complexion passes for white and some of her relatives live as white people. Her character is rooted in her strong sense of pride, justice, and order, and she suffers from living with her husband Ramsey. Fern continually repeats to herself the phrase "*I have been a dutiful wife*" in order to endure humiliations such as her husband's demand that she refrain from washing herself before he returns home and sleeps with her. Jebediah Dickenson's arrival deeply shakes Fern, perhaps because his extreme intelligence seems to her incompatible with his low breeding. Fern becomes obsessed with him and goes so far as to admit to her friends that she feels "as if [she] belong[s] to him." Fern thinks about Jebediah frequently for the rest of her life.

Ramsey Elston

Fern's husband, Ramsey Elston, is a profligate gambler who loses Fern's money and stays away from home for long periods of time. One of his quirks that most infuriates his wife is that he insists that she go without bathing before he sleeps with her.

Anderson Frazier

Anderson Frazier is a Canadian pamphlet writer who interviews Fern Elston in August of 1881. He converts to Judaism in order to marry a Jewish-American woman, and he writes a series of pamphlets entitled *Curiosities and Oddities about Our Southern Neighbors*, which focus on blacks who used to own other blacks as slaves.

Gloria

Henry's slave Gloria is Stamford's lover until she tires of him and takes up with Clement.

Jamie

Moses' son, Jamie, is a fat boy full of mischief. He escapes to Washington, D.C., with his mother.

Hiram Jinkins

Hiram Jinkins is a name shared by a father and son from Louisiana. Both are irascible and mysterious.

Meg Jinkins

Meg Jinkins is a married woman from Louisiana with whom Counsel has a one-night sexual encounter.

Barnum Kinsey

A poor white slave patroller with a drinking problem, Barnum has a good heart, but he lacks the courage to stand up to others. He tries to encourage tolerance and fairness towards slaves, but his companions Travis and Oden bully him for this.

Loretta

Caldonia's maid, Loretta, is a loyal house slave who protects her mistress carefully.

Louis

William Robbins's half-black son, Louis, eventually marries Caldonia when she is a widow. He has a traveling or lazy eye and is close with his father when he is young. He often tries to sound impressive about topics that he does not understand, and he never realizes that Calvin is in love with him.

Luke

Luke is a kind slave boy who befriends Elias.

Reverend Wilbur Mann

Jebediah's former master, Wilbur Mann is a brutal and bad-tempered preacher.

Clara Martin

Winifred's cousin, Clara Martin, becomes deathly afraid of her slave Ralph after she hears a story of a slave cook who puts ground-up glass in her mistress's food. This fear is related to her sexual attraction to Ralph, and it persists and intensifies throughout her lifetime.

Minerva

Minerva is John and Winifred Skiffington's slave, although they treat her like a daughter. When Minerva moves to Philadelphia and gets married, however, she resents Winifred for hanging posters which imply that Minerva is her property.

Valtims Moffett

Valtims Moffett is a preacher who holds services for slaves in exchange for a one-dollar fee. He lives with his wife and her sister and enjoys the fact that they constantly fight over him.

Moses

Moses is a powerful man whom Henry chooses as his first slave and overseer. William Robbins purchases Moses from a French prisoner, separating him from his wife and traumatizing him. Moses neglects and beats his second wife, Priscilla, and he maintains order on the plantation by intimidating and punishing those who disobey him. Moses is extremely loyal to Henry during Henry's lifetime, even after Henry abruptly begins to treat him as a slave and not a friend.

Elias points out that Moses is "world-stupid," by which he means that Moses does not know north from south and cannot negotiate life outside the plantation. This description pinpoints an important aspect of Moses' character, which is that he thrives only within the system that he knows. Moses is a very effective overseer, but his world begins to turn upside down when he becomes intimate with Caldonia. He grows restless and expects to marry Caldonia, and when he sees that this will not happen, he becomes depressed and then attempts to run away.

Calvin Newman

Calvin Newman is Caldonia's brother. He has homosexual desires and is in love with his schoolmate Louis, but he spends much of his life celibate, looking after his mother Maude. Calvin is an abolitionist, and he feels guilty about the fact that his family owns slaves, but he does little to act on his convictions. He lives in Washington, D.C., but never sees New York, as is his dream.

Maude Newman

Maude Newman is Caldonia's manipulative mother, whose great desire for privilege and power over others leads to her obsession with the "legacy" of slaves that she owns. Out of fear and disgust with her husband's plan to free his slaves, she poisons him with arsenic. Shortly after he dies, she takes her slave Clarke as her lover, perhaps because she enjoys having someone totally her power.

Tilmon Newman

Caldonia's father, Tilmon Newman, is a free black man who wishes to free all of his slaves at the end of his life. Before he is able to do so, however, his wife Maude murders him.

Mary O'Donnell

Mary O'Donnell is an Irish woman living in New York who receives the package with William Robbins's slave Rita inside.

Sheriff Gilly Patterson

Winifred's father, Gilly Patterson, precedes Skiffington as the sheriff of Manchester County.

Winifred Patterson

See Winifred Skiffington

Oden Peoples

A Cherokee slave patroller, Oden Peoples is a rough and brutal man. He specializes in maiming slaves as punishment for disobedience or attempted escape, and he seems to enjoy this work. After Henry pays him for cutting off a third of Elias's ear, for example, Oden offers to do the rest for free.

Philomena

The mother of William Robbins's mixed-race children, Philomena is an unhappy black woman who wishes to live in Richmond. She cultivates the desire to live there after hearing that even slaves have slaves in the city. Philomena finally comes to Richmond to live only after the Union Army burns it to the ground.

Priscilla

Priscilla is Henry's slave and Moses' wife. She is jealous and resentful of Moses for "years of abuse and rejection," but she escapes to Washington, D.C., under his arrangements and seems to prosper there.

Ralph

Clara Martin's slave Ralph is a harmless and loyal old man with rheumatism. He moves to Washington, D.C., after Clara dies.

Rita

William Robbins's slave Rita is close friends with Mildred, and she watches over Henry as his second mother when Augustus buys Mildred's freedom. Rita is so attached to Henry that she is unable to leave him when he is freed, and Augustus ends up shipping her in a box to New York.

Ethel Robbins

William Robbins's wife, Ethel, is horrified by and depressed about her husband's second family with Philomena.

Patience Robbins

Patience Robbins is the daughter of William Robbins and Ethel.

William Robbins

The wealthiest man in Manchester County, William Robbins is an intimidating and ambitious person obsessed with power and control. His grandfather was a stowaway on a ship from Bristol, England, and Robbins's fortune is self-made. He knows how to dominate others and pursue his sense of entitlement. Because Henry is an industrious worker with great respect for his master, Robbins grows to respect Henry as a son, and he is responsible for fostering Henry's own ambition and desire for power over others. In fact, Robbins needs Henry because he fears he is losing his mind, and Henry acts as an intermediary between Robbins and his black family. The fact that Robbins's intense blackouts occur when he returns from his visits to his black lover, Philomena, suggests that this relationship is part of the reason that Robbins is mentally ill. Philomena is not the first black woman with whom Robbins has children, however. In fact, Robbins has two children by a slave on his own plantation. After Henry dies, Robbins blesses the marriage of Caldonia and Louis.

Sam

Sam is a slave of William Robbins who has his ear cut off after he runs away for the second time. He scares slave children, including Henry, with the ear hole, and Henry remembers it long afterwards.

Belle Skiffington

From a well-to-do family in Raleigh, Belle Skiffington is Counsel's wife and the next-to-last person to die of smallpox on their plantation.

Carl Skiffington

Carl is John Skiffington's father, and he lives with Skiffington and Winifred.

Counsel Skiffington

John Skiffington's cousin, Counsel, is a racist and ambitious man who becomes increasingly greedy and ruthless after he travels to Texas and claims to find God. He and his wife give John a slave, Minerva, as a wedding gift, and he continues to be a symbol of the slave-holding ethos. Counsel is too proud to live with his cousin for more than a brief period, and he becomes increasingly disgusted with John's idea of justice.

Sheriff John Skiffington

Sheriff of Manchester County, John Skiffington is a religious man who does not like the idea of owning a slave, though he willingly does his work, which supports the institution of slavery. He tries to be just in his role of maintaining order, but he goes to great lengths to prevent slaves from running away and fails to ensure that free blacks are treated fairly. In some ways, this is the inevitable result of the legal system he is charged with upholding, but it is also due to Skiffington's feelings that blacks are inferior to whites. He is attached to his slave Minerva as though she were his daughter, but he also has sexual feelings for her (about which he feels guilty) and he will not allow her to become a free woman.

Winifred Skiffington

Giles Patterson's niece from Philadelphia, Winifred marries Skiffington and tells him that she does not want slavery in her life. Although she treats her slave Minerva like a daughter and lives with her in Philadelphia, paradoxically, she never accepts the idea that Minerva could be a free woman.

Stamford

Stamford is Henry's slave and a lover of younger women. When he was twelve, an older slave told him that the way to survive slavery is to be sexually active with young females, and so he becomes obsessed with them. He develops a commitment to help children in need, and later in life, he and his wife Delphie found the Richmond Home for Colored Orphans.

Stennis

Darcy's loyal slave, Stennis, is a large black man who helps his master buy and sell free black people.

Tessie

The oldest child of Elias and Celeste, Tessie lives to be ninety-seven years old and keeps the doll her father makes for her until she dies.

Thomasina

Thomasina owns the boardinghouse where Counsel stays while he is Skiffington's deputy. She has an affair with Counsel, and she cries and trembles after they make love.

Ray Topps

Ray Topps is the representative from Atlas Life, Casualty, and Assurance who keeps returning to the plantation attempting to sell Caldonia a policy on the slaves.

Augustus Townsend

Henry's father, Augustus Townsend, is William Robbins's slave until he buys his own freedom from the profits he makes as a woodcarver. Augustus hates the institution of slavery, and he and his wife are involved in the Underground Railroad, helping slaves reach freedom in the North. Even after Oden Peoples sells him back into slavery, Augustus refuses to act as a slave. His final act of resistance is to begin to walk north after he is sold, but this results in his death. His son Henry owns slaves, which is a great disappointment to Augustus, and he never recovers from it; even when he visits Henry's plantation, Augustus refuses to stay under the same roof as his son.

Caldonia Townsend

Caldonia Townsend is Henry's wife and later his widow. She means well towards the slaves, and they generally like her, and she has ideas about being a kind and tolerant mistress. Although she occasionally stops to reconsider what is happening to them as masters and slaves, she never has any plans to free them and prefers to think of her role as a benevolent mistress who helps her slaves lead good lives. Caldonia is deeply in love with Henry, and her relationship with Moses is due in no small part to the fact that she misses her dead husband. Caldonia has strong feelings for Moses, but she never sees him as more than a slave.

Henry Townsend

Henry Townsend is a bright, industrious, and ambitious black man who works his way to become the master of a successful plantation and a slave owner. He admires his master, William Robbins, and courts his favor even as his father, Augustus, is working terribly hard to free Henry and bring him home. They become increasingly close, and Henry cultivates himself in Robbins's image. For example, Henry treats Moses as his friend and equal until Robbins tells him that this is wrong. Henry can be a cruel and effective master, such as when he has the outer rim of Elias's ear cut off and then realizes with glee that the most effective way of chaining Elias to the plantation is to allow him to marry Celeste. Despite his great intelligence, Henry never fully understands why his father is so opposed to slavery, and he wishes to be remembered as a prosperous slave owner.

Mildred Townsend

Augustus's wife, Mildred Townsend, is a forthright woman who is caught in the battle between her son and husband. She hates slavery as much as Augustus, but she does not turn away from Henry when he becomes a slave owner. When she takes in Moses and attempts to help him, Mildred reveals her resourceful character and strong sympathy for slaves.

Harvey Travis

Harvey Travis is a vicious slave patroller with a Cherokee wife. He is jealous and resentful of people like Augustus who he feels have some kind of advantage over him (Augustus, for example, is a much better woodworker), and he responds with cruelty towards them.

Hillard Uster

Hillard Uster is a poor man from Georgia who buys Augustus Townsend for fifty-three dollars and shoots him when Augustus refuses to be his slave.

Hope Uster

Hope Uster is a poor white woman from Georgia who is with Augustus Townsend when he dies.

TOPICS FOR FURTHER STUDY

- The narrator of *The Known World* makes reference to the corruption and bias involved in formulating U.S. Census figures. Research the history of the U.S. Census from 1830 to the present day, particularly as it relates to issues of race, and then give a class presentation summarizing your findings. What was the purpose of the census, and how has it changed? How has race been defined, and why? How have the ethics of census-taking changed, and what are the continuing difficulties? Describe the major changes in government policy regarding the census. Include visual aids in your presentation.

- The novel makes reference to the fate of the children of Elias and Celeste, who survive into the twentieth century. Choose one of those characters, or invent one of their grandchildren, and write a short story that focuses on him or her. How does your character's ancestry affect his or her life?

- Jones uses a point of view that jumps back and forth in time and renders the reader omniscient. Write an essay discussing this formal or stylistic convention and its relationship to a particular theme or set of themes in the novel. As you do your research, you may want to consider other movements and genres that might have influenced Jones's narrative technique. You may want to consider also the novel's references to other authors, such as John Milton, and their significance to *The Known World*.

- Read a scholarly work of history, published by a university press, which deals with slavery in antebellum Virginia or another southern state. Then write a book review. In order to do this assignment, you will need to read a variety of reviews in a historical periodical such as the *William and Mary Quarterly*, studying their style and format. Be sure to state your book's specific area of inquiry and to focus less on synopsis than on the fundamental concepts of the work and its strengths and weaknesses.

Beth Ann Wilford
Beth Ann Wilford is Clarence's wife and the mother of eight children.

Clarence Wilford
Clarence Wilford is a poor white slave patroller to whom Travis sells a cow.

Saskia Wilhelm
A Dutch woman who elopes with a scoundrel, Saskia Wilhelm transmits smallpox indirectly to Counsel Skiffington's plantation.

Thorbecke Wilhelm
Thorbecke Wilhelm is Saskia's no-good husband who sells her to a brothel.

Willis
Willis is a brick marker whom Darcy kidnaps and sells to schoolteachers in North Carolina.

Zeddie
Zeddie is Henry's cook, the second slave he purchases.

Zeus
Zeus is Fern Elston's loyal house slave.

THEMES

Slavery in the Antebellum South
Perhaps the predominant theme in *The Known World* is the nature of the power and distinction that human beings desired to hold over one

another in the southern United States during the period leading up to the Civil War. The novel's central subject, African American ownership of other African Americans as slaves, encourages the reader to concentrate not only on the relationship between particular races, but on the fundamental desire to own other people. Blacks like Henry may have fostered their desire to own slaves based on their experience with white masters, but they do not necessarily want to become white or act as though they are white. The novel is intent on probing many different types of master-slave relationships that are defined in terms more complex than skin color or race.

The novel's many subplots bring various types and forms of inter-human ownership to the fore, starting with Henry's role as a master. As an ambitious young man trying to cultivate himself in his master's image, Henry associates the ownership of slaves with prosperity and success in general. At first, he does not even seem to believe that he is different or separate from his slaves, which is why he sees no problem with wrestling with Moses in the mud. He begins to think and act as though he is superior to slaves, however, after Robbins and Fern indoctrinate him in this convention. Other characters, such as Caldonia, by contrast, see the role of master rather differently, associating it less with economic prosperity than with paternalism. In other words, Caldonia believes that she will help and protect the slaves under her care, guiding them to a good life as they could not manage alone. Meanwhile, characters like Harvey Travis reveal that their conception of slavery is based on cruel and petty feelings of jealousy and hatred.

Despite revealing a great diversity in how various people conceptualize slavery, however, the novel reminds the reader that an institution which reduces people to property is always immoral and always fueled by the desire for superiority and control. Sometimes characters express the notion of control in terms of order and stability; Robbins, John Skiffington, and others worry that any breakup of the system of slaveholding will result in chaos and disorder. Even in these cases, however, the novel reveals the grim reality of slavery by displaying the violence and injustice that are its inevitable results. From Henry's decision to have one third of Elias's ear cut off to Counsel's order to cut

Moses' Achilles tendon, the horror of slavery never recedes from the surface.

Ownership and Love

Another central theme in Jones's novel pertains to the connection between personal ownership and love or sex. The novel frequently draws attention to characters whose ideas of superiority, slavery, and property intersect with their intimate relationships and desires, including affairs between masters and slaves. Slaveholding characters, Robbins, Caldonia, and Maude, consummate relationships with one of their slaves, while Fern, Skiffington, and Clara Martin have a strong desire to do so.

For their part, slaves such as Minerva, Philomena, and Moses, either seem indifferent to a relationship with their masters or view it as an opportunity to rise on the social ladder. Moses' relationship with Caldonia sparks his desire for freedom, and he comes to see it as a pathway to a different life. In chapter 10, the narrator says that Moses wants to have sex with Caldonia not to satisfy his lust, but "because he needed to be able to walk through that back door again without knocking." Meanwhile, Fern's statement that she feels as though she is Jebediah Dickinson's "property" seems to be her way of saying that she is in love with him. Skiffington and Winifred's relationship with Minerva is another example of the way in which slavery is tied to love—both parental love and (for Skiffington) erotic love—but the fact that Minerva abandons Winifred in Philadelphia suggests that love between slaves and masters is flawed, problematic, and unequal.

Justice in an Inequitable System

The quest for justice is enacted, in a sense, by the subplot about John Skiffington. A religious man with a strong sense of fairness, Skiffington attempts to reconcile slavery with justice, but he is doomed to failure because he cannot control his subordinates and because he believes in or at least supports a fundamentally unjust legal system. The final scene of the novel, in which Skiffington shoots Mildred Townsend without provocation, is a climax to this subplot that reveals that Skiffington cannot police Manchester County without resorting to violence and inequity. Skiffington cannot provide Mildred with justice any more than, for example, Robbins can be fair to his true love Philomena, because both men treat black people as inferior, as property.

COMPARE & CONTRAST

- **1850s:** According to the 1850 U.S. Census, 3,638,808 African Americans live in the United States, and of those, 3,204,313 are held as slaves.

  Today: According to the 2000 U.S. Census, 34,658,190 to 36,419,434 African Americans live in the United States, where slavery is illegal.

- **1850s:** Vast numbers of African Americans live in poor and desperate circumstances. Many slaves are treated harshly and malnourished, while free blacks often have difficulty finding work and live in fear of being sold into slavery.

  Today: Many African Americans continue to struggle with poverty; by the end of the twentieth century, blacks are three times as likely as whites to be poor.

- **1850s:** Political and cultural tensions between the northern and southern United States are rising and soon lead to the bloody Civil War.

  Today: There is debatably a sharp cultural divide between conservative and liberal areas of the United States.

- **1850s:** Pro-southern president Franklin Pierce, who has a charming personality but is somewhat incompetent in his duties, fails to calm the rising tensions that result in the Civil War.

  Today: As of late 2006, President George W. Bush, who is related to Franklin Pierce through his mother, is increasingly unpopular, in large part because of the disastrous aftermath of the U.S.-led invasion of Iraq.

STYLE

Flashbacks and Nonlinear Narrative

Although much of *The Known World* focuses on events stretching from Henry's death to Skiffington's death, the novel does not progress in a strictly chronological order. Instead, it frequently jumps back and forward in time as it pieces together a wide-ranging story that includes key episodes from characters' pasts and futures. Jones sometimes jumps ahead to the twentieth century in a single sentence, for example, when he refers to the fate of Celeste and Elias's children, and he focuses at length on episodes from Henry's youth.

This nonlinear storytelling technique has the effect of weaving a tapestry of history around the reader. Events across a long range fit together in provocative ways that emphasize that historical periods are more closely connected than might appear. Henry's desire to be a slaveholder is rooted in his boyhood experience, and Elias's children carry their direct experience of slavery well into the twentieth century. The novel blurs the divide between mid-nineteenth-century events and lives with those generations later, implying that the institution of slavery and the practice of owning or controlling other human beings has a very long history and affects events and people long after the institution itself is made illegal.

History and Authority

Jones's novel carefully develops a sense of historical reality by relating many specific details about Manchester County as well as the wider political and social context of the novel's characters. Referring to scholarly books published by university presses and sets of figures from the U.S. Census, the book appears to make frequent use of historical authorities. Such information lends the appearance of historical accuracy, and often it provides the basis for implied conclusions about the impact and import of events in the novel upon later generations. Although these references seem to involve a close acquaintance with the historical circumstances of the era, however, they are fictional; they are not based on scholarly research. Jones creates figures and references in order to suit his goals as an author and imbue his work with a sense of accuracy, gravity, and authority.

HISTORICAL CONTEXT

The Laws and Politics Connected to Slavery

Some works of historical fiction, such as the 1936 novel *Gone with the Wind*, have romanticized the southern antebellum period and the period leading up to the Civil War. *Gone with the Wind* represents antebellum Georgia as a place of gallantry and prosperity, and such romantic imagery extended to Virginia and other southern states. In fact, however, the era was marked by rising political tensions and severe human rights abuses due to the institution of slavery.

Through the early nineteenth century, the North and South in the United States became increasingly disparate. While industrial manufacturing and urbanization were dominant features of the northern economy, the South remained a predominantly agricultural area which depended on slave labor. Slavery was prohibited in the North, the home of a growing abolitionist movement that worked for the eradication of slavery, but the system was a fundamental part of southern life. Slave patrollers had the authority to beat, maim, and kill slaves who violated the slave codes, those guidelines that stripped slaves of fundamental human rights. For example, slave codes prohibited slaves from reading, testifying in court in cases involving whites, and having sexual relations with white women. The codes also prohibited slaves from gathering for religious services without a white person present, a stipulation which resulted from the Nat Turner Rebellion of 1831, since Turner claimed that God inspired him to lead slave revolts. Slaves were frequently malnourished, separated from their families, raped, tortured, and murdered.

Although it is not a highly publicized phenomenon, many free blacks owned slaves in the early-nineteenth-century South. Many, perhaps most, owned family members in order to keep them close, since some states, including Virginia, required that manumitted slaves leave the state. Some purchased slaves with the intention of freeing them. There is evidence, however, that some blacks owned slaves in order to profit from them and their labor.

After the United States purchased Mexican land in 1845, then invaded and conquered much more between 1846 and 1848, major disputes arose over whether new western and southwestern territories would allow slavery. The discovery of gold in California and the accompanying rise in westward migration made the question more urgent. The Compromise of 1850 temporarily eased tensions by allowing residents in the New Mexico Territory to vote on whether it would outlaw slavery and conceding that southern slaveholders could claim fugitive slaves from northern states.

During the 1850s, disputes over the fate of the new territory of Kansas led to violent confrontations, and political parties became increasingly divided along northern and southern sympathies. The Supreme Court's 1858 Dred Scott decision, which declared that blacks were not entitled to constitutional rights, had a number of effects, including strengthening northern opposition to slavery. Abraham Lincoln became known for his opposition to the spread of slavery to new territories (though he did not favor abolition), and his election to the presidency in 1860 led to the secession of seven southern states. Four additional states, including Virginia, seceded after the Confederate Army overtook Fort Sumter in South Carolina. The Civil War took hold, and in 1863 Lincoln emancipated slaves in Confederate territory.

CRITICAL OVERVIEW

Jones's first novel has been widely reviewed and roundly praised. John Vernon writes in the *New York Times Book Review*: "Among the many triumphs of *The Known World*, not the least is Jones's transformation of a little-known footnote in history into a story that goes right to the heart of slavery." Edward B. St. John, meanwhile, highly recommends the novel in *Library Journal*, writing that it is "A fascinating look at a painful theme." Vanessa Bush of *Booklist* agrees, emphasizing the elegance of Jones's prose: "This is a profoundly beautiful and insightful look at American slavery and human nature." Laurance

COSTUMES
DES AFFRANCHIES ET DES ESCLAVES.
Aux Colonies.

Freed black slave woman with her slaves, who gather fruit in baskets (© Hulton Archive / Getty Images)

Wielder of the *Virginia Quarterly Review* praises Jones's "imaginative powers," while Kyle Minor of the *Antioch Review* compliments the novel's "thoroughly contemporary structure that dispenses with linear narrative in favor of disjointed juxtaposition."

Some reviewers have expressed frustration with Jones's style and the mystery surrounding the impulse of black characters to own slaves. For example, Trudier Harris-Lopez writes in *Crisis*: "I found the narrative to be simultaneously engaging and exasperating." The novel proved its enduring popularity, however, when it went on to become a National Book Award finalist and then win the 2004 Pulitzer Prize for Fiction. *The Today Show* selected *The Known World* for its book club, and because of the novel, Jones won the IMPAC Dublin Literary Award, the National Book Critics Circle Award, and a Lannan Foundation Literary Award.

CRITICISM

Scott Trudell

Trudell is a doctoral student of English literature at Rutgers University. In the following essay, he argues that, in The Known World, *slavery is a deeply rooted ideological system which results in communities and generations of people unable to relate to others except in terms of power and ownership.*

Beginning and ending with scenes that establish Moses' alienation from Henry and Caldonia, Jones's novel dwells on the isolating relationship between black slaves and black masters. It closes with an image of Moses crippled, either failing to see Caldonia or unwilling to look at her, and it opens with a sentence that places Henry on an equal line with white slaveholders:

> [Moses] was thirty-five years old and for every moment of those years he had been someone's slave, a white man's slave and then another white man's slave and now, for nearly ten years, the overseer slave for a black master.

Moses, whose name is a reference to the mediator between God and man in the Bible, is intimate with both Henry and Caldonia. He gives advice to Henry and wrestles with him in the mud as though they are equals, and he has a sexual relationship with Caldonia after Henry's death. In both cases, however, Moses' masters put him in his place when they refuse to free him or treat him as an equal. If the overseer Moses is the instrument of communication between those who think of themselves as gods and the common slaves, he nevertheless remains firmly on the slave side of the equation.

Moses' humiliations are significant because they highlight the profundity of the gulf between slave and master, the inescapability of the slaveholding ethos as it was inscribed into antebellum southern society. For Jones, slavery is not simply a means of keeping one race of people subservient to another—although this was an important part of its function. It is an economic and cultural way of life at the basis of southern society, and it affects all types of relationships between all races. *The Known World* is an exploration of the manifestations of the slaveholding ethos within individual minds and between members of a community, and one of its central implications is that slavery is an ideological legacy which remains influential many generations after manumission.

Jones articulates his view of the essence of slavery, first, by implying that even in the antebellum South, the idea that some people are property did not necessarily depend on race. As a legal system, slavery is powerful and effective

WHAT DO I READ NEXT?

- Jones's 2006 short story collection, *All Aunt Hagar's Children*, focuses on African Americans living in Washington, D.C. Some of his richly drawn characters struggle with feelings of isolation and depression, while others harbor dreams of a different lifestyle away from the hectic city.

- In Charles Johnson's 1990 novel *Middle Passage*, which is set in the 1830s, a newly freed young black man accidentally embarks on an illegal slave ship headed for Africa. His views about women and race evolve through his adventures with the tyrannical captain and mutinous crew.

- *The Adventures of Huckleberry Finn* (1883), by Mark Twain, is a famous American realist examination of antebellum black-white relations, including the search for freedom.

- Langston Hughes, one of the most influential African American writers of the twentieth century, published his first book of poetry, *The Weary Blues*, in 1926. These striking poems combine the traditional rhythms of African American culture with the innovations of literary modernism.

- *American Slavery, American Freedom* (1975), Edmund S. Morgan's superb work on Virginian history before U.S. independence, details how the ideas of freedom from British rule and individualism became paired and reconcilable to the institution of slavery.

in separating even members of the same racial group into a hierarchy of power. Most free blacks, even former slaves, are indoctrinated by the ideology of slavery enough to long to be masters themselves. Henry expresses his faith in this system when he tells his father, "Thas how a master feels," betraying a conviction that masters truly are better than slaves. Slavery may have developed as a method of forcing African captives to work and suffer for white people's gain, but by the mid-nineteenth century, it has become something much more insidious than this.

Of course, race remains an extremely important factor in most characters' understandings of inferiority and superiority, including tiny shades of difference in skin color or heritage. Some poor white or Native American characters, such as Harvey Travis and Oden Peoples, consider free blacks vastly inferior to themselves, although in point of fact Travis despises Augustus less because of the color of his skin than because Travis is jealous of his woodworking skills. Fern Elston's mother, meanwhile, suggests that individual worth is related not only to race but to a strict hierarchy of skin tone: "'Marry nothing beneath you,' [Fern's] mother always said, meaning no one darker than herself." Fern does not follow her mother's advice, however, and race is not the determining factor in her finely tuned understanding of cultural superiority: "But it had never crossed Fern's mind to pass as white. Not caring very much for white people, she saw no reason to become one of them."

Slavery reveals or inspires a desire to own others which extends far beyond the color line, therefore, and complex cultural factors determine who is a master and who is a slave in various situations. It is easy to have sympathy with Fern when she expresses disdain for white people, since her snobbery is a natural reaction to the inequitable, hierarchical system in which she lives. All her life she has been indoctrinated with the idea that some people are property, and those who are not need to act in a different or superior manner. Education is the key to Fern's understanding of self-worth and superiority, which is why William Robbins chooses her to alter Henry's mental state from a slave to a master. Robbins believes, perhaps correctly, that knowledge, poise, and manners hold the key to reinforcing the divide between slave and master that will ensure Henry's success as a domineering slave-driver.

Fern's absorption of the idea that humans are separated into categories of power and property, however, results in severe psychological trauma. She is close with her friends and generous with her time and advice, but she is very troubled when it comes to sexual relationships. Obsessed with being "*dutiful*" to her husband, Fern allows Ramsey to humiliate her as though this is a necessary condition of sexual intimacy.

> **SLAVERY IS A DISEASE WHICH HAS MUTATED INTO A VITAL FORCE THAT MEDIATES THE MOST BASIC PROCESSES OF COMMUNITY INTERACTION IN MANCHESTER COUNTY, EVEN AMONG THOSE WHO HAVE BEEN MANUMITTED FROM IT."**

She holds her degradation as a kind of trophy of her nobility and purity, which is why she asks for the phrase "Dutiful Wife" to be inscribed on her tombstone. Furthermore, she describes her love for Jebediah Dickinson by stating that she is "his property," even though she is the one who legally owns him. The fact that Fern is unable to conceptualize human love except as an interaction based on ownership and property is likely due to her internalization of the slaveholding ethos that runs so strongly through her community.

Others understand slavery on what seem to be different terms. Caldonia and Winifred and John Skiffington believe that owning a slave is an opportunity to offer this person a holy and a good life. To Counsel's confusion and consternation, the Skiffingtons treat Minerva as their daughter, and they seem to meet her needs and treat her fairly. Caldonia, meanwhile, tries to act in a manner which she considers kindly to her slaves. She visits them frequently, asks that they be given the occasional holiday from backbreaking labor, and allows the children more food when she hears that they have been stealing. Jones stresses emphatically, however, that these poses of benevolence are not only harmful and hypocritical, since supposedly kindly masters continue to profit from their slaves, but infuriating and disrespectful. This is why Minerva finds Winifred's advertisement stating that she "Will Answer To The Name Minnie" so offensive, why she refuses to see Winifred after she marries, and it is why many of Caldonia's slaves run away. The slaves tend to receive Caldonia's gestures of benevolence cordially, but they understand the cruelty and superiority that lurk behind their mistress's pretense of compassion.

In fact, Caldonia and Winifred's false generosity is not so different from William Robbins's view that the institution of slavery is the community's principal guarantor of prosperity and stability. Robbins, a fierce and ruthless slave driver, does not care to indulge in any compassion towards his slaves, but he believes that slavery is good for everyone because it ensures stability and safety; brutality is simply a means to an end for him. It is easy for the reader to see the flaw in Robbins's worldview because of the blatant horrors that he permits in its service, but his viewpoint is influential and, indeed, dominant in Manchester County. The reader develops a certain amount of sympathy for the man charged with implementing Robbins's desire for order, namely John Skiffington, but by the end of the novel, it is clear that Skiffington's desire for justice is hopelessly flawed and dependent on brutality as well.

Perhaps the key insight that Jones expresses through his analysis, however, is not so much that the institution of slavery is inevitably horrific—few would claim otherwise in this day and age—but that it is a system which seeps into every corner of southern life, from culture and education to politics and the law. Slavery is about much more than race, or even social control; it cultivates a desire to control other people and treat them as property. Robbins is no less a master because he spends so much time with black people and has a second family with a former slave, and Caldonia is no less a master because she mediates her impulse to control others through a pose of kindness and compassion. Sexual or intimate relationships, from Fern and Ramsey to Caldonia and Moses, are inextricable from feelings of power and ownership. Even the character most vehemently opposed to slavery, Augustus, tries (too late) to teach his son of its evils by posing as a master and beating Henry until his shoulder is broken. Slavery is a disease which has mutated into a vital force that mediates the most basic processes of community interaction in Manchester County, even among those who have been manumitted from it.

What is *known* about the world of the antebellum South, therefore, is that it is rooted in a cultural, legal, and economic system which cannot be eradicated simply by freeing the slaves. As Jones suggests with his narrative technique, which makes huge, omniscient jumps across decades and even centuries, the issues of the novel bear on widely divergent historical periods. Tessie, Elias and Celeste's child, continues to hold and treasure the doll her father made her, a physical relic of Elias's slavery and suffering and a metaphor for the continuing influence of slavery, nearly one hundred years after it is made. By making reference to academic studies of slavery through the 1990s, Jones implies that the cultural implications of such a powerful ethos seem likely to last even longer than that. Slavery is more than a horrific and exploitative set of rules that used to govern race relations. It is, to use Maude's term, a "legacy" so internalized and far-reaching during its heyday that it is hard to imagine the end of its influence. The novel implies that slavery's central ethos, that one should seek power and ownership of other human beings, is ingrained not only in U.S. history but into contemporary U.S. society, among people of all races.

Source: Scott Trudell, Critical Essay on *The Known World*, in *Novels for Students*, Thomson Gale, 2008.

Sarah Anne Johnson

In the following interview, Jones discusses "what inspires his stories, how themes evolve and his writing process."

In *The Known World*, Edward P. Jones takes on the rarely explored phenomenon in our national history in which freed slaves turned around and purchased slaves of their own. The novel, which won the 2004 Pulitzer Prize and was a National Book Award finalist, tells the story of Henry Townsend, a slave who was purchased and freed by his father. Henry works hard to acquire land and then purchases slaves to work the land.

This compelling story roams seamlessly between the past, present and future in the characters' lives, weaving together the stories of freed and enslaved African Americans, whites and Native Americans to offer a deeper understanding of the complexities and injustices heaped upon the world by the institution of slavery.

The Known World undercuts the idea that freeing slaves provided them with the same freedom enjoyed by white Americans. In his writing, Jones often reveals the realities behind such myths. In his short-story collection *Lost in the City* (short-listed for the National Book Award), for example, he looks beyond the shiny tourist image of Washington, D.C. He reveals the Washington that he grew up in, a city in which poverty, hardship and misery were an everyday reality, a city in which ordinary people lived beautiful and complicated lives.

> HOPEFULLY, SOMEWHERE ALONG THE LINE I HAVE CREATED JUST A LITTLE BIT OF THE WORLD THAT I HAD KNOWN ONCE UPON A TIME."

Jones is low-key about his literary success, pleased with the fact that people are willing to buy his books, but he's not banking on anything. He's currently working on a collection of stories built around minor characters from the stories in *Lost in the City*. In a telephone interview, he discussed what inspires his stories, how themes evolve and his writing process. He offered this advice to writers: "I think the only thing you can do really is read and write and read and write some more."

[Sarah Anne Johnson:] William Faulkner said: "I don't know anything about inspiration, because I don't know what inspiration is—I've heard about it, but I never saw it." Where do you find your inspiration?

[Edward P. Jones:] You just wake up one morning with some image or some words in your head, and you go on from there. You try to build a world around whatever image you woke up with. The first thing that set me off with *The Known World* was the image of Henry Townsend on his deathbed in the first few pages. You have to figure out how he got to be in the bed and who's in the room with him. Then you branch out even further and further until finally you have all the pages that are in the book right now.

[Sarah Anne Johnson:] In writing the stories that make up Lost in the City, *did you start with the idea of doing a collection?*

[Edward P. Jones:] Some of the stories have been published someplace else, but even with that, without even knowing it, part of me knew that they would be part of one book. I never write a story here and a story there. That's certainly not the thing that I'm doing now with this new collection of stories. [For *Lost in the City*], I had an idea that things would start with the youngest character in the stories, and that's what happens, all the way to the very oldest person. Hopefully, somewhere along the line I have created just a little bit of the world that I had known once upon a time. Of course, it wasn't enough, and that's one of the reasons I went along and started creating another collection of stories. When I finished *Lost in the City*, I thought that that was all there was, and then time went on and I found that there was more to say. There was a crossover from one story to another.

[*Sarah Anne Johnson:*] *Many of the stories are about struggling for spiritual survival in the midst of the harsh realities of an inner-city environment. What drew you to this theme?*

[Edward P. Jones:] Those are things that I never think about. The characters come first, and I say whatever I need to say in order to make people understand what kind of people they are. I'm not really a very spiritual person myself, but I find that I'm having to write about people who are. I think it's the way that I started out in life and it's difficult to let go of all that.

[*Sarah Anne Johnson:*] *When you sit down to write a novel, do you sit down and write from start to finish and then go back and rework it?*

[Edward P. Jones:] I try to, but sometimes you get up and you know in a general way what you want to do but the details don't come to you. So I sometimes found myself going to a part of the book where I was rather inspired, so that there wouldn't be a day where I hadn't done anything. Some days there was just nothing I wanted to say.

[*Sarah Anne Johnson:*] *Why did you decide to set* The Known World *in the fictional town of Manchester, Va., rather than an actual town?*

[Edward P. Jones:] My plan had been ... to read all these books on slavery and use that as background. I also was going to go visit this friend of mine in Lynchburg, Va., and use his county as the setting. I never got around to reading the books or going down to see him in the end, so when the day came for me to start working, I knew I wasn't going to take time off and go visit him. So, I decided that I would invent [the setting]. Then I could say whatever I wanted. If I used a real place, I'd be confined. If you say, as I do, that the place where all the judicial records were kept burnt down in 1912, it has to be true. Using a fictional town gave me the leeway to make those statements, and it let me lead into this whole thing about the coming Civil War. I could give this reason for why Manchester County no longer exists, that it was brother against brother, as it were.

[*Sarah Anne Johnson:*] *How did you create the historical data about Manchester County, and how does that data serve your narrative?*

[Edward P. Jones:] You just make it up. I had to sit there and ask myself, "How many white people and how many slaves?" It couldn't be too many, but it was the largest county in Virginia at that time, so it had to be enough. I was aiming to add a sense of truth to the fiction.

[*Sarah Anne Johnson:*] *You begin this novel with Moses at the end of his workday, and end with him broken down in his cabin. How did you choose to begin and end this way?*

[Edward P. Jones:] There are certain things that you have a feeling about. It just seems that that's where it should've begun and where it should've ended. I don't have any real idea that I can point to. When laying it all out there, that's just the way it had to be.

[*Sarah Anne Johnson:*] *Why did you think it important to show the point of view of a character whose experience of America does not live up to the promise of America?*

[Edward P. Jones:] This country is built on a lot of myths. I mention ... discouraged and homesick immigrants ... [going back to their countries]. Now I've never heard of people doing that, but I'm sure, this world being what it is, there must've been people like that. From the first pages, I mention this Irish guy who went back.

The country moves along forever and ever on a certain plane where all the bad stuff is wiped away. Last year I happened to see this PBS special on Benjamin Franklin. They had mentioned that Franklin's role as a diplomat in France and in England was almost as important as all the fighting that was being done in America, but the country wanted the world to see it as having been built on the fighting. Franklin's role was downplayed to the point where you have to go digging for what he did.

[*Sarah Anne Johnson:*] *That goes back to what you were saying about wanting to write about the Washington, D.C., that you grew up in. It's the underside of what's on the postcards.*

[Edward P. Jones:] That's a problem with the country now. It's why things still spin in a bad way, because people don't want to confront this stuff. It reminds me that many years ago, maybe 30 years ago, I came across this record by Dick Gregory. He was giving one of his funny talks. There was a woman in the audience who

A row of original brick slave cabins stand on the grounds of Boone Hall Plantation in Mount Pleasant, South Carolina (© Lee Snider | Photo Images | Corbis)

stood up and said, "Mr. Gregory, don't you have anything good to say about America?" And he said, "If I'm dying of cancer, I don't want the doctor to tell me how good my teeth are." Talking about good teeth is fine, but there are a lot of major problems going on that started a long time ago.

[*Sarah Anne Johnson:*] *The women in* The Known World *take on powerful roles. Caldonia Townsend takes over running the plantation when her husband dies. Fern Elston educates the black kids and Alice creates transformative art. Where did you find your inspiration for these dynamic women?*

[Edward P. Jones:] There are such women nowadays, and these women can't be the first ones. There must've been women like that before. I'm not doing anything extraordinary with them. I don't have some woman running for the Senate in Virginia in 1855—that would be ridiculous. You have women who, within the scheme of things, are able to stand up and assert themselves. Fern teaches William Robins' kids and she knows

that she has a certain power with that, so when she's abused on the road by the slave patroller, she knows she can go to [Robins]. I didn't think that the women today came on the scene today. There were believable precedents for them.

[*Sarah Anne Johnson:*] *What inspires the events in your novel that could be called supernatural or superstitious, such as spontaneous combustion, or the cow whose milk supply came back? What does the story gain from these elements of magic?*

[Edward P. Jones:] I don't necessarily believe in that kind of stuff, but I'm writing about people who do, so I have to be true to those beliefs. I realized that I was putting in everything that I had learned in life. I grew up with my mother talking about a woman she knew when she was a little girl who ate dirt, so I used that. In the '70s, I had friends who were going to law school and they would tell me about the cases they were reading about. One was about a man who'd sold a cow to someone thinking that the cow didn't give milk. Then one day the cow started giving milk again, so the guy went to court to try to get the cow back, because he believed that he'd sold a cow without milk, and now that it was a cow with milk, they should go back on the deal.

[*Sarah Anne Johnson:*] *Eudora Welty said, "I don't write for my friends or myself, either; I write for it, for the pleasure of it. I believe if I stopped to wonder what so-and-so would think, or what I'd feel like if something were read by a stranger, I would be paralyzed." How do you perceive the audience for your work when you're writing?*

[Edward P. Jones:] You don't write for anybody but yourself. If you like it at the end of the day, then you go on to the next part of it. You shouldn't sit around thinking what that guy out there on the plains in Iowa would think about it. There's only one person you should try to please, and that's yourself.

[*Sarah Anne Johnson:*] *What would you say to new writers working on their first stories or novels?*

[Edward P. Jones:] I've been rather fortunate. You hear stories about people who work for years and years and years and then they have to go through 15 or 20 people before someone says yes. I haven't had that experience. The first time around, people said yes.

I will say, if you're writing to be recognized and to be paid, then you're in it for the wrong reasons. If you write because you're compelled to write, then that becomes the only reward you should look for. I'd probably be doing this even if there weren't any people out there willing to buy the stuff. It goes back to the first question about what you do, which is to continue writing and reading and writing and reading.

Source: Sarah Anne Johnson, "Untold Stories: An Interview with Edward P. Jones," in *The Writer*, Vol. 117, No. 8, August 2004, p. 20.

SOURCES

Bush, Vanessa, Review of *The Known World*, in *Booklist*, Vol. 100, No. 2, September 15, 2003, p. 211.

Harris-Lopez, Trudier, "Novel Look at a Largely Unknown World in Antebellum Virginia," in *Crisis*, Vol. 110, No. 5, September-October 2003, p. 53.

Jones, Edward P., *The Known World*, Harper Collins/Amistad, 2003.

Minor, Kyle, Review of *The Known World*, in *Antioch Review*, Vol. 63, No. 1, Winter 2005, p. 190.

St. John, Edward B., Review of *The Known World*, in *Library Journal*, Vol. 128, No. 13, August 2003, pp. 132–33.

Vernon, John, "People Who Owned People: Two Historical Novels Deal with the Peculiar Institution of Slavery and its Power to Distort Human Life," in *New York Times Book Review*, August 31, 2003, p. 9.

Wielder, Laurance, Review of *The Known World*, in *Virginia Quarterly Review*, Vol. 80, No. 1, Winter 2004, p. 271.

FURTHER READING

Kofie, Nelson F., *Race, Class, and the Struggle for Neighborhood in Washington, D.C.*, Routledge, 1999.
   The results of Kofie's three-year ethnographic case study develop a scholarly perspective on relationship between poor African Americans, the Nation of Islam, and the police in Washington, D.C. This community's struggle to deal with an open-air drug market offers insight into the difficult situation of the black poor across the U.S. capital.

Koger, Larry, *Black Slaveowners: Free Black Slave Masters in South Carolina, 1790–1860*, University of South Carolina Press, 1985.
   This erudite historical analysis of black slave owners focuses on South Carolina, a state which was similar to Virginia in this regard. Koger challenges the notion that African Americans held slaves primarily for humanitarian reasons or to be near their relatives, drawing out the fundamentals of the southern caste system during this era.

Patton, Venetria K., *Women in Chains: The Legacy of Slavery in Black Women's Fiction*, State University of New York Press, 1999.
   Patton's book explores the theme of motherhood among African American female authors. Suggesting that the legacy of slavery is to paint black women as breeders, not mothers, Patton argues that black female authors reverse and subvert this historical tendency by consistently portraying black women as motherly figures.

Rothman, Joshua D., *Notorious in the Neighborhood: Sex and Families Across the Color Line in Virginia, 1787–1861*, University of North Carolina Press, 2003.
   Rothman's scholarly investigation of interracial sexual relations in Virginia from Thomas Jefferson's family to the Civil War is a helpful complement to some of the issues of miscegenation raised in *The Known World*.

Schwarz, Philip J., "Emancipators, Protectors, and Anomalies: Free Black Slave Owners in Virginia," in *Virginia Magazine of History and Biography*, Vol. 95, July 1987, pp. 321–22.
   Schwarz provides a brief analysis and description of the practice of free black slaveholding as it was practiced in Virginia.

Solomon, Deborah, "Questions for Edward P. Jones: Prize Writer," in *New York Times Magazine*, October 10, 2004, p. 17.

  In a brief interview with Jones, Solomon asks him about his mother and his reaction to winning the Pulitzer Prize.

The Lord of the Rings

J. R. R. TOLKIEN

1954-1955

The Lord of the Rings, by John Ronald Reuel Tolkien, first published in three parts during 1954 and 1955, is sometimes thought of as the first adult fantasy novel, although as a form it has affinity with the old heroic romances that inspired its author. Tolkien was a professor of Anglo-Saxon at Oxford and a scholar of such texts as *Beowulf*. His mythic quest novel, pitting a small hobbit as a hero against the Lord of Evil, holds a unique place in twentieth-century fiction: it is popular culture and enduring literature at the same time. It is a story about how goodness prevails, even in times of confusion and war, when people of integrity hold together. From the first, the book evoked strong, subjective reactions. In the fifty years following its publication, commentators learned to take an objective look at it.

Tolkien knew there was a hunger for heroic myth in the modern world, but he was surprised by his vast success. He would be even more overwhelmed at the games, toys, and films spawned by the novel, but he would understand the urge to proliferate what he had done. He hoped to sketch out a giant mythology that others could appreciate and add to, and they have. Not only has the fantasy industry grown up around the book, but also a demand for more details about his imaginary world, Middle-Earth. His son, Christopher, carried on, editing and publishing Tolkien's unfinished manuscripts. The amount of Middle-Earth history and chronicles published since the

J. R. R. Tolkien *(© Bettmann / Corbis)*

author's death is fourfold in volume to *The Hobbit* and *The Lord of the Rings* put together. Tolkien demonstrates that mythic stories speak to the human spirit in every age.

AUTHOR BIOGRAPHY

John Ronald Reuel Tolkien was born on January 3, 1892, in Bloemfontein, South Africa, of English parents, Mabel Suffield and Arthur Tolkien. His younger brother, Hilary, was born in 1894. In 1895, their mother took the children to England for a holiday, and while they were gone, their father died of rheumatic fever in South Africa. Mabel Tolkien was suddenly a widow in Birmingham, England, with two small children and very little income. She found a cottage in the country for the boys in Sarehole, Warwickshire, and the setting's effect on Ronald was deep. This was his ideal English countryside before industrialization, a hobbit landscape of villages and carts, an old brick mill, and lots of trees.

His mother was his first teacher, and from her, Ronald learned a love of languages and botany. He also loved fairy tales, adventure stories, and drawing. Meanwhile, she became a Catholic, to her family's dismay. This choice cut her off from their financial and emotional support, but Tolkien was proud of his mother's religious strength all his life. His strong Catholic faith came from her.

At the age of seven, he entered King Edward's School in Birmingham, and the family moved there. After two years, both boys were enrolled in a Catholic school, and the local priest, Father Francis Xavier Morgan, became the boys' guardian. Because Ronald needed a more intellectual training, his mother enrolled him again at King Edward's on scholarship.

Mabel Tolkien died in 1904 of diabetes when Ronald was twelve. Though the orphans boarded with an aunt, Father Francis became their only real family. At King Edward's, Tolkien formed his first club, the TCBS (Tea Club and Barovian Society) with four close friends who all shared an interest in ancient languages and medieval studies. Tolkien even then was writing verse and inventing his first languages. The group dreamed of contributing something new to the world. This club helped him find a voice for his life work.

At the age of sixteen, Tolkien fell in love with nineteen-year-old Edith Bratt, another orphan in his boarding house. Father Francis forbade Tolkien to see or write to her until his twenty-first birthday, at which time they became engaged.

At Oxford, Tolkien studied comparative philology and ancient literature and went on inventing languages. When World War I broke out, he enlisted as a second lieutenant in a signaling corps, marrying Edith in 1916 before he left for France and the Battle of the Somme. In the trenches he began scribbling bits of his mythology, and when he returned to England to recuperate from trench fever, he continued his "Lost Tales," the germ of *The Silmarillion*.

After the war, Tolkien worked on staff at Oxford, then taught at Leeds University for three years, before settling as professor of Anglo Saxon at Oxford and raising his family of four children, John, Michael, Christopher, and Priscilla. His habit of inventing stories for the children led to *The Hobbit*, a children's story, published in 1937. In the same year, he began the sequel, *The Lord of the Rings*, which turned out to be for adults and wove in much of his

MEDIA ADAPTATIONS

- Tolkien collaborated with composer Donald Swann in *The Road Goes Ever On: A Song Cycle*, the book and CD of poems from *The Lord of the Rings* set to music by Donald Swann in 1967 and published by HarperCollins in 2003. Piano scores are beautifully illustrated with Tolkien's tengwar (elvish writing) and with comments on the elvish languages. Tolkien himself approved this arrangement. As of 2007, this production was available from Amazon.com and Amazon UK.

- *The Lord of the Rings* (Part One) was released in theaters as an animated film by Ralph Bakshi in 1978, produced by Saul Zaentz's Fantasy Films and distributed by United Artists. It includes the story up to Helm's Deep. The generally acknowledged critical failure of this version did not hurt its financial return. It led to Jackson's desire to do the live-action film. As of 2007, this version was available from Amazon.com.

- *The Return of the King* was released for television in 1980 as an animated film by Rankin-Bass to complete Bakshi's attempt. Warner Brothers released the Bakshi and Rankin-Bass versions along with Rankin-Bass's *The Hobbit* as a three-part series, *The Hobbit*, *The Lord of the Rings*, and *The Return of the King* on VHS and DVD. As of 2007, this version of *The Hobbit* was available on Amazon.com.

- *The Lord of the Rings* was read and sung by National Theatre and Royal Shakespeare Company actor Rob Inglis. It was produced in a CD format by HarperCollins in 1981, a complete production of fifty-one hours. As of 2007, Amazon.com made this version available.

- *The Lord of the Rings* appeared as a BBC Radio production. The abridged thirteen CDs included twenty-six half-hour shows dramatized by Brian Sibley with Ian Holm as narrator. As of 2007, this version could be ordered from Amazon.com.

- *Realms of Tolkien Images of Middle-Earth*, with illustrations by famous Tolkien artists, was produced by Harper Collins in 1996. Fifty-eight full-page color plates are included by artists such as Alan Lee, who influenced the look of *The Lord of the Rings* movies.

- *The Lord of the Rings*, the film trilogy on DVD (2002–2005), was produced by New Line Cinema. It includes: *The Fellowship of the Ring*, *The Two Towers*, and *The Return of the King*. Directed by Peter Jackson and starring Ian McKellan, Elijah Wood, and Kate Blanchett, this elaborate adaptation shot in New Zealand won awards for special effects and art design. The in-depth DVD appendices with Tolkien experts and detailed explanations of how the film was made are as impressive as the film. As of 2007, this version was available from Amazon.com and in bookstores.

- One of many video games based on Tolkien's novel, *The Battle for Middle-Earth II* (2006) was produced by Electronic Arts. As of 2007, it was available in video game stores.

- *Map of Tolkien's Middle-Earth*, with text by Brian Sibley and illustrations by John Howe, is a fold-out with booklet published by HarperCollins in 2003. This version is very helpful in recreating the landscape of the stories and, as of 2007, was readily available in bookstores.

---

mythology (published 1954–1955). *Farmer Giles of Ham* was published in 1949; "The Homecoming of Beortnoth Beorhthelm's Son," in 1953; *The* Adventures of Tom Bombadil in 1962; *Tree and Leaf* in 1964, and *Smith of Wootton Major* in 1967.

The American campus cult of Tolkien began in the 1960s, and Tolkien spent the last years of his life, too famous and busy to finish his great work of mythology. Edith died in 1971, and he died in 1973, at the age of eighty-one in Bournemouth, England. His son Christopher became his literary executor, publishing his unfinished work between 1975 and 1996.

Some of the awards Tolkien won are the International Fantasy Award for *The Lord of the Rings* in 1957; Fellowship in the Royal Society of Literature, 1957; Commander, Order of the British Empire, 1972; Gandalf Grand Master Award of the World Science Fiction Society for lifetime achievement, 1974; Gandalf Award for *The Silmarillion*, 1978; Locus Award for *The Silmarillion*, 1978; and the Mythopoeic Fantasy Award for *Unfinished Tales*, 1981.

PLOT SUMMARY

The Fellowship of the Ring

BOOK ONE

The action takes place in Middle-Earth (Earth) at the end of the Third Age. The story opens in the Shire, the peaceful country of the hobbits, who are a small race, half the size of humans. At his eleventy-first birthday party, the hobbit Bilbo Baggins stages a spectacular departure from the Shire: he puts on a magic ring that he had found in his previous adventures (told about in *The Hobbit*) and disappears before the eyes of the guests. This is his joke, a way of escaping pesky relatives and a life that has become burdensome. He longs to travel again and return to Rivendell, home of the elves, and then settle down to write his memoirs.

He leaves his hobbit hole at Bag End, all his belongings, and the magic ring (at the wizard Gandalf's insistence) to his heir and nephew, Frodo Baggins. Some years later, Gandalf returns with alarming news: the magic ring is the One Ring of the Dark Lord, Sauron, who is trying to find it so he can control Middle-Earth. Sauron had fooled the elves into forging rings of power for every race; then he forged the One Ring to rule them all. The nine rings of men and seven of the dwarves are held by Sauron. Only the three elven rings are unsullied, used by the elves to preserve Middle-Earth. The One evil Ring was cut off Sauron's finger in a war and lost till Bilbo got it from the creature Gollum on his

adventures. Sauron knows the Ring is in the Shire, and so Frodo must leave with Sam, his servant, and if Gandalf does not show up to guide them (he does not), they must at least meet Gandalf later at the inn in Bree. Frodo is joined by his two friends, Merry and Pippin, and the four hobbits journey towards Bree by indirect ways, because they are being chased by Black Riders (the ghostlike Ringwraiths), servants of Sauron, who are always seeking the One Ring.

The hobbits take a detour through the Old Forest. There they meet Tom Bombadil who saves them from Old Man Willow and the barrow wights. When they finally get to Bree, Gandalf is still missing, and they do not know what to do. Gandalf has been delayed getting to Frodo because Saruman, the head of his order of wizards, has been corrupted by the Dark Lord. Saruman tempts Gandalf to join the dark side and, when he refuses, imprisons him. It takes some time for him to escape; Gandalf does not catch up with Frodo until Rivendell.

At the inn, Frodo accidentally slips on the Ring, becoming invisible. This immediately draws the Ringwraiths to him, for wearing the Ring puts the wearer into the world of shadow. The hobbits meet a strange man called Strider who says he is a Ranger from the north and friend of Gandalf. The Black Riders attack the inn, so they decide to trust Strider as a guide.

Strider takes them through the wilderness towards Rivendell, an elf haven. The Black Riders catch them halfway at Weathertop, a ruined fort, and wound Frodo with a magic knife, causing him to hover between life and death. His companions rush him to Rivendell where Lord Elrond can save him. As they cross the Ford of Bruinen, Gandalf causes a flood that temporarily drowns the Black Riders.

BOOK TWO

Frodo wakes up in Rivendell, healed by Elrond, though Gandalf says the wound will never heal completely. The hobbits rest, meet Bilbo and Gandalf again, and spend time singing and celebrating with the elves, lost in the wonder of their celestial land. Here Strider is revealed as Aragorn, the last heir of the Numenorean throne. He is a man betrothed to the elf maiden, Arwen, daughter of Elrond.

Elrond holds a council and invites representatives from all the free peoples of Middle-Earth.

There it is decided that the only way to destroy Sauron and evil is to destroy the Ring itself. The Ring cannot be used, for it is a power that corrupts everyone around it. The hobbit Frodo is elected to be the Ringbearer and eight companions are chosen to go with him: three other hobbits, Gandalf the wizard, Aragorn the future king, Gimli the dwarf, Legolas the elf, and Boromir the warrior of Gondor. They are called the Fellowship of the Ring.

The Fellowship is blocked making its way over the Caradhras mountain pass, so they turn and reluctantly go under the mountain through the mines of Moria, a dark place with many orcs or goblins. Gimli the dwarf finds the great underground city of Dwarrowdelf in ruins and his people extinct due to their greed in mining mithril, elf silver. The dwarves had awakened an ancient demon, a balrog, and the company also meet this balrog whom Gandalf fights, falling with it into the deeps of the Earth. The fellowship, grief-stricken, makes its way to Lothlórien, the greatest remaining elf kingdom. They are followed by the creature, Gollum, from whom Bilbo originally took the Ring and who miserably has been seeking it ever since. The Lady Galadriel, elven queen of great magic, gives presents and warns of treachery within the Fellowship.

Indeed, Boromir tries to take the ring from Frodo with the intention, he thinks, of using it to defend his city of Minas Tirith from the Dark Lord. The Ring has started corrupting the Company with a desire for power. Frodo puts on the Ring to escape Boromir and resolves to go on alone, but loyal Sam follows him. Meanwhile, Boromir is killed by orcs, and Merry and Pippin are captured and carried off. Aragorn, Gimli, and Legolas follow to rescue the remaining hobbits and leave Frodo and Sam to go to Mt. Doom.

The Two Towers

BOOK THREE

After Boromir's death, the Fellowship is split. Aragorn, Gimli, and Legolas chase the orcs who have captured Merry and Pippin. They leave Frodo to his own quest. Aragorn's party runs into the Riders of Rohan, the warriors of the plain, led by Eomer. Eomer's men have already destroyed the orcs in battle, and Merry and Pippin have escaped into Fangorn Forest. In Fangorn, the hobbits meet Treebeard, an ent, or walking tree, who herds and rules the forest.

Treebeard laments that the evil wizard, Saruman, has cut down the trees of the forest for his war furnaces. Merry and Pippin rouse the ents to go to war, and they march towards Saruman's stronghold in Isengard.

When Aragorn's party enters Fangorn, they find not the hobbits, but the resurrected Gandalf, now Gandalf the White, who has been sent back from death to finish his task. He takes Aragorn and the others to the capital of Rohan to rouse the king, for war is about to break out on two fronts: one at Isengard, the fortress of the traitor, Saruman, and the other in Gondor with the army of the Dark Lord himself. Gandalf seeks to set up an alliance of free peoples to be ready.

Theoden, King of Rohan, is in bondage to Saruman who has put a spell on him. Gandalf breaks the spell, and once he has regained his strength, Theoden leads his warriors to the fortress of Helm's Deep with Eomer, Aragorn, Gimli, and Legolas to defend his people from Saruman's army. Just as Saruman's orcs are about to defeat Theoden, Gandalf appears at dawn with more men of Rohan, and the orcs of Isengard are defeated. Men chase the orcs underneath trees which have mysteriously appeared overnight on the plain. The orcs do not come out again. These are the walking trees of Fangorn Forest who play a part in the battle and who have destroyed the stronghold of Isengard.

Theoden, Gandalf, and the others march to Isengard and find Merry and Pippin with Treebeard, guarding Saruman and the ruins. Gandalf tries to get Saruman to come back to the allies, but Saruman refuses, so Gandalf breaks his magic staff. Pippin mischievously looks into a palantir, a seeing stone, revealing himself to the Dark Lord and confusing Sauron into thinking that Saruman has captured the hobbit with the Ring and that the Ring is thus at Isengard. This diverts his attention and buys the allies some time as Gandalf rides with Pippin to Gondor to rouse the Gondoreans. He leaves Aragorn at Rohan with Theoden's forces, ready to march for the Gondor front when he sends word.

BOOK FOUR

Sam and Frodo are lost on their way to Mordor to destroy the Ring. In the middle of the night, the creature Gollum is found near them, searching for the Ring. They ponder whether to kill him or bind him, but Frodo has pity on him, as Bilbo had. Gandalf had praised Bilbo's pity for sparing Gollum's life, saying that Gollum had some important part to play before the war was over. Now, Gollum becomes their guide into Mordor. Without Gollum's help, they could not have passed the Dead Marshes or found the Black Gate, entrance to Mordor. Frodo pities Gollum because he once bore the Ring, and now Frodo understands how the Ring destroys, for it is destroying him. It is becoming heavier and more evil the closer to the Dark Lord it gets. Frodo tries to save the schizophrenic Gollum, appealing to the hobbit nature he once bore, by calling him Smeagol, his former name when he was a hobbit like Frodo. Gollum tells them they cannot go through the Black Gate; they must go through a secret path that only he knows. Sam, however, remains skeptical of Gollum, naming his split personality, Slinker and Stinker.

While going through Ithilien, they meet Captain Faramir of Gondor, Boromir's brother, who is out on patrol with his men. Faramir finds out their secret mission but nobly does not stop them, because he learns how his brother fell from the evil influence of the Ring. The hobbits hear from Faramir that Gondor—the last Numenorean stronghold—is all that holds the Dark Lord from overrunning Middle-Earth. Faramir gives the hobbits provisions, and they continue on with Gollum to Cirith Ungol, a secret pass into Mordor.

The cave at the top of the pass is the lair of Shelob, the monstrous spider, which Gollum counts on to kill the hobbits so he can get the Ring. In the evil dark, Frodo pulls out the phial of Galadriel, containing starlight, which temporarily frightens Shelob away. But she bites Frodo, and Sam, thinking his master dead, wounds Shelob and escapes. He leaves behind the body of his master, taking up the Ring to continue the quest. When orcs come, he puts on the Ring to become invisible and, overhearing them speak, realizes that his master is not dead, only paralyzed. The orcs take Frodo, unconscious, to the tower of Cirith Ungol, and Sam cannot leave him but follows to see what he can do.

The Return of the King

BOOK FIVE

As Gandalf rides into the country of Gondor on his horse, Shadowfax, with Pippin,

they see the beacons on the mountaintops lit, one after the other, as a signal that Gondor calls for aid in battle. They hurry to the capital city of Minas Tirith to speak to the Steward of Gondor, Denethor, the father of Boromir and Faramir. Minas Tirith is the city of the Numenorean kings of old, built on seven levels into the mountain. It is on the point of collapse, and Denethor is half mad from the loss of his son, Boromir, and from looking into a palantir to spy on the Dark Lord. He is suspicious of Gandalf and has heard rumors of Aragorn, the rightful heir to the throne. Gandalf urges him to prepare for war and counsels that Rohan will come to their aid.

Meanwhile, the remaining Rangers of the North and Elrond's sons come to Aragorn in Rohan, with the message that he must now fulfill his destiny and earn his kingship by taking the Paths of the Dead. Aragorn has looked into one of the palantirs and revealed himself to the Enemy, filling Sauron with fear that the heir of the kings still lives with the sword that cut off the Ring from his finger, reforged now as Anduril, the Flame of the West. Aragorn hopes to provoke Sauron into a hasty attack, before his full strength forms.

Eowyn, sister of Eomer, falls in love with Aragorn, who gently refuses her because he is betrothed to the elf maiden, Arwen. Eowyn, in despair and in hope of military renown if she cannot have love, disguises herself as a warrior and secretly takes Merry with her to ride to Minas Tirith with the men of Rohan. Aragorn and his kin, as well as Gimli and Legolas, ride through the haunted mountains, the Paths of the Dead, to find their own way to Minas Tirith where the battle will be. An army of ghosts follows them. The ghosts are warriors who had broken their oaths to Aragorn's ancestor, and now, to find rest, they must follow him to fight for Gondor.

In Minas Tirith, Denethor sends Faramir on a hopeless mission to retake a post from the enemy. Faramir is wounded and thought to be dead by his father, who in his madness would burn them both alive in the tombs of their fathers. Pippin warns Gandalf, who saves Faramir, but Denethor dies.

The Siege of Gondor is in full swing, and the city ready to fall to Sauron's armies, though Gandalf commands what Gondorean troops there are. At dawn, they hear the horns of Rohan blowing; the horse lords have come to lift the siege. In the ensuing battle, the Chief Ringwraith on a winged beast attacks Theoden. Eowyn, disguised, defends her uncle and lord. The Ringwraith taunts her that no man may kill him. She reveals that she is a woman and kills his beastly steed. Together she and Merry finish the Chief Ringwraith as well. Theoden dies, and the allies are outnumbered, until suddenly, Aragorn and his ghost army show up to rout the enemy, for the time being.

Aragorn is allowed into Minas Tirith and accepted as the future king because he is able to heal the wounded, especially Faramir, Eowyn, and Merry. Then Gandalf comes up with a bold plan to attack Mordor directly, even though they are outnumbered, to divert the attention of Sauron and give Frodo more time to complete his mission. All the army of the West moves south to the Black Gate and fights an orc army that will surely win.

BOOK SIX

Frodo awakens in the tower of Cirith Ungol, thinking the enemy has taken the Ring. Sam, tricking the orcs into killing each other, climbs the tower and sets Frodo free, returning the Ring to him. They set off towards Mt. Doom. Frodo and Sam struggle on through the desolate land of Mordor with little food and water, and little hope. Sam has to assume leadership, as Frodo is weak and delirious from carrying the Ring. The Eye of Sauron is diverted to Aragorn's army at the Black Gate.

Sam carries Frodo on his back the last part of the journey up Mt. Doom. Suddenly, Gollum reappears and fights Frodo for the Ring. Sam guards Gollum while Frodo goes to the brink of the volcano to throw in the Ring. At the last moment, Frodo cannot destroy the Ring. Gollum escapes Sam and attacks Frodo who puts on the Ring to become invisible, but Gollum will not let go and bites the Ring off Frodo's finger. Gollum, triumphant, dances for a moment with the Ring on the brink, then trips and falls into the fiery chasm with it. The mountain erupts, and Sam leads Frodo out to a spot on the mountain to await death together, their mission accomplished.

Meanwhile, at the Black Gate, the Captains of the West are foundering until the giant eagles come to aid them. In the middle of this chaos, an earthquake topples the towers of the Black Gate and darkness covers the land. Gandalf knows this means that Frodo's mission has been successful, and the reign of Sauron has ended. Gandalf calls down one of the giant eagles and rides on its back to Mt. Doom, rescuing Sam and Frodo from the erupting volcano.

Aragorn is crowned king, and the Fourth Age of Men begins. Faramir weds Eowyn, and Aragorn weds Arwen, who must give up her elven immortality to live a mortal life. Her place on the last elven ship to leave Middle-Earth is given to Frodo whose wound will never heal. After the hobbits return to the Shire as heroes, they rid the Shire of the evil men who had crept in during Sauron's time, and Sam becomes the new mayor. When Frodo finishes his memoirs, he takes the last elven ship with Gandalf, Galadriel, Elrond, and all the elves to the Blessed Lands of the West.

Appendices

Appendices cover material from the mythology which Tolkien could not fit into the novel. Appendix A tells the history of Numenorean Kings, the history of Gondor, and the tale of Aragorn and Arwen. Appendix B is a chronology of the Ages of Middle-Earth. Appendix C contains family trees of the hobbits. Appendix D describes the Calendars of Middle-Earth. Appendix E explains the pronunciation and alphabets of Tolkien's invented languages for Middle-Earth. Appendix F is a fuller explanation of the languages of various races of Middle-Earth: elves, men, hobbits, orcs, ents, and dwarves.

CHARACTERS

Aragorn

Also called Strider, Dunedan, Elessar, and Estel, Aragorn, son of Arathorn, is a long lived Numenorean man, heir of Isildur and the throne of Gondor. He is raised by Elrond in Rivendell, where he falls in love with Elrond's daughter, Arwen. He wanders Middle-Earth in disguise as a Ranger, helping Gandalf keep track of the doings of the Enemy. He is suspected by the hobbits at first because of his rough appearance, but once they get to Rivendell where Strider the Ranger is known as Aragorn, the heir of Isildur, they form a different opinion, because he takes on his true, noble appearance. He guides the hobbits from Bree to Rivendell and becomes one of the Fellowship. He is later crowned King of Gondor by Gandalf. A wise, resourceful, and humble man, worthy of being king, he is called Estel by the elves, meaning hope. Elessar refers to the green Elfstone jewel presented to him by Galadricl. Duncdan means one of the Northern Rangers, last of the Numenorean men in the north.

Bilbo Baggins

Bilbo is a hobbit of the Shire who first finds the Ring and takes it from Gollum in the tunnels of the Misty Mountains (as explained in *The Hobbit*). Hobbits are Halflings, three to four feet tall, peaceful, and fond of food and drink and a good pipe. They have hairy feet and go barefoot. Bilbo is a fun-loving and clever trickster, good at riddle lore. His greatest act is his pity in sparing the life of Gollum, who becomes important in the quest to destroy the Ring. The Ring abnormally prolongs Bilbo's life. He gives it reluctantly to Frodo and retires to the elves in Rivendell where he writes songs and his memoirs. Bilbo was fortunate in being relatively untouched by the Ring's evil. His elven sword, Sting, whose blade turns blue when orcs are near, and his precious chain mail of mithril, are given to Frodo.

Frodo Baggins

Frodo is Bilbo's nephew and heir. Frodo is more aristocratic and noble than the other hobbits. He is well read in the lore of Middle-Earth and speaks Elvish. He becomes the main hero, whose task is to destroy the Ring of evil so Sauron will not control Middle-Earth. He is wounded by a Ringwraith, and the wound never completely heals. The evil Ring nearly drives him mad, and he is unable to throw it into Mt. Doom at the last minute. He is followed throughout his adventure by his faithful servant, Samwise Gamgee, and by the creature Gollum, both character doubles for Frodo, showing his good and bad potential. Like the wounded King Arthur, Frodo does not exactly die but is allowed to leave in the last ship of the elves for the Blessed Lands as a reward for his great sacrifice to Middle-Earth.

Tom Bombadil

Tom is a nature spirit of the Old Forest who looks clownish in his bright blue jacket and yellow boots. He speaks in rhyme, saving the hobbits from Old Man Willow and the barrow wights. He and Goldberry, his lady, entertain the hobbits and help them get to Bree. Tom is called a "master" of the forest, one of the oldest beings of Middle-Earth, and the only character not interested in the Ring or Sauron.

Boromir

Boromir, son of Denethor, is son of the ruling Steward of Gondor. Boromir is a hearty warrior, good but rash, a man of action. Though chosen as one of the Fellowship to help Frodo, he is overcome by lust for the Ring that he thinks will help defend his beloved city of Minas Tirith. He wants to give it as a mighty gift for his father to use in fighting Sauron. After he scares Frodo away, he is killed by orcs, trying to protect the other hobbits. He carries a horn that he blows at time of need.

Meriadoc Brandybuck

Meriadoc, or Merry, is a hobbit of the Shire. He is a Bucklander, one of the more independent hobbits, considered a bit outlandish because Bucklanders boat on the river and go into the Old Forest. Merry has maturity and more lore of the world than most hobbits. He is paired with Pippin, his cousin and friend, and considered the older and steadier of the two. He becomes squire to King Theoden and a hero on the battlefield of Pelennor Fields when he kills the chief Ringwraith.

Denethor

Denethor is Steward of Gondor, who holds the throne until the return of a king. Denethor is from the failing line of Numenorean men, ruling over the capital city, Minas Tirith, about to be destroyed by Sauron. He is a proud and stubborn man, a tragic hero, who means well but lacks sound judgment. In his desperation he has looked into a palantir, or seeing stone, and spied on the Enemy. This has made him mad. He irrationally favors his son, Boromir, over his son, Faramir and sends Faramir on a suicide mission. He kills himself out of despair, believing all is lost with Boromir dead and Faramir wounded. He sets himself on fire, as though already dead himself, leaving the city to fend for itself in its darkest hour.

Elrond

Elrond is Halfelven, the son of an elf and human. He is Lord of Rivendell or Imladris, an elven stronghold protected by magic. Aragorn was hidden and raised here by Elrond for protection as the last surviving heir to Gondor's throne. Many of the precious treasures of Middle-Earth, such as the shards of Narsil, the sword that cut off the Ring from Sauron's finger, are preserved at Rivendell. Elrond bears one of the three great rings, Vilya, the blue stone of air. The rings preserve and protect Middle-Earth. Elrond has chosen immortality, as his daughter, Arwen, chooses mortality when she marries Aragorn. Elrond is one of the wisest leaders, a friend of Gandalf, committed to preserving Middle-Earth from the Dark Lord, whom he fought in the previous age. He hosts the Council of all free peoples to decide the fate of the Ring.

Eomer

Eomer is nephew and heir of King Theoden of Rohan, who is banished with his men when Theoden falls under the spell of the evil counselor, Wormtongue. Eomer is loyal to the king and is recalled when Gandalf cures Theoden. Eomer is a brave warrior and fights at Theoden's side at Helm's Deep and on the Pelennor Fields. He becomes friends with Aragorn, and when his uncle dies in battle, he succeeds him as King of Rohan. The ethic of the Rohirrim is exhibited by Eomer on the battlefield when he sings and laughs in the face of despair.

Eowyn

Lady Eowyn is the beautiful and slender sister of Eomer and niece of King Theoden, who treats her as a daughter. Eowyn and Eomer are close as brother and sister, but he councils her always against fighting in the war. She is a proud shield-maiden, trained to fight, and fears being stranded in a woman's inactive life. She falls in adolescent love with Aragorn, who gently refuses her. Though Theoden leaves her to rule the people while he goes to battle, she disguises herself as the warrior Dernhelm and rides with Merry into war. She is wounded defending her uncle from the Chief Ringwraith and cured of her wounds by Aragorn; afterwards, she marries Faramir.

Faramir

Faramir, younger son of Denethor, is a Ranger of Ithilien, guarding Gondor from the spies of Mordor on the border. He is wiser than his brother, Boromir, more like Aragorn or Gandalf in nature. He captures Sam and Frodo on their way to Mordor but nobly lets them go

and helps them towards their goal, thus succeeding where his brother failed, as he does not take the Ring. After the wars, Aragorn makes Faramir the Steward of Gondor, and he weds Eowyn, thus cementing the alliance between Gondor and Rohan.

Galadriel

Galadriel, elven queen of Lothlórien with the golden hair, is the most powerful elf left in Middle-Earth. She is tall, beautiful, and wise. She sees past, present, and future in her mirror. She bears one of the three rings of power, Nenya, the ring of adamant, ruling water. The Lady of the Wood presents important gifts to the Fellowship for their success. Galadriel was one of the ancient elves who came to Middle-Earth to protect and teach men, but she refused to obey the gods when the elves were ordered to go back to Valinor, land of the gods. Because she helped defeat Sauron and refused the temptation of the Ring when Frodo offered it to her, she was allowed to go finally to the Blessed Lands on the last ship with her consort, Celeborn, and Gandalf, Elrond, Bilbo, and Frodo.

Samwise Gamgee

Samwise is a hobbit of the Shire, servant of Frodo, and his companion on the quest. Sam is Frodo's humble gardener; his devotion to his master is so absolute that he never thinks of himself or of stealing the Ring. He has a lower class dialect and sense of humor; he is cheerful, a good cook and storyteller, and he composes songs and loves to be with the elves. Sam is in only one way less admirable than Frodo. He sees the worst in Gollum and does not have Frodo's pity or understanding for the ruined creature, thus provoking Gollum's worst side at the wrong time. Without Sam, Frodo could not have completed his journey. Tolkien thought Sam more interesting in character than Frodo, who had to be more noble and rarefied as the main hero.

Gandalf

Gandalf, called Mithrandir or Grey Pilgrim by the elves, is one of the five wizards who are Maiar (angelic beings) sent to protect Middle-Earth. Gandalf has the appearance of an old man; he begins as the humble Gandalf the Grey, clothed in a grey robe and pointed hat, traveling from one land to another, like Aragorn, his friend, keeping an eye on things in the quiet before the Dark Lord begins his war. He wears one of the three rings of power, Narya the red fire, the kindler that helps him rouse all the peoples to join together. Gandalf is the wisest teacher, the kingmaker, like Merlin to Arthur. He is betrayed and imprisoned by Saruman the White, the head of his order, who has been corrupted by looking into a palantir. Gandalf falls to his death fighting the Balrog in Moria but, being one of the immortals, is resurrected and comes back to finish his task as Gandalf the White, replacing Saruman. He rides Shadowfax, the fastest horse in Middle-Earth; bears the elven sword, Glamdring; and carries a magic staff that creates light in dark places. He is a little stern and inscrutable in manner, but kind at heart. He is not allowed by the higher powers to interfere with Middle-Earth matters directly but seeks to defeat evil by inspiring and teaching those around him. When his task is done, he leaves Middle-Earth on the last elven ship for the Blessed Isles.

Gimli

Gimli is the son of Gloin, one of the dwarves from Bilbo's adventures. He is part of the Fellowship that sets out from Rivendell, representing the dwarf folk. Gimli carries an axe and is a fierce fighter. He is stubborn and irascible, but makes friends with Legolas, though dwarves and elves usually detest each other. His cousin, Balin, is Lord of Moria, the underground dwarf kingdom the company passes through. Gimli is loyal to Aragorn, following him even to the Paths of the Dead. He also becomes passionately devoted to Galadriel after passing through Lorien, obtaining the gift of three gold hairs from her head.

Gollum

Gollum, the slimy and twisted creature, was once a hobbit called Smeagol. He killed his friend Deagol, who found the Ring in the river. Gollum choked his friend and ever after makes an involuntary swallowing noise, "gollum." Gollum uses his invisibility to steal things, but eventually he is outcast from his kind, hating the light of day and hiding away in caves. The Ring prolongs his miserable life, until it falls in the cave, and Bilbo picks it up. Gollum, like the Ringwraiths, searches ever after for the Ring, secretly following Frodo and Company. Frodo lets Gollum be his guide to Mordor against Sam's judgment. Sam names Gollum's split personality "Slinker" and "Stinker," the whining victim and the malicious aggressor. Nevertheless, it is Gollum who finishes the quest by falling into Mt. Doom with the Ring. It was this prediction of Gandalf's, that Gollum had some part to play, that stayed Frodo's hand from killing him earlier.

Legolas

Legolas is a woodland elf, one of the Fellowship, son of Thranduil, king of the Mirkwood elves. Legolas has attributes of his kindred—he can see farther than humans, is intuitive, and walks lightly above the ground. He is agile and a good fighter, using bow and arrows. Elves are immortal but can be killed in battle. He becomes best friends with a dwarf, Gimli, which is unheard of, for the two races typically detest each other. Legolas sings the glories of trees and forests; Gimli of mining in caves. They stick by each other in battle.

Merry

See Meriadoc Brandybuck

Pippin

See Peregrin Took

Saruman

Saruman is the White Wizard, the head of the Order of Wizards, who becomes corrupt. Saruman lives in Isengard in the tower of Orthanc, studying the lore of Middle-Earth. He is seduced to the side of the Dark Lord when he looks into a palantir. He does not understand that he is a tool of Sauron. He turns Orthanc into a war factory, making explosives and breeding orcs or warrior demons (called Uruk-hai) that are more terrible than the Dark Lord's. His orcs bear a white hand on their armor. Saruman's main weapon is his voice, which can bend others to his will. He attempts to seduce Gandalf to the dark side, saying they will be partners with Sauron. He stirs up war, sending out his armies against Rohan. He is defeated at Helm's Deep. Gandalf breaks Saruman's staff, but he slinks off to do what evil he can in the Shire as Sharkey. Eventually, he is killed by his own minion, Wormtongue.

Sauron

Sauron, the Dark Lord of Mordor, is the evil Enemy of Middle-Earth. He was once a Maia (angel) and lieutenant of Melkor, the Valar (god) who fell. When Melkor was destroyed, Sauron

TOPICS FOR FURTHER STUDY

- Research the stages of the quest in Part I of Joseph Campbell's *The Hero with a Thousand Faces*. Write a paper applying those stages to Frodo's quest in *The Lord of the Rings*. Does Frodo fit the average quest pattern? How does he make the Atonement with the Father? How does he cross the return threshold? If you can make a case for Sam going farther than Frodo on the quest by accomplishing the step called The Master of Two Worlds, then do so.

- Discuss with your classmates what makes Aragorn fit to be king. Is it because he is Aragorn, son of Arathorn, the wielder of the heirloom sword, Anduril, or is it his leadership ability? Name Aragorn's abilities as a leader. List the qualities, such as courage, and then find examples in the book that substantiate that quality. Based on hints from the book, imagine how his reign will change Middle-Earth. How will he solve problems? Do research to find an historical king who had similar qualities or circumstances and write a report on kingship in history and in fantasy.

- Research the role of women in Anglo-Saxon society and comment on Eowyn's desire to go to war. Were women trained to fight with weapons? Were men and women equal in that society? Give a report on your findings or write a poem or short story on Eowyn's Dream of Glory. Imagine she is a young girl on the threshold of life, dreaming of her future.

- Summarize the differences between book and film versions of *The Lord of the Rings*. Watch the DVD commentaries of the Jackson film and give a report on how the writers adapted the story for film. Did Jackson do a good job as director? What would you have done differently if you were making the film? Which version, book or film, do you like better and why? Comment in general on what one must do to adapt a novel to film.

- Compare the elves in Tolkien's story to other stories of fairies and elves. How are Tolkien's elves distinctive? Why do they leave Middle-Earth at the end of the Third Age? Find drawings of elves and fairies to illustrate your points. Create a fairy scrapbook with comments interspersed with illustrations. Do this as a group project, then present it to the rest of the class.

- How was World War I, the war in which Tolkien participated, similar to and different from the War of the Ring? Were battle conditions and movements the same? Were the codes of war the same or different? Which were the best warriors in Middle-Earth and why? Does Tolkien paint war realistically or unrealistically? What does the novel show readers about the effectiveness of war as a solution? Create a research journal with the answers, giving examples from the novel and history.

---

arose to take his place. He fooled the elves into creating the rings of power, and then he created the One Ring to rule them all. He controls the nine rings of men, the seven of the dwarves, but the three elven rings are hidden from him. In the Third Age, Sauron has no visible shape but dwells in Mordor, building a great army in the wasteland around Mt. Doom. All his power has been poured into the One Ring, which was cut off his finger by Isildur, Aragorn's ancestor, in the Second Age. Sauron appears in the palantir only as a fiery eye that does not sleep but can see everything in Middle-Earth. He is served by the Nazgul, or Ringwraiths, the ghosts of the kings of men, and by orcs, the demons who are corrupted elves. He is immortal, so when he is destroyed in one form, he takes another when he regains strength. The Third Age and Sauron's power are destroyed when the Ring is destroyed.

Theoden

Theoden is King of Rohan, land of the horse lords or Rohirrim. His hall, Meduseld, is something like a Viking hall with its armed warriors. Rohirrim are men (speaking Anglo-Saxon and living in that kind of culture), not as noble or long lived as the Numenoreans, but with a long and honorable warrior tradition. Theoden is bewitched into senility by Saruman, letting Wormtongue, Saruman's lackey, make his decisions for him. When Gandalf breaks the spell on him, he takes action as the noble chieftain he is, a model to his men, calling on the Rohirrim to rally. Aragorn fights at his side at Helm's Deep, and in turn, Theoden goes to the aid of Gondor, where he falls on Pelennor Fields in full honor. His niece, Eowyn, is wounded trying to save him, and his nephew, Eomer, succeeds him as king.

Peregrin Took

Peregrin Took or Pippin, hobbit of the Shire, cousin of Merry (Meriadoc Brandybuck) is the comic relief. The Tooks are considered adventurous for hobbits. Lighthearted and mischievous, Pippin causes trouble to the Fellowship by being curious at the wrong times: he rouses the Balrog in Moria and looks in the forbidden palantir. Pippin becomes squire to Denethor and helps save Faramir's life in Minas Tirith when Denethor tries to burn him on his own funeral pyre.

Treebeard

Treebeard is an ent, or treeherder. An ent is a tree that can walk, taking care of the other trees who are not awake. The ents are sad because they have lost their entwives, who left them eons ago, preferring gardens to forests, and there are no more entings, or descendents. Treebeard speaks slowly because ents are long lived and think slowly. He is a friend of Gandalf but becomes an enemy of Saruman, who is destroying the trees. Pippin and Merry convince the ents to go to war. The ents destroy orcs and dismantle the stones of Isengard, Saruman's stronghold.

Arwen Undomiel

Arwen, called the Evenstar of her people, is an immortal dark-haired elf-maiden, daughter of Elrond. She foregoes her immortality to marry Aragorn and ennoble his line of kings in the Fourth Age. Elrond has forbidden their marriage until Aragorn overcomes the Enemy and takes the throne. She is Galadriel's granddaughter and makes a banner for Aragorn to carry into battle.

THEMES

Providence

The Lord of the Rings demonstrates the theme of Providence, the medieval doctrine that holds that God works out everything to a right end. The righteous prevail. The attacks of the Dark Lord ultimately unite the free peoples of Middle-Earth and bring back a golden age with the rightful king. Gollum, a nasty character who tries to defeat the quest, is the one who actually destroys the Ring and achieves the quest. Gandalf falls to his death, only to arise as the more powerful Gandalf the White. Tolkien does not name God directly, but the work suggests that a divine justice rules Middle-Earth. Gandalf tells Frodo that the Dark Lord does not know everything: "Behind [Bilbo's finding the Ring] there was something else at work, beyond any design of the Ring-maker.... Bilbo was *meant* to find the Ring, and *not* by its maker." Gandalf convinces Frodo he is also meant to have it, and since it is a divine mission given to Frodo, he must be worthy and capable of taking on the quest.

Power Corrupts

The One Ring is the Ring of Power, and it destroys everyone who tries to possess it. Thus, Tolkien implies that since the Ring embodies the Dark Lord, it is the desire for power over others that corrupts. Frodo unconsciously tests each main character for strength of integrity. He offers the Ring to Tom Bombadil, Gandalf, Aragorn, Elrond, and Galadriel. They all refuse, showing they are just. Boromir fails the test by trying to get the Ring from Frodo, but his brother Faramir passes by refusing it. The desire for the Ring destroys Gollum, Saruman, and Denethor. Sam is able to carry it without harm because of his devotion to his master. Frodo is strong until the last minute when he is unable to part with the Ring on his own. The Ring of Power is shown to be untrustworthy and deceiving, a symbol of lust for domination that must be actively refused by every good soul.

The Haunting Sense of History

The sense of history alive in the present, an elegiac feel of a more glorious past slipping away, is present in every culture of Middle-Earth through songs and legends. It is the end of the Third Age, and readers are reminded of the fading power of the elves, who are leaving Middle-Earth; the lost kingdom of Numenor, sunk like Atlantis, and the continued failure of that line of men in Gondor; the fewer numbers and strength of the Rohirrim; the fall of Khazad-dum, the great Dwarf city; and the growing threat to the Shire, that had always been safe. Faramir calls Gondor "Men of the Twilight." None of the races is able to keep their precious heritage intact, with the threat of war ever present.

Friendship as the Basis of Strength

Friendship is not to be underestimated, for though the Allies are fewer than the armies of the Dark Lord, they are bound in love and loyalty, a unity that counts for more than numbers. Individual initiative is not prized, as in modern action films. Teamwork and loyalty are the key virtues. Friendship is evident in the bond between the hobbits, especially Frodo and Sam, who only make it up Mt. Doom together; and in the Fellowship of the different races of Middle-Earth, who accompany and support the Ringbearer. It is the alliance of good people and of friends that overcomes the Enemy. It takes everyone working together, everyone a hero, to outsmart and defeat evil. Community is a corollary of the friendship theme—what binds the different lands together in internal harmony and tradition, such as the Shire, Rivendell, and Rohan. Each land is shown to enrich the fabric of the whole of Middle-Earth. Diversity and interdependence are values that Gandalf stands for, as he rides through the countryside, rousing each group to support the other.

Courage Against the Odds

Courage against overwhelming odds is a theme Tolkien lifted from Norse sagas. He loved heroes like Beowulf, whose honor and fame lived on, even though he faced unbeatable foes and died to save his people. The brave heart that endures is noble in victory or defeat. Heroism does not depend on size or gender (e.g., the hobbits are Halflings, and Eowyn is a woman) or outcome (Theoden dies honorably in battle). Frodo is constantly worried that he will not have enough courage to carry out what he knows must be done, but he finds it within himself at each crisis. Tolkien's heroes have to face their fears, not just walk through their parts.

War Does Not Defeat Evil

Though Gandalf urges an assault on the Black Gate, he explains that evil is not defeated through war: "I still hope for victory, but not by arms." War is a necessary evil, a self-defense, but it does not stop Sauron. As Faramir explains to Frodo, warfare is not the ultimate solution; it destroys both sides. Frodo's quest to destroy the One Ring of Power is ultimately an internal moral battle and is fought on that high ground: the message is that people must be willing to sacrifice domination for the good of all.

Heroism Depends on Free Will

Although Providence rules Middle-Earth, each character must choose the good out of free will. Frodo was meant to have the Ring and go on the quest, but he did not have to accept the burden. At each stage of the quest, he has to choose whether to go on. At Amon Hen, Frodo contends with the Eye of Sauron and Gandalf's voice, each urging him on a different course. These are in his mind, symbolizing the power of good and evil in each person. "Suddenly he was aware of himself again. Frodo, neither the Voice nor the Eye: free to choose." Frodo chooses the good for himself.

Evil Defeats Itself

The Dark Lord loses because he is not as imaginative as the good characters who have a larger viewpoint—the good of the whole. The Dark Lord does not imagine the allies would seek to destroy the Ring; he imagines they want power, as he does. The demonic orcs always outnumber the allies, but they are quarrelsome, envious, hateful, ambitious, and suspicious. Evil is often shown to be a corruption of the good, insubstantial in itself. For instance, Sauron himself was once, like Satan, an angelic being of light. The orcs were once elves. Gollum was once a hobbit. Tolkien seems to have it both ways, making evil an external and internal force, an active malice and a mere distortion of good. Boromir, for example, is a good man who falls because of the outer temptation of the Ring, but he is attracted to it from his own inner weakness as well.

The Spoiling of Nature Is Demonic

Tolkien dearly loved the world of unspoiled nature, especially trees. He hated the industrialization of the modern world that was destroying nature. Saruman's war factory at Orthanc demands the stripping of trees from Fangorn Forest, and the revenge of the trees, under Treebeard, is perhaps his desire to see balance in nature restored. The Land of Mordor is a

Ian McKellen, as Gandalf the White in the 2001 film version of J. R. R. Tolkien's The Lord of the Rings: The Fellowship of the Ring, *directed by Peter Jackson* (The Kobal Collection. Reproduced by permission)

barren land of ash and waste, not unlike a land destroyed by war or industrialization.

The Desire to Create Is Divine

The creative urge in humans, who according to Tolkien's belief are made in the image of God, is explored in the race of elves, who are actually glorified humans. Their desire to make Middle-Earth beautiful and abundant is seen in their civilizations among trees and river valleys that preserve all that is good and beautiful. Tolkien sees the making of fantasy itself as an elven craft, a vision of how things are and could be.

STYLE

Fantasy Novel

Fantasy is a type of story that takes place in a non-existent world, often used to comment on the contemporary world, as is the case with this novel. Tolkien has been credited with the invention of modern fantasy, though of course, the fantastic itself is an ancient mode of storytelling (seen for example in *The Arabian Nights* and the *Odyssey*). Though some critics deny that modern fantasy is literature, Tolkien saw the genre as belonging to that category of literature which has to do with a spiritual journey and serious purpose. He defined this type of literature in his essay "On Fairy Stories." The fantasist engages in what he called subcreation, making an alternative world, in order to help readers see in enriched form what is already in this world. The story provides consolation through a eucatastrophe (happy ending), and that is important because it mimics grace and denies a final victory by evil.

Heroic Romance

Tolkien himself did not call *The Lord of the Rings* fantasy; he called it mythic or heroic romance. A myth is a story of creation and the gods. Tolkien's complete mythology of Middle-Earth, told in *The Silmarillion* and the appendices of the novel, is felt in the background of the novel's action, giving it its large scope. Readers

COMPARE
&
CONTRAST

- **1950s:** The cold war persists between the United States and the Soviet Union. The novel reminds readers of World War II, which ends in 1945. Readers see parallels between Sauron and Hitler and between Rohan, Gondor, the Shire, and the Western Allies, Britain, the United States, and France.

  Today: Readers see a parallel between the novel and President Bush's war on terrorism, with Bush as either Aragorn saving Middle-Earth or as Sauron trying to dominate Iraq. About.com. posts a doctored photo of Bush with the Ring of Power on his finger sitting at his desk in the Oval office (politicalhumor.about.com).

- **1950s:** Edmund Wilson and other critics attack Tolkien for his handling of female characters, saying there are almost none, and the few portrayed are stereotyped.

  Today: The Girl-Power effect increases in Hollywood in the 2000s after the example of the movie *Alien* with an independent female lead. Fantasy heroines, such as Xena, Buffy, Wonder Woman, and Princess Leia, are popular draws in film and video games.

- **1950s:** Deforestation is still accepted as a necessary price for urban progress in Great Britain and elsewhere in the world, with only a relatively small number of vocal opponents.

  Today: The total woodland of Great Britain is 2.5 percent of its land area, with 45 percent of the ancient and semi-natural woodland that existed after World War II lost since that time. The government of the U.K. has a policy to increase woodland planting by 5,000 hectares a year.

---

are aware that the story takes place in the Third Age, that two more glorious ages have preceded and one lesser one follows without magic in it. These are the imagined early cycles of the Earth, the ages of heroes. Heroic or epic stories concern the legendary heroes of any culture. The romance, or long tale with supernatural elements such as demons and magicians, is the form of the tale often chosen for telling about heroes (such as *Beowulf* in Anglo-Saxon literature). The epic tale (e.g., *Odyssey*) concerns heroes who save or renew a civilization in crisis, and it has certain conventions that Tolkien uses freely; for instance, the ornate weapons and architecture and customs of each place exhibiting the nature of the character or country. The hobbits are armed from the weaponry in the mounds of the Numenoreans, which is a reference to a superior, lost culture behind their own small Shire. Heroic characters, such as Theoden, Boromir, Legolas, Gimli, and Eomer, are more types than realistic portraits. They frequently engage in long conversations that are set pieces, such as at the Council of Elrond. The book is also constructed around Tolkien's invented languages (fourteen in all), which are peppered throughout as names, place names, songs, poems, and legends. Names and words are thus not so much symbols, as direct invocations of lost races or heroes, evident in the song of Earendil, for instance, in which the hero becomes a star, whose light Frodo holds in physical form in the phial of Galadriel, to guide him. As a linguist, Tolkien knew the rules of languages and could make whole cultures out of the roots of his invented words. His genius in naming places and characters conveys the sense that they exist. Tolkien gives the book the weight and feel of history. The story appeals to many modern readers because it has blended elements of many genres; it is finally a novel because the events are treated at length as everyday reality. Tolkien carefully coordinates all details, like the phases of the moon and the dates.

The Quest Journey

The Lord of the Rings is structured as a quest journey. The omniscient third person narrator tells the story, basically around the journey of Frodo's quest through the fantastic world of Middle-Earth (Earth in its imagined ancient history) to Mount Doom and back again, but there are digressions; for instance, through the Old Forest where they meet Tom Bombadil. The digressions do not detract from the tightly woven and unified plot. The narrator is perfectly aware of the importance of the events ending the Third Age, and so each episode, whether told chronologically or picked up out of sequence, is handled with suspense that moves the plot in the direction of the climax of the Ring's destruction. The narrator's formal and archaic sounding English, heroic and prophetic in tone, helps provide authority to his vision, almost giving the feel of scripture.

The publisher insisted it was too expensive to make one novel of a million words and a thousand pages, so the three separate novels were created, based on Tolkien's divisions of the work into six books. Each title covers two books. The first two books have a linear structure—the forward journey of Frodo and the Fellowship. "The Two Towers" begins the more intricate interlaced structure in which Tolkien hops from one group of characters to another, after the Fellowship breaks up. Some have seen this design as a flaw, contrary to modern novels that intercut more closely between stories, as happens in film. Possibly Tolkien was influenced by medieval literature in his design. In any case, the interlace works to build suspense: he follows Aragorn and Gandalf for a while, then backtracks to pick up Frodo and Sam. The starting and ending point of the journey is the Shire, the home of the hobbits. Like the usual mythic journey, the starting point is a version of everyday reality, the mundane hobbit life in the foreground. By the time the hobbits reach the Old Forest, however, they have crossed the boundary into a magic world where trees can sing and Tom, the nature spirit, is there to save them.

HISTORICAL CONTEXT

Tolkien, the Philologist

Tolkien's thinking was historical; a professor of Anglo-Saxon, Tolkien was immersed in the study of languages and old sagas. Using his knowledge of linguistic laws, he created his own languages with logical morphological changes. The Elven tongue Quenya was inspired by the Finnish language in *The Kalevala*, and the Elven tongue, Sindarin, was similar to Welsh. These imagined languages are the basis of his Middle-Earth mythology, for he said he had to invent people to speak his languages. The languages are so complex that linguists still study them, and people try to learn them. From the invented languages and the meanings of the roots of those words, he reconstructed missing parts of the Earth's history, as it might have been, with all the various races of beings: hobbits, dwarves, elves, men, ents, gods, orcs, demons, dragons. The novel is an epic, set as Tolkien saw it, in the imagined pre-history of the present Earth (called Middle-Earth after the name of the Earth in *Beowulf*).

The Four Ages of Middle-Earth

Tolkien follows the scheme of four cosmological ages as in Greek mythology, with the First Age of Middle-Earth, a golden age (retold in *The Silmarillion*); the Second Age, a silver age, declining in value but still glorious with the civilization of Numenor (Atlantis). The sinking of Numenor, and the Last Alliance of Men and Elves when the One Ring was cut from Sauron's hand ends the Second Age. The Third Age, the time of the novel, is a nostalgic time in which beings look back to earlier glory. The elves are still on Earth, preserving it with their rings of power, but Sauron, the Dark Lord, is looking for his lost Ring and threatening once more to destroy Middle-Earth. The wizard Gandalf is a Maia, or angelic being, sent to Earth to help rouse the races to defeat Sauron. With Sauron's defeat, the elves leave, and the Fourth Age of the rule of men begins with Aragorn's reign. Though the Fourth Age starts with a golden time ruled by the true king, it is implied that this will be an Earth more like the present one, without magic.

World War II

The novel was begun in 1937 and was written largely during World War II (1939–1945). Many commentators and readers have seen a parallel between Sauron and Adolf Hitler, and the Ring of Power is sometimes thought of as the atomic bomb that ended the war, like Mt. Doom exploding when the Ring was thrown in. Tolkien has repeatedly denied the intention of such allegory. In the Foreword to the second edition, he states that his story is not an allegory, but has "applicability." A mythic story is universal and should be relevant to any time, for the same principles apply, age after age.

Nevertheless, Tolkien's experience in the trenches of World War I, where many of his friends were killed, and his son Christopher's experience in World War II certainly weave in the flavor and concerns of the first half of the twentieth century. Tom Shippey credits Tolkien with being a twentieth-century author depicting evil in a new, impersonal way that fits the angst of his generation. He calls it "the wraithing-process" where one becomes gradually emptied of a moral responsibility. In a modern age, no one seems personally responsible for evil; it is decentralized and administered by wraith-like people who have lost their will (e.g., the Ringwraiths).

Critique of Modernism

Tolkien's myth, though not set in the contemporary world, is clearly a critique of modernism, and perhaps the best way he knew to stage such a critique was to set the story in ancient times. Modernism, from Tolkien's perspective, is not just free form in literature, but a way of thinking, cut loose from traditional roots and values. His disgust with the pollution caused by industrialism, for instance, which values money over the environment, vents itself in the episode of Saruman's cutting down trees for his war furnaces. It has been said that the tremendous popularity of *The Lord of the Rings* is due to its reference to an older, more traditional world where humans have clear relationship both to the spiritual and natural worlds, thus satisfying generations of readers who long for an alternative vision of life.

The Inklings

Tolkien and his friends, C. S. Lewis and Charles Williams, were part of a group of Oxford dons who met together in the 1930s and 1940s to read their writing aloud to one another. Their club was called The Inklings, and many fantasy books came out it, such as *The Lord of the Rings* and the Narnia books. These men were generally opposed to modernist writers and thinkers, having more religious, philological, philosophical, and theological interests. Tolkien was a devout Catholic, and though he did not write specifically about his religion, it informs his myth and values.

CRITICAL OVERVIEW

When *The Lord of the Rings* was published in three parts, one at a time during 1954 and 1955 (*The Fellowship of the Ring*, *The Two Towers*, and *The Return of the King*) it garnered a mixed reception. Reviewers loved it or hated it. It was not taken seriously by the literary establishment, for there was nothing comparable in modern fiction: the work was the first modern adult fantasy novel. Edmund Wilson was one of those intellectuals who found it repulsive, and as quoted in *The Tolkien Scrapbook* in his article for *Nation* in 1956, Wilson calls it "juvenile trash," a fantasy for its own sake. He claims it is written by an amateur who does not understand literary form and that the hero undergoes no real temptations. One can feel Wilson wanting to quickly stamp out the enthusiasm of the few before it is fanned into a flame.

W. H. Auden, the well-known English poet (also quoted in *The Tolkien Scrapbook* and in the same year in the *New York Times Book Review*), supported Tolkien's work, calling the book "a masterpiece of its genre" and describing it as a heroic quest. He further asserts Tolkien succeeds, as Milton does not, in representing the good as a fuller, more imaginative reality than evil. Comparison of *The Lord of the Rings* by admirers to great epic literature irked scholars such as Wilson.

Tolkien's friend and fellow Inkling, C. S. Lewis, defended the work. In "Tolkien's *The Lord of the Rings*," Lewis calls it "lightning from a clear sky," and he argues that it should be taken seriously as a moral depiction of good and evil, that the book is full of the experience of his generation who lived through World War I. He asserts that myth is a valuable tool for understanding the world.

Neil Isaacs, in his essay "On the Possibility of Writing Tolkien Criticism" in *Tolkien and His Critics*, points out that the popularity of the book gets in the way of its being taken seriously as literature. He refers to the fact that in the 1960s Ace Publishing came out with an illegal paperback version, and *The Lord of the Rings* became an overnight cult favorite on American college campuses. Some critics felt that an adolescent craze cannot be literature and assumed interest would die out.

Fifty years after its first appearance, *The Lord of the Rings* was widely viewed as serious

Dominic Monaghan as Merry, Elijah Wood as Frodo Baggins, Billy Boyd as Peregrin 'Pippin' Took, and Sean Astin as Sam Gamgee in the 2001 film version of The Lord of the Rings: The Fellowship of the Ring, *by J. R. R. Tolkien* (New Line | Saul Zaentz | Wing Nut | The Kobal Collection)

literature. The work serves as the foundation of the popular fantasy industry and prompted whole areas of critical investigation, such as Tolkien Studies and Middle-Earth Studies. It appealed to something vital in so many people that T. A. Shippey, in his 2001 study *J. R. R. Tolkien: Author of the Century*, claimed Tolkien as the most important author of the twentieth century, over such giants as James Joyce.

CRITICISM

Susan Andersen

Andersen is an associate professor of English literature and composition. In this essay, she considers whether Tolkien's popular fantasy is an enduring piece of literature.

As Tolkien himself was aware, readers love or hate *The Lord of the Rings*. Not since Dickens has popular fiction been responded to so intensely by so many. According to Tom

Shippey in *J. R. R. Tolkien: Author of the Century*, the novel was first in polls as the most read book in the twentieth century, after the Bible. Through innovations in both content and form, Tolkien created a saga that satisfied the modern hunger in many for new myths—those heroic tales perpetuated in every culture that speak of the power of humans in the universe. The War of the Ring, nevertheless, set off a critical war over whether Tolkien's novel is worthy of the status of timeless literature. The mounting evidence suggests yes.

It is hard to remember how fresh *The Lord of the Rings* was, after fifty years of imitations based on the formula it made famous: a wizard, a king, elves, demons, and a quest to save the world from evil. What remains new? Tolkien adds surprising turns to old motifs and invents a new genre to do it: the fantasy novel. His is the familiar realm of Faery, but no one had ever before seen any beings like his elves. The world of the Ring deals with good versus evil but has modern applicability with its theme that power

WHAT
DO I READ
NEXT?

- *The Hobbit* (1937), Tolkien's first hobbit book preceding the action of *The Lord of the Rings*, tells about Bilbo's adventures in finding the Ring, his friendship with Gandalf, the riddle contest with Gollum, and the slaying of Smaug, the dragon. The book is more light-hearted than *The Lord of the Rings*, because it was written for children, but it is enjoyed by readers of all ages.

- Tolkien's mythology of Middle-Earth, *The Silmarillion* (1977), gives the background of *The Lord of the Rings*. Published posthumously from his father's notes by Christopher Tolkien, it tells the creation myth and the First Age of the Valar or gods, the creation of the First-Born or Elves and how they left Valinor for Middle-Earth with the divine jewels, the Silmarils. Also included are the war with the first Dark Lord, Morgoth and the story of Numenor (Atlantis) and its fall. Finally, the Tale of the Rings of Power is the bridge to the Third Age. The style is formal and terse, a little difficult to read; details are left undeveloped, as in the oral tradition.

- John Gardner's *Grendel* (1971) tells one of Tolkien's favorite tales, the Beowulf story, from the monster Grendel's point of view. It imagines the origin of evil, explaining Grendel's misery and why he decides to teach men a lesson by terrorizing the Danes. Grendel believes life is meaningless until he finds his place in the story of the hero, Beowulf. Without a monster, there can be no hero, so in order that men may have something to live by, Grendel must die. Gardner is a masterful writer, one able to show through his tale why humans need fantasy.

- T. H. White's *The Once and Future King* (1958) is based on Malory's story of King Arthur but with a different slant. This book is the basis of the musical *Camelot*. Merlyn turns Arthur into several different animals to teach him their secrets. Arthur is trained to be a just king in an unjust world. White, a medieval scholar, explored good and evil through his characters.

- Ursula K. Le Guin's classic *The Earthsea Trilogy* includes: *A Wizard of Earthsea* (1968); *The Tombs of Atuan* (1970); and *The Farthest Shore* (1972). Written originally with teenagers in mind, these books are enjoyed by a general audience. The story centers on the Wizard Ged, also called Sparrowhawk. He begins using magic as a peasant boy and becomes in maturity the Archmage of Roke. Ged's magic works by the power of true naming. The story and settings are powerful, and the style is clear and easy to read.

- C. S. Lewis's *The Chronicles of Narnia* series (1950–1956) includes seven titles, all pertaining to four children who discover a magic land called Narnia. There are talking animals, fauns, a witch, and the heroic lion, Aslan. The children return many times to Narnia, becoming Kings and Queens and fighting battles between good and evil.

- Frank Herbert's *Dune* (1964) is the first in the Dune series of science fiction novels. Herbert's novels present a complex, multilayered universe of human societies spread out over galaxies. It is 8,000 years into the future and the coin of the realm is mélange, a spice drug that expands consciousness. Paul Atreides is a young prince who becomes leader of the empire through his ability to know the future.

- George R. R. Martin's *A Song of Ice and Fire* series (1996–2005) includes four of seven planned books that combine Martin's knowledge of the historical Wars of the Roses and elements of fantasy. There is not the same poetry as in Tolkien's writing; the style is more explicitly spelled out but has the same kind of magic pull. There is great character depth and intricate political intrigue. Magic is in the background. A lot of violent twists of the plot create constant suspense.

> WHETHER MAKING UP LANGUAGES OR USING THEM, TOLKIEN HAD THE EAR OF A BARD. HE IS REGARDED BY MANY AS THE SHAKESPEARE OF MODERN FANTASISTS."

corrupts. It is a fantastic world but told as if it were an everyday reality. The spectacle of two child-like hobbits toiling up Mt. Doom, telling themselves that they are like heroes of old who "had lots of chances, like us, of turning back, only they didn't," puts the heroic and homely together. The hobbits realize they are still part of the One Great Tale: "Don't the great tales never end?" asks Sam.

However, Tolkien would have been the first to deny that he invented anything new. He and his friend C. S. Lewis shared a love of medieval and Norse literature. They were immersed in the beauties of *Beowulf*, *The Eddas*, and *The Kalevala*, and they lamented that such stories were no longer being written. They loved this literature's magic—the magic of elves and wizards and dragons. Tolkien dignified the world of Faery by changing the popular, tiny, and cute fairies into the tall powerful elves who protect Middle-Earth. But even more, he desired the magic of the telling itself. Tolkien said in his essay "On Fairy-Stories" that he wanted stories with "beauty that is an enchantment, and an ever-present peril; both joy and sorrow as sharp as swords." The passages describing Galadriel's farewell to the Fellowship; Boromir's funeral boat going over Rauros Falls; the first appearance of a Ringwraith in the Shire: these are the sharp swords he means.

Perhaps an even greater urge was to have stories that placed human beings in a cosmic context. So often, realistic stories of the trials of modern life give no release or solution. They make humans seem small and hopeless, victims from within and without. Fairy-story or myth (Tolkien used the terms interchangeably) overcomes limitation and satisfies, he writes in the same essay, the "primordial human desires," such as surveying the depths of space and time. In *The Lord of the Rings*, readers are aware of the passage of history and of history's vastness, stretching back into the dark initiations when the cosmos began. Frodo knows, for example, that he is living in the Third Age, that he is working with the principle players of that age to uphold Middle-Earth: Gandalf, Galadriel, Elrond, and Aragorn. Furthermore, as Joseph Campbell explains mythic stories help people realize their human potential: "the hero is symbolical of that divine creative and redemptive image which is hidden within us all, only waiting to be known and rendered into life."

Tolkien's novels are the most accessible of his body of work, though the lesser part of what he called his mythology for England, which he created, purged of grosser elements found in older mythology. Norse and Germanic stories had a certain raw brutality and revenge motive that he omitted. Middle-Earth is filled with the values of his own religion, Catholicism, presented in a nonreligious and universal light: friendship, brotherhood, loyalty, love, sacrifice, peace. Modern literature, by contrast to Tolkien's fantasy, records the lack of these in gruesome detail. Tolkien sought, against the prevailing pattern, to create a world where these values were once more vital.

In his essay "On Fairy-Stories," Tolkien asserts that the right of the human artist is to be a "sub-creator," inventing worlds that are a "shared enrichment" of the readers' own, helping them understand how this one could be better. Fairy-story, he said, is a "natural branch of literature," producing a profound transformation in the reader, a catharsis or purification of the highest sort, which includes recovery, escape, and consolation.

Recovery, Tolkien believed, is the ability to regain a clear view of things, to regain innocence. This recuperation cannot be achieved if one embraces the dark expectations of realistic fiction, with the ironic tone of a John Steinbeck or Ernest Hemingway. Tolkien's book may seem naïve, tiresome in its elaborate details of the long journey and endless landscapes, its ornate language, its predictable character types (Saruman, the evil magician; Aragorn, the king in exile). Yet Tolkien explained that myth demands an adult mind but a child's heart. For instance, readers may see the threat of industrialism clearer using Treebeard's point of view, the joy of small pleasures in a hobbit's bath-song, the wonder of elves in Sam's voice when he spots Gildor's band in the Shire.

Consolation is next. The deep friendship of Frodo, Sam, Merry, and Pippin and their amusing antics on the frightening journey cheer readers' young hearts, and the fact that elves show up at the right time with their song, waybread, and phials of starlight, gives what Tolkien called consolation, the eucatastrophe or happy ending. Tom Bombadil, who comes running in his blue jacket and yellow boots, speaking in rhyme, to save the hobbits from Old Man Willow, is not escapist or childish, for his assistance assures readers of life's essential goodness, the working of all events toward some good end. Even the twisted Gollum unwittingly destroys the Ring, in spite of his intentions. C. N. Manlove's accusation that the happy ending is not real, because there is no price paid for it, is belied by Frodo's wound that will never heal. Sacrifice is a theme of the book—Gandalf's, Aragorn's, Frodo's, Sam's, Arwen's, Eowyn's, and so on.

Finally, fantasy serves for escape, not a bad thing for Tolkien. The depiction of so-called real life, which presents a prison to human beings, with its dulling materialism and pollution, should be escaped. Why is a machinegun or motorcar more real than a dragon, he asks his readers. The fairyland of Lothlórien is a memory for Gimli, which as Galadriel says, "shall remain ever clear and unstained in your heart, and shall neither fade nor grow stale." The memory of the good is necessary for doing good.

According to Tolkien in "On Fairy-Stories," the successful fantasy or alternative world is a subset of the primary world, of human needs and desires; therefore, it has to ring true, to be truthful, no matter how many Balrogs or Ringwraiths there may be, or it would not relevant to readers' lives. Hobbits may not exist in the real world, but the feeling of being small and having to fulfill an impossible task does. The desire to meet a wise wizard like Gandalf is, according to Jungian psychology, symbolic of the desire to know the wisdom of the deepest self. The desire to speak to other creatures and species and races is also innate, according to Tolkien. Treebeard allows readers to know the hearts of trees. Shadowfax, the archetypal horse, allows readers knowledge of the hearts of horses. Aragorn is the model leader that resides in the human heart, and readers feel relief in seeing him.

Tolkien's prose, as Ursula Le Guin has rightly noticed, is "like poetry in that it wants the living voice to speak it, to find its full beauty and power, its subtle music, its rhythmic vitality." Many people read the book aloud, and doing so brings out its power, for it has the power of the oral tradition to which Tolkien was keenly attuned. Listening readers are then swept along on an inner vision based on the rhythms and tone. Le Guin notes how "the narrative moves in balanced cadences in passages of epic action, with a majestic sweep reminiscent of epic poetry." The "vagueness" that offends C. N. Manlove is not due to poor writing, but to Tolkien's debt to an older tradition. Epic poems are composed in charged, formulaic phrases, allowing listeners to fill in the gaps with their imagination. The vagueness (for example in "'Dark is the water of Kheled-zâram, and cold are the springs of Kibilnala, and fair were the many-pillared halls of Khazad-dum in Elder Days before the fall of mighty kings beneath the stone'"), could seem embarrassing, but the precise description of the many-pillared halls is not missed when Tolkien is calling it up through the power of naming.

Complaints about Tolkien's ineptness with character, plot, and style may come from expectations that the novel should be more modern; readers with these expectations may not remember or know that in the epic tradition from which Tolkien drew, the characters are archetypal; the language, formulaic and suggestive, like music; the dialogue long-winded; the detail of shields, swords, history, lineage, all excessive. As to the charge that Tolkien's writing is amateur, a bloodless imitation of the grand style, one is reminded of C. S. Lewis's remark, quoted in Carpenter's biography of Tolkien, that the author was no mere scholar, for with his invented elvish languages like Sindarin and Quenya, "he had been inside language." He knew it from the roots up. Shippey's thesis in *The Road to Middle-Earth* is that Tolkien was qualified to carry on in the footsteps of the Beowulf poet: his linguistic scholarship and art are all of a piece.

Myth is a cauldron of story, Tolkien said, always boiling, to which each teller can add something. He saw himself as part of an ongoing tradition. The oddity is that he had to defend writing fantasy when it is the oldest form of storytelling. Poul Anderson remarks, "At least

Viggo Mortensen as Aragorn in the 2003 film version of The Lord of the Rings: The Return of the King *(New Line Cinema | The Kobal Collection | Pierre Vinet)*

since Homer, probably earlier and certainly not only in the West, until recent times, fantasy was the mainstream of literature." Tolkien rightly perceived that the world was starved for it. As Orson Scott Card noted, "*Ulysses* can be taught. But Lord of the Rings can only be read." This assertion implies a definition of literature as something so vital, it does not need to be studied or taken as a pill for the mind; it can be enjoyed and absorbed. Terry Pratchett agrees: "The Lord of the Rings opened me up to the rest of the library."

One cannot dismiss this novel as non-literary on the ground of its being juvenile or popular. One cannot judge its status from lesser imitations. Joseph Campbell points out that mythology is not manufactured: it is spontaneously resurrected from the psyche. Tolkien could call up archetypes through the magic of his invented languages. He said in his essay that "It was in fairy-stories that I first divined the potency of the words and the wonder of the things, such as stone, and wood, and iron; tree and grass; house and fire; bread and

wine." Whether making up languages or using them, Tolkien had the ear of a bard. He is regarded by many as the Shakespeare of modern fantasists.

Source: Susan Andersen, Critical Essay on *The Lord of the Rings*, in *Novels for Students*, Thomson Gale, 2008.

C. S. Lewis

In the following essay, Lewis asserts that the characters in The Lord of the Rings *are not simply black or white. He also expands on Tolkien's use of characters to explore the themes of heroism and the use of mythic storytelling. In addition, he elucidates another theme in the work: "that the fate of the world depends far more on the small movement than on the great."*

When I reviewed the first volume of this work, I hardly dared to hope it would have the success which I was sure it deserved. Happily I am proved wrong. There is, however, one piece of false criticism which had better be answered: the complaint that the characters are all either black or white. Since the climax of Volume I was mainly concerned with the struggle between good and evil in the mind of Boromir, it is not easy to see how anyone could have said this. I will hazard a guess. "How shall a man judge what to do in such times?" asks someone in Volume II. "As he has ever judged," comes the reply. "Good and ill have not changed ... nor are they one thing among Elves and Dwarves and another among Men."

This is the basis of the whole Tolkinian world. I think some readers, seeing (and disliking) this rigid demarcation of black and white, imagine they have seen a rigid demarcation between black and white people. Looking at the squares, they assume (in defiance of the facts) that all the pieces must be making bishops' moves which confine them to one color. But even such readers will hardly brazen it out through the two last volumes. Motives, even on the right side, are mixed. Those who are now traitors usually began with comparatively innocent intentions. Heroic Rohan and imperial Gondor are partly diseased. Even the wretched Sméagol, till quite late in the story, has good impulses; and, by a tragic paradox, what finally pushes him over the brink is an unpremeditated speech by the most selfless character of all.

There are two Books in each volume and now that all six are before us the very high architectural quality of the romance is revealed. Book I builds up the main theme. In Book II that theme, enriched with much retrospective material, continues. Then comes the change. In III and V the fate of the company, now divided, becomes entangled with a huge complex of forces which are grouping and regrouping themselves in relation to Mordor. The main theme, isolated from this, occupies IV and the early part of VI (the latter part of course giving all the resolutions). But we are never allowed to forget the intimate connection between it and the rest. On the one hand, the whole world is going to the war; the story rings with galloping hoofs, trumpets, steel on steel. On the other, very far away, two tiny, miserable figures creep (like mice on a slag heap) through the twilight of Mordor. And all the time we know that the fate of the world depends far more on the small movement than on the great. This is a structural invention of the highest order: it adds immensely to the pathos, irony, and grandeur of the tale.

This main theme is not to be treated in those jocular, whimsical tones now generally used by reviewers of "juveniles." It is entirely serious: the growing anguish, the drag of the Ring on the neck, the ineluctable conversion of hobbit into hero in conditions which exclude all hope of fame or fear of infamy. Without the relief offered by the more crowded and bustling Books it would be hardly tolerable.

Yet those Books are not in the least inferior. Of picking out great moments, such as the cockcrow at the Siege of Gondor, there would be no end; I will mention two general, and totally different, excellences. One, surprisingly, is realism. This war has the very quality of the war my generation knew. It is all here: the endless, unintelligible movement, the sinister quiet of the front when "everything is now ready," the flying civilians, the lively, vivid friendships, the background of something like despair and the merry foreground, and such heavensent windfalls as a *cache* of choice tobacco "salvaged" from a ruin. The author has told us elsewhere that his taste for fairy-tale was wakened into maturity by active service; that, no doubt, is why we can say of his war scenes (quoting Gimli the Dwarf), "'There is good rock here. This country has tough bones.'" The other excellence is that no individual, and no species, seems to exist only for the sake of the plot. All exist in their own right and would have been worth creating for their mere flavor even if they had been irrelevant. Treebeard would have served any other author (if any other could have conceived him) for a whole book. His eyes are "filled up with ages of memory and long, slow, steady thinking." Through those ages his name has grown with him, so that he cannot now tell it; it would, by now, take too long to pronounce. When he learns that the thing they are standing on is a hill, he complains that this is but "a hasty word" for that which has so much history in it.

How far Treebeard can be regarded as a "portrait of the artist" must remain doubtful; but when he hears that some people want to identify the Ring with the hydrogen bomb, and Mordor with Russia, I think he might call it a "hasty" word. How long do people think a world like his takes to grow? Do they think it can be done as quickly as a modern nation changes its Public Enemy Number One or as modern scientists invent new weapons? When Tolkien began there was probably no nuclear fission and the contemporary incarnation of Mordor was a good deal nearer our shores. But the text itself teaches us that Sauron is eternal; the war of the Ring is only one of a thousand wars against him. Everytime we shall be wise to fear his ultimate victory, after which there will be "no more songs." Again and again we shall have good evidence that "the wind is setting East, and the withering of all woods may be drawing near." Every time we win we shall know that our victory is impermanent. If we insist on asking for the moral of the story, that is its moral: a recall from facile optimism and wailing pessimism alike, to that hard, yet not quite desperate, insight into Man's unchanging predicament by which heroic ages have lived. It is here that the Norse affinity is strongest: hammerstrokes, but with compassion.

"But why," some ask, "why, if you have a serious comment to make on the real life of men, must you do it by talking about a phantasmagoric never-never-land of your own?" Because, I take it, one of the main things the author wants to say is that the real life of men is of that mythical and heroic quality. One can see the principle at work in his characterization. Much that in a realistic work would be done by "character delineation" is here done simply by making the character an elf, a dwarf, or a hobbit. The imagined beings have their insides on the outside; they are visible souls. And Man as a whole, Man pitted against the universe, have we seen him at all till we see that he is like a hero in a fairytale? In the book Éomer rashly contrasts "the green earth" with "legends." Aragorn replies that the green earth itself is "a mighty matter of legend."

The value of the myth is that it takes all the things we know and restores to them the rich significance which has been hidden by "the veil of familiarity." The child enjoys his cold meat, otherwise dull to him, by pretending it is buffalo, just killed with his own bow and arrow. And the child is wise. The real meat comes back to him more savory for having been dipped in a story; you might say that only then is it real meat. If you are tired of the real landscape, look at it in a mirror. By putting bread, gold, horse, apple, or the very roads into a myth, we do not retreat from reality: we rediscover it. As long as the story lingers in our mind, the real things are more themselves. This book applies the treatment not only to bread or apple but to good and evil, to our endless perils, our anguish, and our joys. By dipping them in myth we see them

more clearly. I do not think he could have done it in any other way.

The book is too original and too opulent for any final judgment on a first reading. But we know at once that it has done things to us. We are not quite the same men. And though we must ration ourselves in our rereadings, I have little doubt that the book will soon take its place among the indispensables.

Source: C. S. Lewis, "The Dethronement of Power," in *Tolkien and the Critics*, edited by Neil D. Isaacs and Rose A. Zimbardo, University of Notre Dame Press, 1968, pp. 12–16.

SOURCES

Anderson, Poul, "Awakening the Elves," in *Meditations on Middle-Earth*, St. Martin's Griffin, 2001, p. 26.

Auden, W. H., "At the End of the Quest, Victory," in *A Tolkien Scrapbook*, edited by Alida Becker, Running Press, 1978, p. 44; originally published in *New York Times Book Review*, January 22, 1956.

Campbell, Joseph, *The Hero with a Thousand Faces*, Princeton University Press,1949, pp. 4, 39.

Card, Orson Scott, "How Tolkien Means," in *Meditations on Middle-Earth*, St. Martin's Griffin, 2001, p. 160.

Carpenter, Humphrey, *J. R. R. Tolkien: A Biography*, Houghton Mifflin, 2000, p.138.

Isaacs, Neil D., "On the Possibility of Writing Tolkien Criticism," in *Tolkien and the Critics: Essays on J. R. R. Tolkien's "The Lord of the Rings,"* edited by Neil D. Isaacs and Rose A. Zimbardo, University of Notre Dame Press, 1968.

Le Guin, Ursula K., "Rhythmic Pattern in *The Lord of the Rings*," in *Meditations on Middle-Earth*, St. Martin's Griffin, 2001, pp. 102, 103.

Lewis, C. S., "Tolkien's *The Lord of the Rings*," in *Of This and Other Worlds*, edited by Walter Hooper, Collins, 1982, p.112.

Manlove, C. N., "J. R. R. Tolkien (1892–1973) and *The Lord of the Rings*," in *Modern Fantasy: Five Studies*, Cambridge University Press, 1975, p. 194.

Pratchett, Terry, "Cult Classic," in *Meditations on Middle-Earth*, St. Martin's Griffin, 2001, p. 80.

Shippey, T. A., *J. R. R. Tolkien: Author of the Century*, Houghton Mifflin, 2000, p. 125.

Tolkien, J. R. R., *The Lord of the Rings*, Houghton Mifflin, 1994.

——, "On Fairy-Stories," in *The Monsters and the Critics and Other Essays*, edited by Christopher Tolkien, George Allen & Unwin, 1983, pp. 109, 116, 132, 138, 143.

Wilson, Edmund, "Oo, Those Awful Orcs," in *A Tolkien Scrapbook*, edited by Alida Becker, Running Press, 1978, p. 55; originally published in *Nation*, April 14, 1956.

FURTHER READING

Carpenter, Humphrey, *The Inklings: C. S. Lewis, J. R. R. Tolkien, Charles Williams, and their Friends*, Houghton Mifflin, 1979.

Carpenter interweaves biographical background about the three friends with actual reconstructions of meetings of the Inklings, a club of Oxford professors and writers who read their work aloud to one another. In this circle, Tolkien tested drafts of *The Lord of the Rings*.

———, *J. R. R. Tolkien: A Biography*, Houghton Mifflin, 1987.

Carpenter is able to take the seemingly boring life of a professor and illuminate it as the rich leaf mold of an artist's inner world. He integrates the main events of Tolkien's life with the themes and content of his books. This is the official biography; Carpenter was given unrestricted access to papers and interviewed friends and family. It is very entertaining, a glimpse into both the internal and external life of an Oxford don.

Carpenter, Humphrey, and Christopher Tolkien, *The Letters of J. R. R. Tolkien*, Houghton Mifflin, 2000.

The letters of Tolkien illuminate like no commentator can the richness of the novel. This collection is like another appendix based on readers' questions with many details of the story further developed. His letters explain his background myths and the characters' fates in the novel.

Haber, Karen, ed., *Meditations on Middle-Earth*, St. Martin's Griffin, 2001.

In this anthology, major science fiction and fantasy writers, such as Ursula Le Guin, Raymond Feist, Poul Anderson, Terry Pratchett, George R. R. Martin, and many others, tell how they discovered Tolkien and how he inspired their desire to write. The book is informative in many directions at once, giving deep insights into Tolkien's work and its legacy, as well as into the creative process of writing fantasy. The book was nominated for the 2002 Hugo and Locus awards.

Hammond, Wayne G., and Christina Scull, *J. R. R. Tolkien: Artist and Illustrator*, Houghton Mifflin, 1995.

Tolkien is recognized as an illustrator as well as a writer, and though his own drawings appear in books and calendars, many have never been published before this publication. This fascinating book shows the range of his subjects and how he used drawings and maps to think out his stories. Such details as coats of arms and Numenorean fabric design are included.

Perkins, Agnes, and Helen Hill, "The Corruption of Power," in *A Tolkien Compass*, edited by Jared Lobdell, Open Court, 2003, pp. 55–65.

This article discusses how even the desire for power corrupts the characters in *The Lord of the Rings*. The authors conclude that the theme is timely because the demand for power in contemporary politics continues to increase from all sides, and the dangers need to be spelled out. The other articles in this anthology are equally helpful.

March

GERALDINE BROOKS
2005

Geraldine Brooks and her husband moved in the 1990s to a small town in Virginia that appeared to have been part of the battlefield of the Civil War. Brooks found bullet holes in the nearby church and unearthed a Union soldier's belt buckle in her yard. The town had been predominantly abolitionist and Quaker but was situated in a Confederate state. The clash of interests in the area along with its history sparked Brooks's interest in the war, especially in the ideals for which each side fought.

Her study brought her to Louisa May Alcott's classic novel *Little Women* (1868) and an interest in the part of the story that was left out: John March's experiences in the war. In her novel *March* (2005), Brooks envisions what happens to Mr. March after he leaves his family to serve as a chaplain for the Union army. As she imagines the story of the March family, Brooks adds a more somber tone to her depiction of the idealistic father and the harsh truths he must face about the institution of slavery and the fight to abolish it. The novel traces twenty years in March's life, chronicling his journey from innocence to experience as he discovers the darkness at the heart of humankind and in his own soul.

AUTHOR BIOGRAPHY

Geraldine Brooks was born in Sydney, Australia, in 1955. She attended Sydney University and in

Geraldine Brooks *(© Rune Hellestad | Corbis)*

1983 earned a master's degree in journalism at Columbia University in New York. While living in Sydney, she worked as a reporter for the *Sydney Morning Herald.*

Brooks served as a correspondent for the *Wall Street Journal* during the late 1980s and 1990s, covering stories in the Middle East, Africa, and the Balkans, and in 1990 during the Persian Gulf War. During this time, she was able to study the world of Muslim women, an experience that inspired her first non-fiction book, *Nine Parts of Desire: The Hidden World of Islamic Women* (1995). The book was highly praised for its realistic portrait that provides impressive insight into the lives of these women. Her second non-fiction work, *Foreign Correspondence: A Pen Pal's Journey from Down Under to All Over* (1998), is a memoir of her childhood in Sydney, Australia, and of the important effect that international pen pals had on her sense of self.

Brooks turned to fiction in 2001 with the critically acclaimed novel, *Year of Wonders: A*

MEDIA ADAPTATIONS

- As of 2007, an audio version of the novel, read by Richard Easton, was available from Audiobooks America. No film versions had been made.

Novel of the Plague (2001), which dramatizes the effects of the bubonic plague on an English town in the seventeenth century. The subsequent novel, the Pulitzer Prize-winning *March* (2005), cemented her reputation as an important figure in the literary world.

In addition to the Pulitzer, Brooks has won several awards. She received the Hal Boyle Award, Overseas Press Club of America in 1990, for the best daily newspaper or wire service reporting from abroad. In 2005, the *Washington Post* named *March* one of the five best novels of the year. In 2006, Brooks received a fellowship from the Radcliffe Institute of Advanced Study at Harvard University.

In 1984, Brooks married fellow Pulitzer Prize winner, Tony Horwitz. As of 2007, the couple had one son.

PLOT SUMMARY

Chapter One: Virginia Is a Hard Road

March opens with lines from a letter written by John March, a forty-year-old company chaplain for the Union army, on October 21, 1861, to his wife, Marmee, and to his daughters, after the Battle of Ball's Bluff in Virginia. March is exhausted but has promised to write her everyday. He admits that although he misses her comforting hand, he does not want her there, and he will not write her the truth about the war.

March watches the burial party collect bodies, claiming, "I had no orders, and so placed myself where I believed I could do most good," praying with the wounded. He recalls that during the battle, he tried to help a young Union soldier cross the river to safety, but the boy was shot in the process and drowned. Some of the men, including March, made it to an island in the river where March now thinks about the day's events and the rotting bodies that surround him. As he makes his way to the army field hospital, he recognizes that it is Clement's house.

Chapter Two: A Wooden Nutmeg

When he was eighteen, March peddled trinkets and books throughout Virginia. At one plantation, he met a slave named Grace who impressed him with her regal manner and beauty. She brought him into the kitchen for a meal and later to meet the master, Augustus Clement, who took an immediate liking to March and his passion for learning. Clement invited him to stay as long as he liked and peruse his well-stocked library. The two men talked long into the night about the books that they had read, enjoying each other's company.

The next day, March met the frail Mrs. Clement who had not been well since a fall from her horse. March noted Grace's kind treatment of her mistress, to whom she read every afternoon. Mrs. Clement explained that Grace was born on the plantation and was given to her as a wedding gift. Grace later told him that Clement sold her mother south soon after she was born.

That evening March and Mr. Clement discussed slavery, the latter insisting that slaves should be treated decently but not trusted because they are prone to such vices as "laziness, deceit, debauchery, [and] theft." He considered them children, "morally speaking," who occasionally needed to be whipped "for their good, as well as [their masters]." When Clement convinced March that slaves benefit "from the moral example of the master," March felt fortunate to be "even briefly, a part of this higher way of life."

After Prudence, the cook's daughter, showed aptitude and interest in learning to read, March drew some letters in the ashes of the hearth, which frightened Grace. She explained to March that for the past ten years teaching a slave to read had been against the law. Later, however, Grace reconsidered and asked March to teach Prudence to read.

March, who had always yearned to be a teacher, was touched by Grace's request and considered raising the issue with Clement. One evening, when March asked him whether one of his slaves could be taught to handle some of the

accounts at the plantation, Clement reproached him, insisting that educating a slave would inspire a violent rebellion. The next morning, March decided to begin teaching Prudence surreptitiously a few nights a week.

During the next two weeks, Prudence proved herself to be an apt pupil as March became a capable teacher. One evening, after drinking too much wine, March kissed Grace who then warned him that "it's not wise" to do so. Later, he was awakened by Clement's manager who discovered evidence that he had been teaching Prudence. Grace took responsibility and as a result was cruelly whipped, which March was forced to observe.

Chapter Three: Scars

March writes his next letter to his wife on November 1, 1861, thanking her for her letter and a parcel that she has sent. He thinks back to his wanderings after he left the Clement estate and remembers one day praying in a church. Outside the window, slaves were being auctioned. When the pastor called for donations for missions into Africa to a congregation that ignored the injustices occurring just a few feet away, March was sickened by the hypocrisy and left. During the next year, March made good money on his sales, which eventually he invested and turned into a sizable fortune.

At present, he works with a surgeon at the Union camp and offers comfort to dying men. Only three hundred and fifty are left out of more than six hundred. He discovers that Grace is helping the surgeon and tending to Clement, who has become a feeble old man. She explains that after his wife died, Clement refused to give Grace up, and later she admits that he is her father. After Clement's son was disfigured in a hunting accident, Clement started a slow decline in health. March's feelings of guilt and lust for her overwhelm him and the two embrace.

Chapter Four: A Little Hell

While he is stationed outside Harper's Ferry, March writes Marmee on January 15, 1862, about his position as chaplain and about how some soldiers with a stricter religious attitude are perplexed by his unconventional beliefs. He explains that the previous night, as they were poised for battle, he gave a sermon on John Brown and his abolitionist activities.

March remembers the first time he met Marmee, in her brother's church where he had been invited to speak. When he saw her in the congregation, he was immediately struck with her intensity and intelligence. That evening at dinner with her and her brother, March discovered that their zeal for reform matched his own.

As he waits for the fighting to begin near Harper's Ferry, March sees many injustices. A major commands troops to burn a town after one of his men is killed there. When March criticizes the action, the major refuses to speak to him further. March later finds soldiers harassing a woman and her daughter and destroying her property. When he reports them, the colonel barely responds. The colonel then suggests that March resign his post because he "can't seem to get on with anyone." When March resists, the colonel insists, noting that the surgeon has seen him with Grace. The colonel wants him reassigned to the "problem of the contraband," the displaced former slaves. March is worried that he will bring shame to Marmee if she discovers his relationship with Grace, and so he agrees.

Chapter Five: A Better Pencil
March thinks back to his relocation to Concord, where Marmee is staying with her invalid father, under the pretext of searching for an investment. His uncle had found him a young man who had invented a better pencil. March stayed with the Thoreaus and their son, Henry David Thoreau, a taciturn person who felt most at home in nature.

One evening, Mrs. Thoreau, an ardent abolitionist, invited Ralph Waldo Emerson, his wife, and Marmee, who was a friend of her daughters, for dinner. After Emerson rebuked Marmee for endangering her father with her abolitionist activities, Marmee flew into a rage, insisting that Emerson was doing little to help the plight of blacks. March was shocked by her outburst and thought that she needed a man to help her govern her temper.

That night, March came across Marmee in the woods. She broke down as she told him that the slave she was trying to help was caught and branded. March's attempts at consolation led to a consummation of their feelings for each other. Less than two weeks later they were married, and within nine months, Marmee gave birth to Margaret, the first of their four daughters.

Chapter Six: Yankee Leavening
March writes to Marmee on March 10, 1862, while aboard the *Hetty G*, a federal ram boat,

on his way to Oak Landing, a southern plantation that is now being run by Ethan Canning, an Illinois attorney. Canning has a year's lease on the property, which he is trying to restore and make profitable. When Marsh arrives, he finds the plantation in utter disarray. The cotton fields are overgrown, and the house has been picked clean by federal soldiers and rebel irregulars. After finding a sick boy and rescuing a man whom Canning had confined in a well for punishment, March confronts Canning about the treatment of the ex-slaves on his property, none of whom is being paid for his labor.

Canning explains that there is no doctor available to treat the sick, and the man whom he punished had slaughtered a hog and fed it to his grown sons who then joined the Confederates. The 167 ex-slaves on the plantation need to be fed, and so they all must work, he insists, to harvest the cotton crop. Their pay will come after the cotton is sold. March determines to contact abolitionists in Concord and Boston to help fund the running of the plantation. He feels guilty about not being able to help: He has lost his fortune, which has impoverished his family and has caused him a tremendous sense of guilt.

Chapter Seven: Bread and Shelter
March thinks back to the time when he and Marmee were newlyweds and when he renovated their home, which included a space in which slaves could hide on their way north to Canada. They spent a good deal of time with Emerson and Thoreau. One evening, Marmee lost her temper with March's aunt over the issue of slavery. Later, they heard a speech by John Brown, the famous abolitionist, who spoke at a Concord church. Brown stirred Marmee's passions, and she and March invited him back to their home where he outlined his Adirondack project, which helped indigent blacks become landowners. Prodded in part by his jealously over his wife's attentions to Brown, March turned over his fortune to Brown for his project. The land Brown bought proved, however, to be worthless, and much of the money was rerouted into arms.

With their finances depleted, March was forced to sell off his possessions and move to a smaller home. Aunt March and Marmee had another heated argument, which caused the former to refuse to talk to the family for ten years. When March confronted Marmee about her temper after she lashed out at him, she agreed that it had gotten out of hand and resolved to work on controlling her emotions. Ten years later, when Jo ran into Aunt March on the street, Jo charmed the elderly woman who hired her as a companion. Meg had already acquired a position as a governess to help out with the family's finances.

Chapter Eight: Learning's Altar

March writes to Marmee from Oak Landing, on March 30, 1862, the day the cotton ginning begins. He tells her that he has set up his schoolhouse and that the workers are enthusiastic learners. Later, March goes to town to get news of the war and comes across a group of Union scouts. One causes a young black child, Jimse, to scald his hand. March takes the child back to the plantation, followed by the child's mother Zannah, and dresses his wound. He is later told that Zannah never speaks because her tongue was cut out by two whites who had molested her. March notes his absolute pleasure in teaching, even though it is exhausting work.

Chapter Nine: First Blossom

On May 10, 1862, March writes to Marmee that all are rejoicing on the plantation this day because the cotton has been safely shipped to market, and they have received packages from Concord, filled with clothing, food, and medicines. When payment arrives, Canning has little left after handing out wages to the blacks. But some of the workers bring him high quality cotton that they had saved and hidden from the soldiers, which enables Canning to pay his expenses. That night, March celebrates with the workers.

Chapter Ten: Saddleback Fever

The next morning March awakes with saddleback fever, so called because the return of health is only temporary before the fever strikes again. Canning and the workers nurse him back to health. When he recovers, Canning tells him that the Union army is reducing the number of soldiers in the nearby town. They all now fear that the Confederates will try to take the land and return the workers to slavery. March, however, refuses to leave, even though Canning warns him that the Confederates kill abolitionists.

Chapter Eleven: Tolling Bells

March recalls the details of John Brown's raid on Harper's Ferry and his resulting martyrdom in the North. The incident, however, had a negative effect on blacks in the South and caused a slowdown of the number of escaped slaves on the Underground Railroad. He remembers when they hid a young, pregnant girl for a few weeks. One evening, when March and Marmee were out, the constable came to look for the girl but Beth, one of their daughters, sent him away. A year later, war was declared, and during an impromptu sermon given to a group of young men preparing to leave, March decided to join them in their fight.

Chapter Twelve: Red Moon

March's fears are realized when one evening, Confederate soldiers raid the plantation. March hides while Canning is captured and tortured. One of the soldiers threatens to kill a worker if March does not come out of hiding, but March's fear holds him back, and the soldier decapitates the worker, which fills March with overwhelming guilt. The soldiers burn the buildings and round up several black men, women, and children and leave with them along with Canning, who has had both knees shattered by bullets. March follows at a safe distance, wondering how he can ever face his family and endure his shame.

After the group arrives at camp, March tries to help Zannah when a soldier attacks her as she tries to save her child. Jesse, one of the workers, stops him, insisting "Now ain't no time to make a move." He tells March to wait with him until nightfall when they might have a chance to free some of the workers.

Chapter Thirteen: A Good Kind Man

Jesse explains that he "put a little something" in the corn liquor the soldiers stole from the plantation and that they will wait until the men feel its effects. When the first soldier, sickened by the liquor, goes off into the woods, Jesse kills him and takes his weapons. March refuses to kill the next one but takes the saber from Jesse so that he can free the workers. He overhears the soldiers planning to ransom Canning, but the latter insists that he has no family to pay for him. Just as a soldier is about to kill Canning, March rushes out from his hiding place and insists that he has a fiancée. Canning, however, admits that the woman died of consumption a year ago. Determining that he will decide their fate in the morning, the major orders March and Canning tied up.

Soon, after most of the soldiers have fallen into a drunken sleep, he sees Zannah, whom Jesse had helped to escape, cut the other captives' ropes. A cracking branch draws fire from one of the guards and the others awaken and recapture the workers, but not before killing some, including Canning, and wounding March. After March lies unconscious for a time, Zannah appears and tells him that she is the only one who got away. March loses consciousness again, and when he awakes, he finds himself in a Union hospital. A nurse tells him that Zannah risked her life to bring him there.

Chapter Fourteen: Blank Hospital

The narrative switches to Marmee's voice after she has received a note from Blank Hospital in Washington, informing her that March is gravely ill. As she sits by his bedside, waiting for him to regain consciousness, she thinks that "it was folly to let him go" and that he should not have left his family. She also blames him in part for plunging the family into poverty.

When she first sees him in the hospital, she does not recognize him due to his emaciated, broken body, which is suffering from fever and pneumonia. When he wakes, he is delirious, ranting about people and events that she does not recognize. She can only make out his cries for forgiveness.

Chapter Fifteen: Reunion

The next morning Marmee tries to find someone in the hospital to care for her husband, but the number of patients overwhelms the small number of staff. She has an argument with a cold, curt nurse and ends up throwing a bowl of soup in her face. Marmee recognizes that if March is going to survive, she will have to care for him. An orderly who has observed the row directs her to the nurse who knows more details about what happened to March. The nurse turns out to be Grace, who has cared for him since he arrived in the hospital. When she observes the intimate interaction between March and Grace, Marmee suspects that he has been unfaithful to her.

Chapter Sixteen: River of Fire

When March is too weak to speak to her and allay her fears about Grace, Marmee finds herself living in the home of the hospital surgeon and his wife, who have grown to love her as their own daughter. Grace tells Marmee of the history Grace and March have together, her words

striking Marmee "like a fist." Marmee recognizes the deception of his letters and understands that he lost his first position because he had been caught with Grace. She is incensed that this woman is providing the truth about her husband and her marriage. When Marmee insists, "He loves you," Grace explains that he loves only the "idea" of her, of a liberated black woman. Marmee wonders whether she will be able to forgive him "for the years of silence, and the letters filled with lies."

Chapter Seventeen: Reconstruction

Grace tells Marmee that March's distressed spirit is preventing him from recovering and that Marmee must find a way to help relieve his guilt and to convince him that he is needed at home. Marmee thinks about how he has failed her "in so many ways" and wounded her profoundly, but soon she becomes convinced that whatever it costs her, she will bring him home. Gradually, March's condition improves to the point that he is able to tell Marmee about everything that happened to him as she tries to fill him with hope for the future. March, however, insists that he needs to do more to help others who are suffering in the war, a sentiment Marmee recognizes as his effort to assuage his own guilt over his actions on the plantation. She accuses him of being proud and insists that his duty now lies with his family. March admits that he despises himself. Later, Marmee recognizes that she still loves him.

Chapter Eighteen: State of Grace

March's voice returns, expressing the guilt he feels over the lives that have been lost. He learns that Beth has come down with scarlet fever and that Marmee has been called back to Concord to tend to her. In a note she leaves for him, she reiterates the family's need for him and implores him to return to them as soon as possible. After March expresses the hope that he can work with her to help the injured, Grace tries to convince him to stop wallowing in his guilt. When he insists that she cannot know how he feels, she tells him that she had played a part in the accident that caused Clement's son's death, after the latter tried to have sexual relations with her. She tells him that he must learn to live with his guilt as she has with hers. She insists that blacks must learn to manage their own destiny and that he should go home where he can help prepare northern whites to see blacks as equals. March understands that his daughters, and not Grace, need him now.

Chapter Nineteen: Concord

March returns home, feeling like an imposter since he has changed so radically, and finds that Beth has recovered. He still pines for Grace, however, recognizing that he will never see her again. Surrounded by his loving family, March decides, "I would do my best to live in the quick world, but the ghosts of the dead would be ever at hand."

CHARACTERS

John Brown

John Brown is based on the famous abolitionist who raided the armory at Harper's Ferry and was subsequently hanged. He is passionate about his cause and gives stirring speeches to his followers. He does not appear to be a good business man, however, when he loses the fortune that March has given to him.

Ethan Canning

Ethan Canning is an Illinois attorney who has leased Oak Landing, the southern plantation where March comes to teach ex-slaves. When March arrives, he observes Canning's cruel treatment of his workers. Yet March soon discovers a more complex side to the man. Canning explains that his quite realistic fear of ruin causes him to force the blacks to work continuously. He recognizes that the neglected crops as well as the constant threat from rebels may cause the plantation to fail.

He reveals a basic decency as he is influenced by March's own. March notes a kinder side to Canning, describing him as open to suggestion, fair-minded, and grateful for the hard work of his laborers. Canning allows the workers time off to attend school and to share in the goods sent by northern abolitionists. He also warns March to leave when the Union army reduces its troops in the nearby town, knowing that they habitually kill abolitionists. His courage emerges when he refuses to tell the soldiers where to find March and is tortured and later when he dies as a result of trying to save March's life.

Augustus Clement

Augustus Clement, a well-educated southern plantation owner, is generous to March upon his arrival, insisting that he stay as long as he likes. Clement enjoys discussing books and ideas with the younger man. Clement appears to be a decent, intelligent man who treats his slaves well, but when March presses him on the issue of emancipation, Clement reveals his racism. He considers blacks to be children who need the firm hand of a white master to keep them in line. His cruel nature is evident when he sells Grace's mother as soon as Grace is born and when he orders Grace whipped for asking March to teach Prudence to read.

Grace Clement

The biracial daughter of August Clement, Grace Clement appears proud when March first meets her, but she soon proves that she is aptly named. March commends her neat appearance and intelligent, well-spoken manner. Her kind treatment of Mrs. Clement and later of Mr. Clement almost appears too good to be true, especially when she refuses to leave the latter even after he has ordered her beaten. Readers see her, however, through March's eyes; she appears saintly to him, an idea, as Grace notes, of Africa itself and of the promise of equality. She tries to force him to see by the end of the novel that she too has faults. She was involved in the accident that disfigured Clement's son, who had tried to rape her. Grace suggests she might have caused the gun to discharge and admits that she rejoiced in his death.

Mrs. Clement

Mrs. Clement, Augustus Clement's wife, has been an invalid since a fall from a horse and since then has been terrified of the world. She has accepted Grace as a constant companion and feels a real affection for her, although she also feels complete ownership of her.

Ralph Waldo Emerson

Based on the historical person, Ralph Waldo Emerson is a well-known writer and philosopher. He and his wife are good friends of the Thoreaus, with whom March stays for a time. Emerson's unwillingness to speak out against slavery causes Marmee to lose her temper with him. Later, however, he becomes more active in his condemnation of the slave system.

Jesse

Jesse, one of the workers who initially escapes the Confederates after they raid the plantation, reveals his intelligence when he spikes his moonshine with poison, knowing the soldiers will take it. He also shows his kindness and courage when he tries to save March's life.

Aunt March

Aunt March, March's sister, is a cold, unforgiving woman who refuses to speak to the March family after Marmee loses her temper with her. She relents, however, revealing a softer side when she runs into Jo one day and decides to hire her as a companion. Later, she shows her generosity and capacity to forgive when she gives Marmee money to go to Washington to care for March. She speaks her mind, as does Marmee, and sees the reality of situations behind the idealistic surface; she is the only one who upbraids March for deciding to enlist.

Beth March

Painfully shy Beth March, one of the four March daughters, shows great courage when she stands up to the local sheriff who comes looking for a runaway slave.

Jo March

Jo March, one of the four March daughters, inherits Marmee's temper. She shows her good heart, though, when she cuts her beautiful hair to raise money for Marmee's trip to Washington to care for March.

John March

John March is an idealist, with firm convictions, especially his commitment to abolitionism. He also is a nonconformist who is not afraid to show his independence in thought and action. This side of his personality is revealed in his style of preaching. He rejects the traditional Calvinist sermons full of fire and damnation and also the idea of original sin. His God is more personal. He dismisses the rituals of organized, conventional religion. He aspires to aid and give comfort to soldiers, but his earnestness and honesty often cause them more consternation than comfort. A Union corporal to whom he complains about some soldiers' rough treatment of southerners notes, "your duty is to bring the men comfort. . . . And yet all you seem to do is make people *un*comfortable."

March is a kind and loving father and husband, although his acceptance of traditional male and female roles causes him to try to restrain his wife's emotions and behavior. He is also generous, placing his desire to help the abolitionist cause above his desire for material comfort. His strong moral sense is triggered by the hypocrisy he perceives in churchgoers who can raise money for African missions but ignore the sale of blacks outside the church door. When he enlists in the Union army, he displays the courage of his convictions. He becomes confused, however, when his firm set of beliefs is shaken by the realities of the war. Aunt March thinks him a fool when he enlists, a sentiment shared to a lesser degree by Marmee. March's ideals sometimes blind him to the consequences of his actions.

Margaret Day March

See Marmee March

Marmee March

Margaret Day March, called Marmee, has a sometimes explosive temper, which she unleashes on those whom she thinks insult her or her convictions. Her passionate nature and zest for life attract March, even though her temper troubles him. She is as devoted to the abolitionist cause as he is, and like him she has the courage to act on her beliefs, serving as a conductor on the Underground Railroad. She is intelligent, quickly picking up on the nuances of an argument, and self-assured. Her unconventional opinion of women's rights is sometimes contradicted by her husband. She does, however, succumb at times to the pressure to conform, as she notes in her quiet acceptance of March's determination to go to war.

Prudence

Prudence is the cook's daughter on the Clement plantation. When she shows a quick mind and a strong desire to learn, March teaches her to read, which is against the law. When they are discovered, Grace takes responsibility and is whipped for it.

Henry David Thoreau

Based on the historical person, Henry David Thoreau is a young man when March stays with the Thoreau family while courting Marmee. Thoreau would rather be walking by his beloved Walden Pond than sitting in the parlor exchanging pleasantries with guests.

Mrs. Thoreau

Mrs. Thoreau, Henry's mother, is a passionate abolitionist. She and her husband are good friends with Marmee and the Emersons.

Zannah

Zannah is a young female ex-slave at Oak Landing, who has had her tongue cut out by two white men after she refused their sexual advances.

TOPICS FOR FURTHER STUDY

- Read Stephen Crane's *The Red Badge of Courage* and compare its theme of bravery and cowardice to that in *March*. Does Brooks raise any new points about what defines these terms and the effect that the acknowledgement of cowardice has on an individual? Write a comparison and contrast paper on the two novels, focusing on the authors' treatment of this subject.

- The flashbacks in the novel would be difficult to depict in film. How would you solve this problem? Write a section of the novel that includes a scene from the present and one from the past as a screenplay, noting how you would make a smooth transition between the parts.

- Research the subject of race relations in the North during the Civil War. How did attitudes towards blacks compare with those in the South. Did those attitudes change significantly immediately after the war? Present a PowerPoint presentation on your findings.

- Write a short story that focuses on the March family five years after the end of the novel. How do you envision March dealing with his guilt? Would he and Marmee be able to regain the strong relationship they once had?

She displays a fierce love for her son Jimse. She also shows great strength and courage when she carries March to the Union hospital.

THEMES

A Woman's Place

Both Marmee and Grace suffer from the restrictions placed on American women during the nineteenth century. The difference is Marmee, a middle-class white woman, is able to voice her objections. She notes how difficult it is for women to gain a meaningful education, that they "are subjected to a course of study [music, drawing, languages] that is stultifying, oppressive, crippling rather than enhancing to [their] moral integrity and intellectual growth." They are not allowed to engage in arguments or show any strong emotion. Marmee tries to ignore this tradition but is criticized for doing so, especially by her husband. When they first marry, she determines that if she has daughters, she will raise them to be free spirits.

Marmee tries without much success to control her emotions and actions. When she gets angry at Emerson's apparent lack of conviction regarding the abolitionist cause, March wonders, "who could have imagined this gently bred young woman to be so entirely bereft of the powers of self-government." He determines that it is his place to teach her to stay within feminine boundaries, noting "perhaps...a husband's gentle guidance could assist her in the battle against such a dangerous bosom enemy." He wonders "what sort of wife, what sort of mother" would she be if she were allowed to give free vent to her emotions. Yet the irony is lost on him when he enjoys her passionate nature as it turns sexual in the woods. Looking back on their relationship, he thinks, "I tried to teach her something about *her* new place, giving her to understand, with gentle hints and loving guidance, that what might be considered lapses born of high spirits in a young maiden were in no way proper in one who was now a mother and a wife." The tacit assumption is that it is the male's prerogative and responsibility to educated the female, that he has the superior awareness and knowledge.

Marmee recognizes the limitations of her power to break out of traditional roles. Facing Jo's similarly intense temper, Marmee justifies her refusal to curb her daughter by declaring "the world would crush [Jo's] spirit soon enough." Later, she regrets keeping quiet about her feelings regarding March's enlistment. She claims, "It was folly to let him go," but she recognizes that "one is not permitted to say such a thing; it is just one more in the long list of things that a woman must not say." She insists, "I only let him do to me what men have ever done to women: march off to empty glory and hollow acclaim and leave us behind to pick up the pieces." Those pieces include her sense of betrayal when March lies to her about the reality of the war and his relationship with

March is based on the novel Little Women, *by Louisa May Alcott, pictured here* (© Bettmann / Corbis)

Grace. His need to protect her from the truth suggests both his hypocrisy and his assumption that she is incapable of handling it. Brooks adds a nice touch of irony in the fact that March works so hard at trying to free blacks from slavery, while at the same time he is blind to restrictions placed on his own wife. While working on behalf of slaves, he does not examine his own patriarchal and paternalistic thinking.

Rebellion against Tradition

March rebels against traditional religious practices and beliefs when he rejects the notion of original sin and finds more spirituality in nature than he does in a church. Marmee, although restricted by convention, is also able to exercise some resistance to social dictates about the behavior of women. She has grown up with the freedom to voice her opinions, an urge that does not appear to have been checked by her parents. She rejects the traditional education offered to women and has learned on her own about a range of subjects that conventionally would

be considered in the realm of male knowledge (that information only appropriate for men to know).

Marmee also refuses to give in to her husband's desire to put her in her place. After her outburst at Aunt March, she insists to him, "You stifle me! You crush me! You preach emancipation, and yet you enslave me, in the most fundamental way." She asserts her right for equality when she asks, "Am I not to have the freedom to express myself, in my own home? . . . I am your belittled woman, and I am tired of it," insisting, "I will not be degraded in this way." Marmee does go too far in her tirade, however, when she strikes March, but her words address the real issue of female inequality during the period and of women's early efforts to break free of traditional roles.

STYLE

Literary Reinvention

Brooks wrote *March* after imagining what happened to the absent father in Louisa May Alcott's classic novel *Little Women* during his experiences as a chaplain among the Union forces during the Civil War. She borrowed plot details and scenes from the first novel as she created a story for Mr. March, who does not have a voice in Alcott's novel. Brooks's novel is darker in tone and presents a more complex study of its main character.

Both novels begin with a letter from Mr. March to his family. In Alcott's novel, the March daughters are gathered around Marmee as she reads the letter, and in Brooks's, March is writing it from a remote military camp. Part One of Alcott's novel ends with March's return home after a serious illness, focusing on his appreciation of his daughters' development into womanhood. The rest of the novel continues the story of that development as the March daughters successfully overcome their individual character flaws.

Brooks includes March's homecoming, but this version is much more ambiguous than the first. Marmee's voice at the end of *March* reinforces the link to the previous work but also emphasizes the darker vision of the latter as she learns of and must come to accept the radical changes in her husband. Brook refuses easy solutions or lessons; she focuses on the horrors of war and its effects on those who participate in it.

In all, Alcott's novel is a sentimental, woman-centered depiction of the inner world of family life, while Brooks's novel emphasizes the man's outer world of war and work.

Mixture of Fictional and Non-fictional Characters

Brooks's novel is a historical fiction. It combines historical figures, such as Ralph Waldo Emerson and Henry David Thoreau, with fictional characters, some of whom are borrowed from Alcott's novel. Brooks creates an historically based picture of life in Concord, Massachusetts, in the mid-nineteenth century, and she also depicts the complicated experience both northerners and southerners faced during the Civil War, a conflict waged mostly in the southern states. Brooks incorporated bits of Bronson Alcott's letters into the novel as well as those by Thoreau and Emerson, along with other pieces of their writings. The famous authors were Alcott family friends just as they are depicted to be in Alcott's and Brooks's novels. In combining fact and fiction, in elaborating on the original fiction of Louisa May Alcott, Brooks is able to convey in her novel a broader and admittedly different perspective on the Civil War experience and the cause of abolition.

HISTORICAL CONTEXT

The Civil War

The American Civil War lasted four years (1861–1865), the bloodiest conflict in U.S. history, which claimed 600,000 American lives, more than all wars fought between 1865 and 2007 added together. It broke out between northern states, the Union, and the southern states, the Confederacy, when the South seceded from the Union. The causes of the war were complex and involved political, economic, and social issues. The southern states had increasingly tried to separate themselves from the North since the Revolutionary War, a movement that escalated sharply after 1820 when the newly formed western territories began to deal with the question of slavery and faced being admitted to the Union as either slave or free states. The concern about keeping the number of states even on both sides was coupled with increasingly vocal objection by abolitionists in the North, which caused the South to be even more eager to have equal representation in Congress.

When Abraham Lincoln was elected in 1860, South Carolina seceded from the Union, followed by Mississippi, Florida, Alabama, Georgia, Louisiana, and Texas. The war began on April 12, 1861, when P. G. I. Beauregard led an attack on Fort Sumter, South Carolina. Soon after, Arkansas, North Carolina, Virginia, and Tennessee joined the other Confederate states. Jefferson Davis (1808–1889), a U.S. senator, became president of the Confederacy. Robert E. Lee became commander of the Confederate Army, and Ulysses S. Grant led the Union army.

The Underground Railroad

The Underground Railroad was a network of hidden routes and safe houses that led from southern states to Canada, Mexico, and overseas. Abolitionists worked along the routes during the nineteenth century to help escaped slaves reach freedom. During the first part of the century, approximately one hundred thousand slaves escaped from the South. Along the secret routes, these escaped slaves found refuge and provisions in safe houses called "stations." Church congregations and other spiritual groups played a major part in helping slaves escape, especially Quakers, Congregationalists, Wesleyans, and Reformed Presbyterians. In an effort to combat the growing Underground Railroad network and assist slave owners in recapturing their slaves, the Fugitive Slave Law was passed in Congress, making it illegal to assist escaping slaves. This law further infuriated those northerners who believed slavery is immoral; many of these people refused to obey the new law.

John Brown and Harper's Ferry

John Brown (1800–1850), a radical abolitionist, led a raid on the federal armory in Harper's Ferry, West Virginia, on October 16, 1859. He and twenty-one men captured several buildings of arms, intent on arming a slave revolt in the South. They were unable to escape with the arms, however, as they became surrounded by locals and the militia. Within two days, most of the raiders had been killed or captured, including two of Brown's sons. Brown was found guilty of treason and was hanged, a martyr for some and a traitor for others. The raid stirred both pro- and anti-slavery passions in the North and in the South and helped propel the country into the Civil War.

A Union soldier with his family (*MPI / Getty Images*)

Transcendentalism

March is referred to in passing as a transcendentalist, a follower of transcendentalism, the philosophical movement that rose in New England during the nineteenth century. Its most prominent proponents were Ralph Waldo Emerson (1803–1882) and Henry David Thoreau (1817–1862). American transcendentalism was a form of philosophical romanticism that first emerged in Europe in Immanuel Kant's *Critique of Practical Reason* (1788). The philosophy was also expressed by certain romantic poets, for example, Samuel Taylor Coleridge (1172–1834) and William Wordsworth (1770–1850).

Emerson's *Nature* (1836) explains the philosophy, which poses that the natural world cloaks a spiritual one beyond it. Permeating nature are signs of what Emerson called the Oversoul, the metaphysical divine agency behind all creation. Transcendentalism asserts that the material world is a code or manifestation of the transcendent spiritual realm beyond it. Followers of this philosophy believe that they have direct connection to deity, often felt most clearly out in nature.

Emerson believed that humans should trust themselves since God can speak through them. This sense of spiritual democracy is expressed somewhat indirectly in Thoreau's works, especially *Walden* (1854), along with a call to live simply and close to nature.

CRITICAL OVERVIEW

March, which received widespread positive reviews, won the Pulitzer Prize in 2006. Writing in *Publishers Weekly*, one reviewer calls the novel "luminous," "affecting," and "beautifully written" as it "drives home the intimate horrors and ironies of the Civil War and the difficulty of living honestly with the knowledge of human suffering." Brooks's characters, the review claims, "speak with a convincing 19th-century formality, yet the narrative is always accessible," an assessment echoed by a reviewer for the *Economist*, who asserts that "the novel's voice captures well the flowery, elegant prose of a bookish 19th-century reverend." However, Marta Segal Block in *Booklist* argues that while "the nineteenth-century writing style is accurate and entertaining, . . . it may be too ornate for some readers. The best moments in the narrative are the peeks inside the mind of the long-suffering Marmee."

Christina Schwarz, in her review for the *Atlantic Monthly* writes, "Brooks's narrative is remarkably tight. Whereas much literary fiction wallows in digression, here every scrap of information propels the story forward." Schwarz praises the "vibrant elucidation of the idea at the heart of this novel" that humans and "the loftiness of [their] undertakings are inherently 'clouded' and 'murk-stained.'" An article in *Kirkus Reviews* finds "the morally gray complications" of March's work with the freed slaves "the novel's greatest strength," but concludes that while "the battle scenes are riveting, the human drama [is] flat."

Thomas Mallon, in the *New York Times Book Review*, also finds fault. Mallon points out that the subjects of war and slavery prompt "the author and her characters toward a prolonged moral exhibitionism." While he gives credit to the work as "nicely researched," Mallon concludes, the novel "makes a distressing contribution to recent trends in historical fiction, which . . . seems to be returning to its old sentimental contrivances and costumes."

WHAT DO I READ NEXT?

- Brooks takes the absent father from Louisa May Alcott's *Little Women* (1868) and creates his story in *March*, focusing on his Civil War experiences. Alcott's work chronicles the lives of his wife and children in Concord, Massachusetts, as they wait for March to come home.

- Brooks's historical novel *Year of Wonders* (2001) imagines the devastation of the plague on an English town in the seventeenth century and on a young housemaid's struggles to survive.

- Stephen Crane's classic novel *The Red Badge of Courage*, originally published in 1894, documents the horror of the Civil War and examines the complex ways that the participants responded to it. In his characterization of Henry Fleming, a young Union soldier, Crane explores questions of honor, cowardice, and humanity.

- Charles Frazier's *Cold Mountain* (1997) presents the tale of a Confederate soldier named Inman, his turncoat journey home from the Civil War battlefields, and his bittersweet reunion with the woman who has waited for him. The novel cuts back and forth between Inman's difficult journey that tests his physical as well as his emotional strength and Ada's tale of her own struggles to survive on a farm without a man to help her.

- *The Odyssey*, an ancient Greek epic attributed to Homer, relates the adventures of its main character Odysseus as he travels home after fighting in the Trojan War. His journey is a difficult one, and his wife awaits him on the island of Ithaca. Readers may want to use Richard Lattimore's fine translation, *The Odyssey of Homer* (1999), which is available in a Perennial Classic edition.

Many critics praise the historical accuracy of the novel and its creative link to Louisa May Alcott's *Little Women*. Daniel Shealy in the *New England Quarterly*, for example, writes that Brooks "weaves a novel out of both real and fictional characters, creating a tapestry of nineteenth-century American life during the Civil War that both pays homage to its famous literary predecessor and establishes itself as an excellent work of historical fiction." He concludes, "her fictional March family can stand proudly next to Louisa May Alcott's earlier creation." Anita Sama in *USA Today* insists that "the novel stands on its own." She determines that "imaginative extrapolations, done successfully as in *March*, illuminate the original works and allow tangential characters to claim their own full lives."

The reviewer for the *Economist* writes that Brooks "researched with great historical thoroughness," and though the "ceaseless goodness" of March and his family "does grow a little oppressive, Ms. Brooks merely imbues her pages with the same perfume that rises from Alcott's account of the saintly Marches." The reviewer finds that "the text is anything but sentimental about the civil war itself, whose stench and waste is depicted with brutal clarity" and predicts, "Alcott fans will find *March* both respectful and sufficiently full in its own right that it might have thrived without piggy-backing on" *Little Women*. The review concludes: the novel "enhances rather than appropriates its sister work from 1868. Louisa May Alcott would be well pleased."

CRITICISM

Wendy Perkins

Perkins is a professor of twentieth-century American and British literature and film. In this essay, she explores the difficult journey from innocence to experience.

In Geraldine Brooks's Pulitzer Prize-winning *March*, the title character goes off to war with the best of intentions: to offer aid and comfort to the Union soldiers who are engaged in the good fight for emancipation. John March is certain that he will be able to help in this noble cause and that it ultimately will be successful because its moral imperative cannot be questioned. As he faces the reality of war, however, his faith in humanity and himself is tested. Indeed, March's journey to war and back again becomes a painful trek from innocence to experience. During the first few months after his enlistment, when his idealistic vision begins to cloud, he admits, "I hope to go back.

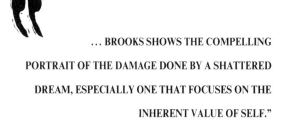

"... BROOKS SHOWS THE COMPELLING PORTRAIT OF THE DAMAGE DONE BY A SHATTERED DREAM, ESPECIALLY ONE THAT FOCUSES ON THE INHERENT VALUE OF SELF."

To my wife, to my girls, but also to the man of moral certainty that I was that day [I enlisted]; that innocent man, who knew with such clear confidence exactly what it was that he was meant to do." March discovers at the end of his journey that he will never be able to go back, and this understanding threatens to destroy him.

After serving as chaplain in the Union army for only a brief time, March is told by a soldier who sees his lack of knowledge about how some profit from the war, "Chaplain, you sure is an innocent man." At this point, March is an innocent although he has learned some harsh truths about the conditions of slavery and the fight to abolish it. His first experience with the true injustices of the system comes twenty years before the novel begins. Brooks flashes back to these early years in order to show March's maturation process and the development of his commitment to the abolitionist movement.

When March first arrives at the Clement plantation, he immediately has his notions of blacks tested when he meets Grace, who speaks and dresses with more style and intelligence than the whites in the small New England town where March grew up. He convinces himself that blacks on the Clement plantation have not suffered from the system of slavery after he observes what he thinks is "affection and trust" between Clement and his slaves, especially Grace who is the constant companion of his wife. March is certain that Clement is a kind man, too intelligent and moral to oppress his slaves.

The complexities in Clement's nature, however, begin to emerge during a discussion of the character and habits of blacks. March "winces" when Clement insists that "the only way to keep slaves honest is *not* to trust them." Yet March continues to listen, certain that this wise man will have some intelligent reason for his opinion.

After Clement cites examples of lenient masters who were taken advantage of and sometimes murdered by their slaves, March protests that slavery causes immoral behavior, which is not inherent in the black person's nature. Clement agrees in part with his assessment, insisting that he does not believe that blacks are wicked, but he insists they are just children who do not know any better. Thus, he claims, the system of slavery works because it is the duty of whites to act as "stern father" to teach blacks how to be moral. March is able to accept this judgment since it fits more with his mission to teach and to save souls. He also enjoys Clement's company and his hospitality and wants to believe that the man shows good judgment. (The irony that Clement is literally the father of the slave called Grace is not revealed until later.)

Taken in by a kind of benevolent dictatorship, March "felt fortunate" in Clement's company, "flattered by his attention, overcome by his wisdom, and thrilled to be, even briefly, a part of this higher way of life." His opinion of Clement is tested, however, when March begins to observe the realities of a slave's life. He is pleased when Prudence, the cook's daughter, shows a keen desire and aptitude for reading and does not understand why educating a slave is against the law. When Prudence's mother fears her daughter will be whipped if she is caught, March tries to calm her, insisting that surely her master will allow him to teach Prudence since "he is a scholar and loves learning."

One evening March tests his naïve theory by suggesting to Clement that one of his slaves could help him with the plantation's accounts, March witnesses the racism in Clement's philosophy when the man insists that educating slaves would lead to insurrection and the butchering of whites. March now understands that men like Clement would never give up the power slavery affords them.

March, however, does not foresee the violent response that could erupt if a man like Clement were betrayed, and so March begins to teach Prudence surreptitiously. Once he is discovered, the veneer of wise, paternal oversight is shattered: Clement insists that March has "contaminated" his "property." March, who has begun to see the slaves as individuals rather than types, is appalled that Clement regards "the vivid person of Prudence and the dignity of Grace" as mere property. Subsequently, he blames himself for Grace's savage beating, feeling profound guilt over being "seduced by Clement's wealth and deceived by his false nobility."

His experiences on the Clement plantation cause March to be even more fervent in his belief that slavery should be abolished, a position that inspires him to enlist when the Civil War breaks out. Before the war, he had mixed feelings about the best course for abolitionists to take, especially after John Brown's raid on Harper's Ferry. He admits that his response teetered "on a seesaw between repulsion and admiration." He wondered: "Was ever a course of action more reckless and savage? Was ever one so justifiable, so self-sacrificing? My mind was as confounded as it had been the day I heard the news."

When war breaks out, however, he sees a clearer path for himself and for the country, sure that courage and strength of conviction assure them success. As he faces his first battle, he thinks of his motive for enlisting: "moral greatness had little meaning without action to affect the moral end." This became, he declares, "the great argument that would animate my life; the selfsame argument that has brought me to these wintery ridges." Immediately, however, his idealistic vision begins to cloud when his unit must swim across a river to escape their enemies. March promises a young injured soldier, "I will get you across," but fails, discovering that even the best intentions do not guarantee victory.

As March faces the horror of the battlefield and of the hospital were men die in his arms, he discovers "how often it is that an idea that seems bright bossed and gleaming in its clarity when examined in a church, or argued over with a friend in a frosty garden, becomes clouded and murk-stained when dragged out into the field of actual endeavor."

March regains some of his idealistic vision when he is reassigned to Oak Landing, seeing himself as part of "*this first great experiment of equality.*" When he first arrives and quizzes Canning about the harsh treatment of his workers, the lack of doctors, and the poor living conditions, the latter notes, "you know exactly nothing." Again, March's vision becomes "clouded and murk-stained," this time when he is forced to recognize the economic realities of running such an experiment. His harshest lesson, however, is learned when the Confederates raid the plantation. Still holding on to his belief in the basic humanity of man, he declares to one of the workers, "the Confederate soldier is a hard and desperate fighter, but he is not a savage. There are rules, even in war." The worker gives him "a look that combined pity and exasperation" as he explains that the men he has seen "sure enough don't follow no rules." As March soon discovers, neither he nor the Confederate soldiers follow the rules: They engage in torture, and he cannot summon the courage to stop them.

Daniel Shealy, in his review of the novel for the *New England Quarterly* writes, "Brooks makes this idealistic man grope deeply in the darkness of his own conscience, a battle more intense, more significant, perhaps, than any he witnessed in the war." March blames himself for several tragedies that he witnesses—the soldier who does not make it across the river, the savage whipping of Grace, and the torture of Canning—and comes to believe both he and his idealistic vision have failed. Both Grace and Marmee insist that he is not responsible for the suffering he has observed and convince him to find the strength to live for his family. Yet when he returns home, he declares, "I felt like an imposter," as if "this was the house of another man . . . a person of moral certainty, and some measure of wisdom, whom many called courageous. How could I masquerade as such a one? For I was a fool, a coward, uncertain of everything."

The novel ends with March's resolve "to live in the quick world," but he knows "the ghosts of the dead would be ever at hand." As March hides his face "in the gathering darkness" in his family's parlor, Brooks shows the compelling portrait of the damage done by a shattered dream, especially one that focuses on the inherent value of self.

Source: Wendy Perkins, Critical Essay on *March*, in *Novels for Students*, Thomson Gale, 2008.

SOURCES

Block, Marta Segal, Review of *March*, in *Booklist*, Vol. 101, No. 11, February 1, 2005, p. 938.

Brooks, Geraldine, *March*, Penguin Books, 2006.

Mallon, Thomas, "Pictures from a Peculiar Institution," in *New York Times Book Review*, March 27, 2005, p. 11.

Review of *March*, in *Economist*, Vol. 374, No. 8419, March 26, 2005, p. 84.

Review of *March*, in *Kirkus Reviews*, Vol. 73, No. 1, January 1, 2005, p. 5.

Review of *March*, in *Publishers Weekly*, Vol. 251, No. 51, December 20, 2004, p. 34.

Sama, Anita, "'Little Women' from Father's Point of View," in *USA Today*, March 17, 2005, p. 04d.

Schwarz, Christina, "Finds and Flops," in *Atlantic Monthly*, Vol. 295, No. 3, April 2005, p. 115.

Shealy, Daniel, Review of *March*, in *New England Quarterly*, Vol. 79, No. 1, March 2006, pp. 164, 165.

FURTHER READING

Bial, Raymond, *The Underground Railroad*, Houghton Mifflin, 1999.

> Stirring photographs accompany eye-witness accounts of the perilous journeys taken on the Underground Railroad, the term for a series of sites that operated as safe havens for slaves escaping to freedom in the North.

Foote, Shelby, *The Civil War: A Narrative*, Vintage, 1986.

> In this trilogy that was adapted by Foote and Ken Burns into a popular PBS miniseries, Foote chronicles the historical facts of the war and brings a novelist's sensibility to his characterization of many of those who were affected by it.

Harrold, Stanley, *The American Abolitionists*, Longman, 2000.

> This work, part of the Seminar Studies in History series, traces the abolitionist movement in the United States from its beginnings in the eighteenth century to the end of the Civil War in 1865. Included in the text are analyses of the major issues as well as important documents concerning the movement.

Wagner, Margaret E., and Gary Gallagher, *The American Civil War: 365 Days*, Harry N. Abrams, 2006.

> This book gathers together over five hundred photographs, lithographs, drawings, cartoons, posters, maps, and letters from the war, covering a wide range of subjects, including politics, battles, slavery, and the treatment of women and civilians during this period.

Martian Time-Slip

PHILIP K. DICK

1964

Written in 1962 and titled *Goodmember Arnie Kott of Mars* then serialized in *Worlds of Tomorrow* as "All We Marsmen" in 1963, *Martian Time-Slip* was finally published as a paperback book in 1964. Although not initially a commercial success, it came to be considered one of the best books of Philip Dick's peak period in the 1960s when the author wrote sixteen novels. *Martian Time-Slip* was reprinted several times as Dick's reputation grew and as hit movies were made from his stories, such as *Blade Runner* (1982), *Total Recall* (1990), and *Minority Report* (2002).

Set on the deserts of Mars in 1994, the story is a satire of the business world and suburban life on Earth. In addition, Dick was fascinated with schizophrenia, and in this novel, he explored the nature of reality as a central theme. In *Martian Time-Slip*, Dick shows how what is real is determined by how it is perceived; the same scene is repeated from the points of view of three characters. Union leader Arnie Kott calls upon a repairman, Jack Bohlen, to develop a device for communicating with the nonverbal, autistic child, Manfred Steiner, who has precognition abilities. Kott wants to get the edge in a business deal, but the child projects schizophrenic vibes onto the two men that skew everyone's reality. The "time-slip," therefore, is the nonlinear timeframe. The native Martians, called Bleekmen, recognize the malleability of time and understand the value of Manfred's gifts although the colonists debate the value of keeping "anomalous" children alive. These simple tribal people also

serve as a contrast to the Teaching Machines that spout Establishment-approved information to school children on Mars. From intelligent machines to schizophrenic humans to psychic indigenous observers, this story has nothing to do with Mars, except as a backdrop, and everything to do with the vagaries of human nature on Earth.

AUTHOR BIOGRAPHY

Philip Kindred Dick and his twin sister, Jane Charlotte, were born six weeks prematurely on December 16, 1928, in Chicago, Illinois, to Joseph Edgar, a fraud investigator for the U.S. Department of Agriculture, and Dorothy Kindred Dick. Jane died several weeks later, and the loss of his twin had a residual impact on Dick's life and the themes in his writing. The family relocated from Chicago to the San Francisco Bay Area, but Dick's parents divorced when he was five. He attended high school in Berkeley then briefly attended the University of California at Berkeley. His teen years were plagued by two problems: a serious swallowing disorder that prevented him from eating in public and acute vertigo that gave him the strange sensation of being disconnected from real life. This unnerving feeling contributed to the paranoia that often appears in his writing. For several years he worked in a record store, the only real job he ever held other than writing. His first short story was published in 1952, and he sold his first novel in 1955. By 1958, he had written thirteen novels and eighty short stories, but other prolific periods lay ahead. While he tried to write more mainstream work, his science fiction was the work that got published and gained attention.

Dick became increasingly paranoid and often feared that he suffered from schizophrenia. His concern was expressed notably in *Martian Time-Slip*, the 1964 book that centered on schizophrenia. In February and March of 1974, Dick experienced a series of visions, dreams, and a hallucination involving a "pink light" beam transmitting information directly into his mind. He later used the shorthand "2-3-74" to describe this time period and spent the remainder of his life trying to decipher the meaning of these events. Dick married five times: to Jeanette Martin in 1948, to Kleo Apostolides from 1950 to 1958, to Anne Williams Rubenstein from 1958

MEDIA ADAPTATIONS

- The official website of the estate of the late Philip K. Dick is www.philipkdick.com.

- www.philipkdickfans.com, the former official website for Dick, is now maintained by admirers of science fiction and Philip K. Dick and has many resources and links.

to 1964, to Nancy Hackett from 1967 to 1973, and to Tessa Busby from 1973 to 1976. He had one child with each of his last three wives: Laura, Isolde, and Christopher.

Dick won the Hugo Award in 1963 for *The Man in the High Castle* and the John W. Campbell Memorial Award in 1975 for *Flow My Tears, the Policeman Said*. He died on March 2, 1982, at the age of fifty-three in Santa Ana, California, after a series of strokes followed by heart failure. Posthumously, Dick's work regained popularity, especially after the film adaptations *Blade Runner*, *Total Recall*, *Minority Report*, *Paycheck*, and *A Scanner Darkly*. Dick was inducted into the Science Fiction Hall of Fame in 2005.

PLOT SUMMARY

Chapter One
It is August 1994 in a United Nations colony on Mars where families get rations of water for their home use from a canal, including neighboring families the Bohlens and the Steiners. Jack Bohlen, a repairman, receives a call from his father in New York City saying that he wants to come to Mars to research a real estate deal. Jack copters out to a job and sees along the way Lewistown, the second most successful colony on Mars—the one for the Water Workers' union people who control the canals. The most successful colony is New Israel.

Chapter Two

Arnie Kott, head of the Water Workers' union, enjoys the luxury of a steam bath while discussing with his minions some land in the F.D.R. Mountains. He also complains about the UN demands that he improve the wages of the Bleekmen, the indigenous Martian tribe, who are used as laborers in the mines. Beside a *New York Times* newspaper ad for prospective colonists for Mars, touting the opportunities for those who have only a bachelor's degree and thus cannot get a job on Earth, Arnie sees an article about the Colonial Safety Committee on Mars that irritates him, especially since his ex-wife is on the committee. On his way to see her, his helicopter pilot gets a message asking for aid for some stranded Bleekmen. Jack hears the same emergency call and is the first to arrive and give food and water to the Bleekmen who reward him with a water witch. Arnie's pilot also provides water even though Arnie protests because he does not consider Bleekmen to be people.

Chapter Three

Norbert Steiner, who runs a black-market food operation, goes to Camp Ben-Gurion, a home for "anomalous children," where his son Manfred is a resident. Having an autistic son is considered shameful, but he can talk to Anne Esterhazy, who also has a child at Camp B-G. She tells him about a bill under consideration at the UN that would kill the anomalous children in an effort "to keep the race pure." Although at first horrified by the news, Norbert wonders if such action might be best for children like his son who cannot communicate. The institute's psychiatrist, Dr. Milton Glaub, tells Norbert about a new theory that looks at how autism speeds up time and the possibility of being able to communicate with autistic children if they were able to slow down sights and sounds. Norbert dismisses Milton's ideas as idealistic nonsense. He then goes to a bar where the owner rants about how the freaks like those at Camp B-G should be destroyed. Norbert reveals that his son lives at the camp, and the bar owner becomes angry that Norbert never told him before. In despair from all this conflict, Norbert suddenly decides to kill himself and steps in front of a bus.

Chapter Four

UN policemen come to the Steiner home to tell the family that Norbert has died. Silvia babysits the four Steiner girls and learns of the existence of Manfred. Arnie learns about Norbert's death when he and Anne have lunch together. She then tells him of the possible closure of Camp B-G, and even though he and Anne have a son there, he thinks it is better for Mars not to have a place like Camp B-G. Milton hears about Norbert's suicide, and the implication that he might have said something to drive Norbert to it makes Milton worry about his position. Silvia calls Jack to tell him about Norbert and to ask him to come home early because she is caring for the girls. However, Mr. Yee will not let Jack go and sends him to a job at the Public School.

Chapter Five

Jack is unnerved by the Public School. As he repairs one of the mechanical teachers, he speculates about the function of the Public School within the society on Mars and how people with autism and schizophrenia are feared and rejected. Jack then recalls his own bout with schizophrenia back on Earth. Right before he left for Mars, Jack hallucinated that his boss was a machine and that everything around him was lifeless and mechanical. It was then he realized he was sick and needed help. Jack thinks now that the reason the Teaching Machines make him so uncomfortable is that they remind him of this hallucination.

Chapter Six

Arnie calls Yee and specifically requests that Jack come to repair his encoder device. He thinks about rumors that the UN is buying up some of the F.D.R. Mountains and how they will become very valuable. He needs to know what part of the mountains, so he begins wondering if there might be a precognitive schizophrenic living at Camp B-G who would be able to tell him. An aide tells Arnie to ask Milton. Meanwhile, Otto Zitte sits in a storage shed in the F.D.R. Mountains where Norbert keeps the black-market food. He wonders where Norbert is and why it is taking him so long to return. He thinks about how he ended up working for Norbert after he lost his union membership and failed at his own black-market business. Jack arrives at Arnie's and meets Doreen Anderton, to whom Jack is instantly attracted. Arnie invites Jack to go with him and Doreen to meet Milton for drinks. Arnie explains that he needs to find a precognitive schizophrenic, and Jack reveals that he is himself a schizophrenic. Arnie wants to know if Jack can see the future, but Jack says he cannot. Arnie does not believe him.

Chapter Seven

On his way to meet Arnie, Milton muses about how much money he will make when he is on Arnie's payroll. He assumes Arnie must need his services to deal with an onset of schizophrenia, and he is excited about the large opportunity this presents. Then he learns that Arnie wants to know if he has an advanced schizophrenic at Camp B-G. Milton tells them about Manfred. Arnie becomes convinced that if Jack can build a machine that can communicate with this child, then Manfred will be able to tell them the future. Arnie puts Jack on his payroll, but not Milton. Sitting at the table, Jack begins to have a schizophrenic episode. Doreen notices and takes him away. As they walk, Doreen tells Jack that her brother is schizophrenic, and Jack confides to Doreen about the nature of his visions. He decides to take the job with Arnie, and he vows to keep fighting off his schizophrenia. Later that night, Arnie decides to start up his own black-market food business now that Steiner is gone. Jack considers calling Doreen. He decides against it, but then Doreen calls to ask him over. She assures Jack that she will tell Arnie, who will not object. So Jack goes.

Chapter Eight

Leo Bohlen arrives on Mars. As they spend some family time, Leo asks Jack about his relationship with Silvia and his mental state. He can tell Jack is withdrawn. He wants Jack to go in on the land deal with him, but Jack is not interested. Leo confronts Jack about his affair with Doreen, but Jack says he has everything under control. Silvia, in her drug-induced haze before sleep, wonders why Jack has changed recently and why he is distant from her. Meanwhile, Manfred has a terrifying vision of meat-eating birds and large, wet worms. He tries to run, but the steps give way underneath his feet. He starts to fly up, but the birds eat his head off. He is then standing on a bridge over a sea where sharks try to attack him. He is then strangled with a loop of shark teeth that cuts off his head. He is trapped in a decaying world without a voice. At Arnie's, Doreen is told about a land speculator who arrived on Mars that day, and Arnie expresses excitement about Manfred's potential to help him get ahead of the game and make a fortune.

Doreen is tired and wants to sleep, but Arnie wants sex, and he is the boss.

Chapter Nine

Jack, Leo, and Manfred fly over the F.D.R. Mountains. Leo explains to Jack that the UN is planning to build a huge co-op there, and Leo wants the UN to have to buy the land from him at a huge profit. Leo tells Jack not to share this information. They see some Bleekmen below them, and Jack wonders what it would be like for Manfred to live among them. Jack lands the 'copter and he and Leo drive a stake into the ground, claiming ownership. They notice that Manfred is drawing a picture of what the co-op will look like when it is old and crumbling. He writes the word "AM-WEB" on the building, but only says "gubbish." Jack begins to understand Manfred's visions and how limiting and awful they are. Manfred later has a vision of his own future. He is eighty-three with no teeth or eyes. He sees himself interned at AM-WEB for a hundred and twenty-three years, where most of his body is removed or artificial. When Arnie asks him what he sees, the only response Manfred has is "gubble, gubble."

Chapter Ten

Jack, Doreen, and Manfred are at Arnie's having drinks. Arnie tries to play a tape but has the wrong one. Arnie inquires about Jack's progress with Manfred, but he does not get the answer he wants. Jack has not built the machine, but he does show Arnie Manfred's drawing. He explains what the picture means and relays the information about the co-op that he learned from his dad. Arnie realizes that it is already too late for him to get in on the deal; he has lost out. He seems to take it surprisingly well, and even though Jack feels badly about how things turned out, Arnie does not blame Jack or even want to fire him. Suddenly, Jack, Leo, and Manfred are flying away from the F.D.R. Mountains again. Jack calls Arnie and tells him that he will see him that night, and he somehow knows he will show Arnie the drawing and will tell him everything he knows. He asks Manfred to draw a picture of what will happen that evening, and Manfred draws one man punching another in the eye. Jack drops his father off then watches Manfred change his drawing so one of the men falls and dies. Jack does not know if it will be him or Arnie.

Once again, Jack, Doreen, and Manfred are at Arnie's having drinks. Arnie tries to play a tape but has the wrong one. Arnie inquires about Jack's progress with Manfred, but he does not get the answer he wants. Jack is having a schizophrenic hallucination in which Doreen decays and rots away. He hears only the word "gubble" in his head. He turns up the music very loud to try to clear his head.

It is the afternoon again, and Jack has just dropped off his dad. He and Manfred fly to Doreen's apartment. He tells Doreen that he knows things are not going to go well that night at Arnie's, and Doreen tries to convince him to send Manfred back to Camp B-G and forget the whole thing before he loses his mind, but Jack says he has to go through with it. Jack then goes to the Public School to pick up David, taking Manfred with him.

Chapter Eleven

Once again, Jack, Doreen, and Manfred are at Arnie's having drinks. In this hallucination, Doreen's clothes are infested, and she rips them off her body. Arnie sees her stripping, pulls her to the floor, and they have sex. Doreen can tell something is watching them. It is the afternoon again, and Jack and Manfred arrive at the Public School. Jack realizes that Manfred's presence is leading him into schizophrenia and that he is on the verge of going permanently insane. Meanwhile, Silvia sits in June Henessy's kitchen, gossiping about the Steiner family. June talks about her current affair, and Silvia wonders what it would be like to cheat on Jack and what it would be like if Jack cheated on her. Otto comes to the door selling health food and black-market goods. Silvia is intrigued by him and asks him to come by her house later. Over at Milton's office, Milton is looking over Sam Esterhazy's file. He decides he can get back at Arnie by sending Sam home. Milton tells Anne that Sam can no longer stay at Camp B-G, but she counters by saying that she will cease to object to the closing of Camp B-G if Sam leaves. Knowing her influence, Milton realizes that he is defeated. At the Public School, Jack searches for Manfred. When Jack finds him, Manfred is clearly distressed, and the teaching machines are all saying "gubble." Jack realizes that Manfred's presence has disrupted the entire school system.

Chapter Twelve

It is evening again, and Manfred sits on the floor of Arnie's living room. The sights and sounds are harsh and overwhelming to him. He hears the voice of Heliogabalus, Arnie's Bleekman servant, in his head. To escape the overload, Manfred uses his mind to look into the future, where once again he is two hundred years old and interned at AM-WEB. Everything is falling apart, and the only thing holding it together is Manfred. Arnie inquires about Jack's progress with Manfred, but he is not getting the answer he wants. Jack start to hallucinate; suddenly, the evening is over, and he and Doreen are walking in Lewistown. Doreen is discussing the events of the night that Jack does not remember.

Chapter Thirteen

Otto goes to Silvia's house ostensibly to sell black-market items but also to seduce Silvia, and he succeeds. That same morning, Jack wakes up at Doreen's. Doreen talks about their shaky future with Arnie, assuming that he will fire Jack and dump her once he knows about her affair with Jack. Milton visits Anne in hopes that she can prevent Arnie from harming Jack in his scheme with Manfred. Arnie learns that Helio can communicate telepathically with Manfred. Helio tells Arnie that Manfred's attention wanders because of his dread of his old age and death. Arnie tells Helio that he thinks Manfred can control time. Helio warns Arnie not to hurt Jack. That afternoon, Jack finds out that Arnie bought his work contract from Mr. Yee.

Chapter Fourteen

Otto leaves Silvia's. She feels hatred for him then disgust for herself, but she calls June and tells her every detail. Otto goes back to the mountains to find his storage shed destroyed, his goods stolen, and a warning note from Arnie. Otto swears he will get back at Arnie. Meanwhile, Helio explains to Arnie that he must go on a pilgrimage to the Bleekman sanctuary in the F.D.R. Mountains with Manfred if Arnie wants to be able to go back in time to beat Leo to the land deal. Arnie and Manfred set out in Arnie's car, but Anne and Milton catch up to them trying to plead about Jack. Arnie's goons and Jack arrive in helicopters, and, while everyone is fighting, Arnie drives away.

Chapter Fifteen

With Jack and Doreen hovering overhead in the 'copter, Arnie and Manfred climb up to Dirty Knobby where they bribe a Bleekman priest to let them visit the shrine alone for an hour. Arnie then follows the step-by-step instruction given him by Helio, which includes Arnie's taking a drug and promising Manfred that he will be spared from AM-WEB if Manfred will take them back about three weeks in time. Arnie next finds himself back in his steam room going through the exact same actions as before. He decides not to keep Norbert from killing himself because he wants the black-market business. The only things he will change is getting a deed to the F.D.R. land and getting back at Jack. However, things start changing on Arnie as he experiences schizophrenic symptoms. His paper blurs and is full of "gubbish" and people have no faces. All his attempts to communicate his desire to buy the mountain land fail, and he finally has to get a stake and fly out to make the claim himself.

Chapter Sixteen

Arnie's trip to the mountains is interrupted by an emergency call to assist some Bleekmen. Arnie realizes that the event when he first meets Jack will be repeated. So he asks Jack to step over to the 'copter and then points a gun at him. A Bleekman notices and fires a poisoned arrow into Arnie's chest. Arnie realizes that the Bleekmen knew what would happen the first time they had this encounter and that is why they gave Jack the water witch. Arnie fears he is dying, and, in his mind, Arnie begs Manfred to bring him back to the right time, promising to give up on his revenge and getting the land. Everything goes black, but then Arnie wakes with the priest standing over him. Manfred is gone, but Arnie intends to keep all his promises. He heads to a 'copter, but instead of Jack, Otto comes running towards Arnie and shoots him. Jack arrives, but Otto gets away. Arnie tries to tell Jack this is all just another hallucination, but he dies on the way to the hospital. Jack does not worry about Manfred because he knows it was inevitable that Manfred would join the Bleekmen. Indeed, Manfred finds a tribal group and asks to join them. As he walks away with them, he feels himself transforming. Doreen realizes that with Arnie gone, everything will change, so, despite their feelings, they part, and Jack heads home to his family where he and Silvia agree to give their marriage another try and resume a life of everyday calm and normalcy. A scream draws them to the Steiner house where an old Manfred from the future has stopped by to say goodbye to his mother. He has had a happy life.

CHARACTERS

Doreen Anderton

As Union Treasurer and Arnie Kott's girlfriend, Doreen Anderton is privy to everything that goes on in Arnie's world. Consequently, she meets Jack Bohlen and Manfred Steiner when they are brought into Arnie's schemes. While she is unnerved by Manfred, she is particularly sensitive to Jack's situation because she has a schizophrenic brother. She seems to genuinely love Jack and declares that she is willing to give up all her luxuries from Arnie to be with Jack. Nonetheless, Doreen is practical. When Arnie dies, she knows that everything will change and that there will be nothing to keep her and Jack together. Even though they still love each other, they will not need each other's comfort in the face of Arnie, and she is wise enough to know that Jack needs and wants to go back to his ordinary life with his wife and son.

Bleekmen

The native tribe on Mars, the Bleekmen are described as looking like aboriginal people. They are quite primitive and have an ancient mystical religion. The colonists from Earth use the Bleekmen for cheap labor and treat them as sub-beings. The planned development of the F.D.R. Mountains will force the Bleekmen out of their traditional homeland into the desert and potential extinction, their telepathic and precognitive talents unappreciated, except by Manfred Steiner who finds peace and a home with them.

David Bohlen

The son of Jack and Silvia Bohlen, David Bohlen is a normal boy growing up on Mars. He attends the Public School where instruction is delivered by Teaching Machines. David scores on par with his achievement group, relieving Jack's fear that his son will be a schizophrenic like he is.

Jack Bohlen

Jack Bohlen is an "ex-schizophrenic" and repairman. He and his wife Silvia have one child, David, and lead what would be considered on Mars a normal settler's life. However, Jack constantly worries that the schizophrenia of his early adulthood will come back in which visions distort his image of people into death and rot and machinery. The visions and reality become frighteningly confused, so Jack is desperate to keep his sanity.

Hired out by his employer, Mr. Yee, to labor boss Arnie Kott, Jack is drawn into Arnie's scheme to try to communicate with Manfred. In the process, Jack falls in love with Arnie's girlfriend Doreen and has a brief affair with her. Jack finds comfort in Doreen, who understands his fears because she has a schizophrenic brother. Unfortunately, the association with Manfred fulfills Jack's fears because Manfred's powerful autistic aura projects hallucinations onto others. Jack cares about Manfred and wants to help him, but he cannot seem to gain control over what is happening to him. Fortunately for Jack, Arnie's manipulations cause everything to fall apart before Jack loses his mind permanently. He amicably dissolves his relationship with Doreen and gratefully heads straight back to his home and to normalcy. As a final reward for his good-heartedness, Jack is assured that Manfred will live a happier life, too.

Leo Bohlen

Jack's father, Leo Bohlen is a successful real estate developer in his late seventies from New York City. His business involves acquiring cheap land and reselling it for a large mark-up in price once its value has increased. Jack finds this kind of operation distasteful because he sees it as taking advantage of the less savvy. Leo thinks it is just good business and travels to Mars to scope out a possible bonanza in the F.D.R. Mountains. It is Leo's interest in seemingly worthless property that piques Arnie's curiosity and involves him in unsuccessfully trying to beat Leo to the punch through the time travel that he believes Manfred and the Bleekmen can enable. The result, however, is a schizophrenic time warp in which Arnie loses touch with reality. Leo has "a lot of money and doesn't mind spending it," and he also has a lot of opinions and does not mind sharing them. He is very concerned that his son is treating Silvia well and that their marriage is working. In the end, all that Leo wanted has happened: Jack and Silvia are on stable ground again, and Leo has made another immensely successful deal.

Silvia Bohlen

Jack's wife, Silvia Bohlen is a homemaker disillusioned with her life on Mars. She takes pills to help her sleep at night and pills to wake her up in the morning. She is generally unsympathetic towards other people's problems, but she does help out when she should, for example, when

Norbert Steiner dies and his children need care, yet she resents having to do so. She fantasizes about having an affair, but when she actually does have one with Otto Zitte, she decides it was a horrible mistake and resolves to give her marriage a second chance.

Anne Esterhazy

The ex-wife of Arnie Kott, Anne Esterhazy owns a gift shop in the colony of New Israel and is involved in all the political and social happenings on Mars, taking on many causes. Arnie dismisses her as a "do-gooder" but relies on her insider information and valuable advice nonetheless. They still often collaborate on business deals and are friends. Their son, Sam, born two years after their divorce, lives at Camp B-G because of severe physical deformities and mental retardation, although they claim that he is anomalous and thus qualified to live there. Anne can handle having a son who is anomalous but not one who is retarded. Anne tells Norbert Steiner of the impending bill at the UN that calls for the destruction of anomalous children. This news is so upsetting to Steiner that it contributes to his suicide.

Dr. Milton Glaub

A psychiatrist, Dr. Milton Glaub works part-time at Camp Ben-Gurion, a home for "anomalous children." Milton struggles to make ends meet because his wife cannot control her spending, and this problem makes him eager for a more lucrative situation. When he is disappointed in his hope to get on Arnie's payroll, Milton takes out his anger towards Arnie by threatening to dismiss his son Sam from Camp B-G and send him to an institution on Earth. When this attempt fails because of a counter threat from Anne, Milton at least knows enough to admit defeat. Although Milton tends to think of people in terms of the Freudian behavioral category into which they fall, most of the time he does try to do what is right by his patients. In fact, he attempts to protect Jack when he realizes that Jack is in danger of succumbing to schizophrenia as a result of Arnie's exploitation. Milton cares enough to crawl back to Anne to beg for her intercession on Jack's behalf and then to confront Arnie.

Heliogabalus

A member of the dwindling Bleekman race, Heliogabalus is Arnie Kott's house servant. His is loyal to Arnie and does his duty even though Arnie treats him as if he were an imbecile. Helio is actually very knowledgeable and wise. He is the only one able to discern the true nature of Manfred's autism and what it means for all of them. He can communicate telepathically with Manfred, see what Manfred sees, and understands what Manfred's visions mean and why they are so terrifying to the boy. Helio knows how to help Manfred in ways that no one else can comprehend, and it is Helio who advises Arnic to go with Manfred into the mountains to the tribal mystics to find the answers that Arnie seeks.

June Henessy

Typifying suburban culture, as neighbor, friend, and fellow housewife, June Henessy is the person to whom Silvia Bohlen confides her problems. June has had six affairs, and she keeps her friends well-informed about her extramarital activities.

Arnie Kott

As Supreme Goodmember of Water Workers' Local, Fourth Planet Branch, Arnie Kott is the most powerful man in the union town of Lewistown and one of the most powerful on all Mars. He enjoys his power and flaunts the luxuries with which he surrounds himself. His life is all about money and control. Brusque, quick to anger, and superficial, Arnie, as he insists on everyone calling him, will seek revenge against those who cross or threaten him. Yet he is dependent on his servant Helio for conversation and advice, and he uses people: the minions from the union who do his dirty work; his girlfriend, Doreen; and the Bleekmen who are like annoying animals to him.

Oddly, Arnie values things from the past—he owns the only harpsichord on Mars, listens to classical music, and continues a close relationship with his ex-wife, Anne. Although he is very sexist and disapproves of Anne's "masculine" features, he relies on her good business sense. Their relationship remained so close for a time that they had a son together after their divorce, but the child is born with physical disabilities and must live at Camp B-G. It is through this association that Arnie discovers Manfred's precognitive potential and decides to find a way to tap into this fortunetelling for an advantage in business deals. He hires Jack Bohlen to create a device for communicating with Manfred, but

that leads to both Jack and Arnie suffering schizophrenic hallucinations projected by Manfred.

When Arnie decides to get into the black-market business, he wants a monopoly. So he literally destroys his competition—he steals Otto Zitte's supplies and then has his storage building bombed. In the end, it is this all-or-nothing greed that causes his demise because Zitte shoots Arnie in revenge. Ironically, the hallucinations have caused Arnie to relive the same scene, so he does not even know when his real death actually occurs, and he dies thinking that he has escaped the consequences of his misdeeds once again.

Manfred Steiner

Manfred Steiner is a ten-year-old autistic boy who lives at Camp Ben-Gurion in the Jewish colony with other "anomalous children." He has never spoken a word and does not interact with other people, but Manfred's autism allows him to move through time and to see his own future. Sadly, he sees only horror and destruction, never creation or invention of good things to come. Manfred's world is one of overwhelming sensory stimulation and terrifying visions. When Arnie realizes the potential for gain if he can tap into Manfred's precognition, he hires Jack Bohlen to invent a device for communicating with Manfred. Thus Manfred's life changes as he leaves Camp B-G to be near Jack and Arnie. It is Manfred's drawing of the AM-WEB complex that will be built in the F.D.R. Mountains that verifies Leo Bohlen's claims about upcoming development there. At Arnie's, Manfred meets Heliogabalus, who as a Bleekman can communicate with Manfred telepathically. Helio is able to discern Manfred's fears of the AM-WEB once it is turned into a nightmare of an asylum in Manfred's old age. When Arnie and his schemes die, Manfred asks a group of Bleekmen if he can go off in the desert to live with them. They agree, and Manfred feels "very good, better than he could remember ever having felt before in his life. . . . Manfred Steiner felt something strange happening inside him. He was changing."

Norbert Steiner

Norbet Steiner, Manfred's father, runs a legitimate health food business and a black-market business on the side. He and his wife live with their four daughters next door to the Bohlens and often try to weasel extra water or other favors from their neighbors. Steiner keeps the existence of Manfred a secret because of the shame associated with having an autistic child—it is assumed that the parents of such a child must be defective themselves. Steiner diligently visits his only son but resents Manfred for the burden his disorder has placed on the family. When he learns that Camp B-G may be forced to close, Steiner's emotions become mixed. Faced with the horrifying possibility of having Manfred destroyed or the stress of having to take him home, Steiner commits suicide. This action sets in motion the series of events that make up the story of *Martian Time-Slip*.

Mr. Yee

The calculating owner of a repair company, Mr. Yee is Jack Bohlen's employer. He came to Mars from China for a more profitable business. Yee leases Jack's services to Arnie Kott, hoping for further business with this powerful man and eventually sells Jack's contract to Arnie for a hefty price.

Otto Zitte

Employed by Norbert Steiner in the black-market food business after losing his union card and his own similar business, the ambitious Otto Zitte lets his vices get the best of him. After Steiner's suicide, Zitte has the opportunity to take over the business and use it as a vehicle for preying upon lonely housewives. With his particular talent for seduction, Zitte manages to get even Silvia Bohlen into bed. His scurrilous new world comes to a sudden halt, however, when Arnie, out of greed and jealousy, destroys Zitte's stash of goods. In a rage of vengeance, Zitte finds Arnie and shoots him.

THEMES

Human Interdependence

Dick's plot in *Martian Time-Slip* is something akin to the idea of six degrees of separation in that he uses the death of Norbert Steiner to set in motion a series of events that entangles the lives of characters who are seemingly unrelated. The message is that everyone living on Mars (or elsewhere), whether they like it or not, is dependent on everyone else. The patients in the home for anomalous children are dependent on the those who believe that these children's lives have value. The colony is dependent on Arnie and the

TOPICS FOR FURTHER STUDY

- *Martian Time-Slip* is largely concerned with schizophrenia. What is schizophrenia? Manfred is autistic. What is autism? Divide the class into two groups and have one group look up the definition of schizophrenia and research its treatment. The other group can do the same for autism. Then the two groups can share what they have learned and discuss whether Dick gives an accurate portrayal of these disorders.

- Why do you think that Dick set *Martian Time-Slip* in 1994 instead of a time much farther into the future? Could Dick have really expected Mars to be colonized by that time? Do many science fiction writers use the distant future or is Dick's short-term choice common? Research and discuss with a partner.

- Write a report on the latest findings about Mars. What are NASA's plans for exploration? Are there plans to send humans to Mars in the near future? Has there been or is there water on Mars? Could the atmosphere support human life? Your report might include photographs of Mars.

- Using specific information from *Martian Time-Slip*, describe the Bleekmen in words or a drawing.

- Prepare a written point-by-point comparison of the lifestyle and treatment of the Bleekmen as compared to the treatment of aborigines in Australia by white people. Do some research on aborigines and make references to *Martian Time-Slip* also. While preparing this assignment, you may find it useful to watch the Australian film *Rabbit-Proof Fence* (2002), which deals with related subject matter and is based on fact.

plumbers' union for its water. Arnie is dependent on Jack and Manfred to enable him to make his fortune, and Jack is dependent on Arnie's good graces to stay employed. Doreen is dependent on

Arnie for her lifestyle, while she and Jack are temporarily dependent on each other for emotional support. The colonists are dependent on the Bleekmen for a labor source. The Bleekmen, whose prior culture has almost disappeared with the coming of the colony, are dependent on the colonists for their livelihood and survival. Connections are made between good and bad people, and, as often happens in a Dick novel, the characters who survive are generally aided by some system of knowledge involving faith—not scientific but ancient like the paranormal understanding of the Bleekmen, whom Jack respects but Arnie despises. Perhaps that is why Jack survives and Arnie does not.

Political and Financial Maneuverings

As a satire on the business world and post–World War II life in the United States, the colony in *Martian Time-Slip* is a place established purposely for the capitalistic exploitation of consumers. Traveling to and living on Mars is almost a business gimmick, an artificially created market. Those who settle there are motivated much as the pioneers who settled the American West were. Like Jack, those who settle on Mars are trying to escape their former lives, or, like Arnie, they are trying to find new opportunities and riches. However, instead of the classic image of the wholesome, hard-working pioneer families, the colony is populated with stereotypes of the worst of American suburbia. These grasping, social-climbing colonists use scarce water for gardens instead of farming, trade with the black market or become black marketers, and have illicit affairs frequently. Their lives are designed and directed by the industrialists. Even the children are programmed to continue buying into the Establishment view through the cultural propaganda set forth by the Teaching Machines. Meantime, the web of the United Nations and its participating members complicates the governing of the colony with competition and bureaucracy.

Concern with Reality

Individuals face common problems in a shared reality, but they cope with their problems according to each person's psychological make-up. It is tough enough to coexist when people are on the same plane, but when someone is living in a different reality, such as autistic Manfred or schizophrenic Jack, the human commonalities seem more tenuous. For Jack, who is trying to keep his grip on the real world, the question becomes Dick's major theme: How does one tell the real world from the Twilight Zone when the borders keep moving? Furthermore, how does one maintain humanity and compassion when machines and hate dominate?

Dick concludes that there cannot be only one reality. Everything is a matter of perception and relativity. Time is relative. Personal realities collide in the shared world such as when recently balanced Jack is once again unbalanced by Arnie's manic scheme. Jack's only hope for survival is to wait it out until the shifting sands beneath his feet settle into place, until the difference between reality and appearances becomes clear again.

Manfred's precognitive and telepathic abilities are not so much a talent as a curse because his reality is so different from that of the people around him. Critics often note that a hallmark of Dick's novels is the compassionate attitude he takes towards his characters and the empathy he evokes for them. Certainly Dick conveys the pain Manfred feels from his alienation, his inability to get in step with the others. Helio asks the following regarding Manfred: "Who can say if perhaps the schizophrenics are not correct? Mister, they take a brave journey. They turn away from mere things, which one may handle and turn to practical use; they turn inward to *meaning*. There, the black night-without-bottom lies, the pit." Trying to escape reality leads only to further unreality, but Dick sometimes thought that a schizophrenic withdrawal into oneself could be the safest course of action in a hostile environment.

Characters

A recurring theme in Dick's works is the value of the ordinary person. A typical Dick character, like those of Charles Dickens, has an ordinary job and an ordinary life. Real heroes, and the heroes of Dick's stories, are the people who are not given exceptional talents or genius but who manage to cope nonetheless. Facing life without advantages, position, or wealth is a harder path in Dick's estimation, yet the small triumphs achieved by the average person with perseverance, honesty, and kindness lay the foundation of society. Jack Bolton is this type of character in *Martian Time-Slip*. He has an everyday job as a repairman. He is married, has a son, and lives in an ordinary neighborhood like the rest of the

Dick's depiction of the Bleemen aboriginal tribe was influenced by the work of French sociologist Emile Durkheim, pictured here (Courtesy of The Library of Congress)

colonists on Mars. The one exceptional thing about Jack is his recovery from schizophrenia, but that starts to regress when he makes contact with Arnie and Manfred and leaves his ordinary world to work with Manfred for Arnie. He even cheats on his wife with Doreen. The result is almost disastrous, but it is Jack's basic decency that saves him and sends him home to his wife and his normal life.

STYLE

Symbolism

Three symbols in *Martian Time-Slip* are of particular note. First of all, is the Martian deserts. They are not intended to represent the topography of Mars as much as to convey the cultural desert, the ethical and spiritual poverty of the people of the colony. Mars is a dreary place where those who had hoped to escape the

problems on Earth will only find more problems as they are dehumanized by their environment. Second, the proposed building in the F.D.R. Mountains, the one Manfred identifies as AM-WEB, is a symbol for the grandiose plans that people make which fall apart, particularly those government projects that seem to be the latest great idea but turn into colossal mistakes. Manfred is able to draw pictures of the building as it ages and turns into a horrible place—no longer the trendy new apartment complex with gardens and shopping centers, but a decrepit asylum where his life will be a nightmare. Finally, the Bleekman Heliogabalus symbolizes the higher consciousness that escapes most ordinary people. Helio is unaffected by Arnie's exploitations, not because he is too primitive to understand what is happening, but because he is above such pettiness. Helio is sensitive enough to recognize telepathically Manfred's talents. With these symbols Dick adds to the satiric nature of his novel by using the setting to represent the emptiness and ineptitude of 1960s American ambitions and by using the seemingly brutish Bleekman as a contrast to the truly insensitive humans around him.

Satire

In literature, satire is an indirect attack upon a person, idea, or cultural practice through the use of wit, sarcasm, or irony. The intent is to expose foolishness and perhaps instigate change without resorting to rage. Vices and abuses are held up for ridicule. Satire has been an important device in literature since the ancient Greeks and has continued as an effective medium in the hands of Shakespeare, Cervantes, Swift, Dryden, Pope, and Fielding, among others, during what is called the golden age of satire in the seventeenth and eighteenth centuries. In the nineteenth century, satire became a gentler criticism as practiced in England by William Thackeray, Charles Dickens, Oscar Wilde, and George Bernard Shaw. In the United States, Washington Irving, James Russell Lowell, Oliver Wendell Holmes, and the masterful Mark Twain continued the tradition. Perhaps the best known satirists of the early to mid-twentieth century, both British and American, are Sinclair Lewis, James Thurber, Aldous Huxley, Evelyn Waugh, W. H. Auden, Philip Roth, and Joseph Heller. Toward the end of the twentieth century and into the early 2000s, the most well-known satires may have been cartoons, for example *Doonesbury* and *The Simpsons*.

COMPARE
&
CONTRAST

- **1962:** The Civil Rights Act prohibits discrimination on the basis of race, creed, national origin, or sex, but this prohibition against discrimination is not reflected in *Martian Time-Slip* in which the native Martians are treated badly.

  1994: Denny's restaurant chain agrees to pay more than $54 million to thousands of black customers who have been refused service or have been forced to wait longer or pay more than white customers in one of the largest and broadest settlements following passage of the Civil Rights Act.

  Today: The U.S. Commission on Civil Rights continues to report on investigations concerning charges of discrimination at polling places and anti-Semitic harassment, as well as to check on the status of desegregation in elementary schools.

- **1962:** Dick writes *Martian Time-Slip*, in which the United States and Russia both have colonies on Mars in cooperation with the United Nations. But, in real life on Earth, 1962 is the year of the Cuban Missile Crisis in which the United States and the Soviet Union come very close to nuclear warfare.

  1994: American President Clinton visits post-Soviet Russia, and Russian troops participate as United Nations peacekeeping troops in the Serbian conflict.

  Today: Russia and the United States are the primary partners in the International Space Station that orbits the Earth, continuing to expand its size and facilities for scientific research.

- **1962:** John Glenn is the first American to orbit the Earth; only seven years later, humans land on the Moon. At the same time, NASA approves the sending of a probe to photograph Mars in 1964.

  1994: In *Martian Time-Slip*, a colony of humans on Mars was several years old in 1994, but in reality 1994 was the year after the end of the 337-day Mars Observer mission, launched in 1992 to make a detailed study of the planet's geology, geophysics, and climate. The spacecraft was lost due to a malfunction.

  Today: The Mars Reconnaissance Orbiter, which spent two years looking for signs of past or present water in 2005 and 2006, is serving several years as a data relay station for future missions.

Dick uses satire in *Martian Time-Slip* to make his point about financial and political maneuvering in U.S. society. Big business as represented by the co-op runs lives as well as manipulates deals and uses political clout for its own gain, just like major corporations everywhere are thought to do. Further, Dick's depiction of Arnie Kott and the Water Workers' Union is a satirical dig at U.S. labor unions. The most precious commodity on Mars is water, yet the Water Workers themselves waste water in ways that suggest derision and excess as a means of flaunting power and privilege. The epitome of a corrupt union boss, Arnie always has eager henchmen to call upon to

do his dirty work. Education takes a slap, too, in the form of the Teaching Machines that spout out nothing but Establishment propaganda. Dick is criticizing the white, standardized education of the 1950s and 1960s for being a one-size-fits-all treatment that reinforced stereotypes and did not consider diversity or any kind of innovation. In addition, *Martian Time-Slip* satirizes most the vapidity that Dick sees as suburban life in the United States of his time.

Nonlinear Time and Multiple Realities
Typically, Dick incorporates into his stories an outside force that affects how a character

experiences reality. In *Martian Time-Slip* the outside force is Manfred and his contagious schizophrenia. Jack says of Manfred's illness: "It is the stopping of time. The end of experience, of anything new. Once the person becomes psychotic, nothing ever happens to him again." That is why the same scene is repeated, each time from a different perspective. Dick is asking which reality is real, and he is introducing the idea of nonlinear time, of short-term stasis. Since Manfred sees only the worst and any change is only for the worse, then stopping time seems like a good way to avoid change. Unfortunately, it appears that stasis means spiritual death if not physical death as well. So who will make the first move towards starting time again? Will anyone come out of the revolving door of the time slip? Arnie does not make it. Manfred is lifted into a new reality by the Bleekmen, and Jack finds himself able to walk out of the door, released by the death of Arnie and the exit of Manfred.

HISTORICAL CONTEXT

Science Fiction

Although science fiction was a form used by nineteenth-century European and English authors, most notably in Mary Shelley's *Frankenstein* (1831) and the works of Jules Verne and H. G. Wells, it is largely an American genre. Science fiction became a distinct form of writing in 1926 with the launching of the magazine *Amazing Stories* whose stated purpose was to publish stories based on science. The genre also includes fantasies and utopias, set in any time period, not just the future. In the early years, many of the stories were about space exploration, but thanks to the editorship of John W. Campbell at *Astounding Science Fiction*, which began to publish in 1930, eventually branched out into plots that were concerned with the effects of technology on individuals and society. From this emphasis came writers such as Isaac Asimov and subjects such as robots, alien cultures, alien and human interaction, and the consequences of nuclear warfare. After the United States used the atomic bomb in World War II, science fiction writers were taken more seriously and their works entered the mainstream. In two years' time, two new science fiction magazines were founded: *Fantasy and Science Fiction* (1949) and *Galaxy* (1950). Their emphasis on debunking science

fiction stereotypes with satire and humanism greatly influenced the field, and it was with these magazines that many of the notable science fiction novelists of the second half of the twentieth century got their start. Often, a novel would first be serialized in a magazine before being picked up by one of the book publishing houses, as was the case with Dick's *Martian Time-Slip*. In Britain, science fiction returned with the establishment of the magazine *New Worlds* and the publications of writers Brian Aldiss and J. G. Ballard, the latter being one of the first writers of the New Wave movement in science fiction. New Wave authors were more sophisticated and metaphorical in style and more concerned with the psychological impact of modern social trends. An anti-utopian pessimism crept into this genre that had started with optimism about the future. After the 1970s, anthropology and cosmology were added to the mix as well as a number of fine works by women such as Ursula K. Le Guin and Doris Lessing. Later, the impact of the computer triggered a whole new group of works exploring the interaction of humans and computers. Long a favorite of the motion picture and television industries, producing such cultural icons as *Star Wars* and *Star Trek* among many, many others, science fiction is definitely an established and respected genre in American literature.

Labor Unions

American labor unions were initiated among skilled crafts workers in the late eighteenth century to protect their jobs against less trained people. In the 1830s, unions became more concerned with larger social and economic matters. However, by the time the American Federation of Labor was founded in 1886 by Samuel Gompers (Readers may note there is a Samuel Gompers Field near Arnie Kott's settlement), the unions were focused on collective bargaining in regard to wages and working conditions, not on transforming the capitalist system. Eventually, the labor unions became very powerful politically as they lobbied the government and endorsed candidates. In the early 1960s, when Dick wrote *Martian Time-Slip*, the number of U.S. union members was growing because of the development of public employee unions, although the percentage of all workers that were unionized was starting to drop because the labor force was shifting to service jobs and away from manufacturing and manual jobs, where the bulk of the unions exist for craft or industrial workers. Nonetheless, Dick grew up and lived in a time when the money, power, and influence of labor unions were huge, and corruption among union bosses was legendary. For example, Jimmy Hoffa was the head of the Teamsters Union from the mid-1950s to the mid-1960s and was suspected of having ties to the Mafia. In 1964, Hoffa was convicted of attempted bribery of a grand jury member and was sentenced to fifteen years in prison. Released in 1971, he disappeared in 1975 and is believed to have been murdered by rivals. It is this element of American culture that Dick transferred to Mars with the colonists and which resulted in the character of the plumbers union boss, Arnie Kott, complete with henchmen and dirty tactics.

CRITICAL OVERVIEW

Martian Time-Slip was written during a particularly prolific period in Dick's life and is considered one of the best novels of his early career. However, in the many reviews and analyses of Dick's long list of works, *Martian Time-Slip* is frequently left unmentioned. Some critics tend to write about his works in total, noting common themes and style rather than singling out a particular book. Still, *Martian Time-Slip* garners some attention for its unique qualities. It is a novel that Bernadette Lynn Bosky and Arthur D. Hlavaty, writing about Dick for the *St. James Guide to Science Fiction Writers* state "skillfully combines 1950s social satire and metaphysical uncertainty."

Lawrence Sutin in *Divine Invasions: A Life of Philip K. Dick* asserts that *Martian Time-Slip* "is a brilliant novel of ideas and a humane and hilarious look at life on Earth's struggling colonies on Mars." Also noting the humor in the novel, Neil Walsh, writing for the *SF Site*, notes that Dick's inconsistent writing style, which "reads like a translation from another language" may have contributed to the "very funny moments" in *Martian Time-Slip*.

While Dick's writing style may have been inconsistent in this view, Walsh applauds the quality of Dick's structural technique: The repetition of the same scene from different perspective, Walsh says, "is an odd setup, but the payoff is stunning. . . . Which interpretation of reality is really real? Are any of them? It's a chilling,

haunting, beautiful piece of writing." Similarly, Douglas A. Mackey in a Twayne Publishers study of Dick concludes that in *Martian Time-Slip* "Dick effectively utilizes multifocal viewpoints to comment on the nature of the schizophrenic experience and its implication for our evaluation of 'normal' experience."

Emmanuel Carrère in *I Am Alive and You Are Dead: A Journey into the Mind of Philip K. Dick* points out that the "genius misfit" character of Manfred in a "staple of Dick's fiction." Carrère feels that Dick allowed Arnie Kott to die thinking that he was he was just in an alternate reality and that he would wake up and find himself okay because Dick was a "merciful creator" who wanted to let Kott be consoled, yet die in the real world rather than someplace potentially worse. Carrère conjectures that Dick "liked writing the end of this novel. It reassured him. Illusion and reality were clearly separated; the survivors walked on the terra firma of the koinos kosmos [a shared world of universal order, beauty, and ultimate truth]."

Another Dick scholar, Merritt Abrash in "Elusive Utopias: Societies as Mechanism in the Early Fiction of Philip K. Dick" comments that Dick usually does not "pay respect to a machine" in his novels, but he does in *Martian Time-Slip*. Abrash explains that Dick uses the Teaching Machines to make "his most profound statement about the gap between the device with utopian potential and the actual attainment of utopia." The Teaching Machines seem to be an improvement over human beings not only functionally but "in terms of ability to relate to them"; however, it turns out that the machines were "devised not to break through to a new and better form of education, but to strengthen existing social values." Abrash concludes that "as always with Dick, utopian potential is submerged beneath the kind of self-serving practicality associated with the 'establishment.'"

The extent of the criticism available since the resurgence of interest in Dick's literary career is testimony to his importance in the world of science fiction and the admiration he garners from scholars and fellow authors alike. Even though Dick died relatively young, he left behind an enormous body of work that was not fully appreciated in his lifetime but is likely to be examined and enjoyed for a long time to come.

WHAT DO I READ NEXT?

- A story about hunting down renegade artificial human life forms, "Do Androids Dream of Electric Sheep?", written by Dick in 1968, was the basis of the film *Blade Runner* and reissued as a book in 1982 as *Blade Runner* when the movie was released.

- *Player Piano* (1952), Kurt Vonnegut's first novel, is like *Martian Time-Slip* in that it is a satire on the way machines control society and the rebellion that calls for the return to a more natural life.

- Somewhat similar to *Martian Time-Slip*, *The Space Merchants* (1952), by Frederick Pohl and Cyril Kornbluth, depicts an America where huge corporations rule, there is a voiceless working class, and there are plans to colonize Venus.

- *Selected Stories of Philip K. Dick*, published by Pantheon in 2002, contains the original "The Minority Report" on which the Spielberg movie is based, the two short stories on which *Screamers* and *Total Recall* are based, as well as twenty other stories that demonstrate Dick's varied talent.

- An admirer of Dick and a famous science fiction writer in her own right, Ursula K. Le Guin published *The Left Hand of Darkness* in 1984, and a new edition came out in 2001. This novel tells the story of a human emissary to another galaxy and his subsequent involvement with an alien culture.

CRITICISM

Lois Kerschen

Kerschen is an educator and freelance writer. In this essay, she discusses Dick's decision to leave 1960s elements in his 1994 setting, which results in some dated material in this science fiction story.

Although science fiction can be set in any time period, readers usually expect science fiction to be set in the distant future. *Martian Time-Slip* is a little different, just as Dick himself was a different sort of science fiction writer. Dick actually wanted to be a mainstream novelist, but he could not seem to find a way into that realm. Consequently, he often used futuristic or space settings to give a story the veneer of science fiction when in truth it had a mainstream plot that could have been set anywhere. *Martian Time-Slip* is a satire of American business and suburban living; consequently, Dick retained much that pertained to 1962, the year the story was written, in this tale set in 1994.

Dick set his 1960s story in the future so that he could satirize his own times without being too obvious, yet not so far in the future that the comparisons to the 1960s would be missed. Philip Purser reports, after a 1974 interview with Dick for the *London Daily Telegraph*, that Dick's better novels "are set forward only a decade or two so that the ideas come bumping hard at you." True, Dick could have achieved his satire in a very distant future, but then he would have had to think up new technology for his futuristic world. It was easier to use familiar objects in his foreign world so that the focus can be on the satire and not on gadgets.

When it came to technology, Dick did not allow for many advances in thirty-two years, even though he vastly overestimated the speed of the space program by placing colonies on Mars starting in 1988. In 1962, when *Martian Time-Slip* was written, space travel was only beginning with the first orbit of the Earth. Perhaps Dick knew that the plan was to walk on the Moon in 1969 and assumed that going to Mars was just a hop, skip, and a jump away from the moon landing. Arnie's list of black-market items in chapter three includes typewriters and tape recorders. There are references to tapes, spindles, encoders, and recorders in several other places in the book as well. Tapes were an exciting innovation in the 1960s but seem antiquated for a 1994 setting and for readers in the twenty-first century.

Scattered throughout the book are references to articles from everyday life in the 1960s. For example, in chapter five, Lou's wife Phyllis turns on the "hi-fi," a term that may not even be recognizable to anyone born after 1970. A "hi-fi" was a high fidelity phonograph machine that played records. Records had been in use since the invention of the phonograph in the late

SINCE COMMUNISM WAS SO STRONG IN THE 1960S, IT WAS EASY FOR DICK TO ASSUME THAT COMMUNISM WOULD STILL BE A DOMINANT FORCE IN WORLD AFFAIRS JUST THIRTY YEARS LATER."

nineteenth century, but after the 1960s recordings moved rapidly through a series of technological advances such as eight-track tapes, Beta tapes, cassette tapes, compact discs, and other electronic devices.

Also in chapter five, Jack thinks back to when he left Earth, leaving his job and selling his Plymouth, an automobile that was still in production in 1994 but which was discontinued in 2001. Two pages later, Jack is asked why he is not cashing his paychecks. In an age in which most salaries are paid through direct electronic deposit to an employee's bank, the idea that Jack would have to manually deliver his paycheck to the bank certainly dates that detail of the story. In addition, in chapter twelve, there is a reference to Helio reading *Life*, a magazine that appeared in 1883 and was an American institution through the 1960s, but ceased publication in 1972. Although *Life* reappeared as a monthly magazine with limited production between 1978 and 2000, starting in 2004 the logo was attached to a weekend newspaper supplement. So Helio could have been reading a copy of *Life* in 1994, but it would have been a quite different publication from what Dick knew in 1962.

Since communism was so strong in the 1960s, it was easy for Dick to assume that communism would still be a dominant force in world affairs just thirty years later. So, in chapter two he writes, "I know a bunch of Communist officials from Russia and Hungary, big boys, was over here around a week ago, no doubt looking around." While communism still existed in 1994, it was no longer the established form of government for Russia or Hungary. Four pages later, mention is made of the "big powers back home, China and the U.S. and Russia and West Germany." In chapter six, there is a reference to the Soviets. West Germany and the Soviet Union did not exist in 1994. To Dick's credit,

he was not too far off to mention these countries because the Berlin Wall came down only five years earlier in 1989 with the reunification of East and West Germany following soon thereafter. The Soviet Union then broke apart in 1991.

Concerning autism, Dick was writing about the disorder under the errant assumptions of his time. In chapter three he states that "To have an autistic child was a special shame, because the psychologists believed that the condition came from a defect in the parents, usually a schizoid temperament." This idea was largely touted by Bruno Bettelheim, a leading child psychiatrist at the University of Chicago from 1944 to 1973. Bettelheim thought that autism in children resulted from emotional deprivation from a cold mother and an often absent father. Dick must have been aware of this theory and gives evidence that he was familiar with Bettelheim's "Joey: A 'Mechanical Boy,'" a famous 1959 article written for *Scientific American* about a boy who believed himself to be a robot. In chapter 10, Arnie says, "I read about a kid who thought he was a machine." Bettelheim's theory about autism was eventually discredited once it was learned that autism is not a form of schizophrenia but is a neurological disorder that hinders developing skills in social interaction and communication. In the early 2000s research intensified as the frequency of cases of autism continued to increase ten to fourteen percent each year.

Furthermore, the racial and sexual attitudes exhibited by the characters in *Martian Time-Slip* are taken directly from the time period in which the book was written. Leo Bohlen say the Bleekmen look like aboriginal Negroes. It was not long after the book was written that the term "Negroes" was replaced in common usage with black or African American. Of course, Dick could not anticipate changes in English usage, but "Negroes" does sound strange to younger readers who are not accustomed to hearing or seeing the term and it immediately signals outdated material. In like manner, the sexist remarks made by Norbert and Arnie may leave young readers wondering what the problem is with marrying a woman who has a master's degree. Older readers may likely remember a time before the 1970s when fewer women went to college, and suburban housewives were expected to devote themselves entirely to domestic matters and their husbands, and leave jobs, money matters, and decisions to their husbands. Arnie can be written off as just a macho jerk when he never notices anything about a woman except her looks, and when he criticizes Anne for being "overly masculine," but the aura of sexism hangs over the whole book. Just the fact that Dick calls the Martian natives Bleek*men* instead of Bleeks or Bleekers or some other non-sexist term dates the book.

Dick never explains how the colonization of Mars was made possible. Of course, the science of this science fiction novel was not important to him. He wrote a satire filled with questions about schizophrenia and just happened to place the story on Mars without being overly concerned if the setting was plausible. So the reader is left to wonder how humans conquered the problems of the toxic soil on Mars that gives off radiation, gravity (.375 that of Earth), temperature (average -81 degrees Fahrenheit), and atmosphere (mostly carbon dioxide, which is lethal to humans). There is a brief mention of adjusting to the air, but it is made with the casualness of someone asking about adjusting to the altitude on Pike's Peak. True, Mars is the only planet in the solar system that has any potential for colonization, but such plans would probably require an artificial atmosphere in an enclosed area and protective gear like an astronaut's suit for going outside.

Dick is not like Jules Verne or H. G. Wells, at least not in *Martian Time-Slip*. Purser reports that Dick said, "We've got to lock on to the present. Only those who can escape the past are free to seek new solutions." So Dick wrote about the present in his futuristic book to show that old, traditional practices may need changing if society is to truly have a better future. Otherwise, all that will result is the past rehashed. Thus, anyone expecting robots more advanced than the tape machines in the costumed contraptions called Teaching Machines, anyone expecting sophisticated computerized systems, highly imaginative technology or time machines will be disappointed with *Martian Time-Slip*. On the other hand, readers of this book will find unique time sequences in the plot and time travel via the mind, food for thought about life and what matters most, and an interesting perspective on shaping one's own reality.

Source: Lois Kerschen, Critical Essay on *Martian Time-Slip*, in *Novels for Students*, Thomson Gale, 2008.

Jason Koornick

In the following review, Koornick remarks on the place of Martian Time-Slip *in Dick's career and its message about the human mind. Koornick also outlines what he considers to be the critical elements in the novel.*

Martian Time-Slip is truly an anomaly in the science fiction genre. While it has many elements of a typical sci-fi novel, including a title highly suggestive of the genre, the main focus of *Martian Time-Slip* is on the intracies of the human mind with a heavy focus on the introverted world view of the schizophrenic.

The story takes place on the fledling Martian colonies in 1994 and its main character is Jack Bohlen, a skilled repairmen and recovering schizophrenic who still suffers flashbacks. The colonies on the planet are in a period of transition as the fate of the planet is decided by the UN. Jack gets caught up in the frantic business affairs of Arnie Kott, head of the powerful Plumbers Union who isn't afraid to use his power & money to further his goals, often at the expense of others.

Much of the novels psychological (and classic Dick) elements lie with an autistic boy named Manfred Steiner. The son of Jack's neighbor, Manfred boards in a clinic for autistic children who can't communicate with the people around them. Kott discovers that this boy has psychic powers and hires Jack to develop a system to communicate with the boy. Kott's motivations are to foresee the UN's use of Martian land so he can buy and resell the vast desert wasteland for a profit.

Jack's schizophrenic tendencies are exaggerated around the boy with whom he is hired to communicate. Manfred projects his world view to those around him and has a profound influence on the realities of the other characters. Philip Dick creates an incredible and thought-provoking explanation for the way that the schizophrenics experience time in *Martian Time-Slip*. By offering the readers glimpses into Manfred's and Jack's schizophrenic episodes, one is able to view their situation from a different viewpoint, one that sees time as relative and can foresee the decay of modern society.

There are many classic Dick episodes in *Martian Time-Slip*. Among them are Dick's fascination with decay and the long-term triumph of chaos over order (of which only Manfred is able to prophecize), the use of a business deal gone bad as a major element of the plot and the outward projection of personal realities onto the shared world. The main character is a normal person who gets caught up in the twisted schemes of a selfish businessman, only to find his own perceptions of reality crumbling.

Written in 1962 and published in 1964, *Martian Time-Slip* is an important novel in Dick's career and according to some, one of his best. The science fiction aspects of this novel are secondary in importance to the questions Dick is raising about the human mind. The stark Martian landscapes provide the setting but the situations and the characters have little to do with space travel or futuristic science commonly seen in the genre. Instead *Martian Time-Slip* focuses on the problems of human existence and personal psychological issues in the face of common and shared realities.

Martian Time-Slip was written during an interesting period of Philip Dick's career. In 1962, he had already been accepted into the science fiction community and was trying to hit it big with a mainstream novel. Written in the same period as *The Man In The High Castle*, Dick was working with ideas that would bring him mainstream acceptance. Both *The Man In The High Castle* and *Martian Time-Slip* deal less with the fantastic elements of science fiction and more with the internal struggles of the individual and how they relate to their world. With *Martian Time-Slip*, Dick was hoping to reach a much broader audience than those used to seeing his stories in pulp magazines and Ace Doubles.

Unfortunetly for him and in our favor, Phil was always able to make more money writing science fiction and after these novels, he would give up his hope for mainstream success and stick to the genre that he had the most success—science fiction. Of course one of Phil's greatest contributions to the genre is that he was able to use the freedom of science fiction to express ideas of philosophy, religion and psychology that were normally found in literature and other "mainstream" writing.

Some have called *Martian Time-Slip* one of PKD's greatest novels. In this reviewer's opinion, the strongest elements of this novel are (especially compared to his other works):

1. A consistent flow from beginning to end. The novel progresses at a slow pace at first but rises to the climax, keeping the reader's attention to the finish.

2. Less reliance on weird hallucinations and nightmarish delusions. While these elements are definitely present in *Martian Time-Slip*, they generally occur in a context which makes their effect stronger and meaningful.

3. The use of Mars as a backdrop and setting for the story is tasteful and relevant. As in many PKD stories, the threat of inevitable settlement (in this case, it could be war, collapse of government or extinction) looming in the background plays a major role in the actions of the characters and their psychological profile.

4. A fascinating look into the mind of the schizophrenic. Dick's fascination with the way that a schizophrenic views the external world is very apparent in *Martian Time-Slip*. His attempt to scientifically explain this psychological phenomenon is clever and an expression of PKD's doubts about his own reality.

What this reviewer found difficult about *Martian Time-Slip* is the sluggish pace of the first half. Instead of the book grabbing the reader's attention from the beginning, it slowly builds and finally rewards the reader with a glimpse at Jack Bohlen's and Manfred Steiner's schizophrenia. The initial part of the book introduces the main characters and sets up the situations that develop later in the novel. We meet typical Dick characters like Jack Bohlem, Mr. Yee and Arnie Kott who are involved in rather ordinary jobs and lives. The only exception is the older Mr. Steiner who is faced with a severe case of depression.

The events surrounding Steiner's suicide are rather irrelevant to the story of *Martian Time-Slip*. This novel is like other PKD novels in that it incorporates a few unrelated elements into a single story. This book is able to hold its own however and doesn't wander nearly as much as some of his other lesser works.

All in all, this reviewer was most impressed with the subtleties of *Martian Time-Slip*. It's avoidance of unbelievable and fantastic futuristic adventures works in its favor. The characters are faced with very recognizable and realistic dilemmas. The reactions of characters like Jack Bohlen to circumstances beyond his control are heartfelt and lend more credibility to the characters in this novel than some of PKD's other novels. This reader is able to sympathize with the trappings of Manfred Steiner who is forced to live in a world which he could see decaying. His psychic gifts of telepathy and foresight are a curse when his version of reality is so far removed from the world he lives in. The sense of alienation is expressed eloquently in *Martian Time-Slip* and Dick is playing with a powerful emotion to which everyone can relate in some way.

Martian Time-Slip is a novel which does not try to be more than a sum of its parts. It is an enjoyable and quick read that is not as bizarre and twisted as some of PKD's other novels but manages to incorporate these elements in an effective manner. This book would be recommended to a more seasoned reader of PKD, rather than as an introduction to the author. Among the reasons are a rather slow-paced first half and a story which doesn't represent the author at his best. Instead it is a novel which would be most appreciated by a reader who has tasted PKD's best flavors and is ready to sample the subtler aspects of his style.

Source: Jason Koornick, "*Martian Time-Slip*," in *philipkdickfans.com*, 2007, pp. 1–3.

Carl Abbott

In the following chapter excerpt, Abbott examines the ways in which the homesteading experience of the American West has been recreated by writers in depicting planetary colonies. In particular, Abbott discusses Dick's treatment of a successful settlement on the Mars frontier that shows the disaster as much as the triumph.

When writers such as Philip K. Dick and Ursula K. Le Guin wrote about homesteading in ways that questioned simple stories of success through perseverance, they were situating their ideas in this changing context of American historiography and also reflecting specific historical writings of the 1950s and 1960s that were probing beneath the surface of the western myth to find uncomfortable and incongruous realities. Novelist and essayist Wallace Stegner in *Beyond the 100th Meridian* (1954) and historian Walter Prescott Webb in "The American West: Perpetual Mirage" (1957) documented the fundamental inhospitality of the arid West and the problems that arose when eastern expectations came westward. In Webb's memorable phrase, the western mirage defied eastern farming practices and technological solutions such as dry farming and irrigation. Literary scholar Henry

Nash Smith, whose *Virgin Island* (1950) was one of the most influential works of post-World War II scholarship, analyzed the many ways in which the dream of a welcoming, garden-like continent had misdirected both political decisions and popular culture. Indeed, these scholars argued, expectations of individualism ignored the deep dependence of western settlers and communities on outside institutions. ...

Dick was correct that homesteading viewed realistically is a hard fit with American narratives of growth, for close examination of the historical experience shows as much disaster as triumph. Settlement from the eastern US has repeatedly washed across the high plains into the Rocky Mountains, lingered a decade or two, and then washed back. One generation of failure began with the Homestead Act of 1862, expanded with the first transcontinental railroads, and crashed in the drought and depression of the 1890s. More generous land laws and European hunger for American grain during World War I attracted another ambitious generation, who hit trouble in the 1920s and disaster in the 1930s. World War II, farm subsidies, and energy exploration subsidies fueled a third generation of ambition that crested and crashed in turn in the 1980s and 1990s.

Towns grew, perhaps even prospered, but they also failed. From the Texas Panhandle to the Dakotas is now a region of declining agriculture, aging population, and few in-migrants (see Frey). Just as the western American mountains are specked with the ghost-town remnants of the mining frontier, the plains are slowly taking back small-farm towns, while regional centers struggle to keep young people from the attractions of Denver, Seattle, or Minneapolis. Some areas actually peaked in population in the 1890s, others in the 1940s or 1950s. Jonathan Raban has chronicled the process of ambition and decline in eastern Montana in *Bad Land*, and Larry McMurtry fictionalized the experience of Texas in *The Last Picture Show* (1966). William Least Heat-Moon has explored the thinning human imprint in central Kansas in *PrairyErth*. Geographers Frank and Deborah Popper aroused consternation and fascination when they noted that 388 western counties in 1980 supported fewer than six people per square mile, the shorthand for frontier conditions. Their proposal—really a metaphor—was to slowly return unneeded lands to a preagricultural ecology as a Buffalo

Commons, pointing out that the extensive tracts of National Grasslands were the result of a similar process following the 1930s. The made-up title *Pilgrims without Progress,* the banned book that supposedly encompasses the Martian settlement experience in Dick's *Stigmata,* would not be a bad summary for much of homesteading history.

Martian Time-Slip describes a superficially more successful Mars, but one in which the hopes of a family frontier have given way to the worst of 1960s suburbia, with many of the details taken directly from the popular suburban critique of the 1950s and 1960s that Scott Donaldson incisively summarized in *The Suburban Myth.* The Martian homesteaders/householders that we see might as well be in San Bernardino County. They use water from the Martian canals for gardens rather than commercial agriculture. Husbands have second jobs as machinery repairmen of black-market merchandisers, while wives carry on sexual affairs in the afternoons. There are ads for automatic farm tractors, but no picture of how they might be used. There is also agribusiness, represented by a "ranch" in an area purchased by a Texas oil tycoon and administered by Texas (but, joke on Texas, it is really a dairy farm).

Meanwhile, the way to make money is through land speculation. The father of one of the homesteaders arrives unexpectedly from Earth with plans to buy land in the arid F.D.R. Mountains: "It was the last gasp of hope springing eternal in the old man; here there was land selling for next to nothing, with no takers, the authentic frontier which the habitable parts of Mars were patently not." In fact, the father is not a deluded romantic but a shrewd insider, attracted by an inside tip about a planned government facility that will cause the value to skyrocket. He wouldn't need his son's warning: "Don't commit yourself, because it's a known fact that any Mars real estate away from the part of the canal network that works—and remember that only about one-tenth of it works—comes close to being outright fraud."

Dick's 1960s Mars novels are satirical assaults on postwar American culture, with similarities to Kurt Vonnegut's *Player Piano* (1952) and Frederick Pohl and Cyril Kornbluth's *The Space Merchants* (1953) and *Gladiator-at-Law* (1955), but they are also critiques of the nation's past. They are positioned both chronologically and conceptually between the historians and critics of the 1950s, who pointed out the misunderstandings inherent in the agrarian myth, and those historians of the 1980s and 1990s who emphasize conquest, environmental devastation, and the corrupting effects of land monopoly. Dick's version of homesteading coincides with the ideas of numerous writers who have pointed out that the enterprising family of the homesteading West was caught from the start in a web of political and economic institutions beyond its control (see, for example, Dubofsky, Davis, Lukas, Robbins, and Worster). If it existed at all, the agrarian family utopia of nineteenth-century American aspiration and twentieth-century nostalgia was, at most, a brief moment in a process dominated by big institutions and capital.

Source: Carl Abbott, "Homesteading on the Extraterrestrial Frontier," in *Science Fiction Studies,* Vol. 32, No. 96, July 2005, pp. 251, 253–54.

Emmanuel Carrère

In the following excerpt, Carrère says that Dick wondered what it was like to be psychotic and then described the condition with his novel Martian Time-Slip. *This excerpt discusses how other characters in the book become like the one character Manfred, yet Dick allows the plumber to escape the confusion of illusion and reality through death.*

Soon after finishing *The Man in the High Castle,* Dick wrote a novel called *Martian Time-Slip,* in which, with considerably more earnestness than Huxley had after his mescaline trip, he asked himself the question, What does it feel like to be psychotic?

The story, which begins with a suicide whose effects ripple outward and touch every character at some point in the course of the novel, turns around land speculation on Mars, Earth's somewhat neglected colony, where labor union fiefdoms and United Nations concessions vie for control and influence. In an effort to get the jump on the competition, the chief of Mars's powerful Water Workers Union, an erstwhile plumber, would like to take a peek into the future. An ingratiating psychiatrist tells him of a new theory that holds that autism, and schizophrenia in general, is a derangement of the individual's sense of time. What distinguishes the schizophrenic from other people, according to the theory, is that the schizophrenic gets the whole picture all at once, whether he wants it or not: the entire reel of film that normally passes before people's eyes frame by frame unravels in a rush. Causality doesn't exist for the schizophrenic; he lives in a world governed by a principle of acausal connection that Wolfgang Pauli called "synchronicity" and that Jung, replacing one enigma with another, tried to use to explain the phenomenon of coincidence. Like someone on LSD or like God—insofar as one can know the nature of His *idios kosmos*—the schizophrenic dwells in an eternal present. All of reality comes rushing headlong at him as though he were in a never-ending car wreck. Accordingly, the psychiatrist tells the plumber, the schizophrenic has access to what we call the future. With this the ex-plumber has heard all he needs to and turns to that staple of Dick's fiction, the genius misfit, in this case a recovering schizophrenic and jack-of-all-trades capable of repairing everything from toasters to helicopter blades—a highly valued skill on Mars, where spare parts are exceedingly hard to come by. The plumber wants him to rig up a machine that will let him enter into mental contact with an autistic child named Manfred and extract precious information about the future from the boy's mind.

The repairman accepts the job reluctantly, fearing it will bring back painful memories of his own schizophrenia and force him to confront the question he has been trying to repress for years, ever since he left Earth: what was it he really saw that day he sat across the desk from his company's personnel manager and the man appeared to him as an assemblage of gears and electric circuitry? A hallucination or a vision, a psychotic breakdown or a sudden glimpse of true reality, stripped of its facade? Nevertheless, he grows attached to Manfred, eventually deciding, in the plumber's words (and with the same optimism that Dorothy felt with regard to her sister, Marion), that "it must be like fairlyland, in there, all beautiful and pure and real innocent."

A serious mistake, of course. Soon strange things start to happen. A Bruno Walter recording of a Mozart symphony becomes a hideous jangle of sound; the bodies of other people seem to split open as if in an accelerated process of organic decay. The entire objective universe in which the characters move about becomes progressively invaded by that of Manfred, who sucks them into his nightmarish reality, a place of absolute entropy, a land of death. The concept

of the "tomb world" had fascinated Phil ever since he first came across it in essays by the Swiss psychiatrist Ludwig Binswanger. The schizophrenic, Binswanger believed, lives (if one can call it living) in a world of eternal death in which everything has happened and at the same time is still happening, in which nothing more can ever happen. This "tomb" swallows up anyone who approaches it; it is waiting there to engulf everything and everyone.

All the characters in the novel become Manfred; no one can speak except to produce the desolate noises that are his response to the world. "I kept on going," the horrified repairman tries desperately to explain, looking for someone who I could still talk to. Who wasn't like—him." The ex-plumber gets his wish and travels through time, but it's Manfred's time that he travels through, the time of the tomb world, and the voyage turns hellish. His once-faithful secretary has become a predatory monster, everyday objects have taken on sharp, angry edges, the coffee he drinks tastes bitter and poisonous. A mask of empty darkness hangs in the air above his face and begins to descend on him. Now he realizes that never again will he see the living world he so foolishly left behind; he knows he will die in Manfred's autistic world—which he does.

It is hard to imagine anything more horrific than dying in someone else's nightmare, and Dick, merciful creator that he was, rescues the ex-plumber from this fate and grants him a kinder, and at the same time more ironic, demise. The hideous spell is lifted and the ex-plumber emerges from the tomb world, only to be killed by a minor character from one of the novel's subplots. As he is being rushed to the hospital in the throes of death, he can't believe what's happening to him and starts to laugh, because now he figures he knows the routine: he is still trapped in one of those fucked-up schizophrenic universes where first you get killed for no reason and then you wake up. That's what's going to happen to him, he thinks: he'll wake up and find himself back in his own reality. And as he's lying there thinking all this, he dies, this time for good.

Perhaps it's better this way, the repairman concludes. Phil thought so too, for two reasons: first of all, the ex-plumber dies consoled by the thought that he is not dying and, second, he dies in the real world, not in a place where things far worse than death can happen.

Phil liked writing the end of this novel. It reassured him. Illusion and reality were clearly separated; the survivors walked on the terra firma of the *koinos kosmos*. The repairman continues to have his doubts, for no one is ever cured of schizophrenia. "Once a person becomes psychotic," he tells himself, "nothing ever happens to him again. I stand on the threshold of that."

Me too, Phil thought. Perhaps he was standing on that same threshold. Perhaps he had always been there.

Source: Emmanuel Carrère, "Idiocy," in *I Am Alive and You Are Dead: A Journey into the Mind of Philip K. Dick*, translated by Timothy Bent, Metropolitan Books, Henry Holt, 2004, pp. 82–84.

Brian W. Aldiss

In the following essay, Aldiss identifies and explains the three webs that are integrated into Dick's novels and how they are used in Martian Time-slip: *the web of civilization, the web of human relationships, and the web connecting all the good and bad things in the universe. In addition, Aldiss discusses the comic effects and dark wit in the book.*

Arnie Kott is on his way back into a schizoid variant of the recent past:

> The trail levelled out and became wider. And all was in shadow; cold and damp hung over everything, as if they were treading within a great tomb. The vegetation that grew thin and noxious along the surface of the rocks had a dead quality to it, as if something had poisoned it in its act of growing. Ahead lay a dead bird on the path, a rotten corpse that might have been there for weeks; he could not tell.

The setting is Mars, which is now partly colonized. Colonists live along the water system, where conditions of near-fertility exist.

This web of civilization is stretched thin over utter desolation. There is no guaranteeing that it can be maintained. Its stability is threatened by the Great Powers back on Earth. For years they have neglected Mars, concentrating dollars and man-hours on further exploration elsewhere in the system; now they may interfere actively with the balance of the colony.

Behind this web exists another, even more tenuous: the web of human relationships. Men and women, children, old men, bleekmen (the autochthonous but non-indigenous natives of Mars) all depend, however reluctantly, on one

> THIS IS THE MALEDICTORY CIRCLE WITHIN WHICH DICK'S BEINGS MOVE AND FROM WHICH THEY HAVE TO ESCAPE: ALTHOUGH ALMOST ANY CHANGE IS FOR THE WORSE, STASIS MEANS DEATH, SPIRITUAL IF NOT ACTUAL."

another. When poor Norbert Steiner commits suicide, the effects of the event are felt by everyone.

Behind these two webs lies a third, revealed only indirectly. This is the web connecting all the good and bad things in the universe. The despised Bleekmen, who tremble on the edge of greater knowledge than humanity, are acutely aware of this web and occasionally succeed in twitching a strand here and there, to their advantage; but they are as much in its toils as anyone else.

These three webs integrate at various coordinate points, the most remarkable point being AM-WEB, a complex structure which the UN may build some time in the future in the F.D.R. Mountains. The structure is visible to Steiner's autistic son, Manfred, who sees in it an advanced stage of decay. Its function in the novel is to provide a symbol for the aspirations and failures of mankind. The structure will be a considerable achievement when completed; which is not to say that it is not ultimately doomed; and part of that doom may be decreed by the miserable political and financial maneuverings which form one of the minor themes of this intricately designed novel.

Martian Time-Slip comes from the middle of one of Dick's most creative periods. *The Man in the High Castle* was published in 1962. In 1963 came *The Game-Players of Titan* and then, in 1964, *The Simulacra*, *The Penultimate Truth*, *Clans of the Alphane Moon*, and the present volume. Although Dick is a prolific author, with some thirty novels appearing in fifteen years, his production rate is modest when compared with many other writers in the prodigal field of SF.

One of the attractions of Dick's novels is that they all have points at which they interrelate, although Dick never introduces characters from previous books. The relationship is more subtle—more web-like—than that. There is a web in *Clans of the Alphane Moon*, made by the "world-spider as it spins its web of determination for all life." The way in which Mars in the present novel is parceled up between various nationalities is reminiscent of the parceling up of Earth into great estates in *The Penultimate Truth*, and *The Game-Players of Titan*. The horrifying corrupt world of Manfred's schizophrenia, the realm of Gubble, reminds of the tomb world into which John Isidore falls in *Do Androids Dream of Electric Sheep* or of one of the ghastly fake universes of Palmer Eldritch in *The Three Stigmata of Palmer Eldritch*. When Jack Bohlen, in the first few pages of the novel, awaits the arrival of his father from Earth, change is about to creep in; and change is often paradoxically embodied in someone or something old, like the Edward M. Stanton lying wrapped up in newspaper in the back of Maury Rock's Jaguar, in the opening pages of *We Can Build You.*

Such building blocks are by no means interchangeable from book to book; Dick's kaleidoscope is always being shaken, new sinister colours and patterns continually emerge. The power in the Dickian universe resides in these blocks, rather than in his characters, even when one of the characters has a special power (like Jones's ability to foresee the future in *The World Jones Made*), it rarely does him any good.

If we look at two of the most important of these building blocks and observe how they depend on each other for greatest effect, we come close to understanding one aspect of Dickian thought. These blocks are the Concern With-Reality and the Involvement-with-the-Past.

Most of the characteristic themes of SF are materialist ones; only the concern-with-reality theme involves a quasi-metaphysical speculation, and this theme Dick has made peculiarly his own. Among his earliest published stories is "Imposter" (1953), in which a robot believes himself to be a man; the faking is so good that even he cannot detect the truth until the bomb within him is triggered by a phrase he himself speaks. Later, Dickian characters are frequently to find themselves trapped in hallucinations or fake worlds of various kinds, often without knowing it or, if knowing it, without being able

to do anything about it. In *The Man in the High Castle*, the world we know—in which the Allies won World War II and the Axis Powers lost—is itself reduced to a hypothetical world existing only in a novel called *The Grasshopper Lies Heavy*, which the victorious Japanese and Germans have banned.

And it is not only worlds that are fake. Objects, animals, People, may also be unreal in various ways. Dick's novels are littered with fakes, from the reproduction guns buried in rock in *The Penultimate Truth* which later are used, and so become "genuine fakes," to the toad which can hardly be told from real in *Do Androids Dream of Electric Sheep*? and the androids masquerading as human in the same novel. Things are always talking back to humans. Doors argue, medicine bags patronize, the cab at the end of *Now Wait for Last Year* advises Dr. Eric Sweetscent to stay with his ailing wife. All sorts of drugs are available which lead to entirely imaginary universes, like the evil Can-D and Chew-Z used by the colonists on Mars in *Palmer Eldritch*, or the JJ-180 which is banned on Earth in *Now Wait for Last Year*.

The colonists in *Martian Time-Slip* use only the drugs available to us, though these are generally at hand—in the very opening scene we come across Silvia Bohlen doped up on phenobarbitone. Here the concern-with-reality theme is worked out through the time-slip of the title, and through the autistic boy, Manfred.

Manfred falls into the power of Arnie Kott, boss of the plumbing union which, because water is so scarce, has something of a stranglehold on Mars (a typical piece of wild Dickian ingenuity). Arnie worries a lot. He asks his Bleekman servant, Helio, if he has ever been psychoanalyzed.

> "No, Mister. Entire psychoanalysis is a vainglorious foolishness."
> "Howzat, Helio?"
> "Question they never deal with is, what to remold sick person like. There is no what, Mister."
> "I don't get you, Helio."
> "Purpose of life is unknown, and hence way to be is hidden from the eyes of living critters. Who can say if perhaps the skizophrenics are not correct? Mister, they take a brave journey. They turn away

from mere things, which one may handle and turn into practical use; they turn inward to meaning. There, the black night-without-bottom lies, the pit."

Of course, there are many ways of falling into the pit, one of which is to have too much involvement-with-the-past. In a published interview with Philip Purser, Dick admits to a fascination with the past, quoting lines of Henry Vaughan, "Some men a forward motion love / But I by backward steps would move . . . " Whilst saying how much he enjoys the junk of the past, Dick adds, "But I'm equally aware of the ominous possibilities. Ray Bradbury goes for the Thirties, too, and I think he falsifies and glamourises them" (Daily Telegraph Magazine, 19th July 1974).

Arnie Kott has an innocent fascination with objects of the past—he possesses the only spinet on Mars. In the same way, Robert Childan's trading Mickey-Mouse watches and scarce copies of Tip Top Comics to the victorious Japanese (in *The Man in the High Castle*) is represented as entirely innocuous. Trouble comes when the interest with the past and all its artifacts builds into an obsession, like Virgil Ackerman's Wash-55, a vast regressive babyland which features in *Now Wait for Last Year*.

And this is indeed where Dick parts company with Ray Bradbury, and with many another writer, in or out of SF. If he sees little safety in the future, the past is even more insidiously corrupting. So dreadful is Manfred's past that you can die in it. The past is seen as regressive; one of the most striking Dickian concepts is the "regression of forms" which takes place in *Ubik*, that magnificent but flawed novel in which the characters try to make headway through a world becoming ever more primitive, so that the airliner devolves into a Ford trimotor into a Curtis biplane, while Joe's multiplex FM tuner will regress into a cylinder phonograph playing a shouted recitation of the Lord's Prayer.

In *Martian Time-Slip*, the involvement-with-the-past is general, as well as being particularised in Manfred's illness. Mars itself is regarded by Earth as a has-been, and is patterned with has-been communities based on earlier versions of terrestrial history. Here it is especially difficult to escape damnation.

With the past so corrupting, the present so uncertain, and the future so threatening, we might wonder if there can be any escape. The secret of survival in Dick's universe is not to attempt escape into any alternate version of reality but to see things through as best you can; in that way, you may succeed if not actually triumphing. The favoured character in *Martian Time Slip* is Jack Bohlen, whom we last see reunited with his wife, out in the dark garden, flashing a torch and looking for someone. His voice is business-like, competent, and patient; these are high-ranking virtues in the Dickian anthropology. It is significant that Jack is a repairman ("an idiot who can fix things," says Kott)—a survival-rich job, since it helps maintain the status quo. Similar survivors in other novels are pot-healers, traders, doctors, musical instrument makers, and android-shooters (since androids threaten the status quo).

The characters who survive are generally aided by some system of knowledge involving faith. The system is rarely a scientific one; it is more likely to be ancient. In *Martian Time-Slip*, it is the never-formulated paranormal understanding of the Bleekmen; Bohlen respects this vague eschatological faith without comprehending it, just as Kott despises it. The *I Ching*, or *Book of Changes*, the four-thousand-year-old Chinese work of divination, performs a similar function in *The Man in the High Castle*, whilst in *Counter-Clock World*, Latta Hermes randomly consults the Bible, which predicts the future with an alarming accuracy. In both Dick's two early masterpieces, *Time-Slip* and *High Castle*, this religious element—presented as something crumbling, unreliable, to be figured out with pain—is well-integrated into the texture of the novel.

Dick's next great book, *The Three Stigmata of Palmer Eldritch*, was written very soon after *Martian Time-Slip*, and the two are closely related, not only because Mars is in both cases used as a setting. To my view, *Eldritch* is a flawed work, over-complicated, and finally disappearing into a cloud of quasi-theology; whereas *Martian Time-Slip* has a calm and lucidity about it. But in *Eldritch* we also find an ancient and unreliable meta-structure of faith, in this case embodied in the ferocious alien entity which fuses with Eldritch's being.

> Our opponent, something admittedly ugly and foreign that entered one of our race like an ailment during the long voyage between Terra and Prox . . . and yet it knew much more than I did about the meaning of our finite lives, here; it saw in perspective. From its centuries of

vacant drifting as it waited for some kind of life form to pass by which it could grab and become ... maybe that's the source of its knowledge: not experience but unending solitary brooding.

So muses Barney Mayerson. Jack Bohlen desperately needs a transcendental act of fusion; he is estranged from his wife, sold by his first employer, threatened by his second, invaded by the schizophrenia of the boy he befriends. He sees in this mental illness, so frightenly depicted in the book, the ultimate enemy. From this ultimate enemy come the time-slip of the title and that startling paragraph which seems to condense much of the feeling of the book and, indeed, of Dick's work in general, when Bohlen works out what Manfred's mental illness means:

> It is the stopping of time. The end of experience, of anything new. Once the person becomes psychotic, nothing ever happens to him again.

This is the maledictory circle within which Dick's beings move and from which they have to escape: although almost any change is for the worse, stasis means death, spiritual if not actual.

Any discussion of Dick's work makes it sound a grim and appalling world. So, on the surface, it may be; yet it must also be said that Dick is amazingly funny. The terror and the humor are fused. It is this rare quality which marks Dick out. This is why critics, in seeking to convey his essential flavour, bring forth the names of Dickens and Kafka, earlier masters of ghastly comedy.

Martian Time-Slip is full of delightful comic effects, not least in the way in which Steiner and the lecherous Otto Zitte ship illegal gourmet-food items from Earth in unmanned Swiss rockets. Dick's fondness for oddball entities and titles is much in evidence, notably in the surrealist public school, where the Emperor Tiberius, Sir Francis Drake, Mark Twain, and various other dignitaries talk to the boys. Below this easy-going humour lies a darker stream of wit. Arnie Kott's terrible and fatal mistake of believing that reality is merely another version of the schizoid past is also part of the comedy of mistakes to which Dick's characters always dance.

There is a deeper resemblance to the works of Dickens and Kafka. Dick, like Dickens, enjoys a multi-plotted novel. As the legal metaphor is to *Bleak House*, the world-as-prison to *Little Dorrit*, the dust heap to *Our Mutual Friend*, the tainted wealth to *Great Expectations*, so is Mars to *Martian Time-Slip*. It is exactly and vividly drawn; it is neither the Mars as adventure playground of Edgar Rice Burroughs nor the Mars as parallel of Pristine America of Ray Bradbury; this is Mars used in elegant and expert fashion as metaphor of spiritual poverty. In functioning as a drearnscape, it has much in common with the semi-allegorical, semi-surrealist locations used by Kafka to heighten his Ghastly Comedy of bafflement. Staring at his house in the meagre Martian desert, Bohlen smiles and says, "This is the dream of a million years, to stand here and see this."

Dick's alliance, if one may call it that, with writers such as Dickens and Kafka makes him immediately congenial to English and European readers. It may be this quality which has brought him reputation and respect on this side of the Atlantic before his virtues are fully recognized in his own country.

Source: Brian W. Aldiss, "Dicks Maledictory Web: About and Around *Martian Time-Slip*," in *Science Fiction Studies*, Vol. 2, No. 5, March 1975, pp. 42–47.

SOURCES

Abrash, Merritt, "Elusive Utopias: Societies as Mechanisms in the Early Fiction of Philip K. Dick," in *Clockwork Worlds: Mechanized Environments in Science Fiction*, edited by Richard D. Erlich and Thomas P. Dunn, Greenwood Press, 1983, p. 119.

Bettelheim, Bruno, "Joey: A 'Mechanical Boy'," in *Scientific American*, Vol. 200, March 1959, pp. 117–26.

Bosky, Bernadette Lynn, and Arthur D. Hlavaty, "Philip K. Dick: Overview," in *St. James Guide to Science Fiction Writers*, 4th ed., edited by Jay P. Pederson, St. James Press, 1996.

Carrère, Emmanuel, *I Am Alive and You Are Dead: A Journey into the Mind of Philip K. Dick*, translated by Timothy Bent, Bloomsbury Publishing, 2005, pp. 83, 84.

Dick, Philip K., *Martian Time-Slip*, Vintage Books, 1964.

Mackey, Douglas A., *Philip K. Dick*, Twayne Publishers, 1988, p. 55.

Purser, Philip, "Even Sheep Can Upset Scientific Detachment," in *London Daily Telegraph*, No. 506, July 19, 1974, pp. 27, 29.

Sutin, Lawrence, *Divine Invasions: A Life of Philip K. Dick*, Carroll & Graf, 2005, p. 117.

Walsh, Neil, "*Martian Time-Slip*: A Review," in *SF Site*, www.sfsite.com/12bpkd71.htm (accessed November 8, 2006.)

FURTHER READING

Apel, D. Scott, ed., *Philip K. Dick: The Dream Connection*, Impermanent Press, 1999.

This book contains over eight hours of interviews with Dick, a number of supplementary essays by leading critics and contemporaries of Dick, and a little-known short story by Dick about his mystical experiences.

Bukatman, Scott, *Terminal Identity: The Virtual Subject in Postmodern Science Fiction*, Duke University Press, 1993.

This book is a collection of essays about science fiction, the relationship of technology to human culture, and authors such as Philip K. Dick and many others who have tackled social issues in this genre.

Carrère, Emmanuel, *I Am Alive and You Are Dead: A Journey into the Mind of Philip K. Dick*, translated by Timothy Bent, Bloomsbury Publishing, 2005.

A fellow science fiction writer of note, Carrère really gets into Dick's head as he provides literary criticism in a cultural and personal context in this examination of Dick's life and works.

Sutin, Lawrence, *Divine Invasions: A Life of Philip K. Dick*, Carroll & Graf, 2005.

Although there are other biographies of Dick, *Divine Invasions* is generally considered the best. Originally published in 1981, it was reissued in 2005 to complement the release of the film *A Scanner Darkly*, which is based on Dick's book of the same name.

Warrick, Patricia S., "The Labyrinthian Process of the Artificial: Philip K. Dick's Androids and Mechanical Constructs," in *Philip K. Dick*, edited by Martin Harry Greenberg and Joseph D. Olander, Taplinger Publishing, 1983, pp. 189–214.

In this essay, Warrick investigates the variety of portrayals that Dick gives to answer the questions of "What is human?" and "What only masquerades as human?" In addition, there is a question about whether and when electronic devices menace or help humans.

Picture Bride

YOSHIKO UCHIDA

1987

Picture Bride, first published in 1987, is the story of a young Japanese woman who leaves, what she believes to be, the confines of her small village and heads for the broader horizons of the United States in the early decades of the twentieth century. Waiting for her is her future husband, a man whom she has never met. She has seen a picture of him and has heard stories of his prosperity, but she knows little else about the man, who has also only seen a photograph of her. Theirs is a typical story of the times in which Japanese bachelors ventured forth to the West Coast of the United States, hoping to find wealth, to buy a house, and then to send for a woman to marry. In most cases, both the men and the women were not fully prepared for the challenges of moving away from the security and comfort of their native country. Many of these new immigrants were caught off guard by the cultural and racist antagonism waiting for them in their adopted country, as well as the awkwardness of marrying a complete stranger.

Picture Bride begins as the protagonist, Hana Omiya, is sailing toward the United States to meet for the first time a man called Taro Takeda. Hana's heart and mind are afire with imagined possibilities. Unfortunately, by the end of the story, many of Hana's and Taro's dreams are unrealized. They have watched friends die. Others have given up and returned to their native land. When World War II breaks out, Hana and Taro are detained in prison camps, their material possessions reduced to the

Yoshiko Uchida *(Photograph by Deborah Storms. Courtesy of the Bancroft Library, University of California, Berkeley)*

contents of four suitcases. This is all they can show for their thirty years of hard work. They are mistrusted by non-Japanese people, their neighbors, employers, and government leaders. How will they find the strength and courage to begin again?

Although a prolific writer, Yoshiko Uchida wrote only one novel for adult readers, *Picture Bride*. The work was reprinted many times over the years. Despite the traumatic events presented in this novel, the story ends on a hopeful note, encouraging readers to cheer for the protagonist's seemingly endless supply of courage.

AUTHOR BIOGRAPHY

For a long time, Yoshiko Uchida was the only author who focused on the Japanese-American experience. She was a prolific writer of mostly juvenile works who won many awards.

Uchida was born in 1921 in Alameda, California, the daughter of Japanese immigrants. She and her sister, Keiko, lived relatively

comfortable lives because their father was one of the few Japanese immigrants who held a secure job. Uchida's early life included writing, which she began at the age of ten. After graduating from high school at the age of sixteen, Uchida attended the University of California at Berkeley. She was in college when the Japanese attacked Pearl Harbor in 1941. The internment that Uchida writes about in her novel *Picture Bride* is based on personal experience, as she and her family were interned for three years in these prison camps, first in California at the Tanforan Racetrack and later at Topaz, in the Utah desert. Uchida was released in 1943 from Topaz so she could attend Smith College, where she eventually earned a master's degree in education.

After college, Uchida taught elementary school for awhile, then she took on a variety of clerical positions and began to spend more and more of her time writing. At first she wrote Japanese folktales, and in 1955, she won the Children's Spring Book Festival Award for her collection *The Magic Listening Cap*. In 1972, she earned a notable book citation from the American Library Association for *Journey to Topaz*, Uchida's first account in fiction of the Japanese-American internment camp experience. In 1983, the *School Library Journal* and the New York Public Library named Uchida's children's book *The Best Bad Thing* the best book of the year. Awards were presented in 1985 for another of Uchida's children's stories *The Happiest Ending* by the Bay Area Book Reviewers, the Child Study Association, and the San Mateo and San Francisco Reading Associations. In 1988, the Japanese American Citizens League honored Uchida with an award for her life's achievements.

In her lifetime, Uchida published over thirty books, most of them written for children. She died in 1992 in California.

PLOT SUMMARY

Chapters 1–9
Twenty-one-year-old Hana Omiya, the protagonist of Uchida's *Picture Bride*, is on the ship that is taking her from Japan to the California coast as this story begins. It is some time in November of 1917, and Hana has decided to leave her village of Oka for a new life in the United States. She is heading toward Taro Takeda, whom she has promised to marry although she has never

met him. Taro lives in Oakland. Their marriage has been arranged through Taro's uncle and Hana's parents. Hana encouraged this union so she might escape the drudgeries of becoming a Japanese farmer's wife. Taro is ten years older than Hana and allegedly the owner of a thriving business.

When Hana first hears of Taro Takeda, she imagines that a life as his wife might be less confining than her prospects in an arranged marriage in her own small village. So she decides to take advantage of this unknown man's need for a wife. She ventures out alone for the first time in her life and endures the long ocean journey. As she spends the cold days on the ship, she fantasizes about her future life as the wife of a merchant. She is hopeful that her life will be leisurely, with simple luxuries. At the end of the trip, she is eager to begin her new life.

Waiting for her is Taro Takeda, the first of many disappointments that diminish Hana's dreams. Taro is much older than he appears in the picture he sent her, and Hana begins to wonder, upon meeting him, if she has made a mistake. Taro takes Hana to his friends, Kiku and Henry Toda. Hana will stay with the Todas until the wedding. Kiku is also a picture bride and completely understands the challenges that lay ahead for Hana.

With Kiku Hana begins to realize how much she must change in order to fit into the American culture. Hana's clothes are all wrong, she notices. She has nothing but kimonos to wear. Even her shoes must be changed. Kiku helps Hana make these fashion transitions by offering her some of her clothing. Kiku's warm personality makes Hana feel more relaxed. Hana also relishes the idea of privacy, when Kiku offers Hana a separate bedroom to use. It is the first time that Hana has ever slept alone. Kiku explains that Americans consider privacy a necessity, which stands in stark contrast to the overall communal atmosphere of Japanese life.

On the following Sunday, Taro takes Hana to his church. Taro is a Christian and very much involved in the Japanese church they attend. Reverend Okada is the head of this church and a friend of Taro's. During the sermon, Reverend Okada mentions the challenges the Japanese congregation must face in this new land, a place that is not always welcoming to Japanese faces. Hana is surprised to hear this. After the service, Taro introduces Hana to some of his other friends, including Dr. Sojiro Kaneda and Kiyoshi Yamaka, a man close to Hana's age who shows immediate interest in Hana. Hana is flattered by Kiyoshi's attention and finds that she too is attracted to him.

After lunch, Kiyoshi drives Hana and Taro to Taro's shop. Hana is shocked by the shabbiness of the store, another one of her disappointments. After eating dinner with the Todas, Hana exposes her disappointment to Kiku. Kiku tells Hana not to build her dreams so big. They are living in a country that does not trust or like them, Kiku tells Hana. She then reminds Hana that she has come to make Taro happy and that Hana should make the best of it. Kiku worries about Hana and also notices the attraction between Hana and Kiyoshi. Kiku works to make Hana's wedding beautiful and to hurry its occurrence. The wedding is scheduled to take place in two weeks.

Hana reluctantly adjusts to married life. She also becomes active in Taro's business, giving it the so-called woman's touch, which means that she cleans and organizes the place. She also learns to deal with customers as Taro prepares her to take care of the store while he is away on business. Before he leaves for a trip to the countryside with Dr. Kaneda and Reverend Okada, Taro asks Kiyoshi to stop by the shop to check on Hana while he is gone. Hana and Kiyoshi's relationship blossoms during the visit. They are unafraid of showing interest in each other. Hana even cries and admits that she wishes she and Kiyoshi had met under different circumstances. "If only we had met in Japan," Hana laments. They agree that they cannot allow the relationship to develop into a sexual one, but they will enjoy one another's friendship. Hana admits that Kiyoshi makes her feel happy and alive for the first time since she has come to the States. When she tells Kiyoshi that she wants him to be her friend for as long as she lives, she realizes that "for that brief moment, Taro did not even seem to exist."

On New Year's Day of 1918, Hana prepares a Japanese feast. She dresses in her kimono and is complimented by her guests for her cooking as well as for her looks. During the meal, Kiyoshi touches his hand to her thigh. Henry Toda notices the flirtation between Kiyoshi and Hana and remarks on it. Later, after the guests are gone, Taro reminds Hana that she is married to him and must pay special attention only to him. That night, he tells Hana that he wants a child.

A few weeks later, Taro again leaves Oakland with Dr. Kaneda and the minister to visit Japanese farmers and to take them needed merchandise. While Taro is gone, Kiyoshi visits with Hana, who invites him up to her apartment for lunch. Kiyoshi kisses Hana, and she almost succumbs to her passion but finally tells Kiyoshi that they cannot do this to Taro. When Taro returns, a customer comments on the fact that the store was closed at noon while Taro was away. Taro suspects the worst of Hana and Kiyoshi, despite Hana's denial. By autumn of that year, Hana is pregnant by Taro. She hopes the baby is a boy, a gift to Taro to make up for Hana's lack of love for her husband.

The great influenza epidemic has infected the city. Because Hana is pregnant, she cannot join other church members who are caring for the sick. But when she hears that Kiyoshi has caught the flu, she rushes to the clinic to see him. The next day, Dr. Kaneda tells Hana that Kiyoshi has died. A few days later, Hana comes down with the flu. In her weakness, she loses the baby.

Chapters 10–17

It is now 1920, and Hana and Taro have had a baby girl, Mary, who is six months old. Taro has been looking for a better place for them to live and raise a child and brings the news that he has found a house for them to rent. The narrator declares that Hana has become familiar with the racial prejudice against Japanese people, and although she does not understand why this hatred exists, she asks Taro to confirm that the people in the neighborhood he has chosen will accept them. He assures her, even though he is not certain.

Shortly after Hana and Taro move into their new home, four men appear at their door, and they suggest that Hana and Taro are not welcomed in the neighborhood. Taro stands up to the men, and Hana feels proud of her husband, realizing what a good man he is.

Kiku shows up, surprising Hana with the news that Henry is planning on moving to the country to become a farmer. Kiku is distressed. She does not think of herself as a country woman and is not looking forward to the prospects of all the hard work that a farm would require. But Henry has lost his job, and he is attracted to the idea of being his own boss. Kiku admits that she has decided to go with her husband and to try to make a good life with him. Hana is sad to see Kiku leave.

After Kiku leaves, Hana becomes more involved in Taro's church. She becomes the treasurer of the Women's Society. One day, the superintendent of the Sunday school comes to her and asks for a loan. Believing that the loan will go to pay for the Sunday school, Hana lends him the money without question. Later, she learns that the superintendent has taken his wife and gone back to Japan, using the money to pay for their tickets. Kenji Nishima, a young seminary student and assistant to the superintendent, takes full responsibility for this theft and promises to donate his personal savings to repay the loan. Hana also wants to help, so she calls Kiku's old employer, Mrs. Ellen Davis, to ask for a job as a cleaning woman. Ellen is the wife of a surgeon, who has also lost a son. She is very nice to Hana and appreciates Hana's work.

Taro hears that Kenji Nishima is not doing very well. He suggests that Hana make Kenji some good Japanese food and take it to Kenji's dormitory. When Hana arrives, she discovers that Kenji is missing. Hana and the minister's wife find Kenji hiding in the attic. Hana later suggests to Taro that they take Kenji into their home and help nourish him both physically and psychologically. Kenji is overwhelmed with guilt about his former boss who stole money from the church, and he is homesick, lonely, and exhausted from school work and church responsibilities. Taro is a little suspicious of Hana's desire to help Kenji, but he agrees to allow the young man into his home. Hana admits that part of the reason for her wanting to take care of Kenji is to give him the life that Kiyoshi missed.

When Ellen hears that Hana is taking care of Kenji, she immediately raises Hana's salary. She also suggests that in order to help Kenji, who has become quite despondent, Hana should give Kenji something to do. One day when Kenji asks to take Hana's daughter to a neighborhood park, Hana reluctantly allows him to do so. Although Kenji comes home late, Hana is impressed with how he has cared for the young girl. It is through Mary that Kenji finds new life and begins to heal. Unfortunately, at this same time, Hana notices that her husband is becoming withdrawn. Hana discovers that Taro is not doing well financially. The owner of his shop has increased the rent, and Taro does not have the money to pay him. Business has been off, and he has no savings. Hana devises a plan, knowing that Ellen will loan them money. But she must make Taro believe this is not a loan but rather that Taro is working for the money. So she asks Ellen to hire Taro to paint her house, which Ellen does. In the meantime, Hana takes care of Taro's shop and makes changes that increase business. Taro is so impressed with Hana's business sense that he suggests that she stop working for Ellen and become his assistant in the shop. Hana is delighted.

Chapters 18–23

Hana's daughter, Mary, is now ten years old. Mary begs her parents to take a summer vacation, something they have never done. Taro finally gives in, as he decides that it would be nice to visit the Todas who are running a successful farm in the valley. Kiku is also thriving in the farming environment and has given birth to two sons, Jimmy and Kenny. At the farm, Taro relaxes, as the families reunite. There are late night horse-drawn wagon rides and family singing fests, activities common to the Todas but unique for Hana, Taro, and Mary. Hana is impressed with the healthy condition of her friends, who are tanned and strong. The Todas, Hana feels, have created a world uninhibited by racial prejudice, a place that nourishes Kiku's and Henry's spirits. When Hana and Taro return to their home, Hana tries to keep her mind invigorated by her experiences on the farm, but she soon feels confined in the city by restrictions silently and subtly imposed by the surrounding white culture.

Reverend Okada announces that he is returning to Japan before his children are too old to remember how to speak Japanese. Kiyoshi Yamaka is assigned to the minister's position. Okada's leaving makes Hana wonder about her daughter, who, as she grows older, seldom speaks Japanese. Hana, by contrast, seldom speaks English. Hana realizes that her world and that of her daughter's are growing apart.

When Mary turns sixteen, she becomes more aware of her differences from the white population. She is embarrassed by her parents who are more connected to Japan than to the United States. She shuns them publicly. When she goes to college, she eventually shocks her parents by dating Joseph Cantelli, a white boy. One morning, Hana and Taro wake up to discover that Mary is gone. She has eloped with Joseph. Time passes and Mary announces that she is pregnant. She and Joe are living in Nevada and will soon move to Utah, where Joe has been offered a new job. Mary sends occasional letters to her parents, but she misses none of her Japanese roots. Unlike Hana, Mary enjoys being in the company of white people and likes being associated with all things American. Hana writes to tell her daughter that she will come to help her with the birth of the new baby, but Mary politely turns down her mother's offer. Hana is devastated.

Chapters 24–35

This section of the novel begins with the announcement of Japan's involvement in World War II. Taro hears the news on the radio and cannot believe it. Even so, Taro believes that this will make no difference in his own world, his life in the United States. Shortly after, however, FBI agents appear at Dr. Kaneda's home and announce that the doctor must go with them to be interrogated. Dr. Kaneda never returns home. Later, Kenji Nishima learns that the doctor has been sent to a detention camp in Montana. Rumors begin to spread that all Japanese people living along the West Coast might be uprooted. Hana and Taro begin to prepare for the possible evacuation, selling their furnishings and possessions for much less money than they are worth. As the rumors become more supported by evidence, Taro liquidates his entire inventory in the shop. Announcements are made about all first-generation Japanese immigrants, who are told they should sell everything except what can be contained in two suitcases for each family member. When Mary hears of this news, she sends a letter to her parents. She welcomes them to come live with her in Nevada, but she also tells them that she thinks they would be more comfortable with their friends. She suggests that since her parents are not citizens, they may be unsafe wherever they go. In other words, Mary suggests that her parents go along with the evacuation, "At least in the camps you would be with your friends," Mary writes. Hana understands that Mary is suggesting that it would be better if they did not travel to Nevada. Besides, Mary adds, she and Joe will probably be moving to Utah soon. Hana and Taro decide to go wherever the U.S. government tells them to go.

Meanwhile, Henry Toda has decided to sell his farm. Before leaving, one night, he packs up some Japanese treats for Dr. Kaneda. It is late, and Henry hears a noise outside. He goes to investigate and is shot and killed.

The day has finally arrive. Kenji Nishima comes to help Hana and Taro pack their suitcases onto Ellen's car. Ellen will drive them to what is called Tanforan, an old race track near San Francisco that has been converted into a camp for all the relocated Japanese immigrants. Hana and Taro are assigned a room, which is actually a stall in a quickly renovated horse stable. Kenji helps the couple find beds and clean the room. Later Taro finds scraps of wood and makes a skimpy table and benches. The walls are thin, so there is little privacy and only scant heat. As they settle in, Hana receives a telegram from Kiku, reporting Henry's death.

As time goes by, Hana learns to adjust to her new surroundings. The woman next door, who is loud and nosey, actually turns into a friend, helping Hana by telling her when it is best to go take a shower and how to improvise with found materials. On the other side of Hana's stall is a widow, Mrs. Mitosa, who has a young daughter, Sumiko, about the same age as Kenji Nishima. Hana and Taro both realize that Sumiko would make a fine wife for Kenji, and they begin their matchmaking scheme. Kenji also helps Henry out of his depression by putting Taro to work as a carpenter, making small utensils and carrying cases for some of the inhabitants of the camp.

By August, Hana and Taro hear the rumor that everyone at Tanforan is going to be sent to Utah. The only good aspect of this is that Hana and Taro hold onto a dream that as their train passes through Salt Lake City, they might see Mary and Joe, and their new baby Laurie. As they prepare themselves for the move, Hana and Taro are greeted by Kenji, who announces that he has asked Sumiko to become his wife. The wedding will be held before they leave Tanforan. Sumiko asks Taro to give her away at the marriage ceremony. Hana, as she sits in the makeshift church, watching Taro walk Sumiko down the aisle, thinks that Sumiko represents the daughter that Taro and she never had. Shortly after the wedding, everyone packs up, preparing for their journey to Topaz, a detention camp built in the Utah desert.

Hana's train passes through Utah at night. By midnight, they stop at Salt Lake City, just long enough for them to see Mary and Joe for a few minutes. They exchange a few words, and Mary gives her parents pictures of Laurie, Mary's daughter. They did not bring Laurie because it was so late and very cold. Before the train pulls out of the station, Hana and Taro convince Mary that they are all right and that their living conditions are not so bad. Hana hides her tears until Mary is out of sight.

When the sun rises, the passengers look at the scenery around them, feeling somewhat hopeful as they pass through small towns. They are on a bus now, and when they enter a desolate area, with vegetation thinning out until it practically disappears, they discover that this is where they will live. Crude barracks have been set up in the middle of the desert. The barracks are surrounded by high barbed-wire fences.

Dr. Kaneda sends Taro a letter. After reading it, Taro concludes that Dr. Kaneda has lost all interest in living. Taro too is depressed. He finds little to do and next to nothing to live for. Kiku is not faring much better, especially since President Roosevelt has declared that all citizens, no matter what their ethnic background, have the right to enlist in the military. Kiku's sons are debating whether to enlist and go to war. One night they inform Kiku that they are leaving.

Meanwhile, Taro has found a new simple interest after having found an old Indian arrowhead in the sand. He talks to Hana about going back to California one day and beginning a new business. Hana's mood lightens when she hears Taro talking about the future. But one night, while Taro is out walking, a guard mistakes his actions around the fence and shoots and kills Taro.

Mary, Joe, and Laurie come to the camp once they hear that Taro is dead. Hana refuses to leave with them. She will stay with Taro, who is buried in the desert, until she can take his body home with her. As Hana says good-by to Mary, she hears someone calling to her. It is Kiku, who has been transferred to the Topaz camp. The story closes with Hana and Kiku walking arm in arm across the camp, and Kenji telling his new wife, Sumiko, that she is not to worry about Hana and Kiku, because they are both strong women.

CHARACTERS

Joe Cantelli

Joe Cantelli is a young college instructor, whom Mary meets when she is in school. Joe is the first white man Mary dates. Joe and Mary eventually elope, are married in Nevada, and have a daughter,

Laurie. After Joe comes into Mary's life, Mary cuts herself off from her parents and their Japanese culture. Joe offers his home to Mary's parents after they are interned; however, Mary does not encourage her parents to accept Joe's offer, and Joe does not insist.

Laurie Cantelli

Laurie Cantelli is the baby girl born to Mary and Joe. Laurie does not make an appearance in this story until Taro's death. At Taro's funeral, Hana sees her granddaughter for the first time.

Ellen Davis

Ellen Davis is the good-hearted wife of a surgeon and one of the few white people who befriend the Japanese characters in this story. Ellen employs Hana and also provides work for Taro. She transports Hana and Taro to the internment camp and give them certain provisions to make their stay more comfortable. She does not in any way protest their internment. She supports Hana as best she can, usually by giving her money. She treats Hana humanely, without degrading her, when Hana works as a cleaning woman in Ellen's house.

Doctor Sojiro Kaneda

Wise Dr. Sojiro Kaneda is a friend of Taro's and a big supporter of the Japanese community. He treats many of the immigrants without expecting pay and often helps them with psychological problems as well as physical ailments. Dr. Kaneda was married, but his wife died of tuberculosis. He is a stabilizing member of the community, even during most of his internment.

When Kiyoshi Yamaka dies from influenza, Dr. Kaneda walks to Hana's house to break the sad news. He understands how much Kiyoshi means to Hana. Kaneda is the helpful one in the midst of trouble and confusion as the new immigrants attempt to adjust to changes in their lives. But in the end, after spending years in the internment camps, Kaneda loses his faith and determination. Right before Taro is shot, Taro receives a letter from Kaneda, espousing his own defeat. This depletes Taro's reserve to stay strong. At the end of the story, there is no further information given, and readers do not know Kaneda's fate.

Mrs. Mitosa

Mrs. Mitosa lives in the horse stall next to Hana's. She is a widow when she comes to the camp and has a daughter, Sumiko, who is close to Kenji Mishima's age. A quiet woman, Mrs. Mitosa suffers from asthma. When the Japanese prisoners are taken to the desert in Utah, she has trouble breathing because of the dust. She is taken to the hospital. Because she needs medical treatment beyond the scope of the camp, she is transferred to a facility in Salt Lake City, thus giving her daughter and Kenji an opportunity to leave the camp to attend to her.

Sumiko Mitosa

Sumiko Mitosa, the daughter of the widow Mrs. Mitosa, is attracted to Kenji Nishima and begins a relationship with him. When the couple marries, Taro gives Sumiko away, as if he were her father. Hana watches Taro walk down the aisle with Sumiko and wishes that her own daughter, Mary, were more like Sumiko.

Kenji Nishima

Kenji Nishima is first introduced when he is shamed by the actions of his boss, the superintendent of the Sunday school at Taro's church. Kenji, a seminary student, is overwhelmed by the guilt of the superintendent's actions, as well as by the responsibility as a student and as a practicing leader of the church. He is lonely and homesick, not psychologically or physically well. Hana suggests that she and Taro take Kenji into their home so she can nourish Kenji back to health.

Upon his recovery, Kenji is permanently grateful to Hana and Taro and counsels Hana on several occasions on how to deal with Taro when Taro is being difficult. Kenji is even more supportive when they are all transferred to the internment camps. Kenji helps Hana and Taro with their luggage and setting up their room, and helps Taro get over his depression. Before their internment, Kenji becomes the head of the church. While imprisoned, he continues his leadership role. By the end of the story, Kenji is happily married, supposedly the last factor in ensuring his future peace of mind.

Reverend Okada

Reverend Okada is the head of the church when Hana first arrives in California. He, like Dr. Kaneda, often ministers to the Japanese immigrant population, both in the city and in the country. Okada is a generous man, who counsels his parishioners on many subjects, including how to overcome the challenges they face among white Americans.

Okada announces, toward the last part of the novel, that he is going back to Japan with his wife and children. He had come to California on a temporary basis, wanting to help the immigrants to establish a church and a community of support. He wants to take his family back to Japan before his children forget what it means to be Japanese. He leaves before the war breaks out. Hana reflects on his departure and realizes it is too late for her to instill Japanese qualities in her own daughter, which Hana regrets.

Hana Omiya Takeda

Hana Takeda is the protagonist of this novel. When the novel begins she is on her way to the United States. She has decided to take up an unknown man's offer of marriage rather than spend the rest of her life in her small Japanese village.

Hana is determined to make her life better than that of her sisters. She is pretty and intelligent and has received an education higher than many of her Japanese peers. She sets off for United States alone, unafraid (and also unaware) of all the challenges that lie ahead of her.

Beginning full of beautiful dreams, Hana quickly becomes disappointed with what she finds on the West Coast. Instead of a young man waiting for her, she finds a man who is middle aged. Instead of a life of leisure, she finds that she must work as a shopkeeper and a cleaning woman. Instead of welcoming arms, she finds racial prejudice. However, Hana has a seemingly unending supply of courage and fortitude. But she does not assimilate well into her new country, unable to learn the English language sufficiently to express her deepest thoughts to anyone who does not speak Japanese, including her daughter. But she is considered, by her friend Kiku, a Japanese jewel. Hana is graceful, tactful, and artful. She is a good wife, in spite of the fact that she falls romantically in love with a man closer to her age. She is a nurturing mother who thinks about her daughter's needs above her own. And she does not chastise her daughter when Mary makes is quite obvious that she does not want her mother in her life.

Although she does not love Taro at first, Hana does learn to respect him. She often defers to Taro, even though she has good ideas of her own. She understands his confusion when he is caught between the more conservative ways of traditional Japanese life and the customs of their adopted country. Hana often tries to smooth the path so Taro has a more comfortable life.

Hana arrives in the United States an innocent, unsuspecting person, living more on idealized hopes than in reality; however, by the end of the story, she is wise and strong enough to figure out any challenge. Hana is tried by a series of calamities and survives, despite considerable hardship.

Mary Takeda

Mary Takeda, Hana and Taro's only child, was doted upon as a child and was obedient and thoughtful. However, the more Americanized Mary becomes, as she grows older, the less she wants to do with her ancestral roots. She is so embarrassed by her parents that when her mother comes to Mary's high school to deliver a costume for a presentation, Mary quickly shoos Hana out the back door. Later, Mary does not tell her parents about her feelings for Joe, and the couple elopes in the middle of the night, leaving only a note behind to explain. She never calls her parents after she leaves, and she seldom writes. When she does send a letter, she often deters her parents from coming to visit her. Mary states that she sees very few Japanese people in Nevada, and she likes it that way. Mary refuses to bring her daughter, Laurie, to the train station to meet Hana and Taro as they pass through the town on their way to the new internment camp; Mary makes excuses for leaving Laurie at home. After Taro dies, Mary regrets that she never allowed Taro to meet his granddaughter. By the end of this story, Hana does not seem to mind as much that Mary is missing from her life.

Taro Takeda

Taro Takeda is in his thirties when this story begins. He is hopeful that the "picture bride" he has sent for will make him a good wife. He is pleased with Hana's looks and style when he first meets her but must soon remind her that she is to focus her attentions only on him, as Hana falls in love with another man.

Taro is a businessman, but not a terribly successful one. He gets by but his skills are not as sharp as Hana's, who quickly evaluates his lack of success and begins to turn around his business. Hana finds that Taro has a good heart and is willing to protect his family at all cost. He is not the romantic partner that she had hoped for, but Taro does his best to provide for Hana and Mary.

TOPICS FOR FURTHER STUDY

- Compose letters from a prospective Picture Bride and her intended future husband. Write two sets of three letters, one answering the other. In these letters describe yourself. For one letter, you might, as the prospective husband, tell your Picture Bride what kind of work you do and what you expect from her as your wife. Then respond as the Picture Bride, telling your future husband what you expect from him. You can write these letters in a serious tone or use your comedic side and make the whole series funny. Read the letters to your class.

- Create two display charts or slide shows for your class. On one display, show a typical wardrobe for a Japanese man and woman for the early period of the twentieth century. Learn the Japanese names of the different pieces of clothing. On the other display, present a wardrobe for an American man and woman contemporary to those same times. Use actual photographs to make the display more informative.

- Conduct research on the Internet or in your local library about the Japanese internment camps. Collect photographs and details of daily life for a teenager in one of the internment camps. Put together a display that shows what a typical day might have been like. Include information on the weather in different seasons, the landscape, what kind of classes children attended each day, what chores they did, what kinds of food they had, and a description of the living quarters. Present this information to your class.

- Watch the movie *Picture Bride* (1994, original screen play by Kayo Hatta). Though this movie is not based on Uchida's novel, it has the same subject matter. How do the stories compare? What emotions are explored in each version? Is internment a part of both stories? Are the endings similar? In what ways do the main characters differ? Present a short synopsis of the movie to your class and explain how the movie compares to the novel.

Eventually Taro learns to trust and respect Hana's gifts and includes her in his business transactions. As their daughter grows up and moves away, Taro and Hana's relationship grows closer. Although Taro becomes depressed after spending more than a year in detention, the suggestion is he pulls himself out of it before he is murdered. The story suggests that the guard misconstrues that Taro is trying to escape. Instead, Taro may have merely been out in the desert at night because he loved both the stars and the small treasures he found in the sand. Tragically, Taro is shot and killed, leaving his wife to fend for herself.

Henry Toda

Henry Toda is a good but somewhat unpolished man. He is a hard worker and a heavy drinker. Henry tends to say what is on his mind and is the first one to voice what everyone else has noticed, that Hana and Kiyoshi are attracted to one another. Henry is married to Kiku, Hana's best friend. When Henry is fired from his job as janitor at a local bank, he decides that he is tired of having to depend on the whims of the white people around him and wants to go out to the valley and work as a farmer and eventually own his own land. This is exactly what he does. He has two children while living in the country and since these boys are U.S. citizens, Henry buys land in his sons' names. He has completely turned his life around when the order for internment comes. Henry must sell his farm way below what it is worth. Tragically, Henry is shot right before the family gathers their belongings and leaves for the internment camps.

Jimmy Toda

Jimmy Toda is one of the sons of Henry and Kiku. He and his brother are the opposite, in many ways, of Hana's daughter Mary. When Hana visits the Toda farm, she sees how unrestricted Jimmy and Kenny are in comparison to Mary. While they are in the internment camp, however, Jimmy and Kenny are as restricted as everyone else. They decide to leave the camp the only way they can, by enlisting in the army.

Kenny Toda

Kenny is one of the sons of Henry and Kiku. Kenny, like his brother, Jimmy, enlists in the army in order to leave the internment camp. There is no mention of what becomes of Jimmy or Kenny after they leave the camp.

Kiku Toda

Kiku Toda was a picture bride several years prior to Hana's arrival in California. Kiku perfectly understands everything that Hana is going through in moving from Japanese culture to her new life in the United States. Kiku is like Hana's big sister. She helps dress Hana in western-style dresses and makes Hana's wedding gown. When Kiku leaves to live on a farm, she offers her old job (cleaning woman to Mrs. Davis) to Hana. Unable to become pregnant while living in the city, Kiku gives birth to two boys once she is living in the country. The country has made Kiku's life fertile in many ways. Contrary to what Kiku anticipated at the prospect of being a farmer, the country has brought vibrancy back into her life. She is so happy that Hana is somewhat jealous of Kiku's new life. When they are relocated, Hana and Kiku are sent to different camps. However, by the end of the story, Kiku is transferred to Topaz. The suggestion is that everything will be all right, despite all the hardships both of these women have faced.

Kiyoshi Yamaka

Handsome Kiyoshi Yamaka is immediately attracted to Hana upon first seeing her. Hana returns his attention, and the two of them confess their feelings for each other. Yamaka wishes they had met under different circumstances and pursues Hana quietly whenever Taro is out of town. Hana pledges her love to him, though she will not go as far as giving in to her sexual passions for him. Kiyoshi succumbs to influenza that sweeps the United States after World War I. He represents the romantic love that Hana never fully experiences.

THEMES

Culture Clash

Uchida's *Picture Bride* is a story of culture clash as experienced by the protagonist, Hana, in her coming-of-age adventures as she adjusts to living in the United States. In California, Hana finds that everything about her seems to be out of place. Her clothes are all wrong; her language is not understood; even the smell of her favorite foods annoys others. Her intelligence is belittled because she speaks a foreign language and cannot fully express herself, and her fine Japanese graces are mocked because they are different from American manners. Everything that she has learned, everything that she has cherished about her Japanese culture comes under suspicion in the United States.

Hana knows that in order to get along better with the majority of the people around her she must adapt to her new culture. However, she is torn between wanting to fit in and wanting to hold onto her Japanese heritage. But even part of what is most dear to her, her daughter Mary, slips away from her because Hana refuses to relinquish her Japanese ways. Hana loves her Japanese culture, but the more she clings to it, the farther away her daughter moves. Mary represents the opposite of Hana. Mary wants all things American. Mary wants nothing to do with her parents' Japanese culture, so she pushes herself away from her parents and even from the West Coast, where many Japanese people live. Mary even tries to remove herself further by marrying a man with European ancestors and then giving birth to a biracial child.

Hana points out the culture clash in her husband, Taro, who wants Hana to be more submissive to him, as most Japanese women of her time were taught to be. Yet Taro also wants Hana to internalize American culture as he encourages her to learn English, to be married in a gown that reflects American fashion tastes, and to relinquish her Japanese mannerisms, such as bowing to guests and uttering typical traditional Japanese phrases upon inviting guests into their home. This same clash is exhibited in Hana's daughter. Though Mary wants to dress in a Japanese kimono to celebrate International Day at her school and asks her mother to bring the kimono to the school and to help her and the other students dress themselves properly, she is so embarrassed by her mother that she sends Hana out the back doors of the school and does not invite her mother to attend the presentation. Mary, in other words, is willing to dress in a Japanese costume, but she still wants to distance herself from being Japanese.

Dreams versus Reality

As Hana sails from Japan to the United States, her mind is filled with pleasant dreams about the future. She imagines her new life in California will be everything that her life in her small Japanese village is not. As she lands on the shores of the West Coast, her dreams begin to fade. This pattern of idealizing the future only to be disappointed by the reality continues throughout the story as her fantasies come face to face with actual circumstances. Taro is not the dashing, young lover she envisioned. He is not a wealthy merchant. Hana will not have a life of leisure. She will lose the man she truly loves and will never have a son. One by one, her hopes are dashed, as Hana faces each new challenge. Once she finds a comforting dream, reality rushes in. She envisions a son, and her daughter turns into someone she hardly knows; she anticipates a close community, and her neighbors are cold-hearted, closed-minded people. Even her adopted country, which she assumes stands for freedom, actually turns into a racial and prejudicial prison. She barely gets to know her grandchild, and her husband is murdered. In spite of all her disappointments, however, somehow Hana finds the courage and patience to dream again. As the story ends, readers cannot help but believe that with the help of her friend Kiku, Hana finds the strength to dream again and to try to make her new dreams come true.

Romantic Love versus Friendship

Twice in this story, Hana must choose between romantic or sexual love and friendship. Hana realizes that she does not love Taro. She goes through with the marriage to him, though, because she has promised to do so. She is disappointed by his age, his looks, and his status. However, over time, Hana realizes that Taro is a good man. Taro works hard, protects his family, and stays true to Hana, even though he knows that Hana does not love him. Taro is not the lover Hana anticipated, but he has a good heart and does not fail Hana. So despite the lack of romantic love, the couple develops a deep friendship.

Just the opposite develops between Hana and Kiyoshi Yamaka. Kiyoshi is immediately attracted to Hana and she to him. They are closer in age than Hana and Taro, and Hana finds Kiyoshi more physically appealing. Although Hana knows it is wrong for a married woman to be attentive to another man, she cannot help herself. She regrets she did not meet Kiyoshi in different circumstances. She is also flattered that such a handsome man would pay attention to her. Although they flirt with each other and kiss, Hana's propriety prevents her full expression of her sexual attraction. She resists making love to Kiyoshi because it would be wrong. An extramarital affair with Kiyoshi would hurt Taro. So she stops Kiyoshi's physical advances. Still she cannot stop her love for him. With Kiyoshi, Hana experiences a situation that is the opposite of her relationship with Taro. She loves Kiyoshi but only allows their relationship to develop as a friendship.

Parent and Child Relationship

Hana and Taro are very pleased when their daughter, Mary, is born. Taro, especially, had wanted a child to confirm his relationship to Hana. When they are blessed with a child, Taro extends his budget so that he can provide a home that is better suited for raising a child. They dote on their daughter and have hopes that their love of her will be reciprocated.

Mary, by contrast, has little emotional attachment to her parents. She is embarrassed by their foreignness and seems selfish in her decisions as an adult. She focuses on moving away from reminders of her Japanese heritage and is all but outright rude when her parents suggest that they want to be part of Mary's new life as a wife and mother. However, Mary is herself a devoted parent. She is more protective of her daughter, refusing to bring her out in the middle of the cold night, than she is concerned that her parents meet their first grandchild when Hana and Taro pass through Salt Lake City on their way to the second internment camp. After Taro dies, Mary regrets her actions toward her parents. She wishes she had taken her daughter to the train station so her father could have at least seen his only granddaughter. She also wishes she had been more like the daughter that Taro wanted. Although it is too late for Mary to show affection for her father, she does try to amend her ways with her mother. As it turns out, it is too late even to do so, as Hana has come to accept Mary's lack of interest in her. Too much has happened. Besides Hana has, in many ways, replaced Mary with Kenji, who has looked

Japanese Americans line up at mealtime at an internment camp in Puyallup, Washington (© Seattle Post-Intelligencer Collection; Museum of History & Industry / Corbis)

after Hana, and Kenji's wife, Sumiko, who asks Taro to represent her father and walk her down the aisle when she is married. The narrator relates that in the end, Hana turned to Kenji, who "comforted her most. He had been through the darkest moments of life with her and knew her needs best." In contrast, Mary seems an "outsider, not knowing quite how to behave in the closeness of the Japanese American community," and she "felt ill at ease among her mother's friends."

Racism

The novel dramatizes the racist views of white people concerning the Japanese. Differences are not explained and accepted but rather incite hatred, suspicion, and segregation. Racist feelings intensify as the story continues. In one incident, neighborhood men visit Taro. Ashamed of their feelings, they lie to Taro, telling him that other neighbors are troubled by Taro and his

family living in their community. They are asked to leave their home merely because they are Japanese. The white people do not explain why they are afraid of Hana and Taro. Instead, they make Taro and Hana feel uncomfortable, hoping that they will decide that they are unwelcome and move away.

A similar racism occurs in the countryside, where Kiku and Henry have bought a farm. They have worked hard and charge lower prices than the white farmers do. This undercuts the white farmers' businesses, so the white farmers do their best to scare the Japanese farmers off their land, going as far as to murder Henry.

President Roosevelt's Executive Order 9066, which demanded that all Japanese people living on the West Coast be interned, was racist in its assumption that after the attack on Pearl Harbor any Japanese American might well be an enemy. The paranoid government feared that some of

COMPARE
&
CONTRAST

- **1940s:** According to the 1940 U.S. Census, the population of Japanese Americans in the United States totals 285,116. Most live in Hawaii or in California.

  Today: Japanese Americans are not singled out in the U.S. Census. They are grouped under a general category of people who are of Asian descent. There are about 7 millions Asian Americans living in the United States. The majority live in New York, California, and Hawaii.

- **1940s:** About 120,000 Japanese American citizens living along the West Coast are sent to internment camps following the 1941 Japanese attack on Pearl Harbor for what the government calls security reasons.

  Today: Many Arab Americans in the United States are detained by the U.S. government for what are termed security reasons after the

terrorist attacks of September 11, 2001. From 2002 through 2006, approximately five hundred Muslims arrested in Afghanistan and elsewhere are detained at a U.S. detention camp at Guantanamo, Cuba, because they are suspected by the Bush administration of being possible al-Qaeda or Taliban operatives. The majority are held without being charged or having access to legal counsel. In June 2006, the U.S. Supreme Court rules against the Bush administration, stating that prisoners at Guantanamo are subject to protections guaranteed by the Geneva Convention.

- **1940s:** By the end of World War II, the economy of Japan is devastated and must be supported by the United States.

  Today: Japan's economy is growing. Its success is partly the result of the U.S. market for Japanese electronics and automobiles.

---

the Japanese might be spies or might assist the Japanese government in its war against the United States. That fear generalized to judging all Japanese by the possible risk posed by some.

STYLE

Timeframe Divisions

Picture Bride is divided into large periods of time. Each section presents a specific time period in Hana's life. The first section is devoted to 1917 and 1918, a time when there were numerous picture brides. During this time, many women came to the United States, prepared to marry men they had seen only in a photograph. These women, like Hana in Uchida's story, had big dreams about the United States and their new lives in what they believed to be a prosperous country. Like Hana, many of these women lost their ideal hopes when they faced the man

behind the photograph. As Kiku comments in this story, most men sent photographs taken when they were much younger. Many of these men also exaggerated their financial status in order to attract the best wife. Many of these women had no idea of the hardships that faced them.

The second segment, 1920 to 1921, depicts Hana as a new mother and as the victim of racism against Japanese. Having a child makes Hana and Taro more aware of the society around them, the people and the community in which their daughter will grow up. This section also introduces Kenji, a young man who is a significant character in the rest of the novel, a sort of surrogate son for the child that Hana and Taro lose.

The third part covers the 1930s. During these years Mary matures. As she grows up, she distances herself from her parents because she wants to be American and not be identified as Japanese. Eventually, Hana realizes she cannot maintain a relationship with her daughter.

The final section deals with World War II and the concurrent internment of Japanese Americans. In this part of the story, the hardships suffered by Japanese Americans during the war is dramatized.

Using this historical timeframe, Uchida follows Hana's coming-of-age development within a particularly hostile environment. The novel gives a fictionalized portrait of what it was like to be Japanese in the United States before and during World War II.

Autobiographical Novel

Much of Uchida's fiction is based loosely on her own life. She and her family were interned during the war at the Tanforan Camp in California and in the Utah camp called Topaz. The author draws from this experience from her life to tell the fictional story of Hana and Taro.

Omniscient Point of View

The novel is related from the point of view of an omniscient narrator, meaning that the narrator depicts what happens from many different points of view but is also able to reveal the thoughts of more than one character. Much of the story is told from the perspective of the main character, Hana. The reader sees and feels what Hana sees and feels. But there are moments when the reader is also aware of the thoughts of Hana's husband, Taro, and Hana's daughter, Mary. Other times, the narrator relates the thoughts of Kiku, Hana's friend. The omniscient point of view allows the reader to gain different perspectives, thus giving a more extensive view of the subject matter.

HISTORICAL CONTEXT

World War II and Japanese Internment

After the Japanese attack on Pearl Harbor on December 7, 1941, President Franklin D. Roosevelt ordered (through Executive Order 9066) the arrest of Japanese Americans, primarily those living on the West Coast. Violating the basic rights of citizens, as provided by the U.S. Constitution, President Roosevelt ordered the U.S. military to build detention camps and then to transport Japanese American citizens and legal aliens to the make-shift quarters. Roosevelt reportedly did so in the name of national security. It has been estimated that 120,000 Japanese Americans were

incarcerated, most of them under the age of eighteen. According to the Report of the Commission on Wartime Relocation and Internment of Civilians, some students were released to go to college or to enlist in the U.S. Army. However, a large number of people were held in these camps until World War II ended. This means some people spent up to four years in these camps. No one in these camps was given the benefit of due process. They could not protest these illegal laws that sent them to prison.

In 1980, when the commission published its results, it was declared that none of the detainees had been proven to be a spy, which had been the government's stated reason for the detention. Rather, the commission concluded the detention of Japanese Americans was the result of racism and wartime hysteria. Eight years later, Congress passed the Civil Liberties Act of 1988, which stated that an injustice had been done to the Japanese Americans and suggested that these people were owed a presidential apology and a token sum of $20,000, paid to every detainee.

There were ten major designated relocation camps, most located in isolated and desolate desert or swampland areas: Tule Lake and Manzanar in California; Minidoka in Idaho; Topaz in Utah; Heart Mountain in Wyoming; Granada in Colorado; Rohwer and Jerome in Arkansas; and Poston and Gila River in Arizona. In addition, there were several temporary so-called assembly areas (such as the Tanforan Race Track) and many isolation centers, totaling over twenty different camps. Tule Lake in the mountains of California was reserved for those people suspected of or convicted of crimes. Also, many who would not sign oaths of loyalty to the United States ended up at Tule Lake.

Japanese Immigration to the United States

In 1869, Japanese immigrants came to California to work at the Wakamatsu Tea and Silk Farm Colony. Their plan to grow tea and to produce silk, however, proved unsuccessful. Most of these Japanese immigrants landed either in Hawaii or in one of the West Coast cities, such as San Francisco, Portland, or Seattle. The U.S. Census of 1870 shows that there were fifty-five Japanese people living in the United States. By 1880, that number had increased to 148. Ten years later, thanks to an agreement between Japan and Hawaii, more Japanese people were allowed to immigrate, and by

A group of Japanese picture brides set sail to meet their new husbands *(© Bettmann / Corbis)*

1890, 2,038 Japanese were in the States, over half of them living in California. These numbers continued to grow as the Japanese gained a reputation for their skills in agriculture and their willingness to work hard. In 1900, the census calculated that there were 24,326 Japanese in the United States, of which only 410 were women. However, in 1907, supremacist organizations, agitated local farmers, and some politicians came together to create a law that reduced Japanese immigration, limiting new Japanese arrivals to women and children. Many of the women who came from Japan arrived as picture brides. Then a permanent halt to Japanese immigration occurred when the U.S. Congress passed the Immigration Act of 1924, which prohibited new immigrants from Japan. This act was in effect until 1952.

Most immigrants lived and worked in Japanese communities. Immigrants opened shops that sold Japanese goods or worked in various industries such as agriculture, fishing, mining, and the railroads. Many Japanese families banded together in cooperatives, which helped them gain power and wealth. There were many successful Japanese businesses just before the bombing of Pearl Harbor, but the subsequent internment of Japanese Americans in most cases led to the loss of homes and businesses.

Picture Brides

Although the concept of picture brides continues in the early 2000s (for example, catalogues of women from such places as the Philippines and Korea can be found in circulation in the United States), the term as used in the early part of the twentieth century mostly referred to Asian women who were willing to emigrate, usually to Hawaii or to the West Coast of the States.

Typically, Asian men traveled to the United States first, setting up some form of employment, either as factory workers or agricultural laborers. Some men were able to save money and develop their own businesses. Entering into an agreement with a matchmaker back home, which usually involved a relative of the man speaking to the relatives of the picture bride, the future husband waited for his bride with her picture in hand, hoping to match the image to the newly arrived woman upon. Picture brides were popular with the Japanese. In Japan, arranged marriages were common, and this tradition made the Japanese amenable to the idea of picture brides. Marriage based on love was not common among the Japanese.

Many future husbands surprised their picture brides by being older than they represented themselves in their photographs, since having another picture taken beyond the one they used for their passports was time consuming and expensive. Many of these men also exaggerated the amount of their personal wealth in order to lure a good woman. Picture brides offered stability for these men. Wives helped in the home with cleaning and cooking, thus providing a better home life for their husbands. Many picture brides also earned money, by either working in the fields with their husbands or taking on domestic jobs in other people's homes. The children from these marriages were another labor and income resource for the family. Employers encouraged the practice of picture brides because they commonly believed stability in the home equated with stability in the labor force.

It should also be noted that according to a report from the Center for Comparative Immigration Studies at the University of California, San Diego, some of the picture brides were actually prostitutes looking for a better life.

CRITICAL OVERVIEW

Picture Bride has not drawn much critical attention. Uchida is best remembered for her children's books, which often contain similar subject matter as her one adult novel, which is the internment of Japanese Americans during World War II. Uchida's work is often credited with giving visibility to Japanese American internment.

In "Prejudice and Pride: Japanese Americans in the Young Adult Novels of Yoshiko Uchida," Danton McDiffett comments on themes that run

through most of Uchida's books, including her *Picture Bride*. McDiffett writes that Uchida, an American citizen who experienced the hardships of a Japanese-American internment camp, writes about "the prejudice against Japanese Americans, even before the attack on Pearl Harbor electrified opinion against them." Her books, McDiffett states, "continue to show the upheaval, sorrow, confusion, and anger spawned by the American government's undeniably racist actions." "Yoshiko Uchida's novels," McDiffett concludes, "provide well-written, interesting, and historically accurate accounts of a period in US history that is both pivotal and shameful. They are especially worthy of study today as the world shrinks due to technology and travel and students in all parts of the US become ever more likely to encounter people of other countries and other cultures."

In their review of *Jar of Dreams*, one of Uchida's children's books, Nancy Livingston and Catherine Kurkjian, writing for *Reading Teacher*, state that "Uchida writes with passion about the heart-breaking events and challenging experiences that her people faced during World War II." As many other people have pointed out about Uchida's life work, the reviewers state: "The author's intentions were to give those in succeeding generations a sense of the past as well as a sense of the strength of spirit of these survivors."

Reviewing another children's book by Uchida, *The Invisible Thread*, a book also about the Japanese-American internment situation, Carol Fazioli, for the *School Library Journal*, comments that "Uchida tells her story without bitterness or anger."

CRITICISM

Joyce Hart

Hart is a published author and freelance writer. In this essay, she explores differences between the protagonist's ideal son and daughter and the relationship she has with her real son and daughter.

In the novel *Picture Bride*, Uchida's protagonist, Hana, struggles throughout the second half of this story in her relationship with her daughter, Mary. Mary is Hana's only child, for Hana miscarried a son previous to Mary's birth. The loss of Hana's son causes great emotional strain on Hana. She takes his death as a sign that she has done something wrong. As time passes,

WHAT DO I READ NEXT?

- Uchida's *Desert Exile: The Uprooting of a Japanese American Family* (1982) tells of the real experiences of her own family during World War II. In this book, Uchida covers the history of her family before and during the war, including her family's confinement in the Topaz internment camp in central Utah.

- Joy Kogawa's *Obasan* (1994) relates the story of a Japanese-American woman named Naomi who decides to explore her past, which forces her to confront how her mother disappeared from her life when she was just a little girl. Naomi grew up in Canada, which also interned Japanese immigrants during World War II.

- Hisaye Yamamoto's short story collection *Seventeen Syllables* (revised edition, 2001) tells about growing up as a Japanese American. Her stories explore the acculturation process and the hardships of living in an internment camp.

- *The Loom and Other Stories* (1991), a collection of short stories by R. A. Sasaki, tells about Japanese-American experiences in the San Francisco area in the late twentieth century.

- Set in the 1950s, Cynthia Kadohata's coming-of-age novel *Floating World* (1989) follows the experiences of a Japanese-American family as they move from one town to another in search of work. Olivia Ann Osaka, a teenager, is the focal character, who is forced to continually make up a new life each time her family takes to the road.

Hana learns to heal herself. One way she does this is to take in the seminary student Kenji Nishima. In helping Kenji to regain his health, Hana feels forgiven for any wrongs she may have done. This sense of forgiveness does not last long though. As her daughter Mary matures, Hana watches the teenage girl pull away from her. The

> THROUGH BOTH SUBTLE AND NOT SO SUBTLE ALLUSIONS TO KENJI AND SUMIKO, THE AUTHOR SETS UP A REFLECTION BETWEEN THE IDEAL AND THE REAL AS SHE COMPARES THE SON AND DAUGHTER THAT HANA DREAMED OF HAVING AND THE CHILDREN THAT HANA BORE."

loss of Mary is devastating for Hana, as Mary purposefully removes herself from Hana's influence. Unlike the death of Hana's son, regarding which Hana achieves a sense of closure, Mary's rejection of Hana is ongoing. In an attempt to heal her heart and soul, Hana takes a greater interest in Kenji, who becomes a surrogate son for Hana. Later in the story, when Kenji falls in love, Hana, at least on a psychological level, adopts Kenji's new bride, Sumiko, as a surrogate daughter. Through both subtle and not so subtle allusions to Kenji and Sumiko, the author sets up a reflection between the ideal and the real as she compares the son and daughter that Hana dreamed of having and the children that Hana bore.

Hana endures many tragedies in this story. She falls in love with a man who is not her husband and then sees him die. She also loses her husband. Other losses include her connections to her Japanese culture, her home, her dignity, and most of the material wealth that she and her husband acquire over the course of their marriage. But the most devastating loss in Hana's life comes through the loss of her children. The first child that she loses is her son. The miscarriage of her son is linked, at least in Hana's mind, with her love for Kiyoshi Yamaka, the handsome young man who takes an interest in Hana the first time he sets eyes on her. Hana is equally attracted to Kiyoshi and invites him into her life. She tells him that she is saddened by the bad timing of their meeting. Hana wishes they had met before she promised herself to Taro. They admit their love of one another and are unable to conceal their affection in front of Taro and their other acquaintances. But when Kiyoshi wants to express his love for Hana on a physical level, when he wants to make love to her, Hana realizes they have gone too far. So she stops him. This, however, does not stop her love from further development. She tells Kiyoshi that she will love him forever. Unfortunately, Kiyoshi dies shortly after this, and so too does the baby boy that Hana is carrying. In this way, Kiyoshi and the baby boy are linked. Hana believes that the loss of her son is the price that she must pay for her illicit love of Kiyoshi. She had wanted to give birth to this son as a tribute to her husband, Taro. Hana thought that the son would make up for her transgressions (her love of Kiyoshi) and the subsequent pain that love caused Taro. With the death of her son, this chance vanishes. Hana has to carry the guilt, which is quite intense, until Kenji Nishima comes into her life.

Kenji is a student like Kiyoshi was, but Hana's interest in Kenji is quite different from the sexual attraction she felt for Kiyoshi. In some ways, Kenji represents Kiyoshi, though. Both are young, lonesome, and starved for attention and nourishment. When the opportunity arises that signifies an urgent need in Kenji's life, Hana offers herself and her home by way of supporting and nurturing the young man. Kenji becomes a symbol of two of Hana's losses—Kiyoshi and the miscarried baby boy. It is through her nourishing of Kenji that Hana, in at least a metaphoric sense, resurrects the lives of Kiyoshi and her son. What she was not able to give to Kiyoshi and to her son, Hana offers to Kenji. She finds the means to feed Kenji physically, emotionally, and spiritually, so that Kenji rises from his illness and is filled with zeal. Hana believes that if she is successful in saving Kenji, she will be forgiven for having loved a man who was not her husband and for having miscarried Taro's son.

Even with Kenji's return to health, however, Hana's troubles are not over. Although she carries her next pregnancy to term and gives birth to a daughter, this child rejects her mother in a different way. Mary, as she matures into her teenage years, begins to notice that she is different from most of her peers. There is something about her face that does not completely match the faces of the students who have European ancestors. When she looks around at the blonde-haired and blue-eyed young girls, she does not see a reflection of herself. She tries to fit in, but something holds her back. What bars her from completely assimilating into the white American culture is epitomized by her mother. Hana comes to represent, for Mary, everything that the young teenage does not want to be. Hana talks in what is a foreign language for Mary. When Hana tries to speak English, the language which Mary uses fluently, words come out twisted and broken, tainted by a thick accent. Mary is ashamed of her mother, as if her mother were dirty and crude. So Mary attempts to separate herself from everything Japanese. Everything Mary has tried to do so far, though, has not worked. No matter how clearly she enunciates her words, no matter how much effort she puts into her studies, she is still identified as Japanese. So Mary tries something new. She becomes enthralled with a young white man, not so much for who he is but for what he is. He is an European American, and he wants her.

Mary does not prepare her parents for her departure. She does not tell them that she has changed her dating habits, tossing aside her Japanese boyfriends to date Joe. Joe merely appears at the door one night; the relationship blossoms; and one day Hana wakes up to find Mary has eloped. As the story develops, Mary moves farther and farther away. First, there is the physical distance as Mary moves out of the state. Then there is the emotional distance as Mary turns down Hana's offer to come help with the delivery of Mary's first baby. Despite these rejections from Mary, Hana never fully awakens to the reality of Mary's rejection of her. Hana continues to hope that one day Mary will return and that Hana will see her only grandchild. But this does not happen until the end of the story, when more tragedies have struck Hana, and when it may be too late.

In the meantime, Hana turns more directly to Kenji. When Hana and Taro are commanded to leave their home and turn themselves in at the internment camp, it is Kenji who helps them with the transition. Whereas Mary has turned her back once again, telling her mother that she thinks her parents would be more comfortable in the camps than they would be in Mary's home. In contrast, Kenji, who also is interred, makes sure that all the comforts that he can muster are given to Hana. He helps carry her suitcases. He finds the room where she will stay. He helps bolster Taro's spirits when Hana is concerned that Taro is depressed. Kenji makes sure that

Hana survives, just as Hana had once done the same for him. Although Kenji and Hana are close to the same age, Kenji acts as Hana's son, and Hana loves him as a son in return.

This surrogate mother-son relationship is further developed when Hana matches Kenji with a bride. This is one of the first things that Hana thinks about when she becomes aware of the daughter of the widow who lives in the room next to hers. Sumiko Mitosa is a quiet young girl who dotes on her mother, caring for her through her mother's bouts of asthma. Sumiko is everything that Hana's own daughter, Mary, is not. Sumiko has escorted the older woman to the camps, where she does everything she can to make her mother comfortable. Sumiko is not ashamed of her Japanese heritage, and Hana wants to unite Sumiko with a good Japanese-American man—Hana's surrogate son, Kenji. Later, when Sumiko asks Taro to give her away at her wedding, the psychological adoption of Kenji and Sumiko as Hana's son and daughter is complete. "At last," Hana thinks as she watches her husband walk Sumiko down the aisle, "you are the father of the bride."

Mary makes her first real appearance back in her mother's life at the end of the story. It is her father's death that pulls Mary in, and of course it is too late. Her father is buried in the desert. Hana, although she stands before Mary, is psychologically absent. For her part, Mary feels like an outsider in the midst of her mother and her mother's friends. Mary attempts to persuade her mother to come live with her. Even Mary's husband, Joe, pipes in, telling Hana, "You shouldn't stay in this godforsaken place alone." Mary's and Joe's efforts, though, are wasted on Hana. She is not alone. She has her memories of Taro, and, of course, she has Kenji and Sumiko, who have been there with her throughout the long journey of hardships. In essence, Hana tells Joe and Mary, thanks but no thanks. What she really says is: "We must learn to forgive and to be forgiven, Mary. I had to learn that too." In other words, the case is closed. Hana has healed her heart, and now Mary must do the same. But Hana has washed her hands of Mary's healing. Instead she tells Joe that he must help Mary. Hana is moving in a new direction. She no longer hungers to be Mary's mother. Instead, the story closes with Hana, accompanied by Kenji and Sumiko, walking to pay their respects at Taro's grave, as any widow and good son and daughter would do.

Source: Joyce Hart, Critical Essay on *Picture Bride*, in *Novels for Students*, Thomson Gale, 2008.

Bryan Aubrey

Aubrey holds a Ph.D. in English. In this essay, he discusses the prejudice faced by Japanese Americans from the 1920s to the 1940s and how this is reflected in Picture Bride.

What is most sobering about Yoshiko Uchida's simple but tragic tale *Picture Bride* is how closely it follows an unsavory aspect of mid-twentieth century American history. Japanese people who settled on the West Coast did experience prejudice on the part of white people. Federal laws were passed discriminating against Japanese Americans, and Japanese Americans throughout the Pacific Coast region were rounded up and sent to concentration camps shortly after the Japanese bombed Pearl Harbor in 1941. As a Japanese American herself, Uchida is an authority on the matter. Just like Hana and Taro in the story, Uchida and her family spent several years at a miserable camp, ironically called Topaz, the Jewel in the Desert, in Utah. It is with an unpleasant start that people in the early 2000s realize that such things did indeed happen on U.S. soil, and within the lifetimes of the grandparents of young readers of *Picture Bride* in the early twenty-first century.

Poor Hana, the naive Japanese girl who in 1917 takes the boat to California to marry her picture groom—she has only seen a photograph of him—does not know what she is in for. At first her disappointment centers on her husband-to-be, who looks older than his thirty-one years and is already balding and whose drab shop in a run-down part of the city does not resemble in the slightest the smart store Hana had imagined he would own. Hana is a resourceful woman, however, and she soon adapts to her husband and to their limited financial resources. Harder to adapt to, however, is the resentment they as Japanese people face from the white residents, since they can do little to change it other than making sure that their lawn is always neatly cut and no soy barrels that might betray Japanese occupancy litter their yard.

Unfortunately for Hana, she has arrived and will live for the next quarter of a century through what might be called the high tide of prejudice on

> IN HER STRAIGHTFORWARD, UNADORNED PROSE, UCHIDA CAPTURES THE BEWILDERING AND PAINFUL EXPERIENCE OF THE PACIFIC COAST JAPANESE-AMERICAN COMMUNITY FOLLOWING THE JAPANESE ATTACK ON PEARL HARBOR ON DECEMBER 7, 1941."

the part of the majority whites against anyone who happened to be Japanese or of Japanese descent. Examples from the period are not difficult to find. Under the Alien Laws of 1913 and 1920 passed in California, people who were ineligible to become U.S. citizens were not permitted to own land. This is why in the novel Taro is not permitted to own his store; eventually he gets around the problem by putting it in the name of his daughter, who, having been born in the United States, is automatically (according to the Fourteenth Amendment) a U.S. citizen. The Alien Laws were aimed principally at Japanese farmers, since white farmers feared that they would not be able to compete economically with the Japanese, who employed more efficient agricultural techniques. In the novel, when Taro visits a Japanese-American farming community, he notes how hard the farmers work, and he comments that this enables them to sell their produce for less than their white counterparts. His friend Dr. Kaneda explains that this accounts for the prejudice the Japanese face: "As long as we are an economic threat, we are going to be hated. It's as simple as that." Kaneda, the community activist, cannot help but feel indignant about this, and he sounds a note that becomes a constant theme in the novel—the fundamental decency of the Japanese people who are being unfairly discriminated against: "And yet why should our farmers be hated for being frugal and working hard to make an honest living?"

The ban on Japanese becoming naturalized U.S. citizens was upheld by the Supreme Court in 1922, and two years later, an immigration law effectively ended Japanese immigration to the United States. In *Picture Bride*, the injustice of laws such as these is conveyed powerfully through the reactions of the innocent Hana,

who finds it hard to believe that such unfairness can exist in the United States. "We Japanese are a peril to this enormous country?" she asks in disbelief after Taro informs her that the newspapers write about how Asians are threatening the jobs of white Americans and use phrases such as "yellow peril" to describe it.

This is just one of the many unpleasant surprises that have awaited the innocent Hana in her new country from the very beginning. For example, when her new friend Kiku Toda tells her that her husband Henry works at the bank, Hana naively assumes that Henry must be a banker or at least a teller or clerk. She is surprised to learn that he is in fact a janitor; the reader guesses what Hana does not yet know: many immigrant Japanese must work at jobs far below their true skills and capabilities simply because white employers will not give them an opportunity to do more. (Later, Henry is fired by the bank and given no reason for his dismissal; the reason of course is clear to readers.)

As the story unfolds, the hurtful slights and more serious discrimination against Japanese Americans accumulate in a steady stream. Taro speaks of how when he first came to the United States, he was humiliated at school because of his poor English skills. (He worked hard to master English, a skill which Hana never seems to acquire.) When Taro tries to rent a house he is refused many times by white landlords who offer the flimsiest of excuses to justify shutting him out. Then there is the delegation of neighborhood whites who report a complaint about the presence of Japanese on the block; they do not have the courage to admit that they are the ones who are complaining, and when asked they can point to nothing that Taro and Hana have actually done to offend anyone. This is racism pure and simple, based not on what a person does but what he or she is. Later, when Hana's daughter Mary, who was born in the United States and is an American citizen, is growing up, she is advised by the staff at the city swimming pool that she would not "enjoy" swimming there, a thinly veiled way of saying she is not welcome. There may not have been an outright ban on Asians using the pool, but there was a de facto segregation that was understood by everyone.

Very occasionally, the discomfort felt by the Japanese Americans is due simply to the unfamiliarity of white people with Japanese culture.

When Hana is asked by the streetcar conductor to move to the rear, this is only because of the pungent smell from the pickled radish she is carrying. Hana is so familiar with the smell she does not even notice it, but to the whites it is an unpleasant odor. However, the cultural and racial misunderstandings usually have a darker coloring. Even after some years living in the United States, Hana never goes to a store without wondering if the clerks will ignore or humiliate her simply because of her race, and she will not speak to a white person unless she is spoken to first, for fear of being rebuffed. This has the effect of wearing her down. "It was as though she were going through life pressed down, apologetic, making herself small and inconspicuous, never able to reach out or to feel completely fulfilled." Some Japanese Americans are pushed beyond the breaking point by the discrimination and other difficulties they face, like the Sunday School superintendent who gets into debt and becomes so desperate that he steals church funds in order to pay for his and his wife's passage back to Japan. Another example is Kenji Nishima, who has a nervous breakdown due in part to the pressures of studying at the seminary in an unfamiliar language; he recovers only due to the kindness of Taro and Hana, who take him into their home.

The pervasive irony of the situation is that the Japanese Americans in the novel want only to be ideal American citizens; they are almost without exception presented as responsible, hardworking, moral people. The advice Taro and Hana give to Mary is typical of the collective aspiration of the Japanese American community. They tell their daughter she must study hard "so she would become a law-abiding citizen, who would one day be accepted and integrated into the fabric of white American society." These are not people who show any desire to preserve their Japanese culture to the exclusion of American culture. They want to assimilate into the mainstream. This is made abundantly clear early in the novel: Henry Toda changed his name from Hisakazu to Henry to make it easier for white people to remember; when Hana first puts on Western clothing, Taro compliments her by saying, "You look like a real American lady," and the narrator adds, "that being the highest compliment he could bestow"; Taro wants an American-style Christian wedding, rejecting "the stiff formality of a Japanese wedding with a doll-like bride, bewigged and so heavily encrusted with powder that the groom scarcely recognized her," and when he and Hana have a daughter they give her an American first name, Mary, adding a Japanese middle name, not the other way round. Also, it is emphasized many times that a large number of Japanese Americans are devout Christians, like the vast majority of white Americans. This contrasts with the Buddhism common in Japan, which has been the only religion Hana has known before she came to the United States. The other common religion in Japan, Shinto, is mentioned only once, and that is when Taro states categorically that he wants none of the traditional Shinto rituals at his wedding.

The reward that these attractive, pleasant folk receive from their new country is to be sent to concentration camps. This may be a blunt way of putting it, but the mass "evacuation" (to use the euphemism favored by the U.S. government at the time) of Japanese Americans in 1942 is not something that is easy to gloss over. It takes up the final third of *Picture Bride* and produces its final tragedy, the cruel and senseless death of Taro, shot by a security guard at the camp because the guard thinks, mistakenly, that he is trying to escape.

In her straightforward, unadorned prose, Uchida captures the bewildering and painful experience of the Pacific Coast Japanese-American community following the Japanese attack on Pearl Harbor on December 7, 1941. The account given in *Picture Bride* of those events is historically accurate to the smallest details. For example, in the novel, Dr. Kaneda is taken away by the FBI on the night of December 7, and this reflects what actually happened on that night. The FBI began to round up all the Japanese-American community leaders. Within forty-eight hours, 1,291 of those leaders were in custody; most of them were treated as enemy aliens and quickly sent to internment camps. This was in spite of the fact that no formal charges were made against them and no evidence ever surfaced to indicate that any of them had engaged in any subversive activities. The historical truth is that Japanese Americans were peace-loving people who presented no threat to the U.S. war effort. As the novel shows, initially they hoped that Americans would not see them as the enemy, but these hopes were soon dashed and they found themselves being herded into camps policed by armed guards.

Newspaper articles published at the time reveal something of the ugly attitudes that were held by whites on the West Coast toward Japanese Americans. The journalist Arthur Caylor made regular contributions to the *San Francisco News* in 1942, and an article by Caylor published on April 29, 1942 began as follows:

> When the war is over and the Japanese come back to Japtown . . . they're likely to discover that Japtown doesn't live here anymore. Indeed, the Japanese—aliens and citizens alike—may find that San Francisco has grown cold-shoulderish to their return at all.
>
> For there seems to be a sub-surface meeting-of-minds if not an actual campaign among certain influential groups, some of them official, to extend the cleanup Japantown campaign in such a way as to build a Japanese wall around this once tolerant and international city.
>
> Just as some governors have been swearing to High Heaven that no Japanese shall come into their states, b'gosh, so certain San Franciscans begun voicing the slogan that the Japanese shall never come back.

It was attitudes such as these that made mass "evacuations" of Japanese Americans possible without protest from anyone. The procedure was that the internees were first taken to a local, temporary camp, before being sent to a more permanent camp, many of which were built on Native American reservations in remote locations. Living conditions at Tanforen, the converted race track south of San Francisco where Taro and Hana are first sent, were as described in the novel. This is confirmed by *Citizen 13660*, a memoir published in 1946 by Miné Okubo about her experience in Tanforen. The title refers to the number ascribed to her by the authorities, just as Taro and Hana are given the family number 13453. When government bureaucracies take over, people are reduced to mere numbers. Okubo describes the demoralizing discomfort of living at Tanforen, just as Taro and Hana experience it: curfews, daily roll calls, white camp police patrolling, looking for contraband, lack of privacy, infestation of rodents, and continual lack of hot water for washing. Conditions at the permanent camps were no better. This was acknowledged at the time by the War Relocation Authority, a government body created in March 1942, in a report issued in May 1943. This report is notable for the self-congratulatory tone with which it begins:

> During the spring and summer of 1942, the United States Government carried out, in remarkably short time and without serious incident, one of the largest controlled migrations in history. This was the movement of 110,000 people of Japanese descent from their homes in an area bordering the Pacific coast into 10 wartime communities constructed in remote areas between the Sierra Nevada Mountains and the Mississippi River.

The phrase "controlled migrations" is of course a euphemism for forced removal and incarceration, while the phrase "wartime communities" is a euphemism for internment camps. However, further down in the report, the War Relocation Authority is honest enough to describe what the camps are really like:

> The physical standards of life in the relocation centers have never been much above the bare subsistence level. . . . the environment of the centers—despite all efforts to make them livable—remains subnormal and probably always will be.

The fictional characters Taro and Hana in *Picture Bride* could certainly testify to that.

Source: Bryan Aubrey, Critical Essay on *Picture Bride*, in *Novels for Students*, Thomson Gale, 2008.

Helena Grice

In the following essay, Grice gives a critical analysis of Uchida's work.

Yoshiko Uchida is known for her work documenting the hardships of Japanese American life during World War II and in the postwar era. Over the course of her career Uchida published more than thirty books, including nonfiction for adults and fiction for children and teenagers, but her reputation in critical circles largely rests upon her autobiographical story *Desert Exile: The Uprooting of a Japanese-American Family* (1982).

The daughter of Japanese immigrants, Yoshiko Uchida was born in Alameda, California, in 1921. Uchida's father had a secure job with an international trading company, and her parents provided their two daughters with financial security and a rich education. Uchida traveled to Japan when she was twelve but found that she felt little connection with her ancestral land, especially since she could not read the language. The struggle of living with conflicting ethnic identities, however, became a prevalent theme in her writing. Uchida's high-school experience included her first encounter with institutionalized racism: she found that Japanese American pupils were routinely excluded from school activities and social functions. Uchida worked hard in high school and graduated early, which enabled her to enroll at the University of California, Berkeley, at sixteen.

Everything changed, though, during World War II, when Uchida and her family and thousands of other Japanese Americans were sent to internment camps. On 7 December 1941, the day Japan bombed Pearl Harbor, Uchida's father was taken away for questioning by the FBI. She and her family were initially sent to a makeshift detention center at Tanforan racetrack in California, where they were forced to live in horse stables. They were later transferred to Topaz Detention Center in the Utah desert. Although this center was supposedly built for the purpose of housing families, conditions were actually even more denigrating than at the racetrack. Nevertheless, the Topaz Detention Center became "home" for three long years. The experience of internment understandably had a profound effect on Uchida and formed the basis of much of her fictional and autobiographical writing.

In 1943 Uchida was allowed to leave the camp in order to study for a master's degree in education at Smith College, in Massachusetts. She became a teacher and later took various office jobs before becoming a writer in New York. In 1952 Uchida received a fellowship to go to Japan to collect folktales, a trip that resulted in the publication of several collections of stories. Unlike her earlier trip to Japan, this one enhanced

her knowledge of, and made her keenly aware of her connections with, her ancestral culture.

For Uchida, writing was always a way of life. She once said: "I was writing stories when I was ten, and being the child of frugal immigrant parents, I wrote them on brown wrapping paper which I cut up and bound into booklets . . . I also kept a journal of important events which began the day I graduated from elementary school . . . By putting these special happenings into words and writing them down, I was trying to hold onto and preserve the magic as well as the joy and sadness of certain moments of my life, and I guess that's really what books and writing are really about." This approach to writing is especially evident in her works about internment, including autobiographical narratives such as *Desert Exile, Journey to Topaz: A Story of the Japanese-American Evacuations* (1971), *Journey Home* (1978), and *The Invisible Thread* (1987).

Uchida's *Desert Exile* is one of several important autobiographical works about the Japanese American internment experience. Other important books are Miné Okubo's *Citizen 13660* (1946), Monica Sone's *Nisei Daughter* (1953), and Jeanne Wakatsuki Houston's *Farewell to Manzanar* (1973). Uchida, Okubo, Sone, and Wakatsuki were all internees at camps across the American West during childhood or adolescence, and they all portray internment as a pivotal moment in the formation of their identities.

Desert Exile differs significantly from works such as *Citizen 13660* and *Nisei Daughter* because there is no framing preface that describes the damaging effects of internment upon the author. Perhaps a preface was considered unnecessary because *Desert Exile* appeared much later than other autobiographical accounts of internment, and therefore setting up the narrative may have seemed unnecessary. Instead, at the end of the autobiography there is an epilogue in which Uchida discusses her internment experience from a wider viewpoint.

Uchida devotes the early part of her story to establishing her family's relatively harmonious life in America. The first two chapters deal with her life in Berkeley, California, and with the issue of her Japanese American identity. At this time Uchida sees little conflict within her hyphenated identity. She expresses this lack of conflict in the way she writes about cultural activities such as eating: "While Keiko and I were still having our toast and steaming cups of cocoa on Sunday mornings, Mama would cook a large pot of rice to be eaten with the food she had prepared the night before." While unavoidably acknowledging the Japanese influence upon her life, Uchida also stresses the importance of her Americanness: "In spite of the complete blending of Japanese qualities and values into our lives, neither my sister nor I, as children, ever considered ourselves anything other than Americans. At school we saluted the American flag and learned to become good citizens."

Pearl Harbor and its immediate effects are the subject of the third chapter. The harmonious family life Uchida establishes at the beginning of the book is shattered by the abrupt internment of the family. At this point Uchida emphasizes the loyalty she and other Japanese Americans felt to the United States, which serves to question the need for internment: "We tried to go on living as normally as possible, behaving as other American citizens. Most *nisei* had never been to Japan. The United States of America was our only country and we were totally loyal to it. Wondering how we could make other Americans understand this, we bought defense bonds, signed up for civilian defense, and cooperated fully with every wartime regulation."

Uchida's discussion of internment and its consequences is politically astute and engaged. The rise in anti-Japanese sentiment in America that culminated in internment is located by Uchida within a wider history of anti-Asian feeling, legislation, and exclusions: "At the time California already had a long history of anti-Asian activity, legitimised by such laws as those restricting immigration and land ownership." She cites the history leading up to the events of 1941-1945, quotes senators' views on the Japanese American issue, and names the amendments to the Constitution that were flouted throughout the internment episode. In fact, Uchida asserts that the state's treatment of Japanese Americans undermined the very institution of citizenship. She observes that Japanese Americans "realized that the deprivation of the rights of one minority undermined the rights of the majority as well." Throughout the book Uchida attempts to persuade her readers to see the actions of the United States in a negative light, and she makes a clear and detailed case against the government.

The latter part of the autobiography, chapters four through eight, deals with internment itself, including evacuation, the move to Tanforan Assembly Center, and the move to Topaz. Uchida's tone describing her family's displacement is one of cutting, condemning sarcasm: "I wondered how much the nation's security would have been threatened had the army permitted us to remain in our homes a few more days." Emphasizing the loss of individual identity caused by internment, she wryly tells readers that "we became Family Number 13453." While autobiographies usually document the *formative* moments in the life of the teller, *Desert Exile* actually charts the *deformative* moments of the internment experience and its aftermath. The very title of the work signals Japanese Americans' relegation to the edges of the country geographically and politically, and the subtitle, *The Uprooting of a Japanese-American Family*, denotes the destruction of personal, social, and familial structures.

Significantly for Uchida, personal healing does not come through telling her story. As she says in her epilogue to *Desert Exile*, "If my story has been long in coming, it is not because I did not want to remember our incarceration or to make this interior journey into my earlier self, but because it took so many years for these words to find a home." The autobiographical form ultimately allowed Uchida to integrate her personal story with political comment for practical purposes: "I wrote," she says, "for all Americans, with the hope that through knowledge of the past, they will never allow another group of people in America to be sent into a desert exile ever again." *Desert Exile* emphasizes the responsibilities of memory, and not simply because the past provides an important cautionary tale for America. Of the younger generations of Japanese Americans, Uchida says, "We must provide them with the cultural memory they lack."

Uchida also discusses the importance of her visit to Japan after World War II ended. This experience made her turn to her Japaneseness as an alternative to an American identity she desired but was disallowed. She explains: "My experience in Japan was as positive and restorative as the evacuation had been negative and depleting. I came home aware of a new dimension of myself as a Japanese American and with new respect and admiration for the culture which made my parents what they were. The circle was complete." Uchida's earlier assertions of her desire to be American and her relatively successful attainment of an American identity contrast strongly with her adoption of the Japanese side so wholeheartedly here. The message seems to be that if Japanese Americans remain outside the mainstream of American society, it is not because of their continuing affiliation with Japan, but because America has rejected them as Americans equal with other American citizens.

Uchida's narrative is supplemented by photographs that almost tell their own story apart from the narrative. There are preimmigration photographs of Uchida's family, establishing origins, and pictures of Uchida's family and community in America, group pictures that establish order, community, stability, and continuity. Then, there are images of anti-Japanese headlines that mark a shift from internal and subjective viewpoints to an external and objectified view of the community. These images are followed by pictures that represent disintegration, including photographs of the internment camp in stages of dilapidation, as well as a distant view of Topaz, showing the distancing and depersonalizing effects of internment.

Although *Desert Exile* is undoubtedly the most famous of Uchida's books, her 1987 novel *Picture Bride* has also received significant critical attention, and it has become widely taught in high schools. *Picture Bride* is a book with a wide chronological sweep, as the story takes place between 1917 and 1943, encompassing World War I, the Great Depression, and World War II. Uchida's narrative emphasizes the racism endured by Japanese Americans during these years. The novel opens with the young female protagonist, a twenty-one- year-old Japanese woman named Hana Omiya, traveling to the United States to meet her husband-to-be, Taro. The daughter of a samurai, Hana is a "picture bride," a woman who was contracted to marry a Japanese American man after the exchange of pictures (and sometimes letters). This practice solved a dilemma faced by Japanese American men: at the time, Japanese American men were forbidden from marrying white American women in many parts of the country, and there were relatively few single women of Japanese descent living in America. The practice also provided a potentially exciting travel opportunity for young Japanese women. Hana is excited when she arrives in America, but she soon learns that her life in America will be very different from what she had anticipated.

Hana and her husband run a store in Oakland, California, and they struggle to survive amid their community's prejudice and overt discrimination. Additionally, Taro, who is much older than his wife, has his own prejudices and stubbornness, and his business is failing. Hana is a resilient woman, however, and her will and strength win out. Through Hana's story Uchida skillfully documents the history of Japanese Americans in the harsh environment of mid-twentieth-century America.

Uchida was also an accomplished writer of children's stories. Two of her many children's works bear particular mention for giving voice to aspects of the Asian American experience. *A Jar of Dreams* (1981) was written for older children or young adults, and it relates the story of an eleven-year-old girl, Rinko, the daughter of a Japanese barber living in California during the Great Depression. Rinko and the rest of her family witness and experience the racist abuse of her father by white Californians, who feel that, as a Japanese immigrant, he is taking much needed jobs and resources away from them. This racist treatment escalates until Rinko's pet dog is killed, and Rinko's father and uncle eventually confront the perpetrators of this act. Rinko and her brother secretly watch the confrontation, which ends with the white businessman backing down. Meanwhile, Rinko is introduced to her Japanese aunt, who has come to visit. Rinko's aunt acts as the unifying presence in the narrative, as she introduces her family to their Japanese heritage by practicing Japanese customs and by helping each person cope with his or her difficulties in America. Through these narrative strands Uchida explores the problems Japanese immigrants face integrating into the majority culture and the conflicting demands placed upon people of "hyphenated" ethnicity. Told from an adolescent viewpoint, the story is able to introduce these issues in ways that are appropriate for a young readership.

Uchida's *The Bracelet* (1993), written for children up to eight years of age, takes up similar racial themes. This story addresses the experience of internment from the perspective of a Japanese American child named Emi. When the United States goes to war with Japan, Emi and her family are forced to live in a detention camp. Consequently, Emi is separated from her best friend, Laurie. When the time comes to say goodbye, Laurie gives Emi a bracelet as a symbol of their lasting friendship. Emi soon experiences all of the harshness and deprivation of the detention camp, where her family is forced to live in a stable. Then, while Emi is trying to adjust to her new existence, she discovers that her bracelet is missing. Although she is initially upset, Emi soon realizes that the bracelet is immaterial, as her relationship with Laurie will endure.

Yoshiko Uchida made it her life's work to demonstrate the injustice of the internment of Japanese Americans during World War II. Through her writing for adults and for children, she described the experience from a variety of perspectives, both autobiographical and fictional, making her position clear. Yet, the internment issue also formed part of a larger message. Particularly telling in this regard is Uchida's description of her mission as a writer of children's stories: "I try to stress the positive aspects of life that I want children to value and cherish. I hope they can be caring human beings who don't think in terms of labels—foreigners or Asians or whatever—but think of people as human beings. If that comes across, then I've accomplished my purpose."

Source: Helena Grice, "Yoshiko Uchida," in *Dictionary of Literary Biography*, Vol. 312, *Asian American Writers*, edited by Deborah L. Madsen, Thomson Gale, 2005, pp. 304–309.

SOURCES

Caylor, Arthur, "Behind the News with Arthur Caylor," in *San Francisco News*, April 29, 1942, http://www.sfmuseum.org/hist8/caylor1.html (accessed January 27, 2006).

Fazioli, Carol, Review of *The Invisible Thread*, in *School Library Journal*, Vol. 49, No. 11, November 2003, p. 83.

Livingston, Nancy, and Catherine Kurkjian, Review of *Jar of Dreams*, in *Reading Teacher*, Vol. 57, No. 1, September 2003, p. 102.

McDiffett, Danton, "Prejudice and Pride: Japanese Americans in the Young Adult Novels of Yoshiko Uchida," in *English Journal*, Vol. 90, No. 3, January 2001, p. 60.

Okubo, Miné, *Citizen 13660*, Columbia University Press, 1946.

Relocation of Japanese Americans, War Relocation Authority, May 1943, http://www.sfmuseum.org/hist10/relocbook.html (accessed January 27, 2006).

Uchida, Yoshiko, *Picture Bride*, University of Washington Press, 1987.

———, *Picture Bride and Related Readings*, Glencoe McGraw Hill, 2000.

FURTHER READING

Harth, Erica, ed., *Last Witnesses: Reflections on the Wartime Internment of Japanese Americans*, Palgrave Macmillan, 2003.

With racism against American Muslims rising in the United States, this book provides insights into the consequences of fear and hatred brought against a particular ethnic group. The essays in this book were written by Japanese-American descendants of those interned in U.S. camps during World War II. These voices, long silenced by the shame that was associated with the internment, provide insights into the long-lasting effects of racial prejudice.

Inada, Lawson Fusao, ed., *Only What We Could Carry: The Japanese Internment Experience*, Heyday Books, 2000.

Sponsored by the California Historic Society, this book contains essays, poetry, art, biographies, and government documents concerning the internment of Japanese Americans during World War II.

Ng, Franklin, *The History and Immigration of Asian Americans*, Routledge, 1998.

Professor Ng provides a comprehensive study of the history of immigration and the challenges imposed on Asian Americans who came to the United States. Immigrants from China, Japan, and Korea were some of the first to come to this country. Ng's book also covers later immigrants, such as those from Vietnam, Thailand, and other southern Asian countries.

Robinson, Greg, *By Order of the President: FDR and the Internment of Japanese Americans*, Harvard University Press, 2003.

The background of President Franklin D. Roosevelt's decision to intern over 100,000 Japanese Americans has only been briefly accounted for in most history books that deal with World War II. In Robinson's book, letters, memos, diary entries, and government documents written by the president are used to explain why an otherwise humanitarian leader decided to deprive Japanese Americans of their civil rights.

The Rainbow

D. H. LAWRENCE

1915

In September 1915, one month after Methuen first published *The Rainbow*, Scotland Yard confiscated more than one thousand copies of it from the publisher and printer. Later that year the novel was successfully prosecuted for obscenity. Not until 1924 was D. H. Lawrence able to find an American publisher for *The Rainbow*. Eventually, the work came to be considered one of Lawrence's finest, due especially to its intricate study of the tensions that often exist between men and women. Covering the pre–World War I period from about 1840 to 1905, the novel explores the relationships between three generations in the Brangwen family, describing in the process the emergence of English society from the Victorian period and its entrance into the modern period. Lawrence shows how characters are determined in part by the time and place in which they live, and he also dramatizes how they struggle to reconcile conflicting feelings and impulses. Lawrence shows how feelings cannot be conveyed adequately by conventional language, and his poetic prose style also illustrates the importance of imagery in conveying meaning to the text.

AUTHOR BIOGRAPHY

David Herbert Lawrence was born on September 11, 1885, in the mining town of Eastwood in the English Midlands. His parents were John Arthur

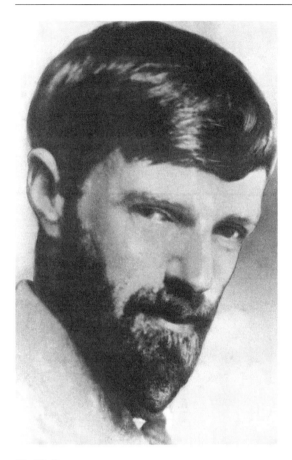

D. H. Lawrence *(Edward Gooch / Getty Images)*

Lawrence, a coal miner and the model for Walter Morel in *Sons and Lovers* (1913), and Lydia Beardsall Lawrence, a former schoolteacher and the model for Gertrude Morel in the same novel. Lawrence grew up in Eastwood and lived there for twenty years. Those years were difficult for him due to health problems that plagued him from birth, impoverished living conditions, and his parents' constant fighting. His autobiographical novel *Sons and Lovers* chronicles those troubled years along with his intense attachment to his mother and his first romantic involvements. Eastwood and the events of his early life appear in other works as well, including his first novel, *The White Peacock* (1911), his masterpiece, *Women in Love* (1920), and his most controversial novel, *Lady Chatterley's Lover* (1928).

After completing a two-year teacher-training course at University College, Nottingham in 1908, Lawrence began a teaching career at a school in Croydon, a London suburb. During this period, he continued his childhood friendship

MEDIA ADAPTATIONS

- Ken Russell directed a film version of *The Rainbow* in 1989, starring British actors Sammi Davis as Ursula, Glenda Jackson as Anna, and Paul McGann as Anton. This version omitted the stories of the first two generations of the Brangwens, focusing on Ursula's coming of age.
- In 1988, the BBC produced a television version with Imogen Stubbs as Ursula and Martin Wenner as Anton. This version also focused on Ursula's life.

with Jessie Chambers, who encouraged him to continue writing. She became the model for Miriam in *Sons and Lovers*.

Lawrence escaped the tedium of teaching by writing and soon had his short story, "Odour of Chrysanthemums," published. A year later, in 1911, his first novel, *The White Peacock*, was published, followed by *The Trespasser*, in 1912. That year Lawrence met Frieda Weekley, the German wife of a professor at Nottingham University College and distant cousin of the famous World War I flying ace, Manfred von Richthofen (1882–1918), who was known as the Red Baron. Frieda introduced Lawrence to the writings of German psychologists, including that of Otto Gross, which had an important influence on Lawrence's work.

Frieda left her husband and three children in 1912 and traveled with Lawrence to Europe. Financial problems prompted him to write book reviews and essays while he continued work on his poetry, novels, and short stories. He was not noticed in the literary world until the publication of his third novel, *Sons and Lovers*, which after negative early reviews for its sexual themes gradually gained acclaim.

Lawrence and Frieda married in 1914 and moved to the English coast of Cornwall, where Lawrence tried to set up an artist commune. During the next few years, Lawrence worked on *The Rainbow* (1915) and *Women in Love* (1920), the novel that cemented his reputation as one of England's finest writers.

When they were forced to leave Cornwall after being suspected of collaborating with a German spy ring, Lawrence and Frieda traveled extensively in Europe and the United States, settling for a time in an artist colony in Taos, New Mexico, where he continued to write. His last novel, *Lady Chatterley's Lover*, was banned in the United States and England soon after its publication in 1928. On March 2, 1930, Lawrence died in Vence, France, at forty-four after a long battle with tuberculosis.

PLOT SUMMARY

Chapter I: How Tom Brangwen Married a Polish Lady

The Rainbow opens with a general description of the Marsh Farm in the English Midlands and of the generations of the Brangwens who have lived there. The men were well satisfied on the land, with which they had an intimate connection, but the women "looked out from the heated blind intercourse of farm-life, to the spoken world beyond." The women craved a better life, if not for themselves, then for their children.

The narrative shifts to 1840, when a canal is constructed across the Marsh Farm and soon after, a colliery and the Midland Railway appear. During this period, Alfred Brangwen and his family live on the farm and prosper from the development of the nearby town. Alfred's youngest son Tom becomes the focus of the narrative as he is sent off to school with his mother's hopes of his becoming a gentleman. Without an aptitude for book learning, however, Tom fails miserably at academics.

When his father dies, seventeen-year-old Tom takes over the running of the farm. After he has sex with a prostitute, he becomes confused about his feelings. The experience increases his desire to be with a woman, but the "nice" girls terrify him and the "loose" ones offend him. He begins to drink heavily to escape his constant dreams of women. One day Tom meets a gentleman who inspires in him a curiosity about the outside world.

When Tom is twenty-eight, he meets Lydia Lensky, a Polish widow who has become a housekeeper for the local vicar, and her four-year-old

daughter, Anna. He feels "a curious certainty about her, as if she were destined to him." He is attracted to her "fineness," and she, to his directness and confidence. They soon agree to marry.

Chapter II: They Live at the Marsh

The two are nervous about marriage. Each is attracted to the other, but they also feel their foreignness to each other. After they marry, Tom is afraid to give himself to Lydia completely, somehow fearing her power. During their first months together, he vacillates between a fierce desire for her that allows him to give himself up to her and a fear that she might leave him, which fills him with anxiety. He often feels that she intentionally keeps separate from him, which enrages him and prompts his desire to destroy her. Yet eventually they come together, losing themselves in each other.

When Lydia gets pregnant, she withdraws from him again, and Tom spends evenings in the local pub. He also turns to Anna, Lydia's child, with whom he eventually forms a deep bond. Initially, however, Anna resents Tom's intrusion into their lives and rejects him. Gradually, as her mother withdraws further into herself, Anna turns to Tom for comfort and companionship. Lydia becomes depressed during her pregnancy, filled with memories of her first husband's death and the loss of her first two children to diphtheria. Tom comforts the frightened Anna during her mother's labor. Lydia and Tom forge a stronger bond after the birth of their son.

Chapter III: Childhood of Anna Lensky

Though Tom and Lydia have a son, Anna remains his favorite. Tom and Lydia's relationship follows the same pattern of coming together and separating. When he cannot reach her, he drinks more heavily and transfers his attentions to Anna, whom he takes weekly to the cattle market. One evening, however, Lydia confronts Tom, complaining of his distance, and after the two discuss what they need from the other, they are able to unite and find entry "into another circle of existence," a "complete confirmation" into a more satisfying life.

Chapter IV: Girlhood of Anna Brangwen

Prompted by a desire to make her a lady, Tom sends nine-year-old Anna away to school in a nearby town. Anna has a difficult time at school due to her sense of superiority and her need to keep her distance from others. She does, however, form an attachment to her mother's friend, Baron Skrebensky, a Polish exile who is now vicar of a country church in Yorkshire, who represents to her a romantic world of lords and kings.

When she is sent to a young ladies school in Nottingham, Anna determines to adapt to the habits and style of the girls whom she meets there, but she still finds it difficult to establish any friendships and becomes unsure of her sense of herself. She prefers her life at home, where she and her family are "a law to themselves, separate from the world."

When Anna is eighteen, she meets her twenty-year-old cousin Will Brangwen, who has taken a job at a nearby town. After an awkward beginning, they are soon drawn to each other and begin a passionate relationship. Tom, who has become jealous of Anna's attentions to Will, tries to talk them out of marriage, but Anna angrily insists that Tom is not her father and so has no right to deny her, which cuts him deeply. Later, after Tom finally agrees, Anna tries to reestablish a bond with him, but he now feels separate from her. Yet after they marry, Tom enjoys helping the couple set up house.

Chapter V: Wedding at the Marsh
The Brangwen men enjoy their drink at the wedding, especially Tom, who makes a heartfelt toast after the ceremony, extolling the virtues of married life. After Anna and Will retire to their cottage, several of the men, including Tom, sing carols outside their window.

Chapter VI: Anna Victrix
After the wedding, they spend days together, lounging in bed. Anna returns to the world first, which Will resents along with his growing dependence on her. She becomes impatient with his continual need to be with her and so tells him to find something to do. He becomes filled with a dark anger in response and pulls away from her, sometimes treating her cruelly. Other times they come together in a perfect union.

Anna becomes jealous of his love for and attention to the church. When she ridicules his beliefs, trying to force him to find explanations for the rituals, he fails, and so his passion for his religion fades. He hates her for forcing him into this state, and the two engage in frequent, vicious battles of will. He tries to control her actions; she rebels against his authority. Yet after their fights, she fears she will lose him and so comes back to him. They continually move back and forth between union and conflict, yet his dark side is always present. He tries to assume the role of master of the house, but she will not acknowledge him as such, jeering at his attempts, which fills him with black rage.

When Anna becomes pregnant, Tom intervenes and brings the two back together. Their battle of wills, however, continues, and Anna banishes him to another bedroom for a few nights each week so that she can sleep in peace. When they have a girl, Ursula, Will claims the child, but Anna becomes victorious in the sense of her motherhood. She soon is pregnant again, which fills her with an ultimate sense of satisfaction.

Chapter VII: The Cathedral
Anna and Will visit Baron Skrebensky and his new wife and then visit Lincoln Cathedral, a church that meant a great deal to Will when he was a boy. During the visit, Will is caught up in religious ecstasy, renewing his old spiritual passions, while Anna feels only a sense of being closed in, cut off from the world. When she calls attention to the carved gargoyles and what she considers to be their separate, defiant wills, she begins to destroy his "vital illusions," and he becomes disillusioned with the power of the church. He still loves the church as a symbol but is unable to reach the same heights of spiritual ecstasy again.

As Anna becomes lost in the bliss of mothering her child, Will finds a measure of peace in the nearby church, teaching Sunday school and playing the organ. Their relationship continues to be tumultuous.

Chapter VIII: The Child
Ursula and Will form a strong bond, especially when a year later, Anna gives birth to a second child, Gudrun. Anna falls into "a kind of rapture of motherhood" and soon has two more children. Ignored by Anna, Will spends evenings in town. One night, he tries to seduce a young woman, but after some passionate moments, she resists him. When he returns, Anna responds to his new air of confidence, and her passion for him returns. Now with his intimate life fulfilled, Will turns to public life and starts teaching carpentry.

Chapter XI: The Marsh and the Flood
When Ursula is eight, Tom drowns when the canal breaks and floods the farm. He has been out drinking, and when he returns home, he can scarcely walk. When he tries to put the horse up

for the night in the shed, he is caught in the rising water and falls, losing consciousness when something strikes his head. After his death, Ursula and Lydia become close as she tells her granddaughter stories of her homeland and of her husband.

Chapter X: The Widening Circle
Ursula feels the burden of watching over her younger siblings. When she is sent to school, she becomes obsessed with becoming a lady. She also develops a passion for the church that is similar to the one her father had.

Chapter XI: First Love
At sixteen, Ursula becomes confused about her feelings toward religion, which pit the material world against the spiritual. In the midst of this confusion, she begins a relationship with Anton Skrebensky, a young solider in the army and son of Baron Skrebensky, which redirects her passions from the spiritual to the physical. She is attracted by his relaxed self-assurance, and they soon become lovers.

During her uncle's wedding, Ursula and Anton have an argument about nationalism, Ursula insisting on the primacy of the individual over the country. Later, when they dance, she feels as if he is weighing her down and runs off to dance under the moon. When they reunite, their passion becomes a battle of wills until Anton reluctantly gives himself up to her. Soon the Boer War breaks out in Africa, and Anton leaves to join the fight.

Chapter XII: Shame
While at school, Ursula forms an attachment with one of the teachers, twenty-eight-year-old Winifred Inger. She is attracted to her beauty as well as her sense of independence. During a swim class, the two caress underwater, and soon after Winifred invites Ursula to tea. After she arrives, she persuades Ursula to go for a swim, and the two naked women share an intimate embrace. They soon become inseparable, and Winifred introduces Ursula to new ideas and philosophies, including those concerning the emerging women's movement.

Ursula's Uncle Tom invites her and Winifred to his home in Yorkshire for a visit. Ursula, whose feelings for her friend are waning, hopes she will marry him. While there, she recognizes the affinity between her uncle and Winifred, determining that they both devote themselves to abstractions—

Tom to the industrial machine of the colliery, and Winifred to the cause of womanhood—which repulses her. Winifred and Tom soon marry.

Chapter XIII: The Man's World
At home, Ursula is disgusted by her mother's complacent breeding and determines to follow a nontraditional path. After her father refuses to allow her to take a teaching position on the other side of London, he finds her one in an elementary school in the nearby town. She looks forward to giving "all her great stores of wealth to her children," which "would make them *so* happy." Yet she finds her hopes dashed on her first day when she meets her "bossy" coworkers and feels shut up in her stuffy classroom jammed full of fifty-five children. Ursula quickly feels out of place and overwhelmed, not knowing how to teach the students.

While Ursula enjoys a sense of independence from her parents when she is paid after her first week, her visions of teaching appreciative students are quickly dashed when she is unable to control the class. Mr. Harby, the superintendent, bullies the children and her, constantly berating her for her poor performance in the classroom. She recognizes that to survive, she must turn the children "into one disciplined, mechanical set, reducing the whole set to an automatic state of obedience and attention." After Mr. Harby's continual humiliation of her in the classroom, Ursula turns on one unruly, smug child and beats him, which in turn, breaks something in her. Yet as a result, she is able to gain control of the children.

She and Maggie, one of the teachers at the school, become friends, which helps Ursula endure the tedium she experiences there. Maggie, who is an active member of the suffragette movement, inspires Ursula's desire for independence. She thinks about Anton but determines that "he had not been strong enough to acknowledge her."

Chapter XIV: The Widening Circle
When Ursula spends a weekend at Maggie's home, Maggie's brother falls in love with Ursula and proposes marriage. Ursula rejects him. Her father soon takes a position as instructor for the County of Nottingham, and the family becomes involved in the bustle of moving. When she is given a going-away present by her colleagues at her elementary school, she softens toward them, including Mr. Harby.

Chapter XV: The Bitterness of Ecstasy

Ursula returns to college and passes her first exams at the end of the year. During her second year at college, the glamour begins to wear off, and she is filled with a sense of disillusionment. Though she has not seen Anton for two years, her thoughts return to him, and she convinces herself that she loves him. When he returns home on leave for six months, they resume their relationship and soon consummate it. They declare their love for each other, and Ursula is caught up in the realization of her sensual nature.

But when he asks her to marry him, she refuses. He later presses her, however, and she finally agrees. During the next few weeks, she begins to drift away from him and the two argue about his nationalistic feelings. She admits that he no longer satisfies her, which enrages him to the point of madness.

Ursula gets the news that she failed her exams and so will not receive her bachelor's degree. She cannot decide whether she should become Anton's wife or a "spinster, school-mistress." She tells a friend that she loves Anton but that she does not care about love and admits that she is confused about what she does care about. Fearing her uncertainty, she determines that she will go through with the marriage, but at the last minute, she backs out. Anton immediately proposes to his colonel's daughter, and the two are married two weeks later before they sail to India.

Chapter XVI: The Rainbow

During the next few weeks, Ursula is filled with apathy. When she discovers that she is pregnant, she writes Anton, asking his forgiveness and agreeing to marry him. She decides that childbearing is the appropriate role for her. One day while walking, a group of horses chase her menacingly as she runs from them. When she returns home, she falls into a feverish state for two weeks and miscarries. She recognizes that she cannot be bound to Anton and soon gets a letter from him informing her that he is married. As she is recovering, she looks out her window and sees a faint vast rainbow in the sky, which fills her with a sense of hope for the future.

CHARACTERS

Anna Brangwen

As a child, Anna Brangwen exhibits the same kind of foreignness, separateness, and sense of superiority as does her mother, except on the farm. She has an indomitable spirit that she carries over to her adulthood. Her strong sense of independence and desire for freedom emerge when she refuses to allow Will to dominate her. She can also be quite selfish, however, regarding her own needs when she tries to destroy her husband's passionate connection to the church. Anna wants to be the only interest in Will's life, but she then gets irritated when he hovers over her. She devotes herself passionately to child-rearing but seems to lose interest in her offspring when they become adolescents.

Gudrun Brangwen

Gudrun Brangwen's character is not well developed, except as a confidant for her sister Ursula. She shows remarkable artistic talent but is shy and withdrawn.

Lydia Brangwen

Will is attracted to Lydia Brangwen's "fineness" and her self-possession before he marries her. After the marriage, her separateness frustrates him when she will not give herself up to him. The deaths of her first husband and especially of her first two children cause a part of her to withdraw into herself. Yet she is generous and needy enough to eventually open up to Tom. Her sense of superiority also causes her to keep herself separate from others. She regarded people she met in Poland as cattle, and the English are too foreign, and so she keeps to herself. Her capacity for love is shown in her attention to her children and in her reaction to Tom's death, which devastates her.

Tom Brangwen

Tom Brangwen, who becomes stepfather to Anna, has a generous and kind nature with a zest for life. Although he sometimes yearns for a life outside the intimate world of the Marsh Farm, he recognizes that he is well suited to his world. Like all the Brangwen men, he tries to exercise his will over his wife, but he is not as insistent as the others. His gentleness and patience eventually win Lydia over, and the two find satisfaction in their marriage.

Tom also shows his generous nature when he accepts Anna as his own child. One of the most moving scenes in the novel occurs when he comforts her when she is terrified by her mother's labor. Later, he puts aside his sorrow over losing her to Will and helps furnish the couple's new home. He shows his loyalty and good sense when he stands by her when she fights with Will but also tries to get her to reconcile with him.

Ursula Brangwen

Ursula Brangwen exhibits the strongest sense of individuality and desire for freedom of all the Brangwens. Ursula shows great tenderness for her sister and love for her father, until she feels that he betrays her trust when he strikes her for misbehavior. She is open to new experiences and initially idealistic about her success with them. In the face of failure, she shows her resilience when she does not become bitter. That same openness saves her from despair after her miscarriage and enables her to focus, with hope, on the future.

Will Brangwen

Will Brangwen has a passionate nature that is revealed in his love for the church and his desire for Anna. Yet when Anna rejects him, the darkness within him surfaces and he becomes filled with rage, which causes him to lash out at her. He also has a strong will, which, coupled with his conventional ideas about sex roles, prompts him to feel that he has the right to demand that Anna obey him. He is initially indifferent to the outside world, but when he is offered a position in Nottingham, he emerges from his interior life and becomes active in the community.

Mr. Harby

Mr. Harby is Ursula's narrow-minded superintendent at the grammar school. His main goal is to have complete control over his staff and over the children. His pettiness is triggered when he is crossed in any way; he retaliates by trying to humiliate the offender. He also exhibits a cruel streak and evil spirit in his dealings with the children.

Winifred Inger

Winifred Inger attracts Ursula with her independent spirit and combination of masculine and feminine qualities. She proves herself to be morally vacant, however, and so makes a good match with Uncle Tom.

Maggie

Maggie, a young school teacher, befriends Ursula when they both teach at the grammar school. Maggie, who is never developed as a character, is devoted to women's suffrage. She and Ursula drift apart after Ursula rejects her brother's proposal of marriage.

TOPICS FOR FURTHER STUDY

- Read Lawrence's *Women in Love* and compare its treatment of sexual relationships to those in *The Rainbow*. Does Lawrence raise any new points about the tensions that arise between men and women? Does Ursula change in her attitude toward male and female roles? Is Gudrun's attitude similar to or different from Ursula's on the subject. Write a comparison and contrast paper on the two novels, focusing on this subject and your answers to these questions.

- Investigate the English educational system in the beginning of the twentieth century. Look at factors such as class size and the issues of discipline and determine whether Ursula's experiences at her grammar school are realistic. Prepare a PowerPoint demonstration on your findings.

- Although it does not figure prominently in the novel, British industrialization is an important backdrop, especially in the Ursula chapters, as a representation of destructive power of mechanization. Research the development of industrialization in Great Britain, especially in the area of coal mining, and prepare a report on your findings.

- Write a poem or short story that focuses on the problematic interaction between a man and a woman.

Anton Skrebensky

Anton Skrebensky, the baron's son and a young soldier in the British army, is Ursula's first lover. She is attracted to his confidence but pulls away when he tries to dominate her. He has strong nationalistic feelings, especially about Britain's colonialism, which eventually cause Ursula to reject him as a mate.

Baron Skrebensky

Baron Skrebensky, who immigrated from Poland, is Lydia's friend. He is proud of his heritage and so does not assimilate well into the town where he serves as vicar.

Uncle Tom

Tom is detached like his mother but does not have her capacity for love. His elegant exterior hides a corrupt and egocentric nature.

THEMES

Education

Lawrence mistrusted many institutions, including schools, which he felt were concerned more with the group than the individual. Ursula's traumatic experiences in the grammar school illustrate the problems he faced in the system when he taught for a time after earning his certificate. Ursula enters her classroom with idealistic fervor, certain she will make a positive impact on her students' lives. Her intention is soon thwarted by the reality of the educational system in England at the beginning of the twentieth century that crammed fifty-five students into a classroom in which the primary directive was to control the children as a group.

Ursula finds the structure of her school as rigid and inflexible as the air in the prison-like classroom. Instead of "being the beloved teacher bringing light and joy to her children," Ursula learns that her primary job is to keep order, for "if you can't keep order, what good are you?" She finds that the children have not been addressed as individuals who have independent minds that need nurturing; instead they must be compelled "into one disciplined, mechanical set, reducing the whole set to an automatic state of obedience and attention, and then . . . commanding their acceptance of various pieces of knowledge." Their teachers have inadvertently trained the children to try to find ways around the system, and when they are caught, they are beaten into submission. Ursula learns to adapt to this atmosphere, but it causes something to break inside her, revealing the damage done not only to the students, but to the faculty who operate in this oppressive atmosphere.

Colonialism

Lawrence also takes a swipe at colonialism through the character of Anton Skrebensky and his interaction with Ursula. When Anton tries to convince Ursula that his position in the military is

vital, he insists that he would welcome going to war because he "would be doing something" and that "it's about the most serious business there is." When she presses him about England's presence in India, one of its colonial territories, he argues that the army needs "to back up" the British who want to live there because they represent the nation. Ursula insists on viewing the British as individuals not as a nation, asserting people's right to act independently.

Lawrence believed that the primary goal behind nationalism was materialism rather than any noble ideal to civilize underdeveloped lands. Therefore the good of the community becomes "a formula lacking in all inspiration or value to the average intelligence." Thus the "'common good' becomes a general nuisance, representing the vulgar, conservative materialism at a low level." This is the general conclusion Ursula comes to about the army's goal in India, a cause to which Anton has devoted himself.

When she encourages him to define his nationalistic feelings, he admits, "I belong to the nation and must do my duty by the nation." His response betrays his inability to find an authentic self, which Ursula notes when she tells him, "it seems to me . . . as if you weren't anybody—as if there weren't anybody there. . . . You seem like nothing to me." Ultimately, Ursula rejects him because he cannot separate himself from the group and establish a separate sense of self.

STYLE

Recurrent Motifs

Lawrence employs recurrent motifs in the novel that help link the Brangwen generations and reinforce its main themes. Motifs are details, objects, or phrases that recur throughout the work and add cohesion and thematic emphasis. The canal that cuts across Marsh Farm at the opening of the novel signals the beginning of the industrial age in the previously undisturbed, pastoral Midlands, which becomes part of the world that Ursula rejects in the closing chapters of the novel. The canal also represents the sense of separation that all three generations experience, especially in their sexual relationships. Sometimes the main characters strive to maintain a separation between themselves and their spouses or lovers; at other times, they feel an overpowering need

COMPARE
&
CONTRAST

- **Early 1900s:** The New Woman becomes a label for those women who challenge gender-specific notions that limit female participation in the workplace or any other position beyond the traditional one of wife and mother. The New Woman is perceived to be a threat to the established social organization and to the patriarchal arrangement of the family.

  Today: Women have the opportunity to work inside or outside the home or both. However, those who choose to have children and a career face difficult time management problems due to often inflexible work and promotion schedules.

- **Early 1900s:** Modernist writers during this period reflect Britain's growing sense of disillusionment with the tenets of Christianity. Many question the existence of God.

  Today: Britain's population has grown increasingly secular in the past one hundred years; many church buildings are razed or sold for other uses because congregations are so small they cannot maintain them.

- **Early 1900s:** The Boer War, beginning in 1899 and lasting until 1902, is fought between the British Empire and two independent African republics: the Orange Free State and the South African Republic (Transvaal Republic). The republics are destroyed after they surrender to Britain.

  Today: The war with Iraq, which begins with the U.S.-led invasion of the country in 2003, evolves into a civil conflict between two main groups, the Sunni and Shia Iraqis. More than 3,000 U.S. troops and an estimated 650,000 Iraqis are killed, along with casualties among other groups.

to join together in pursuit of a perfect union. In his narration of the dual nature of separation, signified by the canal, Lawrence highlights the often warring impulses that emerge in sexual relationships.

The rainbow, which Lawrence chose as the title of the novel as well as the dominant image at its close, appears in symbolic form earlier in the novel, first as a doorway that Tom and Lydia walk through, signaling their passage to a more settled union, as "she was the doorway to him, he to her." The doorway becomes a clearer symbol of the rainbow at the end of the Anna Victrix chapter, when Anna's doors opens "under the arch of the rainbow." Here the rainbow suggests Anna's passage into the complete satisfaction of motherhood. Its final appearance comes at the end of the novel as Ursula recovers from her miscarriage. Here the rainbow becomes her ambiguous but hopeful vision of the future, unencumbered by the traditional roles of wife and mother, as she is ready to find satisfaction

in whichever direction she chooses. These three visions of the rainbow reveal different stages in the characters' lives and provide images of fulfillment for them.

HISTORICAL CONTEXT

Modernism
This term, associated with an important artistic movement that emerged at the beginning of the twentieth century, was reflected in Western literature, painting, music, and architecture. The modernist period in Britain reached its peak in the second and third decades and in the United States in the 1920s. Modernist British and American literature reflected the growing sense of disillusionment with traditional social, political, and religious doctrines during this period.

This age of confusion, redefinition, and experimentation, in large measure propelled by the disillusionment caused by World War I, produced one of the most fruitful periods in British letters. Writers such as D. H. Lawrence, Virginia Woolf, and James Joyce helped create a new form of literature that repudiated traditional literary conventions. Prior to the twentieth century, writers structured their works to reflect their belief in the stability of character and the intelligibility of experience. Traditionally, novels, stories, and poetry ended with a clear sense of closure as conflicts were resolved and characters gained knowledge about themselves and their world. Modernist authors challenged these assumptions as they expanded the genre's traditional form to accommodate their characters' questions about the individual's place in the world.

The characters in works by these authors reflect their authors' growing sense of disillusionment along with new ideas in psychology, anthropology, and philosophy that became popular in the early part of the century. Freudianism, for example, began to be studied by these writers, as they explored the psychology of their characters and recorded their subjective points of view. Lawrence's works focus on the tensions between men and women against a backdrop of social and political upheaval.

The New Woman

In the last half of the nineteenth century, cracks began to appear in the Victorians' seemingly stable universe. In 1859, Charles Darwin's *Origin of Species* heightened ongoing debates on religious ideology and the development of human beings. In 1867, Karl Marx published the first volume of *Das Kapital*, which challenges notions of class structure and the economics involved. These men of ideas inspired Victorians to question accepted morality and faith in the age in which they lived. During this period, feminist thinkers contributed to the erosion of traditional social mores as they engaged in a rigorous investigation of female identity as it related to all aspects of a woman's life. Any woman who questioned traditional female roles was tagged a New Woman, a term attributed to novelist Sarah Grand, whose 1894 article in the *North American Review* identified an emergent group of women. John Stuart Mill's essay *The Subjection of Women* and such plays as George Bernard Shaw's *Mrs. Warren's Profession* helped make a case for gender equity in education, the workforce, and in the franchise. Some legislations passed by Parliament, for

example, the Married Woman's Property Law, also empowered women and heralded a new age.

Mill equated the institution of marriage to the institution of slavery. He rejected the notion that motherhood should be the ultimate goal for all women and argued that social convention norms do not reflect innate ability. Mill argued both in his essays and in the House of Commons for the perfect equality between men and women in all social matters. Lawrence's works enter into this dialogue, exploring a woman's place inside and outside the traditional courtship and marriage plots repeatedly enacted in Victorian novels.

CRITICAL OVERVIEW

In 1915, shortly after the British publication of *The Rainbow*, the novel was successfully prosecuted for obscenity. Evaluating the initial response, many scholars have come to believe that it was censored because of Lawrence's anti-war stance and his wife Frieda's German heritage. The 1924 American edition of *The Rainbow* fared better; however, many early reviews were negative, focusing on what readers claimed was its shocking sexuality and promotion of lewd behavior. After Lawrence's death in 1930, opinions about the novel began to turn, aided by positive assessments from E. M. Forster and Arnold Bennett. The novel came to be considered one of Lawrence's finest.

Many early reviews of the novel were negative, due to its unusual style and its focus on sexuality. Perhaps one of the more generous was penned by J. C. Squire in a 1915 review of the book for the *New Statesman*. Squire claims: "Its author has a strain of genius, but in this novel he is at his worst. It is a dull and monotonous book which broods gloomily over the physical reactions of sex in a way so persistent that one wonders whether the author is under the spell of German psychologists." Squire insists that he does not agree with the court's decision to censure the novel, but he finds the focus on sexuality disturbing, claiming that it becomes "so tedious that a perusal of it might send Casanova himself into a monastery, if he did not go to sleep before his revulsion against sex was complete."

A much later but still negative assessment is given by Kingsley Widmer in his article on Lawrence for the *Dictionary of Literary Biography*.

WHAT DO I READ NEXT?

- Lawrence's *Women in Love* (1920), considered as the sequel to *The Rainbow*, chronicles Ursula's and Gudren's often troubled relationships with men as they struggle to find a sense of individuality within those relationships.

- Lawrence's most controversial novel, *Lady Chatterley's Lover* (1928), focuses on the stagnant marriage of an upper-class couple and explores the consequences of infidelity.

- *The Awakening*, published in 1899, is Kate Chopin's novel of a young woman who seeks to reconcile the roles of artist and wife and inevitably suffers the consequences of trying to establish her independence.

- In the play *A Doll's House* (1879), Henrik Ibsen examines the childlike role of a nineteenth-century wife and mother and the disastrous effects the limitations of that role have on her marriage. *A Doll's House* is available in a 2004 edition from Kessinger Publishing.

- Kate Millet's *Sexual Politics* (1969) studies the history and dynamics of feminism.

Widmer also finds fault with the novel's focus on sexuality, writing, "The direction of *The Rainbow* may be summarized as an erratically desperate effort to sanctify the erotic in an increasingly anomic society." He adds that it fails "because of bad writing, indifferent dramatization, and fervent inchoherences." Widmer does, however, admit to "its provocative ideas, powerful moments, and intriguing issues." The few scenes he finds effective include Tom's comforting of Anna in the barn while Lydia is in labor and Tom's drunken speech about marriage after Anna's wedding.

Widmer's assessment, however, is not typical of contemporary evaluations of the novel. Paul Rosenzweig, in an article on the book for *The D. H. Lawrence Review*, writes that "Both the pioneering sense of character in *The Rainbow* and its intricacy of form organic to such characterization are now largely appreciated." He finds the novel to be "Lawrence's most carefully written and most revised work" and notes that "the intricate structure of the novel as a whole has [also] been increasingly appreciated." Rosenzweig argues that the first part "has a rhythmic beauty in its characterization and structure" and finds a "thematic appropriateness of the structural split" between the narratives of the first two generations of the Brangwen family and the third. "The subsequent changes in the form and characterization" of the second half, he insists, fit harmoniously with the first.

In his article comparing the novel to a film version, G. B. Crump writes, "Lawrence's *Rainbow* may be his most controlled yet fully realized and satisfying work." He states that this "remarkable act of imagination" is "a pivotal work" in the author's career. Crump claims that Ursula's story becomes "a vivid, complex female *bildungsroman*" and that "The harrowing depiction of her experiences at the Brinsley Street School... ought to be required reading for every prospective teacher." He praises "the extraordinary connectedness of Lawrence's universe," concluding that the central theme, "humanity's fortunate fall from instinctive being into spiritualized mental consciousness" is displayed in "the widening circle structure of the narrative" of the three generations. Crump also praises Lawrence's characterizations, especially those of Tom and Lydia, whom he depicts "with a passionate concreteness and immediacy unmatched almost anywhere in his work." This assessment reflects late twentieth-century appreciation of Lawrence's work in general and this novel in particular.

CRITICISM

Wendy Perkins

Perkins is a professor of twentieth-century American and British literature and film. In this essay, she considers how the search for identity triggers tensions in sexual relationships.

In much of his work, D. H. Lawrence examines and illuminates the psychological forces that create conflict between men and women. In one of his most celebrated novels, *The Rainbow*, the already complicated interchanges between men

> THE PROBLEM OF MAINTAINING A SENSE OF SELF SEPARATE FROM THE SELF THAT MERGES WITH THE OTHER DURING SEXUAL UNION BECOMES MORE COMPLICATED FOR ANNA BRANGWEN WHEN SHE MARRIES WILL, WHO TRIES TO FORCE HER TO DEFINE HERSELF EXCLUSIVELY BY HIS TERMS."

and women are exacerbated by the need for individual fulfillment. The three generations of the Brangwen family struggle to define themselves as individuals and as part of a union with a sexual partner. The process of discovering their own needs involves complex questions of self-definition and redefinition. Through contact with their spouses and lovers, they reevaluate gender roles, raising questions regarding contradictory desires to dominate, to submit, and to gain equality. They also raise questions about the links between these desires and human sexuality.

The characters' exploration of different routes to self-knowledge—isolation, male/female relationships, female/female relationships, and relationships with community—uncover traditional roles as well as such marginalized identities as the liberated woman and the lesbian. In *The Rainbow*, Lawrence traces the chronological development of his characters' growing awareness of themselves and their relation to their world. One of the focal points in the progression of the generations is the woman's need for a separate identity countered by the man's increasing will to control her.

The unnamed Brangwen men and women who open the novel share a "blood-intimacy" with the land. The men's vision of themselves rests on this intimacy and so they are content. The women, though, are not satisfied with defining themselves exclusively in a physical sense and thus "[look] out from the heated, blind intercourse of farm-life, to the spoken world beyond" and "[strain] to listen." They, however, are ultimately restricted by convention to their lives on the farm.

Lydia Brangwen, with her foreignness and sense of detachment, encourages the drive for

independence and a connection to the outer world in her female offspring. She tries to resist Tom's insistence that she lose herself to him in a marital union so that she can maintain her sense of separateness and her Polish heritage and thus a sense of self. Ultimately, however, she cannot ignore the blood-intimacy that connected previous generations of Brangwen men and women.

Lawrence insisted that this desire for blood-intimacy with a mate was an integral part of the self and therefore should not be denied. In a June 2, 1914, letter to his friend, A. W. McLeod (as quoted in Jack F. Stewart's "Dialectics of Knowing in *Women in Love*"), Lawrence writes that "the source of all life and knowledge is in man and woman, and the source of all living is in the interchange and the meeting and mingling of these two: man-life and woman-life, man-knowledge and woman-knowledge, man-being and woman-being." After they establish intimate unions, characters in the novel come to recognize their mates as a part of themselves. Yet since the self in this sense can be known only in relation to the other, knowledge of self can never be complete or absolute.

The problem of maintaining a sense of self separate from the self that merges with the other during sexual union becomes more complicated for Anna Brangwen when she marries Will, who tries to force her to define herself exclusively by his terms. The two share a satisfying sexual intimacy, but when Anna turns outside their relationship in an effort to complete her identity, her husband, who is aptly named, tries to exert his will upon her. "His hovering near her, wanting her to be with him . . . irritated her beyond bearing" and so she turns to domestic concerns that do not involve him. When Will tries to interfere, Anna angrily insists, "you're not going to stop me doing it." He however "seemed to expect her to be part of himself, the extension of his will," and so he tries to "[assert] his position as captain of the ship." When Anna refuses to recognize him in this role, he seethes and withdraws from her.

Although a new, more independent woman began to emerge at the close of the nineteenth century, Anna chooses the traditional route, motherhood, as a way of defining herself. Her maternal role fulfills her completely as it allows her to maintain a sexual relationship with Will as well as an independent self as mother. Eventually, her husband is able to relax his will to dominate her, and the two enjoy a more harmonious balance, although this balance is never consistent as they struggle to find identity inside and outside their marriage.

As Ursula tries to define herself and find a fulfilling life, she tries different roles and tests various relationship, none of which satisfies her. Initially, she finds a sense of completion when she and Anton consummate their relationship, but she recognizes that it is "limited and so defined against him." When she feels "the weight of him sinking, settling upon her, overcoming her life and energy," she resists the urge to give herself completely to him. In response, Anton tries to "exert all his power over her." He determines that "if he could only set a bond round her and compel her . . . Then he would have her, he would enjoy her. . . . when she was caught."

While Anton is called away by his army duties, Ursula is free to explore a separate life, one that tests traditional notions of a woman's role. First, she becomes involved in an intimate relationship with Winifred Ingar, but that ends when she rejects Winifred's inability to act in an authentic manner. Insisting "on the right of women to take equal place with men in the field of action and work," Ursula then enters into "the man's world" of employment, rejecting the "herded domesticity" and complacency of her mother's "breeding." That avenue fails as well, however, when Ursula discovers that in order to be a successful teacher, she must suppress her individuality to the demands of the educational system.

Unable to find fulfillment in the outer world, Ursula turns again to Anton and agrees to marry him. After learning of his devotion to British colonialism, "her soul began to run by itself," and she tells him, "I'm against you, and all your cold, dead things." By the end of the novel, Ursula is alone, having rejected Anton's overpowering masculinity, as symbolized by the horses that threaten her in the closing scenes, and having miscarried.

Lawrence leaves his ending, along with Ursula's fate, unresolved, refusing to offer a solution to the warring impulses of the conscious and physical selves. Ursula's own understanding of her needs is left incomplete since these tensions cannot be resolved. Yet Lawrence's refusal to privilege one option over another for her suggests multiple possibilities, as reflected in the optimistic symbol of the rainbow at the end of the novel. With this closing image, Lawrence gives Ursula, as well as his readers, the hope that the quest for

> MUCH OF THE WRITING IS REDUNDANT AND INFLATED; THE STORY IS OFTEN RAGGED AND UNREALIZED; THE THEMES ARE FREQUENTLY SHIFTING AND MURKY. AN OBVIOUS FAILURE OF FICTIONAL CRAFT, THE NOVEL MAY HAVE BEEN ADDITIONALLY DEFEATED BY ITS OVERLY AMBITIOUS GOAL OF EXPLAINING THREE GENERATIONS IN ENGLAND AS THEY PASS THROUGH MAJOR CHANGES IN SOCIAL VALUES AND PASSIONAL RELATIONSHIPS."

an authentic self may be achieved by finding an ultimate balance between the need to establish a sense of independence and the instinctive desire to experience a blood-intimacy with a sexual partner, if not permanently, than at least in fleeting moments of unity.

Source: Wendy Perkins, Critical Essay on *The Rainbow*, in *Novels for Students*, Thomson Gale, 2008.

Kingsley Widmer

In the following excerpt, Widmer gives a critical analysis of Lawrence's work.

One of the most widely discussed and renowned twentieth-century authors, D. H. Lawrence remains intriguing and problematic in terms of his biography, his writings, and his prophetic role. In his relatively short life, he was a prolific author of fictions, poetry, travel essays, speculative polemics, and other works. His writing, it is widely agreed, ranges from extremely good to extremely bad. He was, and continues to be, a provocative figure.

Lawrence's origins were unusual for a British writer of his time. Born into the working class in the industrial Midlands—his father was a lifelong coal miner—he was as a boy frail, hypersensitive, and bright. Physically and psychologically marred by his restricted background and by parental conflict, he gradually rebelled. In a strongly class-conscious society, the working-class youth became a school-teacher and an aspiring writer. By his middle twenties he had been published and critically recognized as a lyric poet and prose fictionist. He soon abandoned teaching, middle-class aspirations, and the social-sexual decorums of his time. In a famous love affair, he fled to the Continent with another man's wife. Most of Lawrence's remaining years until his death in his early forties were marked by frequent travel, a socially marginal lifestyle, grave illness, and intense art and argument. Declassed and deracinated, he had become something of a bohemian-artist cynosure and an obsessive sexual and social critic-prophet against his times.

Much of Lawrence's writing is autobiographical, though some of his best works are not directly so. One of his earliest stories, "The White Stocking" (originally written about 1907 and revised for his first story collection, *The Prussian Officer and Other Stories*, 1914), shows some of his significant powers. This tale about a young lower-middle-class married couple probes, in a heightened realist manner, some of the emotional extremity underlying even a positive relationship. Though loving her young man, the young woman has erotically played with her sexually predatory middle-aged factory boss before her marriage— "perverse desire." He had once pocketed at a party a white stocking she had "mistakenly" taken with her for a handkerchief, a metaphor for her sexual flaunting. After her marriage, the roué sends her a gift on Valentine's Day, which she keeps secret from her husband. However, when she receives another the following year, she flauntingly confesses the gifts to her sedate husband. Enraged, he strikes her in "his lust to see her bleed, to break and destroy her." Chastened, she returns the roué's gifts, and she and her husband renew their tender love, with the now-tested male dominant. The extremes of erotic hungering and hatred, the warring polarities of male and female, have been briefly but acutely exposed. In Lawrence's uniquely uncondescending dramatization of passional struggle in ordinary life, the deep and complex "anguish of spirit" of otherwise apparently simple people is revealed.

This powerful tale is essential Lawrence. But his first novel, *The White Peacock* (1911), by contrast, is stilted and slight. This slow-paced account of the genteel romances of provincial adolescents—which shams indebtedness to early George Eliot and Thomas Hardy (and lesser late-Victorian fiction)—is narrated by an insufficiently characterized middle-class youth, Cyril Beardsal. It loosely centers on the decline of Cyril's farmer friend, George Saxon, who marries down (a pub girl) and within a few years becomes a depressive and defeated drunk. In the course of the narrative, an odd digressive concern with homoeroticism crops up. "I admired the noble white fruitfulness of his form," Cyril says of George and an obsessively remembered nude swim. He recalls how they rubbed each other dry: "the sweetness of touch of our naked bodies one against the other was superb." In "indecipherable yearning," Cyril always remembers that the young male "love was perfect for a moment, more perfect than any love I have known since, for man or woman." No more is done with it here, but homosexuality becomes an ambiguous issue through much of Lawrence's fiction.

Also striking, and inconsistent with the prevailing tone of the novel, is the brief tale of Annable, a local gamekeeper. This intellectual outsider is an educated ex-parson, once married to a noble lady and since become a misogynist and apocalyptic prophet. He provides the novel's entitling metaphor by describing a showy white peacock in a graveyard "perched on an angel...as if it were a pedestal for vanity. That's the soul of woman—or it's the devil." The peacock dirties the angel—"A woman to the end, I tell you, all vanity and screech and defilement." We learn from young Cyril that the embittered keeper "was a man of one idea—that all civilization was the painted fungus of rottenness." His counter to the falsity, in one of the earliest declarations of what was to be Lawrence's famous doctrine: "be a good animal, true to your animal instinct." He is also a first-run for Mellors, gamekeeper-lover of Lady Chatterley in Lawrence's final novel.

This early crude snapshot of the Lawrence prophet is cast aside with Annable's death in the middle of the book. The rest of *The White Peacock* consists mostly of sentimental adolescent posturings, florid descriptions of nature, and stilted cultural allusions from post-1890s fashions. The novel also reflects what were probably Lawrence's mother's lower-middle-class snobberies and hatred of drinking men. (Indeed, Lawrence rushed a prepublication copy to his mother as she lay dying; she is reported not to have responded.) In his early twenties Lawrence was still trapped by the need to present his mother's puritanic-genteel values. Not surprisingly, then, women dominate all the relationships in the novel, with the males clearly defeated. Many critics have seen this slight fiction as a provincial exercise in late-Victorian quasi-eroticism, though a more essential Lawrence may be recognized in the touches of homoerotic misogyny and prophetic rage.

Lawrence's next novel, *The Trespasser* (1912), is also weak. He wrote most of it while a schoolteacher in the London suburb of Croydon (1908–1911), after pushing through to a teaching certificate at Nottingham (he had previously worked as a clerk in a surgical appliance factory and assisted in hometown schools). Perhaps some of the claustrophobic emotions in the novel should be related to the painfully slow dying of his mother in 1910 and to his own grave respiratory illness which followed. The book may have been further weakened by Lawrence's inappropriate desire to produce something for popular success. The basic materials for the novel came from an uninsightful schoolteacher friend, Helen Corke, who gave Lawrence her autobiographical manuscript recording a destructive love affair. His adaption covers a few days in the life of a near-middle-aged music teacher, Siegmund, whose adulterous affair with the semifrigid younger Helen concludes with his guiltily hanging himself.

The writing is labored, burdened with poetically inflated statements ("their thoughts slept like butterflies on the flowers of delight"), and heavy with Wagnerian overtones of doomed love. More than half the narrative describes five days of a love tryst on the Isle of Wight, with drawn-out claustrophobic scenes of erotic rituals. These emphasize the resentful fluctuations in feelings between the lovers, mostly induced by the antisexual, willful, and sentimentally righteous woman. Though inadequately backgrounded and developed, these scenes do carry an essential Lawrence theme: the frigidly erotic woman "rejected the 'animal'" in her short-circuited sensuality, leaving the man feeling like a "balked animal." But the man, too, appears inadequate—narcissistic, priggish, and full of resentful self-pity. The scenes with Siegmund's embittered wife and rejecting children also lack dramatic depth, and the irony that Siegmund's wife is unaffected by her husband's death and takes a lover herself seems stock. Lawrence's insights do not rise here above the maudlin writing.

Quite different is Lawrence's intensely realized third novel, *Sons and Lovers* (1913). Paul Morel in this novel provides Lawrence's first largely autobiographical character. The highly self-centered Lawrence only haltingly arrived at the autobiographical emphasis. Issues derived from his relations with his domineering mother and righteously willful girl friends usually took priority. Generally, Lawrence's fictional world, as well as his life, remained woman-dominated—and rebelled against. However, to center the issues of Lawrence and his fictions in the Oedipal, and especially in the reductive and self-insulating notions of psychoanalysis, seems needlessly narrow.

Sons and Lovers, the linear story of the Lawrence-like Paul Morel, moves from the early married life of Paul's parents, Gertrude and Walter, to Paul's desperate outcastness after the death of his mother when he is twenty-four. The novel is less about the mother and son than a whole way of life, although Lawrence does appear to have been influenced in his final (third) draft of the novel by the roughly Freudian views of the woman he then lived with, Frieda von Richthofen Weekley. He acknowledged some of that emphasis in a letter in which he speaks of many emotionally crippled mother-lovers, like his protagonist. However, he reasonably insisted that this was only a part-truth (and he failingly attacked Freudianism in his later *Psychoanalysis and the Unconscious*, 1921, and *Fantasia of the Unconscious*, 1922—two of his many syncretistic religious essays). Most essentially, *Sons and Lovers* is a novel of provincial family life—a major type of nineteenth-century fiction—with a lower-class and sexual emphasis. Its shape and texture insist on showing its characters as part if not parcel of a whole way of life and culture, not just as psychological cases.

Class ideology and repressions are at issue. No doubt speaking for Lawrence, Paul says of his social ambivalence: "from the middle classes one gets ideas, and from the common people, life itself, warmth." His mother, bitter in her marriage to an improvident coal miner, objects because she desperately wants her sons "to climb into the middle classes." The mother's social ambitions, as well as Paul's mother-fixation, provide much of the basic conflict. As a rising clerk for a surgical appliance firm, as a promising conventional designer, and as a priggish and "superior" young man shedding his social origins, traditional restrictions, friends, and girls, Paul follows his mother's aspirations. His creator had partly gone that route and then rebelled; after teaching, Lawrence turned toward declassed and deracinated bohemianism, becoming the adversary artist-prophet as dissident bourgeois—a role he maintained for the rest of his life.

Paul's rejection of his pit-working, beer-swilling, wife-beating father—who is presented as crude but sensuously and rebelliously immediate—is social as well as psychological. The mother-dominated, sickly, sensitive son chooses the genteel aspirations of his mother in opposition to much of the world in which he grew up. This petty bourgeois feminization causes Paul's alienation, and part of his desperation, at the novel's end.

The marriage between the ill-matched Gertrude and Walter had early turned into a "deadlock of passion" and produced an embittering social as well as psychological conflict. The puritanic daughter of an autocratic father, Gertrude had become dominant in her marriage—"she was her father now"—and undermined the working-class husband. She transfers her erotic and social passions to her sons. The eldest, William, an aspiring gentleman-clerk in London, trapped between his mother's sense of disciplined ambition and a love-hate relation with a frivolous girl, dies in his early twenties; then the guilty mother foists her devotion on her next son, Paul, engendering the same kind of emotional and social anxieties in him.

Walter's scenes, in spite of the antagonistic feminization of the author, suggest a harsh but warm masculine world, with the public house and its male camaraderie his chapel. The matey miner lives a life antithetical to that of his moralistic, chapel-going (Congregational) wife. Her Protestant ethos of self-denial, sexual repression, impersonal work, disciplined aspiration, guilt, and yearning for conversion-escape, not only defeats her already industrially victimized coal-miner husband but also contributes to the defeat of several of their sons. Understanding the social religious matrix seems crucial to understanding other aspects of *Sons and Lovers* as well. Too much of the critical discussion of Miriam Leivers, Paul's farm-girl love for seven late-adolescent years (derived from Lawrence's girl friend Jessie Chambers, a schoolteacher and later an embittered memoirist) focuses on her conflict with Gertrude for Paul's emotional allegiance. But Paul does not finally reject Miriam because of the disapproval of his jealous mother but because Miriam so totally

represents the anxious Protestant sensibility. Acutely delineated as antisensual (see, for example, the fine graphic scenes with the swing and the pecking chickens), Miriam is too "fussy," too religiously earnest for "higher things," too burdened with puritan "proud humility" and a Christian "martyr" psychology. She thus quite lacks sexual passion, humor, irony, openness, and, as Paul repeatedly insists, the richer sense of life recognized in spontaneous feelings. Finally, driven in her twenties by Paul's overdue insistence, she gives herself sexually as a "sacrifice." Paul's tortuous break with the righteously suffering-demanding Miriam, who demonstrates Nietzschean "slave morality," cannot be defined by the Oedipal but by the provincial Protestant ethos, so dominant in Anglo-Saxon countries of the period.

Though sexually backward, Paul also has an affair—a profane love in contrast with his love for the sacral Miriam—with Clara, an older woman (a thirtyish feminist factory worker separated from her blacksmith husband Baxter Dawes). Partly delineated as an erotic "somnambule"—an early example of Lawrence's repeated Sleeping Beauty motif—Clara had never awakened into passional life with her husband. She is aroused by Paul, who demands her submission in a different way. The eroticism becomes for him a conversion experience, "the baptism of fire in passion"—one of Lawrence's most obsessive themes. The erotic transformation is "the something big and intense that changes you when you really come together with somebody." Clara, as is usual with women in Lawrence, is appalled by "the impersonality of passion" and wants Paul to be more sentimentally personal. But the erotic transformation seems crucial for Paul, producing a heightened sense of immanent life. Thus, "having known the immensity of passion," they also know "their own nothingness" as part of a larger awareness of the impersonal flow of vital life. The desire-negation, eros-nihilism dialectic briefly adumbrated here becomes the central Lawrencean doctrine.

The break with Clara in part depends on Paul's emotional bond with his mother. Paul's mother slowly dies of cancer—her son finally aids in euthanasia—during the time of the love affair. However, the abrupt end of Paul's relationship with Clara also results partly from her demand for more security, her guilt toward her husband, Paul's self-centered social ambitions, and more obscure motives, including Paul's ambiguous relation to Clara's husband. A crude but pathetic character similar to Walter Morel, Baxter in frustration has brutalized his wife. He also thrashes Paul after the priggish youth has helped get him fired and taunted his manliness. Yet "they had met in an extremity of hate, and it was a bond." So Paul becomes a friend of the "sulking" Baxter, gives him money and help in finding a job, and finally insists on turning Clara back to him. This curious twist suggests guilt, homoeroticism, and a placation of the father-masculine world. It also allows Paul to again escape the female power.

Another power seems to be at work in *Sons and Lovers*. Paul is always "fretting" with himself, engaged in a never fully conceptualized internal warfare not adequately explainable by the social tensions and familial discord. Sickly from the start, he has long shown signs of "slow suicide." As more generally with Lawrence, Paul's death wish seems larger and deeper than any specific analysis, such as Oedipal despair, can account for. In "Derelict," the concluding chapter of *Sons and Lovers*, Paul's longing for annihilation goes beyond its ostensible cause in the death of his mother. Having turned Clara back to her husband and made a final rejection of the claustrophobic Christian Miriam, Paul "whimpers" for his dead mother and yearns for the final darkness. In a letter written after he had completed the novel, Lawrence characterized his protagonist as in a "drift toward death." Is this reversed in the concluding sentence of the novel when Paul turns away from the darkness represented (rather than caused) by his dead mother, "towards the faintly humming, glowing town, quickly"? Towns were usually negative images for anti-industrial Lawrence. But some readers ingeniously emphasize the older meaning of the novel's last word, *quickly* (that is, *lively*), to argue for the hopefulness of the conclusion. After all, Paul has achieved passional transformation and has perhaps partially transcended his Oedipal curse. Yet given the whole pattern of the novel, as well as the last chapter (and Lawrence's related works), the most sensible conclusion might be that Paul Morel has lost more than he has won. *Sons and Lovers* may be viewed as considerably story of defeat.

But the crucial experience of the story may be less Paul's progress or defeat than Lawrence's intense portrayal of the life of the lower-class provincials, executed with psychological complexity and without condescension. This portrayal includes not only the coal miner's conflict-ridden family but also life on the Leivers' farm, work in the factory, and the struggles of courtship. While the writing in *Sons and Lovers* is, typically for Lawrence, erratic because of instances of redundancy, inflated statements about feelings, and cursory handling of some important developments (such as Paul's loss of religion), the novel displays unusual sensitivity to the felt fabric of provincial life.

Some critics suggest that this power of the novel derives from its autobiographical basis, but Lawrence's too personal perspective also accounts for some evident weaknesses. The authorial persona is often described in embarrassingly narcissistic ways, while the other Morel children, though crucial to the family theme, are insufficiently developed. Also, there is little critical perspective on Paul's callow artistic views and antifeminist prejudices. Even the later Lawrence reportedly thought his treatment of Walter Morel too biased from the maternal perspective. *Sons and Lovers* falteringly records only part of Lawrence's struggle for a fuller critical consciousness of his background.

The writing of his third novel more or less coincided with drastic changes of consciousness in Lawrence's life. By 1912 he had given up the conventional and restricted life of a schoolteacher. He took a financial risk hoping to live on the income from his writing. (He had to have the help of patrons on several occasions.) After abortive relationships with several women, he ran off to the Continent the spring of 1912 with Frieda von Richthofen Weekley, the upper-class, German-born wife of a former college teacher of his. A combination of the maternal and bohemian, Frieda precipitously abandoned three children to go with Lawrence. The romance placed drastic demands on both. In what became a famous love affair, Lawrence personally dramatized several themes of his love stories, such as his belief that a deep passion requires a cross-class (and often a cross-ethnic and cross-cultural) mating. Does one thus escape some of the Oedipal-incest fears? One certainly thus engages in a relationship marked by considerable conflict, as was true of Lawrence and Frieda, whose marriage was formalized in 1914 and more or less maintained until his death. The two felt themselves to be, as

Lawrence's lovers usually do, in self-exile from the staid communities they had violated and fled in their passion.

Because of his sense of personal liberation, as well as financial need, Lawrence was extremely productive in the following years. Staying first in Germany and then in remote places in Italy, he and Frieda returned to England before World War I. Though outraged at the war, which he saw as an expression of the death wish of Western civilization (and during which he sometimes had to endure police surveillance because of his German wife and his own antipatriotism), he unhappily remained in England for its duration. He completed a variety of essays, plays, sketches, poems, and stories. He had become an established literary figure, though his finances remained precarious and his way of life more or less that of a marginal bohemian.

Among his early writings, the novella *Daughters of the Vicar* (written in 1911) may be considered representative of Lawrence's strengths and weaknesses. Using what was to be one of his favorite devices, he presents contrasting portraits of two sisters: Mary, the dutiful, repressed, and socially successful; Louise, the passional, unconventional, and erotically successful. The tale is an argument for personal liberation and harshly portrays the destructive middle-class Christian (High Church) milieu. With a mixture of realism and caricature, Lawrence savages the vicar's family in their snobbish, genteel poverty and repression. Mary pursues a cerebral clergyman, an Oxfordian with a church sinecure and other financial means, a cold and morally rigid "little abortion" of a man. Denying her erotic existence ("she *would* not feel"), Mary expediently marries him and produces the fussy little monster's children. She had "sold herself," "murdering" what was best in herself, and is filled with "general destruction" which will be directed "towards charity and high-minded living." Thus she commits the crimes of conventional and antipassional Christian moral love.

Sister Louise discovers herself rebelling against such morality in a commitment to passion and thus achieves purposeful character. She pursues, with difficulty, a sensitive, declassed coal miner, Alfred, who has bookish and musical proclivities and is "polarized" emotionally by his strong-willed, widowed mother, with whom he lives. Thanks to Louise, Alfred struggles, after his emotional collapse at his mother's death, from

"great chaos" to a "wonderful" responsiveness, partly elaborated in Lawrence's heavy prose of passion ("lightening," "seared," "fiery anguish," "torment," "utter darkness," "agony of chaos," "glowing," "eternal," "kind of death," "swooning," etc.). Alfred's breakthrough is the emotional liberation of the repressed and requires a social-class violation. The story concludes with the snobbish and nasty rejection of the lovers by the vicar and his wife. The lovers plan to flee to the colonies; such are the social consequences of the realization of passion against the social-moral order. While *Daughters of the Vicar* is sometimes awkward in its caricatures and insistent abstract metaphors of the emotions, it is sharp in its contrasts of class and in its deployment of the dialectics of eroticism.

Another novella, *Love Among the Haystacks* (perhaps written shortly before *Daughters of the Vicar* but first published posthumously in 1930), shows one of Lawrence's simplest erotic patterns. Contrasting brothers, one a victim of "inflamed self-consciousness," the other a more confident mother's boy, discover themselves in a rural-ritualistic scene. They work the harvest haystack, respond intensely to the physical scenery (as is usual in Lawrence), jealously fight in a show of their erotic turmoil, and that night in the hayfield achieve sexual consummations—the confident brother with a "wildcat" foreign governess from a nearby vicarage, the emotionally tortured brother with the humble wife of a migrant worker ("both were at odds with the world"). Erotic realization required for each an alien partner. The brothers achieve not just coitus but also a sacramental heightening—what Lawrence here and elsewhere describes as the conversionlike experience of "wonder"—which gives a vibrant sense of inner and outer life.

More often, Lawrence's fictions present erotic recognition as anguished. In one of his best-known early short stories, "Odour of Chrysanthemums" (the materials and themes were also utilized in Lawrence's best play, *The Widowing of Mrs. Holroyd*, published in 1914), he combines a "realistic" study of working-class domesticity with a poetic heightening. The recurrent metaphor of the "wan flowers," along with Lawrence's usual fire and darkness imagery, reveals failed passion. The burdened and resentful pregnant wife ends up ritually preparing the corpse of her husband, killed in a mine accident. Her epiphany—"death restored the truth"—is that theirs had been an erotic failure and she had been "fighting a husband who did not exist." The righteously rigid wife had defeated the passional individuality of the man. The balancing forces of death and eros fuse in the haunting odor of failure.

The story might also be viewed as the compensatory other side—the woman's failure exposed—of the Walter-Gertrude conflict in *Sons and Lovers*. Additional variations on that autobiographical material appear in other pre-World War I stories of mining life. In the brief "A Sick Collier," a devoted and hardworking miner husband is properly "polarized"—a key Lawrence term for male-female passional balance—with his superior wife. But he is undermined by a painful and enduring injury. Desperate to join his mates in manly pursuits, he is restrained by his wife and breaks down into mad shouts that the pain is her fault and he wants to kill her. The story ends with his sobbing self-pity and his wife's fear that his sick pay may be stopped because of his derangement. Once the collier has lost his manly role, the balance of the marriage is destroyed. Lawrence often insisted on purposive maleness.

"Strike-Pay" loosely focuses on a miner who loses his money, witnesses the accidental death of a navvy, and goes "home vaguely impressed with the sense of death, and loss, and strife." Thus aware of the "greater" strife in life, he for once manages to win the lesser "battle" of domesticity, asserting his manhood against his mother-in-law and wife. The wife submits to the Adamic authority: "She attended to him. Not that she was really meek. But—he was *her* man. . . . "

In yet another of these early working-class stories, "A Miner at Home," Lawrence deploys his vivid sense of domestic reality to show the harsh disagreement between a husband and wife over his going on strike. In "Her Turn," a more comic version of the domestic battle of wills, a well-matched couple fights over whether he will share his strike compensation with his wife or use it only for masculine assertion. She counters by spending all their savings to fix up the home, thus forcing him to share his strike pay with her. From the same period, "Delilah and Mr. Bircumshow" concerns an unassertive bank clerk who has been defeated by his wife. She clipped "this ignoble Samson . . . from instinct," but by depriving her husband of his sense of masculine purpose, she has deprived herself of what passion they had. These minor stories are informed—perhaps overinformed,

some might suspect—by the endless domestic conflict of Lawrence's Eastwood mining-family childhood. The sense of struggle between man and woman is at the center of much of Lawrence's work.

One of the most powerful of the early short stories is "The Christening." With a perception of family life alien to that of the sentimentalist, Lawrence reveals the kinship bond as one of proud hatred. The family of a retired and declining but still autocratic miner show their domestic scars: the painfully sensitive older daughter is a sickly schoolteacher; the son is a rough bully; the younger daughter resentfully mothers her bastard child by a man she despises. The ritual of baptism for the child certifies a larger bastardy as the legacy of disintegrating authority. The vague officiating clergyman feels overwhelmed by the patriarch—the New Testament by the Old (Lawrence's usual preference)—and the slobbering, self-willed wreck of a miner preaches to the preacher and names the bastard for himself while denying mere earthly fatherhood. His children harden themselves in emotional bastardy, finding his very blessing a curse. He concludes by joyously praising life—"The daisies light up the earth"—but his children sullenly shrink back. There has been generation without regeneration within the wrecked power of the old dispensation.

Nearly a dozen lesser early stories by Lawrence struggle with erotic torments. "The Shadow in the Rose Garden" plays bitter ironies on the traditional romance imagery of the rose. On her honeymoon, a woman unexpectedly meets her former lover in a rose garden. But he is now a lunatic incapable of even recognizing her. Her crude husband, now aware that his wife has been sexually possessed before, reacts with hatred. In the rather brittle "The Witch a la Mode" a guiltily adulterous young man is "accidentally" burned in his inflammatory love for a dangerous modern woman. In the slight "The Overtone" the issue is a woman's sexual revulsion for her husband. The fervid "New Eve and Old Adam" has a vaguely defined upperclass urban couple in conflict, with the old, Adamic male longing for a unity of the flesh and total commitment from the modern, willful Eve, who will not tolerate such subordination. In the mawkish "The Old Adam" a Georgian aesthete living in the home of a middle-class couple emotionally dallies with the wife, improbably wins a fistfight with the burly businessman husband—this drives the repentant wife back to the husband—and in a kind of homoerotic transfer becomes "close friends" with his rival. For Lawrence, modern love was indeed perplexed.

"A Modern Lover" is one of a group of stories which relate sexual repression to social class, with the woman defeating passion; Muriel and Cyril here are a version of Miriam and Paul in *Sons and Lovers*. Class more clearly dominates the archly heavy "The Shades of Spring," in which a superior young man, now married, visits his former love, who still longs for his intellectual companionship but has settled for a second-best lover, a gamekeeper. In the slight "Goose Fair" a middle-class young man is passingly tempted by a second-best, a goose girl, but ends in "bitter" submission to the "superior" girl. In the finest of these tales, "Second Best," a young woman desperately decides to settle in love for a man of lower social class. In an unconsciously symbolic act, she brings a dead mole—image of the blind unconscious—to the second-best swain. Throughout his work, Lawrence employs metaphoric animals to represent emotional issues. In "Second Best" social class disparity is overcome by the dark unconscious and ritualistic propitiation, though agony continues in the erotic submission.

After spending time in Germany with Frieda before World War I, Lawrence wrote four stories drawing on German military life, his first reach beyond provincial English materials. In "Once" (1913), a rather forced Maupassant-type erotic tale which may have had its origin in Frieda's experience (she was from a military family and had numerous affairs), a demimondaine tells her current love of an exciting past escapade in which a stranger, a handsome aristocratic officer, came to her bed—a scene with crushed rose petals, gold chains, and other old-fashioned sexual fantasy decor. But the story's tone seems disapproving of the woman's sexual insatiability and search for "sensation." Lawrence, usually very serious about the erotic, frequently contrasts the search for sexual sensation with deeper passion. As he wrote in one of his polemics, "sex in the head, no real desire."

"The Mortal Coil," also brittle in manner, tells of an aristocratic young officer with gambling troubles who is brought to a sense of mortality by the accidental death of his mistress. A better story, "The Thorn in the Flesh," links the

breakdown of authority with the breakthrough of passion. A young army recruit, driven to physical revolt against demeaning treatment, flees. He goes to his girl friend, a servant on an estate, and experiences for the first time a "furious flame of passion." Thus sexually liberated, in contrast to his military condition, he has a new sense of being. In the awkward ending, he is recaptured, but we are led to believe that a truer authority, the local baron (Frieda's father?) has responded with manly sympathy and will help the awakened youth.

No such easy escape weakens the most powerful of the stories drawing on German military life, "The Prussian Officer" (the original, and sardonically better, title, "Arms and Honour," was replaced by an editor). Again the story turns on a violent conflict between a harsh officer and an unconsciously rebellious soldier, but here the covert emotional bond appears homosexual, especially on the side of the cruel, aristocratic captain. (As Lawrence wrote in a letter of this period: "soldiers get their surplus sex and their frustration and dissatisfaction into their blood and *love* cruelty.") After much brutalization, the innocent youth strangles the tormenting officer, flees into the countryside, and wanders about deliriously until he dies. The concluding image of the captain and his orderly side by side in the mortuary emphasizes the irony of union in death for vicious authority and desperate rebel. But the dominant experiences of the story emphasize the obsessional intensification of love-hate feelings and suggest that the consequent alienation and guilt—repeatedly elaborated with scenic images—reveal the desire for annihilation. This, like several of Lawrence's best later fictions, explores the psychological dialectics of destructiveness. The violated innocent's intensification of desire becomes a death-longing.

In summary, of the early (pre–World War I) Lawrence fictions, one novel, *Sons and Lovers*, clearly stands out. The novella *Daughters of the Vicar* is not his best writing but displays some of his characteristic social and erotic insights against the milieu of Christian class morality. Although the early stories have a scattering of interesting descriptions and perceptions, especially around issues of erotic conflict, three tales particularly stand out: "The White Stocking," "The Christening," and "The Prussian Officer." These stories not only display the vivid intensity of scene and emotional conflict but also the erotic-nihilistic dialectics which characterize Lawrencean sensibility.

After finishing *Sons and Lovers*, one of Lawrence's many writing projects was an ambitious novel-saga of provincial life with such provisional titles as "The Sisters" and "The Wedding Ring." This project soon split into two loosely linked but quite different long narratives which became *The Rainbow* (published in 1915) and *Women in Love* (published in 1920). Because it was suppressed, partly by historical accidents, for obscenity in Britain and used in a morally tendentious way by several critics, *The Rainbow* has received more attention than it merits. Much of the writing is redundant and inflated; the story is often ragged and unrealized; the themes are frequently shifting and murky. An obvious failure of fictional craft, the novel may have been additionally defeated by its overly ambitious goal of explaining three generations in England as they pass through major changes in social values and passional relationships.

About half of *The Rainbow* centers on the adolescence of one third-generation, middle-class girl, Ursula. Her forbears were Midlands farmers of long heritage. The first detailed figure, Ursula's grandfather Tom, a youngest child, combines the sensual and transcendent in his "desire to find in a woman the embodiment of all his inarticulate, powerful religious impulses." In a language heavy with images of heat, flame, and other expressions of transfiguration, Lawrence presents some of Tom's struggle to break through his tormenting sexual repression. Finally he achieves a partial victory by means of his late marriage to Lydia, a mid-thirtyish Polish exile widow with a young daughter, Anna. Lydia's exotic foreignness (a trait that recurs in many Lawrence fictions and was important in his life) excites Tom but also makes for uncertain possession, which drives him to rages and drinking. In Lawrence's insistent (and sometimes unconsciously self-parodying) sanctification of the erotic, woman continues to represent for man the transcendent "unknown," part of the process for heightening passion to "eternal knowledge." Tom sees his marriage as "his Gethsemane and his Triumphal Entry in one" (the obscene puns may not be intentional), his sex with his wife as "blazing darkness" (among other oxymorons), and his intense subjectivity as his "transformation, glorification, admission" into a religious state. The actual sex is vague and the relationship apparently both impassioned and strained.

There are a few effective scenes: Tom's comforting stepdaughter Anna in the barn while her mother is giving birth; his drunken speech at Anna's wedding where the sacramental eroticism takes a seriocomic turn ("a married couple makes one Angel"); and other touches here and there. But Tom drops out of the narrative, ten years before his accidental death in a flood (to be answered by the rainbow?). Surprisingly, we then hear that he had been part of "the old brutal story of desire and offerings and deep, deep-hidden rage of unsatisfied men against women," which had not been dramatically developed.

The sexual burning and perplexity pass on to Anna, who has had to fight against her stepfather Tom to achieve sex and marriage with her cousin, Will Brangwen. Part of Anna's self-discovery occurs during the famous surrogate sexual scene in which she and Will shuck corn sheaves in the moonlight. This second generation's more self-conscious battle of male-female wills plays out in metaphors of heat, birds, unfolding plants, and arching cathedrals (further foreshadowing of the rainbow promise?). The marriage bed again becomes "the core of living eternity," but the passions turn into warfare in which "there could only be acquiescence and submission," temporarily salved by the "tremulous wonder of consummation." Anna overcomes Will when she relinquishes "the adventure to the unknown" for compulsive breeding (nine pregnancies) and a "violent trance of motherhood." She forces Will into a resigned "darkness in which he could not unfold." His aspirations as a religious artist are reduced to a hobby of making church repairs while he earns a living doing mechanical design work (and later teaching crafts in the schools). He principally services the female will and family. We later learn that Anna and Will were never "quite defined as individuals."

The third generation engages in an even more perplexing, and certainly more self-conscious, struggle to relate the erotic to "a sense of the infinite." As an adolescent, the oldest child Ursula takes up with a maternal cousin, Anton, an on-and-off love for the rest of the novel. But Ursula does not really like Anton, except for the physical satisfaction he provides ("her sexual life flamed into a kind of disease"). Her dislike is not surprising, since Lawrence defines Anton as essentially conventional, a "conservative materialist" and statist who goes off to the Boer War as an engineering officer. "His soul lay in the tomb. His life lay in the established order of things."

With Anton away, Ursula works as a primary-school teacher for several years. In vivid scenes in the realistic mode (unlike much of the rest of the novel), Lawrence draws on his own teaching experience to show suppressed rage at the trivializing, regimented, and sometimes mean labors of doing a "collective inhuman thing"—compulsory schooling. Ursula finally escapes from teaching and takes her amorphous romantic yearnings to a university, where as a student she soon becomes disillusioned with that "apprentice shop" for "making money," that "commercial shrine" and "slovenly laboratory for the factory." She eventually flunks her exams.

While teaching, Ursula engages in a lesbian relationship with another teacher, Winifred Inger, taking up "the perverted life of the elder woman." (Lawrence uses *perverted* to describe any sexual situation he does not approve of.) But to Ursula's combined relief and disgust, Winifred calculatingly ends up marrying Ursula's uncle, Tom Brangwen, Jr. Though inadequately described, this coal-mine industrialist is presented as "perverted" in a larger sense, dehumanizing lives in his "putrescent" eagerness to serve "Moloch," the industrial machine. (Socially bad people almost always have bad sex in Lawrence's works.) Later Lawrence continues the ideologizing by having Ursula, rather improbably, make Nietzschean denouncements of bourgeois society as enslaved to "money-interest" and other false doctrines ("only degenerate races are democratic").

Returned from the war, Anton seems to Ursula an establishment degenerate. She lives with him for a brief time, searching through sexuality for a "consummation" which includes "the infinite." The sex seems to be good—Ursula "entered the dark fields of immortality"—but not good enough to bridge the split between "passion" and "the social self." Finally, Ursula finds Anton even sexually insufficient, and she becomes a predatory "harpy," insatiable and out to destroy his maleness. Anton, "his will broken," flees from her to a conventional marriage and a job as an Indian colonialist.

The final chapter of *The Rainbow* puts pregnant Ursula in a field with threatening horses (a semifantasy scene, the horses are apparently metaphors for masculinity). Frightened, she becomes ill and soon miscarries. Although now

the modern experienced and alienated woman, she still seeks a man "from the Infinite," though realizing that she dangles between the lost organic world of her forbears and an unacceptable present order which is disorder. "She grasped and groped to find the creation of the living God, instead of the old, hard barren form of bygone living." The concluding image of the Old Testament rainbow (repeatedly foreshadowed) gives an uncertain promise of a transcendent dimension and richer life.

The direction of *The Rainbow* may be summarized as an erratically desperate effort to sanctify the erotic in an increasingly anomic society. In spite of its provocative ideas, powerful moments, and intriguing issues, Lawrence's fourth novel stands as a largely failed work because of bad writing, indifferent dramatization, and fervent incoherences.

In the better-crafted *Women in Love* we still follow Ursula (and get a few details about Anna and Will, and even a casual reference to Anton), but the fifth novel is not in any important sense a continuation of the fourth. The materials of the narrative have drastically changed; so has Lawrence, his outlook altered by World War I into a new sophistication and hardness. The England at issue is no longer rural and marital but industrial and bohemian. In *Women in Love* even the old industrial ethic, as embodied by paternalistic mine owner Thomas Crich, is being replaced by the highly rationalized functionalism of his willful son Gerald; the patriarch is being replaced by the new "industrial magnate." Will Brangwen's religious art in *The Rainbow* has been replaced by his daughter Gudrun's modernist sculpture, by the modernist, antihumanist artist Loerke, by primitive art objects, and the like. In *Women in Love* social and sexual relations are also different and exacerbated. The "bitterness of the war," Lawrence wrote of the novel, though the story takes place prior to the war, provides a pervasive sense of personal and cultural "crisis" in the "passionate struggle into conscious being," which is the theme of the work.

Rupert Birkin, obviously the Lawrence persona, enters the Brangwen story as Ursula's lover and then husband. The narrative covers the love affairs of the sisters Ursula and Gudrun over a period of slightly less than two years, but their lovers, Birkin and Gerald, displace the sisters as the main focus. As Lawrence writes of his Birkin-self, "his way of seeing some things vividly and feverishly, and of his acting on this special sight" and his intense dialectical struggle with problems of consciousness give the fiction some of its power. But the novel also suffers from Birkin-Lawrence's tendency to make abstract statements about tortured subjectivity, a weakness compounded by the awkward conception of the character as a thirtyish, misanthropic school inspector with a substantial income. Birkin lacks solid personal background and social reality behind his upper-bohemian way of life.

Another difficulty with Birkin derives from the half-covert issue of bisexuality. *Women in Love* ends, after the suicide of Birkin's friend Gerald in the Tyrolean Alps while the two couples are on vacation, with Birkin promisingly married to Ursula yet still longing for an "eternal union with a man too." In a canceled opening section of the novel (first published in 1963 as "Prologue to *Women in Love*") Birkin's homosexual side is emphasized in overwrought prose about his "affinity for men," since he has "the hot, flushing aroused attraction" for alien males who "held the passion and the mystery to him." The partly obscured homosexuality dominates several scenes in the novel, especially the wrestling bout between Birkin and Gerald (in the chapter entitled "Gladiatorial"). Homosexuality also explains some of the peculiarities of Birkin's ostensibly heterosexual conflicts with Ursula.

Such ambivalence may underlie such key doctrines of Lawrence's, here and elsewhere, as "Desire, in any shape or form, is primal, whereas the will is secondary, derived." The discovery, and maintenance, of passional desire—the main affirmation of life in a world of smashed values—requires one's protecting desire from the corruptions of willed behavior, be it industrial, social, intellectual, or artistic. *Women in Love* repeatedly focuses on conflicts, within a character and between characters, of desire against will.

Desire, it should be noted, takes some nastily extreme forms. Birkin, for example, emphatically tells Gerald that "a man who is murderable is a man who in a profound hidden lust desires to be murdered." What happens is what one desires. This absurd generality comes from Lawrence's turning "desire" into an all-encompassing absolute. It may be argued, as apparently the novel

intends, that a variant of Birkin's statement applies to Gerald, whose final weakness of desire in his willful struggle with Gudrun becomes suicidal. Even here Lawrence claims larger application since Gerald is the "messenger" of the "universal dissolution into whiteness and snow," the modernist apocalypse without any rainbow promise.

Yet Lawrence's dogmatism with his vitalistic doctrines is not always simpleminded. For striking example, Lawrence gives the negative character Hermione, Birkin's mistress before Ursula (and the author's angry personal caricature of a cultured upper-class lady), some of his doctrinal gestures, such as an insistence on the "spontaneous" over the "self-conscious." Then he has Birkin attack this claim to vitalistic values as "the worst and last form of intellectualism, this love ... for passion and the animal instincts." Ironically, Lawrence thus provides what was to be one of the major attacks on Lawrence's own doctrines.

Birkin nonetheless serves as spokesman for Lawrence's persistent recasting of the Nietzschean dialectic. This includes having a passionate "sensuality" (distinguished from the merely cerebral "sensuous" or "sensation") as the Dionysian necessity for true being and culture, the "great dark knowledge" (perhaps Lawrence's most notorious phrase). In *Women in Love*, various forms of the dark knowledge are presented in terms of a piece of African sculpture, responses to a modernist painting, several episodes with animals, and symbolic scenery. Lawrence's prophetic purpose pervades almost all.

Lawrence makes many of his points by antithesis, and much of the novel is less about desire than about nihilism. Birkin (and Lawrence, as we know from his other writings of the time), shows a raging misanthropy: "mankind is a dead tree"; his "dislike of mankind ... amounted almost to a disease"; he "abhors humanity"; "Man is a mistake, he must go"; and on and on. Most of the characters are denounced as well as revealed as profoundly destructive (Hermione, Gudrun, Gerald, Loerke, et al.). Social scene after social scene—London bohemia, the colliers' Saturday night, the cultured wealthy at Hermione's country house, the Crich family wedding—is savaged. The dominant technological commercial order, especially as represented by Gerald Crich, receives sweeping condemnation for its essence, not just its wrongs; it depends on a fundamentally inhumane will, the reduction of people to "instrumentality" and "the substitution of the mechanical principle for the organic." The resulting social order shows "pure organic disintegration and pure mechanical organization. This is the first and finest state of chaos." The only authentic alternative is individual awareness and flight.

Lawrence's erotic dialectic, in this argumentative fiction, develops out of, rather than in spite of, this destructive ordering and the nihilistic conclusions. The Birkin-Ursula courtship becomes a "passion of opposition." Explicitly not a love ethic in any usual sense (like that which belongs to despised Christianity), the "strange conjunction" that Birkin demands is "not meeting and mingling ... but an equilibrium, a pure balance of two single beings; as the stars balance each other." No doubt Birkin's individualist stance partly reflects a fear of merger with woman. Lawrence repeatedly and vehemently rejects usual sentimental courtship—elsewhere he scornfully calls it "adoration love"—and demands that passion be "stark and impersonal." Such love precariously intertwines with hostility.

While Lawrence's Birkin claims equality in the relationship, clearly one star is more powerful than the other; Ursula, reasonably enough, repeatedly characterizes her lover's demands as male bullying. Birkin's claim to go "beyond love" reveals considerable misogyny. Woman, as "man-to-man" lovers (Gerald and Birkin) know, "was always so horrible and clutching," full of "a greed of self-importance in love. She wanted to have, to own, to be dominant"—"the Great Mother of everything." Thus Birkin justifies the protective "conjunction between two men," such as the *Blutbruderschaft* he demands of Gerald. In the scene in which Birkin stones the reflection of the moon on a pond, he intends to shatter the nature goddess Cybele, "the accursed Syria Dea!" Ursula insists on interpreting his action as a demand for love. It is certainly a demand for submission. He wants "the surrender of her spirit," something even beyond the "phallic," for which she must forgo her "assertive *will*." The woman twists even that to her purposes: she "believed that love was *everything*. Man must render himself up to her. He must be quaffed to the dregs by her. Let him be *her man* utterly, and she in return would be his humble slave. ... " In these conflicting erotic ideologies, mating becomes a kind of permanent warfare.

Curiously, Birkin grants of his transcendental passion that his "spirituality was concomitant of a process of depravity." In Ursula's affectionate surrender in the Sherwood Forest night scene Birkin's ambivalently domineering eroticism apparently takes the form of anal sexuality ("the darkest poles of the body" found "at the back and base of the loins"). How this relates to the "star-equilibrium" of Lawrencean love remains obscure. But the suggestive courtship, presented in intense and even witty scenes, remains provocative, as does the larger passional pathos in which the man desperately quests for "his resurrection" (part of an admitted "religious mania"). Whether the resurrection is momentarily achieved by the "bestial," by female submission, or by male-female warfare for heroic equilibrium, the consequences seem to be an asocial marriage with the couple in isolated flight.

By a not-always-clear antithesis, the Gudrun-Gerald love affair becomes a more deathly battle of wills as they struggle to master each other. Their passion becomes "disintegrating," driving Gerald to self-murder and Gudrun to a man-hating perversity. She takes up with Loerke, a gnomish and nasty German-Jewish modern artist whose "corruption" becomes hers as well. (Lawrence displays some conventional British anti-Semitism here and elsewhere.) For Lawrence, the talented Gudrun and Loerke represent modernist culture in its decadent subservience to the antihuman chaos brought on by industrialism and the war. Through them Lawrence mounts a modernist attack on modernism.

In *Women in Love* one sister finds an affirmative passion and the other a destructive twisting of passion, but neither achieves traditional marriage. The old world is dead in the most intimate as well as largest senses. The relationship of Ursula and Birkin depends on their being "disinherited"—deracinated, declassed, defamilied—though the protagonist, like Lawrence, retains wistful utopian longings for male bonding and even a new community ("I always imagine our being really happy with some few people"). Utopianism was the other side of Lawrence's nihilism. But the issues in *Women in Love*, as Lawrence's dialectics and overreaching metaphors suggest, can have little possible resolution. Erotic perplexity continues. And so does cosmic perplexity: as Birkin says near the novel's end, "Whatever the mystery which has brought forth man and the universe, it is a non-human mystery ... man is not the criterion." So human efforts, erotic and other, provide only a momentary stay against the nothingness. This awareness is the deep modern disenchantment, but even so, it can intensify the possibilities of passional realization, which may be taken as the final moral of *Women in Love*.

This novel is Lawrence's most thoroughly wrought long fiction (though as balanced narrative it may not match *Sons and Lovers* and *Lady Chatterley's Lover*, and for perfection of craft and insight it does not equal the best of the short fictions). Its force comes from Lawrence's combination of perplexed dialectics and vivid metaphoric scenes. Among the latter: the fatal water party at the Crichs'; Gerald's willfully fighting his horse; Hermione's smashing Birkin; the stoning of the reflection of the moon; the rabbit's scoring Gudrun's arm; and Gerald's death in the snow. The display of subterranean motives intensifies these scenes. The dialectics work similarly: Birkin's arguments with Gerald carry homoeroticism as well as anti-industrialism; the lovers' quarrels involve metapsychology as well as courtship; the erotic doctrines concern cultural nihilism as well as sexuality. Such intensification provides much of Lawrence's distinctive quality.

Lawrence's subsequent novels lack much of this force. . . .

Source: Kingsley Widmer, "D. H. Lawrence," in *Dictionary of Literary Biography*, Vol. 36, *British Novelists, 1890–1929: Modernists*, edited by Thomas F. Staley, Gale Research, 1985, pp. 115–49.

T. H. Adamowski

In the following essay, Adamowski explores the theme of otherness in The Rainbow *as it relates to the characters' view of themselves and their relationships with others. The author maintains that Lawrence strikes a precarious balance between a sense of distance and togetherness among the characters that is crucial for a healthy sense of the self.*

D. H. Lawrence has a place among those who have contributed, despite themselves, to the idiom of mid-century cant. Be yourself, fulfill yourself, find your true self—Lawrence worked this vein before the colliers of identity succeeded, in our day, in working it out. His language has become part of the common speech of a psychotherapeutic culture. Like the language of Erik Erikson, an attack on cant that has seen itself absorbed by the enemy, Lawrence's pivotal terms—the "true self" and the "crisis of identity"—have become lost in

> WE MAY GO THROUGH OUR DAILY EXISTENCE AMONG OTHER PEOPLE IN A KIND OF FALSE SECURITY, ALL OF US 'HUMAN,' ALL OF US IDENTIFIABLE PERSONS, BUT THERE COME MOMENTS OF EPIPHANY WHEN THE PERSON VANISHES AND THE OTHER APPEARS."

the generality of everyday use and misuse. They have now become, surely, linguistic tics.

Like Erikson, Lawrence sought to avoid simple-mindedness by means of the context in which he placed the key notions of his own therapeutic discourse. In his case, the self, in its truth, recognized its own limitations. Where contemporary reference to the "true self" (whatever that may be) becomes cant is in its sentimental refusal to consider the implications of what Lawrence called, in *Psychoanalysis and the Unconscious*, the dimension of "abysmal otherness," a dimension that if properly understood by many "encounter" therapists might make them despair of their profession: "When I stand with another man, who is himself, and when I am truly myself, than I am only aware of a Presence, and of the strange reality of Otherness. There is me, and there is *another being*." When Lawrence writes of the need for being "in touch" and for "togetherness," it is never a sentimentalized coincidence, a boundary-less intimacy, that he has in mind; for he maintained a clear perception of the existence of other people in all of their self-enclosed fullness, forever closed to our desire for infiltration into the heart of their being:

> When she has put her hand on my secret,
>   darkest sources, the darkest outgoings,
> when it has struck home to her, like a death,
>   'this is *him*!'
> she has no part in it, no part whatever,
> it is the terrible *other* . . .

This "darkness unfathomable and fearful, contiguous and concrete" of the Other is the measure of my self:

> I shall be cleared, distinct, single as if burnished in silver,
> having no adherence, no adhesion anywhere,

one clear, burnished, isolated being, unique,
and she also, pure isolated, complete,
two of us, unutterably distinguished, and in
unutterable conjunction.

It is with this notion of "otherness" and its manifestation in *The Rainbow* that I am concerned.

I want to indicate how that notion may serve
in assisting us to understand the relationships
that exist in the novel among the following: the
very notion of a core to the self, the sensitivity of
book towards distance and conflict among
selves, and the moments during which they
seem to come into a kind of harmony with each
other. In the Anglo-Saxon world, we are not
often comfortable with what we feel to be the
unnecessary portentousness of the words "self"
and "other," and we prefer to discuss simply the
relationships among certain characters in novels.
The very terms "self" and "other" we find too
suggestive of an entire nexus of continental jargon,
indicative, perhaps, that the person who employs
them has come down with a case of what Arthur
Koestler once called the "French flu."

If I use these terms it is because I think that
in their very abstractness they suggest better
than do the more familiar forms of Anglo-
Saxon jargon the concern of Lawrence with
what men and women *are,* "inhumanly, physio-
logically, materially." They are less vulnerable to
the "psychologizing" that comes all too easily to
the consideration of *characters.* The latter suggests a multiplicity of discrete persons, each with
a certain set of typical feelings, intentions,
motives, interests, that is, I think, of marginal
significance in Lawrence's vision of human reality. That vision, although it includes the psychological texture of individuals, also attempts to
see "beneath" psychology, so to speak, to the
ground upon which it rests. In his concern with
what we are *beyond* the "old stable ego of the
character," his concern with a condition by
whose action "the individual is unrecognizable,"
Lawrence is less a psychological than an ontological novelist.

In Lawrence's fiction the quality of the otherness of the Other makes itself felt as an attention to the distance between selves. When, for
example, Tom Brangwen enters the bedroom of
Lydia, after the birth of their child, Lawrence is
careful to indicate that this is not that moment of
rapport or empathy between husband and wife
that the conventional wisdom often suggests for
their first meeting after the birth of a baby: "She

was beautiful to him—but it was not human. He
had a dread of her as she lay there. What had she
to do with him? She was other than himself."
Lawrence adds that Lydia looks at her husband
"impersonally," and the suggestion is that this
inhuman, impersonal quality of Lydia has been
revealed to Tom in an immediate intuition, as a
certain feeling of dread that goes over him. This
beautiful, non-human, dread-evoking quality of
Lydia is, in fact, her otherness. It is the index of
separation between them. She is the "subject" of
an experience, child-bearing, that is hopelessly
out of his reach but that has made itself felt, if
not thought, in her husband. In his essay "Love,"
Lawrence refers to otherness as being "unthinkable," and it is with this pre-reflective quality
that I am here concerned. We know that there
is otherness, and we know it because we cannot
know the Other. In the sudden coincidence of
non-knowledge and dread that pass over Tom,
Lawrence locates otherness. Tom cannot know
the experience that makes Lydia so beautiful to
him, and that beauty is itself an experience that
fills him with the knowledge of his necessary
ignorance. We may go through our daily existence among other people in a kind of false
security, all of us "human," all of us identifiable
persons, but there come moments of epiphany
when the person vanishes and the Other appears.
The conventional wisdom, including the pieties
of psychology, pertain only to that "humanized"
everyday world in which we think we can understand each other to the extent that we can know
our roles, our habits, and the varieties of stereotyped behavior by which we compose ourselves.

Lawrence finds in the reflective order the
domain of "personality," and, in "Democracy,"
he tells us that the personality is a mask, a "persona," that we pick out from a storehouse of
socially and historically established roles. The
masks of the self hide us from ourselves as much
as they do from others: "This is the self-conscious
ego, the entity of fixed ideas and ideals, prancing
and displaying itself like an actor." These ideas of
the self are a kind of vaccine against otherness.
They serve to immunize us against the dread we
might feel to know that opposite us stands not
simply Mr. Jones, the shy businessman, but,
rather, a self that I am not, a center of synthesis
that may include me as an item within that synthesis of its experience that it is at all times forging.
Alone in her body, free for a moment from any
idea of herself, Lydia appears simply as a discon-
certing presence to her husband. What can she

possibly have to do with him, caught as she is within an experience that is hopelessly alien to his own? It is this inviolable gap between the Self and the Other that, Lawrence believes, gives the lie to the comforting notions of empathy, identification, intimacy, what have you, that exist as possibilities for the *personae* who, now and again, try on each other's masks.

The proof of the complexity of Tom and Lydia—of their "virtue" if you wish—is their capacity to realize and tolerate this gulf. Neither is content to seek the patronage of a personality in order to hide from the otherness of the Other. Lydia is the "active unknown facing him," the "awful unknown next his heart." Nor is Brangwen first made aware of otherness in his encounter with Lydia, for he experiences it as well with the "small withered foreigner of ancient breeding" whom he meets at an inn before his marriage. After his marriage, he senses it in the woman whom Alfred Brangwen loves: "She was about forty, straight, rather hard, a curious separate creature."

This alertness to the distance between selves is not limited to Tom's experience of Lydia. She, too, is moved by the "impersonality" of their relationship: "She did not know him, only she knew he was a man come for her." Lydia is aware of an intention (a man has come for her) and of an unknowable subject who presides over it. The "face and the living eyes" of Tom are less important for her than is the masculine presence that is the line of demarcation between them. She perceives Tom's separateness most forcefully when she sees his naked corpse: "She went pale, seeing death. He was behond change or knowledge, absolute, laid in line with the infinite. What had she to do with him?" That final question is one that Lawrence often uses to suggest a character's recognition of otherness (we recall it in the mind of Tom, earlier). Its presence here implies not that death is the privileged moment of the revelation of distance but that it is the *ratification* of a feeling we always have that the Other is "inviolable, inaccessibly himself." The marriage of Tom and Lydia is free of the kind of conflict that we find in that of Will and Anna, yet, as close as they are, Tom realizes that they "must for ever be such strangers, that his passion was a clanging torment to him. Such intimacy of embrace, and such utter foreignness of contact!"

The inaccessibility of the Other, what Joyce Carol Oates, in writing of Lawrence, has recently called "the absolute mystery of the Other which cannot be guessed and cannot be absorbed into the human soul," is not, of course, of the same order as that of the *things* of the world that we also perceive as distant from us and that we can know only as a set of spatio-temporal relations. The Other, on the contrary, is felt in all of his subjectivity in relationship to our own. We feel that alien subjectivity as a point of reference towards which the world is flowing; and it is a point that may include us in its organization of the world as well as a point with which we can never coincide. "How awfully distant and far off from each other's being we are!" Lawrence writes in a poem that celebrates the closeness of lovers. Apart from certain privileged moments of harmony (that I discuss below), we experience the Other, no matter how much there is of love between us, as an ultimately alien being.

In his account of Anna and Will, Lawrence insists upon this matter of the "distinctiveness" of selves. They are not simply characters with like and different tastes and feelings. Anna first sees Will as a kind of animal: "It was a curious head: it reminded her she knew not of what: of some animal, some mysterious animal that lived in the darkness under the leaves and never came out, but which lived vividly, swift and intense." Later, when his voice fills the church with song, she laughs uncontrollably at this manifestation of the "Will-ness" of Will Brangwen: "Her soul opened in amazement." Her laughter is bizarre only if we assume that we must always place others into certain categories, here that of "tenor." But Will is first a series of sounds, and this primal fact of him is more than Anna can bear. There is even something funny to her in the sight of "his knees on the praying cushion." The others in this congregation are no such burden for her. They do have a place in the church as worshippers, *personae* without distinction. But in Will Anna sees a kind of contradiction between the fact of a human presence and that collective mask that makes all the worshippers so familiar to her. It strikes her as very funny, and she cannot stop laughing. Her laughter seems to have a conservative impulse, seems meant to put Will, in his disturbing otherness, outside of all relationship to her, and to make of him a funny *thing* (knees on a cushion, loud sounds). Anna fails, of course, and Will and his ringing voice force her to see the world differently and make her aware that it offers a different aspect to a different pair of eyes: "In him the bounds of her experience were transgressed: he was the hole in the wall, beyond which the sunshine blazed on an outside world." He can open the world to her by the force with which his distinctive presence to the world makes itself felt in Anna as a perspective that is not her own. They were, Lawrence writes, "strangers, yet near." Near, because the Other is not a thing but a self; strange, because the Other is a self that is not her own.

When they work and love in the moonlit cornfield we see the same "alien intimacy" between them as we saw in the relationship of Tom and Lydia. Will cannot "quite overcome" with his kisses, the distance between them. They are "separate, single." "Why was there always a space between them; why were they apart?" Only the rhythms of their work bring them together. Later, after their marriage, Anna feels this space even more acutely than Will: "How unnatural it was to sit with a self-absorbed creature. ... Nothing could touch him—he could only absorb things into his own self." Abysmal otherness is not simply an occasion of wonder and love but also of doubt, fear, and hate in the observing self. We see both modes in the relationship of Ursula and Anton Skrebensky.

When Ursula walks into the living room and sees Skrebensky, she is struck by his "self-possession." "He seemed," Lawrence tells us, "simply acquiescent in the fact of his own being, as if he were beyond any change or question." Ursula will come to realize that the self must be in question, and in *Women in Love* the peculiar instability of Rupert Birkin will fascinate her; but for now she senses and is drawn to that self-possessed otherness of Anton. What first arouses her is that she could "know her own maximum self, limited and so defined against him." Another student of otherness, Sartre, has written that the "road of interiority passes through the Other," and Lawrence would agree. Ursula experiences herself as female in "supreme contradistinction to the male" in Skrebensky.

But after he returns from Africa that maleness seems to have vanished, and instead of being able to assist Ursula in her task of self-definition Anton exists as a check to all of her yearnings: "He seemed made up of a set of habitual actions and decisions. The vulnerable, variable quick of the man was inaccessible." He has, in other words, acquired his *persona* and become a modern-young-man. Indeed, Ursula can now know

him almost as if he were an invariant and stable thing. He has lost his human quick and become other to himself. There are, we can say, forms of otherness within the self. They include that alteration of the self that comes with the betrayal of the *quick* to the *idea* and that extraordinary quick itself, that we can never get hold of, that we try to personalize, and that is always there behind our masks.

ii

I have suggested that Lawrence is a novelist concerned not with the psychology of character but with the ur-form of human reality that is prior to any psychic container filled with "traits" and motives ("a set of habitual actions and decisions"). He is concerned with "another centre of consciousness" than that of the psychologist. This other center is a "dark" self, a pre-cognitive, pre-reflective self that we can never "know" but that we may experience as it suddenly transfigures us:

> Over [Will] too darkness of obscurity settled. He seemed to be hidden in a tense, electric darkness, in which his soul, his life was intensely active, but without his aid or attention. His mind was obscured.

This "other" self is a body-self, and in the essays on the unconscious, Lawrence speaks of it in physiological and electrical metaphors as a relationship among plexuses and ganglions, electrical circuits and poles. In any consideration of Lawrence's view of otherness, this body-self is crucial because the absorption of the "person" by the body cuts us off entirely from the Other (we are each condemned to our own flesh, each of us ending in our fingertips) and also offers us, paradoxically, a hope of release from the solitary confinement of individuality. If allowed to develop "naturally" (and not under the paralyzing glance of a too-soon-awakened cognitive eye), the solar plexus and the lumbar ganglion, the cardiac plexus and the thoracic ganglion will teach us about the Self and the Other and the relationship that must hold between them. Lawrence does not, of course, lament the individuality of the self. Far from it. He celebrates it. But his insistence on defining human relationships by reference to individualized body-selves confronts him with a problem similar to that faced by Wilhelm Reich, another therapist of the self who sought to make the body function "naturally" in the hope of bringing it into rapport with others. A concern with the uniqueness of the self always runs the risk of making the Other appear to be either inessential or an eternal adversary. The electrical metaphors of *Fantasia of the Unconscious* (reminiscent, at times, of certain of Reich's metaphors) reveal this problem insofar as they suggest the need for a kind of circuit between the Self and Other by which the integral, isolate individuality of each may be transcended. Lawrence need almost to invent a "current" of rapport dependent upon a space between selves that "invites" the leap of spark from one to other.

As long as we remain "egos," beings of the idea, Lawrence argues that there will be "really no vital difference between us." But the individuals themselves "stay apart forever and ever." This distance, open to the dangers I have mentioned, leads Lawrence to offer the vision of a fusion of *desires* (not of individuals themselves) in a "fourth dimension," a kind of earthly paradise, where "she who is the other has strange-mounded breasts and strange sheer slopes, and white levels." In the intertwining of desires, the strangeness of the Other is always present. Lawrence wants no "messy" notions of mental or, God forbid, corporeal fusion. In the fourth dimension we stand in awe of the strangeness of the Other; it becomes the symbol of all that we feel lacking in ourselves. But outside of the earthly paradise, in our world of three dimensions, that strangeness may be the occasion of terrible conflicts with the Other. These are not simply psychological rivalries. It is much more intense than psychological conflict, perhaps because it occurs, in Lawrence's view of it, at a pre-cognitive level.

Consider Tom's torment as he feels himself become an object of indifference to his pregnant wife. Lydia seems to have fallen out of common, everyday space we inhabit and that makes our otherness tolerable, into the urgency of her bodily self; and for Tom it is as if she denies his existence: "He felt he wanted to break her into acknowledgment of him, into awareness of him. It was insufferable that she had so obliterated him. He would smash her into regarding him." It is typical of Lawrence to write in this almost lurid way about what might first appear to be only the banalities of life. But they are banal only if we assume that such moments are perfectly transparent to us and if we no longer see in them that there is always a relationship between two selves in which one is made more intensely aware of otherness by an intensification of Other's bodily experience. It is not that Lydia refuses to be

aware of her husband, if, by "aware," we mean that she does not see him or look at him. The everyday life goes on as usual in that Tom works, walks in the house, sits at the table; Lydia performs her domestic duties, serves him his dinner. Yet there is a difference. Lydia, in a fullness of identity with herself, as a harbor of new life, stands somehow apart from Tom. She is elsewhere at the very moment that she is there before him. This "elsewhere" is to be found in the interplay of selves and not "persons" (in the sense in which Lawrence speaks of "personality"). The reaffirmation of Lydia's "otherness" is, here, the locus of the elsewhere. The desire to break into this elsewhere leads Tom into a frustration and rage that is revealed in the violent desire to "break" and to "smash" this self-enclosed Other into seeing him. He must flee to the inn "to escape the madness of sitting next to her when she did not belong to him, when she was as absent as any other woman in indifference could be." At moments like these one's integrity, one's otherness, becomes so overwhelming that it seems to affect those near one as a kind of nihilation of them.

Tom experiences this sense of his own nihilation when Lydia speaks of Poland and of her first husband. As in the matter of pregnancy, one may first be tempted to describe such episodes as an example of Laurentian jargon or luridness, if one approaches them as if Lawrence were writing about mere "reminiscences." Why all the fuss and bother? Lawrence's point is that insofar as we are beings who possess memory and can reminisce we are always sealed off from memories that we do not share. The Other has a past that is formally akin to my own having a past and, at the same time, it is a past that is not mine. Again, the point is that Lawrence is concerned with man's ontological makeup. The presence before Tom of a Lydia who has her own past makes Tom feel inessential to her, a mere "peasant, a serf, a servant, a lover, a paramour, a shadow, a nothing." He knew then that he had "nothing to do with her." To speak of her memories in this way, is a sign of Lydia's distance from her husband. At another time it may make her attractive, for it is also a tempting gap-to-be-bridged (whether or not this is possible) as well as a proof of exclusion.

Lydia is herself offended by the particular form that Tom's self-enclosure can take. She sees in him "a solid power of antagonism to her," and it "irritated her to be made aware of him as a separate power." In these moments of antipathy to him, Lydia has recourse to a radicalization of separation. She "lapses" into a "sort of sombre exclusion, a curious communion with mysterious powers ... which drove him and the child nearly mad." It is as if they engage in a kind of psychic duel with one another ("It was his turn to submit"), in which now Lydia, now Tom, is master or slave of the other partner.

In Will and Anna we see conflict raised to incandescence. On the day after their marriage, they remain in bed until nightfall, in a "core of living eternity," a "timeless universe of free, perfect limbs and immortal breasts." But eventually the spirit of Anna, like that of Lycius in Keats' "Lamia," begins to pass "beyond its golden bourn/ Into the noisy world almost forlorn." She wants, that is, to give a tea-party. Again, the commonplace becomes a motive for a kind of ontological homicide: "He was sullen. But she blithely began to make preparations for her tea-party. His fear was too strong, he was troubled, he hated her shallow anticipation and joy." Lawrence says of Will that "now he must be deposed." He mopes around the house and gets on his wife's nerves; " ... the futility of him, the way his hands hung, irritated her beyond bearing. She turned on him blindly and destructively, he became a mad creature, black and electric with fury." Will is a man who relishes the eternal "moment," whether it be architectural or erotic, while Anna is able to move comfortably in more mundane patterns of existence. But Lawrence is insistent that such "preferences" be seen properly. The newlyweds do not become blindly destructive and electric with fury because they have different tastes. The quarrel is not between rival tastes but between that which accounts for such tastes, between, that is, mutually exclusive bloodstreams roused to fury by their inability to coalesce.

Problems arise when husband and wife insist that the love between them be perfect, and Lawrence argues that this is, in principle, impossible except in a "third land," because "the individualities of men and women are incommensurable." Will's solution to the individuality of his wife is to become "unaware of her. She did not exist. His dark, passionate soul had recoiled upon itself ... " His aim is to "annihilate" Anna if he cannot coalesce with her. It is to turn Anna and her party into things of the external world, not to see her as a Self but to brush against her and her

party-plans as one brushes against a table. One doesn't say "excuse me" to things. Anna feels his terrible self-sufficiency when she sees in Will the proof of her own nothingness: "His intelligence was self-absorbed. How unnatural it was to sit with a self-absorbed creature, like something negative ensconced opposite one." He is "negative" in that he negates the world by making it a function of his own indifference. And Anna feels her own mastery drained away into this human blotter who "absorb[s] things into his own self."

This see-saw of nihilation is present throughout the novel. In the cathedral it is first Will who denies Anna: "Brangwen came to his consummation" in the world of "this timeless consummation ... " that is the church. Anna "resented his transports and ecstacies," for they made this world "not quite her own." In her turn, and despite her own love of the church's beauty, Anna becomes "the serpent in [Will's] Eden," forcing him out of his ecstasy into a world of details, *her* world of gargoyle faces, so different from the multiplicity of undifferentiated particulars in which Will loses himself. Later, when Anna finds her own ecstasy in dancing, pregnant, "before the Lord," Will can make her "flinch" by his very presence in the room. The presence of Will signals the fact of a different perspective than her own, and it scandalizes her to feel that perspective as it tilts her world into its direction. Anna's dance is, of course, intended as a kind of gesture of nihilation, a magical attempt to "annul" Will, to dance his "non-existence."

These patterns of conflict continue, with certain qualifications, into Lawrence's account of the life of Ursula. When she meets Skrebensky, after his return, Ursula feels that "every movement and work of his was alien to her being." She recalls how, in his youth, he was "near to her": "She thought a man must inevitably set into this strange separateness, cold otherness of being." But Ursula allows her first sense of Skrebensky as a "set of habitual actions and decisions" to go cloudy, in a kind of bad faith. Once again they become lovers, but soon Lawrence sounds the dirge of conflict between them.

Anton is simply unable to match that white-hot passion that makes Ursula "available" to the ministrations of the moonlight: "He felt himself fusing down to nothingness, like a bead that rapidly disappears in an incandescent flame." It is Ursula's rapport with her sister in the sky that causes Anton to "disappear." It is an error to suggest, as does Frank Kermode, that Ursula is to be judged here by reference only to Lawrence's uneasiness with respect to "frictional" sexuality, "the salt destructiveness of all the powers that are hostile to living sex." Theirs is not the conflict between "fell and mighty opposites" that we see in other relationships in the novel (or between Ursula and Birkin in *Women in Love*). Ursula's "lust" in these passages is a result of Anton's "modernism" more than it is of a flaw in her.

Thus, when they make love under the moon, Anton is a prey to a "beaked" Ursula who gives him a "harpy's kiss." The imagery of castration is perfectly appropriate here, but it has no relationship to the cruder claims of Lawrence's alleged sexism. Better to say that Anton has castrated himself, or that, having abandoned his body to an ego, he deserves what he gets from the passion of a woman who can find no boundary against which to measure herself. Anton's commonness makes him passive to this "prowling" female who "held him pinned down at the chest, awful. The fight, the struggle for consummation was terrible. It lasted till it was agony to his soul, till he succumbed, till he gave way as if dead . . . " At breakfast, the morning after his encounter with this "fearful thing," the Other, he is "white and obliterated."

Their battle is not simply a result of the differing sexuality of each, for we see such conflict in relationships among characters who are better "matched" sexually. But sexuality is the privileged "content" with which to fill this "form" that is the conflict between individuated selves. Sexuality is, first, a corporeal matter, and Skrebensky is eager to displace it onto a social plane, that of marriage. He is scandalized by, and terrified of, Ursula's ability to give herself up to this inflammation of the body that is sexuality. He simply stands in ignorance before her, unable to meet this being who shouts, as the sea washes over her feet, "'I want to go, I want to go.'" All he sees, all he knows, is her alien being, her otherness, for he is on the plane of reflection, that is, he is self-conscious. He is *aware* of his fear and of her passion, not "lost" in passion and beyond reflection. Her "beaked mouth" goes to the "heart of him," of this Prometheus *manqué,* who receives the punishment of the beak for having been unable to appropriate the fire of the dark gods.

iii

I have suggested that Lawrence's insistence on the integrity of individual selves accounts for the emphasis in his work on the distance between selves as well as on the liability of conflict between them. Yet this necessary distance also acts as a call to harmony with the Other. Lawrence does not wish so to lock his individuated selves within themselves that no hope of rapport between them is possible. This rapport should not, however, be understood as a fusion of some kind that dissolves individual uniqueness and creates an identity between selves. One recalls the effort, in philosophy, of Merleau-Ponty to posit an *intermonde* by which he hoped to resolve the dilemma created by Sartre's vision of endless conflict between Self and Other. Lawrence calls his own *intermonde* the "third land where the two streams of desire meet":

> The individual has nothing, really, to do with love. That is, his individuality hasn't. Out of the deep silence of his individuality runs the stream of desire, into the open squash-blossom of the world. And the stream of desire may meet and mingle with the stream from a woman. But it is never *himself* that meets and mingles with *herself*. . . .

In the Hardy study Lawrence describes desire as a lack of that which we feel would complete us:

> And desire is the admitting of deficiency. And the embodiment of the object of desire reveals the original defect of the defaulter. So that the attributes of God will reveal that which man lacked and yearned for in his living. And these attributes are always, in their essence, Eternality, Infinity, Immutability.

Man, for Lawrence, is, as it were, a desire to be God, to be that is, completed, whole, and stable. It is when the streams of desire meet that the tensions of otherness disappear, and we attain to what Lawrence calls "another circle of existence." This other circle is repeatedly described in terms of perfection, completeness, and wholeness; and attains it with the Other.

In *The Rainbow* Lawrence does not limit the imagery of perfection to moments of sexual desire, although these are the finest and, perhaps, the only real moments of the mingling of the two streams. Given this emphasis on the isolation of the self within its own integrity, it seems reasonable to assume that the self will wish to get outside of itself, outside of what it experiences as incomplete existence (everywhere around it, in persons and things, is evidence of existence other than its own). To achieve this transcendence of the Self by entering into relationships with the Other is a risky business. The Other is moved by the dictates of her own experience, and we have seen the friction that may result from these rival perspectives on the world. Therefore the self may try to find its completeness in non-human experience. In *The Rainbow* we see such attempts to flee one's partial existence by means of flight into the ecstasies offered by religion, art, and knowledge.

Consider Ursula's initial infatuation with the college. "She was on holy ground," Lawrence writes. Ursula wants a union in which she will be one part of a whole that includes her as a part and that gives her intelligibility and stability. The academic paraphernalia of the college offers her the illusion of a share in its *being*. Its gothic arches take her back to the "cloistral origin of education", and she would prefer that the faces of her fellow students be more than those of English students of the early twentieth-century: "... she wanted their faces to be still and luminous as the nuns' and the monks' faces." She would like to be no more than a student-in-a-timeless-college, and she loves to pass along the corridors with books in her hand and to hurry into lecture rooms, all as if she were a simple determination of the spirit of the academy. The college offers her a spurious eternity: "Here, within the great whispering sea-shell, that whispered all the while with reminiscences of all the centuries, time faded away, and the echo of knowledge filled the timeless silence." The professors in their gowns are not "ordinary men who ate bacon and pulled on their boots," but were, instead, the "black-gowned priests of knowledge." When she looks out of the classroom window, she sees the world "remote, remote." Ursula has allowed herself to become lost in an *unio mystica* in which she no longer acts but performs the gestures that reveal her as an academic being, a prefabricated self.

She experiences more important and complex forms of timelessness with Anton: "At the touch of her hand on her arm, his consciousness melted away from him. He took her into his arms, as if into the sure, subtle power of his will, and they became one movement, one dual movement ..." But, as we have seen, she does not really find with Anton that equilibrium that Birkin will call "star-polarity." Looking at Skrebensky, she wishes to "lay hold of him and tear him and make him into nothing." Since she cannot rid him of his "will," that reflective faculty that gnaws away at spontaneity, she is tempted to tear apart the body that reveals it. In their second affair she can, by passing over in silence her first feeling of dismay at the sight of him, know a "perfect" moment; but it is

one that finds its order corroded by her awareness of her bad faith. In the "utter, dark kiss that triumphed over them both, subjected them, knitted them into one fecund nucleus of fluid darkness," we see the kind of union in the third land to which Lawrence referred. Out goes "the light of consciousness," to inaugurate the reign of darkness and the transfiguration of integers into a "nucleolating of the fecund darkness." But there is no long-term hope for the renewal of such moments. Ursula always sees Anton for what he is, and she must make him suffer for her awareness of his limitations.

This possibility of union with either another person or with an experience is available also to Will and Anna. Their love for each other offers the first possibility, while Will's feeling for beauty and Anna's for maternity offer instances of the second. In the cathedral at Lincoln, "'before' and 'after' were folded together, all was contained in oneness. Brangwen came to his consummation." Anna, on the other hand, loves to be "the source of children," an essence, one might say, that precedes other existences: "This was enough for Anna. She seemed to pass off into a kind of rapture of motherhood, her rapture of motherhood was everything." These are resting places, the church and the infant, analogous to Ursula's idealized academy. One harmonizes with others across certain mediations: art, biology, knowledge. Lawrence does not mean to suggest that we should not have these experiences. They are, of course, revelations of one's individuality. They become dangerous only insofar as they prevent us from attempting to find rapport with unmediated Others, with beings of flesh and blood who stand before us.

For three days after their marriage, Will and Anna seem to have entered the third land. Lawrence describes them as being "immune in a perfect love." In their cottage, on the first day, there was between them "a great steadiness, a core of living eternity. Only far outside, at the rim, went on the noise and destruction. Here at the centre the great wheel was motionless, centred upon itself. Here was a poised, unflawed stillness that was beyond time ..." In time move individuated persons. It is the place of otherness. But as they lie in each other's arms, "complete and beyond the touch of time or change," the lovers find the interworld where Self and Other can, by a mingling of the desire for each other, "complete" themselves. They are at the "centre where there is utter radiance and eternal being" and where individuals become a new being that is the cause of itself. Thus the religious imagery that clothes them with divinity.

One must speculate on the reasons for Lawrence's choice of sexuality as the privileged place. In sexuality there is a reciprocal incarnation of selves into body-selves. It is as if, in un-sexual moments, there is always some vestige of personality that hides us from ourselves. And in the everyday world, even at those moments when our otherness shines through our *personae*, it is as if the tasks of living (the tea party, for example) are there to reveal otherness as a series of incommensurable choices of action. Sexuality, however, closes the body in on itself. Action-in-the-world has no call on it, and the ideas we harbor of our selves are given the lie by the resurrection of that pre-ideational body that we always are "behind" our ideas. Desire flows through the body and washes away reflection, and all that is left is this pre-reflective "lack" that is the meaning of desire and that is the lack of the Other there before us, returned to her own body. Desire is there on the surface of the body as it touches the desired and desiring "other" body. In this reciprocity of "ignorance," when, as Lawrence once said of the true self, the self "is not aware that it is a self," Will and Anna can be the still and silent hub of an everturning world. It is important also to be clear that at such "perfect moments" otherness is not destroyed. In the reciprocal incarnation of sexuality, there is a reciprocal tolerance of otherness, for it is the Other that one needs to complete oneself. Each lover is the desire for and lack of the beloved.

Tom and Lydia are less self-conscious beings than Will, Anna, and Ursula. They do not have the mediated resting-places that we have seen as being important to the latter. They are left to themselves, knowing distance, conflict, and union only with each other. In their relationship we also see the timeless moments, as, for example, in that "elemental embrace beyond their superficial foreignness" that unites them and in which Tom "let himself go from past and future, [and] was reduced to the moment with her." When, in mutual presence, Tom and Lydia shed the reflectiveness that knows past and future, there is left only the touch that is mindless of everything but its own fullness-in-contiguity with the touch of the beloved. As he lies in bed with this woman to whom he was drawn by her distinctiveness and from whom he was cut off by that distinctiveness, Tom

> was silent with delight. He felt strong, physically, carrying her on his breathing. The strange, inviolable completeness of the two of them made him feel as sure and as stable as God. Amused, he wondered what the vicar would say if he knew.

But when Lydia gets up, takes out a "little tray-cloth," sets a tray and speaks of Poland, time begins once more to move. The union is gone as the temporal woman does her chores and speaks of her memories. It is the time of conflict again: "Again he had not got her." Later, after another night when time had come to a stop, Lydia arises in the morning, foreign, and makes Tom "uneasy again. She was still foreign and unknown to him." When the stream of desire flows back to its source, the Other again stands before him and against him.

Lawrence's invulnerability to the charge of cant, whatever his contribution to its vocabulary, lies in his refusal to back off from his vision of otherness. The morning always returns, and the world's pressure is always there. Timelessness is, in fact, contingent on the temporal order, and if his individual selves can be redeemed from conflict it is only on the ground of this fundamental possibility of conflict to which they must inevitably return. There is no way of being "true to oneself" that does not involve the Other. One must always be prepared to acknowledge the existence of experience that can not be reduced to one's own and that may be felt as a kind of laceration of our own experience. One can, I think, raise serious objections to Lawrence's "solution" to the tension of this necessary distance between the Self and the Other, but first it is necessary to understand that his proffer of a third land is intended to respond to his clear perception of this "strange reality" that we have to admit if we wish to claim integrity for the self. Have your individuality, your uniqueness. It is yours by right. Only understand, he implies, that what it entails may appear as a frightening solitude that can be transcended only by first accepting it.

Source: T. H. Adamowski, "*The Rainbow* and 'Otherness,'" in *D. H. Lawrence Review*, edited by James C. Cowan, Vol. 7, No. 1, Spring 1974, pp. 58–77.

SOURCES

Crump, G. B., "Lawrence's *Rainbow* and Russell's *Rainbow*," in *The D. H. Lawrence Review*, Vol. 21, No. 2, Summer 1989, pp. 187, 188, 199, 200.

Lawrence, D. H., *The Rainbow*, Penguin, 1995.

Rosenzweig, Paul, "A Defense of the Second Half of *The Rainbow*: Its Structure and Characterization," in *The D. H. Lawrence Review*, Vol. 13, No. 2, Summer 1980, pp. 150, 151.

Squire, J. C., "Books in General: *The Rainbow*," in *New Statesman*, Vol. 6, No. 137, November 20, 1915, p. 161.

Stewart, Jack F., "Dialectics of Knowing in *Women in Love*," in *Twentieth Century Literature*, Vol. 37, No. 1, Spring 1991, p. 63.

Widmer, Kingsley, "D. H. Lawrence," in *Dictionary of Literary Biography*, Vol. 36: *British Novelists, 1890–1929: Modernists*, edited by Thomas F. Staley, Gale Research, 1985, pp. 115–149.

FURTHER READING

Brown, Homer O., "The Passionate Struggle into Conscious Being," in *The D. H. Lawrence Review*, Vol. 7, No. 3, pp. 275–90.
Brown explores the characters' quest in *The Rainbow* for a sense of identity, especially one that relates to the outside world.

Jackson, Dennis, and Fleda Brown Jackson, eds., *Critical Essays on D. H. Lawrence*, G. K. Hall, 1988.
This collection includes an overview of the critical reception of Lawrence's works as well as an article on expressionism pertaining to *The Rainbow*.

Roberts, Warren, and James T. Boulton, eds., *The Letters of D. H. Lawrence*, Cambridge University Press, 2002.
Lawrence was a prolific letter writer, and in his letters he discusses his works in progress, outlines main themes, and explains his philosophy.

Sagar, Keith, *The Life of D. H. Lawrence: An Illustrated Biography*, Chaucer Press, 2004.
Sager focuses on important biographical events that influenced Lawrence's work. What makes this book an added plus is that it contains 170 pictures, some in color and many of which have not been published previously.

The Tenant of Wildfell Hall

ANNE BRONTË

1848

The Tenant of Wildfell Hall, by Anne Brontë, is one of the first modern feminist novels. It tells the story of a young wife during the Regency period in England (1800–1830) who runs away from her drunken, adulterous, verbally abusive husband, an act virtually unheard of at this time in history. Brontë is the youngest sister of the famous Charlotte Brontë and Emily Brontë and although her poetry and novels have never received the same attention, she was arguably the pioneer of her family. Brontë's use of realism—unlike the gothic romances of Charlotte and Emily— was a precursor to the literary traditions of the late nineteenth and early twentieth centuries.

The Tenant of Wildfell Hall was a wildly popular and controversial novel when it was published in 1848. Critics then and later criticized the uneven characterization, but it was Brontë's progressive ideas about the rights of women that caused an uproar in the mid-1800s. Some considered the novel unfit for women to read. *The Tenant of Wildfell Hall* has interest for readers in the early 2000s because of its insight into the historical roles of men and women and for the ways it illustrates how marriage has changed and how some things—such as domestic abuse—have not.

Anne Brontë *(Time Life Pictures | Mansell | Time Life Pictures | Getty Images)*

AUTHOR BIOGRAPHY

Anne Brontë was born January 17, 1820, the sixth and last child of Patrick and Maria Branwell Brontë. She was born in the village of Thornton in West Yorkshire, England, but the family moved to Haworth just a few months later so that her father could take a higher paying position as the local parson. Brontë's mother died before her youngest daughter was two years old. Their aunt, Elizabeth Branwell, came to live with the family and cared for the children. She and Anne were particularly close as Aunt Branwell was effectively the only mother the girl remembered having. The two eldest daughters, Maria and Elizabeth, died when Anne was only four. Growing up, Anne was closest to her sister Emily, and together they made up stories about the imaginary land of Gondal. Charlotte and her brother Branwell similarly played together, making up stories about a fantasy land named Angria.

Anne Brontë did not attend school until she was fifteen when she took Emily's place at Roe Head School. She was acutely homesick but, unlike Emily, she endured being at school and worked hard because she believed an education would give her the means to support herself. Her first known poems were written during her two years at school. She worked as a governess for the Ingham family at Blake Hall in 1839 and then, in 1840, for the Robinson family of Thorp Green, near York, where she stayed for five years. Her poetry expresses her homesickness and unhappiness with her appointment. Brontë captured her experience as a governess in her novel *Agnes Grey* (1847), which depicts a young governess trying to manage spoiled children.

While at home between the two jobs, Brontë met her father's new curate, William Weightman. Her writings of this time suggest that she fell in love with him, but there is considerable scholarly debate over this point. If true, her feelings were hidden and almost certainly unrequited. Weightman and Aunt Branwell both died in 1842, and Brontë grieved through her poetry. In 1843, Brontë's brother Branwell joined her at Thorp Green to tutor the Robinson's son. Brontë resigned her post in June 1845—Branwell was dismissed soon thereafter for having an affair with Mrs. Robinson.

In 1845, with all four Brontë siblings at home and out of work, Charlotte, Emily, and Anne reached an agreement to secretly publish their poems. *Poems by Currer, Ellis, and Acton Bell* was published the following year. (The sisters used pseudonyms that preserved their initials but obscured their sex.) *Agnes Grey*, Brontë's first novel, was published in 1847 and her second, *The Tenant of Wildfell Hall*, was published in 1848. During this time, the family's health was deteriorating. Branwell drank himself to his grave by September 1848. Many contend that Branwell, in part, inspired the character of Mr. Huntington. Emily died of tuberculosis in December 1848. Brontë was also ill and, seeing her own death coming, she asked Charlotte to take her to Scarborough, a favorite place of hers near the sea. Anne Brontë died there on May 28, 1849, at the age of twenty-nine. She is buried there, while all the other Brontës are buried in the family vault in St. Michael and All Angels' Church, Haworth.

MEDIA ADAPTATIONS

- *The Tenant of Wildfell Hall* was first adapted to television by the British Broadcasting Corporation (BBC) in 1968. It was directed by Peter Sasdy with a script by Christopher Fry and starred Janet Munro as Helen Huntington. The BBC aired this miniseries in four parts from December 28, 1968, through January 18, 1969. It is three hours long and available in limited quantities on VHS from the United Kingdom.

- The BBC produced another adaptation of *The Tenant of Wildfell Hall* in 1996. The script was adapted by Janet Barron, and the production stars Tara Fitzgerald as Helen Huntington. Mike Barker directed this highly rated adaptation. It is two and a half hours long and was originally aired in three parts. It is available on VHS from Twentieth-Century Fox (released 1997) and BBC Warner (released 2000). DVD availability is limited to Europe.

PLOT SUMMARY

Volume I

TO J. HALFORD, ESQ.

The Tenant of Wildfell Hall begins with a letter from Gilbert Markham to his brother-in-law and friend, Jack Halford. Halford and Gilbert had a quarrel when Halford revealed a secret, and Gilbert did not return the favor. Gilbert promises to make amends and tell Halford his biggest secret although it is a long story.

CHAPTERS I–V

In the autumn of 1827, a widowed young woman named Mrs. Graham takes up residence at the derelict Wildfell Hall. Rose Markham and her mother visit, hoping to learn more about this stranger, but she is evasive. Rose's older brother Gilbert cannot stop himself from staring at her in church and a few days later his hunting takes him near her house where he saves her son from falling out of a tree. Their first meeting is awkward because she is so suspicious of him.

Mrs. Graham pays a return visit to the Markhams where she gets into several arguments. Mrs. Markham chides her for spoiling her son because she will not let anyone else watch him. Then she and Gilbert quarrel about the strengths and weaknesses of men and women. She declines an invitation to the family's Guy Fawkes Day party on November 5th. At the party, the guests gossip endlessly about Mrs. Graham. Gilbert flirts with his sweetheart, Eliza Millward, the vicar's daughter. After the party, Mrs. Markham chastises her son for showing Eliza affection because she does not think Eliza will be a good wife for him.

At the end of November, Rose and Gilbert visit Wildfell Hall and learn that Mrs. Graham earns her living by painting landscapes—and she signs a false name to the paintings to hide her location. A mysterious man comes to visit, but Mrs. Graham sends him away before her guests see who he is. Gilbert accidentally uncovers a painting of a dashing young man, which annoys Mrs. Graham. But she apologizes to Gilbert for her temper, and they part on good terms.

CHAPTERS VI–XII

Throughout winter, Gilbert and Mrs. Graham—now Helen—run into each other and have many pleasant conversations. In March, Gilbert meets Frederick Lawrence, his neighbor, on the road to Wildfell Hall. Lawrence expresses surprise because he thought Gilbert did not like Helen. Gilbert has changed his mind, but he mistakenly believes Lawrence to be in love with Helen. Lawrence laughs. In mid-May, Gilbert, Rose, Fergus, Jane, Richard, Mary, Eliza, Helen, and Arthur make the day-trip out to the seaside. Gilbert enjoys talking with Helen while they walk and even follows her when she slips away to sketch. Gilbert realizes that Eliza's chatter annoys him and that he may be falling in love with Helen.

In June 1828, Gilbert tries to give Helen a new book, but she refuses to take it without paying because she does not want to encourage his affections. Gilbert is crushed but promises that he will not make any advances on her favor. She takes the book as a gift on those terms, and they part as friends. Not long after

Gilbert's affection shifts from Eliza to Helen, scandalous gossip about Helen emerges and spreads rapidly among her neighbors. People whisper that she is involved with Lawrence and her child even looks like him. Gilbert refuses to believe the slander, but Mrs. Markham thinks there might be some kernel of truth. He visits Wildfell Hall the following week to lend Helen a book. They walk in the garden, and he asks her for a rose, which she gives him. Realizing his intentions, Helen implores him to be her friend or end their acquaintance. Gilbert reluctantly agrees and leaves, running into Lawrence on the road. They quarrel about why Lawrence is traveling to Wildfell Hall, but Reverend Millward interrupts them.

Back at home, Rose tells Gilbert to stop visiting Helen and soon thereafter Reverend Millward arrives. He has just returned from Wildfell Hall where he told Helen the gossip circulating and asked her to correct her conduct. He says she took the news badly, which causes Gilbert to immediately rush back to Wildfell Hall. He tells Helen he believes none of the rumors and that he loves her. Helen offers to explain her secrets to him the following day. Gilbert leaves reluctantly. Lingering outside, he chances to see Helen walking arm-in-arm with Lawrence. This view seems to confirm the rumor after all.

CHAPTERS XIII–XV

Gilbert pours himself into his work and avoids meeting Helen. He rides toward the nearby town one day and meets Mr. Lawrence along the road. Lawrence tries to talk to him, but Gilbert is so angry that he strikes him with his horsewhip, cutting open his head and knocking him to the ground. After Gilbert makes sure Lawrence is still alive, he starts to leave, then he returns to offer help. Lawrence refuses, and Gilbert goes on to town, leaving Lawrence lying on the damp ground. When Gilbert returns home, Rose tells him that Lawrence has had a terrible accident. She urges him to visit Lawrence, who may be on his deathbed, but Gilbert refuses, sending Fergus instead. Helen finally catches Gilbert and asks him why he did not meet her to hear her story. They argue, and she leaves, but Gilbert grows curious. He visits her the next day and reveals why he is angry. Helen gives him her diary by way of explanation.

CHAPTERS XVI–XIX

The next twenty-nine chapters are told from Helen's perspective, via her diary. Her story begins June 1, 1821, seven years earlier. Helen is eighteen years old and lives at Staningley manor with her uncle and aunt, Mr. and Mrs. Maxwell. She reflects upon her latest visit to town, meaning London. Mrs. Maxwell has introduced Helen to some older men, but Helen is only interested in the dashing Mr. Huntington. One of the older suitors, Mr. Boarham, proposes, but Helen refuses him. The next day, she visits her uncle's friend Mr. Wilmot and Huntington is among the guests. He pays special attention to Helen, which distresses her aunt. Mrs. Maxwell tries to dissuade Helen from forming an attachment to Huntington, but Helen believes she can reform him.

A party comes to Staningley in the autumn of 1821, including Huntington, Lord Lowborough, Boarham, Wilmot, Annabella Wilmot, and Milicent Hargrave. Helen is excited to see Huntington, but he confuses her by flirting with Annabella. She is brought to tears one evening when Annabella sings a song about lost love. Helen flees to the library to cry, and Huntington follows her, declaring his love and asking her to be his wife. Mrs. Maxwell comes upon them kissing, and Helen assures her aunt that she has not yet given her assent.

Volume II

CHAPTERS XX–XXIII

Helen is very happy the next day but she tells Mr. Huntington that her aunt and uncle will only let her marry a good man. He promises her to be better than he has been. Later, Helen talks with her aunt, declaring that she will reform Huntington when she is his wife. But at church that day, Helen observes Huntington's wandering attention and boredom. Nevertheless, she tells her uncle she will marry the man, and Christmas is settled upon for the wedding day, three months hence. Milicent is surprised at this engagement while Annabella declares her intention to become Lady Lowborough. Later that day, Huntington tells Helen a long story about how he and his friends mistreated Lord Lowborough while the lord struggled with a gambling problem and alcoholism. Helen is appalled at Huntington's lack of compassion. Before the end of the day, Annabelle and Lowborough are engaged as well.

Eight weeks into her marriage, February 1822, Helen is beginning to feel a little disenchanted with her husband. Huntington hurried through their honeymoon on the continent and, once home at Grassdale Manor, implored Helen to be less religious so that she could give him more of her heart.

CHAPTERS XXIV–XXVII

In April, Helen and Huntington quarrel after he tells her about an affair he had with a married woman when he was younger. Helen thinks to herself, "for the first time in my life, and I hope the last, I wished I had not married him." Restless with country life, Huntington makes plans to go to London. He and Helen make up, and she accompanies him. She returns to Grassdale Manor a month later. Huntington stays behind to finish some unspecified business. He keeps delaying his return and reports in his letters that Milicent is engaged to his friend Mr. Hattersley. Milicent writes to Helen that Hattersley tricked her into the engagement, but Milicent was too timid to speak out against him. Huntington finally returns home at the end of July, ill from too much debauchery. He recovers after a few days and plans to have their friends come and visit in September: Lord and Lady Lowborough, Mr. and Mrs. Hattersley, Mr. Grimsby, and Walter Hargrave, their neighbor. Annabella and Huntington flirt together, distressing both Lowborough and Helen. A month into the visit, Helen sees Huntington and Annabella talking at the piano with hands intimately clasped. Helen is upset, but Huntington convinces her that it means nothing.

CHAPTERS XXVIII–XXXII

By Christmas 1822, Helen and Huntington have a son, who is named Arthur after his father. Helen is delighted to be a mother, but Huntington is jealous of the time and affection Helen devotes to the baby. A year later, Helen is glad to see Huntington take an interest in little Arthur but fears that her son will take after his father. In the spring, Huntington says he is returning to London without Helen or the baby. He is gone from March through July during which time Helen visits with the Hargraves for company even though she finds Mr. Hargrave annoying. Huntington is more ill this time when he returns home than he was the previous summer but a trip to Scotland to hunt refreshes him.

In March 1824, Huntington sneaks off to London while Helen is visiting her ill father. Huntington returns in July and soon thereafter Helen's father dies. Huntington will not let her go to the funeral because he wants her at home with him. In September, their friends visit again. Grimsby and Hattersley encourage Huntington to drink heavily, and the three men behave riotously and rudely to the rest of the company. A week into the visit, Milicent urges Helen to talk to her younger sister Esther about being very careful in her choice of a spouse. Hattersley complains to his wife that he wishes she would be firmer with him. His concerns show him to be more introspective than Huntington. Mr. Hargrave wishes to tell Helen some terrible news about her husband, but she refuses to hear him.

CHAPTERS XXXIII–XXXVII

One night, Helen comes upon her husband outside. At first he is delighted, then surprised, and he demands that she return to the house. His affection puts Helen in a good mood for the evening. Two nights later, Helen discovers her husband and Annabella in the shrubbery outside, kissing and exchanging endearments. Later Helen asks him if he will permit her and their son to leave, but he refuses. Helen struggles the next day to behave normally. She makes her enmity known to Annabella, who begs Helen not to tell Lowborough. Helen declares that she will tell no one but not because Annabella asks it of her. A few weeks later, Hargrave declares his affection to Helen, who is offended. He apologizes later, but their conference is observed by Grimsby and Hattersley, whose looks imply they believe something is going on between them.

After their guests leave, Helen and Huntington grow accustomed to their estrangement even as they continue to live in the same house. Helen is distressed that two-year-old Arthur seems to cling to his father more than his mother. In May, Hargrave renews his declaration of love to Helen and is again rebuffed. Esther knows they have quarreled and is concerned that they remain friends. Helen is very annoyed by Hargrave. In November, he again tries to convince her to return his affection and, angered, Helen tells him he is selfish and should leave her alone. He soon leaves for Paris, and Helen is relieved.

Volume III

CHAPTERS XXXVIII–XLIV

A year later, September 1826, Helen and Huntington's friends return for a visit joined by Mrs. Hargrave and Esther Hargrave. Two weeks into the visit, Lowborough finally catches his wife at her infidelity, and they leave the next day. During the rest of the visit, Helen is appalled to see Huntington teaching their four-year-old son how to behave like his father—drinking and swearing. She determines to leave Grassdale. Hargrave again renews his love declaration to Helen. Grimsby spies him gripping her hands and soon Huntington bursts into the room and confronts them. Helen's name is cleared by Hargrave's reluctant confession.

In January 1827, Huntington takes Helen's diary from her and reads it, discovering her plan to escape. He immediately confiscates all of her money and valuables and burns many of her painting tools. Helen's plans are dashed because she cannot afford to support herself and her son on the tiny allowance Huntington gives her. In March, Huntington leaves for London, and Helen works to break her son of the bad habits his father has taught him. Helen's brother, Frederick Lawrence, visits and agrees to aid Helen in leaving Grassdale. Helen councils Esther to be careful about whom she chooses to marry and to not marry for love alone. Milicent and her husband visit Grassdale, and Hattersley tells Helen that he is weary of Huntington and that she is better off not having him at home. Helen encourages his resolution to give up drinking and be a better husband and father.

Huntington returns to Grassdale in September and tells Helen he is hiring a governess for their son. Helen dislikes Miss Myers and soon resolves to leave Grassdale, even though she is penniless. In early October 1827, she and Rachel secretly pack a few boxes and, with Benson's help, send them ahead to the coach-office. Rising early in the morning, Helen, Rachel, and little Arthur flee Grassdale in a hired coach. Helen disguises herself as a widow and travels under an assumed name, Mrs. Graham. After a day-long journey, they arrive at Wildfell Hall, the childhood home of Helen and her brother, which Rachel also remembers. Lawrence reports to Helen that Huntington is looking for her. They get settled at Wildfell Hall although Helen finds her new neighbors to be nosy.

CHAPTERS XLV–XLIX

The story returns to the present time, summer of 1828. Gilbert hurries to Wildfell Hall the morning he finishes Helen's diary. He and Helen reconcile, but she tells him that they can never see each other again. He implores her to change her mind, and she finally consents that he may write to her in six months time, after she has moved to a new place. Gilbert leaves and visits the ill Mr. Lawrence, who is surprised to see Gilbert, but they reconcile their differences. Gilbert cannot talk to anyone about Helen's story for fear of word getting back to Huntington. Helen moves two months later, and Gilbert visits with Lawrence to hear about her. He also warns his bachelor friend against pursuing Jane Wilson for a wife because she is cold-hearted underneath her charming veneer and hates Helen. Lawrence is offended at Gilbert's impertinence but soon cuts off his visits to Ryecote Farm.

In November 1828, Eliza visits the Markham home to tell Rose, Gilbert, and Fergus that Helen is not a widow but has actually run away from her husband. Gilbert is shocked and hurries to Woodford Hall where Lawrence tells him that Helen has returned to Grassdale Manor to attend her ill husband, who has been abandoned by everyone else. Huntington has fallen from his horse and has internal injuries. Less than a week later, Lawrence shares another letter from Helen: Huntington is no longer delirious but is still unwell. Helen fears for Esther's happiness because her mother continues to push her to marry. With Helen's permission, Gilbert tells the truth to Rose, who spreads it to their neighbors. Two weeks later, Gilbert learns from another letter that Huntington's illness has returned. Hattersley and his family come to visit when they hear that Huntington is near death. Huntington is frightened and will not let Helen leave his side. He dies on December 5, 1828.

CHAPTERS L–LIII

Lawrence leaves immediately to attend the funeral. Gilbert worries that the difference in social standing between him and Helen may yet keep them apart. He resolves to wait until the six months are up at the end of February to write to Helen. But near the end of January, Helen's uncle dies. Gilbert cannot write to her because he does not know the address for Staningley, and Lawrence will not tell him. In early December

1829, Eliza tells Gilbert that Helen is getting remarried to none other than Hargrave then laughs at him as he is overwhelmed with her news. Gilbert takes off the very next day for Grassdale, arriving at the church just as the newlyweds emerge. But it is Lawrence and his bride, Esther Hargrave who have been married that day and not Helen and Hargrave.

Gilbert travels to Staningley to see Helen. Near the manor he learns from his fellow travelers that Helen has inherited her uncle's estate and is now wealthy. Standing outside the manor gates, Gilbert decides they are too different in station, and he must leave her alone. A carriage drives by and Arthur spots Gilbert. Helen invites him into the house where he meets Mrs. Maxwell. When Gilbert and Helen are alone, they renew their declarations of affection for each other and make plans to get engaged and then marry. Helen and Gilbert marry eight months later, in August 1830.

CHARACTERS

Benson
Benson is a servant at Grassdale Manor. He helps Helen, Arthur, and Rachel flee from Mr. Huntington.

Mr. Boarham
Mr. Boarham is Mrs. Maxwell's friend and one of Helen's suitors, but Helen refuses his marriage proposal because he repulses her.

Master Arthur Graham
See Master Arthur Huntington

Mrs. Helen Graham
See Mrs. Helen Huntington

Mr. Grimsby
Mr. Grimsby is Mr. Huntington's friend. He lives for drinking, hunting, and gambling and is the only one of Huntington's friends who does not marry. He is eventually killed in a barroom brawl.

Mr. Jack Halford Esq.
Jack Halford is Rose's husband and Gilbert's friend. *The Tenant of Wildfell Hall* is framed as a series of letters from Gilbert to Halford.

Miss Esther Hargrave
Esther, the youngest Hargrave, is a friend to Helen. She is pretty and vivacious but suffers pressure from her mother and brother to marry quickly. She listens instead to Helen's advice: "When I tell you not to marry *without* love, I do not advise you to marry for love alone—there are many, many other things to be considered." At the end of the novel, she marries Helen's brother, Mr. Lawrence.

Miss Milicent Hargrave
See Mrs. Milicent Hattersley

Mrs. Hargrave
Mrs. Hargrave is mother to Walter, Milicent, and Esther. She is tightfisted and pushes her daughters to marry wealthy men while doting excessively on her son.

Mr. Walter Hargrave
Walter Hargrave is the older brother of Milicent and Esther. He is spoiled but still more of a gentleman than his friends, Huntington, Hattersley, and Grimsby. Hargrave falls in love with Helen, but his love is egocentric and he annoys Helen. He eventually marries a plain but rich woman who is disappointed in him when his charm wears off, revealing his selfish and careless nature.

Miss Helen Hattersley
Helen is the first child of Milicent and Ralph Hattersley. She is a few months younger than Helen's son Arthur.

Mrs. Milicent Hattersley
Milicent Hattersley is Annabella's cousin and Helen's friend. Her gentle, yielding nature attracts the eye of the rakish Mr. Hattersley, who claims her as his fiancée almost against her wishes. Much like Helen, she is unhappy in her marriage for the first several years. Hattersley is often physically and verbally abusive. Milicent nevertheless believes that he is a good man and will eventually come around. When he does, they are very happy together. They have several children.

Master Ralph Hattersley
Ralph is the second child of Milicent and Ralph Hattersley.

Mr. Ralph Hattersley Esq.

Mr. Hattersley is Mr. Huntington's friend. For the first few years of his marriage, Hattersley continues to live a profligate lifestyle, but as he sees Huntington's health decline, he reforms his ways. Hattersley turns to his wife and family. He no longer goes to London to party, instead keeping busy at his country manor with farming, breeding cattle and horses, and hunting. He, his wife Milicent, and their sons and daughters live very happily thereafter.

Master Arthur Huntington

The son of Helen and Arthur Huntington, Master Arthur Huntington is a cheerful little boy and innocently aids in bringing Gilbert and his mother together.

Mr. Arthur Huntington

Arthur Huntington, Helen's husband, is handsome and charming but also irresponsible and selfish. Huntington regularly overindulges in drinking and gambling and has several affairs with other women, including Annabella Lowborough and Miss Myers. Huntington tires of Helen's pressure to reform and takes to spending several months a year in London or on the continent without his wife or son. Huntington takes no interest in Arthur except to be jealous of the attention Helen gives to the baby instead of to him. Even in the face of death, at the end of the novel, Huntington is childish and fearful, unable to seek solace in piety. Brontë, in the character of Huntington, has painted the portrait of a unmanly gentleman.

Mrs. Helen Huntington

The heroine of Brontë's novel, Mrs. Helen Huntington courageously leaves her depraved husband to save her son from his father's influence. Helen is a religious and extremely moral person. As a young wife, she naively believes that she can cure Huntington of his profligate lifestyle and that he will welcome the change. When their marriage falls apart, Helen continues to stay at the house because Huntington has not given her permission to leave. She refuses the advances of Mr. Hargrave and Gilbert because she is still married. Hargrave's persistence offends her but refusing Gilbert is more difficult because she returns his loves; however, her piety makes it impossible for her to betray her marriage vows.

Helen loves literature—an interest she shares with Gilbert. She also loves to write in her diary and record events in great details, making the direct, first-person presentation of half of the novel possible. As a character, Helen has one glaring flaw: her infallibility. Brontë has made Helen too perfect. Even Gilbert, the other central character, is not entirely sympathetic because of his behavior. This excessive perfection gives one the sense that Helen is more acted upon in events than an agent in shaping them.

Mrs. Esther Lawrence

See Miss Esther Hargrave

Mr. Frederick Lawrence

Frederick Lawrence is Helen's brother and Gilbert's neighbor. He and Gilbert have an awkward relationship, even after Gilbert understands Lawrence's true relationship with Helen. Gilbert warns Lawrence not to marry Jane Wilson because he knows that Jane hates Helen and that her charm is all on the surface. Although Lawrence is offended, he takes Gilbert's advice. Lawrence does not approve of Gilbert's attachment to Helen and even goes to some effort to interfere with their acquaintance once Helen leaves Wildfell Hall. At the end of the novel, Lawrence marries Helen's pretty young neighbor, Esther Hargrave.

Lady Annabella Lowborough

Annabella is Milicent's beautiful and vivacious cousin. She marries Lord Lowborough after Mr. Huntington and Helen are engaged. Annabella and Huntington later have an affair. Despite her charm, Annabella is cold and cruel to Helen, whom she views as competition. Lowborough is devastated when he learns of the affair, and he takes their children and lives apart from his wife. Annabella eventually elopes with another man and moves to the continent whereupon her husband divorces her. Annabella's new man leaves her also. She continues to live extravagantly but eventually dies in disgrace and poverty.

Lord Lowborough

Lord Lowborough is a friend of Huntington's who gives up drinking and gambling because he cannot moderate his behavior. He is quiet and morose but sincerely wants a wife to love. He marries Annabella Wilmot but learns after a few years that she is unfaithful. They separate, and he takes their son and daughter with him. Low-borough eventually divorces Annabella when she elopes to the continent with another man. He marries a steady older woman who cares for him and his children, and they live the rest of their lives very happily.

Mr. Fergus Markham

Fergus Markham is Gilbert's younger brother. He is probably a teenager during the narrative and often does and says insensitive things. Fergus grows out of this phase by the time he inherits the family farm from Gilbert and marries a vicar's daughter.

Mr. Gilbert Markham

Gilbert Markham is the narrator of this novel, relating the story by letters to his friend and brother-in-law, Halford. Gilbert is a gentleman farmer, managing his family's business in lieu of his father, who is either absent or dead. Gilbert likes to read and have intelligent conversation, which inevitably draws him to his mysterious new neighbor, the widow Helen Graham. He falls in love with her, and although he senses that she does not want a romance, he is unable to keep himself from declaring his attachment to her. He mistakes Mr. Lawrence for a suitor and becomes insanely jealous, to the extent that he strikes the man a near-deadly blow. The attack is a turning point for Gilbert, who slowly begins to temper his emotions. Helen returns his feelings but refuses to act on them, instead sharing her secret with Gilbert: she is still married. While they are separated for eighteen months, Gilbert undergoes a subtle transformation. His love for Helen both mellows and deepens. He loses his desperation although not his motivation. He cultivates a difficult friendship with Mr. Lawrence. Gilbert also becomes painfully aware of the differences in their social stations as Helen is much wealthier than he is. When they are finally united, these differences pose no barrier. Many critics have commented on Gilbert's character as problematic: He is not an entirely likable and at the least seems undeserving of Helen's love. These incongruities can be explained in terms of Brontë's realistic style.

Mrs. Markham

Mrs. Markham is the mother of Gilbert, Rose, and Fergus Markham. Mrs. Markham tends to go along with neighborhood views, including when the whole community is suspicious of Helen.

Miss Rose Markham

Rose Markham is the middle Markham child. She is a typical young woman, gossiping with her neighbors. Rose marries Jack Halford, the man to whom the narrative of this novel is addressed.

Mrs. Margaret Maxwell

Mrs. Maxwell, Helen's aunt and the only woman Helen has known as a mother, tries to impress upon Helen the importance of choosing a good husband.

Mr. Maxwell

Mr. Maxwell, Helen's uncle, leaves his entire estate of Staningley to her when he dies, making Helen wealthy.

Miss Eliza Millward

Eliza Millward, the vicar's younger daughter, is vivacious but shallow, conspiring with Jane Wilson to spread nasty rumors about Helen after Gilbert spurns Eliza. She later marries a rich tradesman.

Miss Mary Millward

Mary Millward, the vicar's older daughter, is a quiet and reserved woman and the only one besides Gilbert who refuses to believe the rumors about Helen. Mary is secretly engaged to Richard Wilson.

Reverend Michael Millward

Reverend Millward, the local vicar, is a well-meaning busybody. When he retires, he passes on his position to his curate and son-in-law, Richard Wilson.

Miss Alice Myers

Miss Myers is a governess hired by Huntington to come between Helen and her son. Brontë also alludes to a sexual relationship between Miss Myers and Huntington. Miss Myers abandons Huntington when he becomes gravely ill.

Rachel

Rachel is Helen's nurse and has taken care of her since she was a child. She chooses to accompany Helen on her flight from Grassdale Manor rather than stay behind and be tormented by Mr. Huntington.

TOPICS FOR FURTHER STUDY

- Brontë's novel was written and takes place during the early nineteenth century in England. Research the clothing fashions for both men and women of this time and place. What were the differences between the high and low classes? Prepare a ten-minute speech or a detailed visual aid that focuses on a particular area of fashion (such as shoes, jewelry, gowns, or work clothes). Do the clothes look strange to you? Do you see any connection with modern fashion?

- Huntington is an alcoholic who denies he has a problem. Findings from a 2005 survey in the United Kingdom show that 19 percent of men and 8 percent of women drink heavily at least once a week. Research alcoholism and learn what the danger signs of alcohol abuse are as well as the steps one can take to break the addiction. In small groups, design an ad campaign aimed toward raising awareness of teen drinking and directing people where they can get help locally. For your campaign, you can make posters, flyers, newspaper advertisements, and radio or television spots.

- In the early 2000s, domestic abuse remains a serious problem. Abuse does not need to be physical to do damage. Research domestic abuse in its various forms and read several case studies. How does Huntington fit the profile of an abuser? How do Helen and Arthur fit the profile of abused individuals? Write up the Huntington family as a case study in domestic abuse.

- Brontë's characters love to go on walks. Sometimes they stroll in the garden after dinner and sometimes they take longer hikes (for example, out to the sea). Take a walk or hike of you own in a park or other scenic place, taking particular care to observe your surroundings. What do you see that is unique to that particular setting? What do you see that is familiar and unfamiliar? Do you see anything that pleases you? Immediately after your walk (or during a break in the middle of it) sit down and write a poem or story that captures your experience.

- Britain has its own cuisine, although it may not be as famous across the world as French or Italian cuisine. Research recipes for some traditional British foods. Do you see regional differences? How has British cuisine changed? Choose a dish to prepare and bring it to class to share in potluck fashion. Try a little bit of everything and discuss with your classmates what is unusual, what is familiar, what is unpleasant, and what you would like to eat again.

Miss Annabella Wilmot
See Mrs. Annabella Lowborough

Mr. Wilmot
Mr. Wilmot, Mr. Maxwell's friend and Annabella's uncle, is one of the older men who pursue Helen. He seems oblivious to her indifference, which disgusts Helen.

Miss Jane Wilson
Jane Wilson, the only daughter of Mrs. Wilson, is pretty and accomplished at piano, but she can also be small-minded and unpleasant. Jane pursues Mr. Lawrence, hoping to marry him and his money, but Gilbert ruins her chances by warning off Mr. Lawrence. Jane never finds another rich man to marry and lives out her life as a gossipy old maid.

Mrs. Wilson
Mrs. Wilson is the mother of Robert, Jane, and Richard. Her older son Robert manages her home, Ryecote Farm. They are neighbors to the Markhams and the Millwards.

Mr. Richard Wilson

Richard Wilson, Mrs. Wilson's younger son, is quiet and studious, and eventually he graduates from Cambridge. Richard is secretly engaged to Mary Millward, and they marry after he becomes curate to Reverend Millward. Richard succeeds Mr. Millward as vicar.

Mr. Robert Wilson

Robert Wilson, Mrs. Wilson's older son, manages the family's estate, Ryecote Farm.

THEMES

Alcoholism

Alcoholism is a chronic substance abuse disorder. People who suffer from alcoholism are so preoccupied with alcohol that they cannot function normally. In the United Kingdom, as of 2001, alcoholism afflicted 8 percent of the population. In Brontë's novel, Huntington and several of his friends are heavy drinkers. Lord Lowborough and Mr. Hattersley each reform their lives, unlike Mr. Huntington and Mr. Grimsby. Lord Lowborough and Mr. Huntington both particularly seem affected by traditional signs of alcoholism. They drink to excess often and are even driven to the point of drinking alcohol early in the day to help themselves feel better. Lord Lowborough sees that he has a problem and with supreme effort and willpower, overcomes his addiction. Mr. Huntington never really believes he has a problem and gradually sinks into poor health until he is overcome by an internal injury, resulting from a fall from his horse. His son, Arthur, is made ill by the very smell of alcohol, a physiological sign of his psychological abhorrence for the substance that has so altered his father.

Mr. Hattersley, although he drinks heavily with his friends, does not seem to be afflicted by alcoholism as much as by a lifestyle problem. Once he resolves to spend his time in the country with his wife and stay away from London, he becomes a happy man. Mr. Grimsby, by contrast, continues to live an intemperate life, gambling and drinking and eventually dies in a brawl. The message Brontë is sending to her readers is abundantly clear: overindulgence in alcohol leads to ruin whereas moderation or abstinence leads to happiness.

Piety

Piety is the state of being devout, in matters of religion and in matters of social or familial obligations. The daughter of a minister, Brontë was a pious woman who nonetheless struggled with her devotion several times during her short life. In *The Tenant of Wildfell Hall*, pious characters are rewarded. Despite extraordinary hardship as a young woman, Helen is firmly devoted to her religion and its moral precepts. Against all odds, she ends up a rich woman, happily married to a loving husband. After she and Mr. Huntington are estranged but still living in the same house, Mr. Hargrave declares his love to her, but Helen is not the least bit tempted from her loneliness. She dislikes Mr. Hargrave, but she is also offended that he would suggest she violate her marriage vows because those vows were made before God and are sacred. Later, at Wildfell Hall, she also rebuffs Gilbert without hesitation for much the same reason except that this time her choice is much more poignant because she does, in fact, love Gilbert.

Other characters rewarded for piety in this novel include Mary Millward and Richard Wilson, who marry after being secretly engaged. They are regarded by many of their neighbors and relations as dull and uninteresting, but Helen quickly forms a friendship with Mary, drawn to her sensibility and strong moral sense. Mary, like Gilbert, is one of the few people who refuse to believe anything scandalous about Helen without knowing her true background. They sense in her a good nature that is not easily bent to vice. Milicent Hattersley is also rewarded in the long run when her husband reforms his bachelor ways and dedicates himself to his family, his religion, and his home. Although wild as a young man, Mr. Hattersley, by his own declaration, was only waiting for someone to rein him in.

Brontë further emphasizes the importance of piety with her numerous biblical references within the story. It was more common in nineteenth-century Western literature to allude frequently to the Bible because of the central importance this text played in people's lives.

Marriage

In nineteenth-century England, marriage was an extremely important institution. Many women were raised with the understanding that their job, as young women, was to secure a good husband. For some, good was defined variously, as

Visitors stand outside the Brontë family parsonage in Haworth, West Yorkshire. Anne Brontë was living here when she wrote The Tenant of Wildfell Hall *(© Patrick Ward / Corbis)*

rich or loving or handsome or titled. Women were encouraged to marry young and to have children. Although there was pressure on men to marry also, education and business experience were important for middle-class men, so that they could maintain themselves, attract a wife, and support a family. Husbands were often considerably older than their wives.

Once married, a woman was in charge of the servants and the children. Her husband was head of the household and responsible for managing the family's income. In a high-class home, as seen at Grassdale Manor, this responsibility would entail keeping track of rents and inheritance. In a middle-class household, like that of the Markhams, the head managed the family business—in this case, a farm. In Brontë's novel, marriage is first treated by many of the characters as a stepping stone to some greater goal. Mr. Huntington loves Helen's beauty and is perhaps driven by his own reckless nature (reckless because he could have married Annabella, with whom he later has an affair). Helen is misguided by ideas of romantic love and duty

into the delusion that she can repair her husband's conduct. Hattersley declares that he wants a pliant wife who will not interfere with his fun, but the truth that comes out later is that he really wants quite the opposite. Milicent is too shy and deferential to argue against the man who claims her hand. Lowborough wishes to be married to ease his loneliness; Annabella wants to be rich and have a title. Jane Wilson also seeks wealth.

What the reader learns over the course of the novel is that marriage is not an institution to be taken lightly. Helen is the guiding light on this point because although she is firmly against Huntington once they are estranged, she does not leave him until she believes their son is in danger. Also, she returns home to nurse her husband when all others have abandoned him. Her example guides Esther Hargrave toward making a more careful choice in mate, although Esther's delay in marrying angers her family. Gilbert's love for Helen is somewhat tempered by consideration for her hardship and higher status, but these differences are ultimately not an obstacle

COMPARE & CONTRAST

- **1840s:** According to the census, the population of England numbers nearly 15 million people. Approximately 1.5 million—or 9 percent—live in London, the largest city in the world at this time.

  Today: As of 2001, the population of England is 49 million people. London is the most populous city in Europe and is inhabited by more than 7 million people or roughly 7 percent of the British population.

- **1840s:** Personal communication is accomplished face-to-face or by letter-writing. Mass communication is achieved with newspapers, leaflets, and broadsides.

  Today: Cell phones and email are popular ways to communicate. Letter-writing via the postal system is increasingly considered archaic and slow. Mass media is centered on the Internet, television, magazines, and newspapers.

- **1840s:** The population of England is largely Anglican. Small numbers of Jews and Roman Catholics also live in Britain. Alternate religions such as Unitarianism and various other forms of Protestantism are on the rise.

  Today: According to the 2001 census in the United Kingdom, the British population is comprised of 71.6 percent Christians, 2.7 percent Muslim, 1 percent Hindu, 0.4 percent Sikh, 0.3 percent Jewish, 0.3 percent Buddhist, and 0.3 percent other religions. Approximately 15.5 percent of respondents declared no religion, and 7.3 percent declined to answer.

because Helen returns his love. Although *The Tenant of Wildfell Hall* is not a novel written in a romantic style, it is still much about the courtship and marriage plot, about what realistically works and what does not.

STYLE

Epistolary Novel

An epistolary novel presents itself as a letter or collection of letters. The form allows the author to write in the first person of the letter writer and to address a particular reader to whom the letter is addressed. This setup provides certain advantages and allows for greater intimacy in tone. This form gives the novel the semblance of fact; the text is a document and not made up or fiction. The use of letters in a novel is a way around the omniscient narrator, as well, because it permits the narrator to show other characters' points of view. The epistolary form was not unique to Brontë. Letter writing was the most important means of communication in nineteenth-century Britain, after face-to-face contact. This form was used by many authors of fiction from the thirteenth through the nineteenth centuries. The third-person limited omniscient narrator technique became more popular later in the nineteenth century.

The Tenant of Wildfell Hall is narrated in a series of letters between Gilbert Markham and his brother-in-law and friend, Jack Halford. The events of the story take place between 1821 and 1830 while the letters conclude in 1847, seventeen to twenty-six years later. Other documents appear in the novel: Helen's diary is the prime example. Her story as reported in the diary spans Chapters XVI through XLIV. The heart of the novel is told to Gilbert (who is telling it to Halford) through her private diary. Also, at the end of the novel, the author continues to present Helen's experience directly through her letters to her brother, Mr. Lawrence, who shares them and often gives them to

Gilbert. This format allows the author to jump back and forth in time and to jump from one narrator to another.

Allusion

An allusion is an indirect reference to something external to the text, which economically adds another layer of meaning to the text for the reader who recognizes the reference. Brontë's novel is rich with allusion, particularly allusions to the Bible and occasionally to other literature. Her use of biblical allusions enhances her theme of piety by drawing an explicit connection between scripture and its relevance to the story of these characters. For example, in Chapter XX, Helen's aunt tries to impress upon Helen the disparity in virtue between Helen and Mr. Huntington: "how will it be in the end, when you see yourselves parted for ever; you, perhaps, taken into eternal bliss, and he cast into the lake that burneth with unquenchable fire." The burning lake is an allusion to Revelations 20:10 and 21:8. Helen, along with Brontë's contemporary readers would understand this reference and the weight that it carries—Mr. Huntington is, in Mrs. Maxwell's view, beyond Paradise, even if he loves Helen well.

An example of another allusion from *The Tenant of Wildfell Hall* occurs in Chapter XXX when Mr. Huntington is declaring to Helen that he will do what he pleases just as his friend Hattersley does: "he might come home at any hour of the night or morning, or not come home at all; be sullen sober, or glorious drunk; and play the fool or the madman to his own heart's desire without any fear or botheration." The phrase, "play the fool or the madman" is a reference to William Shakespeare's *Twelfth Night* (the fool) and *King Lear* (the madman). Readers who understand this allusion would then grasp the foreshadowing of Mr. Huntington's downfall, like that of the tragic King Lear. If readers know the texts to which an author alludes, then the text at hand gains in meaning by its connection to those other works.

HISTORICAL CONTEXT

King George IV and the Regency Era

The Regency is the name for that period from 1811 to 1820 when the Prince of Wales served as prince regent in place of his father the ill King George III. King George IV reigned from 1820, when his father died, until his own death in 1830 at age sixty-seven. The prince regent was best known for his extravagant lifestyle—hallmark of the Regency era—which angered his father, King George III, who was known to be thrifty and plain. Prince George further upset his parents and Parliament by carrying on a romance with the Roman Catholic Maria Anne Fitzherbert, whom he married in 1785, even though several laws prohibited the union. The couple kept their marriage secret. In 1787, friends of the profligate prince sought and were given a parliamentary grant to pay off George's debts. The prince was forced by his father to marry Caroline of Brunswick in 1795, but after conceiving a child, George and Caroline permanently separated. Fitzherbert remained a part of George's life throughout this period, but their relationship was over by 1811.

George IV was interested in fashion and is known for popularizing seaside spas. He founded King's College London as well as the National Portrait Gallery. He enjoyed food and drink, like Mr. Huntington, and this indulgence eventually took its toll on his health. Late in life, he suffered from mental illness, gout, and mild porphyria (an inherited blood disease). History has come to regard King George IV as a pathetic, bloated, irresponsible figure, not unlike Brontë's villain, Mr. Huntington.

Regency era styles, from fashion to architecture, are marked by elegance. Greek Revival architecture became very popular and women's fashion turned to fabrics that were lighter in weight and color with the French-inspired empire waist. This era was also marked by war—the Revolutionary War in North America and the Napoleonic Wars on the continent.

Queen Victoria and the Victorian Era

Following the brief seven-year reign of George's brother, King William IV, Queen Victoria took the throne in 1837 when she was only eighteen years old. Three years later she married her first cousin, Prince Albert. There are rumors that Albert did not really want to marry Victoria but agreed to it because of her status and pressure from his family. Ultimately theirs was a very happy marriage. Over the course of her long life, there were seven attempts to assassinate or frighten Victoria, all involving guns, but these incidents were generally believed to be attempts at fame rather than due to conspiracy.

Albert died in 1861, devastating Victoria who wore black for the rest of her life. Victoria celebrated her golden jubilee in 1887 to commemorate the fiftieth anniversary of her accession. Ten years later, she celebrated her diamond jubilee, which included recognition that she was then the longest reigning monarch in British history. Victoria died of a cerebral hemorrhage in 1901, aged eighty-one. She was queen for sixty-three years.

The Victorian era was marked by technological and scientific advances such as the Industrial Revolution and Charles Darwin's theory of evolution. Railways were built across the United Kingdom, making cities more accessible to rural populations. Women gained the right to divorce and own property. The clean lines of Regency fashion for women bloomed into larger skirts, more frills, and bustles. The Victorian era is remembered for the strong sense of morality espoused by the queen—probably a reaction to the flagrancy of King George IV. The first world fair—the Great Exhibition of 1851—was held in London. Photography was displayed for the first time there and the glass and steel architecture of the Crystal Palace was a herald of modern architecture. The Great Exhibition was an enormous success, and these massive fairs became a popular attraction in the Western world for the next one hundred years.

CRITICAL OVERVIEW

Brontë's writing talent has long been overshadowed by that of her older sisters, Charlotte and Emily. Although their work was romantic, even gothic, Brontë favored realism in her novels, anticipating the shift in taste that occurred during the nineteenth century. *The Tenant of Wildfell Hall* was a bestseller in its time, famous for its controversial depictions of oppressive and unhappy marriages as well as the heroine's courageous effort to free herself. Brontë's sisters did not approve of her stories, especially Charlotte, who survived all of her siblings and was executor of Brontë's literary estate. This alone may be the reason *The Tenant of Wildfell Hall* went out of print and faded from the minds of the reading public.

The Tenant of Wildfell Hall was published in 1848, just one year before Brontë died. She published her works under the pseudonym Acton Bell, and many assumed she was a man. An anonymous critic for the *Spectator*, in 1848, describes Brontë's subject as "offensive" and her writing as rough: "*The Tenant of Wildfell Hall* . . . suggests the idea of considerable abilities ill applied." The following month, a reviewer for the *Literary World* writes more favorably of Brontë's novel, although this person mistakenly attributes *Wuthering Heights* to Acton Bell. The critic describes the two novels as "crude though powerful productions" and goes on to criticize Brontë's depiction of Huntington, Markham, and other characters as unrealistic. Nonetheless, the review affirms Brontë's talent: "[i]t is the writer's genius which makes his incongruities appear natural." Interestingly, the reviewer also comments on the favorable reception these two novels have received, despite critical condemnation. The reviewer suspects the author to be a "gifted" woman.

Brontë responded to her critics in the second edition preface of *The Tenant of Wildfell Hall*:

> My object in writing the following pages, was not simply to amuse the Reader, neither was it to gratify my own taste, nor yet to ingratiate myself with the Press and the Public: I wished to tell the truth, for truth always conveys its own moral to those who are able to receive it.

She also deflects the question about her sex, stating, "I am satisfied that if a book is a good one, it is so whatever the sex of the author may be." This opinion was fairly radical in a time when works produced by women were more leniently judged than those produced by men. The likelihood of not being taken seriously was a reason for adopting a sexually ambiguous pen name.

Just over fifty years later, critics of the twentieth century also gave *The Tenant of Wildfell Hall* mixed reviews. A reviewer for the *New York Times* considers it "far from unattractive as a story, and full of moral energy and strong ethical purpose." But Walter Frewen Lord, writing for the *Nineteenth Century* in 1903 is disturbed by the casual manner with which the characters dismiss their own brutality toward each other. For instance, Gilbert Markham strikes Mr. Lawrence with a riding crop, nearly killing him, and Mr. Hattersley brutally beats

WHAT DO I READ NEXT?

- *Agnes Grey* (1847) was Anne Brontë's first novel and was probably inspired by her experience working as a governess. In this novel, the title character struggles to control and teach the undisciplined children of her wealthy employers.

- *Jane Eyre* (1847), by Charlotte Brontë, is a famous English novel about a plain governess who captures the interest of her employer, Edward Rochester. But Rochester has a terrible secret.

- *Wuthering Heights* (1847), by Emily Brontë, is a famous romantic story about Catherine Earnshaw and the interloper Heathcliff. They passionately love each other but differences in their social station prevent them from being together.

- *Pride and Prejudice* (1813), by Jane Austen, is about the love and misunderstandings between Elizabeth Bennett and the wealthy Mr. Darcy. Austen was popular in her time and was a literary influence on the Brontës.

- *Oliver Twist* (1837–1839), by Charles Dickens, tells the poignant tale of an orphaned boy who stumbles upon misfortune after misfortune before finally coming into happiness. Dickens focused his writing on the underprivileged, in contrast to many writers of his day.

- *The Awakening* (1899), by Kate Chopin, is a slim novel about a smothered young wife and mother who casts off the constraints of her position as a southern socialite.

- *Best Poems of the Brontë Sisters* (1997), edited by Candace Ward, is a Dover Thrift collection of ten poems by Charlotte, twenty-three poems by Emily, and fourteen poems by Anne. Emily is arguably the best—and most prolific—poet of the three. Anne was also a skilled poet, whereas Charlotte's strength lay more in fiction writing.

- *A History of English Literature* (2000), by Michael Alexander, is a lively and comprehensive examination of a rich literary tradition. Alexander includes a discussion of the ever-changing idea of which works are classics, including what the term classic means.

Lord Lowborough. Lord also criticizes Helen Huntington as entirely too "blameless," which makes her too perfect as a heroine. May Sinclair also complains about Helen's perfection in her introduction to the 1914 Everyman's Library edition of the novel. Sinclair describes the novel as "unspeakably and lamentably dull" but still significant because it is "the first attempt in the mid-Victorian novel to handle the relations of a revolting wife to a most revolting husband with anything approaching to a bold sincerity." It is, in fact, Sinclair declares in conclusion, "the first presentment of that Feminist novel which we all know." Naomi Lewis gives the novel a lukewarm reception in her 1946 review for the *New Statesman & Nation*. She writes, "Virtue, not passion, is the powerful motive of the book," and "The characters have a kind of reality, but they are observed, not felt as the surroundings inevitably are." "But for all the force of its detail, the book is not great," Lewis concludes. In 1970, Louis Auchincloss compares *Wuthering Heights* to *The Tenant of Wildfell Hall*, noting their similar structures (a story within a story) and sometimes strained methods of imparting information (extensive eavesdropping and diary-keeping), and concludes that although they are not very different, the former succeeded and the latter failed. When the form works, it is praised, and, he concludes, when the form does not work, it "is given more than a fair share of the blame." In all, critics have continued to have their reservations about this novel.

CRITICISM

Carol Ullmann

Ullmann is a freelance writer and editor. In the following essay, she discusses the dichotomy of country life and city life in Brontë's novel The Tenant of Wildfell Hall.

Anne Brontë, in her novel *The Tenant of Wildfell Hall*, highlights the distinctions between city life and country life. The contrasts between London, known as Town, and everywhere else in England, which was largely the rural countryside, were important to nineteenth-century lifestyle. People of the upper class visited London during the Season, which was spring, when weather was mild and people were eager to get out of the house after being cooped up all winter. The Season is when Huntington makes his annual trip into London, although he often stays late into the summer as well. Being in London during the Season provided an important opportunity for socializing. During these visits, young ladies had the opportunity to exhibit themselves and attract potential suitors. These were periods also for distant friends and relations to visit, for people to meet new friends and go shopping to see recent fashions and trends. Men did business and looked for wives for themselves or their daughters. Various social events, such as balls and concerts, were hosted to bring people together. During a ball in London, Helen first meets Huntington. They meet again at a private dinner party at Mr. Wilmot's residence in town, another common social function among the upper class.

London began to grow considerably in the 1830s when the first railways were built, making it more easily accessible to those who lived far away. At the beginning of the nineteenth century, London was the most populous city in the world and the largest city in Europe. Although New York City had the distinction to be the world's most populous city a century later, London was still Europe's largest city at the dawn of the twenty-first century. Although London is central to Britain's commerce and identity in the early nineteenth century, the gentry regarded it as "dusty, smoky, noisy, toiling, striving." Once summer began in mid-June, many would retire to country estates for "invigorating relaxation and social retirement." There they would pass their time leisurely, enjoying their homes, tending to their families, corresponding with

> MUCH OF HUNTINGTON'S DEBAUCHERY
> OCCURS WHEN HE IS AWAY IN LONDON OR ON THE
> CONTINENT, UNDERSCORING THE IDEA THAT THE
> COUNTRYSIDE IS HEALTHFUL AND THE CITIES ARE
> CORRUPT."

friends, reading, hunting, and visiting each other. It was common for guests to stay several weeks or even a number of months because of the great effort it took to pack and travel to a distant friend or relation. Thus, for several autumns, the Huntingtons entertain a group of their friends at Grassdale Manor for upwards of two months. Country life is considered to be peaceful, quiet, safe, and wholesome. When Helen returns to Staningley in West Yorkshire after meeting Huntington in London, she writes in her diary, "I am quite ashamed of my new-sprung distaste for country life... I cannot enjoy my music, because there is no one to hear it. I cannot enjoy my walks, because there is no one to meet."

Helen and Milicent, like all upper-class women of their time, go to London to meet eligible bachelors so that they might get married and settled in life as soon as reasonably possible. Unfortunately for both women, they find themselves unhappily married. Until the 1857 Matrimonial Causes Act, which permitted divorce by courts of law rather than by an act of Parliament, divorce was difficult and expensive. Helen and Milicent had no hope of reversing their situation and could only try to change their husbands or find a way to live with them. Much of Huntington's debauchery occurs when he is away in London or on the continent, underscoring the idea that the countryside is healthful and the cities are corrupt. Mr. Huntington's hunting trip to Scotland is the one time he returns home healthier than when he left. His health slowly but steadily suffers from his drinking, which is inextricably tied to the fast life he leads in London. Huntington occasionally brings his debauched lifestyle home to Grassdale Manor in the form of his friends Hattersley and Grimsby. Hattersley, who is also given to physical violence toward his friends and wife, is following a similar path of ruin but saves himself when he sees the irreparable damage Huntington has done to himself. Hattersley breaks from his life in London and retires to the countryside with his family and thereafter the Hattersley family is very happy.

Those who are also brought to ruin by a city lifestyle or mentality are Annabella Lowborough and Jane Wilson. Annabella's death illustrates. She lives a fast and lavish life, estranged from her husband and flirting endlessly with other men. She ultimately finds herself abandoned and impoverished and dies a lonely woman. Jane moves to a country town after her mother's death and settles into a life of gossip and scandal. She never marries because her expectations are higher than her possibility of attainment. Once Jane leaves Ryecote Farm, she does not talk about her childhood home or her older brother Robert, who now runs the farm. She only mentions her younger brother, the vicar. In this way, Jane completely eschews any association with life in the countryside and thus any association with peace, beauty, and true happiness.

Into the early 2000s, British people love their countryside in all of its varieties, from the rocky seacoast to the wooded hills to the wild moorlands and beyond. The government maintains right of way public footpaths that crisscross the island despite the occasional inconvenience these trails may impose on private property. Bicycles and horses are not permitted on footpaths, although wheelchairs and leashed dogs are allowed. These footpaths are important to the British sense of belonging to their landscape. In the region of Yorkshire where the Brontë family lived there is a forty-three mile footpath called the Brontë Way, which runs from Oakwell Hall near the town of Bradford to Gawthorpe Hall near the town of Burnley. This footpath goes by important sites such as Brontë's birthplace in the village of Thornton, Ponden Hall (a gloomy Elizabethan manor that inspired the three sisters), and the village of Haworth where the Brontës lived for most of their brief lives. The north of England is famous for its rough beauty. The heather moors of West Yorkshire, where Haworth is located, are more rustic and wild than many other places in Yorkshire. The Brontës loved their home in Yorkshire and almost never left it. Anne Brontë became quite fond of Scarborough and the seaside in

northeast Yorkshire during her five-year tenure as governess with the Robinson family. This region was likely the inspiration for the setting of Wildfell Hall, which was only four miles inland from the seacoast.

In *The Tenant of Wildfell Hall*, Brontë celebrates the virtues of county life over the corruption of life in the city. Country life is quiet, safe, religious, clean, beautiful, and family-oriented. City life is crowded, dirty, smelly, noisy, secular, and full of vice and distraction. Brontë does not just treat London as having a potential for evil but as the source of evil because everything that emerges from or willingly enters into London is tainted. Helen ultimately finds happiness with Gilbert Markham, a farmer who helps to cleanse Helen of her former woes. Markham's profession puts him in intimate connection with the land. He and Helen deepen their admiration of each other through a quiet portion of the novel where they find each other out on the moors and take long rambles together.

Brontë links as positive the inside and urban as bad and the outside and rural as good. After all, Helen catches Huntington at his infidelity outside. But at Wildfell Hall, Helen supports herself with paintings of the landscape that surrounds her (although the income comes from London). The roses grow outside that Helen gives to Gilbert, twice. The one activity with which Huntington restores his health (other than rest) is hunting. Huntington, to his credit, wants only to be outdoors hunting and sporting when he is at Grassdale. All of the indoor parties, which Helen attends, come to no good.

Brontë uses the names of the different homes in this book to add character to the various locations. Wildfell is the most remote manor in the novel and, as it says in the name, the surrounding countryside is wild and rough. Fell is a Middle English word that means hill. Grassdale is the opposite of Wildfell. Grass gives the impression of civilization and cultivation; dale is another world for a valley. Gilbert and his neighbors live in the district of Lindenhope. Linden is a type of deciduous tree with heart shaped leaves and in mythology it is a symbol of peace for Freyja, goddess of love and fortune. Hope is a word for valley in the northern English dialect. These meanings reflect the roles each landscape plays in the story. Grassdale Manor is Helen's gilded prison and when she escapes, she hides out at Wildfell Hall, beyond the reach of civilization and all the norms that she once knew. Lindenhope is a valley of peace and the place where Helen not only heals but also has the good fortune to fall in love again.

Source: Carol Ullmann, Critical Essay on *The Tenant of Wildfell Hall*, in *Novels for Students*, Thomson Gale, 2008.

Tess O'Toole

In the following essay, O'Toole responds to common criticisms of this novel by suggesting that its structure of epistolary account and diary account work to instruct about the claustrophobic experience of an abusive marriage. O'Toole suggests that "The architecture of Brontë's narrative calls attention to alternative forms of domestic containment," and these forms are imposed by the "natal family" and by "courtship and marriage."

Anne Brontë's *The Tenant of Wildfell Hall* has been singled out most frequently for two elements: (1) its unusually complicated framing device (Gilbert Markham's epistolary account of his relationship with Helen Huntingdon surrounds her much lengthier diary account of her first marriage and flight from her husband) and (2) its strikingly frank and detailed description of a woman's experience in an abusive marriage. These two features of the text, one formal and one thematic, are intertwined in the experience of reading the novel. For, in proceeding through the multilayered narrative and remaining for a surprisingly protracted time in Helen's painful account of her nightmarish marriage, the reader experiences a sensation that might be labeled narrative claustrophobia. The text thus produces an effect on the reader that mimics the entrapment Helen experiences in her marriage.

"The book is painful," Charles Kingsley declared in his unsigned review in *Fraser's Magazine*, sounding a note that would be echoed by many contemporary critics. A notice in the *North American Review* complained that the reader "is confined to a narrow space of life, and held down, as it were, by main force, to witness the wolfish side of [Huntingdon's] nature literally and logically set forth." This language invokes the claustrophobic sensation that I have suggested is exacerbated by the narrative from. The reader's discomfort is likely to extend beyond Helen's diary account of her hellish first marriage, however. The events recounted in the framing narrative—Helen's courtship by and eventual marriage to Gilbert

> HELEN AND FREDERICK'S RELATIONSHIP REMAINS INSULAR, AND IT REMAINS LOCKED WITHIN THE FIELD OF HELEN'S DIARY."

Markham—purportedly provide a happy ending for Helen, released from her disastrous first marriage and free to choose a better mate. But Gilbert is an oddly unsuitable partner for Helen. Though it may be tempting to read the events in the framing narrative as representing a recovery from the events recounted in the embedded one, such a meliorist view is challenged by the fact that the framing narrative finds Helen remarried to a man who, while not the rake that Arthur Huntingdon was, is capable, like Arthur, of violence and cowardice (as evidenced by his vicious attack on Frederick Lawrence, which he does not publicly acknowledge). Gilbert, like Arthur, has been spoiled by his mother and has an inflated ego, and he subscribes to all the standard Victorian stereotypes about female nature and female merit (as evidenced by his behavior toward and descriptions of both the "demon" Eliza Millward, his first flame, and the "angel" Helen).

Gilbert's shortcomings become less critical, however, when attention is shifted from the relationship he describes in his letters to Halford to the one whose forging Helen narrates in her diary—the relationship with her brother Frederick, whom Gilbert perceives as his antagonist and who is his opposite in character. The formal displacement that occurs when Helen's narrative undermines Gilbert's, exceeding it in both length and power, is thus echoed in a displacement of the exogamous romantic plot articulated in his account by the endogamous brother-sister plot contained within hers. The architecture of Brontë's narrative calls attention to alternate forms of domestic containment, one deriving from courtship and marriage, the other from the natal family. Rather than representing these two forms of domesticity as continuous or overlapping, as nineteenth-century novels of family life commonly do, *The Tenant of Wildfell Hall* stresses their disjunctions, an approach that is complemented by the narrative format.

Treatments of *Tenant* as domestic fiction have tended to focus on marital relationships, and hence, when examining the relationship of the framing to the framed narrative, to focus on the differences between Gilbert and Arthur as spouses. The critics I will discuss below, for instance, have suggested that the agenda Helen pursues unsuccessfully in her first marriage, an agenda consistent with prevailing domestic ideology, is realized in her second. It must be acknowledged, however, that the novel's relationship to domestic ideology is an unusually vexed one. In presenting Helen's attraction to her first husband, Brontë daringly implies that her heroine's culturally sanctioned role as the would-be reformer of a sinful man serves as a cover for her sexual attraction to him, but a hellish marriage punishes Helen for succumbing to her desire for Arthur. The novel makes a heroine out of a woman who runs away from her husband; but this transgressive act is sanctioned by a conservative motive: Helen wants to save her son from his father's corrupting influence. The more subversive kind of rebellion enacted by Arthur's mistress, Annabella—a rebellion that does not have a selfless motivation—is severely punished by her society and by the text: "she [sinks], at length, in difficulty and debt, disgrace and misery; and die[s] at last ... in penury, neglect and utter wretchedness." But if Annabella's fate suggests that the novel's critique of domestic ideology has its limits, her role in Brontë's treatment of domestic reform also indicates the limited efficacy of that ideology.

Helen displays the ironic naïveté of a young woman who, subscribing to the ideas about woman's moral influence articulated by Sarah Ellis and others, ardently believes that as her husband's "angel monitress" she can redeem him. While Helen's surveillance of her home and husband accords with the function of the domestic woman posited by Nancy Armstrong in *Desire and Domestic Fiction*, Helen is not nearly so effective as that powerful creature. The futility of her efforts are underscored by Annabella; while Arthur finds his wife's moralizing tedious, he can be kept in line by his mistress's strategy, which depends on his physical desire for her. Annabella's brand of sexual management, ironically, has more pragmatic reach than domestic authority. In this way, Brontë's novel exposes rather than reproduces the myth

of power embedded in cultural constructions of the domestic woman. Helen's friend Millicent may be criticized for failing to provide the sort of moral management her husband needs, but the example of Helen and Arthur suggests that there is a problem with the entire notion of the wife as agent of reform.

The authorial preface to the second edition reiterates on a figural level Helen's frustrated efforts at domestic purification. Just before asserting, "if I can gain the public ear at all, I would rather whisper a few wholesome truths therein than much soft nonsense," Brontë compares herself to a cleaning woman who, "undertak[ing] the cleansing of a careless bachelor's apartment will be liable to more abuse for the dust she raises, than commendation for the clearance she effects." If her commitment to acknowledging unpleasant truths links her to Helen, so too does this indication of the limits of her own success, since Helen's wifely attempts at cleaning up Arthur's act are met with obdurate resistance.

This essay stresses the novel's ambivalent relationship to domestic ideology because some of the best readings of this novel become entwined with it when treating the relationship between Helen's and Gilbert's narratives. Inspired by Brontë's eloquent and compelling defense of a wronged woman, and her invention of a heroine who heroically fights back, N.M. Jacobs, Linda Shires, and Elizabeth Langland have all provided insightful readings of *Tenant* as a protofeminist text. Each of these critics, however, credits Brontë's heroine with the successful moral education of her second husband, maintaining that Gilbert is reformed by his exposure to Helen's text and that their union redeems Helen's disastrous first marriage; in so doing, they risk reinscribing the domestic ideology that it is a part of the novel's accomplishment to problematize. Moreover, each has at some point to ignore, minimize, or recast elements in Gilbert's narrative that qualify a positive account of Helen's second marriage. It is my contention that these elements are linked to a narrative strategy that contrasts Gilbert the suitor, would-be hero of the framing narrative, and Frederick the brother, hero of the framed narrative. The strategy behind the narrative layering is not to show Gilbert's reform and to celebrate a restored conjugal ideal, but to juxtapose siblings and suitors, to poise natal domesticity against nuptial domesticity.

In "Gender and Layered Narrative in *Wuthering Heights* and *The Tenant of Wildfell Hall,*" Jacobs initially seems set to view Gilbert's framing narrative as part of a continuing critique of the domestic, rather than as the site of its recuperation. She notes that the enclosure of Helen's diary narrative within Gilbert's epistolary one mimics not just the division of male and female into separate spheres but also the law of couverture. The fact that Helen's diary has become her husband's possession and that he has the power to bargain with it in a bid to recover his friend's favor reinforces this point, but Jacobs does not pursue that tack. Instead, she sees the relationship between Helen's story and Gilbert's as one that works not to contain her but to educate him. According to Jacobs, the "effect on Gilbert of reading this document—of being admitted into the reality hidden within and behind the conventional consciousness in which he participates—is revolutionary, and absolutely instrumental to the partnership of equals their marriage will become. Its revelations force him outside the restricted boundaries of an ego that defines itself through its difference from and superiority to someone else."

If this were the case, however, then the access to Helen's consciousness which Gilbert's reading of her diary gives him should have altered his behavior and assumptions. Jacobs, however, provides no evidence in support of Gilbert's moral growth. And far from demonstrating any such alteration, Brontë's novel shows us that in the events following upon his reading of the diary, Gilbert is as egotistical and as sexist as he appears in the opening chapters. His immediate response when he has concluded the account of Helen's harrowing domestic drama is pique that the pages detailing her initial impressions of him have been ripped out. While the diary might have restored Helen to his good graces, rendering her once again "all I wished to think her ... her character shone bright, and clear, and stainless as that sun I could not bear to look on", it has not touched his tendency to demonize all attractive women who are not the exalted Helen, as his continued shabby treatment and vilification of Eliza make clear. His unreasonable resentment of Frederick continues, and his egotism is still intact; his pride almost leads him to lose Helen, as he refuses to

make himself vulnerable to learn whether she still loves him. Most disturbing, the violence he exhibited in his attack on Frederick is still manifest in his behavior toward Eliza, the former object of his sexual interest; when she says something that angers him, he responds: "I seized her arm and gave it, I think, a pretty severe squeeze, for she shrank into herself with a faint cry of pain or terror." Thus, there does not seem to be any significant revision in Gilbert's character that would encourage us to disagree with Helen's aunt when she says, "Could [Helen] have been contented to remain single, I own I should have been better satisfied." The absence of growth on Gilbert's part was commented upon by Kingsley, who questioned Brontë's agenda: "If the author had intended to work the noble old Cymon and Iphigenia myths, she ought to have let us see the gradual growth of the clown's mind under the influence of the accomplished woman, and this is just what she has not done." Precisely. We can only assume that Brontë knew what she was about when she chose to include details suggesting Gilbert's persistent limitations.

While Shires concedes those limitations, she maintains that Gilbert and his correspondent Jack Halford are both educated by their reading of Helen's diary: "[The novel] counsels an inscribed male friend that what he may perceive as overly independent female behavior is a strong woman's only way to maintain integrity in a world where aristocratic male dominance can easily slip into abusiveness. It is important that the text addresses a man, for the counter-hegemonic project of the text is not merely to expose a bad marriage but to teach patriarchy the value of female rebellion." Like Shires, Langland views the framing male narrative as one that serves a feminist agenda, though in different terms. Writing in part in response to Jacobs's description of the relationship between Gilbert's narrative and Helen's as one of enclosure, Langland argues in "The Voicing of Female Desire in ... *The Tenant of Wildfell Hall*" that "[a] traditional analysis that speaks of nested narratives is already contaminated by the patriarchal ideology of prior and latter and so cannot effectively question what I wish to question ... the transgressive nature of narrative exchange." Thus she proposes viewing the "narrative within a narrative not as hierarchical or detachable parts, but as interacting functions within a transgressive economy that allows for the paradoxic voicing of feminine desire." Central to her argument is the fact that the text as a whole is structured around an exchange of letters, and that the epistolary exchange is the prelude for an exchange of visits (Halford and Rose to Gilbert and Helen). She argues that an exchange structure is inherently destabilizing and thus can serve a feminist agenda. She does not allow the gender implications built into this particular exchange to give her pause. However, it is surely not irrelevant that the exchange of letters is an exchange between two men, nor that the material exchanged is a woman's story, though this is a point Langland's reading must ignore. It strikes the reader as curious at best that Gilbert would transcribe for another man the contents of his wife's intimate diary, and disturbing at worst that Helen's hellish experience is used for a homosocial end.

The transaction between Gilbert and Halford accords with the model outlined by Eve Kosofsky Sedgwick in *Between Men*, which describes how women are used as instruments with which those economic and affective bonds between men that structure society are forged. Gilbert's revelation of Helen's story to Halford is an act of debt paying. He has fallen out of Halford's favor because he did not respond to his friend's sharing of confidences with equal candor; the story he is telling him now, which is actually his wife's story, will acquit his debt. He instructs Halford: "If the coin suits you, tell me so, and I'll send you the rest at my leisure: if you would rather remain my creditor than stuff your purse with such ungainly heavy pieces,—tell me still, and I'll pardon your bad taste, and willingly keep the treasure to myself." The exchange between Gilbert and Halford is not only an economic one, it is also an emotional one, geared toward a restoration of affection. It is clear that Halford has replaced the women in Gilbert's life for the top spot in his affections. Halford is Gilbert's brother-in-law, and he has taken his sister's place in his affections. When in Gilbert's account he first refers to his sister Rose, he pauses to comment: "Nothing told me then, that she, a few years hence, would be the wife of one—entirely unknown to me as yet, but destined hereafter to become a closer friend than even herself." More intriguingly, Markham refers to his marriage to Helen Huntingdon as "the most important event of my life—previous to my acquaintance with Jack Halford at least." The story wins Gilbert his friend's love again, renewing the affective bond between the two

men that was in danger of dissolving: "I perceive, with joy, my most valued friend, that the cloud of your displeasure has past away; the light of your countenance blesses me once more."

At one point Gilbert contrasts his warm friendship with Halford to his inability to feel that same kind of bond with Frederick Lawrence, Helen's brother: "[U]pon the whole, our intimacy was rather a mutual predilection than a deep and solid friendship, such as since has arisen between myself and you, Halford." His jealousy of Frederick, whom he mistakenly assumes to be Helen's lover, leads to Gilbert's resentment of him and to his violent attack on him. But even after he learns of Frederick's kinship with Helen and of how instrumental he has been in Helen's escape from Huntingdon, Gilbert is unable to forge a connection with him or even to appreciate his merit. The antipathy between the two, much more virulent on Gilbert's side, is significant, for Frederick is a man who will not engage in the sort of transactions over women that Gilbert wishes him to conduct. Frederick, while placing no impediments between Gilbert and his sister, is not willing to play the active role of go-between that Gilbert expects him to play. Gilbert resents Frederick and even considers him morally culpable for not intervening with his sister on his behalf: "[H]e had wronged us ... He had not attempted to check the course of our love by actually damming up the streams in their passage, but he had passively watched the two currents wandering through life's arid wilderness, declining to clear away the obstructions that divided them, and secretly hoping that both would lose themselves in the sand before they could be joined in one." Though Helen sees her relationship to her brother as an end in itself, Gilbert wants the brother to serve as their mediator, to channel the passion whose object and destination is himself.

Such a structure of channeling and mediation is embodied in the novel by gossip, whose central and suspect role in this novel has been elucidated by Jan Gordon: "[G]ossip always appears as a threat to value: it either 'speculates' or exaggerates by 'inflating' ... In short gossip devalues because it has nothing standing behind it. Lacking the authenticity of a definable source, it is simultaneously financially, theologically, and narratively unredeemable." (It is in fact gossip, with Frederick as its unwitting subject, that brings Gilbert and Helen together; gossip's misconstrual of Frederick's wedding as Helen's causes Gilbert to rush to the scene, a trip which ends in his engagement to Helen.) Gilbert implicitly links Frederick's refusal to play go-between with his refusal to gossip when he complains to Halford that "[h]e provoked me at times ... by his evident reluctance to talk to me about his sister." When Helen, on the verge of rejoining her husband, had suggested to Gilbert that he might know of her through her brother, she had specified: "I did not mean that Frederick should be the means of transmitting messages between us, only that each might know, through him, of the other's welfare." In her formulation of the triangle, Frederick is less a mediating term than an apex. Gilbert's contrasting expectation that Frederick will serve as an intermediary is thwarted by the literalism and lack of expansiveness with which Frederick imparts news of Helen: "I would still pursue my habitual enquiries after his sister—if he had lately heard from her, and how she was, but nothing more. I did so, and the answers I received were always provokingly limited to the letter of the enquiry." Significantly, Frederick is a character who resists transmitting gossip. He does not, for example, let the community know it was Gilbert who attacked him. He is most reluctant to gossip about women, a reluctance that baffles and aggravates Gilbert.

Gilbert's conversation with Frederick about Jane Wilson is especially revealing in this regard. His narrative has painted Jane as a social climber who wished to ensnare Frederick. Gilbert takes it upon himself to warn Frederick of the danger Gilbert believes he faces from this predatory woman. Frederick checks Gilbert's desire to gossip about the woman and to slander her: "'I never told you, Markham, that I intended to marry Miss Wilson' ... 'No, but whether you do or not, she intends to marry you.' 'Did she tell you so?' 'No, but—' 'Then you have no right to make such an assertion respecting her.'" As Gilbert continues to press his point, Frederick, who is not interested in Jane, responds with gentle sarcasm to Gilbert's diatribe. While Gilbert is miffed by Frederick's refusal to join him in maligning Jane's character, to engage in this particular kind of male bonding, he comforts himself by reflecting: "I believe ... that he soon learned to contemplate with secret amazement his former predilection, and to congratulate himself on the lucky escape he had made; but he never confessed it to me ... As

for Jane Wilson ... [h]ad I done wrong to blight her cherished hopes? I think not; and certainly my conscience has never accused me, from that day to this." The assumption of his own correct insight into Frederick's attitude, steadfastly maintained in the face of a lack of evidence, and the callous indifference toward the unhappy Jane Wilson are both powerful indicators of Gilbert's self-satisfied nature and the limits of his imagination and his empathy. Significantly, this smug reflection is made by the older Gilbert who has been married to Helen for many years; it thus cautions us not to assume too much about Gilbert's improvement under Helen's tutelage.

Frederick's refusal to gossip about women is in contrast not only to Gilbert's eagerness to gossip about Jane Wilson, but also to Gilbert's sharing of his wife's intimate diary with his male friend. As we have seen, attempts to read Helen's second marriage as an event which redeems the domestic ideal compromised by her first marriage must ignore evidence about Gilbert's shortcomings and the troubling implications of his transfer of the contents of her diary to his friend. It is significant that many of Gilbert's flaws are made visible through interactions with Helen's brother Frederick; this fact should encourage us to think further about the latter's role. For all the famous violence of the domestic scenes in this novel, the most violent moment in the novel is the one in which Gilbert attacks Frederick:

> I had seized my whip by the small end, and—swift and sudden as a flash of lightning—brought the other down upon his head. It was not without a feeling of strange satisfaction that I beheld the instant, deadly pallor that overspread his face, and the few red drops that trickled down his forehead, while he reeled a moment in his saddle, and then fell backward to the ground ... Had I killed him? ... [N]o; he moved his eyelids and uttered a slight groan. I breathed again—he was only stunned by the fall. It served him right—it would teach him better manners in future. Should I help him to his horse? No. For any other combination of offenses I would; but his were too unpardonable.

Gilbert's physical attack on Frederick makes particularly vivid and concrete an opposition between Helen's suitor and her brother that is visible throughout the novel, yet Frederick's importance has been largely overlooked by critics.

Frederick plays an instrumental role in the recuperation of Helen's unhappy history; it is he, not Gilbert, who redeems Helen's faith in humanity after her disillusioning experience with Arthur. She writes in her diary: "I was beginning insensibly to cherish very unamiable feelings against my fellow mortals—the male part of them especially; but it is a comfort to see that there is at least one among them worthy to be trusted and esteemed." Curiously, Frederick is exactly the sort of man the reader who wants a happier, more appropriate second marriage for Helen would expect her to marry. He, not Gilbert, is the gentle, sensitive, and supportive male that Helen has sought. If we are to look for an optimistic, meliorist plot in the novel, it is more likely to be found in the brother-sister relationship than in the husband-wife one. The opportunity for revision and recuperation lies not in the undeniably disappointing Gilbert, so curiously less mature than his bride, but in the brother. Improvement is effected not so much by Gilbert as a replacement for Helen's first husband as it is by her brother as a replacement for her father. Juliet McMaster notes a pattern of generational improvement in the novel's juxtaposition of characters who embody Regency values with those who embody Victorian values. She discusses this distinction primarily with reference to the replacement of the dissolute Arthur, with his aristocratic associations, by the gentlemen farmer Gilbert (elevated to the squirearchy by his marriage to the newly propertied Helen). But that pattern is most marked in the contrast between Helen's irresponsible father and his virtuous son. The framing story is the wrong place to look for a positive alternative to Helen's marriage with Arthur; we must look instead to her diary, to the account of her relationship with Frederick. By shifting attention from the suitor to the brother, we can account for the dissatisfactions of the courtship narrative while revealing Brontë's display of alternate forms of domestic containment. It is Helen's growing relationship with her brother, rather than the burgeoning relationship with Gilbert, that receives the privileged place in her diary after she leaves her husband. The containment of the brother-sister plot within the embedded narrative reflects the turn inward, toward the natal family. The claustrophobic narrative structure, originally linked to an imprisoning marriage, finds an alternate thematic corollary in a potentially incestuous relationship.

II

Poised between Helen's first marriage and her second is the relationship she forges with her brother during her exile. As the person to whom Helen turns for help when she makes her escape, Frederick serves as a buffer between her and the world during her period of disguise. Helen and Frederick's relationship is peculiar for a brother-sister one because they have been raised having only minimal contact with each other. Helen's father, an alcoholic with no interest in daughters, abnegated his responsibility toward her, turning her over to relatives after the death of his wife, while keeping charge of his son. Helen's flight from her husband provides the occasion for building a relationship with her brother that they have thus far not enjoyed. Becoming better acquainted as adults, their relationship is in some ways structurally closer to a courtship relationship than to a brother-sister one. The townspeople, ignorant of Helen's true identity, construe their relationship as a sexual one, and Gilbert sees him as a romantic rival, suggesting, perhaps, the novel's own flirtation with an incest motif. Helen, after all, is fixated on her son's resemblance to the brother she loves. She reconceives her son as the progeny not of her husband Arthur but of her brother Frederick; she says to him: "He is like you, Frederick ... in some of his moods: I sometimes think he resembles you more than his father; and I am glad of it." Helen's flight from her husband's to her brother's house is followed, then, by the realignment of her son's lineage in relation to her natal family. Previously, the son's physical likeness to his father was stressed, and Helen has kept Arthur senior's portrait (which had symbolized her physical desire for him) in order to compare the child to it as he grows. In raising her son, she seeks to instill the character she would create into the body she desired. Finding the embodiment of manly virtue in her brother, she redesignates her son's person as "like Frederick's."

Rather than exploring sexual overtones in the sibling relationship, however, Brontë's novel foregrounds its relationship to domestic reform; Frederick's virtue compensates for their father's neglectful treatment of Helen, and their comfortable relationship, defined by mutual respect, contrasts with Helen's problematic relationships with her husband and her suitor. The implication that the brother-sister relationship has the potential to redeem a compromised domestic sphere bears some resemblance to Jane Austen's employment of the sibling model of relationships as described by Glenda A. Hudson in *Sibling Love and Incest in Jane Austen's Fiction*. Emphasizing the nonsalacious nature of Austen's treatment of incestuous relationships— "In her novels, the in-family marriages between the cousins and in-laws are successful because they do not grow out of sexual longing but are rooted in a deeper, more abiding domestic love which merges spiritual, intellectual and physical affinities"—Hudson argues that for Austen, "the incestuous marriages of Fanny and Edmund, Emma and Knightley, and Elinor and Edward Ferrars are therapeutic and restorative; the endogamous unions safeguard the family circle and its values ... Incest in Austen's novels creates a loving and enclosed family circle." The idea of closing family ranks for protective and restorative purposes can be applied to Helen's turn to her brother. Unlike what we would find in an Austen novel, however, no warm relationship is effected between Frederick and Gilbert through the latter's marriage to Frederick's sister. The brother-in-law whose visit Gilbert eagerly anticipates at the end of the novel is Jack Halford, not Frederick Lawrence. The alternate domestic relationships of siblings and spouses remain quite distinct in Helen's experience, rather than the former fostering marital exchange.

The endogamous quality of the brother-sister relationship is exaggerated in the case of Helenand Frederick: formed during her time in hiding, it is necessarily an insular one which cannot incorporate outsiders. And it coexists with a regressive project in which Helen engages upon her flight from her marital home, for Helen's retreat from her husband is followed by a return to her natal family origins, symbolized by her adoption of her mother's maiden name as her alias and her return to the home in which her mother died. Wildfell Hall, though "no[t] yet quite sunk into decay," is a previous family home that has been exchanged for a more up-to-date one, so she is not only symbolically returning to her family, but returning to a prior stage in the family history.

Together, Helen and Frederick revise their family history. Enjoying frequent contact with her brother, helen reconstructs the family life she was denied as a child. Frederick's supportive and responsible fraternal behavior compensates for the poor behavior of Helen's father. The contrast between Helen's relationship with her father and the relationship she enjoys with her brother bears out claims made by Joseph P. Boone and Deborah E. Nord about Victorian brother-sister plots. They argue that the "[sister's] investment in the brother figure ... originates as a means to combat her own devaluation within the family and society," frequently making up for paternal neglect in particular. They also note that the brother-sister relationship might be used to circumvent problems inherent in a conjugal relationship: "[I]n some cases, the sibling ideal becomes a utopian basis for figuring heterosexual relationships not based on traditional conceptions of gender polarity as the basis of romantic attraction. Theoretically, at least, the idealized union of brother and sister rests on a more egalitarian, less threatening mode of male-female relationship, precisely because the bond is one in which gender difference is rendered secondary to the tie of bloodlikeness, familiarity and friendship." While one might question the assumption that there is something more inherently benign about brother-sister relations than other male-female ones, Helen and Frederick's relationship does seem intended to provide an alternative to the violence and power plays that contaminate the conjugal relationship. Frederick gives her both emotional and practical support and appears to be the only male in the novel who embodies the virtues she seeks in a mate.

Contrary to the case of the brothers and sisters Boone and Nord describe, however, the intimacy of Frederick and Helen is not born and nurtured in the nursery; it is not itself, therefore, cultivated by domestic arrangements. It is, we must suspect, precisely because Frederick and Helen have not been raised together that their sibling relationship presents a strong contrast to the others in the novel, such as that between Gilbert and his sister Rose, who complains of the favoritism with which the sons of the family are treated, and that of Esther Hargrave and her brother, who attempts to pressure her into an unsuitable match. The problem of triangulation within the nuclear family is called to our attention from the first page, when Gilbert commences his account of himself with reference to the competing agendas his mother and father had regarding their son; this is swiftly followed by an exposure to the sibling rivalry between Gilbert and his younger brother as well as that between Rose and her brothers. (The fact that Helen's son is conceived alternately as an improved version of her husband and a younger version of her brother suggests that her family will not be exempt from the kind of triangulation that plagues the Markham family.) Because Helen and Frederick come together as adults, there is no parental mediation to promote rivalry or jealousy. Moreover, due to the early death of his mother, Frederick has not been spoiled by maternal indulgence in the way that both Arthur and Gilbert are said to have been. Thus, their exemplary sibling relationship is also exceptional. While Helen and Frederick's relationship seems to present a model for domestic relations, it is a somewhat utopian one, and its strength, paradoxically, derives from the absence of domestic structures in its formation. Therefore, that model is unable to provide the basis for its own reproduction.

In this respect, Brontë's treatment of the brother-sister motif differs from that of many other nineteenth-century novelists who privilege sibling bonds. Austen and Charles Dickens, for example, both use the sibling relationship as a model for the marital one by having the spouse metonymically connected to the brother (either by being him, as in *Mansfield Park*, or by having a special connection to him, as in *Dombey and Son*). In *Tenant*, this approach is visible only on the margins of the central plot, as, for example, when Helen arranges for Frederick's marriage to Esther Hargrave, the young woman whom she has called her "sister in heart and affection." The marriage of Arthur Jr. and Helen Hattersly, a second "Helen and Arthur" marriage, is also a sort of fraternal/sororal match, since their mothers' closeness has caused them often to play and take lessons together from childhood, as siblings would do. Gilbert and Helen's marriage, however, does not adhere to the sibling paradigm. In the central plot, Brontë keeps the suitor and the brother steadfastly segregated: they are antithetical types and are, consequently, antipathetic to each other. Moreover, Gilbert is rendered analogous not to Helen's brother, but to her son. Using his friendship with little Arthur as a way of accessing the mother, the petulant and immature Gilbert is, as Shires describes him, the "boy child who wants to take possession of the mother." It is Frederick, not Gilbert, whom Helen perceives as Arthur's ideal imaginary parent. This fact reinforces the extent to which Frederick appears to be Helen's only male equal in the novel as well as the only exemplar of manly domestic virtue. Though it is incest that is

traditionally associated with the disruption of normal generational sequence, Brontë reverses this association by figuring generational imbalance in the exogamous relationship.

Brontë's treatment of the sibling motif contrasts not only with Dickens's and Austen's, but, closer to home, with her own sister's. Numerous critics have traced the lines of kinship between *Tenant* and *Wuthering Heights*, which contains the more famous representation of sibling love. Paradoxically, while the incest motif appears less transgressive in *Tenant* than in *Wuthering Heights*—it is where family values are housed—it is less translatable into the social sphere. In Emily Brontë's novel (as in Charlotte Brontë's *Jane Eyre*), the notion of kinship is used to figure the romantic love whose promise is a cornerstone of the domestic ideal. In *Desire and Domestic Fiction*, Armstrong alludes to the strategy behind the kind of romantic identification often associated with incest in the novels of the other Brontë sisters: "In the face of the essential incompatibility of the social roles they attempt to couple [Emily and Charlotte Brontë] endow their lovers with absolute identity on an entirely different ontological plane." Working against a critical tradition that "has turned the Brontës' novels into sublimating strategies that conceal forbidden desires, including incest," Armstrong associates Emily and Charlotte Brontë's fiction with a development whereby "sexuality ... become[s] the instrument of, and not the resistance to, conventional morality." It is not surprising that Armstrong's account does not include Anne Brontë, for, unlike Emily and Charlotte, Anne seems to juxtapose rather than to collapse kinship relations and sexual ones in *Tenant*. This makes *Tenant* a most unusual example of nineteenth-century domestic fiction, a fact that may account for the relative marginalization of Anne's masterpiece within the Brontë corpus.

Helen's relationship to her brother Frederick cannot ultimately solve the problems of contradictions that cluster around the concept of the domestic, for it apparently cannot be brought to bear on other familial relationships, or on anything outside its own circuit. While in *Wuthering Heights* the incestuous longing of Cathy and Heathcliff is replaced by the more socially acceptable (but, as William Goetz points out, sanguinally more affined) marriage of Catherine and Hareton, in *Tenant*, the sibling relationship seems to exist as an end in itself. The sense of narrative claustrophobia described above is the formal corollary of this self-containment. Helen and Frederick's relationship remains insular, and it remains locked within the field of Helen's diary.

Helen's narrative itself is "locked," for, once her diary is turned over to Gilbert, she never again narrates. This means that we have only his word for the success of their marriage. That he is satisfied is clear, but the reader has no firsthand access to Helen's subsequent experience. It also means that in Helen's diary the strongest affective relationship with a man that she describes after leaving Arthur is with her brother, in keeping with Brontë's use of the brother-sister plot to cast a dubious light on Gilbert and his courtship. It is no doubt because the novel privileges Helen's relationship to her brother, the record of which is confined to the embedded narrative, that Gilbert's framing narrative strikes many readers as perfunctory.

But it is more than perfunctory; it is part of a sustained critique of marital domesticity and part of an oppositional structure that segregates the nuptial and the natal forms of domestic containment. Tenant is distinctive in its brilliant use of compartmentalized narratives to reflect this thematic opposition. It is even more distinctive in its refusal to reconcile sexual and kinship relations, and in its willingness to sustain the resulting note of unease.

Source: Tess O'Toole, "Siblings and Suitors in the Narrative Architecture of *The Tenant of Wildfell Hall*," in *Studies in English Literature, 1500–1900*, Vol. 39, No. 4, Autumn 1999, pp. 715–31.

SOURCES

Auchincloss, Louis, "Speaking of Books: The Trick of Author as Character," in *New York Times Book Review*, February 1, 1970, pp. 2, 38.

Brontë, Anne, "Preface to the Second Edition," in *The Tenant of Wildfell Hall*, Oxford University Press, 1992, pp. 3, 5.

———, *The Tenant of Wildfell Hall*, Oxford University Press, 1992.

Lewis, Naomi, "Books in General," in *New Statesman & Nation*, Vol. 32, No. 808, August 17, 1946, p. 119.

Lord, Walter Frewen, "The Brontë Novels," in *Nineteenth Century*, Vol. 3, No. 313, March 1903, p. 489.

Review of *The Tenant of Wildfell Hall*, in *Literary World*, Vol. 3, No. 80, August 12, 1848, pp. 544, 546.

Review of *The Tenant of Wildfell Hall*, in *New York Times Book Review*, May 19, 1900, p. 324.

Review of *The Tenant of Wildfell Hall*, in *Spectator*, No. 1045, July 8, 1848, pp. 662, 663.

Sinclair, May, "An Introduction," in *The Tenant of Wildfell Hall*, by Anne Brontë, Everyman's Library Series No. 685, J. M. Dent & Sons, 1922, pp. v–viii.

FURTHER READING

Alexander, Christine, and Margaret Smith, *The Oxford Companion to the Brontës*, Oxford University Press, 2004.

This book is organized like an encyclopedia, with entries on topics, including names of characters, titles of works, places the Brontës visited, books they read, and more. Alexander and Smith have included the Brontë sisters' father, Patrick, and brother, Branwell, as well.

Barker, Juliet, *The Brontës: A Life in Letters*, Overlook Press, 1998.

Barker's book collects the correspondence of the Brontë family: father Patrick, son Branwell, and three daughters, Charlotte, Emily, and Anne—some of which was not previously published. These letters provide insight into the personalities of a very literary family.

David, Saul, *Prince of Pleasure: The Prince of Wales and the Making of the Regency*, Grove/Atlantic, 2000.

David's biography is an engaging and detailed examination of the life and times of profligate King George IV, who died in 1830. George was known in his day not only as a patron of the arts but also as a drunk and a lecher.

Hawkes, Jason, *Yorkshire from the Air*, Ebury Press, 2001.

This book of aerial photographs captures the beauty of the Yorkshire countryside in the north of England. The Brontë family lived in Yorkshire and were very attached to this landscape of wild moors, rolling hills, grand old manors, historic towns, and seaside villages.

Ulysses

JAMES JOYCE

1922

Ulysses, by James Joyce, is a challenge to understand. It is at once a masterpiece and an anomaly, a novel that stretches the form and content of the genre of which it is a part. At the same time that *Ulysses* uses Homer's *Odyssey* as a major literary referent, the work heralds the end of the nineteenth-century novel as it was commonly understood. It takes readers into the inner realms of human consciousness using the interior monologue style that came to be called stream of consciousness. In addition to this psychological characteristic, it gives a realistic portrait of the life of ordinary people living in Dublin, Ireland, on June 16, 1904. First published in its entirety in France in 1922, the novel was the subject of a famous obscenity trial in 1933, but was found by a U.S. district court in New York to be a work of art. The furor over the novel made Joyce a celebrity. In the long run, the work placed him at the forefront of the modern period of the early 1900s when literary works, primarily in the first two decades, explored interior lives and subjective reality in a new idiom, attempting to probe the human psyche in order to understand the human condition.

Joyce supplied a schema for *Ulysses* that divides and labels the novel's untitled episodes, linking each to the *Odyssey* and identifying other structural and thematic elements. The headings provided in this schema are used in the plot summary below, as is customary in literary analysis of

James Joyce (© *Corbis*)

this work. In the novel itself, there are three sections marked with roman numerals but no other explicit headings. The first line of each episode in the novel appears in small capital letters. The schema can be found in a number of works on Joyce; one of these is *Reading Joyce's Ulysses*, by Daniel R. Schwarz. For explanations of references and parallels to Homer's epic, readers will find Don Gifford's exhaustive work, *"Ulysses" Annotated*, indispensable.

AUTHOR BIOGRAPHY

James Augustine Joyce was born in Dublin, Ireland, on February 2, 1882, the eldest of ten children of John Stanislaus Joyce and Mary Jane Joyce. At age six in 1888, Joyce began his Jesuit education at Clongowes Wood, a boarding school. After that, he attended Belvedere College, a Catholic day school in Dublin. Joyce attended University College in Dublin from 1898 to 1902 and graduated with a degree in modern languages. By this time, he was already writing both poetry and prose sketches. He went to Paris

to study medicine for a year but returned to Dublin when his mother was in the final stage of a terminal illness. He taught briefly and published some stories and poems. Then in 1904, he met and began a lifelong relationship with a semi-literate hotel chambermaid, Nora Barnacle, and shortly thereafter, the couple relocated to the town of Pola on the Adriatic Sea where briefly Joyce taught in a local Berlitz school. The following year, Joyce and Barnacle moved to Trieste, where they made their home for the next ten years, except for a brief time in Rome. Married some years later, the couple had two children, Giorgio and Lucia, both born in Trieste.

As early as 1903, Joyce had begun working on an autobiographical work, tentatively titled *Stephen Hero*, and on his collection of short stories, which was ultimately published as *Dubliners* in 1914. He published a collection of poetry, *Chamber Music*, and then revised and expanded *Stephen Hero* and published it as *Portrait of the Artist as a Young Man*, which was serialized in the magazine *Egoist* in 1914 and 1915. In 1915, Joyce and his wife moved to Zurich, where he worked on *Ulysses*, allowing excerpts from the novel to appear in *Egoist* and a New York magazine, *Little Review*. In 1919, he and his wife returned to Trieste and shortly thereafter settled in Paris.

In 1920, *Little Review* stopped serial publication of *Ulysses*, which was drawing obscenity charges in the United States. It was clear to Joyce that the completed novel could not find a U.S. or British publisher. As it happened, an American expatriate in Paris, Sylvia Beach, published the work with the imprint of her bookshop, Shakespeare and Company. The book appeared, as Joyce requested, on his birthday, February 2, 1922. Seen as scandalous and worthy of suppression, the book created a furor and made Joyce a literary celebrity.

During the 1920s, Joyce underwent a series of eye operations. The next decade was also darkened by the apparent mental decline of his daughter, Lucia, who was committed to an asylum in 1936. Joyce completed *Finnegans Wake* in 1938, which was published the following year to generally hostile reviews. He lived briefly in the French village St. Gérand-le-Puy near Vichy and then moved back to Zurich. He died there on January 13, 1941, after surgery for a perforated ulcer. Nora Joyce lived on in Zurich until her death in 1951.

MEDIA ADAPTATIONS

- An audio book abridgement of *Ulysses*, read by Jim Norton and Marcella Riordan, became available in 1995 from Naxos. The four cassettes are in total five hours long.

- In 1967, Joseph Strick directed *Ulysses*, starring Milo O'Shea in the role of Leopold Bloom. As of 2007, this film was available on DVD.

- In 2006, Odyssey Pictures released *Bloom: All of Life in One Extraordinary Day*, directed by Sean Walsh and starring Stephen Rea as Leopold Bloom.

PLOT SUMMARY

Foreword, District Court Decision, and Letter from Joyce

The 1934 edition of *Ulysses* begins with a Foreword written by Morris L. Ernst, a Random House defense attorney involved in the obscenity case against the novel. Ernst applauds the decision of John M. Woolsey, the presiding judge, to rule against the charge of obscenity and allow the novel to be published in the United States. Ernst claims this judicial decision marks a "New Deal in the law of letters." The attorney explains the complications involved in the definition and application of obscenity and links this release from "the legal compulsion for squeamishness in literature" with the repeal of Prohibition, which occurred also in the first week of December 1933.

Next, Judge Woolsey describes in his opinion Joyce's accomplishment:

> [He] attempted . . . with astonishing success— to show how the screen of consciousness with its ever-shifting kaleidoscopic impressions carries . . . not only what is in the focus of each man's observation of the actual things about him, but also in a penumbral zone residua of past impressions, some recent and some drawn up by association from the domain of the subconscious.

This technique, Judge Woolsey explains, is like "a multiple exposure on a cinema film." In essence, the judge concludes, Joyce's effort was to show how the minds of his characters operate. Woolsey also expounds on the legal meaning of the term, obscenity, as a characteristic in a work intended "to stir the sex impulses or to lead to sexually impure and lustful thoughts." Read in its entirety, he maintains, the novel does not have this effect. Rather, it serves as "a somewhat tragic and very powerful commentary on the inner lives of men and women."

Also included is the April 2, 1933, letter of James Joyce to Bennett A. Cerf, the Random House publisher who decided to print *Ulysses*. Joyce explains the assistance he received from Ezra Pound and from Sylvia Beach, owner of an English bookstore in Paris which first published the novel. He also explains some of the difficulties in the United Kingdom and in the United States regarding the subsequent distribution and sale of this first edition.

I: Telemachia

TELEMACHUS

Early on June 16, 1904, Stephen Dedalus, the Englishman Haines, and Malachi Mulligan, called Buck, have breakfast at the Martello Tower at Sandycove on Dublin Bay which Stephen rents. Irreverently, Buck shaves as though he is celebrating mass and says a mock grace before the three eat breakfast. Buck also alludes to Stephen's "absurd" Greek name. Stephen feels imposed upon by the Oxford student Haines, who was invited by Buck but has been disruptive during the previous night with a bad dream. Though it is Stephen's place, Buck seems to have taken charge, serving the food, taking possession of the key to the tower, and getting money from Stephen for drinks later in the day. Stephen is preoccupied with thoughts of his recently deceased mother, having dreamed of her the night before. Buck goes off for a swim, Haines and Stephen smoke a cigarette, and both Haines and Buck refer briefly to Stephen's theory about *Hamlet*. Haines draws a parallel between the Martello Tower and Hamlet's castle and then asks Stephen about his belief in a personal God. Stephen responds that he is "the servant of two masters . . . an English and an Italian," meaning "the imperial British state" and "the holy Roman catholic and apostolic church." He adds there is a third master, Ireland, "who wants [him] for odd jobs." It is about 8:00 a.m. when Stephen heads off to the boys' boarding school where he teaches. Buck asks that they meet at 12:30 at the pub called the Ship. As Stephen leaves, he promises himself not to sleep at the tower the coming night since Buck has taken it over. Stephen calls him a "usurper." This allusion to the usurper King Claudius in *Hamlet*, as well as several references to Hamlet and to Stephen's brooding depression, all suggest parallels between Stephen and the melancholy prince.

NESTOR

It is 10 a.m., and Stephen is teaching an ancient Greek history class in a boys' school in Dalkey, drilling the students on Pyrrhus and picking on an unprepared student named Armstrong. It is a half-day at school, and the boys are eager to go out on the field and play soccer. Next, Stephen asks the students to read from John Milton's "Lycidas," an elegy on the death by drowning of Milton's friend. Stephen then challenges the students to solve a paradoxical riddle. The class ends, and the students leave in haste, except for one, Cyril Sargent, who remains behind to get help with his math problems. Bending over Cyril, Stephen thinks about how some woman gave birth to this boy and loves him, thoughts associated in Stephen's mind with the recent death of his own mother. Cyril leaves, and Stephen goes to collect his pay from the headmaster, Garrett Deasy, who expresses misogynistic and anti-Semitic views and wants a letter he has written on hoof-and-mouth disease to be published in local newspapers. He gives a copy of the letter to Stephen, asking him to take it to news offices where he has contacts. Mr. Deasy suggests that Stephen will not long work as a teacher. Agreeing that he is more learner than teacher, Stephen leaves with Mr. Deasy's letter, laughing at the headmaster's opinions and reminding himself that he has a date to meet Buck at the Ship pub at 12:30.

PROTEUS

Including very little dialogue, the third episode, which begins at 11 a.m., is the most interior of the first three. In this section, Stephen walks along Sandymount Strand, spending an hour and a half on the beach, thinking about the difference between the objective world and how it appears to his eyes. He spies two midwives, one with a bag in which Stephen imagines there is a miscarried fetus. He considers the possibility of an umbilicus long enough to serve as a telephone line across

which one could phone up navel-free Eve in Eden. He thinks about the conception of Jesus and how, according to the Nicene Creed, Jesus was said to be of the essence of God, not created out of nothing as man was. The wind reminds him that he has to go to the newspaper offices with Mr. Deasy's letter. Briefly he considers visiting his aunt, but then he misses her street. He thinks about being ashamed of his family when he was little. Headed toward the Pigeon House, he thinks of Mary and how her pregnancy was attributed to a bird. He thinks back to Paris and remembers a conversation with Kevin Egan on nationalism. At the edge of the water, he looks back, searching the view for the Martello Tower and again promising himself not to sleep there this night. He sees a dog running toward him followed by a couple who are intent on picking cockles. He thinks about his dream the night before, in which a man with a melon took him along a red carpet. When the couple passes Stephen, he thinks of a poem and writes it down on a scrap of paper torn from Deasy's letter. When he decides to leave the beach, he urinates, picks his nose, and then looks around to see if anyone is observing him.

II: Odyssey

CALYPSO

The fourth episode occurs at the same time as episode one. It is 8 a.m. at 7 Eccles Street, and Leopold Bloom is in the kitchen getting milk for the cat and a breakfast tray ready for his wife, Marion, called Molly, who is still in bed. Leopold loves organ meat and fancies a fried kidney for his breakfast, so he goes around the corner to a butcher to buy one. Back in the house, he fixes toast for Molly, boils water, and sets the kidney to fry in butter. Upstairs, he brings Molly her breakfast and gives her a card and letter. The letter is from Hugh Boylan, called Blazes, and Leopold sees her hide it under the pillow. She asks him what the word, metempsychosis, means. He has received a letter from their daughter, Milly, which he takes downstairs and reads while he eats. Bloom is wearing his good black suit because at 11 a.m. today he is attending the funeral of his friend Patrick Dignam. After breakfast, he goes to the outhouse to defecate. The church bells toll the hour.

LOTUSEATERS

Leopold Bloom heads in a roundabout way to a post office where he picks up a letter from Martha Clifford, with whom he is conducting a clandestine, erotic correspondence using the pseudonym Henry Flower. With the letter in his pocket, he runs into an acquaintance, C. P. McCoy, who talks to Bloom about Dignam's death and asks that Bloom enter his name as an attendant though he will not be at the funeral. Off by himself, Leopold reads Martha's letter and wonders what kind of woman she really is. Like its parallel episode in the *Odyssey*, this episode is full of indolence and repeated references to smoking and opiates, which Leopold associates with the East and with Molly, who is from Gibraltar. He enters All Hallows, the incense-filled Catholic Church, and observes part of the mass. At 10:15 a.m., he heads to the chemist to buy some face cream for Molly. There he thinks of chloroform and laudanum. The cream must be prepared. The chemist asks for the empty bottle, which Leopold has neglected to bring. Leopold buys a bar of soap and plans to return for the cream. Outside, he meets Bantam Lyons, who wants a newspaper so he can check on the Gold Cup horserace scheduled to run this day. Bloom offers his paper, saying he was going to throw it away, and Lyons rushes off to place a bet, misconstruing Bloom's comment for a tip on the long-shot racehorse named Throwaway. Bloom resolves to have a bath, envisioning himself lying back in the water, his penis floating like a flower.

HADES

In a funeral procession from Sandymount to Prospect Cemetery in Glasnevin, north of Dublin, at 11 a.m., Bloom travels in a carriage with Jack Power, Martin Cunningham, and Simon Dedalus. As they leave the village, shop blinds are drawn down and people on the street tip their hats in respect. Bloom notices Stephen walking along and mentions it to his father, Simon Dedalus. Bloom thinks of his own son, Rudy, who died just a few days after birth and would be eleven years old now had he lived. They pass Blazes Boylan and the other men call to him, which secretly embarrasses Bloom, who knows Boylan will visit Molly at 4 p.m. Mr. Power asks about the concert tour, referring somewhat disrespectfully to Molly as "*Madame*." It is 11:20 a.m., and Bloom thinks of Mrs. Fleming coming into 7 Eccles Street to clean. They pass Reuben J. Dodd, the Jewish moneylender, from whom each of them, except for Bloom, has borrowed money. They comment about how Dodd's son almost drowned in the Liffey, and

when a boatman saved him, the father gave him a small bit of money as thanks. Power comments that suicide is the worst death, a family disgrace; Cunningham cuts him off, saying, "We must take a charitable view of it." Bloom sees this as a kindness from Cunningham who knows that Bloom's father was a suicide. At the cemetery, Simon Dedalus cries at the grave of his recently deceased wife, May. A service is given in the chapel and some brief words spoken at the grave. As the mourners disperse, a reporter, Joe Hynes, asks Bloom for his full name and if he can identify a thirteenth man at the gravesite. Bloom cannot name the man in the mackintosh, but he does remember to ask that McCoy's name be added to the list of those present.

AEOLUS

This episode takes place in the *Freeman* newspaper offices. The text here is divided by headlines like those appearing in a newspaper. Bloom gets a copy of the advertisement for Keyes tea and then heads into the *Telegraph* printing room and speaks to the foreman, City Councillor Nanetti, who is in conversation with Hynes about his report on Dignam's funeral. Nanetti wants Bloom to get Keyes to agree to advertise his tea in the paper for three months. Bloom suspects Keyes wants the ad to run only for two months. Bloom goes into the *Telegraph* office, where Simon Dedalus and others are listening to Ned Lambert, who is making fun of a patriotic speech by Dan Dawson. J. J. O'Molloy enters, knocking into Bloom with the doorknob. Stephen Dedalus comes in and hands Deasy's letter to Crawford, who decides to publish it. A group, including Stephen, heads out to a pub, pushing past Bloom as they leave. Bloom wants Crawford to agree to run the Keyes ad for two months rather than three, but Crawford rejects the idea.

LESTRYGONIANS

Bloom goes past a candy store and someone hands him a throw-away announcement of the arrival of an American evangelist. He passes Dilly Dedalus and feels sorry for the motherless child and condemns the Catholic Church for forcing people to have more children than they can afford. He thinks of the term, parallax, recalling his morning discussion with Molly about metempsychosis. Sandwich board men weave their way through the pedestrians, advertising Hely's, one letter on each board. Bloom meets Jossie Breen on the street, his girlfriend from years before, and they talk about Mina Purefoy, who is in protracted labor at the maternity hospital. Repeatedly his thoughts go back to Rudy's neonatal death, to the pain of labor, to the fact that stillborns "are not even registered." As a cloud blots the sun, Bloom thinks about the seasons of life, of Dignam's funeral, and Mrs. Purefoy giving birth. It all seems meaningless to him. Near an optometrist's office, he thinks again about parallax and holds up his little finger to cover the sun; doing so makes him recall an evening walk with Molly and Blazes Boylan, and now Bloom wonders if the two of them were touching then or holding hands. Bloom tosses the announcement into the Liffey.

Eager for his lunch, Bloom leaves one restaurant where the customers are eating rudely and enters Davy Byrne's for a cheese sandwich and glass of burgundy wine. There Nosey Flynn asks about Molly's tour and in mentioning Boylan reminds Bloom of the upcoming meeting between his wife and Blazes. Flynn discusses the upcoming Gold Cup. Two flies stuck together on a window remind Bloom of a time when Molly fed him seedcake out of her mouth and they had sex. There is a big difference between their relationship then and as it is now; he thinks, "Me. And me now." Elsewhere in the restaurant, men gossip about Bloom, about his work, his involvement with the Freemasons, his refusal to sign his name to contracts. As Bloom leaves, Bantam Lyons comes in, whispering about Bloom's tip on the horse Throwaway. Outside, Bloom walks along calculating what he may make if he sells certain ads for the newspaper. Then he spots Boylan on the street and ducks into the National Museum to avoid him.

SCYLLA AND CHARYBDIS

At the National Library, Stephen Dedalus puts forth some of his literary and philosophical views, along with his biographical reading of *Hamlet*, to a circle of men in the director's office. The group includes the Quaker librarian Thomas W. Lyster, the literary critic and essayist John Eglinton, and the poet, A. E. To these men, Stephen suggests that Shakespeare identified with King Hamlet, that he saw in Prince Hamlet a version of his own son Hamnet who died as a child, and that Queen Gertrude is a dramatic version of Shakespeare's own wife, Ann Hathaway. A. E. objects to a biographical reading of the play, asserting that the text of the play ought to

be the focus of any interpretation of it. The librarian Mr. Best comes into the office. Best has been showing Haines the library's manuscript copy of *Lovesongs of Connacht*; the text of *Ulysses* at this point includes a line of music. A. E. is ready to leave, and Eglinton asks if they will meet at Moore's that night for a poetry reading, to which both Buck Mulligan and Haines are invited. Stephen takes his exclusion from these plans as a snub. The literary discussion of *Hamlet* continues with Eglinton suggesting that Shakespeare most identified with Prince Hamlet. A worker enters, asking help from Mr. Lyster for a patron (Bloom) who wants to look at the newspaper called *Kilkenny People*. Stephen continues at length, mapping out supposed evidence in Shakespeare's plays of Hathaway's infidelity. At last, he and Mulligan leave the library, knocking past Bloom as they go out. Mulligan refers to Bloom as "the wandering jew" and also suggests that Bloom is a homosexual and is attracted sexually to Stephen.

WANDERING ROCKS

This long episode contains eighteen vignettes or small scenes that taken together give a sense of pedestrian traffic in Dublin between 3 p.m. and 4 p.m. It begins with the Catholic priest, Father John Conmee, who sets out about 3 p.m. to visit a school in the suburbs to see if Dignam's son can attend without charge. The episode concludes with the arrival of a cavalcade of the king's governor-general at the Mirus Park charity bazaar. These major treks weave through and around smaller scenes, some focusing on the principal characters, some on minor characters, and some on people who in a film would be called extras. Among these characters are a one-legged soldier; the dancing teacher, Mr. Maginni; Mrs. Breen, who earlier spoke with Bloom; and Corny Kelleher, the undertaker who handled the Dignam funeral. Two scenes occur at bookstalls. Stephen Dedalus pauses at a bookcart in Bedford Row and is approached by his sister Dilly who asks him if the used French primer she has bought for a penny is any good. Elsewhere, Leopold Bloom selects the novel *Sweets of Sin* for Molly. At the Dedalus home, Stephen's sister Maggey boils shirts and his other sisters, Katey and Boody, lament the family's poverty. When Maggey says Dilly is out trying to find Simon, Boody responds, "Our father who art not in heaven." Martin Cunningham, who is involved in collecting money for Dignam's son, speaks to the subsheriff about the boy. Molly's arm appears at the second-floor window of the Bloom residence as she tosses a coin to the one-legged soldier who "crutche[s] himself" up Eccles Street. Blazes Boylan steps into a fruit shop and orders a basket to be sent ahead and looks down the open neckline of the shop girl's blouse as he asks to use the telephone. Across town, Boylan's secretary answers the phone and mentions his 4 p.m. appointment with Mr. Lenehan at the Ormond Hotel. Dilly waits in the street for her father and gets a shilling and two pennies from him. Through these and other tiny views of the street traffic, of people on footpaths, crossing bridges, and spitting out of open doors, the governor-general's carriage is spotted or missed as it makes its way out of town.

SIRENS

Two of the sirens in this episode, Ormond Hotel barmaids Lydia Douce and Mina Kennedy, lean out an upstairs window watching the cavalcade go by. The hotel is a meeting place for several groups of characters. Simon Dedalus enters the bar with Lenehan, looking for Boylan who arrives shortly. Elsewhere, Bloom buys stationery so that he can respond to Martha Clifford's letter and then goes into the Ormond with Richie Goulding to have some dinner and spy on Boylan. As Goulding and Bloom order drinks, Boylan leaves with Lenehan, causing Bloom to sob. In the bar, Simon Dedalus, Ben Dollard, and Bob Cowley recall concerts and discuss Molly Bloom's voice. The three sing together for the bar crowd, causing Bloom to think about how he once loaned Dollard evening clothes for a performance. Simon sings "M'appari," from an opera called *Martha*. Bloom listens, thinking about Dignam's funeral, about how music is mathematical, and about how his daughter Milly is not interested in music. The blind piano tuner taps his return to the hotel to pick up his tuning fork. As Boylan drives to Eccles Street and knocks at the Blooms' front door, Bloom hunches over the table, writing secretly to Martha. As he leaves the hotel, Bloom spots Bridie Kelly, a prostitute whose services he has used, and he turns away toward a shop window to avoid being recognized by her. He pretends to study a portrait displayed there of Robert Emmet and to read his last words. As a tram passes, he farts.

CYCLOPS

The Cyclops episode begins at 5 p.m. with a description of a near accident in which a chimney-sweep handles his brush carelessly and almost pokes out the eye of another person who is this episode's unnamed first-person narrator. This speaker, quite distinct in his use of language from the omniscient narrator whose voice appears repeatedly in other episodes, turns to give the sweep "the weight of [his] tongue." Indeed, the weightiness of the language in this episode is due to its pervasive vicious sarcasm and hyperbole. The narrator spies Joe Hynes and the two of them go off to Barney Kiernan's pub where they are joined by the unnamed citizen, who takes the lead in a loud, combative talk about politics, the Gold Cup horserace (which the twenty-to-one long shot Throwaway wins), and other matters, all of which culminates with a verbal attack on Leopold Bloom. The pub is across the street from the courthouse where Bloom has agreed to meet with Martin Cunningham and together travel out to Sandymount to visit Dignam's widow. As Bloom waits for Cunningham to arrive, the circle of drinkers in the pub enlarges, with O'Molloy, Lambert, Nolan, and Lenehan arriving after Bloom. The citizen's narrow-minded nationalistic and racist rant is counterpoised by Bloom's reasonableness and moderation. Bloom, the one non-drinker in the crowd and thus perceived by others to be giving offense on that count, remains broad-minded, able to see more sides to the topics being discussed. In this way he inadvertently arouses the further ire of the citizen who, as Bloom spots Cunningham and leaves, runs into the street, yelling anti-Semitic remarks. Bloom and Cunningham escape into a carriage and pull away. This bombastic, ridiculous episode is complicated by thirty-two dispersed passages of extraordinarily inflated prose that present various styles and describe unrealistically other places and times, such as a courtroom scene, a public hanging, and action being taken in Parliament.

NAUSICAA

A third-person narrator in this episode uses language that parodies a second-rate sentimental novel, beginning with the description of Sandymount Strand and how "the summer evening had begun to fold the world in its mysterious embrace" and Gerty MacDowell, "as fair a specimen of winsome Irish girlhood as one could wish to see" with her "rosebud mouth." Gerty sits apart from her friends, Cissy Caffrey and Edy Boardman, who are playing on the beach and watching younger siblings, Cissy's little twin brothers and Edy's younger brother. Having visited Dignam's widow, Bloom has come to the beach. It is sometime between 4 p.m. and 5 p.m.; his watch stopped at 4:30. In a nearby church, evening mass is being celebrated with prayers to the Virgin Mary. Bloom watches Gerty, and she realizes it, positioning herself so he can look up her dress, exposing her thighs and underpants. With his hand in his pocket, Bloom masturbates, achieving orgasm as fireworks from the Mirus bazaar explode and viewers of the show sigh audibly. Bloom suspects his watch stopped at the very moment when Boylan and Molly engaged in sexual intercourse. Gerty gets up and walks away, revealing her limp.

OXEN OF THE SUN

Said by many, including Joyce himself, to be the most difficult episode in the novel, this inscrutable section presents the evolution of the English language through the parodied idiom of major texts and writers, all of which is divided into nine sections to match the months of gestation. It is 10 p.m. and various medical students drink and discuss rather boisterously a variety of topics related to sexuality and gestation in last delivered of her ninth son. Leopold Bloom is in the room with drunken Stephen Dedalus and others, called "right witty scholars," and while he hears their misogynistic and sacrilegious banter, he does not participate in it. Rather, as Mrs. Purefoy's baby is born, Bloom thinks sadly of Molly and the birth of their son, Rudy, who only lived a few days. Buck Mulligan arrives and takes center stage from Stephen. The nurse tries to quiet the young men, and eventually they decide to leave for a pub. Among the group is Alex Bannon, who speaks about his girlfriend and only gradually realizes she is Bloom's daughter, Milly. Bloom trails along, watching Stephen.

CIRCE

This episode, the longest of the novel at about one hundred and seventy pages, is presented in play format, with stage directions and speakers' names over their lines. It takes place about midnight in Nighttown, Dublin's red-light district, where the drunken Stephen and his buddies go, and Leopold Bloom follows along. The scenes of this play or drama are a series of hallucinations or fantasies, some of which must be induced by fatigue or alcohol. Separated from the young men, Bloom goes into an alley where he feeds a dog some meat he has purchased. This act engenders an hallucination in which Bloom is

questioned and charged by two policemen. Witnesses, including the ghost of Dignam, seem to materialize to accuse him. Bloom heads into Bella Cohen's brothel, seeking Stephen. Inside, Stephen and Lynch are with two prostitutes, Florry and Kitty. Another fantasy or hallucination occurs in which Bloom is tyrannized by Bella Cohen, who accuses him of being less than a real man, a person who deserves to have the virile Boylan cuckolding him. Another prostitute, Zoe Higgins, accuses Bloom of being dominated by Molly. Stephen has an hallucination in which the ghost of his mother rises up and accuses him. This vision terrifies him, and he breaks away and runs outside, Bloom coming out after him. Outside there is a ruckus, and Stephen is knocked unconscious. Police come, but Corny Kelleher is nearby and helps resolve the tension. Abandoned by his friends, Stephen lies on the street, and Bloom looks over him, imagining he sees Rudy.

III: *Nostos*

EUMAEUS

After midnight, Bloom picks Stephen Dedalus up off the street and brushes him off. In this anticlimactic meeting between Bloom and Stephen, described in second-rate prose, the two walk arm-in-arm toward a cabman's shelter, a late-night place where winos and stray loners can find a cup of coffee. In the role of Good Samaritan, as an ordinary older man offering a young man regular kinds of advice, Bloom cautions the not-yet-sober Stephen about drinking too much and about going into Nighttown to the "women of ill fame" without knowing "a little juijitsu."

Along the way, they come across an acquaintance of Stephen, called Corley, who asks for money. Stephen gives him a halfcrown, much to Bloom's disapproval. Stephen remarks he has no place to sleep this night, and Bloom suggests Stephen go to his father's house. The two enter the cabman's shelter, which is operated by a man believed to be Skin-the-Goat Fitzharris, a person involved in the Phoenix Park murders. Here, Stephen and Bloom engage in conversation with a sailor who says his name is D. B. Murphy. When they exchange names, Murphy asks Stephen if he is related to Simon Dedalus. Stephen does not admit kinship, and Bloom offers that it must be a coincidence of names. Bloom looks at a paper and sees an article on the Gold Cup and one on

Dignam's funeral, in which among the attendants listed are a "*M'Intosh*" and a person named "*L. Boom*." Talk turns to Parnell, and Bloom sympathizes more with Parnell and the married Kitty O'Shea than with O'Shea's husband, who Bloom assumes deserved his wife's betrayal. As chairs are inverted on tables, Bloom rises and takes Stephen outside, suggesting that the night air and a walk to Bloom's residence in Eccles Street will do the young man some good. Bloom offers a cup of cocoa at his house, and Stephen accepts. Street cleaners watch the two men go off, arm-in-arm.

ITHACA

This episode is narrated in a question-and-answer format, as might be seen in the dialogues of Socrates. According to Frank Delaney, in *James Joyce's "Odyssey,"* Joyce described this as "the form of a mathematical Catechism." It is 1 a.m. on Eccles Street at Leopold Bloom's residence, and Bloom discovers he does not have the key. He has to drop to the basement level and climb in through a window. Holding a candle, he opens the front door, and Stephen enters. They make their way to the back kitchen where they drink cups of cocoa. Bloom thinks maybe Stephen would be interested in Milly and invites him to stay the night, but Stephen declines. They talk about the Irish and Hebrew languages. About 1:30 a.m., they go out in the back, urinate side-by-side while observing a shooting star, and then separate. In his house again, Bloom sits in the front room, thinking about how he has spent his money on this day, about how his Dublin acquaintances are in bed and Dignam in his grave, about how he wishes he had enough money to buy a little house on the outskirts of town. He has observed evidence in the kitchen, front room, and elsewhere of Boylan's visit, and he thinks of Boylan as one of many suitors for Molly, one in a series. The music for "Love's Old Sweet Song," is open on the piano. At 2 a.m., he goes upstairs to bed, lying down with his feet next to Molly's head and his head at her feet. He kisses her buttocks, and she awakes slightly. He tells her about his day, lying about some details. It has been over ten years since they engaged in sexual intercourse. This episode ends with a big dot, like an oversized period, marking the spot, the conclusion.

PENELOPE

According to Frank Delaney, Joyce described this episode as "amplitudinously curvilinear."

Delaney further explains that the first sentence contains twenty-five hundred words, that there are eight sentences in all, and the episode begins and ends, again quoting Joyce, with "the most positive word in the English language, the word *yes*." Commonly referred to as Molly Bloom's soliloquy, this episode presents in stream-of-consciousness style her drowsy reverie.

Her first sentence begins with her surprise at Bloom's request that she serve him breakfast in bed the next morning, ordering up two eggs before he falls asleep. She wonders if Bloom has reached orgasm during the day. She compares Boylan's aggressive sexual style to Bloom's and then thinks about the Breens' marriage, concluding that hers and Leopold's is better. In the next sentence, Molly thinks about men who have admired her, listing several of them. She wonders if she will get together with Boylan again and thinks of their upcoming concert trip to Belfast. Among her many thoughts, she considers losing some weight and wishes Bloom had a better paying office job. In the third sentence, she thinks about how attractive breasts are and how unattractive male genitals are. She thinks about how Bloom admires her breasts and once suggested she express milk from them into their tea. Molly thinks back to her early years in Gibraltar, and her friend Hester Stanhope. She recalls how lonely she felt after Hester and her husband moved away. She also thinks about Milly and how she got a card from their daughter while Leopold received a letter.

The fifth sentence includes memory of her first love interest, Lieutenant Mulvey, whom she knew in Gibraltar. A train whistles in the distance, making her think of "Love's Old Sweet Song," which she has been practicing for an upcoming concert. In the next sentence, Molly thinks of her daughter, who is studying photography in Mullingar. She thinks about how pretty Milly is, quite like Molly herself was in her teens. Molly senses she is beginning to menstruate and gets up to use the chamber pot. In the seventh sentence, back in bed, Molly muses about Leopold's finances, how she and he have moved several times. She wonders if he spent money this day on other women and wonders how much he offered at Dignam's funeral. She thinks of Bloom's circle of male acquaintances and about Simon Dedalus's good singing voice. She recalls meeting Stephen when he was a little boy. In the eighth sentence, she ponders the fact that Leopold does not hug her any more.

She thinks of Stephen's mother recently dead and of Rudy's death. She thinks about morning and about the possibility of telling Leopold about her sexual encounter with Boylan, her first extramarital involvement. She thinks she will buy flowers for the house, in case Stephen returns. Finally, she thinks of being with Leopold sixteen years earlier at Howth, how he called her "a flower of the mountain" and proposed to her, and how she accepted him:

> I put my arms around him yes and drew him down to me so he could feel my breasts all perfume yes and his heart was going like mad and yes I said yes I will Yes.

Following these memorable lines, the places and dates for the composition of the novel are given: "*Trieste-Zürich-Paris, 1914–1921.*

CHARACTERS

A. E.
The pseudonym of George Russell, A. E. is a highly respected Irish poet. He associates with other established literary people, a group which includes Haines and Mulligan but which excludes Stephen Dedalus, though he wishes to be a member.

Richard Best
Richard Best, a librarian at the National Library, takes part in the Scylla and Charybdis episode discussion of *Hamlet*. His comments represent conventional views of the play.

Leopold Bloom
Leopold Bloom, a thirty-eight-year-old canvasser, lives with his wife Marion at 7 Eccles Street in Dublin. Bloom is an empathetic, sensitive, earthy, sensual person who responds to the weather, to the smell of organ meat cooking, to women he sees on the street, and who puzzles over laws of physical science. He loves his daughter, fifteen-year-old Milly, and still mourns for his son Rudy, who died when he was a baby about eleven years earlier. On June 16, 1904, Bloom attends a funeral, visits a newspaper office and the National Library, has dinner at a hotel, and meets up with Stephen Dedalus in a brothel and invites him home. On this day in Dublin, Leopold Bloom anticipates and dreads his wife's infidelity with Blazes Boylan, yet he himself continues a clandestine correspondence with Martha Clifford and masturbates on Sandymount beach as he watches Gerty MacDowell.

Marion Bloom
Voluptuous Marion Bloom, called Molly, is thirty-four years old and a professional singer. Her father was a British officer, and her mother, Lunita Laredo, was a Spanish Jew. Molly grew up in Gibraltar, and presumably she moved to Dublin with her father sometime in 1886. Since the neonatal death of her second child, Rudy, she has not had a sexual relationship with her husband or any other man, but on this day, while he is away from home, she has a sexual encounter with Hugh Boylan.

Millicent Bloom
Millicent Bloom, called Milly, is the fifteen-year-old daughter of Leopold and Molly Bloom. She lives in Mullingar and is studying to become a photographer. On this day, Leopold enjoys a letter from Milly, in which she thanks him and her mother for birthday gifts.

Hugh Boylan
Hugh Boylan, called Blazes, is Molly Bloom's concert manager. Boylan is a womanizer, a fancy dresser, and man about town. He walks in slick, highly polished shoes and his car jingles through the streets making a sound reminiscent of Molly's bedsprings.

Josie Powell Breen
Josie Breen was years earlier a girlfriend of Leopold Bloom. She is now the wife of Dennis Breen, a paranoid who requires a lot of her attention and care.

The Citizen
This unnamed character, prominent in the "Cyclops" episode, is a vitriolic, narrow-minded nationalist, in favor of a free Ireland and willing to blame social ills on foreigners, especially Jews. In the pub, he verbally attacks Leopold Bloom, who responds logically and withdraws quickly. The citizen is the kind of man who sits around in a pub waiting for someone else to buy him a few drinks and then sounds off in a political harangue.

Martha Clifford
Martha Clifford writes letters to Leopold Bloom, whom she does not know face-to-face, addressing him by his pseudonym, Henry Flower. Martha's

letters indicate that she is poorly educated and not particularly daring in pursuing a sexual relationship with Bloom. Yet she enjoys the titillation of their clandestine correspondence.

Bella Cohen

Bella Cohen is the madam in charge of the brothel that Stephen Dedalus and his friends visit in Nighttown. She is domineering, with a large build. Concerned with appearances, she attacks the rowdy visitors in her establishment.

Martin Cunningham

One of the mourners at Patrick Dignam's funeral, Martin Cunningham takes the initiative to start a collection for Dignam's widow and son. He is sympathetic and kindly, speaking up on Bloom's behalf several times during the day. In the late afternoon, he and Bloom visit Dignam's widow in Sandymount Strand.

Garrett Deasy

Misogynistic, anti-Semitic Garrett Deasy is the headmaster of the boys' school where Stephen teaches history. Mr. Deasy has written an essay on hoof-and-mouth disease and wants it published in local papers. He gives it to Stephen, asking him to present it to the newspaper editors with whom he is acquainted. He suspects that Stephen is not suited to a professional life in teaching.

Dilly Dedalus

Dilly Dedalus, one of Simon's daughters and Stephen's sister, has as much natural intelligence as Stephen has, but she is unlikely to have his opportunities to become learned. Nonetheless, she seeks to become educated and with a penny buys a used French primer in order to study the language. She waits on the street to get a shilling from her father and take the money home to her sisters who are washing shirts there and would have virtually nothing to eat were it not for the soup brought to them by a local nun.

Simon Dedalus

Father of Stephen and four daughters, Simon Dedalus recently buried his wife May and still mourns her. Simon has quite a good singing voice and likes to entertain his drinking friends with funny stories. Born in Cork and once rather successful, Simon has recently had financial problems. During this day, he spends money in pubs, doing nothing to help or protect his daughters at home. Simon is highly critical of Stephen,

and when Stephen is asked if Simon is his father, Stephen demurs.

Stephen Dedalus

Recently home in Dublin from a year or two in Paris where he studied medicine, Stephen Dedalus is an intellectual and would-be poet, a well-read young man who takes himself very seriously and is depressed after his mother's recent death and his ongoing alienation from Ireland and the Catholic Church. A teacher at a boys' school, Stephen spends his time talking about his literary theories and drinking with his friends. At this point in his life, he is aware of having not found his professional place. He dissociates himself from his sisters and is alienated from his father, Simon.

Ben Dollard

A drinking friend of Simon Dedalus, Ben Dollard has a good voice and enjoys singing in pubs. He performs with Simon at the Ormond Hotel.

Lydia Douce

Lydia Douce is a barmaid at the Ormond Hotel. She has a crush on Boylan. She and Mina Kennedy are seen hanging out the second-floor window watching the viceregal cavalcade go by in the streets below.

John Eglinton

A published essayist, John Eglinton spends time in the National Library, where he hears Stephen expound on his theory about *Hamlet*. He finds Stephen over-confident and egotistical.

Richard Goulding

Suffering from chronic back pain, Richard Goulding, called Richie, has dinner with Bloom at the Ormond Hotel. Goulding is the brother of the deceased May Dedalus and thus Stephen's uncle.

Haines

An Englishman who is temporarily staying at the Martello Tower with Buck Mulligan and Stephen Dedalus, Haines has a bad dream during the night of June 15, waking the others by shooting a gun at an imagined tiger. Later, on June 16, Haines, an Oxford student, socializes with Buck and other literati, who exclude Stephen from their circle.

Joe Hynes

A local newspaper reporter, Joe Hynes borrows three pounds from Leopold Bloom but conveniently forgets to pay back the loan. He meets the narrator of the Cyclops episode in the street and accompanies him to Barney Kiernan's pub for a conversation with an unnamed character referred to as the citizen.

Corny Kelleher

Corny Kelleher is the undertaker who officiates at Patrick Dignam's funeral and is later seen in his shop doorway. Corny intervenes on their behalf when Stephen Dedalus and Leopold Bloom get involved with two policemen on the street near Nighttown.

Mina Kennedy

Mina Kennedy is a barmaid at the Ormond Hotel. She and Lydia Douce flirt with their male customers. Blond Mina is more reserved than Lydia. Both women are seen hanging out the second-floor window watching the viceregal cavalcade go by in the streets below.

Lenehan

Lenehan is a sports editor for a local Dublin newspaper. Disliked by Molly Bloom, Lenehan makes fun of Leopold Bloom. He is a friend of Simon Dedalus.

Lynch

An old friend of Stephen Dedalus, Lynch is a medical student. He is involved with the prostitute, Kitty Ricketts.

Thomas W. Lyster

Quaker librarian at the National Library, Thomas Lyster patiently hears Stephen expound on his *Hamlet* theory and is open-minded about it.

Gerty MacDowell

Gerty MacDowell is influenced by romance literature and women's magazines and takes special care of her clothes and skin. She dreams of meeting a strong, handsome man who will marry her. Bloom is sexually aroused by her when he sees her on Sandymount Strand in the Nausicaa episode.

John Henry Menton

John Menton was once Leopold Bloom's rival for Molly. A lawyer by trade, Menton was Patrick Dignam's boss. Menton looks down on Bloom.

TOPICS FOR FURTHER STUDY

- Spend several hours walking around your neighborhood, noting people you see and events as they occur. Later, make a map of your journey and write a story about it.

- Read *Portrait of the Artist as a Young Man* and then write a paper about what you learn in this novel about Stephen Dedalus that helps clarify the portrait of him in *Ulysses*.

- Research patterns of alcohol consumption and alcoholism in Dublin, Ireland. Using whatever statistics you can find, make a graph that shows changing levels of alcohol consumption in three different decades of the twentieth century.

- Read Frank McCourt's novel *Angela's Ashes* and write a paper on how alcoholism affected McCourt's family.

- Do some research on the literary technique of stream of consciousness. Then study a couple of pages of Molly Bloom's monologue and trace the sequence of her thoughts. Write a paper that shows how the sequence of thoughts reveals her personality.

Malachi Mulligan

Popular Malachi Mulligan, called Buck, is a medical student and friend of Stephen Dedalus. Buck is lively, theatrical, and able to satirize anything. He is well-read and tells funny, off-color jokes. Neither Bloom nor Simon Dedalus thinks well of Buck.

J. J. O'Molloy

J. J. O'Molloy is an unemployed lawyer who on this day is unable to borrow money. At Barney Kiernan's pub, he defends Bloom.

Kitty Ricketts

A prostitute with aspirations for a better life, Kitty Ricketts dates Lynch.

George Russell

See A. E.

Florry Talbot

One of the prostitutes at Bella Cohen's establishment, Florry Talbot entertains the medical students who visit the brothel with Stephen.

THEMES

The Modern Hero

Ulysses has as its hero a most ordinary man, Leopold Bloom. So unlike the muscular, militaristic Homeric hero whose name serves as the novel's title, Bloom is gentle, self-effacing, reserved, and peripheralized. Arguably more associated with home than the outer world, even though on this day he spends most of his time out about town, the kindly, other-centered Bloom is first depicted making breakfast for his wife and feeding the cat. He is a caring man, deeply attached to his wife and daughter and continuing to mourn the neonatal death of his son, Rudy. Whereas Ulysses welcomes adventures in strange and threatening places and has a crew of sailors he orders about, Bloom lives an ordinary man's life and is a loner, an outsider, a Jew, a man who thinks about the physical world but chooses not to interfere, a man who lives very much in his body, responsive to women, courteous toward men, sensual in an unobtrusive way. He admires women on the street, wonders sympathetically about a woman in protracted labor, and talks politely to a childhood sweetheart. He helps a blind man cross the street, he tells an acquaintance his hat has a ding in it, and he kindly reminds someone of a loan and does not take offense when the man seems to brush him off.

While the daring epic hero slays the Cyclops and navigates between the rocks of Scylla and the whirlpool of Charybdis, Bloom maneuvers among offensive others, seeking to engage with them peacefully, deferring to others and not taking offense even when he is directly insulted. He dresses in black out of respect for a friend's funeral and gives generously to the collection taken up for the man's widow. While the epic hero is defined by his conquests, his ego, his self-centeredness, Bloom is defined by his small gestures of kindness, his thoughtfulness of others and of the physical world, and his polite social restraint.

Sad about his wife's infidelity, he is resigned rather than defensive or controlling. Though their marriage is sexless, he is not without desire. He becomes aroused while looking at Gerty MacDowell on the beach, but he satisfies his desire privately, without imposing it on her, and his thoughts here and elsewhere inevitably return to Molly, so comfortably is he bound to her. In many ways, Leopold Bloom is the antithesis of the classical Ulysses; he is not a world traveler or an adventurer; he is not larger-than-life, and he is not able to perform extraordinary feats. In this character, Joyce affirms what is extraordinary about an ordinary man's character; he provides a new sense of the heroic, written in the small-scale actions of a twentieth-century urban man, in his kindliness in the face of alienation, in his ability to calmly analyze differences, in his civic decency.

The Artist's Search for a Place in the World

Stephen Dedalus is a would-be poet, a well-schooled young man full of academic theories and familiar texts. In a sense homeless (he rents a place that is usurped by others, he is back in Ireland only temporarily, he has nowhere to sleep in this day), Stephen expresses the discomfort and ennui of a creative spirit who has not yet found his medium or made his mark. Like the young Icarus, the son of the mythological Dedalus, Stephen has yet to test his wings, and perhaps like the mythic son, he may fail when he does. He is hampered, he says, by two masters, the government of England that controls Ireland and the Catholic Church that clutches his conscience. Without the role model of a suitable father, Stephen drifts in Dublin literary society, working at a job that bores him, excluded by literary insiders he wishes to displace. His plight in part results from his age: he is just starting out, and he is at this moment hampered by grief and guilt concerning his mother. On a larger scale, his plight is a product of feeling trapped by a social context which is itself fettered by poverty and alcoholism.

STYLE

Stream of Consciousness

The stream-of-consciousness novel takes as its subject the interior thought sequence and patterns of associations which distinguish characters from one another. According to *A Handbook to Literature*, the stream-of-consciousness novel assumes that what matters most about human existence is how it is experienced subjectively. The interior level of experience is idiosyncratic, illogical, and disjointed and the "pattern of free psychological association ... determines the shifting sequence of thought and feeling." The work of Sigmund Freud (1856–1939) offered a structure and way of understanding different psychological levels or areas of consciousness, and some modern writers, such as Joyce, Virginia Woolf, and William Faulkner, drew upon Freud's theories as they used the stream-of-consciousness style.

In the eighteenth and nineteenth centuries, many English novels focused more on outer rather than inner events, and the plot was usually arranged in a linear fashion (as it is, for example, in Charles Dickens's *David Copperfield*). Typically, when these novels traced the inner thoughts and feelings of characters, they did so within the single idiom of the narrator. In Joyce's handling, the spontaneous flow of thoughts and associations which typify one character is presented in that person's own idiom or voice. In part, what Joyce undertakes in *Ulysses* is to write the novel from the inner world of characters' interior thinking, using their idiosyncratic language patterns.

In his review of the novel, Edmund Wilson explains that whereas earlier novelists presented their characters' inner thoughts in "one vocabulary and cadence," Joyce communicates "the consciousness of each of the characters . . . made to speak in the idiom proper to it." In this way, as Wilson explains, "Joyce manages to give the effect of unedited human minds, drifting aimlessly along from one triviality to another." For the inexperienced reader who brings to the novel expectations based on the nineteenth-century novel, the challenge is huge. Such a reader assumes that the novel will present first things first, that its characters will be introduced, that relationships will be explicit and clear, and so forth. However, in the case of *Ulysses*, the reader must experience the world of the novel from within each subjective consciousness as it is presented.

Autobiographical Novel

Ulysses is, in part, the portrait of Joyce as a slightly older young artist, back from Paris at the time of his mother's death and staying for a while in the Martello Tower rented by his friend, Oliver St. John Gogart. Joyce was educated by Jesuits, and in 1904, he taught in a boys' school in Dalkey, about a mile from the Martello Tower. Among his literary friends, he pronounced all manner of theories, not least of which was his biographical interpretation of *Hamlet*, and, with a fine tenor voice, he pursued a singing career, entering a singing competition and giving a couple of performances in the summer of 1904. The portrait in *Ulysses* of the feckless Simon Dedalus is based on John Joyce, and the Dedalus sisters reside at the same address in the novel that the Joyce family resided in that year: 7 St. Peter's Terrace, Cabra. The choice of June 16, 1904, as the time for this novel honors Joyce's first date with Nora Barnacle, an illiterate hotel maid who became the author's long-time companion and years later his beloved wife. Although Joyce was no longer as young as Stephen Dedalus is portrayed in *Portrait of the Artist as a Young Man*, and Stephen in *Ulysses* has not yet proved himself as a writer and artist, Joyce nonetheless identified closely with Stephen Dedalus. Stephen's moodiness, his egocentrism, and his creative puns and extensive web of literary and religious allusions parallel Joyce's own manner of thinking and speaking and express the author's feelings about Ireland and Catholicism.

Allusion

There are thousands of literary allusions in *Ulysses*, the countless corollaries to Homer's epic being only one constellation of correspondences. One recurrent allusion is to Shakespeare's *Hamlet*. The play is mentioned in the first episode, with comparisons drawn between Stephen's moodiness and the depressed self-absorption of Prince Hamlet and between the Danish castle and the Martello Tower. The allusion to *Hamlet* is prominent also in the Scylla and Charybdis episode, which takes place at the National Library. Here, Stephen Dedalus expounds on his biographical reading of *Hamlet*, basing his theory on suppositional information about Shakespeare's life. The theory, which he admits not believing himself, argues that Shakespeare identified with King Hamlet's ghost, that Prince Hamlet is aligned with Shakespeare's son, Hamnet, who died as a child, and that Queen Gertrude is the equivalent of the unfaithful Ann Hathaway. Using this play as a referent and embedding this theory in the novel, Joyce capitalizes on certain themes well known to

COMPARE
&
CONTRAST

- **1900s:** The eighteenth-century Martello Tower in which James Joyce lives in 1904 is a rented apartment, one of many small defensive forts built along Dublin Bay to defend the island against possible attack by Napoleon.

  Today: The Martello Tower is the site of the James Joyce Museum, a tourist stop for people who want to walk in the footsteps of Stephen Dedalus and Leopold Bloom.

- **1900s:** Ireland is predominantly a one-religion country with 85 percent of its population devout Catholics.

  Today: Still predominantly Catholic, Ireland is increasingly secular, and prohibitions by

  the Catholic Church on reproduction matters are ignored by increasing numbers of Irish people.

- **1900s:** While estimates on Irish consumption of alcohol are unavailable, the pub serves as a daily meeting place where the Irish drink, discuss local matters and politics, and sing along with musicians who gather together informally.

  Today: Between 1992 and 2002, estimates place the consumption rate of alcohol among the Irish as among the highest in Europe at 14.2 liters per adult annually.

---

readers familiar with Shakespeare's play. Parallels are suggested between the deceased King Hamlet, the betrayed husband and father of Prince Hamlet, and Leopold Bloom, who has an unfaithful wife and serves somewhat as a surrogate father for Stephen. There are other allusions to *Hamlet*: Stephen is apparently ousted by the so-called usurper Buck Mulligan (just as Hamlet's ascension to the throne is thwarted by his uncle, Claudius); and the tentative step-father relationship Stephen forms with Bloom may be an inexact reference to Hamlet's uneasy relationship with Claudius. The literary allusion offers a point of departure or contrast by which the present text can be understood. This is a novel much about a son's longing for a father (Homer set it up that way to begin with), and *Hamlet* is a Renaissance referent that also explores this theme. Joyce toys with the ideas of paternity and legacy and examines the forces that disrupt context and inheritance, situating his novel within the classical framework and extending it to Shakespeare's play, among probably hundreds of other well-known and lesser-known texts, all in order to place his novel in a literary tradition of which it is a product and which it aims to reroute. His assumption throughout is that the reader has read as much as he has.

HISTORICAL CONTEXT

Irish Struggle for Independence: From the 1860s to World War I

The term, home rule, refers to an Irish movement for legislative independence for Ireland from the United Kingdom, which began in the 1860s. In 1874, advocates for home rule won fifty-six seats in the House of Commons, and these men formed an Irish party of sorts in Westminster, led by Isaac Butts. Butts was followed by William Shaw in 1879 and by Charles Stewart Parnell in 1880. As Parnell led the movement, advocates for home rule won eighty-six seats in the 1885 parliamentary election and supported the liberal government of Prime Minister William Ewart Gladstone, who introduced the first home rule bill. It was defeated in 1886 in the House of Commons. Gladstone introduced a second bill in 1892, which passed through the House of Commons but was defeated in the House of Lords. The third time such a bill was presented to the House of Commons occurred in 1912 by Prime Minister Herbert Henry Asquith. This third piece of legislation passed the House of Commons, but in the House of Lords, a veto move was used to stall discussion for two years, by which time World War I had begun and Parliament decided to postpone discussion of home rule until after the conclusion of the war.

The Rise and Fall of Parnell

Charles Stewart Parnell is buried in Glasnevin, where in the novel May Dedalus is buried and Patrick Dignam's body is laid to rest. In the Lestrygonians episode, Parnell's brother, John Howard Parnell, is spotted in the corner of a pub, and in the Cyclops and Eumaeus episodes, Parnell is heatedly discussed, Bloom siding privately with Parnell rather than contributing to criticism of him. Indeed, by 1904, Parnell was, in every sense, gone but not forgotten.

Born June 27, 1846, Charles Stewart Parnell was educated at the University of Cambridge and became politically active as a young man when he began supporting the work of Isaac Butts for home rule. Parnell was elected to the House of Commons in 1874, and once there, he pursued an obstructionist policy, using filibusters to stall legislation and bring political and public attention to conditions and sentiments in Ireland. In 1879, Parnell headed the recently formed National Land League, which sought ultimately to remove English landlords from Ireland. When Parnell urged a boycott, he was arrested, and from Kilmainham Prison he issued a manifesto, inciting Irish peasants to refuse to pay their rent to English landlords. After this, he and Prime Minister Gladstone reached what was called the Kilmainham Treaty, in which the no-rent policy was abandoned and Parnell urged Irish people to avoid violence. Parnell was released on May 2, 1882, and just four days later, the chief secretary and undersecretary for Ireland, Lord Frederick Charles Cavendish and Thomas Burke, were murdered in Phoenix Park, Dublin, an event alluded to in the cabstand discussion in the Eumaeus episode and elsewhere in *Ulysses*. Much speculation surrounded the identity of the assassins, since this crime so effectively sabotaged Parnell's new strategy for peace in partnership with Gladstone's resolve to work for reform. Ultimately, the radical militant group, the Irish Invincibles, took responsibility for or was assigned responsibility for the murders. The aftermath was a split between Parnell and Gladstone, culminating in the end of the prime minister's government.

The death knell of Parnell's effectiveness as a leader sounded with the 1889 divorce case brought by Lieutenant William Henry O'Shea, a loyal supporter of Parnell, who named Parnell in an adultery charge. Proven guilty of this extramarital alliance in 1890, Parnell was ruined. He and Katherine O'Shea, who had been lovers for years, were married shortly after the O'Shea divorce was granted, causing further public scandal among both Irish and English, which exacerbated the divisions among the nationalists. Parnell fought in vain for the reunification of the nationalists until his death at Brighton on October 6, 1891. The schism persisted and contributed to the further delay of the discussion of home rule when World War I erupted.

CRITICAL OVERVIEW

Highlighting both the strengths and limitations of the novel, Edmund Wilson's 1922 review in *New Republic* is an excellent starting place for evaluating the critical reviews garnered by *Ulysses*. Wilson applauds the work for its "high genius," and at the same time, he asserts that Joyce "has written some of the most unreadable chapters in the whole history of fiction." Wilson calls Joyce's "technical triumph . . . the most faithful X-ray ever taken of the ordinary human consciousness." Wilson explains that Joyce shows all the ignobility of common people in such a way that readers sympathize with and respect them. According to Wilson, Joyce demonstrates "his extraordinary poetic faculty for investing particular incidents with universal significance." Yet Wilson faults Joyce's work on two counts: first, its form is dictated by the form of the *Odyssey* rather than emerging from its own immediate content; second, his literary imitative parody "interposes a heavy curtain between" readers and the novel's characters.

Frank Delaney described the divide among other critics in the 1920s:

> When the novel appeared . . . there seemed to be only two schools of thought—and criticism. Ford Madox Ford wrote: 'One feels admiration that is almost reverence for the incredible labours of this incredible genius.' But Alfred Noyes suggested that it was 'the foulest book that has ever found its way into print.'

Delaney quotes W. B. Yeats who commented that *Ulysses* amounted to "the vulgarity of a single Dublin day prolonged to seven hundred pages." Delaney also notes that the *Sunday Express* held that *Ulysses* was "The most infamously obscene book in ancient or modern literature"; and the *Daily Express* agreed: "Our first impression is that of sheer disgust."

Milo O'Shea as Leopold Bloom in the 1967 film version of James Joyce's Ulysses *(Ulysses Film Prod / The Kobal Collection)*

It was the Nausicaa episode which brought about the U.S. charge of obscenity and caused the *Little Review* to stop publishing installments of the novel. This decision led to the publication of the novel in France. After that, the furor brought attention to the novel and to Joyce, who was exonerated by the U.S. district court decision that the novel was not prurient. Joyce himself made little money from the novel, but when it "emerged from copyright" in 1992, many presses hurried to print and profit from the novel, as an anonymous reviewer explains in the January 18, 1992, *Economist*. Cyril Connolly in a 1999 issue of *New Statesman* mildly reports on the "revolutionary" technique that made it possible for Joyce "to create a mythical universe of his own." But he points out that Joyce was so much a part of the novel his "clock seemed literally to have stopped on June 16th, 1904."

The degree to which this revolutionary and controversial work came to be accepted is indicated in the widespread celebration of the one hundredth anniversary of what is called Bloomsday, on June 16, 2004. The occasion brought forth festivities, readings, and renewed critical attention for the novel. For example, two articles appeared in *Commonweal*. In one, Robert H. Bell writes of the "the enduring power" of *Ulysses*, which "has become the canonical twentieth-century novel." In the other, which is especially beautifully written, Mark Patrick Hederman describes the festival held in Dublin in 2004 and the new James Joyce Bridge that was opened on Bloomsday in 2004. He notes the irony that the country which initially "condemned and reviled" the work now makes Joyce "an Irish industry." Hederman points to the fact that *Ulysses* "describes the paralysis" of Dublin, depicting how "The twin forces of politics and religion had entrapped the Irish in alcoholism,

WHAT DO I READ NEXT?

- To prepare for reading *Ulysses*, people should first read James Joyce's *Dubliners* and then his *Portrait of the Artist as a Young Man* (both available from Norton [2005]), because *Ulysses* in a sense is the sequel to the collection of stories and the autobiographical novel.

- Originally published in 1930 and reprinted several times by Vintage Books, Stuart Gilbert's *James Joyce's "Ulysses"* is the essential starting place for decoding the novel. Gilbert worked closely with Joyce and got the author's approval for this interpretation of the novel. Gilbert's writing is formal and complex, but it expresses the vision of the novel Joyce himself hoped to impart to readers.

- Richard Ellmann wrote *James Joyce*, the definitive biography of Joyce, published by Oxford University Press in 1983.

- Virginia Woolf's *Mrs. Dalloway* (1925) is a stream-of-consciousness novel about a day in the post–World War I London life of Clarissa Dalloway, wife of a member of Parliament, as she prepares to give a party that night. An excellent annotated edition edited by Mark Hussey appeared in 2005.

---

sexual repression, and poverty." Writing of the improvements in the city and its culture since Joyce abandoned it in 1904, Hederman remarks that Joyce in a sense showed Dubliners the way to embrace "the new century's awareness of human possibility." He concludes that "Joyce's magisterial work ... incorporates the whole of humanity, unconscious as well as conscious."

CRITICISM

Melodie Monahan

Monahan has a Ph.D. in English and operates an editing service, The Inkwell Works. In the following essay, Monahan discusses some reader expectations and how in Ulysses *Joyce surprises with new technique and focus.*

Ulysses is an inordinately complex novel, in part because it unhinges readers' expectations of what a novel is supposed to be. Those who appreciate novels and know something of the form's development in England in the eighteenth and nineteenth centuries come to Joyce's novels expecting certain features with which they are familiar: a recognizable narrator or combination of narrators and a clear point of view; a mostly chronological storyline; a consistent style along with standard mechanical elements such as punctuation and quotation marks; introductory and concluding parts to sections which provide framework and ease comprehension. Without even knowing it, readers may come to Joyce's work with the assumption that the world created within the text is a single, palpable world, one that all the characters in the work inhabit and which readers can recognize and make sense of. (Indeed, in the history of the novel, authors have taken deliberate measures to make the work of fiction appear real and true, often attempting to pass the novel off as an historical record, as in for example Daniel Defoe's *Journal of the Plague Year* or Charlotte Brontë's *Jane Eyre*, in which latter case the first edition title page gives the additional information that the work is "an autobiography edited by Currer Bell.") While there are exceptions, of course, especially in novels that have fantastic elements, the genre typically asks readers to believe that its depiction is a cohesive presentation of the known world. But the stream-of-consciousness technique Joyce uses here suggests multiple worlds and multiple points of view, causing some readers to long for the comfortable singleness of vision a novel such as *Jane Eyre* presents. When such readers come to Joyce's novel, they quickly realize they are facing a work that appears to operate without rules or with the intention of ditching customary rules without explanation, one that seems deliberately opaque, intent on daunting readers, forcing them to rely on outside research and scholarship in order to decode what appears on many pages to be a labyrinth of nonsense. This essay explores some aspects of the quandary *Ulysses* generates in uninitiated Joyce readers and attempts to quell some of that dissonance, also pointing out secondary works that may help readers comprehend and appreciate *Ulysses*.

> JOYCE HERALDS A NEW PERIOD IN THE
> DEVELOPMENT OF THE NOVEL, ONE THAT DIRECTS
> READERS TO CONSIDER HOW SUBJECTIVE
> CONSCIOUSNESS CREATES EACH INDIVIDUAL'S
> PERCEPTION OF THE WORLD. . . ."

First, the narrator. Each of the three major divisions of the novel begins with a page that is blank except for a roman numeral; on the recto of this sheet a colossal letter fills much of the page followed by a much smaller letter or couple of words. These three beginnings are in the omniscient narrative voice readers may expect in a novel. In each beginning, then, readers' first impression may not be unsettling. They might assume that this voice narrates all text that does not begin with a dash, which Joyce uses as a substitute for an opening quotation mark to identify dialogue. Some text is, to be sure, in this narrative voice. But quite soon, for example, in the first episode, Telemachus, with the dream paragraph beginning, "Silently, in a dream she had come to him," the narrator makes some jumps that are so poetically smooth readers might miss the elisions. The narrator describes Stephen Dedalus's dream, describes the sea, and equates the sea with the white china bowl at his mother's bedside. In these steps inward, into the associative pattern of Stephen's mind, readers slide away from the objective omniscient narrator and into the inner reality of Stephen Dedalus. Two pages later, the jumps are neither poetic nor smooth; they seem disruptive. Buck Mulligan puts his arm on Stephen. The text reads: "Cranly's arm. His arm." Who is Cranly and does the pronoun refer to Cranly's or to Buck's arm? These are simple skips compared to those that follow in this long novel, but they indicate the way the narrator can vanish and references occur without explanation. Don Gifford's *"Ulysses" Annotated: Notes for James Joyce's "Ulysses"* explains that Cranly is Stephen's friend in Joyce's previous novel, *Portrait of the Artist as a Young Man* (1916); the assumption is that readers of this novel have read the previous one. Moreover, the stylistic point is that stream-of-consciousness technique presents readers with the associations of the character in whose

mind the connections make a certain sense; no explanation within that technique is allowed to bring readers up to speed. An added complication is that the third-person narrator is not always this voice which begins these divisions; indeed, the third-person voice is clearly different elsewhere in the novel, for example, in the sentimental style of the Nausicaa episode.

Next, the storyline. There are two basic ways of looking at the story that this novel tells: one using the classical model; one focusing on the day in Dublin. Given the title and Stuart Gilbert's book, *James Joyce's "Ulysses": A Study*, the novel is definitely linked to the classical hero and stories about him, the Greek Odysseus, whom the Romans called Ulysses. Joyce knew the parallels to the *Odyssey* would be hard for readers to deduce, so he wrote a schema for the novel and gave it to Stuart Gilbert to elucidate. Gilbert's book is itself a sophisticated academic writing, but it received Joyce's approval and thus presents what the author wanted to have said about the novel's organization. Though the eighteen sections of the novel are untitled, the corresponding titles taken from the *Odyssey* are assigned to them in the schema. Much scholarship examines the Homeric parallels to these episodes, drawing from Joyce's own guideline. The second story is more explicit and accessible: it is the hour-by-hour story of Leopold Bloom's day trip around Dublin on June 16, 1904. It is mainly his story of being away from home, but his story includes the partial stories of other Dubliners who are going about their lives on this day and whose paths crisscross through the hours of daylight and night that follow. An excellent source for visualizing this day's journey is provided in Frank Delaney's *James Joyce's Odyssey: A Guide to the Dublin of "Ulysses,"* which includes historical and contemporary photographs (from the 1900s and the 1980s) of the city along with city maps that explain the route and the spots of local interest where these Joycean Dubliners pause to engage with one another. In his introduction, Delaney remarks that *Ulysses* is for "many, a literary obstacle course." A poetic and colorful writer in his own right, Delaney laments that the novel is "lodged outside the reach of the people about whom it was written." This is true, and yet Delaney is able to deliver Joyce's novel into those people's hands, bringing the Dublin day into focus by introducing readers to the city as it was in 1904 and as it was in the 1980s when Delaney made his photographic tour.

Regarding style, it would take a long and erudite book to identify and explain all the styles Joyce uses in this novel. He makes the style match the subject in many places, as in the Aeolus episode in which Bloom visits the newspaper office and the novel's text is divided by newspaper headings. Elsewhere, Joyce parodies types of styles, as in the women's magazine style of the Nausicaa episode or the far more complex styles mimicking the development of the English language, which he attempts in the Oxen of the Sun episode. The virtuosity and breadth of these styles, the diversity and richness of the figures, puns, jokes, the complicated network of motifs (for example, the play on the word, throwaway, which refers to a horse running in the Gold Cup and a one-page advertisement handed out to pedestrians), all of this requires multiple readings, along with supportive scholarship, to begin to appreciate.

A couple of examples of this virtuosity may serve here. Delaney shows an almost Joycean zest in his appreciation of the puns that appear in the lunchtime Lestrygonians episode, in which Leopold Bloom enters a deli in search of his midday meal. Here is the interior monologue of Bloom as he eyes the display of food: "Sardines on the shelves. Almost taste them by looking. Sandwich? Ham and his descendants mustered and bred there." Delaney exclaims: "Bloom the Jew. Ham. Mustard. Bread. Grrr! Joyce!" For another example, the episode equated with the Homeric Sirens shows how Joyce uses his considerable knowledge of music (he had a trained tenor voice) when he writes about the sounds in the Ormond Hotel. Bloom enters the hotel intent on observing Blazes Boylan who has planned a 4 p.m. assignation with Bloom's wife, Molly. The jingle of Boylan's car after he leaves the hotel, the in-coming tapping of the blind piano tuner returning for his tuning fork, the drunken songs from the bar, the associations that certain songs elicit, and all the street sounds that penetrate this busy meeting place are conveyed in a symphony of language. Here is a description of the two barmaids' hair and what they hear as they lean out the hotel window to observe the viceregal cavalcade as it passes: "bronze from anear, by gold from afar, heard steel from anear, hoofs ring from afar, and heard steelhoofs ringhoof ringsteel." A sound poem, perhaps, but a passage like this may leave some readers feeling lost. Here is a description of one barmaid serving and Simon Dedalus lighting his pipe:

> With grace of alacrity . . . she turned herself. With grace she tapped a measure of gold whisky from her crystal keg. Forth from the skirt of his coat Mr. Dedalus brought pouch and pipe. Alacrity she served. He blew through the flue two husky fifenotes.

There may not be actual music described here, but there are many musical words: tapped, measure, pipe, fifenotes. To see what is happening in this scene is one thing; to appreciate the layers of stylistic choices is another.

The world that makes a single sense in this novel is the world within each consciousness. As Richard Ellmann explains in his insightful and highly readable *Ulysses on the Liffey*, the novel presents "a new odyssey in which most of the adventures occur inside the mind." The interiority of the text can come as a surprise and a hurdle to new Joyce readers, but if they know something of the character beforehand then tracking the idiosyncratic, associative patterns of his or her thoughts can convey the world as that character experiences it. For example, when Boylan walks out of the Ormond Hotel, Bloom, hunching over his dinner, sobs. He experiences the other man's departure as the outward sign of his wife's imminent betrayal; others in the hotel and Boylan himself cannot experience the moment this way. As Joyce shifts the focus inward in this and his other novels, *Portrait of the Artist as a Young Man* and the subsequent highly experimental and even more challenging *Finnegans Wake* (1939), he dramatizes the post-Freudian idea that dominated the modern period, the early decades of the twentieth century. The interior reality of the Joycean text, this stream of thoughts in the consciousness of separate people, asserts the sense that individuals experience, indeed even inhabit, separate worlds. These worlds are defined by the layered and much unconscious nexus of individuals' past experiences, their beliefs, their education, their current situation. The way the character thinks about experience becomes in the stream-of-consciousness novel the plot that is articulated. This interior journey supersedes or blots out an objective reality as fully as Bloom's lifted little finger blots out the sun. Nowhere is this interiority more obvious than in the hallucinatory journey into Nighttown, the Circe episode. Alcohol-induced, fatigue-induced, these surreal fantasies or dreams are the experiences of Leopold Bloom and Stephen Dedalus. It is as though the guilty conscience (what Stephen calls, using Middle English, the "Agenbite of inwit") designs the character's delirium, the most repressed fears or regret surfacing to excoriate the person who harbors them.

In the last analysis, or perhaps more so in the first analysis, readers need to hold on to some notion of why Joyce wrote the novel as he did, some notion of his purpose. In his excellent Preface to *Ulysses on the Liffey*, Ellmann states that Joyce's method was comic:

> He liked comedy both in its larger sense of negotiating the reconciliation of forces, and in its more immediate sense of provoking laughter. Sympathy and incongruity were his gregarious substitutes for pity and terror ... The comic method might take varied forms, malapropism or epigram, rolypoly farce or distant satire, parody or mock-heroics. But all its means must coalesce in a view which ... Joyce was willing to call his faith.

Ulysses is grounded in autobiographical details, many of which Delaney identifies, but it is more than autobiography in every sense. Ellmann cites a September 1920 letter Joyce wrote to Carlo Linatti, in which the author states his intention in writing *Ulysses* and its schema:

> My intention is not only to render the myth ... but also to allow each adventure (that is, every hour, every organ, every art being interconnected and interrelated in the structural scheme of the whole) to condition and even to create its own technique.

So in terms of authorial intention, it seems there were two emphases, among many: first, to use comedy to recreate Dublin on a particular day and in that setting to recreate ordinary Dubliners living their ordinary lives; second, to use myth as a vehicle and an impulse in choosing the diverse styles of that comedy. Joyce heralds a new period in the development of the novel, one that directs readers to consider how subjective consciousness creates each individual's perception of the world and one that invites readers to expand their awareness of literary history in order to see each work of literature in its greater historical and linguistic context, part of a continuum of culture and artistic expression.

Source: Melodie Monahan, Critical Essay on *Ulysses*, in *Novels for Students*, Thomson Gale, 2008.

Cormac Ó Gráda

In the following essay, Ó Gráda questions the validity of Joyce's familiarity with the Jewish community in Dublin and, therefore, the details and makeup of his characters and their surroundings in Ulysses.

> JOYCE'S QUEST FOR VERISIMILITUDE, HIS EAR FOR THE VARIETIES OF DUBLIN ENGLISH, AND HIS EYE FOR DUBLIN FOIBLES AND CHARACTERS, MAKE *ULYSSES* A RICH SOURCE FOR THE HISTORIAN OF IRELAND AND ITS CAPITAL CITY. THE SAME CANNOT BE SAID FOR HIS ACCOUNT OF IRISH JEWRY."

James Joyce left Dublin for good in October 1904 at the age of twenty-two. Dublin, Of course, never left him: "all my books are about Dublin," he liked to say. And the Joyce household's frequent address changes and Joyce's own flâneur habits meant that he knew his Dublin well. In *Ulysses* he wanted "to give a picture of Dublin so complete that if the city one day suddenly disappeared from the earth it could be reconstructed from my book" (as cited in Delany 10; see also Bulson). But how much of the topographical and other detail in *Ulysses* did he carry with him in his head? How much of it relied on letters from home and on the two brief return trips that he made in 1909 and 1912? Such questions are grist to the mill of Joyce scholarship. The same questions have been asked about Leopold Bloom. Critics still debate Bloom's compositional makeup. To some extent, he represented Joyce himself. He was also fashioned in part from Joyce's encounters in Dublin. Joyce's biographer Richard Ellmann has shown that Bloom was the same height and weight as one of Joyce's college friends and that he made a living as a billboard advertiser, like another acquaintance (Ellmann, *James Joyce* 374–75); and Bloom was not an uncommon Jewish name in Ireland.

In their search for Leopold's real-life alter ego, both Ellmann and Louis Hyman, author of *The Jews of Ireland*, canvassed the possible links between Leopold and practically every Jewish family named Bloom in Ireland. Ellmann, prompted by a throwaway remark by Dublin academic A. J. Leventhal on their first meeting in 1952, was fixated for a time on a case involving an Irish Bloom who was party to a suicide pact, while Louis Hyman peppered one of his main informants about fin de siècle Jewish Dublin, Jessie Bloom, with queries by mail about Pesach Bloom (her husband), Solomon Bloom, "one of the Lombard Street Blooms who married a daughter of Levy of Cork," "the Simon Bloom who was involved in the Wexford murder of 1910," Basseh Bloom, "probably a sister of Simon or some near relative," "an A. Bloom who was murdered in his saloon in Chicago in 1899," and the "Jacob Bloom [who] had a daughter named Bertha Jenny who was born in Sligo in 1900." Ellmann and Hyman both made far too much of even the most tenuous connections between Joyce's Bloom and real-life Dublin namesakes. The Simon Bloom murder had taken place in a photographer's shop in Wexford in 1910; for Ellmann, this "presumably" is how Milly, Leopold Bloom's daughter, came to work in a similar establishment in Mullingar. Louis Hyman even speculated whether Leopold was modeled in part on Benny Bloom, listed in the 1901 census as a traveler and still selling holy pictures in Dublin in the 1960s. However, since Benny joined the army at the age of twenty in 1901 and did not return to Dublin until 1916, he seemed an unlikely candidate. All these searches for Leopold Bloom's Dublin cousins turned out to be wild goose chases (Ellmann, *James Joyce* 375; Hyman 173–74).

Joyce lived mostly in the Hapsburg port city of Trieste while writing *Ulysses*. So was Leopold a Dublinized Middle European Jew? Joyce scholars (e.g. McCourt; Hartshorn) also have their answers to this question. Italian writer Italo Svevo, Jewish by birth though a convert to Roman Catholicism, once pleaded with Joyce's brother: "Tell me some secrets about Irishmen. You know your brother has been asking me so many questions about Jews that I want to get even with him" (Ellmann, *James Joyce* 374).

Of course, critics also debate Bloom's Jewishness. On the one hand, it is claimed that he did not qualify by strictly confessional criteria (compare Steinberg; Levitt, "Family of Bloom"). His mother, Ellen Higgins, was a gentile; his father converted in order to marry her; their son Leopold was neither circumcised nor bar mitzvahed; he married out, going through the motions of conversion to Catholicism in the process; he flouted the Jewish dietary laws, and proclaimed himself an atheist. On the other hand, in support of the Jewish Bloom there is the possibility that his maternal grandmother was a Hungarian Jew. But surely what matters most is that Bloom was perceived as (or even mistaken for) Jewish by others: in Cyclops he is dubbed "a new apostle to the gentiles" and the "new Messiah for Ireland" by the anti-Semitic "Citizen." The deity that he rejected was Jewish, and he always wore his Jewishness on his sleeve. For Joyce too, surely Bloom was an Irish Jew.

In part, the ongoing controversy about Bloom's Jewishness springs from rival definitions of Jewishness. But it overlooks a key issue: what was it to be an Irish Jew a century ago? In 1866, the year of Leopold Bloom's birth, Dublin contained no more than a few hundred Jews. The community, scattered thinly throughout middle-class Dublin, was in decline; it recorded only nine births in that year. Its status as a religious community was precarious: an English Jew who often made business trips to the city in the early 1870s was more than once summoned from his hotel on the Sabbath to make up the necessary minyan of ten adult males. The reason for the small size of the Jewish community was not (as the bigoted Garrett Deasy proclaimed in *Ulysses*) that Ireland had "never let them in" (Joyce 30:437–42); it was Irish economic backwardness. Ireland had long been a place of emigration, not immigration. Within a few years, however, the earliest representatives of an inflow that would define Irish Jewry for a century settled in Dublin. Thanks to these immigrants from a cluster of small towns and villages in northwestern Lithuania, Dublin's Jewish population exceeded two thousand by 1900, and it was nearly three thousand by 1914.

The half-dozen or so families that arrived in the 1870s settled first in run-down tenement housing. Some lived in Chancery Lane, not far from St. Patrick's Cathedral, "in a little square wherein stood the police station, joining the other foreigners—Italian organ-grinders, bear leaders, one-man-band operators, and makers of small, cheap plaster casts of saints of the Catholic church." Others lived north of the River Liffey on Jervis and Moore Streets, perhaps in order to be nearer Dublin's only synagogue at St. Mary's Abbey. Conditions were tough: Molly Harmel Sayers, a delicate child born in a Mercer Street tenement in 1878, "survived only because of the tender care bestowed on her by a drunken applewoman."

These plucky newcomers did not remain in the tenements for long. The first movers to the complex of small streets off Lower Clanbrassil Street and the South Circular Road on the southern edge of the city proper, where most of the community would settle, can be inferred from Thom's Directory (a source much favored by Joyce while writing *Ulysses*) and other sources. Harris Lipman and Jacob Davis were living in Oakfield Place by 1880, and Michael Harmel was living in Lombard Street West; Meyer Schindler was a tenant in nearby St. Kevin's Parade a year later. There they found purpose-built family housing, mostly rented out in three- or four-room terraced units. Others quickly followed, and by century's end the Lithuanian-Jewish presence stretched south across the South Circular Road as far as the Grand Canal. Robert Bradlaw, "prince" of the immigrant community, formed its first chevra (or prayer house) in 1883, at number 7 St. Kevin's Parade.

The area became Dublin's "Little Jerusalem." Few streets would ever become completely Jewish, or remain so for long. This was not the East End or the Lower East Side. Nonetheless, the area would boast a significant and unbroken Jewish presence for several decades. There is evidence of some confessional clustering within streets: the analysis of settlement patterns suggests that Jewish householders preferred to live next to Jewish neighbors.

Most of the newcomers, like the unfortunate Moses Herzog in the Cyclops episode of *Ulysses*, made their living as peddlers or credit drapers. This involved selling dry goods on credit to the poor, who were supposed to repay in weekly installments. Naturally, the peddlers became known as "weekly men." There were skilled craftsmen among the Lithuanian (or Litvak) immigrants too—cabinet-makers, shoemakers, tailors, cap-makers—some of whom worked for Jewish employers. But most of the immigrants lived up to the Yiddish dictum that "arbeiter far yennem was for a goy, nicht far a Yid." A few quickly graduated to petty moneylending: the most prominent machers among the first generation of Litvaks were nearly all moneylenders.

The Litvaks arrived with mind-sets formed in the small shtetls of Lithuania. In considering Leopold Bloom's Jewish milieu, this is very important. One hallmark of the Litvak community in the early years was quasi-endemic bickering about ritual and doctrine between factions within the community, and also between the immigrants and the "English" Jews in Ireland before them. In Cork the feuding between the Clein and Jackson factions lasted for years, to the bemusement of the local goyim. Blows and insults were often traded. In the wake of one reconciliation, Cork's rabbi was congratulated on the shalom in the community by the Chief Rabbi, but Cork's request for a new sefer torah was rejected, because the warring parties had beaten each other about the head with the previous one. In Limerick in early 1889 the police were notified when "the Chazan was knocked down, and the book used for the service was carried off." That dispute lasted for several years; in 1901 a row about the ethics of moneylending resulted in another bitter split in the community. In Belfast in November 1912 the defeat of the "English" Mitanglim in an election for the vice-president of the new synagogue (which had been under "English" control from the outset) prompted enthusiastic celebrations by the Litvak Haredim. These tensions were a central feature of Jewish life in Ireland life a century ago, yet, on the evidence of *Ulysses*, Joyce and Bloom were impervious to them.

Both contemporary reports and autobiographical memoirs testify to the Litvaks' intense religious orthodoxy (compare Bloom; Harris; Price). Consider the tragic deaths of Joseph and Rebecca Reuben, whose bodies were found hanging in their house on Walworth Road on a Saturday night in late March 1894. The Reubens were comfortably off, Joseph being a well-stocked wholesale draper. A near relative could offer no explanation for what the Dublin Evening Mail dubbed "the Jewish suicides." However, earlier that day two of Joseph's clients, whom he had accused of theft, had appeared before a civil court. According to the Freeman's Journal's reporter, it was believed that remorse for having brought two co-religionists to court on the Sabbath led to the Reubens' deaths.

According to the late Esther Hesselberg (née Birkahn), who grew up in Cork's "Jewtown" in the 1890s, so observant were Cork Jews that in the early days "nobody carried a handkerchief on the Sabbath." The shul provided spittoons for the "bronchitic baila batim" and Esther's brother related how "those kosher hillybillys were 'dead eye dicks' and never missed their target." In Dublin as in Cork, observant Jews refused to even handle money on the Sabbath, and the shabbas goyim who lit and stoked their fires and boiled their water were left their penny or two on the table or else collected it on a Sunday.

The newcomers from the east, some of them almost penniless on arrival, were not made welcome by their co-religionists already in Dublin.

This was a common pattern wherever East European Jews settled. Indeed, representatives of the mainly middle-class "English" community offered the glazier Jacob Davis, one of the first men (if not the first) to arrive from Lithuania, the considerable sum of £40 (enough then to employ an unskilled worker for a year or more, or about $8,000 in today's money) to betake himself and his panes of glass elsewhere. Long after the establishment of a grand "English" synagogue on Adelaide Road on the south side of the city in 1892, a majority of the Litvak faithful clung to their own rabbis and places of worship. In late 1889, as members of the Dublin "English" community rehearsed their annual show for the Montefiore Musical and Dramatic Club, a group of young Litvaks were establishing reading and lecture rooms in Curzon Street. The latter belonged to "the poorest class," "extremely anxious to raise their educational status," and welcoming gifts of books in English, German, and Hebrew. For a time in the 1900s the Adelaide Road shul suffered the indignity of having to pay a few poor Litvaks to attend in case they were needed to make up a minyan. The most successful of the Litvak men married into the "English" community, but that meant forsaking Little Jerusalem; "they all lived on this side of the system [. . .] and didn't have much to do with the foreigners on the other side."

The immigrants probably did not think much of the native gentiles at first either. Their attitudes towards non-Jews back in der heim were unflattering, to say the least. According to the Encyclopedia Judaica entry on Lithuanian Jewry:

> Lithuania was a poor country, and the mass of its inhabitants, consisting of Lithuanian and Belorussian peasants, formed a low social stratum whose national culture was undeveloped. The Jews, who had contacts with them as contractors, merchants, shopkeepers, innkeepers, craftsmen, etc. regarded themselves as their superior in every respect.

It surely stands to reason that the immigrants brought some of their superiority complexes with them to Ireland and that this conditioned their initial interaction with the host community. There are scattered hints that such was the case. Writer Leslie Daiken, who grew up in Little Jerusalem, recalled an earthy and unpleasant piece of Yiddish doggerel doing the rounds during his childhood, d presumably e r der heim: "Yashka Pandre ligt in drerd, Kush mein tokkes vee a ganze ferd (Jesus Christ lies in s——; kiss my arse the size

of a horse)" (Daiken 19). Yaski (or Yoshke) Pandre was a rude and offensive way of describing Catholics. An unpublished family memoir refers to drunken Galway neighbors in the 1880s as "horrible—all Yoshke Pandres." Much in the same vein is the currency in early twentieth-century Dublin of "laptzies" or "laptseh," a disparaging Yiddish term for gullible gentile clients (Schlimeel). The terms goy and shikse were also in widespread use; in those Jewish households that could afford an (invariably Catholic) domestic servant, she was called the shikse. Jessie Spiro Bloom's mother banned the use of the word in their home by the Grand Canal, but her parents were atypical. Her father shunned the "weekly payment" business because, according to Jessie, "the idea of taking a shilling a week from poor Irish people who were hardly able to repay it repelled him" (Bloom 23).

The immigrant community in the 1880s and 1890s was clannish and resilient and steeped in what economists and sociologists dub "social capital." It was wonderful at caring for its own, quickly establishing a vibrant and exclusive network of clubs and support groups. It was made up of immensely gregarious people, who had fun together. A police report dating the early noted: "They only associate with themselves [. . .] always trading when possible with one another." Chaim Herzog, future president of Israel and resident of Little Jerusalem (where he was known to his friends as Hymie) between 1917 and 1935, concurred. "Physically and psychologically, he remembered, "the Jewish community was closed in on itself. [. . .] Very few Jews mingled socially with non-Jews" (Herzog 9).

Ongoing day-to-day contact between native and newcomer in Little Jerusalem and its satellites in Belfast and Cork would erode such attitudes in due course. Initial suspicions, rudeness, and hostility on both sides gave way to mutual respect and, on occasion, close friendships and intimacy. Children helped to break the ice. Leslie Daiken's mother advised him not to have "anything to do with that rough crowd from the back streets," but he ignored her, and "could not find anything bad about them" (Yodaiken 30).

For most of their existence these Irish Little Jerusalems were successful experiments in multiculturalism. They are warmly remembered as such by both present and former residents of all faiths. Yet, almost certainly, negative stereotypes were still powerfully present on both sides up to

1904, when James Joyce left Dublin. Even in the 1920s it took a long time for "a [Jewish] trader from Hungary with his big red beard and a lot of children" to be accepted by the Litvaks.

The story of Leopold Bloom fits uncomfortably into the setting described here. The first false note concerns Bloom's putative birth in May 1866 at 52 Upper Clanbrassil Street. A Dublin Tourism plaque marks the spot today. Upper Clanbrassil Street links Little Jerusalem proper to Harold's Cross on the other side of the Grand Canal: presumably Joyce chose it with Little Jerusalem in mind. Yet, as we have seen, there was no Little Jerusalem in 1866. And although Peisa Harmel, at one time the wealthiest man in the Litvak community, lived on Upper Clanbrassil Street for a while in the 1880s and 1890s, the street never really formed part of Little Jerusalem. On Lower Clanbrassil Street, to the north of Leonard's Corner, it was a different story. That was "the kosher street where we go to do our shopping [with] foodstuffs that you cannot buy in O'Connor's, Burke's or Purcell's" (Yodaiken 29). But neither Joyce nor his interpreters made the distinction between the two Clanbrassil Streets. Joyce's quest for verisimilitude, his ear for the varieties of Dublin English, and his eye for Dublin foibles and characters, make *Ulysses* a rich source for the historian of Ireland and its capital city. The same cannot be said for his account of Irish Jewry. At a time when it was almost unimaginable for an Irish Jew to "marry out," Leopold Bloom, the son of a Hungarian-Jewish father and an Irish Protestant mother, married a Catholic. What stretches credibility even more is that Bloom could have blended into the immigrant Litvak community described above. Joyce paints a vivid and credible picture of the petty racist jibes inflicted on Bloom by the "Citizen" and others. But had Bloom stepped from the written page into the real-life Little Jerusalem of Joyce's day, his mixed parentage and his marrying out would almost certainly have ensured him a rather cold welcome from that quarter also. Much has been made of Joyce's references to several real-life inhabitants of the Jewish quarter. Louis Hyman identified Moses Herzog, featured in the Cyclops chapter (Joyce 240:31–34), as the peddler who lived at number 13 St. Kevin's Parade between 1894 and 1906. "Poor Citron," with whom Bloom spent "pleasant evenings," was Israel Citron, another peddler, who lived at number 17 between 1904 and 1908. "Mastiansky

[recte Masliansky] with the old cither" in the same passage in Calypso was Citron's next-door neighbor. But it is well known that Joyce lifted these and most of the Jewish names used in *Ulysses* from his copy of Thom's Directory, perpetuating some of the transcription errors in the directory in the process (Hyman 168, 185).

Citron and "Mastiansky," both natives of Lithuania, are supposed to have been Leopold Bloom's friends. But would their English have been fluent enough for nocturnal conversations with Bloom on topics such as "music, literature, Ireland, [. . .] prostitution, diet, the influence of gaslight or the light of arc and glowlamps on the growth of adjoining paraheliotropic trees, exposed corporation emergency dustbuckets" (Joyce 544:11–18)? Bloom's background and upbringing would almost certainly have precluded him from understanding Yiddish, the dominant language in the homes where he spent so many "pleasant times." Rudolph Bloom had attempted to pass on a little Hebrew and some knowledge of the Jewish scriptures to his son, but he was no Yiddish speaker. It is difficult to imagine the immigrants in the 1880s or 1890s switching to English, even if they could, for an outsider like Leopold Bloom.

And whatever about Leopold Bloom himself, it is simply inconceivable that Molly Bloom, that sensuous and earthy shikse, would have been offered the basket-chair normally reserved for Israel Citron when she and Bloom visited the Citron home in St. Kevin's Parade (Joyce 49:205–07). Nor by the same token is it easy to imagine the "funny sight" in the "Lestrygonians" episode of the pregnant "Molly and Mrs. Moisel [. . .] two of them together, their bellies out" on their way to a mothers' meeting (Joyce 132:391–92; Hyman 190). Most likely the pious residents of St. Kevin's Parade or Greenville Terrace would have shunned Leopold and Molly; Leopold for doing the unthinkable and marrying out (insofar as they would have regarded him as Jewish in the first place), and Molly for being the trollop who seduced him. So—to refer to the "Circe" episode of *Ulysses*—Harris Rosenberg, Moses Herzog, Joseph Goldwater, and others of the "circumcised" would have been far from "wail[ing] [. . .] with swaying arms [. . .] in pneuma over the recreant Bloom" (Joyce 444:3,219–25). Nor—given the social distance between the two groups—is it likely that an "English" Jew like Bloom would have been happy to work as a mere canvasser for one of the Litvak "weekly men."

The Litvaks differed from Leopold Bloom in yet another respect: while Bloom, like the Joyce family, were Parnellites in politics, in the early 1900s the Litvaks were still emphatically loyalist. Only a few years earlier they had celebrated Queen Victoria's diamond jubilee in 1897 with gusto, and during the Boer War they sided with the British, while the Catholic Irish tended to be pro-Boer. In the alleyways of Little Jerusalem, Jewish lads had fought "battles of sticks and stones with the Catholic boys, we representing the British and they the Boers [. . .]." When Joseph Edelstein, Jacob Elyan, Arthur Newman, and a few others established the short-lived Judaeo-Irish Home Rule Association in September 1908, they faced considerable opposition within their own community, and their first public meeting in Dublin's Mansion House ended "with several interruptions and a free fight."

Despite the huge literature on the Jewish content of *Ulysses*, and Joyce's reputation for being fastidious—indeed obsessive—about context and geography while writing it, it is hard not to conclude that his portrait of Leopold Bloom owed much more to information garnered during his time in Trieste (1904–1919) than to first-hand contacts with Irish Jews before leaving Dublin at the age of twenty-two. The very different character of Trieste Jewry—more urbane, more middle-class, more integrated, more western than their Dublin brethren—would have suited both Joyce and Bloom well. Though some Ostjuden had reached Trieste in the 1880s and 1890s, in 1910 nearly three-fifths of its Jews spoke either Italian or German as a first language. Bloom's agnosticism would have been more acceptable in a city where one Jew in five had renounced his or her faith, and where a significant proportion of marriages involving Jews were mixed.

Richard Ellmann began to work on his classic biography of Joyce in 1952, and he showed an interest in likely connections Joyce might have had with Irish Jewry from the start. In his quest for the Jewish in Joyce, he was sometimes reluctant to give up the hares he raised. Long after Louis Hyman had proven to him that the "dark complexioned Dublin Jew named Hunter," who rescued Joyce from a fracas outside a brothel in early 1904, was not Jewish at all, Ellmann continued to refer to him as "putative Jewish" (Ellmann, James Joyce 162, 230; Delany 53–54). And the Sinclair twins, William and Harry, whom Joyce met through the writer Padraic Colum, were thoroughly assimilated and only nominally Jewish (Hyman 148–49; Ellmann, James Joyce 579). Culturally and economically, Hunter and the Sinclairs were far removed from the exshtetl Litvaks represented by Moses Herzog, Israel Citron, et al.

Other aspects of *Ulysses* reinforce the suspicion that Joyce knew less of Jewish Dublin before he left in 1904 than his many interpreters suppose. The boycott against Jewish traders in Limerick earlier in that year would surely have been still fresh in Jewish minds on June 16, yet there is no explicit reference to it in the text. Indeed, for all the detailed references to Jewish custom and Jewish Dublin, there is no hard evidence that Joyce knew anybody in the Litvak community well. In his scrupulous identification of the real-life Jews named by Joyce, Louis Hyman, who did more than anyone to clarify what he called the "Jewish backgrounds of *Ulysses*," admitted as much. He evidently did so with reluctance. In the end, Ellmann too implicitly conceded that he had exaggerated the influence Dublin Jewry had on Joyce's creative imagination. Three decades after his first musings about Joyce's interests in Jews and Judaism, Ellmann declared that there was "not much in it" (Ellmann, as cited in Reizbaum, "Sennschrift" 1). It is surely telling that for all Joyce's empathy with the tribulations of Irish and world Jewry, there was no one in the Dublin Litvak community to whom he could address queries from Trieste. None of this, of course, takes away from the genius of James Joyce or *Ulysses*.

Source: Cormac Ó Gráda, "Lost in Little Jerusalem: Leopold Bloom and Irish Jewry," in *Journal of Modern Literature*, Vol. 27, No. 4, Summer 2004, pp. 17–26.

SOURCES

Bell, Robert H., "Bloomsday at 100," in *Commonweal*, Vol. 131, No. 10, May 21, 2004, pp. 15–17.

Connolly, Cyril, "Joyce Remembered," in *New Statesman*, Vol. 128, No. 4464, November 29, 1999, p. 55.

Delaney, Frank, *James Joyce's Odyssey: A Guide to the Dublin of "Ulysses,"* Holt, Rinehart, and Winston, 1981, pp. 9, 10, 18, 21, 89, 166, 176.

Ellmann, Richard, *Ulysses on the Liffey*, Oxford University Press, 1972, pp. xi, xiii, xvii.

Gifford, Don, and Robert J. Seidman, *"Ulysses" Annotated: Notes for James Joyce's "Ulysses,"* University of California Press, 1988, p. 16.

Hederman, Mark Patrick, "{Bloomsday at 100} in *Commonweal*, Vol. 131, No. 10, May 21, 2004, pp. 17–18.

Holman, C. Hugh, and William Harmon, *A Handbook to Literature*, Macmillan, 1986, p. 484.

Joyce, James, *Ulysses*, Vintage Books, 1990.

"Pull Out His Eyes, Apologize: James Joyce and His Interpreters," in *Economist*, Vol. 322, No. 7742, January 18, 1992, p. 91.

Schwarz, Daniel R., "Joyce's Schema for *Ulysses*," in *Reading Joyce's "Ulysses*,*"* St. Martin's Press, 1987, pp. 277–80.

Wilson, Edmund, Review of *Ulysses*, in *New Republic*, July 5, 1922, http://www.tnr.com/doc.mhtml?i = classic&s = Wilson070522 (accessed July 27, 2006).

FURTHER READING

Bulson, Eric, *James Joyce: An Introduction*, Cambridge University Press, 2006.

This introduction presents the essential information that will make reading Joyce's works easier for the beginner.

Emig, Rainer, ed., *"Ulysses": James Joyce*, Palgrave Macmillan, 2005.

This collection of recent essays gives an overview of scholarship on Joyce's novel and the divergent readings the novel has generated. Among the theoretical approaches included are gender and deconstruction.

Homer, *Odyssey*, translated by Robert Fagles, Penguin Group, 2006.

Homer's classical epic of the mythic journey home by Odysseus is translated by Fagles into modern idiom, making this the edition to choose for a first read.

Kertész, Imre, *Kaddish for a Child Not Born*, translated by Christopher C. Wilson and Katharina M. Wilson, Northwestern University Press, 1997.

This whole novel is a single, unbroken interior monologue in which the protagonist, a Holocaust survivor, reflects on his past, his childhood, a failed marriage, and his decision not to have children.

Glossary of Literary Terms

A

Abstract: As an adjective applied to writing or literary works, abstract refers to words or phrases that name things not knowable through the five senses.

Aestheticism: A literary and artistic movement of the nineteenth century. Followers of the movement believed that art should not be mixed with social, political, or moral teaching. The statement "art for art's sake" is a good summary of aestheticism. The movement had its roots in France, but it gained widespread importance in England in the last half of the nineteenth century, where it helped change the Victorian practice of including moral lessons in literature.

Allegory: A narrative technique in which characters representing things or abstract ideas are used to convey a message or teach a lesson. Allegory is typically used to teach moral, ethical, or religious lessons but is sometimes used for satiric or political purposes.

Allusion: A reference to a familiar literary or historical person or event, used to make an idea more easily understood.

Analogy: A comparison of two things made to explain something unfamiliar through its similarities to something familiar, or to prove one point based on the acceptedness of another. Similes and metaphors are types of analogies.

Antagonist: The major character in a narrative or drama who works against the hero or protagonist.

Anthropomorphism: The presentation of animals or objects in human shape or with human characteristics. The term is derived from the Greek word for "human form."

Anti-hero: A central character in a work of literature who lacks traditional heroic qualities such as courage, physical prowess, and fortitude. Anti-heroes typically distrust conventional values and are unable to commit themselves to any ideals. They generally feel helpless in a world over which they have no control. Anti-heroes usually accept, and often celebrate, their positions as social outcasts.

Apprenticeship Novel: See *Bildungsroman*

Archetype: The word archetype is commonly used to describe an original pattern or model from which all other things of the same kind are made. This term was introduced to literary criticism from the psychology of Carl Jung. It expresses Jung's theory that behind every person's "unconscious," or repressed memories of the past, lies the "collective unconscious" of the human race: memories of the countless typical experiences of our ancestors. These memories are said to prompt illogical associations that trigger powerful emotions in the reader. Often, the emotional process is primitive, even primordial. Archetypes are the literary images that grow out of the "collective unconscious." They appear in literature as incidents and plots that repeat basic patterns of life. They may also appear as stereotyped characters.

Avant-garde: French term meaning "vanguard." It is used in literary criticism to describe new writing that rejects traditional approaches to literature in favor of innovations in style or content.

B

Beat Movement: A period featuring a group of American poets and novelists of the 1950s and 1960s—including Jack Kerouac, Allen Ginsberg, Gregory Corso, William S. Burroughs, and Lawrence Ferlinghetti—who rejected established social and literary values. Using such techniques as stream of consciousness writing and jazz-influenced free verse and focusing on unusual or abnormal states of mind—generated by religious ecstasy or the use of drugs—the Beat writers aimed to create works that were unconventional in both form and subject matter.

Bildungsroman: A German word meaning "novel of development." The *bildungsroman* is a study of the maturation of a youthful character, typically brought about through a series of social or sexual encounters that lead to self-awareness. *Bildungsroman* is used interchangeably with *erziehungsroman,* a novel of initiation and education. When a *bildungsroman* is concerned with the development of an artist (as in James Joyce's *A Portrait of the Artist as a Young Man*), it is often termed a *kunstlerroman.*

Black Aesthetic Movement: A period of artistic and literary development among African Americans in the 1960s and early 1970s. This was the first major African-American artistic movement since the Harlem Renaissance and was closely paralleled by the civil rights and black power movements. The black aesthetic writers attempted to produce works of art that would be meaningful to the black masses. Key figures in black aesthetics included one of its founders, poet and playwright Amiri Baraka, formerly known as LeRoi Jones; poet and essayist Haki R. Madhubuti, formerly Don L. Lee; poet and playwright Sonia Sanchez; and dramatist Ed Bullins.

Black Humor: Writing that places grotesque elements side by side with humorous ones in an attempt to shock the reader, forcing him or her to laugh at the horrifying reality of a disordered world.

Burlesque: Any literary work that uses exaggeration to make its subject appear ridiculous, either by treating a trivial subject with profound seriousness or by treating a dignified subject frivolously. The word "burlesque" may also be used as an adjective, as in "burlesque show," to mean "striptease act."

C

Character: Broadly speaking, a person in a literary work. The actions of characters are what constitute the plot of a story, novel, or poem. There are numerous types of characters, ranging from simple, stereotypical figures to intricate, multifaceted ones. In the techniques of anthropomorphism and personification, animals—and even places or things—can assume aspects of character. "Characterization" is the process by which an author creates vivid, believable characters in a work of art. This may be done in a variety of ways, including (1) direct description of the character by the narrator; (2) the direct presentation of the speech, thoughts, or actions of the character; and (3) the responses of other characters to the character. The term "character" also refers to a form originated by the ancient Greek writer Theophrastus that later became popular in the seventeenth and eighteenth centuries. It is a short essay or sketch of a person who prominently displays a specific attribute or quality, such as miserliness or ambition.

Climax: The turning point in a narrative, the moment when the conflict is at its most intense. Typically, the structure of stories, novels, and plays is one of rising action, in which tension builds to the climax, followed by falling action, in which tension lessens as the story moves to its conclusion.

Colloquialism: A word, phrase, or form of pronunciation that is acceptable in casual conversation but not in formal, written communication. It is considered more acceptable than slang.

Coming of Age Novel: See *Bildungsroman*

Concrete: Concrete is the opposite of abstract, and refers to a thing that actually exists or a description that allows the reader to experience an object or concept with the senses.

Connotation: The impression that a word gives beyond its defined meaning. Connotations may be universally understood or may be significant only to a certain group.

Convention: Any widely accepted literary device, style, or form.

D

Denotation: The definition of a word, apart from the impressions or feelings it creates (connotations) in the reader.

Denouement: A French word meaning "the unknotting." In literary criticism, it denotes the resolution of conflict in fiction or drama. The *denouement* follows the climax and provides an outcome to the primary plot situation as well as an explanation of secondary plot complications. The *denouement* often involves a character's recognition of his or her state of mind or moral condition.

Description: Descriptive writing is intended to allow a reader to picture the scene or setting in which the action of a story takes place. The form this description takes often evokes an intended emotional response—a dark, spooky graveyard will evoke fear, and a peaceful, sunny meadow will evoke calmness.

Dialogue: In its widest sense, dialogue is simply conversation between people in a literary work; in its most restricted sense, it refers specifically to the speech of characters in a drama. As a specific literary genre, a "dialogue" is a composition in which characters debate an issue or idea.

Diction: The selection and arrangement of words in a literary work. Either or both may vary depending on the desired effect. There are four general types of diction: "formal," used in scholarly or lofty writing; "informal," used in relaxed but educated conversation; "colloquial," used in everyday speech; and "slang," containing newly coined words and other terms not accepted in formal usage.

Didactic: A term used to describe works of literature that aim to teach some moral, religious, political, or practical lesson. Although didactic elements are often found in artistically pleasing works, the term "didactic" usually refers to literature in which the message is more important than the form. The term may also be used to criticize a work that the critic finds "overly didactic," that is, heavy-handed in its delivery of a lesson.

Doppelganger: A literary technique by which a character is duplicated (usually in the form of an alter ego, though sometimes as a ghostly counterpart) or divided into two distinct, usually opposite personalities. The use of this character device is widespread in nineteenth- and twentieth-century literature, and indicates a growing awareness among authors that the "self" is really a composite of many "selves."

Double Entendre: A corruption of a French phrase meaning "double meaning." The term is used to indicate a word or phrase that is deliberately ambiguous, especially when one of the meanings is risqué or improper.

Dramatic Irony: Occurs when the audience of a play or the reader of a work of literature knows something that a character in the work itself does not know. The irony is in the contrast between the intended meaning of the statements or actions of a character and the additional information understood by the audience.

Dystopia: An imaginary place in a work of fiction where the characters lead dehumanized, fearful lives.

E

Edwardian: Describes cultural conventions identified with the period of the reign of Edward VII of England (1901-1910). Writers of the Edwardian Age typically displayed a strong reaction against the propriety and conservatism of the Victorian Age. Their work often exhibits distrust of authority in religion, politics, and art and expresses strong doubts about the soundness of conventional values.

Empathy: A sense of shared experience, including emotional and physical feelings, with someone or something other than oneself. Empathy is often used to describe the response of a reader to a literary character.

Enlightenment, The: An eighteenth-century philosophical movement. It began in France but had a wide impact throughout Europe and America. Thinkers of the Enlightenment valued reason and believed that both the individual and society could achieve a state of perfection. Corresponding to this essentially humanist vision was a resistance to religious authority.

Epigram: A saying that makes the speaker's point quickly and concisely. Often used to preface a novel.

Epilogue: A concluding statement or section of a literary work. In dramas, particularly those of the seventeenth and eighteenth centuries, the epilogue is a closing speech, often in verse, delivered by an actor at the end of a play and spoken directly to the audience.

Epiphany: A sudden revelation of truth inspired by a seemingly trivial incident.

Episode: An incident that forms part of a story and is significantly related to it. Episodes may be either self-contained narratives or events that depend on a larger context for their sense and importance.

Epistolary Novel: A novel in the form of letters. The form was particularly popular in the eighteenth century.

Epithet: A word or phrase, often disparaging or abusive, that expresses a character trait of someone or something.

Existentialism: A predominantly twentieth-century philosophy concerned with the nature and perception of human existence. There are two major strains of existentialist thought: atheistic and Christian. Followers of atheistic existentialism believe that the individual is alone in a godless universe and that the basic human condition is one of suffering and loneliness. Nevertheless, because there are no fixed values, individuals can create their own characters—indeed, they can shape themselves—through the exercise of free will. The atheistic strain culminates in and is popularly associated with the works of Jean-Paul Sartre. The Christian existentialists, on the other hand, believe that only in God may people find freedom from life's anguish. The two strains hold certain beliefs in common: that existence cannot be fully understood or described through empirical effort; that anguish is a universal element of life; that individuals must bear responsibility for their actions;

and that there is no common standard of behavior or perception for religious and ethical matters.

Expatriates: See *Expatriatism*

Expatriatism: The practice of leaving one's country to live for an extended period in another country.

Exposition: Writing intended to explain the nature of an idea, thing, or theme. Expository writing is often combined with description, narration, or argument. In dramatic writing, the exposition is the introductory material which presents the characters, setting, and tone of the play.

Expressionism: An indistinct literary term, originally used to describe an early twentieth-century school of German painting. The term applies to almost any mode of unconventional, highly subjective writing that distorts reality in some way.

F

Fable: A prose or verse narrative intended to convey a moral. Animals or inanimate objects with human characteristics often serve as characters in fables.

Falling Action: See *Denouement*

Fantasy: A literary form related to mythology and folklore. Fantasy literature is typically set in non-existent realms and features supernatural beings.

Farce: A type of comedy characterized by broad humor, outlandish incidents, and often vulgar subject matter.

Femme fatale: A French phrase with the literal translation "fatal woman." A *femme fatale* is a sensuous, alluring woman who often leads men into danger or trouble.

Fiction: Any story that is the product of imagination rather than a documentation of fact. characters and events in such narratives may be based in real life but their ultimate form and configuration is a creation of the author.

Figurative Language: A technique in writing in which the author temporarily interrupts the order, construction, or meaning of the writing for a particular effect. This interruption takes the form of one or more figures of speech such as hyperbole, irony, or simile. Figurative language is the opposite of literal language, in which every word is truthful, accurate, and free of exaggeration or embellishment.

Figures of Speech: Writing that differs from customary conventions for construction, meaning, order, or significance for the purpose of a special meaning or effect. There are two major types of figures of speech: rhetorical figures, which do not make changes in the meaning of the words, and tropes, which do.

Fin de siecle: A French term meaning "end of the century." The term is used to denote the last decade of the nineteenth century, a transition period when writers and other artists abandoned old conventions and looked for new techniques and objectives.

First Person: See *Point of View*

Flashback: A device used in literature to present action that occurred before the beginning of the story. Flashbacks are often introduced as the dreams or recollections of one or more characters.

Foil: A character in a work of literature whose physical or psychological qualities contrast strongly with, and therefore highlight, the corresponding qualities of another character.

Folklore: Traditions and myths preserved in a culture or group of people. Typically, these are passed on by word of mouth in various forms—such as legends, songs, and proverbs—or preserved in customs and ceremonies. This term was first used by W. J. Thoms in 1846.

Folktale: A story originating in oral tradition. Folktales fall into a variety of categories, including legends, ghost stories, fairy tales, fables, and anecdotes based on historical figures and events.

Foreshadowing: A device used in literature to create expectation or to set up an explanation of later developments.

Form: The pattern or construction of a work which identifies its genre and distinguishes it from other genres.

G

Genre: A category of literary work. In critical theory, genre may refer to both the content of a given work—tragedy, comedy, pastoral— and to its form, such as poetry, novel, or drama.

Gilded Age: A period in American history during the 1870s characterized by political corruption and materialism. A number of important novels of social and political criticism were written during this time.

Gothicism: In literary criticism, works characterized by a taste for the medieval or morbidly attractive. A gothic novel prominently features elements of horror, the supernatural, gloom, and violence: clanking chains, terror, charnel houses, ghosts, medieval castles, and mysteriously slamming doors. The term "gothic novel" is also applied to novels that lack elements of the traditional Gothic setting but that create a similar atmosphere of terror or dread.

Grotesque: In literary criticism, the subject matter of a work or a style of expression characterized by exaggeration, deformity, freakishness, and disorder. The grotesque often includes an element of comic absurdity.

H

Harlem Renaissance: The Harlem Renaissance of the 1920s is generally considered the first significant movement of black writers and artists in the United States. During this period, new and established black writers published more fiction and poetry than ever before, the first influential black literary journals were established, and black authors and artists received their first widespread recognition and serious critical appraisal. Among the major writers associated with this period are Claude McKay, Jean Toomer, Countee Cullen, Langston Hughes, Arna Bontemps, Nella Larsen, and Zora Neale Hurston.

Hero/Heroine: The principal sympathetic character (male or female) in a literary work. Heroes and heroines typically exhibit admirable traits: idealism, courage, and integrity, for example.

Holocaust Literature: Literature influenced by or written about the Holocaust of World War II. Such literature includes true stories of survival in concentration camps, escape, and life after the war, as well as fictional works and poetry.

Humanism: A philosophy that places faith in the dignity of humankind and rejects the medieval perception of the individual as a weak, fallen creature. "Humanists" typically believe in the perfectibility of human nature and view reason and education as the means to that end.

Hyperbole: In literary criticism, deliberate exaggeration used to achieve an effect.

I

Idiom: A word construction or verbal expression closely associated with a given language.

Image: A concrete representation of an object or sensory experience. Typically, such a representation helps evoke the feelings associated with the object or experience itself. Images are either "literal" or "figurative." Literal images are especially concrete and involve little or no extension of the obvious meaning of the words used to express them. Figurative images do not follow the literal meaning of the words exactly. Images in literature are usually visual, but the term "image" can also refer to the representation of any sensory experience.

Imagery: The array of images in a literary work. Also, figurative language.

In medias res: A Latin term meaning "in the middle of things." It refers to the technique of beginning a story at its midpoint and then using various flashback devices to reveal previous action.

Interior Monologue: A narrative technique in which characters' thoughts are revealed in a way that appears to be uncontrolled by the author. The interior monologue typically aims to reveal the inner self of a character. It portrays emotional experiences as they occur at both a conscious and unconscious level. images are often used to represent sensations or emotions.

Irony: In literary criticism, the effect of language in which the intended meaning is the opposite of what is stated.

J

Jargon: Language that is used or understood only by a select group of people. Jargon may refer to terminology used in a certain profession, such as computer jargon, or it may refer to any nonsensical language that is not understood by most people.

L

Leitmotiv: See *Motif*

Literal Language: An author uses literal language when he or she writes without exaggerating or embellishing the subject matter and without any tools of figurative language.

Lost Generation: A term first used by Gertrude Stein to describe the post-World War I generation of American writers: men and women haunted by a sense of betrayal and emptiness brought about by the destructiveness of the war.

M

Mannerism: Exaggerated, artificial adherence to a literary manner or style. Also, a popular style of the visual arts of late sixteenth-century Europe that was marked by elongation of the human form and by intentional spatial distortion. Literary works that are self-consciously high-toned and artistic are often said to be "mannered."

Metaphor: A figure of speech that expresses an idea through the image of another object. Metaphors suggest the essence of the first object by identifying it with certain qualities of the second object.

Modernism: Modern literary practices. Also, the principles of a literary school that lasted from roughly the beginning of the twentieth century until the end of World War II. Modernism is defined by its rejection of the literary conventions of the nineteenth century and by its opposition to conventional morality, taste, traditions, and economic values.

Mood: The prevailing emotions of a work or of the author in his or her creation of the work. The mood of a work is not always what might be expected based on its subject matter.

Motif: A theme, character type, image, metaphor, or other verbal element that recurs throughout a single work of literature or occurs in a number of different works over a period of time.

Myth: An anonymous tale emerging from the traditional beliefs of a culture or social unit. Myths use supernatural explanations for natural phenomena. They may also explain cosmic issues like creation and death. Collections of myths, known as mythologies, are common to all cultures and language, in which every word is truthful, accurate, and free of exaggeration or embellishment.

Figures of Speech: Writing that differs from customary conventions for construction, meaning, order, or significance for the purpose of a special meaning or effect. There are two major types of figures of speech: rhetorical figures, which do not make changes in the meaning of the words, and tropes, which do.

Fin de siecle: A French term meaning "end of the century." The term is used to denote the last decade of the nineteenth century, a transition period when writers and other artists abandoned old conventions and looked for new techniques and objectives.

First Person: See *Point of View*

Flashback: A device used in literature to present action that occurred before the beginning of the story. Flashbacks are often introduced as the dreams or recollections of one or more characters.

Foil: A character in a work of literature whose physical or psychological qualities contrast strongly with, and therefore highlight, the corresponding qualities of another character.

Folklore: Traditions and myths preserved in a culture or group of people. Typically, these are passed on by word of mouth in various forms—such as legends, songs, and proverbs—or preserved in customs and ceremonies. This term was first used by W. J. Thoms in 1846.

Folktale: A story originating in oral tradition. Folktales fall into a variety of categories, including legends, ghost stories, fairy tales, fables, and anecdotes based on historical figures and events.

Foreshadowing: A device used in literature to create expectation or to set up an explanation of later developments.

Form: The pattern or construction of a work which identifies its genre and distinguishes it from other genres.

G

Genre: A category of literary work. In critical theory, genre may refer to both the content of a given work—tragedy, comedy, pastoral—

and to its form, such as poetry, novel, or drama.

Gilded Age: A period in American history during the 1870s characterized by political corruption and materialism. A number of important novels of social and political criticism were written during this time.

Gothicism: In literary criticism, works characterized by a taste for the medieval or morbidly attractive. A gothic novel prominently features elements of horror, the supernatural, gloom, and violence: clanking chains, terror, charnel houses, ghosts, medieval castles, and mysteriously slamming doors. The term "gothic novel" is also applied to novels that lack elements of the traditional Gothic setting but that create a similar atmosphere of terror or dread.

Grotesque: In literary criticism, the subject matter of a work or a style of expression characterized by exaggeration, deformity, freakishness, and disorder. The grotesque often includes an element of comic absurdity.

H

Harlem Renaissance: The Harlem Renaissance of the 1920s is generally considered the first significant movement of black writers and artists in the United States. During this period, new and established black writers published more fiction and poetry than ever before, the first influential black literary journals were established, and black authors and artists received their first widespread recognition and serious critical appraisal. Among the major writers associated with this period are Claude McKay, Jean Toomer, Countee Cullen, Langston Hughes, Arna Bontemps, Nella Larsen, and Zora Neale Hurston.

Hero/Heroine: The principal sympathetic character (male or female) in a literary work. Heroes and heroines typically exhibit admirable traits: idealism, courage, and integrity, for example.

Holocaust Literature: Literature influenced by or written about the Holocaust of World War II. Such literature includes true stories of survival in concentration camps, escape, and life after the war, as well as fictional works and poetry.

Humanism: A philosophy that places faith in the dignity of humankind and rejects the medieval perception of the individual as a weak, fallen creature. "Humanists" typically believe in the perfectibility of human nature and view reason and education as the means to that end.

Hyperbole: In literary criticism, deliberate exaggeration used to achieve an effect.

I

Idiom: A word construction or verbal expression closely associated with a given language.

Image: A concrete representation of an object or sensory experience. Typically, such a representation helps evoke the feelings associated with the object or experience itself. Images are either "literal" or "figurative." Literal images are especially concrete and involve little or no extension of the obvious meaning of the words used to express them. Figurative images do not follow the literal meaning of the words exactly. Images in literature are usually visual, but the term "image" can also refer to the representation of any sensory experience.

Imagery: The array of images in a literary work. Also, figurative language.

In medias res: A Latin term meaning "in the middle of things." It refers to the technique of beginning a story at its midpoint and then using various flashback devices to reveal previous action.

Interior Monologue: A narrative technique in which characters' thoughts are revealed in a way that appears to be uncontrolled by the author. The interior monologue typically aims to reveal the inner self of a character. It portrays emotional experiences as they occur at both a conscious and unconscious level. images are often used to represent sensations or emotions.

Irony: In literary criticism, the effect of language in which the intended meaning is the opposite of what is stated.

J

Jargon: Language that is used or understood only by a select group of people. Jargon may refer to terminology used in a certain profession, such as computer jargon, or it may refer to any nonsensical language that is not understood by most people.

L

Leitmotiv: See *Motif*

Literal Language: An author uses literal language when he or she writes without exaggerating or embellishing the subject matter and without any tools of figurative language.

Lost Generation: A term first used by Gertrude Stein to describe the post-World War I generation of American writers: men and women haunted by a sense of betrayal and emptiness brought about by the destructiveness of the war.

M

Mannerism: Exaggerated, artificial adherence to a literary manner or style. Also, a popular style of the visual arts of late sixteenth-century Europe that was marked by elongation of the human form and by intentional spatial distortion. Literary works that are self-consciously high-toned and artistic are often said to be "mannered."

Metaphor: A figure of speech that expresses an idea through the image of another object. Metaphors suggest the essence of the first object by identifying it with certain qualities of the second object.

Modernism: Modern literary practices. Also, the principles of a literary school that lasted from roughly the beginning of the twentieth century until the end of World War II. Modernism is defined by its rejection of the literary conventions of the nineteenth century and by its opposition to conventional morality, taste, traditions, and economic values.

Mood: The prevailing emotions of a work or of the author in his or her creation of the work. The mood of a work is not always what might be expected based on its subject matter.

Motif: A theme, character type, image, metaphor, or other verbal element that recurs throughout a single work of literature or occurs in a number of different works over a period of time.

Myth: An anonymous tale emerging from the traditional beliefs of a culture or social unit. Myths use supernatural explanations for natural phenomena. They may also explain cosmic issues like creation and death. Collections of myths, known as mythologies, are common to all cultures and nations, but the best-known myths belong to the Norse, Roman, and Greek mythologies.

N

Narration: The telling of a series of events, real or invented. A narration may be either a simple narrative, in which the events are recounted chronologically, or a narrative with a plot, in which the account is given in a style reflecting the author's artistic concept of the story. Narration is sometimes used as a synonym for "storyline."

Narrative: A verse or prose accounting of an event or sequence of events, real or invented. The term is also used as an adjective in the sense "method of narration." For example, in literary criticism, the expression "narrative technique" usually refers to the way the author structures and presents his or her story.

Narrator: The teller of a story. The narrator may be the author or a character in the story through whom the author speaks.

Naturalism: A literary movement of the late nineteenth and early twentieth centuries. The movement's major theorist, French novelist Emile Zola, envisioned a type of fiction that would examine human life with the objectivity of scientific inquiry. The Naturalists typically viewed human beings as either the products of "biological determinism," ruled by hereditary instincts and engaged in an endless struggle for survival, or as the products of "socioeconomic determinism," ruled by social and economic forces beyond their control. In their works, the Naturalists generally ignored the highest levels of society and focused on degradation: poverty, alcoholism, prostitution, insanity, and disease.

Noble Savage: The idea that primitive man is noble and good but becomes evil and corrupted as he becomes civilized. The concept of the noble savage originated in the Renaissance period but is more closely identified with such later writers as Jean-Jacques Rousseau and Aphra Behn.

Novel: A long fictional narrative written in prose, which developed from the novella and other early forms of narrative. A novel is usually organized under a plot or theme with a focus on character development and action.

Novel of Ideas: A novel in which the examination of intellectual issues and concepts takes precedence over characterization or a traditional storyline.

Novel of Manners: A novel that examines the customs and mores of a cultural group.

Novella: An Italian term meaning "story." This term has been especially used to describe fourteenth-century Italian tales, but it also refers to modern short novels.

O

Objective Correlative: An outward set of objects, a situation, or a chain of events corresponding to an inward experience and evoking this experience in the reader. The term frequently appears in modern criticism in discussions of authors' intended effects on the emotional responses of readers.

Objectivity: A quality in writing characterized by the absence of the author's opinion or feeling about the subject matter. Objectivity is an important factor in criticism.

Oedipus Complex: A son's amorous obsession with his mother. The phrase is derived from the story of the ancient Theban hero Oedipus, who unknowingly killed his father and married his mother.

Omniscience: See *Point of View*

Onomatopoeia: The use of words whose sounds express or suggest their meaning. In its simplest sense, onomatopoeia may be represented by words that mimic the sounds they denote such as "hiss" or "meow." At a more subtle level, the pattern and rhythm of sounds and rhymes of a line or poem may be onomatopoeic.

Oxymoron: A phrase combining two contradictory terms. Oxymorons may be intentional or unintentional.

P

Parable: A story intended to teach a moral lesson or answer an ethical question.

Paradox: A statement that appears illogical or contradictory at first, but may actually point to an underlying truth.

Parallelism: A method of comparison of two ideas in which each is developed in the same grammatical structure.

Parody: In literary criticism, this term refers to an imitation of a serious literary work or the signature style of a particular author in a ridiculous manner. A typical parody adopts the style of the original and applies it to an inappropriate subject for humorous effect. Parody is a form of satire and could be considered the literary equivalent of a caricature or cartoon.

Pastoral: A term derived from the Latin word "pastor," meaning shepherd. A pastoral is a literary composition on a rural theme. The conventions of the pastoral were originated by the third-century Greek poet Theocritus, who wrote about the experiences, love affairs, and pastimes of Sicilian shepherds. In a pastoral, characters and language of a courtly nature are often placed in a simple setting. The term pastoral is also used to classify dramas, elegies, and lyrics that exhibit the use of country settings and shepherd characters.

Pen Name: See *Pseudonym*

Persona: A Latin term meaning "mask." *Personae* are the characters in a fictional work of literature. The *persona* generally functions as a mask through which the author tells a story in a voice other than his or her own. A *persona* is usually either a character in a story who acts as a narrator or an "implied author," a voice created by the author to act as the narrator for himself or herself.

Personification: A figure of speech that gives human qualities to abstract ideas, animals, and inanimate objects.

Picaresque Novel: Episodic fiction depicting the adventures of a roguish central character ("picaro" is Spanish for "rogue"). The picaresque hero is commonly a low-born but clever individual who wanders into and out of various affairs of love, danger, and farcical intrigue. These involvements may take place at all social levels and typically present a humorous and wide-ranging satire of a given society.

Plagiarism: Claiming another person's written material as one's own. Plagiarism can take the form of direct, word-for-word copying or the theft of the substance or idea of the work.

Plot: In literary criticism, this term refers to the pattern of events in a narrative or drama. In its simplest sense, the plot guides the author in composing the work and helps the reader follow the work. Typically, plots exhibit causality and unity and have a beginning, a middle, and an end. Sometimes, however, a plot may consist of a series of disconnected events, in which case it is known as an "episodic plot."

Poetic Justice: An outcome in a literary work, not necessarily a poem, in which the good are rewarded and the evil are punished, especially in ways that particularly fit their virtues or crimes.

Poetic License: Distortions of fact and literary convention made by a writer—not always a poet—for the sake of the effect gained. Poetic license is closely related to the concept of "artistic freedom."

Poetics: This term has two closely related meanings. It denotes (1) an aesthetic theory in literary criticism about the essence of poetry or (2) rules prescribing the proper methods, content, style, or diction of poetry. The term poetics may also refer to theories about literature in general, not just poetry.

Point of View: The narrative perspective from which a literary work is presented to the reader. There are four traditional points of view. The "third person omniscient" gives the reader a "godlike" perspective, unrestricted by time or place, from which to see actions and look into the minds of characters. This allows the author to comment openly on characters and events in the work. The "third person" point of view presents the events of the story from outside of any single character's perception, much like the omniscient point of view, but the reader must understand the action as it takes place and without any special insight into characters' minds or motivations. The "first person" or "personal" point of view relates events as they are perceived by a single character. The main character "tells" the story and may offer opinions about the action and characters which differ from those of the author. Much less common than omniscient, third person, and first person is the "second person" point of view, wherein the author tells the story as if it is happening to the reader.

Polemic: A work in which the author takes a stand on a controversial subject, such as abortion or religion. Such works are often extremely argumentative or provocative.

Pornography: Writing intended to provoke feelings of lust in the reader. Such works are often condemned by critics and teachers, but those which can be shown to have literary value are viewed less harshly.

Post-Aesthetic Movement: An artistic response made by African Americans to the black aesthetic movement of the 1960s and early '70s. Writers since that time have adopted a somewhat different tone in their work, with less emphasis placed on the disparity between black and white in the United States. In the words of post-aesthetic authors such as Toni Morrison, John Edgar Wideman, and Kristin Hunter, African Americans are portrayed as looking inward for answers to their own questions, rather than always looking to the outside world.

Postmodernism: Writing from the 1960s forward characterized by experimentation and continuing to apply some of the fundamentals of modernism, which included existentialism and alienation. Postmodernists have gone a step further in the rejection of tradition begun with the modernists by also rejecting traditional forms, preferring the anti-novel over the novel and the anti-hero over the hero.

Primitivism: The belief that primitive peoples were nobler and less flawed than civilized peoples because they had not been subjected to the tainting influence of society.

Prologue: An introductory section of a literary work. It often contains information establishing the situation of the characters or presents information about the setting, time period, or action. In drama, the prologue is spoken by a chorus or by one of the principal characters.

Prose: A literary medium that attempts to mirror the language of everyday speech. It is distinguished from poetry by its use of unmetered, unrhymed language consisting of logically related sentences. Prose is usually grouped into paragraphs that form a cohesive whole such as an essay or a novel.

Prosopopoeia: See *Personification*

Protagonist: The central character of a story who serves as a focus for its themes and incidents and as the principal rationale for its development. The protagonist is sometimes referred to in discussions of modern literature as the hero or anti-hero.

Protest Fiction: Protest fiction has as its primary purpose the protesting of some social injustice, such as racism or discrimination.

Proverb: A brief, sage saying that expresses a truth about life in a striking manner.

Pseudonym: A name assumed by a writer, most often intended to prevent his or her identification as the author of a work. Two or more authors may work together under one pseudonym, or an author may use a different name for each genre he or she publishes in. Some publishing companies maintain "house pseudonyms," under which any number of authors may write installations in a series. Some authors also choose a pseudonym over their real names the way an actor may use a stage name.

Pun: A play on words that have similar sounds but different meanings.

R

Realism: A nineteenth-century European literary movement that sought to portray familiar characters, situations, and settings in a realistic manner. This was done primarily by using an objective narrative point of view and through the buildup of accurate detail. The standard for success of any realistic work depends on how faithfully it transfers common experience into fictional forms. The realistic method may be altered or extended, as in stream of consciousness writing, to record highly subjective experience.

Repartee: Conversation featuring snappy retorts and witticisms.

Resolution: The portion of a story following the climax, in which the conflict is resolved.

Rhetoric: In literary criticism, this term denotes the art of ethical persuasion. In its strictest sense, rhetoric adheres to various principles developed since classical times for arranging facts and ideas in a clear, persuasive, appealing manner. The term is also used to refer to effective prose in general and theories of or methods for composing effective prose.

Rhetorical Question: A question intended to provoke thought, but not an expressed answer, in the reader. It is most commonly used in oratory and other persuasive genres.

Rising Action: The part of a drama where the plot becomes increasingly complicated. Rising action leads up to the climax, or turning point, of a drama.

Roman à clef: A French phrase meaning "novel with a key." It refers to a narrative in which real persons are portrayed under fictitious names.

Romance: A broad term, usually denoting a narrative with exotic, exaggerated, often idealized characters, scenes, and themes.

Romanticism: This term has two widely accepted meanings. In historical criticism, it refers to a European intellectual and artistic movement of the late eighteenth and early nineteenth centuries that sought greater freedom of personal expression than that allowed by the strict rules of literary form and logic of the eighteenth-century neoclassicists. The Romantics preferred emotional and imaginative expression to rational analysis. They considered the individual to be at the center of all experience and so placed him or her at the center of their art. The Romantics believed that the creative imagination reveals nobler truths—unique feelings and attitudes—than those that could be discovered by logic or by scientific examination. Both the natural world and the state of childhood were important sources for revelations of "eternal truths." "Romanticism" is also used as a general term to refer to a type of sensibility found in all periods of literary history and usually considered to be in opposition to the principles of classicism. In this sense, Romanticism signifies any work or philosophy in which the exotic or dreamlike figure strongly, or that is devoted to individualistic expression, self-analysis, or a pursuit of a higher realm of knowledge than can be discovered by human reason.

Romantics: See *Romanticism*

S

Satire: A work that uses ridicule, humor, and wit to criticize and provoke change in human nature and institutions. There are two major types of satire: "formal" or "direct" satire speaks directly to the reader or to a character

in the work; "indirect" satire relies upon the ridiculous behavior of its characters to make its point. Formal satire is further divided into two manners: the "Horatian," which ridicules gently, and the "Juvenalian," which derides its subjects harshly and bitterly.

Science Fiction: A type of narrative about or based upon real or imagined scientific theories and technology. Science fiction is often peopled with alien creatures and set on other planets or in different dimensions.

Second Person: See *Point of View*

Setting: The time, place, and culture in which the action of a narrative takes place. The elements of setting may include geographic location, characters' physical and mental environments, prevailing cultural attitudes, or the historical time in which the action takes place.

Simile: A comparison, usually using "like" or "as", of two essentially dissimilar things, as in "coffee as cold as ice" or "He sounded like a broken record."

Slang: A type of informal verbal communication that is generally unacceptable for formal writing. Slang words and phrases are often colorful exaggerations used to emphasize the speaker's point; they may also be shortened versions of an often-used word or phrase.

Slave Narrative: Autobiographical accounts of American slave life as told by escaped slaves. These works first appeared during the abolition movement of the 1830s through the 1850s.

Socialist Realism: The Socialist Realism school of literary theory was proposed by Maxim Gorky and established as a dogma by the first Soviet Congress of Writers. It demanded adherence to a communist worldview in works of literature. Its doctrines required an objective viewpoint comprehensible to the working classes and themes of social struggle featuring strong proletarian heroes.

Stereotype: A stereotype was originally the name for a duplication made during the printing process; this led to its modern definition as a person or thing that is (or is assumed to be) the same as all others of its type.

Stream of Consciousness: A narrative technique for rendering the inward experience of a character. This technique is designed to give the impression of an ever-changing series of thoughts, emotions, images, and memories in the spontaneous and seemingly illogical order that they occur in life.

Structure: The form taken by a piece of literature. The structure may be made obvious for ease of understanding, as in nonfiction works, or may obscured for artistic purposes, as in some poetry or seemingly "unstructured" prose.

Sturm und Drang: A German term meaning "storm and stress." It refers to a German literary movement of the 1770s and 1780s that reacted against the order and rationalism of the enlightenment, focusing instead on the intense experience of extraordinary individuals.

Style: A writer's distinctive manner of arranging words to suit his or her ideas and purpose in writing. The unique imprint of the author's personality upon his or her writing, style is the product of an author's way of arranging ideas and his or her use of diction, different sentence structures, rhythm, figures of speech, rhetorical principles, and other elements of composition.

Subjectivity: Writing that expresses the author's personal feelings about his subject, and which may or may not include factual information about the subject.

Subplot: A secondary story in a narrative. A subplot may serve as a motivating or complicating force for the main plot of the work, or it may provide emphasis for, or relief from, the main plot.

Surrealism: A term introduced to criticism by Guillaume Apollinaire and later adopted by Andre Breton. It refers to a French literary and artistic movement founded in the 1920s. The Surrealists sought to express unconscious thoughts and feelings in their works. The best-known technique used for achieving this aim was automatic writing—transcriptions of spontaneous outpourings from the unconscious. The Surrealists proposed to unify the contrary levels of conscious and unconscious, dream and reality, objectivity and subjectivity into a new level of "super-realism."

Suspense: A literary device in which the author maintains the audience's attention through the buildup of events, the outcome of which will soon be revealed.

Symbol: Something that suggests or stands for something else without losing its original identity. In literature, symbols combine their literal meaning with the suggestion of an abstract concept. Literary symbols are of two types: those that carry complex associations of meaning no matter what their contexts, and those that derive their suggestive meaning from their functions in specific literary works.

Symbolism: This term has two widely accepted meanings. In historical criticism, it denotes an early modernist literary movement initiated in France during the nineteenth century that reacted against the prevailing standards of realism. Writers in this movement aimed to evoke, indirectly and symbolically, an order of being beyond the material world of the five senses. Poetic expression of personal emotion figured strongly in the movement, typically by means of a private set of symbols uniquely identifiable with the individual poet. The principal aim of the Symbolists was to express in words the highly complex feelings that grew out of everyday contact with the world. In a broader sense, the term "symbolism" refers to the use of one object to represent another.

T

Tall Tale: A humorous tale told in a straightforward, credible tone but relating absolutely impossible events or feats of the characters. Such tales were commonly told of frontier adventures during the settlement of the west in the United States.

Theme: The main point of a work of literature. The term is used interchangeably with thesis.

Thesis: A thesis is both an essay and the point argued in the essay. Thesis novels and thesis plays share the quality of containing a thesis which is supported through the action of the story.

Third Person: See *Point of View*

Tone: The author's attitude toward his or her audience may be deduced from the tone of the work. A formal tone may create distance or convey politeness, while an informal tone may encourage a friendly, intimate, or intrusive feeling in the reader. The author's attitude toward his or her subject matter may also be deduced from the tone of the words he or she uses in discussing it.

Transcendentalism: An American philosophical and religious movement, based in New England from around 1835 until the Civil War. Transcendentalism was a form of American romanticism that had its roots abroad in the works of Thomas Carlyle, Samuel Coleridge, and Johann Wolfgang von Goethe. The Transcendentalists stressed the importance of intuition and subjective experience in communication with God. They rejected religious dogma and texts in favor of mysticism and scientific naturalism. They pursued truths that lie beyond the "colorless" realms perceived by reason and the senses and were active social reformers in public education, women's rights, and the abolition of slavery.

U

Urban Realism: A branch of realist writing that attempts to accurately reflect the often harsh facts of modern urban existence.

Utopia: A fictional perfect place, such as "paradise" or "heaven."

V

Verisimilitude: Literally, the appearance of truth. In literary criticism, the term refers to aspects of a work of literature that seem true to the reader.

Victorian: Refers broadly to the reign of Queen Victoria of England (1837-1901) and to anything with qualities typical of that era. For example, the qualities of smug narrow-mindedness, bourgeois materialism, faith in social progress, and priggish morality are often considered Victorian. This stereotype is contradicted by such dramatic intellectual developments as the theories of Charles Darwin, Karl Marx, and Sigmund Freud (which stirred strong debates in England) and the critical attitudes of serious Victorian writers like Charles Dickens and George Eliot. In literature, the Victorian Period was the great age of the English novel, and the latter part of the era saw the rise of movements such as decadence and symbolism.

W

Weltanschauung: A German term referring to a person's worldview or philosophy.

Weltschmerz: A German term meaning "world pain." It describes a sense of anguish about the nature of existence, usually associated with a melancholy, pessimistic attitude.

Z

Zeitgeist: A German term meaning "spirit of the time." It refers to the moral and intellectual trends of a given era.

Cumulative Author/Title Index

Cumulative Nationality/Ethnicity Index

Subject/Theme Index

Forgiveness
 Humboldt's Gift: 45, 60–61
 March: 142, 144
 Picture Bride: 195–197
Freedom
 Doctor Zhivago: 3, 17–19, 21, 23–27
 The Killer Angels: 65, 73, 79 84, 86
 The Known World: 92, 94–95,
 98–99, 101, 107
Friendship
 Doctor Zhivago: 6, 12, 19
 Humboldt's Gift: 38, 40–41, 47, 49
 The Lord of the Rings: 124, 131–132
 Picture Bride: 181, 189, 204
 The Tenant of Wildfell Hall: 247,
 249, 260, 263–264
Friendship
 Humboldt's Gift: 40
Friendship as the Basis of Strength
 The Lord of the Rings: 124

G

Gay Nineties
 Ulysses: 288–291
Gender Roles
 The Rainbow: 216
Generosity
 March: 143–144
 The Rainbow: 210, 214
Ghost
 Humboldt's Gift: 33, 47, 52, 54
 The Lord of the Rings: 117–118,
 122, 128, 135
 March: 143, 145, 151
 Ulysses: 273, 279, 291
God
 The Killer Angels: 69, 71, 74–75,
 83–84, 86
 The Known World: 93–94, 98,
 103–104
 The Rainbow: 226, 233, 235, 237
**God's Will, Human Will, or
 Chance?**
 The Killer Angels: 74
Greed
 Humboldt's Gift: 35, 47–48, 50–51,
 54
 Martian Time-Slip: 160–162
Grief and Sorrow
 Humboldt's Gift: 32, 34, 41, 47, 49,
 53, 56–58, 61
 The Lord of the Rings: 116, 131,
 134–135
 The Rainbow: 210, 218, 222, 224,
 232, 234–235
 Ulysses: 270–271, 275–276, 278,
 284
Guilt
 Humboldt's Gift: 45–48, 52, 56–61
 March: 139–142, 147, 151
 The Rainbow: 214, 219–221,
 223–224

H

Happiness and Gaiety
 Doctor Zhivago: 4, 20, 25–26
 Humboldt's Gift: 33, 38–39, 41, 45,
 48, 56
 The Killer Angels: 68–70, 72, 75
 The Lord of the Rings: 120, 125,
 131–132, 135
 Picture Bride: 180–181, 188, 201
 The Rainbow: 208–209, 212, 223,
 228, 234
 The Tenant of Wildfell Hall: 242,
 244–246, 249, 252, 256–257, 260
 Ulysses: 290–291
Hatred
 Doctor Zhivago: 4, 9, 24, 26–27
 Humboldt's Gift: 32, 42, 45–46, 49,
 55, 62
 The Killer Angels: 66–68, 73–74,
 80, 85–86
 The Lord of the Rings: 117–119,
 121, 123–124, 128–129, 134
 Martian Time-Slip: 157, 162, 177
 Picture Bride: 182, 190, 192,
 198–199
 The Rainbow: 209, 214, 218,
 220–221, 223–224, 226–229,
 232, 234–235
 The Tenant of Wildfell Hall: 243,
 248–249, 260, 264
 Ulysses: 267, 275, 281, 289, 291
Haunting Sense of History, The
 The Lord of the Rings: 123–124
Heaven
 The Killer Angels: 86
Heritage and Ancestry
 Picture Bride: 186, 188–189,
 196–197, 200–201, 203
Heroism
 Doctor Zhivago: 10, 12, 14, 16, 21,
 24–27
 Humboldt's Gift: 47–48, 54–58, 60
 The Killer Angels: 83, 86
 The Lord of the Rings: 112, 118–120,
 124, 126, 128, 131, 133–135
 The Tenant of Wildfell Hall: 246,
 253–254, 258
 Ulysses: 267, 278, 284, 291
Heroism Depends on Free Will
 The Lord of the Rings: 124
Historical Periods
 The Known World: 102, 106
History
 Doctor Zhivago: 11, 22, 24–27
 Humboldt's Gift: 47–48, 51–52, 54,
 58, 62
 The Killer Angels: 78, 81–82, 84
 The Known World: 90,
 102–103, 107
 The Lord of the Rings: 112, 118,
 123, 126–127, 131–132, 134
 Martian Time-Slip: 171–172, 176

 Picture Bride: 194, 197, 200,
 202–203
 The Tenant of Wildfell Hall: 239,
 252–253, 261, 263
 Ulysses: 269, 276, 281, 283, 286,
 290
The Holocaust
 Humboldt's Gift: 57–58, 61
Homosexuality
 The Rainbow: 216, 218–219, 221,
 224, 226–227, 229
Honor
 Doctor Zhivago: 20
 Humboldt's Gift: 48, 59
 The Killer Angels: 70, 75–76
 The Lord of the Rings: 112,
 123–124
 March: 145
 The Rainbow: 233, 235, 237
 The Tenant of Wildfell Hall: 259
 Ulysses: 291
Hope
 Doctor Zhivago: 2, 4–5, 7, 10–12,
 18–23, 25–27
 Humboldt's Gift: 33–35, 40, 46, 49,
 53, 55, 61
 The Killer Angels: 65–67, 69, 82, 87
 The Lord of the Rings: 112,
 117–119, 124, 133–135
 Martian Time-Slip: 157, 159,
 161–163, 165, 170, 172–173
 Picture Bride: 179–182, 184, 186,
 189–191, 194, 196, 199, 202, 204
 The Rainbow: 207, 209–211, 213,
 217, 221, 232, 235–236
 The Tenant of Wildfell Hall: 241,
 243, 248, 255–256, 260–262
Human Condition
 Humboldt's Gift: 46, 50
 Ulysses: 266
Human Interdependence
 Martian Time-Slip: 161–162
Humiliation and Degradation
 Humboldt's Gift: 35, 50, 55, 58–59
 Picture Bride: 183, 185–186,
 188–189, 194, 198–199
 Ulysses: 270, 291
Humor
 Humboldt's Gift: 33, 46–48, 50, 52,
 54–57, 59–61
 The Lord of the Rings: 115,
 120, 134
 Martian Time-Slip: 166, 172, 174,
 177
 The Rainbow: 220, 223, 225
 Ulysses: 277, 279, 285–286, 291

I

Ideal versus Real
 Doctor Zhivago: 11–12
Idealism
 March: 137, 144, 149, 151